Lecture Notes in Artificial Intelligence   10062

Subseries of Lecture Notes in Computer Science

LNAI Series Editors

Randy Goebel
University of Alberta, Edmonton, Canada
Yuzuru Tanaka
Hokkaido University, Sapporo, Japan
Wolfgang Wahlster
DFKI and Saarland University, Saarbrücken, Germany

LNAI Founding Series Editor

Joerg Siekmann
DFKI and Saarland University, Saarbrücken, Germany

More information about this series at http://www.springer.com/series/1244

Obdulia Pichardo-Lagunas
Sabino Miranda-Jiménez (Eds.)

Advances in Soft Computing

15th Mexican International Conference
on Artificial Intelligence, MICAI 2016
Cancún, Mexico, October 23–28, 2016
Proceedings, Part II

 Springer

Editors
Obdulia Pichardo-Lagunas
Instituto Politécnico Nacional
Unidad Profesional Interdisciplinaria en
  Ingeniería y Tecnologías Avanzadas
México DF
Mexico

Sabino Miranda-Jiménez
INFOTEC Aguascalientes
Aguascalientes
Mexico

ISSN 0302-9743   ISSN 1611-3349   (electronic)
Lecture Notes in Artificial Intelligence
ISBN 978-3-319-62427-3   ISBN 978-3-319-62428-0   (eBook)
DOI 10.1007/978-3-319-62428-0

Library of Congress Control Number: 2017946059

LNCS Sublibrary: SL7 – Artificial Intelligence

Printed on acid-free paper

This Springer imprint is published by Springer Nature
The registered company is Springer International Publishing AG
The registered company address is: Gewerbestrasse 11, 6330 Cham, Switzerland

Preface

The Mexican International Conference on Artificial Intelligence (MICAI) is a yearly international conference series that has been organized by the Mexican Society of Artificial Intelligence (SMIA) since 2000. MICAI is a major international artificial intelligence forum and the main event in the academic life of the country's growing artificial intelligence community.

MICAI conferences publish high-quality papers in all areas of artificial intelligence and its applications. The proceedings of the previous MICAI events have been published by Springer in its *Lecture Notes in Artificial Intelligence* series, vols. 1793, 2313, 2972, 3789, 4293, 4827, 5317, 5845, 6437, 6438, 7094, 7095, 7629, 7630, 8265, 8266, 8856, 8857, 9413, and 9414. Since its foundation in 2000, the conference has been growing in popularity and improving in quality.

The proceedings of MICAI 2016 are published in two volumes. The first volume, *Advances in Computational Intelligence*, contains 44 papers structured into seven sections:

- Natural Language Processing
- Social Networks and Opinion Mining
- Fuzzy Logic
- Time Series Analysis and Forecasting
- Planning and Scheduling
- Image Processing and Computer Vision
- Robotics

The second volume, *Advances in Soft Computing*, contains 44 papers structured into ten sections:

- General
- Reasoning and Multi-Agent Systems
- Neural Networks and Deep Learning
- Evolutionary Algorithms
- Machine Learning
- Classification and Clustering
- Optimization
- Data Mining
- Graph-Based Algorithms
- Intelligent Learning Environments

This two-volume set will be of interest for researchers in all areas of artificial intelligence, students specializing in related topics, and for the general public interested in recent developments in artificial intelligence.

The conference received for evaluation 238 submissions by 584 authors from 32 countries: Argentina, Brazil, Canada, Chile, China, Colombia, Costa Rica, Cuba, Czech Republic, Ecuador, France, Germany, Greece, Hungary, India, Iran, Ireland, Israel, Italy, Macao, Mexico, Pakistan, Russia, Serbia, Singapore, South Africa, Spain,

Thailand, Turkey, Ukraine, UK, and USA. Of these submissions, 86 papers were selected for publication in these two volumes after a peer-reviewing process carried out by the international Program Committee. The acceptance rate was 36.1%.

In addition to regular papers, the volumes contain two invited papers by the keynote speaker Vladik Kreinovich (USA):

– "For Multi-Interval-Valued Fuzzy Sets, Centroid Defuzzification Is Equivalent to Defuzzifying Its Interval Hull: A Theorem"
– "Metric Spaces Under Interval Uncertainty: Towards an Adequate Definition"

The international Program Committee consisted of 140 experts from 26 countries: Australia, Azerbaijan, Benin, Brazil, Canada, Colombia, Czech Republic, Finland, France, Germany, Greece, India, Israel, Italy, Japan, Luxembourg, Mexico, Poland, Russia, Singapore, Spain, Sweden, Switzerland, Turkey, UK, and USA.

MICAI 2016 was honored by the presence of renowned experts who gave excellent keynote lectures:

– Efstathios Stamatatos, University of the Aegean, Greece
– Imre J. Rudas, Óbuda University, Hungary
– Vladik Kreinovich, University of Texas at El Paso, USA
– Genoveva Vargas Solar, Centre national de la recherche scientifique, France

In addition, a special talk was given by Ángel Fernando Kuri Morales, ITAM, Mexico.

The technical program of the conference also featured tutorials presented by Félix Castro (UAEH), Miguel González Mendoza (ITESM), Oscar Herrera Alcántara (UAM), Francisco Viveros Jimenez (CIC-IPN), Alexei Morozov (IRE-RAS, Russia), and Ildar Batyrshin (CIC-IPN), among others. Four workshops were held jointly with the conference: the First International Workshop on Genetic Programming, the 9th International Workshop of Hybrid Intelligent Systems (HIS 2016), the Second International Workshop on Intelligent Decision Support Systems for Industry, and the 9th International Workshop on Intelligent Learning Environments (WILE 2016).

The authors of the following papers received the Best Paper Award based on the paper's overall quality, significance, and originality of the reported results:

First place:	"Author Profiling with doc2vec Neural Network-Based Document Embeddings," by Ilia Markov, Helena Gómez-Adorno, Juan-Pablo Posadas-Durán, Grigori Sidorov, and Alexander Gelbukh (Mexico)
	Prize from Springer: € 400; prize from SMIA: € 400
Second place:	"Using a Grammar Checker to Validate Compliance of Processes with Workflow Models," by Roman Barták and Vladislav Kuboň (Czech Republic)
	Prize from Springer: € 300; prize from SMIA: € 300
Third place:	"Neural Network Modelling for Dissolved Oxygen Effects in Extensive Litopenaeus Vannamei Culture," by José Juan Carbajal-Hernández and Luis P. Sánchez-Fernández (Mexico)
	Prize from Springer: € 200; prize from SMIA: € 200

The authors of the following papers selected among all papers of which the first author was a full-time student, excluding the papers listed above, shared the Best Student Paper Award:

First place:	"Relevance of Named Entities in Authorship Attribution," by Germán Ríos-Toledo, Grigori Sidorov, Noé Alejandro Castro-Sánchez, Alondra Nava-Zea, and Liliana Chanona-Hernández (Mexico)
	Prize from Springer: € 50; prize from SMIA: € 50
	"A Compact Representation for Cross-Domain Short Text Clustering," by Alba Núñez-Reyes, Esaú Villatoro-Tello, Gabriela Ramírez-de-la-Rosa, and Christian Sánchez-Sánchez (Mexico)
	Prize from Springer: € 50; prize from SMIA: € 50

The awards included significant monetary prizes sponsored by Springer and by the Mexican Society of Artificial Intelligent (SMIA).

We want to thank everyone involved in the organization of this conference. Firstly, the authors of the papers published in this book: It is their research work that gives value to the book and to the work of the organizers. We thank the track chairs for their hard work, and the Program Committee members and additional reviewers for their great effort in reviewing the submissions.

We would like to thank the Instituto Tecnológico de Cancún (ITCancún) for hosting the workshops and tutorials of MICAI 2016; particularly we thank Socorro Xóchitl Carmona Bareño, Director of the ITCancún, for her support and generosity. We also want to thank the staff of the Instituto Tecnológico de Cancún for their support in the organization of this conference. We gratefully acknowledge the sponsorship received from Springer for monetary prizes handed to the authors of the best papers of the conference. This generous sponsorship demonstrates Springer's strong commitment to the development of science and their sincere interest in the highest quality of the conferences published in their series.

We are deeply grateful to the conference staff and to all members of the Local Committee headed by Fernando Antonio Koh Puga. We acknowledge support received from the project CONACYT 240844. The entire submission, reviewing, and selection process, as well as preparation of the proceedings, was supported free of charge by the EasyChair system (www.easychair.org). Finally, yet importantly, we are very grateful to the staff at Springer for their patience and help in the preparation of this volume.

October 2016   Grigori Sidorov
                                                   Oscar Herrera-Alcántara
                                                   Obdulia Pichardo-Lagunas
                                                   Sabino Miranda-Jiménez

Organization

MICAI 2016 was organized by the Mexican Society of Artificial Intelligence (SMIA, Sociedad Mexicana de Inteligencia Artificial) in collaboration with the Instituto Tecnológico de Cancún (ITCancún), the Centro de Investigación en Computación del Instituto Politécnico Nacional (CIC-IPN), the Universidad Autónoma de México Azcapotzalco (UAM), the Unidad Profesional Interdisciplinaria en Ingeniería y Tecnologías Avanzadas del Instituto Politécnico Nacional (UPIITA-IPN), and INFOTEC.

The MICAI series website is www.MICAI.org. The website of the Mexican Society of Artificial Intelligence, SMIA, is www.SMIA.org.mx. Contact details and additional information can be found on these websites.

Conference Committee

General Chair

Grigori Sidorov	Instituto Politécnico Nacional, Mexico

Program Chairs

Grigori Sidorov	Instituto Politécnico Nacional, Mexico
Oscar Herrera Alcántara	Universidad Autónoma Metropolitana Azcapotzalco, Mexico
Sabino Miranda-Jiménez	INFOTEC, Mexico
Obdulia Pichardo Lagunas	Instituto Politécnico Nacional, Mexico

Workshop Chairs

Obdulia Pichardo Lagunas	Instituto Politécnico Nacional, Mexico
Noé Alejandro Castro Sánchez	Centro Nacional de Investigación y Desarrollo Tecnológico, Mexico

Tutorials Chair

Félix Castro Espinoza	Universidad Autónoma del Estado de Hidalgo, Mexico

Doctoral Consortium Chairs

Miguel Gonzalez Mendoza	Tecnológico de Monterrey CEM, Mexico
Antonio Marín Hernandez	Universidad Veracruzana, Mexico

Keynote Talks Chair

Sabino Miranda Jiménez	INFOTEC, Mexico

Publication Chair

Miguel Gonzalez Mendoza   Tecnológico de Monterrey CEM, Mexico

Financial Chair

Ildar Batyrshin   Instituto Politécnico Nacional, Mexico

Grant Chairs

Grigori Sidorov   Instituto Politécnico Nacional, Mexico
Miguel Gonzalez Mendoza   Tecnológico de Monterrey CEM, Mexico

Organizing Committee Chair

Fernando Antonio   Instituto Tecnológico de Cancún, Mexico
   Koh Puga

Area Chairs

Natural Language Processing

Grigori Sidorov   Instituto Politécnico Nacional, Mexico
Sofía Natalia Galicia Haro   Universidad Nacional Autónoma de México, Mexico
Alexander Gelbukh   Instituto Politécnico Nacional, Mexico

Machine Learning and Pattern Recognition

Alexander Gelbukh   Instituto Politécnico Nacional, Mexico

Data Mining

Miguel Gonzalez-Mendoza   Tecnológico de Monterrey CEM, Mexico
Félix Castro Espinoza   Universidad Autónoma del Estado de Hidalgo, Mexico

Intelligent Tutoring Systems

Alexander Gelbukh   Instituto Politécnico Nacional, Mexico

Evolutionary and Nature-Inspired Metaheuristic Algorithms

Oliver Schütze   CINVESTAV, Mexico
Jaime Mora Vargas   Tecnológico de Monterrey CEM, Mexico

Computer Vision and Image Processing

Oscar Herrera Alcántara   Universidad Autónoma Metropolitana Azcapotzalco,
      Mexico

Robotics, Planning, and Scheduling

Fernando Martin   Universidad Veracruzana, Mexico
   Montes-Gonzalez

Neural Networks and Hybrid Intelligent Systems

Sergio Ledesma-Orozco   Universidad de Guanajuato, Mexico

Logic, Knowledge-Based Systems, Multi-agent Systems and Distributed AI

Mauricio Osorio   Jose Raymundo Marcial Romero

Fuzzy Systems and Probabilistic Models in Decision-Making

Ildar Batyrshin   Instituto Politécnico Nacional, Mexico

Bioinformatics and Medical Applications

Jesus A. Gonzalez   Instituto Nacional de Astrofísica, Óptica y Electrónica, Mexico

Felipe Orihuela-Espina   Instituto Nacional de Astrofísica, Óptica y Electrónica, Mexico

Program Committee

Juan C. Acosta-Guadarrama   Universidad Autónoma de Ciudad Juárez, Mexico
Fernando Aldana   Universidad Veracruzana, Mexico
Gustavo Arroyo   Instituto de Investigaciones Eléctricas, Mexico
Maria Lucia Barrón-Estrada   Instituto Tecnológico de Culiacán, Mexico
Ildar Batyrshin   Instituto Politécnico Nacional, Mexico
Igor Bolshakov   Russian State University for the Humanities, Russia
Ramon F. Brena   Tecnológico de Monterrey, Mexico
Eduardo Cabal-Yepez   Universidad de Guanajuato, Mexico
Hiram Calvo   Instituto Politécnico Nacional, Mexico
Nicoletta Calzolari   Istituto di Linguistica Computazionale – CNR, Italy
Erik Cambria   Nanyang Technological University, Singapore
Jorge Victor Carrera Trejo   Instituto Politécnico Nacional, Mexico
Maya Carrillo   Instituto Nacional de Astrofísica, Óptica y Electrónica, Mexico
Heydy Castillejos   Universidad Autónoma del Estado de Hidalgo, Mexico
Oscar Castillo   Instituto Tecnológico de Tijuana, Mexico
Felix Castro Espinoza   Universidad Autónoma del Estado de Hidalgo, Mexico
Noé Alejandro Castro-Sánchez   Centro Nacional de Investigación y Desarrollo Tecnológico, Mexico
Hector Ceballos   Tecnológico de Monterrey, Mexico
Gustavo Cerda-Villafana   Universidad de Guanajuato, Mexico
Liliana Chanona-Hernandez   Instituto Politécnico Nacional, Mexico
Stefania Costantini   Università degli Studi dell'Aquila, Italy
Heriberto Cuayahuitl   Heriot-Watt University, UK
Erik Cuevas   Universidad de Guadalajara, Mexico
Guillermo De Ita   Universidad Autónoma de Puebla, Mexico
Asif Ekbal   Indian Institute of Technology Patna, India

Hugo Jair Escalante	Instituto Nacional de Astrofísica, Óptica y Electrónica, Mexico
Ponciano Jorge Escamilla-Ambrosio	Instituto Politécnico Nacional, Mexico
Vlad Estivill-Castro	Griffith University, Australia
Gibran Etcheverry	Universidad de Sonora, Mexico
Eugene C. Ezin	Institut de Mathématiques et de Sciences Physiques, Benin
Denis Filatov	Instituto Politécnico Nacional, Mexico
Juan J. Flores	Universidad Michoacana de San Nicolás de Hidalgo, Mexico
Andrea Formisano	Università di Perugia, Italy
Anilu Franco-Arcega	Instituto Nacional de Astrofísica, Óptica y Electrónica, Mexico
Alfredo Gabaldon	General Electric Global Research, USA
Sofia N. Galicia-Haro	Universidad Nacional Autónoma de México, Mexico
Ana Gabriela Gallardo-Hernández	Universidad Nacional Autónoma de México, Mexico
Carlos Hugo Garcia-Capulin	Universidad de Guanajuato, Mexico
Alexander Gelbukh	Instituto Politécnico Nacional, Mexico
Onofrio Gigliotta	University of Naples Federico II, Italy
Eduardo Gomez-Ramirez	Universidad La Salle, Mexico
Arturo Gonzalez	Universidad de Guanajuato, Mexico
Jesus A. Gonzalez	Instituto Nacional de Astrofísica, Óptica y Electrónica, Mexico
Miguel Gonzalez-Mendoza	Tecnológico de Monterrey CEM, Mexico
Felix F. Gonzalez-Navarro	Universidad Autónoma de Baja California, Mexico
Efren Gorrostieta	Universidad Autónoma de Querétaro, Mexico
Carlos Arturo Gracios-Marin	CERN, Switzerland
Joaquin Gutierrez	Centro de Investigaciones Biológicas del Noroeste S.C., Mexico
Rafael Guzman	Universidad de Guanajuato, Mexico
Yasunari Harada	Waseda University, Japan
Rogelio Hasimoto	Centro de Investigación en Matemáticas, Mexico
Antonio Hernandez	Instituto Politécnico Nacional, Mexico
Yasmín Hernández Pérez	Instituto de Investigaciones Eléctricas, Mexico
Alberto Hernández	Universidad Autnoma del Estado de Morelos, Mexico
Oscar Herrera	Universidad Autónoma Metropolitana Azcapotzalco, Mexico
Dieter Hutter	DFKI GmbH, Germany
Pablo H. Ibarguengoytia	Instituto de Investigaciones Eléctricas, Mexico
Oscar G. Ibarra-Manzano	Universidad de Guanajuato, Mexico
Héctor Jiménez Salazar	Universidad Autónoma Metropolitana, Mexico
Laetitia Jourdan	Inria/LIFL/CNRS, France

Pinar Karagoz	Middle East Technical University, Turkey
Ryszard Klempous	Wroclaw University of Technology, Poland
Olga Kolesnikova	Instituto Politécnico Nacional, Mexico
Vladik Kreinovich	University of Texas at El Paso, USA
Angel Kuri-Morales	Instituto Tecnológico Autónomo de México, Mexico
Mathieu Lafourcade	Le Laboratoire d'Informatique, de Robotique et de Microélectronique de Montpellier (UM2/CNRS), France
Ricardo Landa	CINVESTAV Tamaulipas, Mexico
Dario Landa-Silva	University of Nottingham, UK
Bruno Lara	Universidad Autónoma del Estado de Morelos, Mexico
Yulia Ledeneva	Universidad Autónoma del Estado de México, Mexico
Yoel Ledo Mezquita	Universidad de las Américas, Mexico
Eugene Levner	Ashkelon Academic College, Israel
Rocio Lizarraga-Morales	Universidad de Guanajuato, Mexico
Blanca Lopez	Instituto Politécnico Nacional, Mexico
Tanja Magoc	University of Texas at El Paso, USA
J. Raymundo Marcial-Romero	Universidad Autónoma del Estado de México, Mexico
Luis Martí	Universidade Federal Fluminense, Brazil
Lourdes Martínez	Universidad Panamericana, Mexico
Juan Martínez-Miranda	Centro de Investigación Científica y de Educación Superior de Ensenada, Mexico
Miguel Félix Mata Rivera	Instituto Politécnico Nacional, Mexico
Patricia Melin	Instituto Tecnológico de Tijuana, Mexico
Ivan Vladimir Meza Ruiz	Universidad Nacional Autónoma de México, Mexico
Efrén Mezura-Montes	Universidad Veracruzana, Mexico
Mikhail Mikhailov	University of Tampere, Finland
Sabino Miranda-Jiménez	INFOTEC, Mexico
Raul Monroy	Tecnologico de Monterrey CEM, Mexico
Omar Montaño Rivas	Universidad Politécnica de San Luis Potosí, Mexico
Manuel Montes-y-Gómez	Instituto Nacional de Astrofísica, Óptica y Electrónica, Mexico
Carlos Montoro	Universidad de Guanajuato, Mexico
Eduardo Morales	Instituto Nacional de Astrofísica, Óptica y Electrónica, Mexico
Guillermo Morales-Luna	CINVESTAV, Mexico
Masaki Murata	Tottori University, Japan
Michele Nappi	University of Salerno, Italy
Jesús Emeterio Navarro-Barrientos	Society for the Promotion of Applied Computer Science (GFaI e.V.), Germany
Juan Carlos Nieves	Umeå University, Sweden
C. Alberto Ochoa-Zezatti	Universidad Autónoma de Ciudad Juárez, Mexico
Ivan Olmos	Benemérita Universidad Autónoma de Puebla, Mexico
Sonia Ordoñez	Universidad Distrital F.J. de C., Colombia
Partha Pakray	National Institute of Technology Mizoram, India

Ivandre Paraboni — University of Sao Paulo, Brazil
Mario Pavone — University of Catania, Italy
Ted Pedersen — University of Minnesota Duluth, USA
Obdulia Pichardo-Lagunas — Instituto Politécnico Nacional, Mexico
David Pinto — Benemérita Universidad Autónoma de Puebla, Mexico
Hiram Ponce Espinosa — Tecnológico de Monterrey CCM, Mexico
Soujanya Poria — Nanyang Technological University, Singapore
Héctor Pérez-Urbina — Google, USA
Risto Fermin Rangel Kuoppa — Universidad Autónoma Metropolitana Azcapotzalco, Mexico
Iván Salvador Razo-Zapata — Luxembourg Institute of Science and Technology, Luxembourg
Orion Reyes — University of Alberta Edmonton AB, Canada
Alberto Reyes Ballesteros — Instituto de Investigaciones Eléctricas, Mexico
Carlos Alberto Reyes García — Instituto Nacional de Astrofísica, Óptica y Electrónica, Mexico
Arles Rodriguez — Universidad Nacional de Colombia, Colombia
Alejandro Rosales — Instituto Nacional de Astrofísica, Óptica y Electrónica, Mexico
Horacio Rostro Gonzalez — Universidad de Guanajuato, Mexico
Jose Ruiz-Pinales — Universidad de Guanajuato, Mexico
Chaman Sabharwal — Missouri University of Science and Technology, USA
Abraham Sánchez López — Benemérita Universidad Autónoma de Puebla, Mexico
Antonio-José Sánchez-Salmerón — Universitat Politècnica de València, Spain
Jose Santos — University of A Coruña, Spain
Friedhelm Schwenker — Ulm University, Germany
Shahnaz Shahbazova — Azerbaijan Technical University, Azerbaijan
Patrick Siarry — Université de Paris 12, France
Grigori Sidorov — Instituto Politécnico Nacional, Mexico
Bogdan Smolka — Silesian University of Technology, Poland
Juan Humberto Sossa Azuela — Instituto Politécnico Nacional, Mexico
Efstathios Stamatatos — University of the Aegean, Greece
Josef Steinberger — University of West Bohemia, Czech Republic
Alexander Tulupyev — St. Petersburg Institute for Informatics and Automation of Russian Academy of Sciences, Russia
Fevrier Valdez — Instituto Tecnológico de Tijuana, Mexico
Manuel Vilares Ferro — University of Vigo, Spain
Esau Villatoro-Tello — Universidad Autónoma Metropolitana, Mexico
Aline Villavicencio — Universidade Federal do Rio Grande do Sul, Brazil
Francisco Viveros Jiménez — Instituto Politécnico Nacional, Mexico
Panagiotis Vlamos — Ionian University, Greece
Piotr W. Fuglewicz — TiP Sp. z o. o., Poland

Carlos Mario Zapata Jaramillo	Universidad Nacional de Colombia, Colombia
Ramón Zatarain	Instituto Tecnológico de Culiacán, Mexico
Alisa Zhila	IBM, USA
Reyer Zwiggelaar	Aberystwyth University, UK

Additional Reviewers

Adan Enrique Aguilar-Justo	Dagmar Monett-Diaz
Maria-Yaneli Ameca-Alducin	Alondra Nava-Zea
Andreas Attenberger	Felipe Ojeda-Cruz
Zbigniew Banaszak	Felipe De Jesús Ojeda-Cruz
Grzegorz Bocewicz	Rosa María Ortega-Mendoza
Wojciech Bozejko	Nahitt Padilla
Jose Camargo-Orduño	José Luis Paredes
Esteban Castillo	Carla Piazza
Silvio Ricardo Cordeiro	Edgar Alfredo Portilla-Flores
Víctor Darriba	Claudia E. Ramírez Hernández
Dario Della Monica	Gabriela Ramírez-De-La-Rosa
Saul Dominguez	Francisco J. Ribadas-Pena
Víctor Manuel Fernández Mireles	Francesco Ricca
Helena Monserrat Gómez Adorno	Daniel Rivas
Marcos Angel González-Olvera	Jorge Rodas
Mario Graff	Hector Rodriguez Rangel
César Guerra	Carlos Rodriguez-Donate
Helena Gómez-Adorno	Mariana Rojas-Delgado
Jorge Hernandez Del Razo	Salvador Ruiz-Correa
Geovanni Hernandez-Gomez	Ryan Stansifer
Luis M. Ledesma-Carrillo	Fernando Sánchez
Rocio Lizarraga-Morales	Kazuhiro Takeuchi
Misael Lopez Ramirez	Eric S. Tellez
Adrián Pastor Lopez-Monroy	Alejandro Antonio Torres García
Joji Maeno	Monica Trejo
Navonil Majumder	Yasushi Tsubota
Ilia Markov	Roberto Villarejo
María-Guadalupe Martínez-Peñaloza	Remy Wahnoun
Mariana-Edith Miranda-Varela	Sławomir Wojciechowski
Daniela Moctezuma	Miguel Ángel Álvarez Carmona

Organizing Committee

Local Chair

Fernando Antonio   Instituto Tecnológico de Cancún, Mexico
  Koh Puga

Logistics Chair

Oscar Andrés Cárdenas   Instituto Tecnológico de Cancún, Mexico
  Alvarado

Registration Chair

José Israel Cupul Dzib   Instituto Tecnológico de Cancún, Mexico

Publicity and Event Follow-up Chair

Viviana Nasheli   Instituto Tecnológico de Cancún, Mexico
  Andrade Armenta

Members

Alejandro Filiberto Gómez Pérez
Luis Alfonso Marín Priego
Francisco José Arroyo Rodríguez
Juan Carlos Navarrete Montero
Florentino Chimal y Alamilla
Silverio Hernández Chávez
Juan Antonio Ruíz Velazco de la Garza
Octavio Ramírez López
Rosa Hilda Valencia Ruíz
Elisa Malibé Carballo Guillén
Domingo Ramos Hernández
Enrique Alberto Trejo Guzmán
Sixto Raúl Rodríguez Alvarado
Esmeralda Tepixtle Guevara
Juan Miguel Morán García
Emery Concepción Medina Díaz
Georgina Chan Díaz
Oscar San Juan Farfán, Instituto Tecnológico de Cancún, Mexico

Contents – Part II

Intelligent Learning Environments

Contents – Part I

Social Networks and Opinion Mining

Fuzzy Logic

Invited paper:

Invited paper:

Time Series Analysis and Forecasting

Planning and Scheduling

Best Paper Award, Second Place:

Image Processing and Computer Vision

Robotics

General

Normality from Monte Carlo Simulation for Statistical Validation of Computer Intensive Algorithms

Angel Fernando Kuri-Morales[1]([⊠]) and Ignacio López-Peña[2]

[1] Departamento de Computación, Instituto Tecnológico Autónomo de México,
Mexico City, Mexico
akuri@itam.mx
[2] Posgrado en Ciencia e Ingeniería de la Computación, IIMAS-UNAM,
Mexico City, Mexico
j.lopezp@uxmcc2.iimas.unam.mx

Abstract. The latest AI techniques are usually computer intensive, as opposed to the traditional ones which rely on the consistency of the logic principles on which they are based. In contrast, many algorithms of Computational Intelligence (CI) are meta-heuristic, i.e. methods where the particular selection of parameters defines the details and characteristics of the heuristic proper. In this paper we discuss a method which allows us to ascertain, with high statistical significance, the relative performance of several meta-heuristics. To achieve our goal we must find a statistical goodness-of-fit (gof) test which allows us to determine the moment when the sample becomes normal. Most statistical gof tests are designed to reject the null hypothesis (i.e. the samples do NOT fit the same distribution). In this case we wish to determine the case where the sample IS normal. Using a Monte Carlo simulation we are able to find a practical gof test to this effect. We discuss the methodology and describe its application to the analysis of three case studies: training of neural networks, genetic algorithms and unsupervised clustering.

Keywords: Computational Intelligence · Goodness-of-fit · Iterative algorithms

1 Introduction

CI techniques are usually computer intensive. The particular selection of parameters defines the details and characteristics of the heuristic proper. [For example, the choice of a genetic algorithm's (GA) parameters will define the GA's behavior]. Since the mathematical modeling of such techniques is particularly complex and the possible models are restricted to the set of selected parameters, the validity of the said techniques is, usually, tested from the results of their application. This is done by selecting a suite of problems, pitting the purported method against the problems of the suite and determining its efficacy for such set. This has the inconvenient of "verifying" the algorithm under test via the solution of a set of problems whose nature and number are subjectively determined. By "element" here we will understand the average cost of solving a set of k problems; by "sample" a set of elements of size N (i.e. Nk problems

© Springer International Publishing AG 2017
O. Pichardo-Lagunas and S. Miranda-Jiménez (Eds.): MICAI 2016, Part II, LNAI 10062, pp. 3–14, 2017.
DOI: 10.1007/978-3-319-62428-0_1

are to be solved). It is known that the distribution of the cost of solving problems from *N* samples, for a large enough *N*, will become normal regardless of the distribution of the cost of solving a single problem. It is possible to automatically generate a set of *Nk* unbiased problems, then to face the algorithm with these problems and extract statistically significant conclusions. Using a Monte Carlo simulation we are able to find a practical gof test to this effect which we call the Л Distribution. We discuss the methodology and describe its application. The rest of the paper is organized as follows: in Sect. 2 we make a brief mention of typical gof tests. In Sect. 3 we describe the general methodology to compare two algorithms. In Sect. 4 we describe the Monte Carlo experiment yielding the critical values of the Л Distribution. In Sect. 5 we analyze its application to 3 case studies. In Sect. 6 we offer our conclusions.

2 Popular gof Tests

The gof of a statistical model describes how well it fits a set of observations. Measures of goodness of fit typically summarize the discrepancy between observed values and the values expected under the model in question. For the rest of the paper we assume that the term *Null Hypothesis* refers to the case when all samples come from the same distribution. In what follows we include a brief list of popular gof tests with basic notes.

1. Chi-Squared test. Also referred to as χ^2 test, is any statistical hypothesis test in which the sampling distribution of the test statistic is a chi-squared distribution when the null hypothesis is true. Chi-squared tests are often constructed from a sum of squared errors. Test statistics that follow a chi-squared distribution arise from an assumption of independent normally distributed data, which is valid in many cases due to the central limit theorem. A chi-squared test can then be used to reject the hypothesis that the data are independent [1].
2. Kolmogorov–Smirnov test. This test (K–S test or KS test) is a nonparametric test of the equality of continuous, one-dimensional probability distributions that can be used to compare a sample with a reference probability distribution (one-sample K–S test), or to compare two samples (two-sample K–S test). The Kolmogorov–Smirnov statistic quantifies a distance between the empirical distribution function of the sample and the cumulative distribution function of the reference distribution, or between the empirical distribution functions of two samples. The hypothesis regarding the distributional form is rejected if the test statistic, D, is greater than the critical value obtained from a table [2].
3. Cramér–von Mises criterion. This is a criterion used for judging the gof of a cumulative distribution function F* compared to a given empirical distribution function Fn, or for comparing two empirical distributions. If the value of the statistic T is larger than the tabulated values the null hypothesis can be rejected [3].
4. Anderson–Darling test. This is a statistical test of whether a given sample of data is drawn from a given probability distribution. When applied to testing if a normal distribution adequately describes a set of data. Normality is rejected if the statistic exceeds the required significance level [4].

5. Shapiro–Wilk test. This test utilized the null-hypothesis principle to check whether a sample $x_1,...,x_n$ came from a normally distributed population. The test statistic is called W. The user may reject the null hypothesis if W is below a predetermined threshold [5].
6. Akaike information criterion (AIC). This is a measure of the relative quality of statistical models for a given set of data. Given a collection of models for the data, AIC estimates the quality of each model, relative to each of the other models. Hence, AIC provides a means for model selection. It deals with the trade-off between the gof of the model and the complexity of the model. If all the candidate models fit poorly, AIC will not give any warning of that [6].

In all previous methods the emphasis is in determining whether sample A may be determined NOT to come from the same distribution as sample B. In our case sample A is the distribution of the events and B is Gaussian. What we are looking for is a method which ensures that normality IS attained. That is, given a sample A that it will approximate a normal distribution. This is quite different than being able to ascertain that A does not distribute normally.

3 Methodology

A method yielding solid numerical evidence which allows us to compare two algorithms is as follows.

Algorithm C. Compare 2 Methods

(a) A value of k is selected. Recall that an element is the average cost of solving k problems. Theoretical arguments allow us to conclude that any $k \geq 25$ will suffice.
(b) Select a set of algorithms to compare. For example, assume we wish to compare the behavior of a neural network (NN) trained with back-propagation (say NN1) vs. a NN trained with an evolutionary algorithm (say NN2).
(c) Select an algorithm from the set. Say we pick NN1.
(d) Make $i \leftarrow 1$.
(e) Make $j \leftarrow 1$.
(f) Select problem j to solve from a previously determined reservoir of problems (call it RP). We take advantage that, in general, the problems to solve may be automatically generated so as not to hand-pick a few of them. Then the values of the input variables of the generating function may be randomly assigned and the value of the dependent variable calculated. The input for NN1 then consists of the values of the input variables and NN1 is required to approximate the value of the dependent variable.
(g) Solve problem j with NN1. Calculate the approximation error. This is the "cost" of the solution of the problem j tackled with algorithm NN1.
(h) If $j = k$ go to step (i); otherwise make $j \leftarrow j + 1$ and go to step (f).
(i) Calculate the average cost of solving the last k problems. This is the i-th element of the distribution of costs.

(j) Are the elements normally distributed? If they are go to step l; otherwise make $i \leftarrow i + 1$ and go to step (e).
(l) Calculate the mean (μ_e) and standard deviation (σ_e) of the elements' distribution.
(m) Calculate the mean (μ) and standard deviation (σ) of the **probability distribution of the cost of the problems**: $\mu = \mu_e$; $\sigma = \sqrt{k}\sigma_e$. The two previous equalities are derived from the central limit theorem. They allow us to infer the parameters of the original population of the cost of solving a particular problem from the averaged behavior of the costs involved when solving several ones. It is very important to underline the fact that no assumption is made regarding the distribution of the costs.
(n) Select the desired reliability of the bounds we are to obtain. For example, assume it to be 0.8. We shall obtain bounds on the behavior of the cost (c) of solving a problem with reliability better than 80% from Chebyshev's inequality:

$$P(\mu - m\sigma \leq c \leq \mu + m\sigma) > 1 - 1/m^2 \tag{1}$$

If we select $m = \sqrt{5}$ we have that $P(c_{NN1} \leq \mu_{NN1} + \sqrt{5}\,\sigma_{NN1}) > 0.8$. In other words, the probability that NN1's error of approximation of for any problem is smaller than $\mu_{NN1} + \sqrt{5}\,\sigma_{NN1}$ is better than 0.8. We denote this least upper bound by lub_{NN1}. $\square$

We may repeat the same experiment, for the same set of problems for NN2. And, as above, we will obtain an upper bound on the approximation which is now given by $\mu_{NN2} + \sqrt{5}\,\sigma_{NN2}$. We call this value lub_{NN2}.

Finally we compare lub_{NN1} with lub_{NN2}. If $lub_{NN1} < lub_{NN2}$ then NN1 is better than NN2, in general (within the specified statistical limits).

3.1 Discussion of the Methodology

We may see that this methodology is radically different than the usual one. The results do not depend on a very limited set of selected problems. In that case even when an algorithm's performance is outstanding, one may not extend the conclusion to other environments. In this case, however, the values of lub_{NN1} and lub_{NN2} are solid and apply for the whole set of problems being solved and any of a similar kind. On the other hand, a comparative analysis, along the same lines, may be applied to as many algorithms as desired. That is, this methodology yields a solid and statistically valid method to compare any number of algorithms and is particularly useful in CI, where closed mathematical models of the algorithms are difficult to come by. The whole methodology rests on step (j) of Algorithm C: "Are the elements normally distributed?" Unless we are able to ascertain normality we cannot reached the desired goal. And therefore, the following discussion is basically relevant.

4   The Modified Chi-Squared Distribution (Л Distribution)

The basic idea rests on being able to answer the question: "How probable is it to compute an experimental value of Л larger than ξ (which will denote the "critical value") for a set of data which are normally distributed?"

We divide the observation space in quantiles. Say Q is the number of quantiles, O_i is the number of events observed in the *i-th* quantil, E_i is the number of expected events in the *i-th* quantil and Φ is the minimum number of observations required per quantil. Also let p denote the probability that Л exceeds ξ when data is normally distributed and there are at least Φ events in all quantiles. Then

$$\text{Л} = \sum_{i=1}^{Q} \frac{(O_i - E_i)^2}{E_i} \wedge [\, O_i \geq \Phi \; \forall i \,] \tag{2}$$

Since we require the events distribution to be normal, we may find the intervals (in standard deviations) which we ought to select to ensure that $E_i = 1/Q$. This implies that when the distribution reaches normality $E_i = \sum O_i/Q \, \forall i$. For example, if $Q = 10$ the left and right values of the quantiles and the corresponding area of the normal curve would be as shown in Fig. 1.

Quantil	Left_i	Righ_i	Area_i
1	-5.0000	-1.2815	0.1000
2	-1.2815	-0.8416	0.1000
3	-0.8416	-0.5243	0.1000
4	-0.5243	-0.2532	0.1000
5	-0.2532	0.0000	0.1000
6	0.0000	0.2532	0.1000
7	0.2532	0.5243	0.1000
8	0.5243	0.8416	0.1000
9	0.8416	1.2815	0.1000
10	1.2815	5.0000	0.1000

Fig. 1. Intervals for Q = 10

Л is smaller the closer the events are to the expected normal values. Therefore, if Л $\leq \xi$ we know the data are normally distributed with probability $> 1 - p$ and step (l) of algorithm C above may be reached. Notice that this is quite different from the χ^2 test where the statistics can be used to **reject** the hypothesis that the data are independent. A Monte Carlo Experiment [7] may be designed to find the value of ξ along the following lines.

4.1   Monte Carlo Method to Find Л

1. Set Q, Φ and p.
2. Calculate the intervals for which 1/Q observations in a gaussian bell will be found relative to σ. For example, assume that $Q = 10$. In this case we expect to find 1/10 of the observations between -5σ and -1.2815σ; 1/10 between -1.2815σ and 0.8416σ and so on.

3. The expected value of Л is defined as per Eq. (2).
4. Make an iterative search for the value of Л which satisfies (2). We will explore a set
   of values $Л_i$ for i = 1, 2, ..., m. We need two parameters for this purpose:
   (a) The starting value of Л (call it $Л_0$)
   (b) The increment between $Л_i$ and $Л_{i+1}$ (call it $δ_Л$.)
5. Since we require 5 observations per quantil we need, at least, 50 observations. For
   practical reasons we explore up to 90 observations. We require that the probability
   of finding Л by chance alone will be smaller than $1 - p$. In Fig. 2 we illustrate the
   process for $Л_0$ = 4.0 and $δ_Л$ = 0.05, yielding Л = 3.2.

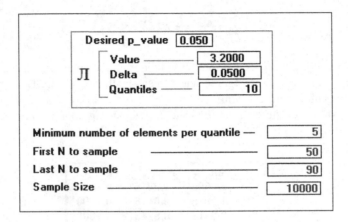

Fig. 2. Parameter settings for Л

The Monte Carlo experiment consists of generating a sequence of 50,...,90
Gaussian samples as illustrated in Fig. 3 and counting the number of observations in
each of the 10 intervals, as illustrated in Table 1. We then calculate the values of Л and
the number of observations per quantil. If $Л < Л_0$ and $|O_i| > Φ$ the sample is com-
pliant. We start by assuming a value of $Л_0$ which is larger than its true minimum value.
From (2) we can see that smaller values of Л will denote better fit to a gaussian
distribution.

Therefore, we start with a "large" value for $Л_0$ and determine its compliance. Larger
values of Л will, intuitively, comply with greater ease than smaller ones. Therefore, the
initial guess for Л is iteratively decremented until the samples do no longer comply with
the conditions of (2). At which point we have determined (with a precision of $±δ_H$) the
lowest compliant value of Л.

To illustrate consider the third item. It reflects a number of observations of 3, 3, 13,
12, 7, 9, 15, 13, 4, 8 for deciles 1–10, respectively. The total number of observations is,
therefore, 3 + 3 + 13 + 12 + 7 + 9 + 15 + 13 + 4 + 8 = 87.

This sample is not-compliant because there are three deciles where the number of
observations is below the required minimum; also because the value of Л is larger than

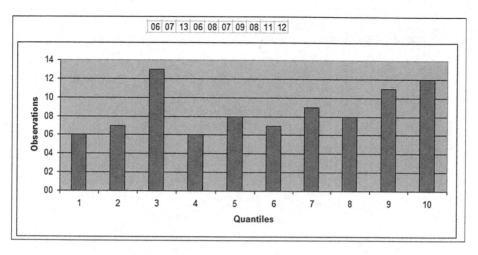

Fig. 3. Observations per quantile for sample 1

Table 1. Monte Carlo experiment

Sample	Л	"x" if not compliant
06071306080709081112	6.4482759	x
10031410080710100906	8.9770115	x
03031312070915130408	20.4712644	x
08070806130509121108	6.9080460	x
05110810040817100509	14.7241379	x
09080909080906071012	2.7701149	
10080808110707071011	2.7701149	
07080710100711090711	3.0000000	
10100909071006071009	2.3103448	
07071109090708120809	3.0000000	
09070810100710110609	2.7701149	

$Л_0$. Samples such as this are produced and analyzed 10,000 times. Then the proportion of compliant samples is calculated. This is done for $n = 50,...,90$. In the Fig. 4 every point corresponds to 10,000 samples.

It may be seen that for all the range ($50 < n < 90$) a value of 3.2 guarantees that the observations are Gaussian with a probability of, at least, 0.95. In other words, given a random sample, a calculated value of Л smaller than 3.2 will guarantee that the observed sample population is Gaussian. The pseudo-code for the algorithm is presented next.

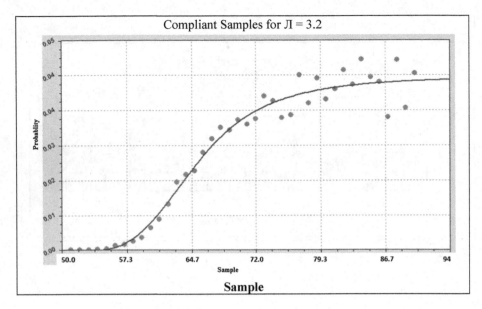

Fig. 4. Proportion of compliant samples for Л = 3.2.

Algorithm G. Ensure data are Normally Distributed.

```
p ←0.95; SS ← 10,000; Л ← 5; δ ← 0.05   ; Initialize parameters
while true                               ; Loop while Л is not tight enough
        NM ← QΦ-1                        ; Minimum observations
        for k =1 to 40
                NM++
                Eᵢ=NM/Q                  ; Expected observations per quantile
                for S = 1 to SS
                        noncompliant ← 0
                        O(i) ← 0 ∀i
                        for i=1 to NM
                                x ← Gauss_01()   ; Normal rand between 0 and 1
                                j ← Quantil(x)   ; j = Quantile number of x
                                O(j) ← O(j)+1    ; Observations in the j-th quantile
                        endfor
                        Лᴛᴇꜱᴛ ← 0
                        MO ← true        ; Minimum observations flag
                        for i=1 to Q
                                if O(i) < Φ
                                        MO ← false
```

```
                              endif
                              Л_TEST  ← Л_TEST  + (O(i) - E_i )²/E_i
                   endfor
               if  MO=false or Л_TEST > ξ
                       noncompliant ++  ; Sample does not comply
                   endif
             endfor
               NC(k) ← noncompliant/SS          ; Prop. of noncompliant samples
         Endfor
         ℓ ← false
         for i=QΦ to NM
           if NC(i) ≤ 1- p
                ℓ ← true                        ; Indicate undesired compliance
             endif
           endfor
         If  ℓ                                  ; See if at least one complied
             Л ← Л - δ                          ; Test a tighter bound
         else
                exit While                      ; Tight upper bound was found
         endif
   endwhile
```

4.2   Critical Values for Л Distribution

Once we have a method to determine the critical values (ξ) of the Л distribution it is possible to get a table of such ξ for different combinations of Q and p. A short table of the calculated ξ s of Л is presented in Table 2.

Table 2. Critical values of the Л distribution

Quantiles	p	ξ
10	0.99	1.90
10	0.95	3.20
10	0.90	4.05
12	0.99	2.95
12	0.95	4.55
12	0.90	5.80
14	0.99	4.10
14	0.95	6.55
14	0.90	8.00

5 Application

We illustrate the application of the method to three case studies. We make a brief description of the problem and present the results. In all cases $Q \leftarrow 10$, $p \leftarrow 0.95$ and $\xi = 3.2$.

5.1 Case Study 1. Training Neural Networks with Different Metrics

Neural networks are very frequently trained with the back-propagation (BP) learning algorithm. BP measures the RMS training error and tries to reduce it iteratively. An alternative, first explored in [8], is to abandon the RMS metric and replace it with alternative ones. In this case BP is no longer applicable and we relied on a genetic algorithm. The defined alternative metrics were MEE [Mean Exponential Error] $(1/S[\sum_S \sum_1^o 10^{|f_i - o_i|}])$; MAE [Mean Absolute Error] $(1/S[\sum_S \sum_1^o |f_i - o_i|])$, Mean Squared Error [MSE] $(1/S[\sum_S \sum_1^o (f_i - o_i)^2])$ and SAE [Supremum Maximum Error] $(\max_{s,i} |f_i - o_i|)$. Where $o \leftarrow$ output neurons, $s \leftarrow$ sample size, $f_i \leftarrow$ expected value, $o_i \leftarrow$ observed value. 2,896 problems were solved (86 batches of 36 problems each were analyzed. Data sets were automatically generated). The relative performances are shown in Table 3.

Table 3. Least upper bound for training metrics

Metric	MEE	MAE	SAE	MSE	BP (MSE)
lub	0.0574	0.0934	0.9504	0.1004	0.1767

The results show that NNs trained with MEE are = $0.1767/0.0574 \sim 30$ times more effective than those trained with BP. Likewise, NNs trained using MEE are ~ 1.7 times better than those trained with MSE [9].

5.2 Case Study 2. Testing Different Breeds of Genetic Algorithms

Four types of GAs and a Hill-Climber were compared: TGA [Holland's Simple GA with eliTism], CHC [Cross Generational elitist selection, Heterogeneous recombination and Cataclysmic mutation GA], SGA [Statistical GA], EGA [Eclectic GA] and RMH [Random Mutation Hill Climber]. 3,312 problems were solved (92 batches of 36 problems each were analyzed. Data sets were automatically generated from constrained functions). The relative performances are shown in Table 4.

Table 4. Least upper bound for GAs

Algorithm	EGA	TGA	SGA	CHC	RMH
lub	0.1186	0.3408	0.3899	0.4206	0.5226

EGA yields minima ~ 2.9 better than those for the classical GA and ~ 4.5 times more efficient than the hill climber [10].

5.3   Case Study 3. Clustering with Different Methods

Four clustering (non-supervised) algorithms were compared; a fifth one (supervised) was included for reference purposes. The non-supervised algorithms were the following: K-means, Fuzzy C-Means, ENCLUS and CBE (Clustering based on Maximum Entropy). Every method has a unique training methodology. CBE was trained using the Eclectic GA (from above). The supervised method was a NN trained with BP. 3,116 clustering problem were solved. The relative performances are shown in Table 5.

Table 5. Least upper bound for non-supervised clustering

Method	CBE	ENCLUS	Fuzzy C-Means	K-Means	NN
lub	0.080	0.130	0.540	0.560	0.074

CBE resulted slightly worse than NN. Such a small difference is remarkable given that supervised methods are much more efficient than non-supervised ones. The comparison between CBE and K-Means (both are non-supervised) shows that CBE is 7 times better than K-Means. It is almost 2 times better than ENCLUS, the second best of all non-supervised methods [11].

6   Conclusions

The statistical analysis of CI methods allows us to establish a solid comparative index between alternative methods aimed at solving the same set of problems. As opposed to typical subjective methods, where no "hard" measure of efficiency is extracted, the critical points of JI (analogous to the critical points of χ^2) give us a number to shoot at. In this methodology all we have to do is solve one problem after another, calculate the values of the resulting samples, calculate JI and stop if JI $< \xi$. We know any method will eventually fulfill the previous inequality, at which point the samples are gaussian. Under a different light, what we are doing is finding the size of the smallest sample which is fully representative of the system under study.

The large number of problems we have to solve is the price we have to pay. In CI, however, this poses no practical problem of concern since computer computation is relatively cheap. This state of affairs, however, does not hold true in other candidate disciplines (i.e. Sociology, Psychology, Economics, etc.) where the sampling process may be expensive and slow. On the other hand, this is a one time only expenditure. Once the superiority of one algorithm over another is established (for a certain p) no discussion is further required.

From the case studies we see that this simple procedure allows us to quantitatively and precisely compare several algorithms of interest. The goodness of any of these is statistically significant and subjective criteria are eliminated.

References

1. Dahiya, R.C., Gurland, J.: Pearson chi-squared test of fit with random intervals. Biometrika **59**(1), 147–153 (1972)
2. Lilliefors, H.W.: On the Kolmogorov-Smirnov test for normality with mean and variance unknown. J. Am. Stat. Assoc. **62**(318), 399–402 (1967)
3. Darling, D.A.: The Kolmogorov-Smirnov, Cramer-von Mises tests. Ann. Math. Stat. **28**(4), 823–838 (1957)
4. Razali, N.M., Wah, Y.B.: Power comparisons of Shapiro-Wilk, Kolmogorov-Smirnov, Lilliefors and Anderson-Darling tests. J. Stat. Model. Anal. **2**(1), 21–33 (2011)
5. Royston, P.: Approximating the Shapiro-Wilk W-Test for non-normality. Stat. Comput. **2**(3), 117–119 (1992)
6. Akaike, H.: AKaike's information criterion. In: Lovric, M. (ed.) International Encyclopedia of Statistical Science, p. 25. Springer, Heidelberg (2011). doi:10.1007/978-3-642-04898-2_110
7. Binder, K.: Introduction: theory and "Technical" aspects of Monte Carlo simulations. In: Binder, K. (ed.) Monte Carlo Methods in Statistical Physics. Topics in Current Physics, pp. 1–45. Springer, Heidelberg (1986). doi:10.1007/978-3-642-82803-4_1
8. Kuri-Morales, A.: Non-standard norms in genetically trained neural networks. In: 2000 IEEE Symposium on Combinations of Evolutionary Computation and Neural Networks. IEEE (2000)
9. Barnard, E.: Optimization for training neural nets. IEEE Trans. Neural Netw. **3**(2), 232–240 (1992)
10. Kuri-Morales, A.F., Aldana-Bobadilla, E., López-Peña, I.: The best genetic algorithm II. In: Castro, F., Gelbukh, A., González, M. (eds.) MICAI 2013. LNCS, vol. 8266, pp. 16–29. Springer, Heidelberg (2013). doi:10.1007/978-3-642-45111-9_2
11. Aldana-Bobadilla, E., Kuri-Morales, A.: A clustering method based on the maximum entropy principle. Entropy **17**(1), 151–180 (2015)

Are Android Smartphones Ready to Locally Execute Intelligent Algorithms?

M. Ricardo Carlos[1], Fernando Martínez[1(✉)], Raymundo Cornejo[2],
and Luis C. González[1]

[1] Facultad de Ingeniería, Universidad Autónoma de Chihuahua,
31125 Chihuahua, Mexico
ricardo.carlos@gmail.com, {fmartine,lcgonzalez}@uach.mx
[2] CONACYT, Universidad Autónoma de Chihuahua, Chihuahua, Mexico
rcornejoga@conacyt.mx

Abstract. Given that thousands of applications are already available for smartphones, we may be inclined to believe that ubiquitous computing is just around the corner, with online processing in these mobile devices. But, how well prepared is current smartphone technology to support the execution of demanding algorithms? Surprisingly, few researchers have addressed the processing capabilities of currently available smartphones. In this paper we investigate some issues in this direction: we employed twelve algorithms for optimization and classification to profile the computational demands they place on current smartphones. For this purpose, we chose twelve devices that go from low to high-end models, from six different makers, and measured execution time, CPU and RAM usage while the devices were running the algorithms.

Keywords: Mobile computing · Optimization algorithms · Classification algorithms · Profiling

1 Introduction

The number of mobile devices in operation has continuously increased during the last decade. According to International Data Corporation (IDC), 337.2 million smartphones were shipped worldwide during the second quarter of 2015. This figure is 11.6% higher than the sales from the second quarter of 2014 [1], and high sales are expected in the future, since short smartphone replacement cycles have been observed worldwide among consumers [2]. United States citizens have short replacement cycles, replacing their smartphones after one year and nine months (while Mexican citizens have longer replacement cycles, replacing their smartphones after three years and three months). Shorter replacement cycles allow consumers to have access to better and faster storage, computing, and sensing capabilities with this type of devices, frequently upgraded by manufacturers. Therefore, these shorter cycles have increased the available computing and sensing capabilities for the mobile device market.

© Springer International Publishing AG 2017
O. Pichardo-Lagunas and S. Miranda-Jiménez (Eds.): MICAI 2016, Part II, LNAI 10062, pp. 15–25, 2017.
DOI: 10.1007/978-3-319-62428-0_2

The integration of sensing technologies (with accelerometers, gyroscopes, magnetometers, GPS, light, and proximity sensors, among others) enables smartphones to see, hear, and feel the user's environment. Therefore, the availability of the information provided by these sensors creates opportunities to infer different types of events for context-awareness, and to create applications for end users, third parties, crowds and groups [3].

Recent research has explored learning algorithms running in smartphones to represent, to some extent, the end users' activities [4]. Inferring and representing the user's activity might have positive implications in different domains such as fitness tracking, health monitoring, fall detection for vulnerable populations, context-aware behavior, and home and work automation [3]. Furthermore, activity recognition has been also explored in businesses and organizations where it is a valuable source of information for decision making processes. Companies have used activity recognition to present targeted advertisements, which are more relevant to their customers' preferences and activities. Similarly, activity recognition can assist with employee management and accounting for employee time. For example, health care companies can track the activities of their employees and improve their critical health processes, based on conflicting or time consuming activities. In crowd and group contexts, activity recognition has been used to track and analyze big data sets to automate tagging events such as traffic, places, emergency events or disasters. Although activity recognition is widely implemented in these three major types of application, only end user applications implement some algorithms in smartphones to recognize activities. Businesses and crowd work applications rely on back-end systems to perform heavy computing algorithms to collect and analyze data.

Machine learning (ML) can be well suited to treat problems of context-awareness for businesses and crowd work. ML capabilities can automatically adapt to the changes in input data created by the user, the available sensors, or environmental factors. Machine learning can also be used to detect malware in smartphones [5], and protect these devices from intrusions. Employing algorithms of this nature has been discussed in the literature, and pre-trained models are already available and deployed [6], but their actual viability to be trained in mobile devices, under normal operating conditions, has not been addressed. Furthermore, it is unclear whether if context-aware mobile applications can be supported with ML algorithms with online processing.

In this paper we address the following relevant open question: are current Android smartphones capable of handling the computational demands of these algorithms?[1] It is our understanding that, frequently, it's taken for granted that smartphones cannot deal with demanding computing tasks, which are left for server side applications. Our contribution in this work is to show how mobile phones perform when classifiers and optimization algorithms are run, to have a better perspective of what smartphones' current capabilities are, and provide some guidance in the implementation of such computing tasks.

---

[1] We chose the Android platform because it represents over 80% of the market share, and this preponderance is expected to remain in the near future [7].

2   Related Work

Mobile phones have evolved extensively, in so manner that today these are not just telephones but multimedia devices and computing nodes with high capabilities. High-end mobile phones have system-on-a-chip (SoC) embedded systems with multi-core ARM processors, with clocks running in the order of GHz, and at least 2 GB of memory. With high performance, low-power, general purpose CPUs, users now expect near PC-like performance and a rich user experience, including high-definition audio and video, high-quality multimedia, dynamic web content, responsive user interfaces, and 3D graphics. In order to meet user expectations, mobile devices must smoothly perform processing tasks at different levels: processor, local I/O, video, memory, cache, communication, application, and interaction with the user. In this section we review some of the benchmarking approaches that target hardware and software systems in mobile phone platforms. Then we present a few works that suggest how applications based on machine learning improve the user experience that fueled our motivation to state the question: are smartphones ready to locally execute intelligent algorithms? As far as we are aware, no previous work has reported how these algorithms perform on mobile phone architectures.

One of the current challenges in social computing is the management of large amounts of data. Indeed, the continuous increase in volume, variety, and velocity of Big Data exposes data centers to an energy utilization problem. Loghin et al. [8] explore the usage of wimpy nodes, mobile phone-like architectures, to achieve some data pre-processing which might help alleviate the storage and processing stress faced by data centers. The authors ran experiments demanding memory, server level communication, and read/write operations on the ARM big.LITTLE technology. The benchmark included Big Data frameworks such as the Hadoop Distributed File System, I/O data processing with Hadoop Map Reduce, and the Parallel Memory Bandwidth Benchmark. Overall performance of mobile phone-like architectures is around four orders below Intel Xeon-based servers. In terms of energy costs Loghin et al. found that, under low processing demands, ARM-based platforms are four times cheaper than Xeon servers but, with peak computing profiles, these servers demand 50% less energy than ARM systems.

One of the changes with the users' lifestyles is that mobile phones allow multitasking. Users can play games while chatting or listening to music, and the concurrent execution of applications increases battery energy usage. To some extent, users consider their mobile device as a repository of running applications. Pathak et al. [9] present *eprof*, a tool to profile the energy demands of applications running on smartphones. Their energy profiler accounts for power draw at hardware components, at program entities, and at the source code level. Five different free applications that require internet connectivity were ran on Android devices. The authors found that running the five applications for about half a minute can invoke 29–47 threads, 200k-6M routine calls, and that it took 0.35%–0.75% of the battery charge. The web browser was also tested using a

Google search, and GPS was used to determine user location. This activity consumes 2000 μAH, distributed among CPU (53%), 3G (31%), and GPS (16%).

The academic interest in studying how energy stored in the batteries of mobile phones is used comes from the direct impact this has on the user's experience. In fact, as demonstrated by Carrol and Heiser [10], the hardware components and services the user interacts with the most are the ones that put the most pressure on battery life. Using micro-benchmarks, the authors characterize power consumption at the system level. The Openmoko Neo Freerunner open source platform allowed them to take physical measurements directly on testing points, available on the main board. Resistors were inserted to measure current, and both current and voltage measurements helped calculate the power demands of CPU, memory, touchscreen, graphics hardware, audio, storage, and various networking interfaces. Their tests integrate such diverse functionality as voice communication, audio and video playback, web browsing, SMS, and email communication, media downloads, and gaming. Their findings indicate that energy is spent the most in Video playback (453 mW), GPS (143 mW), GSM call (1054 mW), SMS (302 mW), email GPRS (610 mW), and email Wifi (432 mW). This level of rich functionality increases the pressure on battery life, and deepens the need for effective energy management.

It can be realized that mobile system designers and computer architects are aware of computing capabilities and processing resources that must allow users to use the smartphone as they wish. Gutierrez et al. [11] considered relevant to measure the performance of interactive applications that are commonly used by users. Representative applications for streaming HD video, gaming, playing MP3 files, and browsing the web, were selected for the benchmark and results were compared against some features of the SPEC CPU2006 benchmark. Generally speaking, the authors found that smartphone applications are far from the SPEC benchmarks. They observed issues with massive application code footprints, missing instruction cache, and poor management of paged memory. An explanation for this level of poor performance of interactive applications is that most mobile applications are developed relying on high level abstractions and calls to shared libraries. This impacts the user's experience.

As illustrated, hardware and software benchmarks have been studied. Battery energy, data processing, application and code performance have been evaluated and characterized in order to inform the designers and architects of future smartphones. This helps envisage robust and high computing performance mobile applications that assist users in their everyday activities. Intelligent applications can keep low resources usage when running location-based systems that make use of the hunger energy consumers like the GSM, WiFi, and GPS sensors [12].

To the best of our knowledge, the stress machine learning algorithms put on mobile phone architectures is not documented in the literature. The next sections describe the experiments and results of running optimization and classification heuristics on smartphones, and our insights from this experience, to address this situation.

3 Experimental Setup

In order to test the processing capabilities of common smartphones, the execution times, memory, and CPU usage were evaluated for seven optimization algorithms and five classifiers, in twelve Android smartphones. The optimization algorithms were run to solve common simple and multi-objective test problems, and the tested classifiers were trained under supervised learning. Each algorithm was run twelve times on each smartphone. Only one CPU core was employed to run the algorithms.

The Android platform was selected because it has represented about 80% of the smartphones in use in the last years [13]. We tested ten mid-range Android devices with up to three years of use, currently the primary phones of their respective owners, as a baseline for the smartphones currently in service. We also a included a more recent high-end model (Samsung S6) and a six years old device (T-Mobile MyTouch), to get an idea of the differences that could be expected for newer and older models. The main characteristics of these devices are summarized in Table 1.

To put in context the capabilities of the smartphones, the same suite of tests was run on a Toshiba P55W-B5224 laptop with 16 GB of RAM and an Intel i7-4510U CPU, using a Java 1.8.0 run-time on a Ubuntu Gnu/Linux x86_64 system (kernel 3.13.0-63-generic SMP), running the algorithms in only one core.

We acknowledge the lack of control in the software installed in the smartphones, and that it can have a significant influence when performing benchmarks. However, the heterogeneity of operating systems, runtimes, and installed applications are inherent to the Android platform. The smartphones had different applications installed, since they were the primary mobile phone for their owners. The manufacturer's kernel and run-time environment were kept in all the smartphones.

Table 1. Characteristics of the smartphones used.

Device	Model	OS	Runtime	CPU cores	RAM	Chipset
1	LG Nexus 4	5.1.1	ART 2.1	Quad 1.5 GHz	2 GB	Qualcomm APQ8064
2	Sony D5316	5.0.2	ART 2.1	Quad 1.4 GHz	1 GB	Qualcomm MSM8928
3	Motorola Moto G	4.4.4	Dalvik 1.6	Quad 1.2 GHz	1 GB	Qualcomm MSM8226
4	Zuum P60	4.2.2	Dalvik 1.6	Quad 1.3 GHz	1 GB	MediaTek MT6582
5	LG D680	4.4.2	Dalvik 1.6	Dual 1.0 GHz	1 GB	Mediatek MT6577
6	Samsung SM-G925I	5.0.2	ART 2.1	Octa 2.1 GHz	3 GB	Samsung Exynos 7420
7	Samsung SM-N900V	4.4.4	Dalvik 1.6	Quad 2.27 GHz	3 GB	Qualcomm MSM8974
8	Samsung SGH-I337M	5.0.1	ART 2.1	Quad 1.89 GHz	2 GB	Qualcomm APQ8064AB
9	Motorola Moto G	5.1.0	ART 2.1	Quad 1.2 GHz	2 GB	Qualcomm MSM8226
10	T-Mobile MyTouch	2.3.4	Dalvik 1.4	Single 1.0 Ghz	768 MB	Qualcomm MSM8255
11	ZTE Blade L3 Plus	4.4.2	Dalvik 1.6	Quad 1.3 Ghz	1 GB	Mediatek MT6582
12	LG Nexus 5	5.1.1	ART 2.1	Quad 2.27 Ghz	2 GB	Qualcomm MSM8974

4   Optimization Algorithms

Four multi-objective algorithms, NSGA-II, a steady-state version of NSGA-II, SPEA2 and PAES, were used to solve the Kursawe test problem with three variables, employing a representation of the chromosome of type Real and a population of one hundred individuals. Crossover, mutation, and selection operations were performed randomly. The maximum number of evaluations was set to 25,000 for all multi-objective algorithms.

Three single-objective algorithms, PSO, Differential Evolution, and Evolution Strategy, were used to solve the Sphere problem with twenty variables. The default parameters used in the framework were kept for each these algorithms: for PSO, the swarm size was set to 50, mutation operations were performed, and was run for a maximum of 5,000 iterations; for Differential Evolution, the population size was 100, crossover and selection operations were performed, and the maximum of evaluations was set to 1,000,000; an elitist Evolution Strategy was evaluated for a maximum of 20,000 times, with $\mu = 1$ and $\lambda = 10$, using bit flip.

These algorithms and the test functions solved with them are frequently found in the literature, and were chosen as a representative sample of the type of calculations performed when working with optimization problems.

The algorithm implementations were provided by the 4.5 version of the jMetal framework, [14]. This framework was chosen because it offers readily available Java implementations of an array of both single and multi-objective optimization and test problems, with Java being the main programming language for the Android platform.

4.1   Results

The average execution times for each algorithm are summarized in Table 2.

The 2015 Samsung S6 was the fastest smartphone. During the execution of the algorithms, the OS reported for it an average CPU usage under 20%. As expected, the oldest phone (T-Mobile MyTouch from 2010), was the slowest (with execution times about 15 times longer than the S6) and had an average CPU usage close to 90%. For the other phones, the CPU usage was between 40% and 60%. The user-installed software running in the background in these devices might affect these results. However, we would expect the differences between devices to remain reasonably similar if we compare all phones with factory settings, due to the hardware specifications.

Hardware is not the only significant factor for smartphone performance, the OS and runtime environment seem to also be relevant for algorithm execution. The algorithms were executed on two Moto G phones with the same hardware, but the one with Android 5.1.0 and an ART 2.1.0 runtime solved the test problems in about half the time. The Samsung SM-N900V (Android 4.4.4, Dalvik 1.6.0) and the LG Nexus 5 (Android 5.1.1 and ART 2.1.0) have the same chipset, yet the first took almost twice the time of the latter to finish the tests. The smartphones with an ART runtime clearly outperformed those with Dalvik, even when the CPU architecture was comparable or equal.

Table 2. Rounded average execution times and standard deviations for genetic algorithms, in seconds.

Device	NSGAII		SSNSGAII		SPEA2		PAES		PSO		ES		DE	
	Avg	Std	Avg	Std	Avg	Std	Avg	Std	Avg	Std	Avg	Std	Avg	Std
1	7.7	0.1	160.6	0.7	41.5	0.5	2.2	0.1	9.4	0.2	11.5	0.3	74.9	0.4
2	8.4	0.6	179.1	1.7	45.3	1.1	2.2	0.1	10.3	0.4	11.6	1.0	55.8	1.4
3	17.6	0.8	354.4	1.0	92.1	1.0	4.8	0.4	22.1	0.4	23.0	0.8	173.6	1.0
4	20.4	0.4	432.6	9.7	110.2	2.4	5.8	0.8	27.2	0.5	27.5	1.0	198.9	1.6
5	18.5	1.5	310.5	3.6	82.9	1.4	4.7	1.0	19.5	2.0	23.6	3.8	151.5	3.2
6	**2.0**	0.0	**35.9**	1.0	**10.7**	0.6	**0.7**	0.1	**2.3**	0.1	**4.0**	0.4	**17.2**	0.3
7	14.2	0.8	232.6	10.5	60.9	1.2	3.7	0.6	15.2	0.7	20.0	1.1	167.1	0.9
8	7.9	1.0	155.7	9.7	34.7	1.1	1.7	0.1	6.2	0.3	8.7	0.5	60.4	0.8
9	9.6	0.1	206.2	0.9	52.3	0.6	2.5	0.1	12.2	0.1	13.1	0.8	65.1	0.3
10	27.7	1.1	536.8	2.2	149.1	1.7	7.4	0.6	31.1	0.9	36.4	1.8	328.1	3.4
11	18.0	0.1	394.6	1.2	104.8	0.8	4.8	0.5	25.3	0.4	23.9	1.4	150.1	0.5
12	3.8	0.1	79.4	4.8	23.2	1.2	1.2	0.1	4.2	0.1	6.5	0.3	42.7	0.3

Memory assignment was not consistent among the smartphones. The T-Mobile MyTouch had a maximum assigned memory under 6 MB, with an average around 3 MB. The S6 had a maximum of almost 50 MB, and an average around 30 MB. The values for the other phones are distributed between those two extremes, with big variations between models. These variations are attributed to differences in the Android OS and runtime versions run in each device.

On average, the laptop required only 12.63% of the time used by the fastest smartphone (with SSNSGAII having the biggest performance difference, requiring only 5.82% of the fastest time, and ES showing the smallest difference, 22.29% of the fastest time).

5   Classifiers

A similar experiment was performed with five classification algorithms. Execution times, memory and CPU usage were evaluated on the Android smartphones for twelve test runs.

The five classifiers employed were: a C4.5 decision tree; KNN, considering fifteen neighbours; a Random Forest with fifteen trees; a support vector machine with a linear kernel; and a multi-layer perceptron, with one hidden layer. The SVM implementation was provided by LIBSVM [15], JSAT [16] provided the other algorithms. These libraries were chosen because they provide Java implementations of the evaluated classifiers.

The data set employed for this experiment consisted of 500 items, labeled for five different categories. These items are histograms obtained from a bag-of-words methodology [17] to classify acceleration signals in one axis. Each item has 250 features, stored as integer values. The classifiers were trained with 60%

of the data and the other 40% was used to test the models. While the same data was employed to train and test all algorithms, it was re-tagged for two categories to be used for the MLP.

5.1   Results

The average execution times for the training of each algorithm on the tested smartphones are summarized in Table 3.

Table 3. Rounded average execution times and standard deviations for classification algorithms, in seconds.

Device	C45		KNN		RFOREST		SVM		MLP	
	Avg	Std	Avg	Std	Avg	Std	Avg	Std	Avg	Std
1	4.54	0.13	5.23	0.08	4.08	0.09	4.21	0.18	11.93	0.29
2	3.2	0.16	4.10	0.12	2.70	0.08	2.97	0.18	12.88	0.28
3	4.35	0.68	6.00	0.52	2.92	0.55	2.41	0.59	30.58	0.72
4	5.04	0.39	6.63	0.29	3.82	0.30	3.59	0.31	31.34	0.39
5	5.54	0.97	7.55	1.14	4.35	0.78	4.48	0.84	27.99	1.91
6	**1.31**	0.09	**1.58**	0.06	**1.21**	0.06	**1.17**	0.06	**6.02**	2.16
7	2.75	0.66	3.21	0.54	2.04	0.50	1.61	0.55	8.56	2.35
8	3.42	0.19	3.68	0.17	2.97	0.23	2.73	0.25	8.04	0.51
9	4.10	0.22	4.96	0.13	3.51	0.09	3.74	0.26	15.41	0.37
10	8.53	0.57	10.90	0.48	5.69	0.50	5.12	0.65	43.93	0.68
11	4.90	0.40	6.13	0.28	3.29	0.31	3.70	0.36	32.28	0.29
12	3.26	0.23	4.43	0.11	2.95	0.12	3.24	0.14	14.25	0.16

The ranking of the smartphones is similar to the one obtained for the optimization algorithms. The Galaxy Note 3 (SM-N900V) had the biggest change in ranking, going from the seventh place in the previous test to almost the top in this one. This big change might be attributed to the owner performing an emergency factory reset, removing some applications that might have been running in the background for our previous test. This noticeable change in performance puts in perspective that the impact of the diversity of conditions found in Android smartphones must not be underestimated.

Except for the SM-N900V, the devices running ART also outperformed those running Dalvik for this test. This finding, together with the performance of the newest device, shows the big advances that are being made in mobile platforms, both in terms of hardware and software.

In this test, unsurprisingly, the laptop also outperformed the smartphones. It required 14.69% of the time used by the fastest smartphone (with MLP having the biggest time difference, requiring 4.32% of the fastest smartphone time).

6   Discussion

Our results show that even modest smartphones can handle low scale applications of optimization and classification tasks.

If we extrapolate execution times to big datasets, or more complex optimization problems, we might quickly run into unacceptable time scales. The current workflow of running the intensive calculations in more powerful machines and just deploying the pre-trained models in smartphones is clearly justified.

The improvement in computing power is clear when comparing the older phones with the more recent ones. If this trend continues, the possibility of smartphones running more complex problems should not be discarded.

We found very noticeable variations in resource usage, which might be caused by both hardware and software differences. For example, CPU utilization was more consistent in some devices (see Fig. 1). This is suspected to be caused by the operating system having to interrupt our process in order to perform some background task. A common situation probably caused by hardware limitations, the number of applications running in the background, the runtime, or a combination of these.

The differences in standard deviation for the execution times are probably related to the previously mentioned situation. And these variations in execution times might have repercussions in the usability of the device, which in turn could play a significant role in the acceptance of the users for applications that run these kinds of algorithms.

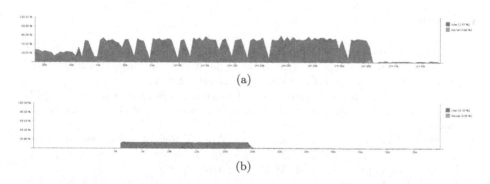

Fig. 1. CPU usage for an execution of NSGAII, for (a) Device 8, and (b) Device 6.

While running the tests, an increase in temperature was felt in most devices, enough to be noticeable when holding the smartphone or having it at rest in the front trouser pocket. This situation, and the impact in battery life, will probably be influential in the choice of the users of using, or not using, applications relying on this kind of processing. A possible solution to these objections could be to schedule the intensive processing to be performed when the smartphone is being charged and is not being actively used by its owner (for example, at night).

7   Conclusions and Future Work

We performed an exploratory evaluation of execution times and resource usage for java implementations of optimization and classification algorithms in Android smartphones. The fastest device took, on average, 6–8 times longer to run the evaluated algorithms than a laptop computer. Considering that the other smartphones were about 7 times slower for optimization tasks, and three times slower for supervised learning, it is clear that the current workflow of deploying only pre-trained models in smartphones is justified if we are working with big datasets or complex problems.

However, the execution times for low scale applications are acceptable, suggesting smartphones might be underused for this kind of tasks. Potential use cases for this type of algorithms include the custom refinement of previously generated models for contextual applications, by performing optimization or training classifiers on data acquired in the specific context of the device's owner. Educational software that can show real life applications of these algorithms are another area of opportunity, with the possibility to put data acquisition and model training, literally, in the hands of students.

As for future work, the lower computational capacity of smartphones might be compensated by performing calculations when the device is charging and not in use. This strategy, and its energetic efficiency, remain to be explored. The viability of distributed computing using smartphones is another possible research topic.

References

1. IDC: Worldwide smartphone market posts 11.6% year-over-year growth in Q2 2015, the second highest shipment total for a single quarter, according to IDC (2015). http://www.idc.com/getdoc.jsp?containerId=prUS25804315
2. Entner, R.: International Comparisons: The Handset Replacement Cycle (2013). http://mobilefuture.org/resources/international-comparisons-the-handset-replacement-cycle-2
3. Lockhart, J.W., Pulickal, T., Weiss, G.M.: Applications of mobile activity recognition. In: Proceedings of the 2012 ACM Conference on Ubiquitous Computing, UbiComp 2012, pp. 1054–1058. ACM, New York (2012)
4. Reyes-Ortiz, J.L., Oneto, L., Samà, A., Parra, X., Anguita, D.: Transition-aware human activity recognition using smartphones. Neurocomputing **171**, 754–767 (2016)
5. Chen, S., Xue, M., Tang, Z., Xu, L., Zhu, H.: Stormdroid: a streaminglized machine learning-based system for detecting android malware. In: Proceedings of the 11th ACM on Asia Conference on Computer and Communications Security, pp. 377–388. ACM (2016)
6. Alammar, J.: Supercharging android apps with tensorflow (2016). https://jalammar.github.io/Supercharging-android-apps-using-tensorflow/
7. IDC: Smartphone Growth Expected to Drop to Single Digits in 2016, Led by China's Transition from Developing to Mature Market, According to IDC (2016). http://www.idc.com/getdoc.jsp?containerId=prUS41061616

8. Loghin, D., Tudor, B.M., Zhang, H., Ooi, B.C., Teo, Y.M.: A performance study of big data on small nodes. Proc. VLDB Endow. **8**(7), 762–773 (2015)
9. Pathak, A., Hu, Y.C., Zhang, M.: Where is the energy spent inside my app? Fine grained energy accounting on smartphones with eprof. In: Proceedings of the 7th ACM European Conference on Computer Systems, pp. 29–42. ACM (2012)
10. Carroll, A., Heiser, G.: An analysis of power consumption in a smartphone. In: USENIX Annual Technical Conference, vol. 14 (2010)
11. Gutierrez, A., Dreslinski, R.G., Wenisch, T.F., Mudge, T., Saidi, A., Emmons, C., Paver, N.: Full-system analysis and characterization of interactive smartphone applications. In: 2011 IEEE International Symposium on Workload Characterization (IISWC), pp. 81–90. IEEE (2011)
12. Papandrea, M.: A smartphone-based energy efficient and intelligent multi-technology system for localization and movement prediction. In: 2012 IEEE International Conference on Pervasive Computing and Communications Workshops (PERCOM Workshops), pp. 554–555. IEEE (2012)
13. IDC: Global market share held by the leading smartphone operating systems in sales to end users from 1st quarter 2009 to 1st quarter 2016 (2016). http://www.statista.com/statistics/266136/global-market-share-held-by-smartphone-operating-systems
14. Durillo, J.J., Nebro, A.J., Alba, E.: The jMetal framework for multi-objective optimization: design and architecture. In: 2010 IEEE Congress on Evolutionary Computation (CEC), pp. 1–8. IEEE (2010)
15. Chang, C.C., Lin, C.J.: LIBSVM: a library for support vector machines. ACM Trans. Intell. Syst. Technol. **2**, 27:1–27:27 (2011). Software available at http://www.csie.ntu.edu.tw/cjlin/libsvm
16. Raff, E.: JSAT: Java statistical analysis tool (2015). https://github.com/EdwardRaff/JSAT
17. Wang, J., Liu, P., She, M.F., Nahavandi, S., Kouzani, A.: Bag-of-words representation for biomedical time series classification. Biomed. Sig. Process. Control **8**(6), 634–644 (2013)

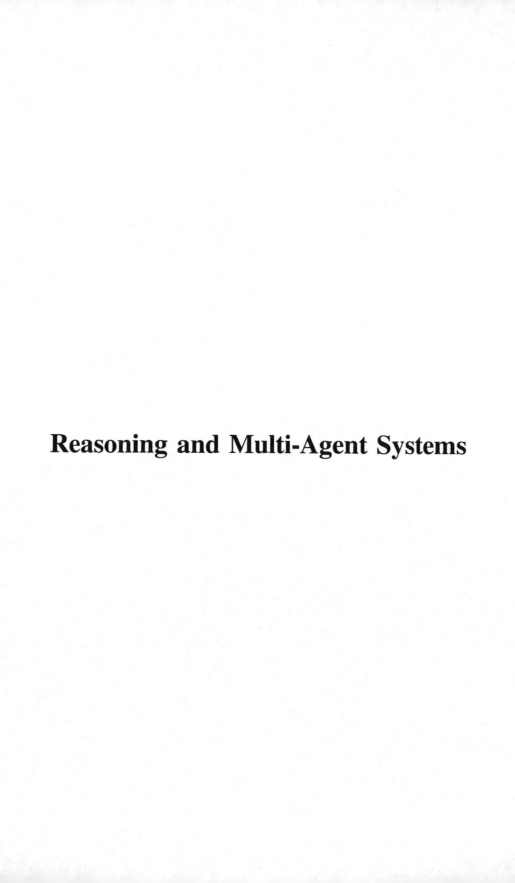

Reasoning and Multi-Agent Systems

Large Scale Reasoning Using Allen's Interval Algebra

Matthew Mantle[✉], Sotirios Batsakis, and Grigoris Antoniou

University of Huddersfield, Huddersfield, UK
{m.e.mantle,s.batsakis,g.antoniou}@hud.ac.uk

Abstract. This paper proposes and evaluates a distributed, parallel ap- proach for reasoning over large scale datasets using Allen's Inter- val Alge- bra (IA). We have developed and implemented algorithms that reason over IA networks using the Spark distributed processing frame- work. Experiments have been conducted by deploying the algorithms on computer clusters using synthetic datasets with various characteristics. We show that reasoning over datasets consisting of millions of interval relations is feasible and that our implementation scales effectively. The size of the IA networks we are able to reason over is far greater than those found in previously published works.

Keywords: Qualitative temporal reasoning · Distributed computing · MapReduce

1 Introduction

Temporal information often exists in a qualitative form, for example *'Alice brushed her teeth before Bob went to bed'*. In this description no quantitative, numeric measurements of time are used, instead events are described in terms of how they relate temporally, one event occured before another. A number frame- works provide formalisms for representing and reasoning over qualitative tem- poral data such as this. One of the most widely used is Allen's Interval Algebra (IA) [3]. IA has been widely used in planning [4] and scheduling [8,10], but also seen application in areas as diverse as medicine [18] and analysis of crime [17].

Recent years have seen rapid growth in the volume of data computing practi- tioners are required to deal. Data from business transactions, web traffic, social media and smart devices is being generated at a scale that creates challenges for analysis, reasoning and querying. Much of this vast data has a temporal aspect. For example, the introduction of sensors and meters into a wide variety of objects has resulted in huge amounts of timestamped data. One open area for investigation is the application of qualitative temporal reasoning techniques to these large scale datasets.

- Many huge datasets contain temporal information that is only available in qualitative form, e.g. those originating in natural language such as social

© Springer International Publishing AG 2017
O. Pichardo-Lagunas and S. Miranda-Jiménez (Eds.): MICAI 2016, Part II, LNAI 10062, pp. 29–41, 2017.
DOI: 10.1007/978-3-319-62428-0_3

media posts, email archives, case notes in electronic medical records. Reasoning over this data e.g. to build a timeline of medical history may only be possible using qualitative techniques.

- Even when the origin of the data is numeric it may be beneficial to represent time qualitatively. For example, in smart homes events such as entering a room are recorded with timestamps. Converting these timestamps to time intervals representing activities such as eating, sleeping etc. would allow for qualitative reasoning. Inferring the relations between these activities could then be used as a basis for scheduling automated tasks.
- Qualitative reasoning is often suited to situations where datasets are incomplete. Data collected from sensor devices is often noisy and records are often missing or incomplete. Rather than discarding records or assigning assumed values, qualitative reasoning frameworks are able to represent indefinite information, allowing them to provide correct (though less precise) solutions [9].

The main contribution of this paper lies in the development of parallel agorithms for qualitative temporal reasoning. An implementation of Allen's Interval Algebra has been developed for use with large scale datasets in a distributed environment. The rest of the paper is organised as follows. Section 2 provides background information on Allen's Interval Algebra and the Apache Spark cluster computing framework. Section 3 describes related work. Section 4 describes our implementation of Interval Algebra for the Spark platform. Experiments and results are provided in Sect. 5, and conclusions and future work in Sect. 6.

2   Background

2.1   Allen's Interval Algebra

Allen's Interval Algebra provides a formalism for qualitative descriptions of time [3]. Specifically, IA is concerned with time intervals. Allen describes 13 possible binary relations that can exist between a pair of intervals. These are shown in Table 1. Six of the relations have an inverse e.g. the inverse of during (d) is contains (di). Where the relation between two intervals is indefinite, a set is used to describe a disjunction of possible basic relations that could hold between the two intervals. For example $X\{b, m, o\}Y$, is interpreted as interval X either happens *before*, *meets* or *overlaps* interval Y. If no information is known, the relation could any of the thirteen basic relations $\{b, bi, m, mi, o, oi, s, si, d, di, f, fi, e\}$, this is denoted by I.

A collection of three or more intervals with relations defined between these intervals can be represented as a directed graph, an *IA network*, where each node is a time interval and the label on each edge is the relation between a pair of intervals. Figure 1 shows an example. For simplicity, loops are not shown and nor are inverses of relations. Plus, for clarity, if there is no information regarding the relation between two intervals, rather than showing a disjunction of all 13 basic relations, I, the label simply is not shown.

Table 1. Allen's basic relations

Relation	Symbol	Inverse	Visual Representation
X *before* Y	b	bi	XXXX YYYY
X *meets* Y	m	mi	XXXXYYYY
X *overlaps* Y	o	oi	XXXX YYYY
X *starts* Y	s	si	XXXX YYYYYYYY
X *during* Y	d	di	XXXX YYYYYYYY
X *finishes* Y	f	fi	XXXX YYYYYYYY
X *equals* Y	eq	eq	XXXX YYYY

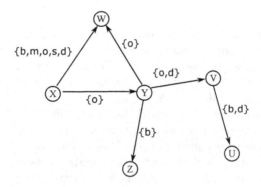

Fig. 1. A simple IA network

Reasoning Using Interval Algebra. The reasoning problem for Allen's algebra involves determining the smallest set of possible relations between all pairs of intervals. This can be viewed as a type of constraint satisfaction problem. A widely used approach for solving such problems, and the one proposed by Allen is path consistency [3], specified by the following formula, and described in more detail below.

$$\forall i, j, k R_s(i, k) \leftarrow R_i(i, k) \cap (R_j(i, j) \circ R_k(j, k)) \qquad (1)$$

Given any three intervals in the network i, j and k, the relation between i and j, and the relation between j and k, imply a relation between i and k. For example, in Fig. 1 the relations $X\{o\}Y$, and $Y\{b\}Z$, imply a relation between the intervals X and Z. Allen provides a table that describes all possible compositions of basic relations [3]. Part of this table can be seen in Table 2. Referring to Table 2 we can deduce that the relation between X and Z, the composition of *overlaps* and *before*, is *before*, $X\{b\}Z$. Given two disjunctive relations R_1 and R_2 the composition of these relations is the union of the composition of each basic relation in R_1 with each basic relation in R_2. In Fig. 1, the relation between Y and U, implied by $Y\{o,d\}V$ and $V\{b,d\}U$ is such an example. Again looking up the compositions of the basic relations in Table 2 and taking the union of the results, the composition of these disjunctive relations is $\{b,o,s,d\}$.

Table 2. Part of the composition table for interval algebra

	b	bi	d	di	o
b	{b}	I	{b,m,o,s,d}	{b}	{b}
bi	I	bi	{bi,oi,mi,d,f}	{bi}	{bi,mi,oi,d,f}
d	{b}	{bi}	{d}	I	{b,m,o,s,d}
di	{b,m,o,di,fi}	{bi,mi,oi,si,di}	{o,oi,s,si,d,di,e,f,fi}	{di}	{o,di,f}
o	{b}	{bi,mi,oi,si,di}	{o,s,d}	{b,m,o,di,fi}	{b,m,o}

The inference of relations places constraints on an IA network. For example, the inference arising from the composition of $X\{o\}Y$ and $Y\{o\}W$ implies the label on the edge (X, W) can be updated to $\{b,m,o\}$. Updating this value is only possible if the newly inferred relation is consistent with the existing relation between the pair of intervals, $\{b,m,o,s,d\}$. Consistency is checked by taking the intersection of the existing relation and the newly inferred relation. Basic relations are pairwise disjoint. Therefore, in the case where the intersection of two sets of possible relations is empty, this denotes an inconsistency in the network.

Reasoning over a temporal network is an iterative process. As new information is added to the network, and relations get updated, these updated relations form the basis for new inferences to be made, and further constrain existing relations. Once $Y\{b,o,s,d\}U$ is added to the network, it is then possible, through the composition of $X\{o\}Y$ and $Y\{b,o,s,d\}U$, to infer the relation between X and U. Therefore, the above path consistency formula is applied repeatedly until a fixed point is reached or an inconsistency is detected.

It is important to note that path consistency does not guarantee the consistency of the entire network [3], it only ensures the consistency of three node subsets of time intervals. As such it provides an approximation. In order to guarentee consistency, we would have to consider consistency between all nodes in a network, *n-consistency* (where n is the number of time intervals in the network). However, the computational complexity of implementing *n-consistency* is exponential with respect to n. An alternative would be to employ backtracking search alongside path consistency, which also has a runtime which is exponential. However, if expressiveness is limited by constructing sub-algebras, there are tractable sets of IA relations for which path consistency is a sound and complete method [11]. Despite path consistency being an approximation, it is a useful one. As Allen [3] states *'it provides us with enough temporal reasoning to participate in these tasks'* (comprehension, problem solving).

2.2 The Apache Spark Framework

Processing large quantities of data is typically accomplished using a cluster computing approach. A large dataset is split, distributed over a number of different machines, and then processed in parallel. Cluster computing frameworks provide programming models for developing distributed applications, as well as handling aspects such as managing resources, load balancing and fault tolerance. The implementation in this paper uses the Apache Spark framework [1]. The Spark API provides many operations that can be executed in parallel. These borrow many ideas from functional programming: *map, reduce, join, filter* etc. A key feature of the Spark framework is the capacity to maintain datasets in memory through a *cache* action [16]. This is especially useful for iterative tasks where the same dataset needs to be visited several times. In the more established MapReduce based frameworks data is written to disk after each *map* or *reduce* action. Spark datasets can be stored in memory allowing them to be easily re-used without this performance overhead. The implementation of a temporal reasoner is such an example. As an existing IA network needs to be merged with newly inferred relations repeatedly, it can take advantage of Spark's caching capabilities.

3 Related Work

When analysing related work, the closely related area of spatial reasoning is also considered. There are examples of frameworks that provide analysis of large scale spatial-temporal datasets. For example, SpatialHadoop [2] is a MapReduce framework designed specifically to work with spatial datasets. It extends the core Hadoop code base to provide spatial index structures and spatial operations e.g. R-trees, range queries, kNN and spatial join [7]. Experiments conducted on datasets consisting of billions of data items show SpatialHadoop offering significant performance advantages over standard Hadoop based implementations. However, SpatialHadoop uses metric point based representations, rather than qualitative ones. There appear to be no examples of qualitative spatial-temporal reasoning over large scale datasets using a distributed computing approach.

There are several examples of applications that provide qualitative spatial-temporal reasoning in a non-distributed environment. GQR (Generic Qualitative Reasoner) [15] is a tool that can reason over any qualitative constraint calculi, including IA. PelletSpatial [12] is a qualitative spatial reasoner built on top of the Pellet reasoner. Both these tools are limited in terms of the size of IA networks they are able to handle. The largest example of temporal reasoning using Allen's algebra appears to be by Anagnostopoulos et al. [5]. Who have successfully reasoned over datasets consisting of 10,000 relations on a single machine using the CHRONOS framework. To our knowledge, the approach taken in this paper is the first attempt to implement an IA reasoner using a distributed, parallel architecture, and to work with larger scale datasets, over 1 million relations.

4   Temporal Reasoning Using Spark

Figure 2, provides an overview of our implementation of Allen's path consistency algorithm using Spark.

The input consists of an IA network. Specifically, the input is a collection of edges in the form (i, R_{ij}, j), where i and j are time intervals and R_{ij} the relation between these intervals. The full set of relations, I, is never used. The composition of I with any other relation always results in I, therefore no useful information can be obtained from inference based on the full set of relations.

The first phase is inference which corresponds to the composition operation in Allen's algebra. This is accomplished via a join between edges with common time intervals. The initial map operation outputs two key-value pairs for each edge in the input, once for the head interval, and once for the tail interval. At this point it is unknown, which, if any of the intervals, will form the basis for the join. In the above example, there is only one join possible, the one between $X\{b\}Y$ and $Y\{b\}Z$. Following the join operation, the actual inference takes place via a map transformation on pairs of edges. A Scala Map is used to implement Allen's composition table. The inferred relation is then deduced by looking-up

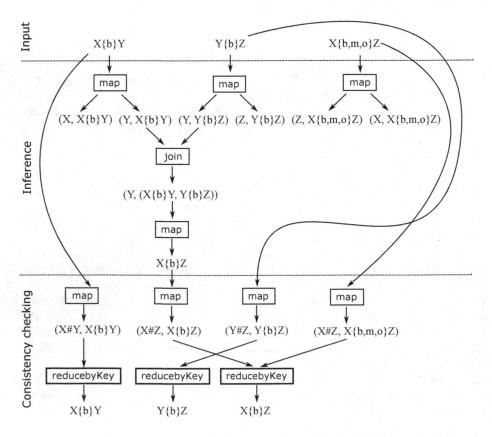

Fig. 2. Overview of temporal reasoning using Spark

the composition of each basic relation in the first edge with each basic relation in the second edge. The outputs of the inference stage are possible new relations between intervals, in this example, again, there is only one output, the edge $X\{b\}Z$. The application then moves onto a consistency checking phase where the output from inference is combined with the initial input. This combined dataset is mapped to key-value pairs where the key specifies a pair of intervals. Edges between the same pair of intervals will be sent to the same reduce process which computes the intersection of these relations for the final output.

The above diagram is a simplification, intended to give an overview of the application. Additional steps and optimisations were implemented as follows:

- It is necessary to add the inverse of each relation into the initial dataset. For example, consider two edges, $X\{b\}Y$ and $Z\{bi\}Y$. It is not possible to perform inference using these edges, as joins can only be performed where the head node of one edge matches the tail node of a second edge. If the inverse of each relation is inserted into the dataset ($Y\{bi\}X$ and $Y\{b\}Z$), inference is now possible. Therefore the transpose of the initial IA network was added as a pre-processing step.
- As mentioned above, path consistency is an iterative process. The two phases, inference and consistency checking are applied repeatedly until no new inferences are made. Algorithm 1 shows an high level overview of the temporal reasoner. Further details on the *inference* and *consistency* operations are provided below.

Algorithm 1. Temporal Reasoning Overview

```
IAnetwork=IAnetwork ∪ IAnetworkᵀ
IAnetwork=consistency(IAnetwork)
count=0
i=1
while IANetwork.count() ≠ count
    count=IAnetwork.count() //the size of the network taking into account new inferences
    newEdges=inference(IAnetwork,i)
    IAnetwork=consistency(IAnetwork ∪ newEdges)
    i++
end while
```

Limiting Duplicates

One problem with a naive implementation is the derivation of duplicate edges. Consider the simple IA network shown in Fig. 3. In iteration 1, it is possible to infer a relation between the time intervals W and Y, and between X and Z. These two new edges ($W\{b\}Y$ and $X\{b\}Z$) will be added to the network. In iteration 2 it is then possible to infer the relation between the intervals W and Z. However, the reasoner will also infer $W\{b\}Y$ and $X\{b\}Z$ again, and add these edges to the network. These duplicates will be removed in the consistency checking phase but they add a significant and unnecessary data in the inference phase and will be inferred repeatedly with every iteration.

Urbani et al. faced a similar problem when reasoning over RDF triples using MapReduce [13]. They limited the joins that were possible based on the distance

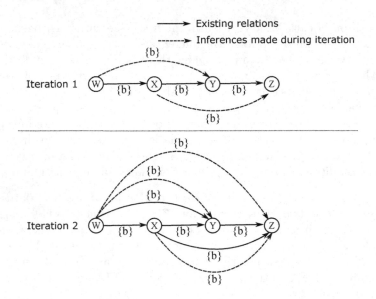

Fig. 3. Derivation of duplicate inferences

between nodes in a graph, specifically on one side of the join only edges with a distance of 2^{i-1} or 2^{i-2} were allowed (where i is the iteration number), on the other side of the join only edges with a distance greater than 2^{i-2} were allowed. The same approach is adopted in our temporal reasoner. In order to implement this, the distance between nodes is stored as part of each edge. When a new relation is inferred, the new edge is assigned a distance that is the sum of the joined edges' distances. During consistency checking the minimum distance is assigned to the reduced edge. The implementation can be seen in Algorithms 2 and 3. It is important to note that duplication still takes place. This is because the same relation can be derived through different joins within the same iteration. In Fig. 3, $W\{b\}Z$ can be inferred twice within iteration 2, through the composition of $W\{b\}X$ with $X\{b\}Z$ and through the composition of $W\{b\}Y$ with $Y\{b\}Z$.

Algorithm 2. Inference

```
inference(iaNetwork, i )
        //iaNetwork: A collection of edges e.g. [(X,{b},Y,1), (Y,{b},Z,1), ...]
        //i: The iteration number e.g. 1
        tailEdges=iaNetwork
                    .filter(edge ⇒ edge.distance=2^{i-1}∨edge.distance=2^{i-2})
                    .map(edge ⇒ (edge.tailInterval, edge))
        headEdges = iaNetwork.filter(edge ⇒ edge.distance> 2^{i-2})
                    .map(edge ⇒ (edge.headInterval, edge))
        joinedEdges = tailEdges.join(headEdges)
        newEdges=joinedEdges.map((key,(tailEdge,headEdge))⇒(
                    tailEdge.headInterval,
                    lookUp(tailEdge.relation,headEdge.relation),
                    headEdge.tailInterval,
                    tailEdge.distance+headEdge.distance
                    ))
        return newEdges
```

Algorithm 3. Consistency Checking

```
consistency(iaNetwork)
    //iaNetwork: A collection of edges e.g. [(X,{b},Y,1), (Y,{b},Z,1), ...]
    keyedEdges=iaNetwork
        .map(edge ⇒ (edge.tailInterval+'#'+edge.headInterval, edge))
    consistentEdges=keyedEdges.reduceByKey((edgeA,edgeB)⇒(
                            edgeA.tailInterval,
                            edgeA.relation ∩ edgeB.relation,
                            edgeA.headInterval,
                            Math.min(edgeA.distance,edgeB.distance)
        ))
    return consistentEdges
```

---

5 Evaluation

The purpose of the evaluation was to investigate the potential and limitations of the algorithms described above. In particular the evaluation was concerned with the issue of scalability and the capacity of the reasoning application to deal with large datasets.

Platform

The experiments were conducted by implementing the algorithms in the Scala programming language using the Apache Spark framework. Some initial experiments were also carried out using the Hadoop MapReduce framework. However, as expected, the algorithms implemented in Spark ran much faster than those in Hadoop. Spark's in-memory caching provided a significant advantage over the Hadoop based implementation. The experiments were carried out using Amazon's Elastic Cloud Compute (EC2) platform. Although EC2 has potential drawbacks such as lack of data locality, virtualised hardware, it is a widely used system as it negates the need for users to build and manage a cluster themselves and provides a typical real-world implementation for a distributed application. For the majority of the experiments a cluster consisting of four machines was used, each with four virtual CPUs and 30GB of memory. One of the experiments focussed on assessing the impact of increasing computing resources. In this case the size of the cluster was varied.

5.1 Experiments

The experiments were conducted using synthetic datasets. The features of each input dataset are discussed under each experiment description.

- **Experiment 1.** A number of time intervals were generated by randomly selecting points on a line for the start and end points. For each time interval, the relation between it and one other time interval was calculated. This gave rise to an input graph with an equal number of nodes (time intervals) and edges (relations between time intervals). Tests were run over datasets consisting of between 2 and 10 million edges.

– **Experiment 2.** Experiment 2 focussed on exploring the effect of increased
  computing resources on reasoning time. An input dataset of 10 million edges,
  generated in the same way as in Experiment 1, was used. The application was
  then run using a cluster size of between 2 and 16 machines.
– **Experiment 3.** Reasoning over an IA network as described in Experiment 1
  does not result in a complete graph. To investigate the worst-case scenario of
  reasoning over an IA network where the relation between every pair of intervals can be inferred, a connected graph consisting of a consecutive sequence
  of time intervals was used. Datasets of between 2,000 and 32,000 relations
  were generated based on this worst-case scenario.

5.2 Results

– Figure 4 shows the results for Experiment 1. The reasoning application
  demonstrates close to linear time performance and even considering the
  relatively small size of the cluster, the application is easily able to cope with
  an input of ten million edges. This is far larger in scale than previous applications that have reasoned over IA networks (limited to 10,000 edges), and
  shows the benefit of a distributed, parallel approach.
– Figure 6 shows the results for Experiment 2, the scalability of the reasoner in
  terms of the number of nodes in the cluster. As would be expected, an increase
  in the size of the cluster results in reasoning time decreasing. Figure 7 shows
  scaled speed-up, a standard metric used when evaluating the performance of
  parallel systems. Ideally a parallelised system should display linear speed-up,
  as we double the number of machines in the cluster the reasoning time should
  half. Apart from an increase with 4 nodes, the application shows sub-linear
  speed-up. However, this is consistent with many other applications running on
  distributed frameworks, and can be explained by the inevitable overheads of
  starting and managing jobs. The number of jobs remains constant regardless
  of cluster size. At some point adding additional nodes has little impact on
  processing time.

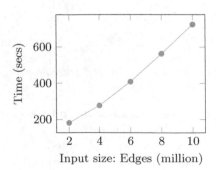

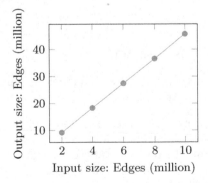

Fig. 4. Experiment 1: runtime as a
function of input size

Fig. 5. Experiment 1: output (number
of inferred edges) as a function of input
size

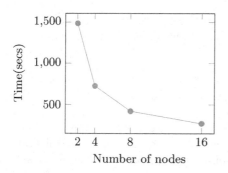

Fig. 6. Experiment 2: runtime as a function of number of nodes

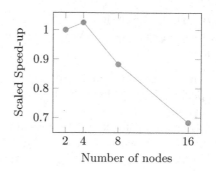

Fig. 7. Experiment 2: scaled speed-up

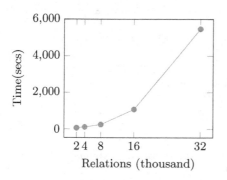

Fig. 8. Experiment 3: runtime as a function of input size (worst-case scenario)

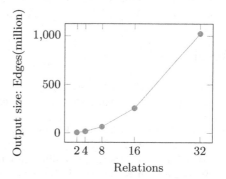

Fig. 9. Experiment 3: output (number of inferred edges) as a function of input size (worst-case scenario)

- The results for Experiment 3, Fig. 8, show two significant differences in the runtime compared to Experiment 1. Firstly, even though the input datasets are considerably smaller, in many cases the runtime is longer. Secondly, runtime does not increase linearly with regards to the input size. These differences can be attributed to the volume of data generated. Figures 5 and 9 show the numbers of generated edges in the corresponding experiments. In Experiment 1, even when reasoning over an initial graph with 10 million edges, the final output is less than 50 million edges. In Experiment 3, a complete graph is generated. For an input size of 32,000 edges over 1 billion edges are generated. Plus, unlike Experiment 1, when generating a complete graph the output does not grow linearly with regards to the input size.

6 Conclusions and Future Work

To our knowledge this is the first attempt to explore the feasibility of large scale reasoning using Allen's Interval Algebra. The results are encouraging. We have shown that, depending on the characteristics of the dataset, it is possible to reason over very large IA networks. Future work will expand the approach to look at:

- The use of real world datasets. The experiments above use datasets with specific characteristics that we have designed. The next step is to work with real world datasets.
- Other areas of qualitative reasoning. The approach described above can be modified to work with other qualitative calculus. For example, Vilain and Kautz's Point Algebra [14] or spatial reasoning using Region Connection Calculus (RCC-8) [6].
- Temporal knowledge bases often feature both qualitative and metric information. We plan to extend the approach described here to reason using both quantitative and qualitative information in large scale datasets.

References

1. Spark. https://spark.apache.org/. Accessed 30 June 2015
2. Spatialhadoop. http://spatialhadoop.cs.umn.edu/index.html/. Accessed 06 July 2016
3. Allen, J.F.: Maintaining knowledge about temporal intervals. Commun. ACM **26**(11), 832–843 (1983)
4. Allen, J.F.: Temporal reasoning and planning. In: Reasoning About Plans, pp. 1–67. Morgan Kaufmann Publishers Inc. (1991)
5. Anagnostopoulos, E., Petrakis, E.G.M., Batsakis, S.: CHRONOS: improving the performance of qualitative temporal reasoning in OWL. In: 26th IEEE International Conference on Tools with Artificial Intelligence, ICTAI 2014, Limassol, Cyprus, 10–12 November 2014, pp. 309–315 (2014)
6. Cohn, A.G., Bennett, B., Gooday, J., Gotts, N.M.: Qualitative spatial representation and reasoning with the region connection calculus. GeoInformatica **1**(3), 275–316 (1997)
7. Eldawy, A., Mokbel, M.F.: Spatialhadoop: a mapreduce framework for spatial data. In: 31st IEEE International Conference on Data Engineering, ICDE 2015, Seoul, South Korea, 13–17 April 2015, pp. 1352–1363 (2015)
8. Focke, R.W., Wabeke, L.O., de Villiers, J.P., Inggs, M.R.: Implementing interval algebra to schedule mechanically scanned multistatic radars. In: Proceedings of the 14th International Conference on Information Fusion, FUSION 2011, Chicago, Illinois, USA, 5–8 July 2011, pp. 1–7 (2011)
9. Iwasaki, Y.: Real-world applications of qualitative reasoning. IEEE Expert **12**(3), 16–21 (1997)
10. Mudrová, L., Hawes, N.: Task scheduling for mobile robots using interval algebra. In: IEEE International Conference on Robotics and Automation, ICRA 2015, Seattle, WA, USA, 26–30 May 2015, pp. 383–388 (2015)
11. Nebel, B., Bürckert, H.-J.: Reasoning about temporal relations: a maximal tractable subclass of Allen's interval algebra. In: Proceedings of the 12th National Conference on Artificial Intelligence, Seattle, WA, USA, 31 July–4 August 1994, Volume 1, pp. 356–361 (1994)

12. Stocker, M., Sirin, E.: Pelletspatial: a hybrid RCC-8 and RDF/OWL reasoning and query engine. In: Proceedings of the 5th International Workshop on OWL: Experiences and Directions (OWLED 2009), Chantilly, VA, United States, 23–24 October 2009 (2009)
13. Urbani, J., Kotoulas, S., Oren, E., van Harmelen, F.: Scalable distributed reasoning using MapReduce. In: Bernstein, A., Karger, D.R., Heath, T., Feigenbaum, L., Maynard, D., Motta, E., Thirunarayan, K. (eds.) ISWC 2009. LNCS, vol. 5823, pp. 634–649. Springer, Heidelberg (2009). doi:10.1007/978-3-642-04930-9_40
14. Vilain, M.B., Kautz, H.A.: Constraint propagation algorithms for temporal reasoning. In: Proceedings of the 5th National Conference on Artificial Intelligence, Philadelphia, PA, 11–15 August 1986, Volume 1: Science, pp. 377–382 (1986)
15. Westphal, M., Wölfl, S., Gantner, Z.: GQR: a fast solver for binary qualitative constraint networks. In: Benchmarking of Qualitative Spatial and Temporal Reasoning Systems, Papers from the 2009 AAAI Spring Symposium, Technical report SS-09-02, Stanford, California, USA, 23–25 March 2009, pp. 51–52 (2009)
16. Zaharia, M., Chowdhury, M., Franklin, M.J., Shenker, S., Stoica, I.: Spark: cluster computing with working sets. In: 2nd USENIX Workshop on Hot Topics in Cloud Computing, HotCloud 2010, Boston, MA, USA, 22 June 2010 (2010)
17. Zaidi, A.K., Ishaque, M., Levis, A.H.: Combining qualitative and quantitative temporal reasoning for criminal forensics. In: Memon, N., David Farley, J., Hicks, D.L., Rosenorn, T. (eds.) Mathematical Methods in Counterterrorism, pp. 69–90. Springer, Vienna (2009). doi:10.1007/978-3-211-09442-6_5
18. Zhou, L., Hripcsak, G.: Temporal reasoning with medical data - a review with emphasis on medical natural language processing. J. Biomed. Inform. 40(2), 183–202 (2007)

Towards the Distributed Logic Programming of Intelligent Visual Surveillance Applications

Alexei A. Morozov[1,2(✉)], Olga S. Sushkova[1], and Alexander F. Polupanov[1]

[1] Kotel'nikov Institute of Radio Engineering and Electronics of RAS,
Mokhovaya 11-7, Moscow 125009, Russia
morozov@cplire.ru, {o.sushkova,sashap55}@mail.ru
[2] Moscow State University of Psychology and Education,
Sretenka 29, Moscow 107045, Russia
http://www.fullvision.ru/actor

Abstract. An extension of the Actor Prolog language with the ability of distributed logic programming is demonstrated. This language extension is developed for experimenting with distributed logic programming and declarative agent approach to intelligent visual surveillance. An approach to resolving the contradiction between the strong typing of Actor Prolog and the independence of software agents is proposed. Remote calls of Actor Prolog predicates are implemented using the object-oriented features of Actor Prolog, translation of Actor Prolog to Java, and the Java RMI protocol. An example of logic program communication based on the remote predicate calls is examined.

1 Introduction

A distributed version of the Actor Prolog language [1,2] described in this paper is intended for experimenting with the declarative agent approach to the intelligent visual surveillance. The concept of the multi-agent programming came to the field of intelligent visual surveillance from Artificial Intelligence [3–8]. The idea of the multi-agent approach to the visual surveillance is in that the intelligent visual surveillance system consists of communicating programs (agents) that have the following properties: autonomy (they operate without direct control from users and other agents), social ability (they can co-operate to solve the problem), reactivity (they perceive the environment and respond to external events), and pro-activity (they demonstrate a goal-directed behavior). Theoretically speaking, the multi-agent approach can provide flexibility, reliability, and openness of the intelligent visual surveillance systems [9,10]. For instance, let us imagine that stages of video analysis are implemented by a set of agents. Then, the visual surveillance system can be easily extended by an additional method of abnormal behavior recognition without modification of its agents and even without suspending its work. One just needs to insert in the system a new agent that can utilize results of other agents and transfer his own results to others.

O. Pichardo-Lagunas and S. Miranda-Jiménez (Eds.): MICAI 2016, Part II, LNAI 10062, pp. 42–53, 2017.
DOI: 10.1007/978-3-319-62428-0_4

In recent decade, the declarative approach to the development of the multi-agent systems is recognized as a basic idea in this research area; a set of excellent declarative multi-agent platforms and languages are developed and implemented [5,7]. Unfortunately, in the framework of the intelligent visual surveillance systems, the agents are to perform very specific operations on big arrays of binary data that are out of the framework of the conventional symbolic processing operations typical for declarative languages. Thus, there is a reason for development of the new means of the multi-agent-programming for experimenting with intelligent visual surveillance systems. The distinctive feature of our approach is in that we implement the intelligent video analysis using the concurrent object-oriented language Actor Prolog and a compiler of Actor Prolog into pure Java [11].

Previously, the object-oriented logic approach to the intelligent visual surveillance was reported in [12–16]. It was demonstrated that the translation of the object-oriented logic language into Java yields a sufficiently fast executable code for real time video analysis and detection of complex patterns of the abnormal people behavior. This approach can be extended to the distributed visual surveillance, because the Actor Prolog language is indeed an object-oriented language and can be easily adapted to the distributed programming framework even without modifications of the syntax. The only problem to be solved is the incorporation into the language the ability of remote procedure calls.

The Actor Prolog language differs from other state-of-the-art Prolog-based agent languages like Jason [17] and 2APL [18] in that it is not based on the BDI model and it does not directly offer high-level features such as planners and agent communication languages that might be expected for a multi-agent language. Actor Prolog is rather a more high-performance object-oriented logic language that is a base for implementation of real time multi-agent application platforms.

The paper is organized as follows. The problem of the contradiction between the strong typing of the Actor Prolog language and the independence of the software agents is discussed in Sect. 2. The type system of the distributed Actor Prolog is considered in Sect. 3. An example of the remote communication between two independent Actor Prolog programs is examined in Sect. 4.

2 The Problem of the Strong Typing in Multi-agent Systems

A term "remote procedure call" is usually associated with the OMG GORBA, Java RMI, or MS DCOM protocols. This meaning of the term is relevant to the topic, because the remote predicate calls are implemented in the distributed Actor Prolog using the Java RMI protocol. At the same time, the term is linked with the general problems of the logic language design and implementation in the context of the agent logic programming.

It is known that interactions between independent agents are very hard to handle for strongly typed object systems [19]. The main problem to be resolved in the course of adapting Actor Prolog to multi-agent paradigm is the contradiction between the strong type system of the language and the idea of independency of the software agents. The strong type system is an important feature of the language and is necessary for generation of fast and reliable executable code [11,13]. The problem is in that one needs to transfer information about the data types between the software units to implement their link and static type-checking. This kind of information exchange between the software agents is definitely undesirable, because it decreases the autonomy of the agents and complicates the agent life cycle. In this paper, another solution of the problem is proposed; the type system of the Actor Prolog language is partially softened to allow a dynamic type-checking (instead of the static one) in some restricted cases linked with the inter-agent communications.

Another problem that is close to the topic, but is still different, is a combination of the object-oriented paradigm and the strong typing. It was recognized earlier, that types are useful for formalizing and maintaining object interfaces, though types are orthogonal to objects and their integration is not a simple deed [20]. The Actor Prolog language supports both types (domains) and classes/objects. A distinctive feature of the language is in that the "object" and "data item" notions were clearly separated in the language [1]. The language has the strong type system that supports various kinds of simple and composite data items like numbers, structures, lists, etc. At the same time, Actor Prolog supports also classes based on the "clauses view" of logic OOP [21]. The instances of classes (so-called "worlds") can be processed like standard Prolog terms; they can be passed as arguments to predicates and can be included in composite terms. However, special rules are used for unification of variables containing instances of classes and special means are to be developed for interchange of these kinds of terms between the distributed agents.

In the Actor Prolog language, different instances of classes are treated always as different entities, that is, unification of two worlds succeeds if and only if these worlds are the same instance of a class. The interface of the class contains all necessary information about its methods including names, arity, flow patterns, and types of arguments. The information about the determinancy/non-determinancy of the methods is also included in the interface. There are three keywords in the languages for the declaration of the determinancy of the methods: *determ*, *nondeterm*, and *imperative*. The *nondeterm* keyword informs compiler that there are no restrictions on the behavior of methods and they can produce several answers in the case of backtracking and/or terminate with failure. The *determ* keyword means that methods can produce just one answer or terminate with failure. The *imperative* keyword imposes the hardest restrictions on the methods: the predicates must succeed and produce one answer; this means that the predicate operates indeed as a usual procedure in an imperative language. All these restrictions are checked by the compiler during the translation of the program.

The description and usage of the class interfaces are complicated a bit in Actor Prolog by the fact that the language supports concurrent processes and two different kinds of method invocations: plain and asynchronous. The processes are a special kind of class instances; they are defined using double round brackets in the class instance constructors [2]. The plain method invocation is a usual predicate call of standard Prolog; the predicate can be invoked in a given world using the "?" prefix. The asynchronous method invocations are indicated by special prefixes "<-" and "<<". Only this kind of predicate calls is applicable for the processes; an attempt to implement a plain predicate call in a concurrent process will always terminate with a failure. The *internal* keyword is introduced in the language to facilitate optimization of the logic programs. This keyword informs the compiler that a given attribute of a class always contains a plain class instance, but not a process, that is important for analysis of predicate determinacy. Obviously, we will focus on the asynchronous method invocations in this paper, because class instances obtained from another logic program are processes that operate concurrently in relation to the invoking logic program.

Ordinarily, a standard static type-checking is implemented in the distributed version of Actor Prolog. The dynamic type-checking is implemented only if a method is to be called in an object (an instance of Actor Prolog class) that is originated from another logic program and is transferred somehow to the logic program under consideration. The verification of the remote predicate call includes the following operations:

1. One checks the name and the arity of the predicate. The predicate with the target name and arity is to be found in the object.
2. One checks the flow pattern of the predicate. The Actor Prolog language supports explicit declaration whether the argument is input or output; the flow directions of all the arguments in the predicate call are checked.
3. One checks so-called structural match of domains of all the arguments (this is a kind of dynamic type-checking).

The structural match of the domains means that graphs representing the data structures belonging to domains have to be equivalent, but not the names of the domains.

3   A Strong Type System in the Distributed Actor Prolog

Let us consider briefly the type system of the Actor Prolog language and the structural matching rules associated with various kinds of simple and compound data types (domains).

Actor Prolog supports the following simple data types: integer, real, symbol, and string. The difference between the integers and real numbers is in that the real numbers contain a dot. The difference between the symbols and strings is in that the symbols are represented by integer codes internally, but not by the text, during the execution of the program. On the syntax level, the symbols are enclosed in apostrophes and the strings are enclosed in quotes. Here is an example of using these built-in data types for definition of user data types:

```
DOMAINS:
Year          = INTEGER.
Height        = REAL.
Color         = SYMBOL.
Message       = STRING.
```

During the structural matching, the integers can match only the integers, the reals can match only the reals, etc. No automatic type conversions are allowed.

Actor Prolog supports so-called numerical ranges and enumerations. A range type can be defined using the integer or real bounds, for example:

```
Hour          = [0 .. 24].
Angle         = [0.0 .. 360.0].
```

The procedure of structural matching checks the exact equality of the bounds of the numerical range types to be compared. The only exception is that the real range bounds can slightly differ in accordance with the real number precision given in the translator options.

An enumeration type can be defined using a set of constants of any simple types, for instance:

```
Hour          = 0; 1; 2; 3; 4; 5; 6; 7; 8; 9; 10; 11; 12.
Color         = 'Red';'Blue';'Green'.
```

The structural match of two enumerations means that these types include the same sets of elements.

Note that a type definition can include a set of names of other types in the language; this is a basic difference of the Actor Prolog type system from analogous type systems in the Turbo/PDC Prolog family [22]. For instance, an argument of the following data type can transmit both integer and real values:

```
Numerical     = INTEGER; REAL.
```

Generally speaking, a type definition can refer to other data types. The structure matching procedure considers all the type definitions and compares the corresponding sets of elements that can include simple domains, literals, and composite types.

There are three kinds of composite types in Actor Prolog, namely: structures, lists, and so-called underdetermined sets [1]. The structure type definition consists of a functor and arguments enclosed in round brackets, for example:

```
AppointedDate = date(Year,Month,Day).
```

The structural matching procedure checks whether two structure domain definitions contain the same functor and the same number of arguments. Then, the structural matching of the types of all corresponding arguments is implemented.

The lists are a separate type in Actor Prolog, but not a kind of the structures. The list type definition contains a name of element type and an asterisk, for instance:

```
Dates          = AppointedDate*.
```

The structural matching procedure checks the types of the elements of the list types.

The definition of an underdetermined set type in Actor Prolog contains an unordered set of named pairs enclosed in braces. Every pair contains the identifier of the pair and the type of the argument, for example:

```
Customer       = {name: STRING, birthday: Date, age: INTEGER}.
```

The structural matching procedure compares the types of all corresponding pairs in the definitions of undetermined set types. The types must contain the pairs of the same names, but the order of the pairs is insignificant.

There are two exotic data types in Actor Prolog: so-called anonymous type "_" and so-called "any set" type {_}. The former type indicates that a predicate accepts terms of any types; it is useful for the definition of read/write procedures, etc. The second data type is used for the definition of predicates/attributes that accept terms of any types, but only in a form of an underdetermined set, for instance:

```
HTTP_ContentParameters = {_}.
```

By the rules of the structural matching, the anonymous type matches only the anonymous type and the "any set" type matches only the "any set" type.

All the rules described above are applicable to both the static and dynamic type-checking. A single difference relates to the structural matching data types that contain class names. The point is that a type definition in Actor Prolog can include the name of a class enclosed in round brackets, for example:

```
MessageHandler = ('MyClass').
```

This type definition means that a term of the *MessageHandler* type can be an instance of the *MyClass* class. This instance can be a plain world or a concurrent process of the class. The definition tells nothing about the concurrent execution of the class instance, but does not prohibit this kind of class usage too. Actor Prolog considers this world data type as a simple one. The compiler of non-distributed Actor Prolog guarantees that a term of this type is an instance of the *MyClass* class or an instance of a class that inherits the *MyClass* class; this rule is softened in the distributed Actor Prolog.

The distributed Actor Prolog checks whether an instance of a class belongs to the class pointed in the type definition only if this class is defined in the same logic program (i.e., it is technically possible to check it). An instance of any external class obtained from another logical agent (program) can be freely assigned to a variable/predicate argument of any type that includes a class name. Thus, the structured matching algorithm allows matching of any world types; the names of classes in the type definitions are simply ignored if the classes are defined in different logic programs (agents).

In distributed Actor Prolog, an instance of a class can be transferred to another logic program somehow and be accepted without the check of the interface if the accepting program expects to accept an instance of some class. A real check of the class interface is to be performed when the accepting program try to invoke a method in the external object. In this case, the structural matching procedure described above is to be performed, that can confirm suitability of the object or yield a runtime error. Obviously, the implementation of this check requires information on the origin of all the objects in the logic program. Thus, distributed Actor Prolog keeps an internal table of all the class instances created during the program execution and transferred outside. Another internal table contains all the objects accepted somehow from other logic programs. These tables allow Actor Prolog to distinguish clearly the instances of own and external classes and use this information in the structured matching algorithm.

Thus, the multi-agent interaction in Actor Prolog is based on the fusion of dynamic and static typing. The static type-checking and standard features of a nominative type system are implemented for all the own worlds like in the conventional Actor Prolog. At the same time, the dynamic type-checking and elements of a structural type system are implemented for all the external worlds. We consider the type system of Actor Prolog as a combined type system. This type system ensures the advantages of the static type-checking for the high-performance code generation and the flexibility of the dynamic type-checking that is necessary for the multi-agent systems programming.

4   An Example of the Logical Agent Communication

Let us consider an example of the remote predicate call. Suppose there are two agents: *Recognizer* and *Observer* (see Fig. 1). These agents should co-operate to search and recognize people in a video scene. Suppose that *Recognizer* controls its own pan-tilt-zoom (PTZ) camera and can identify a person in given co-ordinates. *Observer* can analyze behavior of people and calculate co-ordinates of the persons to be identified. Suppose that these logic programs are different agents that should establish a link dynamically and exchange information to solve the problem.

First, let us define a schema of the *Recognizer* logic program. A logic program that is defined below creates an instance of a class and saves it in a file to be accessible for other programs. Other program can read this class instance and implement a remote call of a predicate defined in the *Recognizer* program. Let the external program transmits co-ordinates of a person to be identified and the *Recognizer* logic programs accept this information and simply print it in the screen for the sake of simplicity.

In accordance with the semantics of the Actor Prolog language, the execution of the program begins with creation of an instance of the *Main* class. In the program under consideration, the *Main* class is an instance of the built-in *Console* class that implements a text window control:

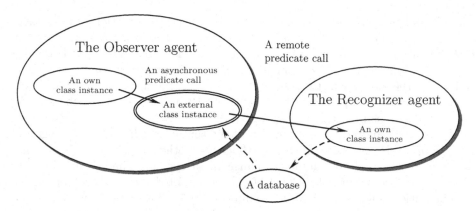

Fig. 1. An example of two co-operating agents. The *Recognizer* agent publishes an instance of a class in the external database. Then, the *Observer* agent obtains this class instance and sends an asynchronous message to this class instance using Java RMI.

```
class 'Main' (specialized 'Console'):
external_file    = ('DataExchange');
[
PREDICATES:
intruder_coordinates(REAL,REAL)     - (i,i);
MODEL:
?intruder_coordinates(X,Y).
```

The *Main* class contains a single slot named *external_file*. The value of this slot is an instance of the *DataExchange* class. The *DataExchange* class implements the data exchange using a built-in database for simplicity, since this is the simplest way of external file control in the Actor Prolog language.

There is a single predicate definition in the *PREDICATES* section. The *intruder_coordinates* predicate has two input real arguments. This predicate is never called directly inside the *Recognizer* logic program, that is why one should indicate in the *MODEL* section that this predicate is to be invoked with two arguments. Otherwise, the translator will discard this predicate during the optimization of the code.

The *CLAUSES* section of the *Main* class contains the definitions of the *goal* and *intruder_coordinates* predicates:

```
CLAUSES:
goal:-!,
      external_file ? insert(self),
      external_file ? save("g:/SharedData.db"),
      writeln("I wait for intruder co-ordinates...").
intruder_coordinates(X,Y):-
      writeln("X=",X,"Y=",Y).
]
```

The *goal* predicate is called automatically during the creation of the *Main* class instance. This predicate inserts the instance of the *Main* class into the *DataExchange* database using the *insert* built-in method and the *self* keyword. Then it records the database content to the file using the *save* built-in method and writes the message in the screen: "I wait for intruder co-ordinates..." The *intruder_coordinates* predicate is to be invoked from outside using the remote call protocol. This predicate simply writes the co-ordinates in the screen.

There is yet another class definition in the text of the *Recognizer* program. The *DataExchange* class inherits methods from the *Database* built-in class that implements a simple database management system. There is a definition of the *Target* domain in the *DOMAINS* section of the *DataExchange* class. This definition is necessary in order to inform the database management system about the type of data to be stored in the *DataExchange* class. It is declared that the *Target* type includes instances of the *Main* class.

```
class 'DataExchange' (specialized 'Database'):
[
DOMAINS:
Target      = ('Main').
]
```

Let us consider the *Observer* logic program. Suppose this program should obtain an instance of an external class from the file and send to this object a message containing co-ordinates of a person to be identified. The *Main* class of this program inherits methods from the *Console* built-in class too.

```
class 'Main' (specialized 'Console'):
file        = ('InternalDatabase');
[
PREDICATES:
send_coordinates('AcceptingAgent')   - (i);
CLAUSES:
goal:-
     file ? load("g:/SharedData.db"),
     file ? find(ExternalObject),!,
     send_coordinates(ExternalObject).
send_coordinates(ExternalObject):-
     ExternalObject << intruder_coordinates(125.009,1107.144),
     writeln("The information is sent...").
]
```

The *Main* class includes the *file* slot that contains an instance of the *InternalDatabase* class. There is a definition of the *send_coordinates* auxiliary predicate in the *PREDICATES* section. This predicate has one input argument that should contain an instance of a class that inherits methods from the *AcceptingAgent* interface defined below. The *goal* predicate acquires information from the external file using the *load* built-in method of the *InternalDatabase* database. Then it takes the *ExternalObject* world from the database and transmits this class instance to the *send_coordinates* predicate. The *send_coordinates* predicate implements an asynchronous predicate call in the *ExternalObject* world and writes the text message in the screen: "The information is sent..." Note that the asynchronous call will be implemented using the remote call protocol, because the variable *ExternalObject* contains an object that originates from another logic program. The dynamic type-checking will be implemented during the call.

The *AcceptingAgent* interface describes methods that are expected to be supported by the collaborator of the *Observer* agent. Note that this interface links up in no way with the classes/interfaces of the *Recognizer* agent:

```
interface 'AcceptingAgent':
[
PREDICATES:
intruder_coordinates(REAL,REAL)     - (i,i);
]
```

The *InternalDatabase* auxiliary class is defined in the similar way as the *DataExchange* class in the *Recognizer* agent. The single difference is in that the *Target* domain includes instances of classes that inherit the *AcceptingAgent* interface.

```
class 'InternalDatabase' (specialized 'Database'):
[
DOMAINS:
Target      = ('AcceptingAgent').
]
```

Let us execute the *Recognizer* logic program. The program will create the *SharedData.db* file in the *g:* disk and write the text in the screen:

```
I wait for intruder co-ordinates...
```

The *SharedData.db* file is text one, because the *Database* class stores the information in a user-readable format. The file contains something like this (the text is reduced):

```
('feffiimuyf2uhb8pqbhesx ... rlp11802mq9vmyzk2o7t4');
```

The alphanumeric code enclosed in the apostrophes and round brackets is a usual Actor Prolog term, namely, a text representation of a class instance. On the technical level, this is an encoded instance of a Java RMI stub that refers to the class instance. Note that this format of data exchange is appropriate for any type of data transfer protocols including E-Mails.

Let us launch the *Observer* agent now. This logic program will read the class instance from the *SharedData.db* external file, implement a remote predicate call in the *Recognizer* agent, and write the text message:

```
The information is sent...
```

The *Recognizer* agent will accept the remote predicate call and write the acquired co-ordinates in the screen:

```
I wait for intruder co-ordinates...
X= 125.009 Y=1107.144
```

This example illustrates the basic schema of agent data exchange in distributed Actor Prolog using the remote predicate calls, dynamic type-checking, and some technical details of the data encoding.

5　Conclusions

The extension of the Actor Prolog language with the ability of distributed logic programming was demonstrated. The idea of a combined type system which provides a new solution of the problem of the strong typing in the multi-agent systems was proposed and examined. This type system ensures the advantages of the static type-checking for the generation of the fast executable code and the flexibility of the dynamic type-checking that is necessary for the multi-agent systems design. It was implemented in the distributed version of the Actor Prolog language that gives new means for experimenting with the multi-agent logic programming. We suppose that these means open new prospects for the development of real time logical multi-agent systems and practical applications of the logic programming in the intelligent visual surveillance.

This research is supported by the Russian Foundation for Basic Research, grant No. 16-29-09626 (please see our Web Site [23] for details).

References

1. Morozov, A.A.: Actor Prolog: an object-oriented language with the classical declarative semantics. In: Sagonas, K., Tarau, P. (eds.) IDL 1999, France, Paris, pp. 39–53 (1999)
2. Morozov, A.A.: Logic object-oriented model of asynchronous concurrent computations. Pattern Recogn. Image Anal. **13**, 640–649 (2003)
3. Russell, S., Norvig, P.: Artificial Intelligence. A Modern Approach. Prentice-Hall, London (1995)
4. Shen, W., Hao, Q., Yoon, H., Norrie, D.: Applications of agent-based systems in intelligent manufacturing: an updated review. Adv. Eng. Inform. **20**, 415–431 (2006)
5. Baldoni, M., Baroglio, C., Mascardi, V., Omicini, A., Torroni, P.: Agents, multi-agent systems and declarative programming: what, when, where, why, who, how? In: Dovier, A., Pontelli, E. (eds.) A 25-Year Perspective on Logic Programming. LNCS, vol. 6125, pp. 204–230. Springer, Heidelberg (2010). doi:10.1007/978-3-642-14309-0_10
6. Gascueña, J., Fernández-Caballero, A.: On the use of agent technology in intelligent, multisensory and distributed surveillance. Knowl. Eng. Rev. **26**(2), 191–208 (2011)

7. Bădică, C., Braubach, L., Paschke, A.: Rule-based distributed and agent systems. In: Bassiliades, N., Governatori, G., Paschke, A. (eds.) RuleML 2011. LNCS, vol. 6826, pp. 3–28. Springer, Heidelberg (2011). doi:10.1007/978-3-642-22546-8_3
8. Kravari, K., Bassiliades, N.: A survey of agent platforms. J. Artif. Soc. Soc. Simul. **18**, 191–208 (2015). http://jasss.soc.surrey.ac.uk/18/1/11.html
9. Vallejo, D., Albusac, J., Castro-Schez, J., Glez-Morcillo, C., Jiménez, L.: A multi-agent architecture for supporting distributed normality-based intelligent surveillance. Eng. Appl. Artif. Intell. **24**, 325–340 (2011)
10. Ejaz, N., Manzoor, U., Nefti, S., Baik, S.: A collaborative multi-agent framework for abnormal activity detection in crowded areas. Int. J. Innov. Comput. Inf. Control **8**, 4219–4234 (2012)
11. Morozov, A.A., Sushkova, O.S., Polupanov, A.F.: A translator of Actor Prolog to Java. In: Bassiliades, N., Fodor, P., Giurca, A., Gottlob, G., Kliegr, T., Nalepa, G., Palmirani, M., Paschke, A., Proctor, M., Roman, D., Sadri, F., Stojanovic, N. (eds.) RuleML 2015 DC and Challenge, Berlin, CEUR (2015)
12. Morozov, A.A., Vaish, A., Polupanov, A.F., Antciperov, V.E., Lychkov, I.I., Alfimtsev, A.N., Deviatkov, V.V.: Development of concurrent object-oriented logic programming platform for the intelligent monitoring of anomalous human activities. In: Plantier, G., Schultz, T., Fred, A., Gamboa, H. (eds.) BIOSTEC 2014. CCIS, vol. 511, pp. 82–97. Springer, Cham (2015). doi:10.1007/978-3-319-26129-4_6
13. Morozov, A.A., Polupanov, A.F.: Intelligent visual surveillance logic programming: implementation issues. In: Ströder, T., Swift, T. (eds.) CICLOPS-WLPE 2014. Number AIB-2014-09 in Aachener Informatik Berichte, RWTH Aachen University, pp. 31–45 (2014)
14. Morozov, A.A., Polupanov, A.F.: Development of the logic programming approach to the intelligent monitoring of anomalous human behaviour. In: Paulus, D., Fuchs, C., Droege, D. (eds.) OGRW 2014, pp. 82–85. University of Koblenz-Landau, Koblenz (2015)
15. Morozov, A.A., Sushkova, O.S., Polupanov, A.F.: An approach to the intelligent monitoring of anomalous human behaviour based on the Actor Prolog object-oriented logic language. In: Bassiliades, N., Fodor, P., Giurca, A., Gottlob, G., Kliegr, T., Nalepa, G., Palmirani, M., Paschke, A., Proctor, M., Roman, D., Sadri, F., Stojanovic, N. (eds.) RuleML 2015 DC and Challenge, Berlin, CEUR (2015)
16. Morozov, A.A.: Development of a method for intelligent video monitoring of abnormal behavior of people based on parallel object-oriented logic programming. Pattern Recogn. Image Anal. **25**, 481–492 (2015)
17. Bordini, R.H., Hübner, J.F., Wooldridge, M.: Programming Multi-agent Systems in AgentSpeak Using Jason. Wiley Series in Agent Technology, 8th edn. Wiley, Chichester (2007)
18. Dastani, M.: 2APL: a practical agent programming language. Auton. Agent. Multi-Agent Syst. **16**, 214–248 (2008)
19. Odell, J.: Objects and agents compared. J. Object Technol. **1**, 41–53 (2002)
20. Nierstrasz, O., Dami, L.: Component-oriented software technology. In: Nierstrasz, O., Tsichritzis, D. (eds.) Object-Oriented Software Composition, pp. 3–28. Prentice Hall, Upper Saddle River (1995)
21. Davison, A.: A survey of logic programming-based object oriented languages. Technical report 92/3, Department of Computer Science, University of Melbourne, Melbourne, Australia (1992)
22. Borland International: Turbo Prolog Owner's Handbook (1986)
23. Morozov, A.A., Sushkova, O.S.: The intelligent visual surveillance logic programming Web Site (2016). http://www.fullvision.ru/actor_prolog/

An Efficient Expert System for Diabetes with a Bayesian Inference Engine

Viridiana Cruz-Gutiérrez$^{(\boxtimes)}$, Mario Alberto Posada-Zamora,
and Abraham Sánchez-López

Benemérita Universidad Autónoma de Puebla,
4 sur 104 Centro Histórico, 72000 Puebla, Mexico
{viricruz,mariop}@rockruz.net, asanchez@cs.buap.mx

Abstract. This article proposes an inference module for an Expert System for diabetes diagnosis. This module is based on a Bayesian Network (BN), which represents knowledge, experience and reasoning mechanisms of a specialist in family medicine of the Mexican Social Security Institute (IMSS). The events and causal relations of the Bayesian Network are obtained from the variables or symptoms of four types of diabetes: Diabetes Mellitus Type I (DMI), Diabetes Mellitus Type II (DMII), Gestational Diabetes (GD) and Prediabetes (PD) or Insulin Resistance. The evidences to build the Bayesian Network were obtained with a first version of a preliminary Expert System (ES) for diabetes; these evidences correspond to a set of 250 selected patients. We present interesting results obtained with this new inference module by comparing both results, those obtained with the preliminary ES and those obtained with the new proposal.

Keywords: Expert system · Diabetes mellitus · Bayesian network

1 Introduction

The field of Medicine has been a discipline that has a powerful technology and software support. The Health Informatics has its origins in the fusion of the communication and information systems, the formal medical languages, the clinical practices guide, the artificial intelligence and the cybernetics [3].

In order to give an accurate Diabetes Mellitus diagnosis, the doctor needs some information like patient's symptoms, and some biochemical criteria [7]. The inexperience of the novice doctors could lead to a wrong diagnosis and can result into non-adequate advices and recommendations, therefore putting the patient on risk; and beacause of that, several Expert Systems have been developed that supports the diabetes diagnosis. Below some examples are given:

Zeki et al. [17] developed a rule-based Expert System that identifies three types of diabetes, and has been tested in the Shahid Hasheminezhad Teaching Hospital affiliated to Tehran University of Medical Sciences.

© Springer International Publishing AG 2017
O. Pichardo-Lagunas and S. Miranda-Jiménez (Eds.): MICAI 2016, Part II, LNAI 10062, pp. 54–64, 2017.
DOI: 10.1007/978-3-319-62428-0_5

Nnamoko et al. [14] presented a FES for a type-2 Diabetes Mellitus that combines case-based and rule-based reasoning. For the development of this Expert System a subset of nine variables was considered.

In [1], Margret Anouncia et al. proposed a rule-based advice diabetes system whose entries are binary data type. The system has demonstrated to be advantageous in some aspects like the accuracy of the diagnosis and the time consumed due to the knowledge representation based on an approximated set.

In [11], a hybrid model is presented in which two techniques were merged: The Bayesian Networks and a multicriteria method for the development of an Expert System. This model has the purpose of assist the Diabetes Mellitus II diagnosis on risk patients. The authors only took three aspects: age, body mass index (BMI) and blood pressure. The entire dataset was taken from a database that describes female Pima American patients.

Even in all the found research about the topic, several characteristics were not considered that involves the Mexican society, so this is the reason why this research focuses on the development of an Expert System with a probabilistic-based inference engine using Bayesian Networks, that supports the Diabetes Mellitus diagnosis on the Mexican society, considering that Diabetes is the leading cause of death for adults. The Bayesian Network design has been built with a dataset of a Fuzzy Expert System Diabetes diagnosis reported in [4].

In the Sect. 2 we detail some concepts about Expert Systems, the probability notion and the uncertainly management. The Sect. 3 describes the development of our proposal and later, in Sect. 4 we present some test that were conducted using the Expert System and the comparison with the results that were reported on the preliminary work [4]. At last, in Sect. 5 we have the conclusions and future work.

2   Basic Concepts

2.1   Expert Systems

The Expert Systems belong to one of the most successful Artificial Intelligence fields; they are also known as Knowledge-based Expert Systems [6].

The Medicine is, without doubt, a very relevant field on which the Expert Systems have found several applications. On sixties, the Stanford University developed MYCIN, a system that supports the doctors on the research and diagnosis of infectious blood diseases. The basic elements of an Expert Systems are:

– The learning or knowledge acquisition subsystem which is responsible for obtaining abstract knowledge (rules, probability spaces, etc.) and concrete knowledge (situations).
– The knowledge base that stores the abstract knowledge.
– The working memory where the concrete knowledge is stored.
– The inference engine who applies the abstract knowledge to the concrete one for giving a statement. The inference process for which by the abstract knowledge we obtain a conclusion is known as deduction.

The Expert Systems knowledge can be obtained by the experience of a human expert and/or knowledge queries available on specialized bibliography; this knowledge could be documented, revised, complemented and used in several places and situations, improving the decision making process [15].

The classical Expert Systems use as model of representation a knowledge base consisting of a set of rules. Their principal disadvantage is the low uncertainty management, due to the inherent stiffness in the inference engine [9] and to the facts or data that could not be know with certitude. This problem could be risky in practical effects, because the statements given by the system could not be completely correct.

The probabilistic Expert Systems use as a knowledge base the probability space structure and the inference engine they use the conditional probabilities. This will lead to a better uncertainty management. Inside the probability space, the most exploited model or knowledge base is the Bayesian Network, which pretends that the probability propagation can be accurate, fast and it does not cause problems with the excessive number of parameters [2].

2.2 Bayesian Networks

A Bayesian Network (or a Belief Network) is a powerful knowledge and reasoning engine representation, because it has a multivariate probabilistic model that links the variables contained in a variable set using a directed graph that shows explicitly a causal influence. Thanks to the probability update mechanism in this type of networks, the Bayes Theorem, the Bayesian Networks are a useful tool for estimating probabilities of new evidences. A Bayesian Network is a causal type of network.

The Bayesian Networks are a formalism based on the probability and graphs theories. A Bayesian Network is defined by:

- A Directed Acyclic Graph (DAG) $G = (V, E)$, where V is the set of nodes of G and E is the set of edges in G.
- A finite probability space (Ω, Z, P).
- A set of random variables associated to the graph nodes and defined in (Ω, Z, P) such that:

$$P(V_1, V_2, \ldots, V_n) = \prod_{i=1}^{n} P(V_i | C(V_i)) \tag{1}$$

Where $C(V_i)$ is the set of causes (parents) of V_i in the graph G.

A Bayesian Network is by that, a causal graph that has been associated with a subjacent probabilistic representation. This representation allows to give a quantitative form to the reasoning made over the graph of the network.

In Artificial Learning, the data recollecting usually involves the compilation of cases, examples or object instances from different types or categories (classes), in such way that for the artificial learning step a model made from this data is created in order to be used for identifying groups or similarity in the data (non-supervised learning); or to predict the class of new object (supervised learning). In the same way a Bayesian Network could be created automatically (by learning) using statistical data (examples). There are two types of learning [13]:

- Parameter learning. Given the structure of a network (graph), we need to find the best parameter set (conditional probabilities) which fits the observed data.
- Structural learning. Without any hypothesis about the network structure, we need to find the one which represents best the observed data when the best parameters had been provided.

By that, given the values of a variable subset (evidence) a Bayesian Network can compute the probabilities of another variable set (query variables).

2.3 Tree Augmented Naive Bayes Algorithm

Tree Augmented Naive Bayes (TAN) [5] is an extended tree-like Naive Bayes, in which the class node directly points to all attribute node and an attribute node only has at most one parent from another attribute node. TAN is a specific case of general Bayesian Network classifiers [10, 16], in which the class node also directly points to all attribute nodes, but there is no limitation on the arcs among attribute nodes (except that they do not form any directed cycle). In practice, TAN is a good trade-off between the model complexity and learnability. Assume that $A_1, A_2, \cdots, A_m$ are m attributes and C is the class variable, the learning algorithm of TAN [8] is depicted as:

Algorithm 1. TAN (D)

Require: a training instance set D
Ensure: the built TAN
1: Compute the conditional mutual information $I_{\hat{P}_D}(A_i; A_j|C)$ between each pair of attributes, $i \neq j$.
2: Build a complete undirected graph in which nodes are attributes $A_1, ..., A_m$. Annotate the weight of an edge connecting A_i to A_j by $I_{\hat{P}_D}(A_i; A_j|C)$.
3: Build a complete undirected maximum weighted spanning tree.
4: Transform the built undirected tree to a directed one by choosing a root attribute and setting the direction of all edges to be outward from it.
5: Build a TAN model by adding a node labeled by C and adding an arc from C to each A_i.
6: Return the built TAN.

---

3 Development of Our Proposal

This section describes the development of the Expert System with a probabilistic inference engine based on Bayesian Networks that is used for the Diabetes diagnosis.

The Fig. 1 shows the proposed architecture for the Expert System. The elements of the architecture are listed below:

- Web app: It is the mechanism in which the doctor introduces the patient's symptoms and their general data.
- Web server: The GlassFish server has been mounted for the Web services implemented in JAX-WS.
- Databases: It stores the input and output data of the Web services (symptoms and diagnosis).
- Web services: It uses a XML standard for the exchange of data between the clients built in different platforms: Web or mobile app.
- Expert System: The principal components of the Expert System are the knowledge base and the inference engine.

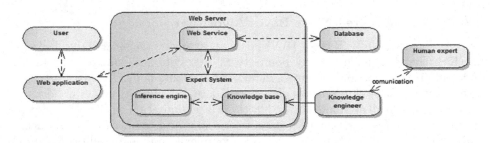

Fig. 1. Architecture for the proposed Expert System

3.1 Knowledge Base

The design of the knowledge base for the Expert System is done with some Knowledge Engineering tools and methods such as:

1. Scope definition and knowledge acquiring:

(a) Identification: The process in which the knowledge engineer learns about the problem situation and the details in a document, the main symptoms for the Diabetes diagnosis.
(b) Understanding: It involves medical bibliography queries, i.e. IMSS procedures books, research papers and personal observations.
(c) Formalization: The process of how organize the knowledge into a matrix representation.
(d) Implementation: The Expert System developed in Java.
(e) Tests: The diagnosis tests were made with the symptoms and data from 80 patients.

2. Knowledge matrix: For the diagnosis, we considered 19 variables that were the most relevant ones in the knowledge base, and they are established by the human expert and the knowledge engineer. It is important to distinguish that all the variables used in the inference engine are present in almost all the Mexican patients.

Table 1. Variables in the knowledge base

No.	Criteria	Values
1	Gender	{Female, Male}
2	Body mass index (BMI)	{Normal, Overweight, Type I Obesity, Type 2 Obesity, Type 3 Obesity}
3	Age	{Child, Adolescent, Adult, Old age}
4	Pregnancy	{No, Yes}
5	Fasting glucose levels	{Normal, Optimum Prediabetes, Diabetes}
6	Glucose tolerance	{Desirable, Intermediate, Elevated}
7	Diabetes family history	{No, Yes}
8	Sedentary lifestyle	{No, Yes}
9	High fat diet	{No, Yes}
10	Tiredness	{No, Yes}
11	Involuntary weight loss	{No, Yes}
12	Increased hunger	{No, Yes}
13	Cholesterol	{Desirable, Intermediate, Elevated}
14	Total blood pressure	{Normal, Medium, High}
15	Hydration/urine frequency	{Normal, High}
16	Previous gestational diabetes	{No, Yes}
17	Overweight newborns at past births	{No, Yes}
18	Congenital malformations at past births	{No, Yes}

3.2 Inference Engine

Two hundred fifty diagnoses and their variable configurations were used in order to build the evidence for the Bayesian Network.

Due to lost values on the diagnosis dataset, it was necessary to preprocess all the data. We present the procedures used in the data preprocessing stage:

1. Scope definition and knowledge acquiring:

- Nearby points mean.
- Linear interpolation.
- Series mean.
- Nearby points median.

2. The values with real numbers that belongs to the fuzzy variable set were discretized according to the linguistic variables considered in the Table 1. The discrete values for each variable were obtained employing the center of gravity (COG) method as a defuzzification process.
3. The diagnoses were made with 21 variables. In order to adapt the data to a new model with 19 variables some of them were merged.

(a) The variable hu replaced the urine frequency and hydration with a new value representing the ratio between these two.

(b) A new variable that represents the total blood pressure level was established. It counts both the diastolic and systolic blood pressure.
(c) The variable representing the vomit existence and frequency was omitted because it only had values on 10% of the diagnoses.

When the evidence was ready for process, the algorithm Augmented Naive Bayes was used to generate the Bayesian Network. The design of the Bayesian Network is shown in Fig. 2.

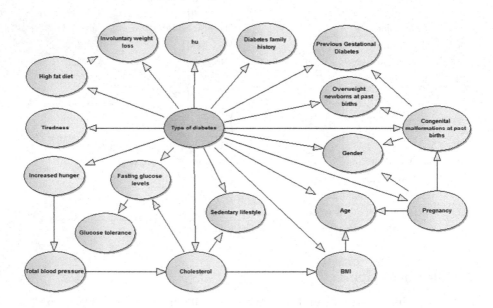

Fig. 2. Design of the Bayesian Network

4   Experiments and Results

The Expert System with the probabilistic inference engine served a group of 80 patients from the Unidad de Medicina Familiar from ISSSTEP. The sample was balanced in terms of the gender of the patients.

For viewing the efficiency of the diagnoses, confusion matrices are shown below [12]. In a confusion matrix we can extract some metrics to understand the distribution and nature of the wrong diagnoses thrown by the engine. In the Table 2 it is presented the confusion matrix with the results of the first fuzzy approach and the Table 3 reports the results from the new probabilistic approach.

According to the Tables 2 and 3 we can obtain the sensibility and specificity for each type of diagnosis from the two approaches. Both measures are shown in Eqs. (2) and (3).

Table 2. Confusion matrix with fuzzy approach

Specialist/FES	No diabetes	Prediabetes	DM I	DM II	GD	Total
No diabetes	12	0	0	0	0	12
Prediabetes	0	13	0	0	0	13
DMI	2	12	8	0	1	23
DMII	1	6	0	10	0	17
GD	2	3	0	0	10	15
Total	17	34	8	10	11	80

Table 3. Confusion matrix with new probabilistic approach

Specialist/FES	No diabetes	Prediabetes	DM I	DM II	GD	Total
No diabetes	12	0	0	0	0	12
Prediabetes	0	13	0	0	0	13
DMI	0	0	21	0	2	23
DMII	0	0	0	17	0	17
GD	0	0	0	0	15	15
Total	12	13	21	17	17	80

As we could observe in the Table 4, the Bayesian Network sensibility is considerably better than the fuzzy sensibility in the last three Diabetes types, this shows that the probability of classifying correctly in all patients is near 100%. While the Bayesian Network specificity is near zero, what it shows is that is a completely healthy patient would not obtain a Diabetes diagnosis from the Expert System.

$$Sensibility = \frac{truePositives}{truePositives + falseNegatives} \quad (2)$$

$$Specificity = \frac{trueNegatives}{trueNegatives + falsePositives} \quad (3)$$

Table 4. Comparation between sensibilities and specificities

Diagnosis	FES sensibility	FES specificity	BN sensibility	BN specificity
No diabetes	1	0.397	1	0.029
Prediabetes	1	0.402	1	0.029
DMI	0.347	0.21	0.913	0
DMII	0.588	0.317	1	0.031
GD	0.666	0.338	1	0.03

Table 5. Test with both approaches

No.	Diagnosis with FES	Diagnosis with BN	Real diagnosis
1	GD 80%	GD 100%	GD
2	GD 76%	GD 97.8%	GD
3	GD 67.9%	GD 100%	GD
4	DMI 67.9%	DMI 99.2%	DMI
5	DMI 88%	DMI 80.2%	DMI
		DMII 19.8%	
6	DMI 95.9%	DMI 99.9%	DMI
7	DMII 71.9%	DMII 99.9%	DMII
8	DMII 81.9%	DMII 90.7%	DMII
		DMII 9.2%	
9	DMII 94.1%	DMII 99.9%	DMII
10	No diabetes 100%	No Diabetes 97.8%	No Diabetes
		DMI 2.1%	
11	No diabetes 100%	No Diabetes 99.5%	No Diabetes
		DMI 0.4%	
12	No diabetes 100%	No Diabetes 99.2%	No Diabetes
		DMI 0.8%	
13	Prediabetes 100%	Prediabetes 52.3%	Prediabetes
		DMI 35.2%	
		GD 12.4%	
14	Prediabetes 100%	Prediabetes 70%	Prediabetes
		GD 25%	
		No Diabetes 5%	
15	Prediabetes 100%	Prediabetes 72.5%	Prediabetes
		No Diabetes 27.5%	

The Table 5 reports 15 tests that were conducted with both approaches; the diagnoses produced by the human expert agree with the ones produces by the two approaches. One important point is that the fuzzy approach does not show more than one diagnosis as the probabilistic approach shows all of the diagnoses in which the probabilities are different from zero.

In the test No. 14, we can observe that the patient has a high probability of having Prediabetes, but as she is pregnant the system shows a 25% probability of having GD. This diagnosis could lead to a set of appropriate advises and cares to take for the patient in order to prevent the development of GD.

For the test case No. 5, the patient has type I Diabetes Mellitus but it is reported the probability of having type II Diabetes Mellitus.

In the test No. 15, the patient has Prediabetes, but we can see that the "No Diabetes" level is near 28%, so the doctor can give a good advice to the patient to prevent the appearing of the first signs of Diabetes.

5 Conclusions and Future Work

In the first prototype of the Expert System, there were considered near 10,000 production rules for the inference engine. These rules depend on the context of the problem and could have a degree of uncertainty, because not every rule is applicable to all the Diabetes Mellitus types. With the Bayesian Network approach, the available variables for the Prediabetes and Non-diabetic diagnoses were incremented.

With this work, we have obtained a very useful and efficient tool because it can give the probabilities of all the types of Diabetes, and this is helpful in the preventive healthcare and this could give more time to the patients to follow a good lifestyle and adopt healthier habits. Even with this, it is possible to correct the medication a patient takes.

It has been detected that numerous works uses only a small subset of all the possible variables they use, this could lead to some risky statements in the diagnosis made by the systems but for some approaches it is demonstrated that their systems actually gives good results but again this depends on the inference engine model used.

As a future work we pretend to release publicly the Expert System with Bayesian inference engine and obtain a bigger dataset that could be useful for having statistical data with respect to the Diabetes Mellitus in Mexico, in order to being used by doctors and nutritionist and they could give recommendations to their patients about their lifestyles.

References

1. Anouncia, M., et al.: Design of a diabetic diagnosis system using rough sets. Cybern. Inf. Technol. **13**, 124–139 (2013)
2. Castillo, E., Álvarez, E.: Sistemas Expertos Aprendizaje e Incertidumbre. Ediciones Paraninfo, Madrid (1997)
3. Coiera, E.: Guide to Medical Informatics, the Internet and Telemedicine. Chapman & Hall, London (1997)
4. Cruz-Gutiérrez, V., Sánchez-López, A.: Un sistema experto difuso en la Web para diagnóstico de diabetes. Res. Comput. Sci. **107**, 145–155 (2015)
5. Friedman, N., Geiger, N., Goldszmidt, M.: Bayesian network classifiers. Mach. Learn. **29**, 131–163 (1997)
6. Giarratano, J., Riley, G.: Sistemas expertos: principios y programación. International Thomson, México (2001)
7. Instituto del Seguro Social: Guía de Práctica Clínica GPC, Diagnóstico y Tratamiento de la Diabetes Mellitus tipo 2. México (2012)
8. Jiang, L., Cai, Z., Wang, D., Zhang, H.: Improving tree augmented Naive Bayes for class probability estimation. Knowl.-Based Syst. **26**, 239–245 (2012)

9. Lahoz-Beltrá, R.: Bioinformática: simulación, vida artificial e inteligencia artificial. Ediciones Díaz de Santos S. A, Madrid (2004)
10. Madden, M.G.: On the classification performance of TAN and general Bayesian Networks. Knowl.-Based Syst. **22**, 489–495 (2009)
11. Menezes, A.C., Pinheiro, P.R., Pinheiro, M.C.D., Cavalcante, T.P.: Towards the applied hybrid model in decision making: support the early diagnosis of type 2 diabetes. Inf. Comput. Appl. **7473**, 648–655 (2012)
12. Morales-Vega, D.: Clasificadores Bayesianos en la Selección Embrionaria en Tratamientos de Reproducción Asistida. Bachelor thesis. Universidad del País Vasco, Donostia (2008)
13. Neapolitan, R.: Learning Bayesian Networks. Pearson Prentice Hall, Upper Saddle River (2004)
14. Nnamoko, N., Arshad, F., England, D., Vora, J.: Fuzzy expert system for type 2 diabetes mellitus (T2DM) management using dual inference mechanism. In: AAAI Spring Symposium Series, pp. 67–70 (2013)
15. Quiroz-Hernández, J.L.: Prototipo de un sistema experto en el diagnóstico de acné. Bachelor thesis. Benemérita Universidad Autónoma de Puebla, México (2000)
16. Xiao, J., He, C., Jiang, X.: Structure identification of Bayesian classifiers based on GMDH. Knowl.-Based Syst. **22**, 461–470 (2009)
17. Zeki, T., Malakooti, M., Ataeipoor, Y., Tabibi, S.: An expert system for diabetes diagnosis. Am. Acad. Sch. Res. J. **4**(5) (2012)

iEnsemble: A Framework for Committee Machine Based on Multiagent Systems with Reinforcement Learning

Arnoldo Uber Junior[✉], Paulo José de Freitas Filho,
Ricardo Azambuja Silveira, Mariana Dehon Costa e Lima,
and Rodolfo Wilvert Reitz

Postgraduate Program in Computer Science - PPGCC,
Federal University of Santa Catarina - UFSC, Florianópolis, Brazil
arnoldo.u.jr@gmail.com, mariana.dehon@gmail.com,
rodolfo.reitz@posgrad.ufsc.br,
{freitas.filho,ricardo.silveira}@ufsc.br

Abstract. The Machine Learning is one of the areas of Artificial Intelligence whose objective is the development of computational techniques for knowledge and building systems able to acquire knowledge automatically. One of the main challenges of learning algorithms is to maximize generalization. Thus the board machine, or a combination of more of a learning machine approach known in literature with the denomination ensemble along with the theory agents, become a promising alternative in this challenge. In this context, this research proposes the iEnsemble framework, which aims to provide a model of the ensemble through a multi-agent system architecture, where generalization, combination and learning are made through agents, through the performance of their respective roles. In the proposal, the agents follow each their life cycle and also perform the iStacking algorithm. This algorithm is based on Stacking method, which uses the reinforcement learning to define the result of the Ensemble. To validate the initial proposal of the framework, some experiments have been performed and the results obtained and limitations are presented.

Keywords: Committee machine · Ensemble · Multiagent Systems · Reinforcement learning

1 Introduction

In the daily life of most people, when there is need to make a decision, often refers to the opinion of others about the problem. This behavior is intended to get more views on the issue of doubt, then, given the different opinions, it is made a decision that is expected to be assertive. This situation is also present in other situations, such as organizing a group to vote on any issue. In this case, it seeks the most different points of view, but through a vote, to express their opinion on something where usually the decision is a simple yes or no, but grounded in a great experience of the subject.

In Artificial Intelligence, specifically in machine learning area, the idea of forming committees, namely the formation of a group that has knowledge about a problem, but

O. Pichardo-Lagunas and S. Miranda-Jiménez (Eds.): MICAI 2016, Part II, LNAI 10062, pp. 65–80, 2017.
DOI: 10.1007/978-3-319-62428-0_6

in a way, its members have opinions and different views to some degree, on the subject, it had its first proposals made in research Ablow, Kaylor and Nilsson in 1965 [22]. In these early works, the general idea was to combine different estimators for final improvement of the classification system. Intensification of research in the area only came later, with the advent of computational evolution and through works such as Hansen and Salamon [14] and Perrone and Cooper [24] which achieved significant improvements in the performance of Artificial Neural Networks (RNA) from the committee use.

The Machinery Committee (known in the literature with the ensemble name) is one of learning techniques, roughly based on the divide and conquer approach. [30] According to this approach, a complex computational task is solved by dividing into several less complex computational tasks and is made later the combination of their results. The division computationally less complex task usually performed by classifies pain, which can have different forms; since the conquest, it is performed by combining the results of classifiers and definition of the final decision. However, for this technique has a good performance, it is necessary that the individual classifiers have good performance, but at the same time, have different behaviors, or have a variety of errors.

Looking in greater detail the procedures for modeling a machine committee, it can be noted that the division task of the problem and his delegation is complex and depends on some decision-makings. This task considers, for example, the dataset partitioning available between the binder and, at the same time considers the training modes and implementation. It also defines the execution parameters, monitor the implementation and get the individual results of the classifiers and can repeat these steps several times. Already the achievement task, i.e., the combination of the results and final decision, it is also complex because it must unite the results, considering certain aptitude classifier that a priori there is no weighting specifying which classifier is more assertive or that should have greater input in the final decision, so a decision to be made and which directly affects the accuracy of the machine committee as a whole.

It must also consider that often in the divide and conquer approach is possible to determine the criteria of the prior problem of division, that is, at design time. However, for some types of problem that is often not possible and divide the problem into subproblems or the division of the possible strategies in different alternatives to solve a certain problem has to be made "on-the-fly" i.e. in runtime, since in some cases not all the problem of invariants are clear or available at design time.

In this context, the theory of agents is proposed as an option to assist in decision making and coordination of the machines committee, following the tasks of "divide and conquer" and providing a way of learning the agents through enhanced. Thus this paper proposes a framework for machines committee using the theory of agents, which intrinsically is the proposal of an algorithm to committee machines based on agents, and also the proposed training of agents by reinforcement learning [32, 33]. In addition to the framework proposal is the objective of the research apply the framework in different case studies and present the results.

2 Problem

Machines committees, such as the name implies, it is the union over a learning machine to generate a solution to a problem. In addition to having the main objective to maximize the generalizability, have two motivating factors: availability of computational resources (to generate the union of various techniques in solving a problem) and the statement made by [37], which shows not existing generic models of machine learning, which on average have better performance than any other model for a class of problems whatsoever [20].

Joining classifiers is not a trivial task, that is, there are several ways to create an Ensemble, performing the training of classifiers and combine their outputs in a final solution. During this process, several decisions must be made to be sought to generalize the model and also to have the coordination to seek a final solution in the minimum satisfactory to the problem. At this point, the theory of agents plays an important role as it allows the training and autonomous decision making of agents, based on their experiences, and provide mechanisms to scale and distribute processing. As for the training of agents, not intended to create a direct relationship between input-output, but to create an increasing learning of the agent in relation to the environment and the result of their actions, that is, action and reward, so the agent behavior It can be modeled by changing their ways, with the goal of a great policy, such as the Q-learning method [36]. Thus one of the main issues of this research is to verify the possibility of moving on maximizing performance machine learning, with the proposal of iEnsemble framework [32, 33]. For this purpose, they are made the framework of the implementation of experiments on case studies, and these compared to the original methods. In the end, the results are presented.

3 Theoretical Reference

The development of the framework iEnsemble based on Committee Machine and Multiagent Systems [2, 5, 6, 8, 21, 27, 32] with Reinforcement Learning Algorithms. The following is a brief summary of the theoretical framework used in this work, to contextualize the reader to the presentation of the proposed model.

The chosen platform is known for JADE (Java Agent Development Framework) [2, 18], which is a framework for developing agent-based applications in accordance with the specifications FIPA (Foundation for Intelligent Physical Agents) for multi-agent systems [11, 27].

3.1 Committee Machine

The Learning Machine (AM) is one of the areas of Artificial Intelligence (AI) whose objective is the development of computational techniques for knowledge and building systems able to acquire knowledge automatically [25]. The acquired learning may take many forms, depending on the nature of the element performance, the component to be optimized and feedback available [26].

The main challenge of learning algorithms is to maximize the learner generalizability from observed data of the problem. Generalization is the ability of a machine to answer satisfactorily the data or samples the input-output mapping not known during the learning process [30]. To obtain satisfactory classifiers with generalizability, various algorithms and approaches to machine learning have been proposed in the literature, among which stands out the machine committee.

The idea of forming committees, namely the formation of a group that has knowledge about a problem, but in a way, has different opinions, to some degree on the subject, it had its first proposals made in Ablow research, Kaylor and Nilsson in 1965 [22]. In these early works, the general idea was to combine different estimators for final improvement of the classification system. Intensification of research in the area only came later, with the advent of computational evolution and through works such as Hansen and Salamon [14] and Perrone and Cooper [24] which achieved significant improvements in RNA performance from the use of Committee.

3.2 Ensemble and Modular

In the literature on machinery committees, some authors refer directly committees machines Ensembles [4], making no differentiation as to the approaches considered Ensemble and cited by Modular [15].

The committee machine can be divided into two categories: ensembles and modular architecture. At first, they combine models as, for example, neural networks, which have individually resolve by itself, the problem as a whole [14], but best results are obtained with the combination. In the modular approach, the problem is broken down into different tasks so that the final solution requires the contribution of all committee members (experts), each with its respective task. The mixture of experts is a modular approach. A representation may be seen the two types in Fig. 1.

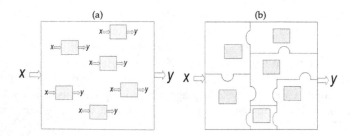

Fig. 1. Types of machines Committees. (A) Ensemble (b) Modular (Source: [1])

In this research work is used to direct relationship Ensembles and committee machines, or used the approach proposed by Bishop [4]. Thus, the term machinery committee not to modular approaches and referenced in the text as Ensemble is adopted.

3.3   Static Structure and Dynamics

As for architecture, machine committees can be classified into two categories [15]:

- Static structures: this structure combination of classifiers is made by an algorithm that does not receive the input signal. Bagging Methods such as [7], Boosting [28] Stacking and [37] are part of the structure [16]:
- Dynamic structures: in this case, the input signal is considered in the algorithm that integrates the outputs of classifiers to form a global output. Approaches involving mixing specialists and their hierarchical version are part of the dynamic structures.

The bagging method was one of the first algorithms used in ensemble. This method is based on resampling of the training patterns so as to obtain different training subsets for each classifier [7].

From a data set, a re-sampling is performed with the same probability of s-harvest for each Ensemble classifier. Data can be repeated between the classifiers, which is called replacement.

Using different sets of training is the main strategy proposed in a Bagging method for generating diversity, but if the classifiers generalize similarly not have a good performance. Thus this method has better performance classifiers to urge learning level because a small change in the training set generates a significant variation in the generalization of capacity [3].

Boosting was proposed by Schapire [28]. In this method, the training of classifiers that make up the Ensemble must be done sequentially. The probability of a given sample to be chosen depends on the contribution of this to the error of classifiers already trained. The most popular version of this method is called AdaBoost. In this approach, each classifier is trained sequentially, and distribution of training data is made taking into account the errors of the previous classifier [3].

The main difference between Bagging and Boosting algorithms is that in the learning data Bagging has a uniform probability of selection and Boosting are selected based on the previous classifier error.

The Stacking method was proposed in [37]. This method operates on the two steps of building an Ensemble: classifying and combining the results. At first, it uses the idea of resampling without replacement when selecting data for training. The second step is done by proposing a classifier which combines the outputs of the first.

Many works are proposed based on Stacking method using similar approaches. [39] extended the method and proposed an approach called ensemble of neural networks, and a neural network as combiner at level 1, in others like Stacking MLR [12] StackingC [3, 29]. The method proposed in the iEnsemble framework is based on Stacking method, where the meta-classifier is performed by Ensemble agent.

3.4   Learning

The supervised learning is based on a set of input and output examples is presented to the classifier. Based on the input data, the classifier performs the processing, and the obtained output is compared with the expected output. If not within the limits, an adjustment is made seeking to minimize the error. A supervised learning example is a backpropagation [15].

Unsupervised learning has a set of expected outputs, i.e., does not have a coach. In this case, the classifier of the input data set and the implementation of classifier directs to an output pattern. Some training quality rules are followed and depending on the results, adjustments to occur classifier parameters. Examples unsupervised learning are Hopfield algorithm and maps of Kohonen.

The reinforcement learning (AR) is based on the existence of critical external environment, which evaluates the defined action, but without explicitly indicate the correct action to be taken [13, 31]. AIR uses a structure of states, actions and rewards as shown in Fig. 2.

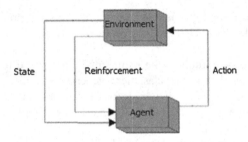

Fig. 2. Reinforcement learning (Source: Adapted from [31])

The agent acts in an environment described by a set of states and can run for each state a set of actions. Each action performed gets strengthened, which indicates the immediate value of the transition state-action-new state. Over time, this produces a learning state-action pairs of sequence and its reinforcements. The goal of the agent is to learn a policy that maximizes an expected sum of long-term [31].

One of the main reinforcement learning algorithms is the Q-learning [36], which seeks to define the es-reap the best action in AR. The main purpose of the Q-learning, shown in Fig. 3, is estimated independently in each state s in which the learner is the value of the function Q (s, a), i.e. Q utility value for the pair (state, action) and from this point, allow to obtain the best action (higher utility value).

```
1:  procedure QLEARNING(r, α_q, ε, γ)
2:      Inicialize Q(s, a)
3:      repeat
4:          Inicialize s
5:          repeat
6:              Selecione a de acordo com a política ε-gulosa
7:              Observe os valores de r e s'
8:              Q(s, a) ← (1 − α_q)Q(s, a) + α_q(r + γ max_{a∈A}(Q(s', a))
9:              s ← s'
10:         until Encontrar um estado final
11:     until Atingir NEp episódios
12:     return Q(s, a)                           ▷ Matriz dos Q-valores
13: end procedure
```

Fig. 3. Q-Learning algorithm (Source: Adapted from [36])

3.5   Ensembles and Agents

The Ensembles have shown better results than individual classifiers to group results, the various models to get a better generalization [23]. A survey on Ensembles can be found in [38].

Some of the early work involving Ensembles and SMA is the case [34]. In this work the SMA is used to run the classifiers distributed and decentralized way, which occurs tam well [10].

[17] extends the use of the agents for detection of intrusion, creating and dynamically changing parameters and creating interaction with the binder. [9] proposes the cooperation of agents to improve the performance of classifiers, and also interact after the combination of results.

4   Framework iEnsemble

The iEnsemble framework has a machinery committee architecture based on SMA. The proposed framework provides: an agent architecture, a model for interaction between these agents, an algorithm for the life cycle of the SMA based on Stacking method, which was named iStacking and base classes package to provide structure development of the ensemble.

The iEnsemble name was proposed because of the union of the theory of intelligent agents and machines committee, giving thus the iEnsemble name whose meaning is Ensemble intelligent, or also, Intelligent Ensemble.

4.1   Model iEnsemble

The model proposed for iEnsemble is shown in Fig. 4.

In this model are presented various interactions between the various classes of agents and possible interaction user with MAS. Each of the classes of agents has a certain function, which will be called in this research paper.

4.1.1   Roles of Agents

The roles of agents that make up the Ensemble is composed of actions and decisions which the agent performs during its life cycle, described as:

- Monitor: This agent is intended to enable user interaction with the SMA. This interaction depends on the situation for which the iEnsemble was created and can occur for many reasons, such as informing a set of parameters, request a result, assist in training;
- Leader: Has the assignment of coordinating the multi-agent system in relation to the results. Among its functions are: to receive information or monitor agent settings made by the user, check the state of SMA, validate structure agents and start agents if necessary and return to monitor the results reported by iEnsemble agent;
- iEnsemble: It has a key role in iEnsemble as coordinates classifiers agents, distributes tasks, gets results and combines. Analyzes the results obtained, if in training

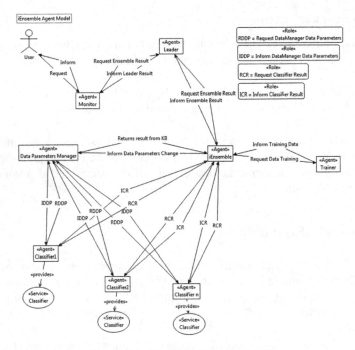

Fig. 4. Model of MAS for iEnsemble

mode, updates its knowledge base through reinforcement learning. If have satisfactory results, return to the Leader agent, otherwise may decide to make additional adjustments to the SMA and request new classification, new combination, and analysis of results;

- Classifier: Responsible for interacting with the iEnsemble and DataParameterManager agent for the initial values for the implementation of classifier algorithm. After interacting with the classifier and run it. Receives the results, analyze the validity through a local knowledge base and communicates the iEnsemble agent;

- DataParametersManager: It has a data knowledge base and parameters used for the problem, as well as the history of what has already been sent to the Classifier and the results. Receives interaction iEnsemble, search their knowledge base and informs classifiers changes in parameters and input data set. If a given classification situation has already been trained or presented to classifiers, returns to iEnsemble results avoiding new presentation;

- Trainer: has the same functions as the Classifier agent running mode, helping, in this case, the generalization of the problem, but differs in learning mode. In this case, it plays a role of returning the set of comparison values and assist iEnsemble in improving their local knowledge.

The actions that the agents will perform and the types of decisions may vary from one ensemble to another as the application situation, but it is aimed to propose a model that allows adapting the changes using the characteristics of the agents.

4.2   Algorithm iStacking

The algorithm for iEnsemble, which can also be regarded as the life cycle of the SMA, was based on Stacking method. In its classic form, the Stacking method has two steps: combining and generalization and follows the representation shown in Fig. 5.

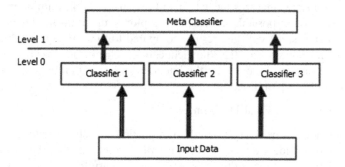

Fig. 5. Stacking model (Source: [1]).

The iStacking is divided into three stages, those made through agents: generalization, combination, and learning. The first stage search to more generalized model, i.e., better search using the training dataset and parameters, using the classifiers for the greatest variety possible. It is worth remembering that search classifier with a good individual performance for the problem, but they, when compared with each other, have a higher error diversity. The second stage is when there is a combination of the results obtained through interaction with the Classifiers agents and classifier goal. This combination is observing the knowledge base of Ensemble agent that acts as classifier goal. Each model iteration, the classifiers are scored according to the results obtained by training and a weight adjustment for the contribution in the final decision is up to date. Still part of the combination. The third step, the learning is done by strengthening the knowledge so far acquired the quality of the results of the classifiers. These steps are best described by the following steps:

Step 1. Generalization:

- iEnsemble search for DataParametersManager DataParametersManager and informs about the parameters and the data set to be used for input;
- iEnsemble demand for classifiers (C) available where $C > 1$;
- Classifiers DataParametersManager informs the input dataset and parameters to be used, i.e. $\forall i$, $i..C$.

- iEnsemble calls on Classifier results. This information comes accompanied by statistics of hits and misses. The iEnsemble feeds the local knowledge base;
- iEnsemble informs DataParametersManagers the parameter modification observing the local knowledge base;
- Step 1 is repeated until no more parameters are changed options and based on the decision of iEnsemble.

Step 2. Reinforcement Learning:

- iEnsemble search in knowledge base current status classification and action taken. It is worth remembering that the classification current state is set according to the case study in question and not necessarily just the return of all the classifiers.
- If encounter a state, analyzes the action and reward. If are in training mode, check the number of other possible actions, and explores, updating the knowledge base (Q and Q table (s, a)) with the results compared to the training value;
- If do not find the state in the knowledge base, check the possible actions and explores one of them by updating the knowledge base (Q table and Q (s, a)) with the result of the exploration.

Step 3. Combination and Final Decision:

- The combination is performed based on the action associated with the state. This action should include the way in which the result was achieved, i.e., what was the strategy adopted for the results. This strategy may vary from state to state, where, for example, can be taken action to compose the result based on a classifier or more, the average proportions of each classifier, and such. The method for combining may vary according to the case study.

5 Application and Result

To validate the previously proposed framework iEnsemble, some experiments were done through the development of applications Ensemble following the iEnsemble model and algorithm.

5.1 iEnsemble World Temperature

At first the preparation of iEnsemble there was a concern in combining stage of the validation of results and training. Thus a case study was defined to allow a relative ease of data acquisition, classification, and return, where the focus of this experiment would be the combination of results and learning Ensemble through reinforcement. In this sense a simple problem has been defined: What is the temperature in a given geographical location by latitude and longitude? The first view is a simple problem, whose solution is the query in any meteorological service and getting results. However, if the same query is made in two separate services, there may be different results. If three more likely to be even more distinctive results, so that the temperature?

To answer this question and to extend this simple problem a little, another issue to the problem was added: What is the temperature for a period (week) future day-to-day at a certain time? So the problem was defined as know the current temperature and the future forecast period at a given time.

Having defined the problem and available iEnsemble framework, it developed a prototype called ieWT, referencing the iEnsemble and added the initial World Temperature, whose translation would be global temperature. This name was chosen because for the geographic coordinates were chosen three capital cities around the world, could be any points. Therefore, cities have been defined: Brasilia, London, and Japan's geographical coordinates were obtained at ground zero of these capitals as official websites of the same.

The state s set to the experiment is pair time of day and city, i.e., s = (time, city). The time was set at 15 s intervals and cities as described above. The action for the function Q (s, a) defined for this problem as the rule percentage share of each classifier in the result, namely, to generate the final temperature. In this case, there may be classifiers that have greater or lesser participation, or also not part of the final result.

There are several available on the web services that provide the temperature through Web services with SOAP and REST technology. Among these services, four were by focusing on the most utilization: Google (browser/Mobile), OpenWeather (browser), Forecast (Mobile) and Apixu (Mobile). In the experiment, training mode, three of the four services are used as binders, and fourth provide the temperature used for comparison. In run mode, the four services are used for classification.

The latter uses a form to interact with the user and display the result of the execution of the prototype. This form can be seen in Fig. 6.

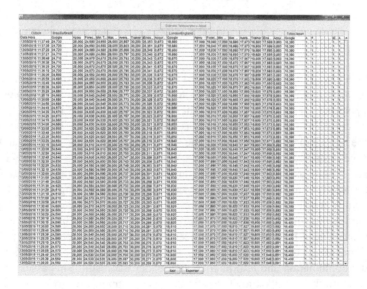

Fig. 6. Form experiment ieWT

In the form of Fig. 6, the following information is presented, in order: date and time, the con-consultations to temperature services, static combinations as average, minimum and maximum, the temperature of training classifier, return the WTAEnsemble and accuracy in relation to training temperature. This first set of data is related to the capital Brasilia/Brazil. After this information is repeated in London/UK and Tokyo/Japan. To return to the user, the agents that make up the ieWT held various communications with each other, until the return to the WTAMonitor. These communication agents made this run of ieWT can be seen in Fig. 7.

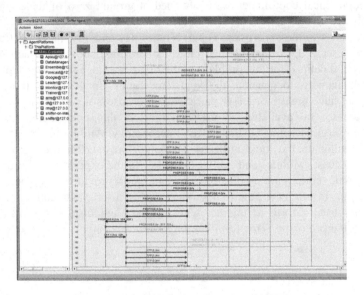

Fig. 7. Communication of agents of ieWT

Figure 7 shows the messages exchanged between the agents during the execution of ieWT. At first the WTAMonitor search for a WTALeader, finding it requests the current temperature for the three capitals. The WTALeader accepts the communication, performs its duties mentioned in Chap. 4, is located at least one WTAEnsemble and executes the application temperature. The WTAEnsemble tells WTADataParameterManager geographical coordinates locates WTAClassifier agents and calls for return temperatures. These ask the WTADataParameterManager geographical coordinates, applying for services to temperature, analyze the return according to the knowledge base and return the temperature to consider valid. The WTAEnsemble receive the returns, if in training mode, check the temperature with WTAClassifierTrainner and updates its knowledge base through reinforcement learning and returns the parameters to match. Otherwise, consult the knowledge base and returns the parameters to match. Performs the combination and returns to WTALeader the result. This assesses whether it is a valid return through its knowledge base if so communicates to WTAMonitor the result, otherwise, repeats the process.

The results obtained by ieWT were evaluated by accuracy. However, for the other experiments, we intend to use the cross-validation stratified 10-fold [19]. As a way of analyzing the accuracy three charts were developed based on feedback from ieWT about the return of WTAClassifierTrainner and are presented in Fig. 8.

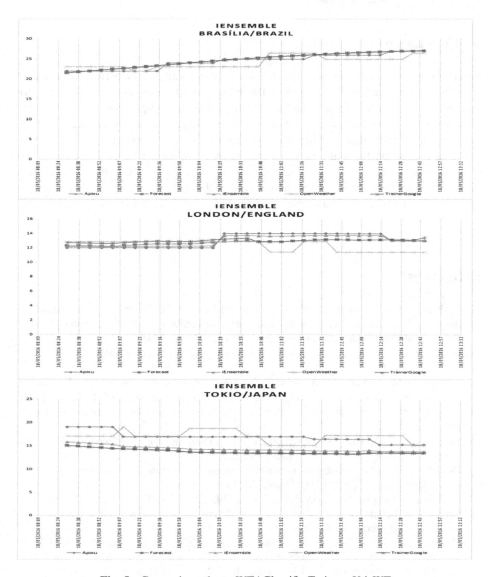

Fig. 8. Comparison charts WTAClassifierTrainner X ieWT

In the first graph due to the little variation of classifiers, the ieWT drew a moni-toring line very close to WTAClassifierTrainer. In the other, there is a greater variation of classifiers, but the WTAEnsemble training period adjusted the confidence weights and during the execution sought to follow the line of WTAClassifierTrainer. The length of time registered in the graphs was divided into two: training and implementation. At first, the iStacking algorithm had to make three classifiers and the fourth classifier was used as a trainer. In the second period, the fourth classifier was only consulted, but their values were not used for training.

6   Conclusion

Based on preliminary results it is possible to observe a satisfactory performance ieWT after the training period, thus reaching the initial goal of achieving a case study to assess the combination of results and the reinforcement learning. Using the framework iEnsemble met expectations and met the necessary requisites for the application and carrying out of tests, thus enabling its application to other case studies.

As a suggestion for future work, more experiments should be made in new case studies to demonstrate the same behavior. Improvements can still be made in the iEnsemble framework, such as the inclusion of techniques of validation 10-fold cross and improvements in the learning algorithm using Deep reinforcement learning and transfer learning.

References

1. Barbosa. B.H.G.: Computação Evolucionária e Máquinas de Comitê na Identificação de Sistemas Não-Lineares. Tese. Belo Horizonte: Universidade Federal de Minas Gerais. Programa de Pós-Graduação em Engenharia Elétrica (2009). 224:il
2. Bellifemine, F., Caire, G., Greewood, D.: Developing Multiagent Systems with JADE, p. 300. Wiley, New York (2007)
3. Bibimoune, M., Elghazel, H., Aussem, A.: An empirical comparison of supervised ensemble learning approaches. In: European Conference on Machine Learning, ECMLPKDD (2013)
4. Bishop, C.M.: Neural Networks for Pattern Recognition. Oxford University Press, Oxford (1995)
5. Bordini, R.H., Hubner, J.F., Woolridge, M.: Programming Multiagent Systems in AgentSpeak using Jason, p. 292. Wiley, Sussex (2007)
6. Bradshaw, J.M.: An introduction to software agents. In: Software Agents, pp. 3–46. MIT Press, Massachusetts (1997). ISBN:0-262-52234-9
7. Breiman, L.: Bagging predictors. Mach. Learn. **24**, 123–140 (1996)
8. Brenner, W., Zarnekow, R., Wittig, H.: Intelligent Software Agents: Foundations and Applications. Springer, Berlin (1998)
9. Calderón, J., López-Ortega, O., Castro-Espinoza, F.A.: A multi-agent ensemble of classifiers. In: Sidorov, G., Galicia-Haro, S.N. (eds.) MICAI 2015. LNCS, vol. 9413, pp. 499–508. Springer, Cham (2015). doi:10.1007/978-3-319-27060-9_41
10. Cervantes, L., Lee, J.-S., Lee, J.: Agent-based approach to distributed ensemble learning of fuzzy ARTMAP classifiers. In: Nguyen, N.T., Grzech, A., Howlett, Robert J., Jain, Lakhmi C. (eds.) KES-AMSTA 2007. LNCS, vol. 4496, pp. 805–814. Springer, Heidelberg (2007). doi:10.1007/978-3-540-72830-6_84

11. FIPA: Foundation for intelligent physical agents. Disponível em. http://www.fipa.org/. Acesso em: 06 mai. 2016
12. Guermeur, Y., Paugam-Moisy, H., Gallinari, P.: Multivariate linear regression on classifier outputs: a capacity study. In: Niklasson, L., Bodén, M., Ziemke, T. (eds.) ICANN 98 Perspectives in Neural Computing, pp. 693–698. Springer, London (1998). doi:10.1007/978-1-4471-1599-1_106
13. Guelpedi, M.V.C., Ribeiro, C.H., Omar, N.: Utilização de Aprendizagem por Reforço para Modelagem Autônoma do Aprendiz em um Tutor Inteligente. Simpósio Brasileiro de Informática na Educação. UFRJ (2003)
14. Hansen, L., Salomon, P.: Neural network ensembles. IEEE Trans. Pattern Anal. Mach. Intell. 12, 993–1001 (1990)
15. Haykin, S.S.: Redes Neurais, 2nd edn. Bookman, New York (2001)
16. Haykin, S.S.: Neural Networks: A Comprehensive Foundation, 3rd edn. Prentice Hall, Upple Saddle River (2007)
17. Helmy, T. et al.: Adaptive ensemble and hybrid models for classification of bioinformatics datasets. Trans. Fuzzy Neural Netw. Bioinform. (2012)
18. JADE: Java agent development framework. Disponível em: http://jade.tilab.com. Acesso em: 5 mai. 2016
19. Kohavi, R.A.: Study of cross-validation and bootstrap for accuracy estimation and model selection. Int. Joint Conf. Artif. Intell. 14, 1137–1145 (1995)
20. Lima, C.A.M.: Comitê de Máquinas: Uma abordagem Unificada Empregando Máquinas de Vetores-Suporte. Tese. Campinas: Universidade Estadual de Campinas. Programa de Pós-Graduação em Engenharia Elétrica e de Computação (2004)
21. Magid, N., Giovanni, C., Bahri, P.: A methodology for the analysis and design of multiagent systems using JADE. Int. J. Comput. Syst. Sci. Eng. Spec. Issue Softw. Eng. for Multiagent Syst. (2006). Murdoch University, Austrália
22. Nilsson, N.J.: Learning Machines. McGraw-Hill, New York (1965)
23. Oza, N.C., Tumer, K.: Classifier ensembles: select real-world applications. Inf. Fusion 9, 4–20 (2008)
24. Perrone, M.P., Cooper, L.N.: When networks disagree: ensemble methods for hybrid neural networks. In: R. J
25. Rezende, S.O.: Sistemas Inteligentes: Fundamentos e aplicações, Barueri, São Paulo (2003)
26. Russel, S.J., Norvig, P.: Inteligência Artificial: A Modern Approach, p. 649. Prentice Hall, Upper Saddle River (2010)
27. Sacile, R., Paolucci, M.: Agent-based manufacturing and control systems, p. 288. CRC Press LLC, Flórida (2005)
28. Schapire, R.E.: The strength of weak learnability. Mach. Learn. 5(2), 197–227 (1990). Kluwer Academic Publishers, Boston
29. Seewald, A.K.: How to make stacking better and faster while also taking care of an unknown weakness. In: Proceedings of the Nineteenth International Conference on Machine Learning, pp. 554–561. Morgan Kaufmann Publishers (2002)
30. Silva, T.C.: Aprendizado de máquina em redes complexas: modelagem, análise e aplicações. Tese. São Carlos: Universidade de São Paulo –USP. Instituto de Ciências Matemáticas e de Computação (2012)
31. Sutton, R., Barto, A.: Reinforcement Learning: An Introduction. MIT Press, Cambridge (1998)
32. Junior, A.U., Silveira, R.A.: HIPS: Um Framework para Escalonamento Distribuído de Processos em Sistemas de Produção Utilizando Sistemas Multiagente. Avances en sistemas e informatica 7, 7–15 (2010)

33. Junior, A.U., de Freitas Filho, P.J., Silveira, R.A.: E-HIPS: an extention of the framework HIPS for stagger of distributed process in production systems based on multiagent systems and memetic algorithms. In: Sidorov, G., Galicia-Haro, S.N. (eds.) MICAI 2015. LNCS, vol. 9413, pp. 413–430. Springer, Cham (2015). doi:10.1007/978-3-319-27060-9_34

34. Villar, S.O.: Ensemble case-based learning for multi-agent systems. Doctoral Thesis, Universitat Autonoma de Barcelona (2005)

35. Vrba, P.: JAVA-based agent platform evaluation. In: Mařík, V., McFarlane, D., Valckenaers, P. (eds.) HoloMAS 2003. LNCS, vol. 2744, pp. 47–58. Springer, Heidelberg (2003). doi:10.1007/978-3-540-45185-3_5

36. Watking, C.J.C.H., Dayan, P.: Q-leaning. Mach. Learn. **8**(3/4), 279–292 (1992)

37. Wolpert, D.: The lack of a priori distinctions between learning algorithms. Neural Comput. **8**, 1341–1390 (1996)

38. Wozniack, M., Grana, M., Corchado, E.: A survey of multiple classifier systems as hybrid systems. Inf. Fusion **16**, 3–17 (2014). Elsevier

39. Yang, B., Braeuning, A., Johnson, K.R., Shi, Y.: General characteristics of temperature variation in China during the last two millennia. Geophys. Res. Lett. **29**, 381–384 (2002)

Exploring Complex Networks with Failure-Prone Agents

Arles Rodríguez[1,2(✉)], Jonatan Gómez[1], and Ada Diaconescu[3]

[1] ALIFE Research Group, Universidad Nacional de Colombia, Bogotá, Colombia
arlese.rodriguezp@konradlorenz.edu.co, jgomezpe@unal.edu.co
[2] Fundación Universitaria Konrad Lorenz, Bogotá, Colombia
[3] Telecom ParisTech, LTCI CNRS, Paris, France
ada.diaconescu@telecom-paristech.fr

Abstract. Distributed data-collection and synchronization is essential in sensor networks and the Internet of Things (IoT), as well as for data-replication in server farms, clusters and clouds. Generally, such systems consist of a set of interconnected components, which cooperate and coordinate to achieve a collective task, while acting locally and being failure-prone. An important challenge is hence to define efficient and robust algorithms for data collection and synchronisation in large-scale, distributed and failure-prone platforms. This paper studies the performance and robustness of different multi-agent algorithms in complex networks with different topologies (Lattice, Small-world, Community and Scale-free) and different agent failure rates. Agents proceed from random locations and explore the network to collect local data hosted in each node. Their exploration algorithm determines how fast they cover unexplored nodes to collect new data, and how often they meet other agents to exchange complementary data and speed-up the process. Two exploration algorithms are studied: one random and one using a stigmergy model (that we propose). Experimental results show how network topologies and agent failure-rates impact data-collection and synchronization, and how a stigmergy-based approach can improve performance and success rates across most scenarios. We believe these results offer key insights into the suitability of various decentralised algorithms in different networked environments, which are increasingly at the core of modern information and communication technology (ICT) systems.

1 Introduction

Sensor networks, server farms and clouds consist of numerous components (e.g. servers, processes, robots) interconnected via (complex) networks. They cooperate and coordinate their actions towards some overall objective, may share common resources, and appear to an end-user as a single system [1]. An important field of study here relates to how fast distributed processes, interconnected via such complex networks, can achieve collective objectives (e.g. data collection,

© Springer International Publishing AG 2017
O. Pichardo-Lagunas and S. Miranda-Jiménez (Eds.): MICAI 2016, Part II, LNAI 10062, pp. 81–98, 2017.
DOI: 10.1007/978-3-319-62428-0_7

synchronisation or processing); and how the particular topological properties of complex networks impact such performance [2–5]. These aspects are key in secure communications [4], logging and machine replication in databases [6]; and, information-processing and consensus-making in sensor networks [7]. A particular challenge here represents data collection from a network's components, both as a stand-alone objective, e.g., in sensor networks, or as an underlying task for data synchronisation. This paper focuses on decentralised data collection in complex networks. Important challenges must be addressed here, as networked components can only act locally and may fail unexpectedly.

Previous works [8,9] have studied data-collection techniques based on failure-prone agents. Analysed approaches included Random walks, Lévy walks and Stigmergy. Agents explored a targeted space based on selected algorithms, in order to collect local information and share it with other agents (that they could meet) [8]. [9] presents agents that collect information from distributed sources and can fail and/or provide unreliable information defining collective information as aggregation of information that agents collect individually. [10] showed how data-collection can be speeded-up by algorithms that favour exploration of new paths and the exchange of new information with other agents. It also showed how mechanisms that favour exploration and achieve faster data-collection are more resistant to failure than those that focus on increasing inter-agent communication. Finally, it showed how stigmergy and pheromone evaporation can help explore new paths, while also allowing to re-explore previous paths in order to recover from failure-related data losses.

In this paper we study this data-collection problem within complex networks (rather than within uniform spaces – studied previously). This is an important difference, since the topology of the network explored has a significant impact on the agents' performance, as they explore, collect and exchange information [11]. As before, agents may fail at different rates; yet we assume accurate data-collection – i.e. when agents are available their information is reliable (as opposed and complementary to [9]). We study two motion algorithms – random and stigmergy. These are similar to the ones defined in [8]; as Lévy walks do not apply to non-directional spaces, like networks. *The objective is to analyse how agent performance* (i.e. how fast all network data is collected) *and robustness* (i.e. how task completion is achieved in the face of agent failures) *depend on the adopted exploration technique, on the network topology and on failure rates.*

The remaining of this paper is organized as follows. Section 2 presents the data collection problem in complex networks; the studied network topologies; and the agents' design. Section 3 details the analysed motion algorithms, while Sect. 4 presents the experimental settings and discusses obtained results. Conclusions and future works are presented in Sect. 5.

2   The Problem of Data-Collection in Complex Networks

The problem studied can be summarised as follows. Agents must explore a complex network (simulated), in order to collect desired data present in the network vertices. Agents move among interconnected vertices based on a predefined algorithm (Sect. 3), collect data from each visited vertex and exchange their data with any agents that they meet at the same vertex. Additionally, agents can fail over time with probability p_f. The aim is to have at least one agent collect all data from the entire network. The parameters of interest are the *speed* of task-completion and the *success rates* in the presence of agent failures, depending on *network topologies, agent motion algorithms* and *failure probabilities*.

The agents' implementation is based on [10]. Each agent is equipped with a set of perceptions $p = \{pheromone, data, current\_node, neighbors, msg\}$; where *pheromone* is a vector in R^n with values in $[0, 1]$, representing the amount of pheromone in the agent's vicinity (i.e. vertices adjacent to the current location) [12]; *data* is the information to collect in the agent's current vertex; *neighbour* returns the *ids* of agents in the same vertex; *msg* stores messages from other agents; and *loc* returns the agent's location (vertex name). Each agent can also perform a set of actions $Actions = \{Move(vertex), Collect, Send(msg), Recv\}$; where $Move(vertex)$ moves the agent to the *vertex* location; *Collect* senses data from the agent's current location and stores it in its local memory; and *Send* and *Recv* enable information exchanges with other agents.

Simulation time is defined via discrete *rounds*. In each round, each agent: senses its local environment (e.g. local data, co-located agents and adjacent vertices); decides on an action (e.g. collect and exchange data, select a neighbouring vertex to move to); and performs the actual action [13,14]. The simulation ends when at least one agent completes the exploration (i.e. collects all the data) or if all the agents fail. The environment is the complex network to be explored.

In short, a *complex network* consists of a large number of interconnected nodes characterized by non-trivial topological properties – i.e. neither purely regular nor completely random; unlike lattices and random networks. Typical features include relative small distances between nodes, high clustering, or power-law degree distributions (i.e. heavy-tailed) [2]. A more formal definition of complex networks is quite difficult to provide; researchers have focused instead on specific topological metrics and on the kinds of node interconnection rules that produce topologies with distinctive properties [11].

In this paper, a complex network is defined as a graph G with a set of vertices V and a set of edges E: $G = (V, E)$. A probabilistic rule defines the way in which vertices are interconnected when constructing the graph [2,11]. Hence, complex networks with different topologies can be generated by using different rules of inter-connection. In this paper we evaluate the main types of network topologies identified in the literature, namely, *Small-World, Scale-free* and *Community* networks (discussed below). We additionally use more regular topologies for comparison, such as *Forest Hub & Spoke, Lattice, Line* and *Circle*.

2.1 Small-World Networks

A *Small-World* network is generated by starting from a regular network (in terms of node interconnections) and then rewiring some of these connections in a random way [15]. This type of network features relatively short paths between any network nodes, even in very large networks. In this paper, we use a Watts-Strogatz model [3,16], with different parameters, to generate Small World networks. We start with a regular ring lattice network with n vertices and k edges per vertex, then rewire each edge with a probability β. The β parameter determines how regular the final network will be: $\beta = 0$ generates a regular network, $\beta = 1$ a random network, and in-between values a Small-World network [15] (Fig. 1).

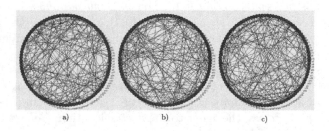

Fig. 1. Small-World networks: $n = 100, k = 4$, (a) $\beta = 0.3$, (b) $\beta = 0.5$, (c) $\beta = 0.9$

2.2 Scale-Free Networks

Scale-free networks are characterised by *degree distributions* that follow a mathematical function known as power-law [17]. The *degree distribution* is the probability distribution of the node degrees over the entire network [18]; where a node's *degree* is its number of links. A power-law distribution implies that node degrees may differ by magnitudes of scale, and hence that a few nodes (called *hubs*) have a disproportionate number of links compared to the average degrees. Notable examples of real scale-free networks include the WWW, email or protein interaction networks. They are highly resistant to accidental failures, but rather vulnerable to targeted node attacks [19].

Scale-free networks can be obtained by starting with sn nodes and η connections. At each step a new node is added and connected via η links to existing nodes, based on preferential attachment (i.e. more likely to connect to nodes with higher degrees) [20]. Namely, the probability to connect to an existing node is defined by $p_i = \frac{k_i}{\sum_j (k_j)}$, where k_i is the degree of node i [16,21,22]. The process is repeated for *steps* times [11]. Figure 2 depicts different configurations showing how the number of connections increases with *eta*.

2.3 Community Networks

Community networks feature structures where nodes can be assigned to different groups, or clusters, that are highly interconnected internally, and have relatively few connections among nodes belonging to different groups [23]. In this paper Community networks were generated using a *n_clusters* parameter to define the number of groups in the network and adding a single connection between

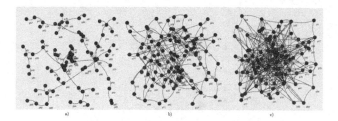

Fig. 2. Scale-free networks: $sn = 4, steps = 97$, (a) $\eta = 1$, (b) $\eta = 2$, (c) $\eta = 4$

nodes of different groups. Each group was generated as a small world network (with its own k, β, and $n = m/n\_clusters$, where m is the number of nodes in the network). Figure 3 shows a Community network with four groups connected either via a central node (selected at random), or via a circle formed by pairs of nodes selected from different groups (also random).

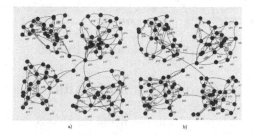

Fig. 3. (a) Community central, and (b) Community Circle network: $n\_clusters = 4, \beta = 0.5, degree = 4$ and $m = 100$

2.4 Forest Hub and Spoke

The *Forest Hub & Spoke* network is based on the Hub & Spoke (or Star) configuration, where all nodes are connected (spokes) around a central node (hub); the forest is then formed by connecting pairs of such Star structures. This type of network ensures high availability and reliable computing services because it allows expansion of individual cloud instances [24]. In this paper, we generate 4 Hub & Spoke clusters of 25 nodes each, as shown in Fig. 4.

2.5 Line, Circle and Lattice

Experimental design includes Lattice, Line and Circle topologies. The purpose of performing experiments with these topologies is to test exploitation and exploration properties of the selected algorithms with a higher diameter (line), a long path length (line and circle), and regular connections (lattice). Figure 5, shows the configurations applied to the experiments each one with 100 nodes.

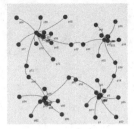

Fig. 4. Forest Hub & Spoke

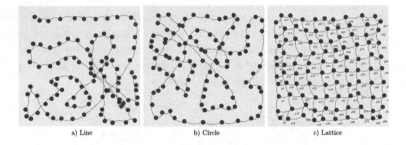

Fig. 5. Line, circle and lattice

3   Agent Motion Algorithms and Failures

After selecting different types of complex networks that represent various topologies, we aim to establish and profile how a determined motion strategy influences the exploration of unvisited vertices, the encounter of other agents and robustness given in terms of completing the task even when agents prone to failure; as all of them are important for data collection.

Each agent implements an algorithm which determines how to sense data from the environment and how to select actions such as motions and communication with other agents. The agent program pseudocode is listed in Algorithm 1. Agent failures are also defined in this program, and produced with a failure probability p_f – e.g., $p_f = 0.1$ means the agent fails on average every 1 out of 10 rounds.

Based on perceptions, agents choose the next vertex to move to based on two possible motion processes: random, which is exploratory; and pheromone-based, which improves exploitation of new paths and agent encounters (which in turn enhances collective exploration).

When following a *random walk* an agent selects its moving direction randomly from the set of vertices adjacent to the current vertex, at each round. A uniformly distributed pseudorandom generator is used for generating the random sequence.

When following a *pheromone-based* movement an agent chooses vertices based on their pheromone load (e.g. in order to find unexplored vertices, or other agents). This algorithm is based on the Ant Colony System algorithm (ACS) [25], using stigmergy, and an adaptation of the *Carriers algorithm* in

---

Algorithm 1. Agent program

 1: Percept p
 2: Action action
 3: round ← 0
 4: **while** *Agent.status* ≠ *Fail* **do**
 5:     $\lambda \leftarrow U[0,1]$ ▷ uniform random number
 6:     **if** $\lambda < p_f$ **then**
 7:         Agent.status ← *Fail*
 8:         **break**
 9:     **end if**
10:     p ← environment.sense()
11:     Agent.move(motionAlgorithm(p))
12:     **if** Agent.hasNeighbors(p.location) **then** Agent.exchange(p.neighbors)
13:     **end if**
14:     round ← round+1
15: **end while**

---

[10]. Initially, all vertices have a pheromone value $\tau_v = 0.5$. As in ACS [25], a random variable $q \in [0,1]$ dictates when to apply an exploitation rule or biased exploration (Eq. 1):

$$dir = \begin{cases} \text{exploitation rule} & \text{if } q \le 0.9 \\ \text{biased exploration} & \text{otherwise} \end{cases} \tag{1}$$

A carrier agent chooses the direction with the *minimum* pheromone amount in its vicinity, looking for uncharted vertices. If more than one vertex has the same *minimum* value a random direction is picked among these.

Biased exploration is a random-proportional rule [25] which gives an agent i a probability of choosing a vertex $p_d(v)$ depending on the amount of pheromone τ_v in its vicinity *neighbourhood(i)* (Eq. 2). *neighbourhood(i)* includes the vertices connected to vertex i. This prevents agents from getting trapped in a confined area (e.g. carriers surrounded by pheromone traces). For carriers $\tau'_v(v) = 1 - \tau_v(v)$.

$$p_d(x,y) = \frac{\tau'_v(v)}{\sum_{(k) \in \text{neighbourhood}(i)} \tau_v(k)} \tag{2}$$

Whenever an agent i moves, at each round t, it updates its internal pheromone value $\tau_{a_t}(i)$ (as in Eq. 3) and also the pheromone amount in its current vertex location $\tau_v(v)$ (as in Eq. 4).

$$\tau_{a_t}(i) = (\tau_{a_{t-1}}(i) + 0.01 * (0.5 - \tau_{a_{t-1}}(i))) \tag{3}$$

$$\tau_{v_t}(v) = \tau_{v_{t-1}}(v) + 0.01 * (\tau_{a_{t-1}}(i) - \tau_{v_{t-1}}(v)) \tag{4}$$

If an agent i, finds or receives new information, then its internal pheromone value is updated to $\tau_{a_t}(i) = 1$. In this case, Eq. 3 decreases internal pheromone value at each round; and Eq. 4 increases the amount of pheromone in the locations that the carrier agent explores.

Passive evaporation is added so as to make explored paths less dominant and allow re-exploration of routes of agents that fail without sharing information [26]. This type of evaporation is performed by the environment rather than by agents and it is applied in all the vertices of the complex network G, using the definition in [27] corresponding to Eq. 5, with evaporation rate $\rho = 0.01$:

$$\tau_{v_i} = (1 - \rho)\tau_{v_{i(t-1)}}, \text{ for}$$
$$\forall_i \in \{V, G = (V, E)\} \tag{5}$$

4 Experiments and Results

Experiments aim to analyse the performance of motion algorithms to solve the data-collection problem in complex networks. We apply metrics of speed, amount of information collected versus time, robustness (in terms of failure resistance) and number of messages sent. Additionally, experimental design provides insights regarding impact of a selected complex network in the agents performance and suitability of motion algorithms to achieve the data collection task in a determined topology.

4.1 Experimental Settings

Each experiment is defined via a combination of: a different complex network topology (Sect. 2), a different agent motion algorithm (Sect. 3), and a different failure probability p_f for all agents. In all cases, the network consist of 100 vertices and is explored by 10 agents (a relation 10 to 1 from vertex to agent). Each experiment was performed 30 times. Agents start from random locations, selected separately for each topology (but the same ones for all 30 repetitions in any one topology). Each simulation stops when one agent collects all the information from all network vertices, or if all the agents fail. We compare the performance of the two movement algorithms (i.e. Random and Stigmergy-based) within different topologies (listed below), and for different failure probabilities starting from zero and by increasing p_f until a value in which most of the experiments fail ($p_f = 0, 0.001, 0.003, 0.005$ and 0.008). The specific parameters used for each complex network topology studied are:

- Lattice: size 10×10;
- Small World: degree 4, $\beta = 0.1, 0.3, 0.5, 0.9$;
- Scale-free: number of steps $steps = 97$, starting nodes $sn = 4$, added links per step $\eta = 1, 2, 4$;
- Community: $\beta = 0.1, 0.3, 0.5, 0.9, n\_clusters = 4$;
- Community Circle: $\beta = 0.1, 0.3, 0.5, 0.9, n\_clusters = 4$;
- Forest Hub & Spoke: $n\_clusters = 4$;
- Line: no specific parameters;
- Circle: no specific parameters.

4.2   Results and Discussion

Agents are evaluated on different criteria in scenarios *with* and *without* agent failure. When agents don't fail ($p_f = 0$) results are analysed terms of the agents' *performance* – i.e. *number of rounds* before the first agent collects all the data. Figure 6 depicts the round numbers for the two algorithms in different network topologies. When agents don't fail, all experiments are ultimately successful. When agents do fail ($p_f > 0$), the agents' *robustness* is evaluated instead in terms of *success rates* – i.e. how often the agents complete the task – and *rate of global data collection* – i.e. how fast the agents collect the data together (rather than individually). Finally, the *number of messages* exchanged among agents is also evaluated, as critical in limited resource environments.

An ANOVA test is also performed for failure-less experiments, to determine whether or not the observed differences between the round number means for the two motion algorithms (Random and Carriers) are statistically significant. The null and alternative hypothesis for a determined topology are the following:

– H_0: round number means for the two algorithms are *equal* for a network G;
– H_1: round number means for the two algorithms are *different* for a network G, indicating a correlation between the algorithm and the round number.

Table 1 shows the ANOVA test results. The *F-value* represents the F statistics – the variation between the round numbers of the two algorithms, in the given network. The *p-val* and *p-wilc* indicate the statistical significance between the results of the two algorithms for all the topologies (since *p_val* < 0.05 and *p_wilc* < 0.05) except for the Community network with a $\beta = 0.5$ and *clusters* = 4 (where *p_val* > 0.05 and *p_wilc* > 0.05; marked as ∗ in Table 1).

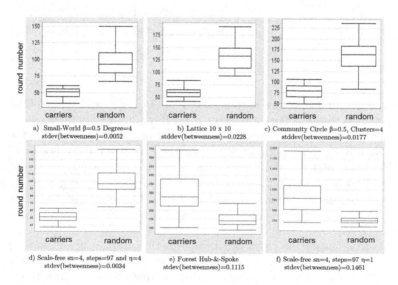

Fig. 6. Box-plot of round number by some selected complex networks with $p_f = 0$

Table 1. ANOVA and Wilcoxon test for carriers vs random, by topology

Topology	F-value	p-val	Dif	p-wilc
Line	111.75	3.806e−15	465	1.824e−6
Circle	248.28	2.2e−16	465	1.822e−6
Lattice 10 × 10	75.996	2.2e−16	465	1.823e−6
Scale-free				
(⋆) $sn = 4, \eta = 1, steps = 97$	91.807	1.476e−13	2.5	2.352e−6
$sn = 4, \eta = 2, steps = 97$	69.922	1.52e−11	465	1.821e−6
$sn = 4, \eta = 4, steps = 97$	128.04	2.2e−11	465	1.822e−6
Forest Hub and Spoke				
(⋆) $clusters = 4$	19.755	3.573e−5	36.5	1.355e−5
Community Network				
$\beta = 0.1, clusters = 4$	47.382	3.952e−9	490	2.21e−6
$\beta = 0.3, clusters = 4$	46.56	5.797e−9	444.5	1.359e−5
(∗) $\beta = 0.5, clusters = 4$	2.304	0.1345	322.5	0.06561
$\beta = 0.9, clusters = 4$	18.228	6.84e−5	474	8.928e−5
Community Circle				
$\beta = 0.1, clusters = 4$	152.07	2.2e−16	435	2.701e−6
$\beta = 0.3, clusters = 4$	144.48	2.2e−16	422.5	9.77e−6
$\beta = 0.5, clusters = 4$	93.448	1.07e−13	465	1.822e−16
$\beta = 0.9, clusters = 4$	121.477	7.472e−16	465	1.823e−6
Small World				
$\beta = 0.1, degree = 4$	126.86	3.149e−16	465	1.821e−6
$\beta = 0.3, degree = 4$	65.385	4.394e−11	465	1.822e−6
$\beta = 0.5, degree = 4$	85.378	5.34e−13	465	1.823e−6
$\beta = 0.9, degree = 4$	144.64	2.2e−16	465	1.817e−6

Hence, based on the round number box-plots in Fig. 6 and the ANOVA test, we can conclude that Carriers are faster than Random agents for most network topologies, when $p_f = 0$. However, as observed in Fig. 6 (and marked as ⋆ in Table 1), Random exploration is faster than the Carriers for the Forest Hub-&-Spoke (Fig. 6(e)) and the Scale-free with $sn = 4, \eta = 1, steps = 97$ networks (Fig. 6(f)). This is probably due to the fact that in these topologies most paths pass through unique large hubs. Therefore, in the Carriers case, these hubs are pheromone-marked very often and hence slow-down agent movement across sub-networks.

We aim to quantify the topological features that impact agent performance. Hence, we tried to identify a correlation between the round number and topological metrics like network diameter, degree distribution, clustering coefficient, and betweenness centrality. We found that the two exception topologies

(Scale-free $sn = 4, \eta = 1$ and *steps* = 97 and Forest Hub-&-Spoke) feature greater values for the *standard deviation of the node betweenness centrality* value – *stdev(betweenness)* – compared to other topologies, as in Fig. 6(e) and (f).

To test this correlation, we generated more Scale-free network instances using the same parameters: $sn = 4, \eta = 1$ and *steps* = 97; and plotted their *log(round number)* versus *stdev(betweenness)*. Indeed, Fig. 7(a) shows the correlation of the betweenness centrality and the round number for all topologies, including the additional Scale-free ones. Since most topologies have relatively low betweenness values (lower than 0.025) compared to the Scale-free cases (greater than 0.05), we only show these cases in Fig. 7(b), for clarity, to highlight that a correlation also exists for these topologies, even if at a different scale. Figure 7(c) shows the same correlation for the Random algorithm, for all topologies; and Fig. 7(d) shows the correlation for both algorithms, for all topologies. The Carriers algorithm seems to feature a stronger relation between the round number and the betweenness centrality, compared to the Random case, with greater betweenness values causing larger round numbers (i.e. lower performance). For system designers, this means that selecting the best agent exploration algorithm depends on the network topology (betweenness centrality); and the selected algorithm may have to change over time, for best performance, as the network topology evolves.

We also evaluated the *global information collected by all agents combined* (rather than by each agent). This is useful for analysing algorithm robustness in case of agent failure, especially for applications where all agents can communicate

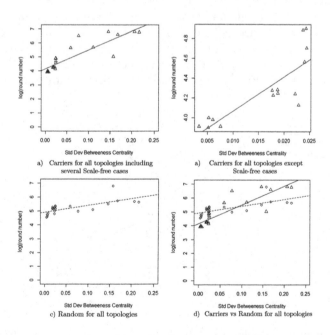

Fig. 7. Correlating the betweenness centrality (std. dev.) to the round number (log)

data collected to a central location, and where a percentage of the complete data suffices (e.g. 90%). Hence, the shape of the function describing global information collected in time is important, with steeper shapes offering better robustness, as data is collected faster, before agents start failing. Global information is measured in each experiment (i.e. given topology, motion algorithm and p_f) by reading the local information collected by each agent, at each round, and calculating the total sum. Figure 8 presents the increase of the global information with the round number for the Scale-free network (generated with parameters $sn = 4, \eta = 1$ and $steps = 97$) for the two algorithms. Each experiment is performed 30 times and the minimum, median and maximum values plotted. Results show that global information is collected faster by Carriers than Random agents – e.g. at round 50, the minimum collected by Carriers is about 90% whereas by Random is only 70%; at round 100, the minimum for Carriers is 97% and for Random about 85%. It also seems that for Carriers the longest time is spent for collecting the last 3% of the data, which causes the Carriers to be slower than Random for collecting all data in this topology (Cf. Fig. 7(d)). This means that in applications where less than 97% of data collection suffices (e.g. some sensor networks) the Carriers can outperform Random agents even for such topologies. Finally, in all cases, the median values approximate the maximum ones much faster for the Carriers than for Random (e.g. round 75 for Carriers and not before round 125 for Random).

Let us now study the cases where agents can fail. Figure 9 provides a histogram of the success rates (a) and the box-plots of messages sent (b), for selected topologies, and $p_f = 0.001$. Figure 9(a) shows that for the Carriers, the topologies most impacted by agent failures are the Scale-free (with $sn = 4, \eta = 1$ and $steps = 97$), where success rates drop to about 60%; and the Forest-Hub-and-Spoke, to about 96.66%. For the Random algorithm, the only impacted topologies are Circle and Line. By comparing these success rates with the round number evaluations (Cf. Fig. 7), we can note that faster data collection favours

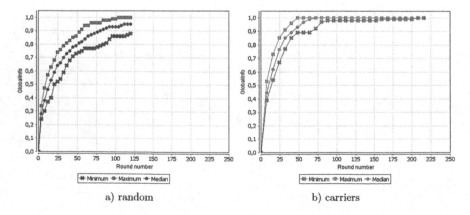

a) random   b) carriers

Fig. 8. Global information collected for Scale-free $sn = 4, \eta = 1, steps = 97$ and $p_f = 0$

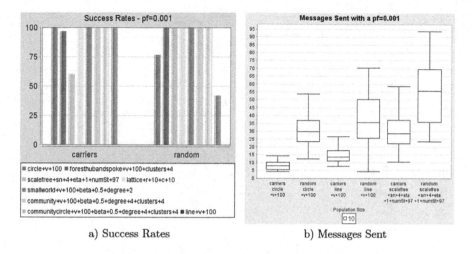

a) Success Rates   b) Messages Sent

Fig. 9. Success rates and messages sent for $p_f = 0.001$

success rates. Figure 9(b) shows a higher number of message exchanges among Random agents compared to Carriers. This could explain the lower success rates for Carriers in topologies that infringe agent circulation (e.g. some Scale-free cases), since agents are less likely to meet and their information is lost when they fail.

Figure 10 shows the global information collected for the topologies most impacted by agent failures (Scale-free and Circle). In both cases, the median reaches 100% faster for Carriers than for Random agents. Also, in the Scale free case where success rates suffer, Carrier agents actually manage to collect all the information together, yet they never meet to share the information and hence no single agent completes. Random agents are slow to explore Line and Circle networks as they move around the same vertices and share the same local information. Hence, when they fail, their information is lost and other agents do not reach the same areas before their own failures.

Figure 11(a) shows that for Carriers with $p_f = 0.003$ the success rate for the Forest-Hub-and-Spoke topology is further reduced, to 43%; and for Scale-free ($sn = 4, \eta = 1$ and $steps = 97$) to 4%. Random agents also start featuring lower success for this Scale-free topology (60%). Community networks start suffering in the Random case, while not being impacted when Carriers are used. For Line and Circle networks, Random exploration becomes severely impaired (less than 10%), while Carriers maintain 100% success rates. The success of both algorithms remains intact (100%) for Small-world topologies.

Figure 11(b) indicates that for the Community network Random agents exchange more messages than Carriers, even with less success rates, signifying that they probably exchange redundant data. Figures 12(a) and (b) show a fast data collection for Carriers, indicating that Carriers are better for exploitation of new vertices in these networks, since they feature higher success rates despite

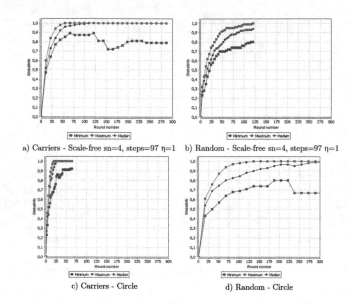

a) Carriers - Scale-free sn=4, steps=97 η=1   b) Random - Scale-free sn=4, steps=97 η=1

c) Carriers - Circle   d) Random - Circle

Fig. 10. Global information collected for Scale-free $sn = 4, \eta = 1$ and $steps = 97$ and Circle, with $p_f = 0.001$

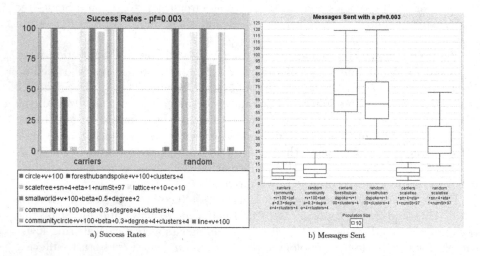

a) Success Rates   b) Messages Sent

Fig. 11. Success rates and messages sent for $p_f = 0.003$

exchanging fewer messages. In the Forest Hub & Spoke network, agents exchange more messages, via the hubs, and the median of global information converges faster to maximum value for Carriers than for Random.

Figure 13 shows success rates for $p_f = 0.005$ in each kind of network, for different generation parameters. Small World (Fig. 13(a)) and Community Circle (Fig. 13(c)) feature the highest success rates compared to other topologies.

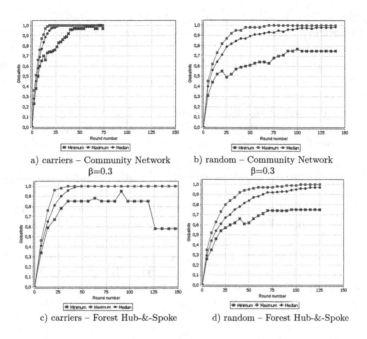

a) carriers – Community Network
β=0.3

b) random – Community Network
β=0.3

c) carriers – Forest Hub-&-Spoke

d) random – Forest Hub-&-Spoke

Fig. 12. Global information collected for community network $\beta = 0.3$ and Forest Hub-and-Spoke, with $p_f = 0.003$

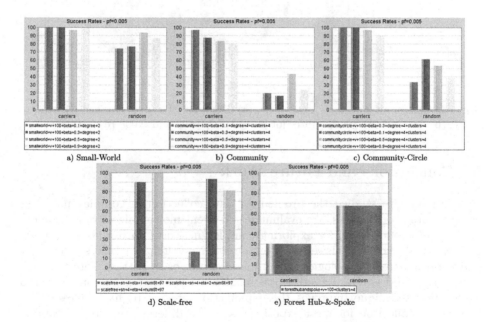

a) Small-World

b) Community

c) Community-Circle

d) Scale-free

e) Forest Hub-&-Spoke

Fig. 13. Success rates for complex networks $p_f = 0.005$

Carriers perform well in all Small World networks, whereas Random performs worse (yet relatively better when Small Worlds are generated with higher beta values – less regular and more random graphs) – Fig. 13(a). Carriers also start to decrease success rates in Community networks (Figs. 13(b) and (c)), especially when clusters are less regular (i.e. greater Beta values). Also, success in Community networks is lower than in Community Circle, for both algorithms, since the clusters are connected through a single central vertex, impeding movement.

For a $p_f = 0.008$, only the Carriers manage to reach success rates of over 70%, for the most failure-resistant topologies: Lattice, Small World (all configurations), Community Circle (all configurations) and Scale Free (4-4-97).

Additionally, a statistic test was performed for the Community network ($\beta = 0.5$) and a $p_f = 0.001$, because there was not a statistically significant difference in terms of round number for $p_f = 0$, while the box-plot for the round number does show a difference (Fig. 14(a)). By taking advantage of the 100% success rates for both algorithms, a Wilcoxon test for round number and a $pf = 0.001$ indicated a $p\_val = 0.0001538$. This means that there is a significant difference between the round number means, with Carriers being faster than Random, when failures occur. For the other failure probabilities success rates decrease faster for Random agents than for Carriers (Fig. 14(b), (c) and (d)).

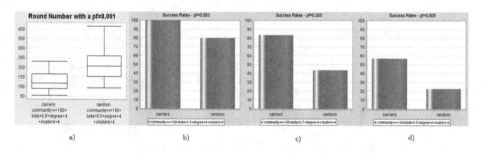

Fig. 14. Community network beta = 0.5. (a) Box-plot of round number with $p_f = 0.001$, (b), (c) and (d) Success rates for $p_f = 0.003, 0.005$ and 0.008 respectively

5   Conclusions and Future Work

In this paper we studied the problem of data-collection in complex networks using failure-prone agents. We evaluated two agent motion algorithms (random and a pheromone-based) for exploring complex networks with different topologies: Small-World, Scale-Free and Community Networks. We also studied several regular network topologies for comparison purposes: Lattice, Forest Hub & Spoke, Line and Circle. Experimental results showed that a pheromone-based exploration technique improves the exploitation of new paths and results in faster data-collection for most experiments in the different topologies. Results also indicate a relation between network topology and data-collection performance, where the differentiating factor among topologies can be quantified as the variance of the *betweenness centrality* among nodes. Namely, the higher the standard deviation of the betweenness centrality of nodes in a complex network, the higher the completion times of the data-collection task in that network.

As shown in [10], the agents' success in completing their collective task relies critically on each agent's motion process. This result was also confirmed here for the case where the space was a complex network (rather than a uniform surface). Also, a faster exploration algorithm provides better resistance to agent failure.

The Carriers strategy is also good for exploitation of new vertices and for reducing the number of messages exchanged. Indeed, the median of the global information collected (by all agents together) was approximated to 100% faster than in the random case, in all the experiments. In the experiments where the random approach was more successful (i.e. Scale-free topology generated with $sn = 4, \eta = 1$ and *steps* $= 97$ parameters; and Forest Hub & Spoke topology) it was difficult for the carrier agents to meet and exchange their local information (as pheromone-marked hubs prevented circulation among sub-networks they interconnected). However, on a global level, carrier agents collect information faster than random agents in all scenarios (even with failures). Small-worlds, Community Circle Networks, Lattice and Scale-free with a degree of 4 (4-4-97) are faster than the other topologies for data collection, for both algorithms (random and carriers), with the Small-world being the fastest topology.

Future work will study various network scales and agent population sizes, and introduce node failures. The case where agents aim to synchronise different data versions among network nodes will also be studied. We believe that obtained results provide key information on the characteristics of different decentralised data-collection algorithms, depending on their application context (e.g. network topology and failure rates). This, in turn, allows system designers to select the best option for their particular application and execution environment, covering a broad spectrum of applications like sensor networks, swarm robotics, server clusters, clouds, systems of systems and the Internet of Things (IoT).

References

1. Tanenbaum, A., Steen, M.V.: Distributed Systems: Principles and Paradigms. Prentice-Hall, Upper Saddle River (2006)
2. Boccaletti, S.: The Synchronized Dynamics of Complex Systems. Elsevier, Florence (2008)
3. Watts, D.J., Strogatz, S.H.: Collective dynamics of 'small-world' networks. Nature **393**, 440–442 (1998)
4. Grabow, C., Hill, S.M., Grosskinsky, S., Timme, M.: Do small worlds synchronize fastest? EPL (Europhys. Lett.) **90**, 48002 (2010)
5. Noh, J.D., Rieger, H.: Random walks on complex networks. Phys. Rev. Lett. **92**, 118701 (2004)
6. Ongaro, D., Ousterhout, J.: In search of an understandable consensus algorithm. Ramcloud.Stanford.Edu (2013)
7. Nedic, A., Ozdaglar, A., Parrilo, P.A.: Constrained consensus and optimization in multi-agent networks. IEEE Trans. Autom. Control **55**, 922–938 (2010)

8. Rodriguez, A., Gomez, J., Diaconescu, A.: Towards failure-resistant mobile distributed systems inspired by swarm intelligence and trophallaxis. In: Proceedings of the European Conference on Artificial Life 2015, pp. 448–455. The University of York UK (2015)

9. Vu, Q.A.N., Hassas, S., Armetta, F., Gaudou, B., Canal, R.: Combining trust and self-organization for robust maintaining of information coherence in disturbed MAS. In: Proceedings - 2011 5th IEEE International Conference on Self-adaptive and Self-organizing Systems, SASO 2011, pp. 178–187 (2011)

10. Rodriguez, A., Gomez, J., Diaconescu, A.: Foraging-inspired self-organisation for terrain exploration with failure-prone agents. In: 2015 IEEE 9th International Conference on Self-adaptive and Self-organizing Systems, vol. 2015, pp. 121–130. IEEE, October 2015

11. Van Der Hofstad, R.: Random graphs and complex networks, vol. I (2016). http://www.win.tue.nl/rhofstad/NotesRGCN.pdf

12. Gray, L.: A mathematician looks at Wolfram's new kind of science. Not. AMS **50**, 200–211 (2002)

13. Balaji, P.G., Srinivasan, D.: An introduction to multi-agent systems. Stud. Comput. Intell. **310**, 1–27 (2010)

14. Russell, S., Norvig, P.: Inteligencia Artificial. Un enfoque moderno. 2da Edición. Prentice-Hall, Madrid (2004)

15. Mori, H., Uehara, M., Matsumoto, K.: Parallel architectures with small world network model. In: 2015 IEEE 29th International Conference on Advanced Information Networking and Applications Workshops, pp. 467–472 (2015)

16. White, S.: Analysis and visualization of network data using JUNG. J. Stat. Softw. **VV**, 1–35 (2005)

17. Barabási, A.: Emergence of scaling in random networks. Science **286**, 509–512 (1999)

18. Gündüz-Öğüdücü, Ş., Etaner-Uyar, A.Ş. (eds.): Social Networks: Analysis and Case Studies. LNSN. Springer, Vienna (2014). doi:10.1007/978-3-7091-1797-2

19. Barabási, A.L., Bonabeau, E.: Scale-free networks. Sci. Am. **288**, 60–69 (2003)

20. Li, L., Alderson, D., Doyle, J.C., Willinger, W.: Towards a theory of scale-free graphs: definition, properties, and implications. Internet Math **2**, 431–523 (2006)

21. Small, M.: Scale-Free Network - MathWorld-A Wolfram Web Resource (2016)

22. Takemoto, K., Oosawa, C.: Introduction to Complex Networks: Measures, Statistical Properties, and Models. Wiley, Hoboken (2012)

23. Girvan, M., Newman, M.E.J.: Community structure in social and biological networks. Proc. Nat. Acad. Sci. U.S.A. **99**, 7821–7826 (2002)

24. Mahmood, Z., Hill, R. (eds.): Cloud Computing for Enterprise Architectures. Computer Communications and Networks. Springer, London (2011). doi:10.1007/978-1-4471-2236-4

25. Dorigo, M., Gambardella, L.M.: Ant colony system: a cooperative learning approach to the traveling salesman problem. IEEE Trans. Evol. Comput. **1**(1), 53–66 (1997)

26. Bell, J.E., McMullen, P.R.: Ant colony optimization techniques for the vehicle routing problem. Adv. Eng. Inform. **18**, 41–48 (2004)

27. Dorigo, M., Stutzle, T.: Ant Colony Optimization, vol. 1. MIT Press, Cambridge (2004)

On the Conception of Intelligent Power Plants Based on Multiple Agent Systems

Raul Garduno-Ramirez[1](✉) and Mónica Borunda[2]

[1] Instituto Nacional de Electricidad y Energías Limpias, Cuernavaca, Mexico
raul.garduno@iie.org.mx
[2] Conacyt - Instituto Nacional de Electricidad y Energías Limpias,
Cuernavaca, Mexico
monica.borunda@iie.org.mx

Abstract. Lately, great efforts have been made to develop effective hybrid power systems, which consist of a mixture of renewable and conventional power plants, energy storage systems and power consumers. The very dissimilar characteristics of these elements, as well as the ever increasing performance requirements imposed to them, makes the design of control systems for power generation plants a remarkably challenging task. A promising approach to provide effective solutions to this problem is by applying the paradigms of Intelligent Agents and Multi-Agent Systems. In this paper, the definition of an Intelligent Multi-Agent System for Supervision and Control (iMASSC) is proposed to create intelligent power plants for either renewable or conventional power generation units. A Multi-Agent System with a generic structure is used instead of a single specific Intelligent Agent. This approach is more realistic in that it takes into account the complexity of current power plants. Later, the community of intelligent power plants, through autonomous and coherent collaboration, will achieve the objectives of the hybrid power system. Hence, the iMASSC model is expected to provide feasible solutions to the operation of modern intelligent hybrid power systems and smart grids.

Keywords: Intelligent agents · Multiagent systems · Intelligent power plants · Hybrid power systems

1 Introduction

Hybrid power generation systems, including both conventional and renewable power plants, aim to properly use both resources in an efficient and sustainable way to supply the ever growing demand of electric energy worldwide. However, the intermittency and non-predictability of some renewable energies make the operation of hybrid power generation systems a challenging task. Achievement of highly effective, reliable, and autonomous operation requires the deployment of intelligent control systems.

Power systems based on conventional power plants have been successfully operated with classical automation and control methodologies so far. The most common control system structure of a power system is that of a hierarchical system, where each power plant is commonly governed with a distributed control system running classical

© Springer International Publishing AG 2017
O. Pichardo-Lagunas and S. Miranda-Jiménez (Eds.): MICAI 2016, Part II, LNAI 10062, pp. 99–114, 2017.
DOI: 10.1007/978-3-319-62428-0_8

control algorithms [1]. This approach is enough to make most conventional power plants fully dispatchable, that is, to make them contribute to control power flows and voltage stability in the power system. However, most renewable power plants are intermittent and not dispatchable; their introduction in a power system can disturb power flows and voltage stability. Classical automation and control methodologies are not enough to control renewable power plants and their interaction with conventional power plants in hybrid power generation systems. Creating power plants, conventional and renewable, that behave as intelligent systems can provide effective solutions to the successful operation of hybrid power systems.

Artificial intelligence emerged and evolved to solve problems with a high degree of complexity [2]. In particular, the Intelligent Agent (IA), and Multi-Agent System (MAS) paradigms were created to perceive their environment, make decisions and act upon the environment. So, these artificial intelligence paradigms can provide solutions to industrial process control problems [3]. In particular, it is believed that the IAs and MASs paradigms can provide the means for power plants and hybrid power systems to behave as intelligent systems, that is, to operate in an autonomous, coherent and goal directed manner.

In this regard, this paper proposes the conceptual model of a generic MAS with which it is possible to create intelligent power plants, from either conventional or renewable power generation units regardless of their very dissimilar behavioral characteristics. Each intelligent power plant will have its own abilities and expertise to cooperate, negotiate or compete with the other plants in the community of intelligent power plants of a hybrid power system. The objectives and goals of the hybrid power system will be satisfied and achieved, respectively, through the autonomous, coherent and goal oriented behavior of the intelligent power plants.

This work is organized as follows. In Sect. 2 the paradigms of IAs and MAS are briefly described in their most general terms from the point of view of information technology. Section 3 presents relevant applications and design issues of MAS for operation and control of power systems and power plants, revealing the scarcity of literature about the design and development of MAS for power plants. In Sect. 4 the functional structure of an intelligent system for operation of power plants is revisited to outline the fundamental distribution of problem solving capabilities required for the agents, as well as, the basic pattern of data and information relationships among them. Section 5 introduces the intelligent multiagent system for supervision and control (iMASSC) for a power plant, either conventional or renewable. This MAS model, not a single IA model as others propose, provides the necessary framework to integrate different technologies in a systematic way to create intelligent power plants. Section 6 introduces the structure of a hybrid power system as a smart microgrid including a community of intelligent power plants. Section 7 lists the future work necessary to build iMASSC prototypes to undertake real-time proof-of-concept experiments within the context of an intelligent hybrid power system. Conclusions are stated in the last section.

2   Intelligent Agents and Multiagent Systems

Real time software systems are an essential ingredient in nowadays control technology. These systems were initially developed with methods created for non-real-time applications, such as real-time structured analysis and design [4] and real-time object-oriented design [5]. However, in order to deal with more demanding and large-scale systems, the agent paradigm was introduced to improve the ability to conceptualize, design and implement increasingly complex software systems [6]. An agent can be defined as an encapsulated software system situated in an environment, capable of perceiving it, perform information-related tasks and act upon the environment in order to meet the design objectives [7].

An agent can be called an intelligent agent (IA) when it has a high degree of operational autonomy. IAs can have beliefs, desires and intentions, as well as precise knowledge [8]. As shown in Fig. 1, the main characteristics of IAs are:

- Reactivity. React quickly to changes.
- Pro-activeness. Look to accomplish their objectives.
- Sociability. Communicate with each other to negotiate, cooperate or compete.
- Autonomy. Able to act by themselves without human supervision.
- Mobility. Are capable of moving to interact with other agents.

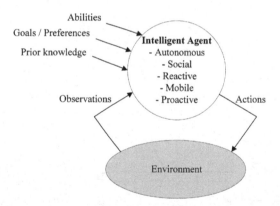

Fig. 1. Intelligent agent.

A Multi-Agent System or Multiagent System (MAS) is defined as a loosely coupled network (organization) of problem solvers (agents) that interact to solve large and complex problems that cannot be individually solved [9]. An agent in a MAS specializes in solving a particular aspect of the larger problem using its own suitable technique [10].

Intelligent agents are highly used in MAS since [11]:

- IAs solve problems that are too big for a single centralized agent.
- IAs interoperate with multiple existing systems to meet the changing needs.

- IAs provide solutions that effectively use spatially distributed information.
- IAs procure solutions with distributed expertise.
- IAs might implement solutions with enhanced performance with respect to computational efficiency, reliability, extensibility, robustness, maintainability, responsiveness, flexibility and reusability.

MAS are organizations of agents and intelligent agents where the interactions between the agents are given through a definition of roles, behavior expectations and authority relationships [12]. Generally, MAS are conceptualized in terms of their structure, i.e., the pattern of information and data exchange relationships, as well as the distribution of problem solving capabilities among the agents, as it is portrayed in Fig. 2. The organizational versatility is crucial since the organizations must be able to adapt to changing circumstances by altering the pattern of interactions among their agents to have the potential to be successful. An open organization is capable of changing dynamically: the information sources, communication links, and components could appear and disappear arbitrarily and unexpectedly. The components may be not known in advance or are able to change over time and may be highly heterogeneous. In open organizations, agents may find dynamically their collaborators depending on the task needs and on the available agents at a given time, forming teams pursuing common goals to achieve the global system coherence [13].

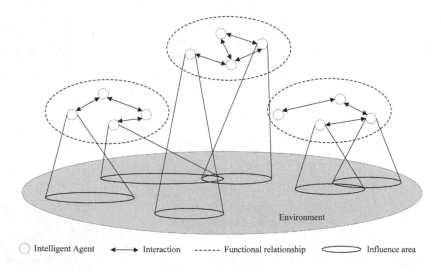

Fig. 2. Multiagent system.

The advantages of MAS based control systems over classical control systems are that they are scalable, flexible, plug and play, fault-tolerant, and suitable for distributed problems. Currently, development of MAS based control systems presents two major design and implementation challenges [14, 15]:

- Engineering design for definition, formulation, description, decomposition and allocation of the overall problem, followed by selection and integration of a suitable group of IAs.
- Engineering implementation to enable agents to achieve global problem-solving coherence; providing the means to communicate and interact, make decisions and take actions, and recognize and bring together disparate viewpoints and conflicting intentions.

The work reported in this paper is mainly concerned with providing answers to the engineering design of a generic MAS intended to create intelligent power plants from either conventional power plants or renewable power plants. Therefore, the process of definition, formulation, description, decomposition and allocation of the overall power plant control problem, followed by the selection and integration of suitable groups of IAs determines the scope of this paper. The engineering implementation of the proposed MAS will be reported in forthcoming papers.

3 Applications of MAS to Microgrids and Power Plants

In general, MAS have been applied to power engineering in many areas, i.e. diagnostics, distributed control, modeling and simulation, monitoring, decision making, automation, protection and maintenance scheduling [16]. There are examples of MAS applications in power systems and power plant control in [18]. Also, a scalable MAS is proposed for control of a large network of power generation, transmission, load and compensation sources in [20], and a multi-agent based power sharing scheme for hybrid power systems is presented in [30]. Regarding power plants, a MAS is applied to improve the heat rate of a fossil fuel power plant in [17] and a MAS to optimally control a power plant based on multiple objectives is designed in [19].

Due to their intrinsic characteristics, MAS have been mainly applied to control microgrids [22–24], which are becoming the new paradigm for structuring power systems. Microgrids are relatively small power systems that are usually integrated by distributed energy sources, loads, storage and control devices, and can operate interconnected or isolated from the main electric grid or power system. Operation and control of microgrids are challenging due to the variety and distribution of their components. For instance, a MAS distributed control implemented in the pilot microgrid of Kythnos Island in Greece is described in [29], a MAS that coordinates steady-state operation of distributed power and load, and provides black start-up capability in islanding operation is presented in [25], and a MAS that aims to achieve optimal energy exchange between power units in the microgrid, the main grid and the local loads is introduced in [26]. An analysis to extend MAS applications for control development in micro/smart grid hybrid systems is done in [27]. A recent survey of MAS applied to microgrid control is provided in [37].

There are several methodologies to design a MAS. The most common design procedure includes: (a) Specify the system and its objectives, (b) Analyze the roles of the agents, and (c) Design the interactions between the agents. The design of a MAS is expressed through its architecture that specifies the information and data exchange relationships, and the specific problem solving capabilities of the agents. Some examples are presented in [38, 39]. Largely, MAS architectures depend on the characteristics of the applications [40]. In particular, there are structures for energy generation and load control [41], forecasting, trading and planning [20], energy management, energy distribution, database management, monitoring [42] and so on [21, 43, 44]. MAS for microgrid operation might exhibit a three-layered architecture [16]:

- A top layer or message handling layer for receiving messages.
- An intermediate layer or behavioral level that defines the tasks to be carried out.
- A bottom layer or functional level for determining the actions agents must perform.

In a three-level MAS for a typical autonomous electricity network, there are distributed energy resource agents, database agents, control agents and user agents [45]. The first level controls the distributed power and load for proper energy management and reliable operation. The second level optimizes power quality and reduces fluctuations. The third level manages and schedules multiple microgrids based on market and scheduling needs [35]. A three-layer MAS made of main grid agents, microgrid agents and component level agents based on a hierarchical coordinated control strategy is proposed in [30]. A MAS architecture with two-layer control strategies in which distributed energy resources and loads are classified, and three types of agents are considered: a regional agent, a local agent and a service agent, for both, grid-connected and isolated modes, is presented in [31]. A MAS with decentralized control architecture for autonomous operation of a microgrid with power electronic interfaces is presented in [32]. A real-time intelligent control and structure based on MAS for microgrids is proposed in [33]. A microgrid energy management framework based on agent-based modelling to increase system performance is proposed in [34]. A MAS architecture for controlling distributed energy resources, where agents are grouped depending on their effect on the environment is presented in [28]. A framework to control active power and frequency to improve stability of a microgrid is presented in [35] and a framework for integration of a microgrid into the grid is presented in [36].

All previous review reveals that most MAS have been designed and implemented to advance and facilitate operation of microgrids. There is a shortage of technical literature about the design and development of MAS for power plants. If prevailing, this state of things will lead to an unbalance in the development of intelligent power systems, smart grids, intelligent hybrid systems, smart microgrids and so forth. Development of intelligent power plants, either conventional or renewable, is crucial to prevent the aforementioned dilemma, and the use of MAS to develop intelligent power plants is the most attractive and promising approach.

4   Intelligent Multiagent System for Supervision and Control of Power Plants

An intelligent system, based on the MAS paradigm, for autonomous operation of fossil fuel power units was proposed in [46]. The two-level hierarchical functional structure of the intelligent system was proposed after three major milestones: (a) The general structure model for industrial batch-process automation [47], (b) The four basic intelligence functions to implement intelligent systems [48], and (c) The principle of increasing precision with decreasing intelligence [49]. System goals were identified using power plant process engineering concepts, and intelligent control systems engineering concepts were used to identify main tasks, as well as to functionally decompose the system. Then, the software engineering agency concepts were used to identify and group agents according to knowledge and purpose interactions. Details of the process followed to define the intelligent system structure can be found in [50].

Now, the structure model of the intelligent system for operation of conventional and renewable power plants is proposed to be also realized as a multi-agent system, yielding the Intelligent Multi-Agent System for Supervision and Control (iMASSC) of power plants. The proposed iMASSC organization is an open superset of functionally grouped agent clusters in a two-level hierarchical system, as it is shown in Fig. 3. The term organization is preferred to emphasize the soft nature of the system structure over a rigid inflexible architecture. The upper level of iMASSC, which is mainly characterized for knowledge-driven processes, performs the supervisory functions needed to provide self-governing operation characteristics, while the lower level of iMASSC, which is mainly characterized for data-driven processes, performs the fast reactive behavior functions necessary for real-time control and protection.

Agents are loosely clustered taking the intelligence functions as guidelines. In that way, the control cluster takes account of the sequence control, regulatory control, protection, and input-output handling agents. The self-awareness cluster is introduced to group the system operating state determination, fault diagnosis, and test assistance agents. The world modeling cluster comprehends the learning, model building, and adaptation agents. The value judgment cluster comprehends the online performance monitoring, control tuning, and reconfiguration agents. The memory cluster is introduced to include the data and knowledge processing agents, as well as the system knowledge and data bases agents. The behavior generation cluster groups the process optimization, sequence generation, and set-point generation functions.

Agent clustering is introduced to simplify the representation and to indicate that the agents in a cluster use closely related system knowledge or data, and have mutual commitments and beliefs. In reality, all agents may coexist as parallel processes with random access to system information. As required for an open system, iMASSC exhibits organizational adaptability mediated by the supervisory execution manger agent and the direct execution manager agent. In principle, the iMASSC organization can adapt to changing circumstances by activating or deactivating agents, incorporating new agents or dismissing old agents, or modifying the pattern of interactions among the current agents. The iMASSC agents should dynamically find their collaborators based on the system requirements at hand and on which agents are present in the organization at any given time. Clusters should be formed adaptively as required.

The system functional decomposition into agents in Fig. 3 is not exhaustive in any way; it shows what is considered a basic set of tasks that should be taken into account to achieve a more general design toward truly intelligent control systems, and how they should be organized. In the spirit of an open system, this set of tasks may be augmented, or decreased, as required by the application at hand. Agents in Fig. 3 are briefly described as follows.

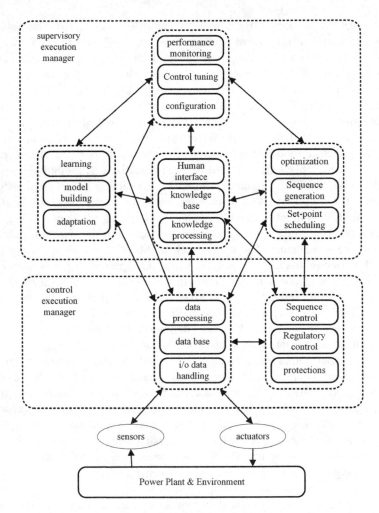

Fig. 3. iMASSC organization.

- Input/output signal handling. Constitute the interface between the control system and the plant instrumentation. Basically, it is responsible for entering and sending contact signals, as well as continuous signals, from and to the process instrumentation at regular intervals or under demand. In a more advanced application it should also implement the dialogs with new intelligent instrumentation. Also can take care of simulating a virtual environment for the entire system by halting actual inputs and imposing arbitrary input values.
- Protection and interlocking. Monitor critical variables to prevent the process entering unsafe operating regions, or shutdown total or partial process when already in unsafe conditions. These functions depend heavily on the physical characteristics, equipment configuration, and protection requirements at different operation stages of the process.

- Continuous regulatory control. Evaluates control algorithms for driving the continuously varying signals in the process according to predefined references.
- Sequence control. Allows the transition between the various operating states of the process. Enables/disables the continuous control functions as required.
- Operating state determination. Evaluates key signals to declare the operating state of the FFPU. This information is to be used by other functions in decision-making and evaluation of permissive conditions.
- Fault diagnosis. Identifies features of faults before occurring, and determines the causes when already occurred. Generates information for fault accommodation.
- Test assistance. Sets and verifies all necessary conditions to perform operation tests from a given catalog of tests.
- Process optimization. Determines the optimal operating conditions by solving optimization problems based on physical principles.
- Operation sequence scheduling. Performs time-sequenced decisions for automatic plant operation, for instance, unit scheduling of power generation based on AGC demands and physical conditions of equipment at the FFPU.
- Set-point scheduling. Generates set-points for the continuous control functions, and limits and threshold values for the sequence control and protection functions according to the different operative stages and optimization routines.
- Performance monitoring. Evaluates behavior of process under control to generate meaningful performance indications for adaptation and optimization.
- Control tuning. Based on performance values decides whether the current control configuration needs to be tuned or not. Performs tuning by updating parameters and knowledge of the direct control scheme if enabled by the human supervisor.
- Control reconfiguration. Based on performance values decides whether a change on the current control configuration should be done or not. Suggest a different control strategy from a given catalog and sets conditions for switching if enabled by human supervisor.
- Learning. Allows the supervisor to build and modify the knowledge and data bases for inferences and decision-making required at both the supervisory and direct control levels based on observations of the input-output behavior of both the process and the control system itself.
- Model building. On line modeling feature to account for plant and environment changes, provides information to be used by the adaptation mechanisms.
- Adaptation. In a broad sense provides the mechanisms to deal with changes in the plant and its environment at the supervisory level, such as updating the operating sequences and nonlinear characterizations required for wide range operation.

What is relevant in the iMASSC structure is the decomposition of the supervision function shown in Fig. 3 into several other tasks, in the form of agents, to provide the control system with the capability to satisfy increasing performance demands keeping the complexity of the system within manageable terms. Also, the software agency concept provides the necessary mindset to integrate very dissimilar technologies in a systematic and harmonious way to achieve a practical and effective system; by making use of the best characteristics each technology has to offer. These models can be advantageously applied to the operation of hybrid power systems.

5   Hybrid Power Generation with iMASSC Equipped Plants

Taking into account the kind of functions to be performed by the intelligent agents in a power plant equipped with iMASSC it is clear that intelligent power plants can be created. Basically, such power plants will perform the four basic functions of an intelligent system: sensory processing, world modeling, value judgment, and behavior generation. Figure 4 depicts a block diagram of a generic power plant, either conventional or renewable equipped with iMASSC. Note that the customary functions of current control systems, such as input/output signal handling, protection and interlocking, continuous feedback control and sequence control constitute the bottom hierarchical level of iMASSC, so little or no change is actually performed at this level in power plants. Nevertheless, all data gathered at this level is available to the top supervisory level of iMASSC. It is this supervisory level which introduces the functions that will provide the power plant with the abilities or characteristics of an intelligent system. While the bottom level functions mainly provide for quick real-time reactiveness of the power plant, the top level functions mainly provide for the goal-oriented behavior and social skills of the power plant.

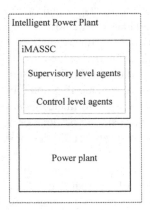

Fig. 4. Intelligent power plant equipped with iMASSC.

As known, a hybrid power system (HPS) incorporates diverse types of power generation sources, usually including renewable sources (wind turbine generators, solar photovoltaic panels, solar thermal plants, geothermal power plants, hydroelectric power plants, etc.), energy storage systems (fuel cell systems, solid state batteries, flywheels, compressed air systems, pumped hydropower, etc.), as well as the more conventional power plants burning some sort of fuel (biomass power plants, diesel motor generators, combustion turbine generators, coal burning power plants, fossil fuel power plants, etc.).

In general, each type of power generation source is an energy conversion system that has its own and defining characteristics regarding supply of primary source of energy, most favorable environmental conditions for more efficient operation, speed of conversion and transient response characteristics, range of electric energy that can be obtained, etc. Therefore, each type of energy conversion system requires control systems specifically designed for it. Nevertheless, all of the power plants must be able to participate and behave properly to provide the electric energy required by the users or loads, that is, power plants of all kinds must have a degree of intelligence enough to follow the guidelines set to get in, generate power and get out of a community of power plants. To carry out the later a smart facilitator or coordinator of operations might be useful. In the proposed structure any system is able to socialize with any other system, nevertheless the coordinator will set goals for their production, pursuing the optimal response of the whole system to the objectives previously set.

A hypothetical hybrid power system is depicted in Fig. 5 to illustrate the structure of a community of intelligent power plants, loads and energy management system. An Intelligent Multiple Agent System for Supervision and Control (iMASSC) is required to create an intelligent power plant from each conventional or renewable plant or energy storage system. An Intelligent Multiple Agent System for Load Control (iMASLC) is required to create an intelligent load or set of loads at the convenience of the power system. An Intelligent Multiple Agent System for Energy Management (iMASEM) is required to create an intelligent Energy Management System for the Hybrid Power System. At the time of writing this paper only the structure of iMASSC has been completely defined. The structures of iMASLC and iMASEM are currently under development and require further elaboration.

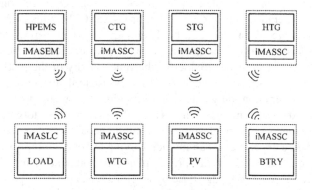

Fig. 5. Hybrid power system with intelligent power plants.

The proposed structure of a hybrid power system as a community of intelligent systems can be realized once the power plants in the system are made intelligent through iMASSC. Each intelligent power plant has its own abilities and expertise to participate, either cooperating, negotiating or competing with the other plants in the community, using the guidelines set for those aims. A key guideline is that the hybrid power system must provide the required power demanded by the loads in an optimal way at any moment. With such guidelines the community of intelligent power plants will show a coherent and goal oriented behavior. Also, the structure is flexible, in the sense that the intelligent power plants can decide whether or not to participate in the activities of the community depending on a variety of reasons, such as environmental conditions, financial issues, physical health circumstances, maintenance and repair programs, etc. Henceforth, to proceed in an orderly manner to ensure the availability, reliability and profitability of the hybrid system, the need for intelligent multiagent systems for energy management and load control was also pointed out, and will be complementary reported after further elaboration.

6   Future Work for iMASSC Development

Development of full iMASSC functionality can be a life-long multidisciplinary project requiring strong and tight collaboration of experts from many fields. Thus, to keep development within bounded time and resources, and to demonstrate the feasibility of the proposed approach, focus should be paid into the development of the essential functions of iMASSC required to create power plants that can be considered to be intelligent systems, that is, to create intelligent power plants. In this regard, there are many challenges and opportunities along the iMASSC research line.

First of all, development of a prototype of iMASSC should be attempted and simulation experiments with a power plant model must be carried out to improve effectiveness. Realization of an iMASSC prototype requires a careful selection of the functions to be developed. As a key requirement at least one function of each one of the four basic intelligence function clusters must be selected to implement the supervisory level of iMASSC. Then, the necessary feedback control, sequence control and protections should be included in the control level of iMASSC. Various challenges need to be solved at this stage. For instance, a hardware-software platform to develop intelligent multiagent systems has to be integrated. This platform should include at least a library of low-level functions to provide for the functionality of the platform, an agent description language to specify the agents and to translate them into executable code, and a language for common knowledge representation across all applications to allow for information exchange among agents. Once the iMASSC prototype is developed simulation experiments must be designed and implemented to demonstrate its intelligent behavior. These experiments can include solving the operation problem for a wide range of changing conditions in the power plant environment, using effectively the information stored in the knowledge base by all functions, arrive to operation solutions with participation of all agents, enhance performance of power plants, etc.

Later, various iMASSC prototypes have to be developed for conventional and renewable generation units to integrate a hybrid power system with intelligent power plants. Nevertheless, to make the hybrid power system practicable, additional intelligent MAS are necessary to be developed. At least an intelligent multiagent system for energy management (iMASEM) and an intelligent multiagent system for load control (iMASLC) are required. Energy dispatch is a crucial problem concerning the mixture of conventional and renewable power generation, and its optimal market-based solution is still open. Also, control on the load side faces multiple factors that must be wisely conciliated to obtain win-win solutions. Closely related to these problems is the definition of suitable performance indexes to measure and compare solutions with multiple competing objectives. Currently, a PC-based distributed platform to simulate a hybrid power system with intelligent power plants is being integrated. Once the hybrid power system development platform is developed, system wide simulation experiments will be carried out. Main experiments will include communication and data security, voltage stability and power flows, system reliability and resiliency, and system autonomy and coherence.

7 Conclusions

This paper introduces conceptual models of a supervision and control system to create intelligent power plants and the structure of a hybrid power system as a community of intelligent power plants. These models are intended to contribute novel solutions to the design of control systems for modern electric power systems, which are nowadays composed from either conventional or renewable power generation units. The proposed models define a reference framework to keep complexity of control systems within manageable bounds. This allows to create goal oriented and coherent communities of power plants, with very dissimilar behavioral characteristics. Therefore, power plants and hybrid power systems consistently achieve highly reliable, effective and autonomous operation. The difference with other approaches is that a Multi-Agent System is applied to each power plant instead of a single Intelligent Agent, providing a framework to create large-scale intelligent power systems.

The presented model of a supervision and control system to create intelligent power plants is based on the paradigms of intelligent agents and multiagent systems from the fields of software engineering and artificial intelligence. The simple typical structure of a multiagent system was extended using the concepts of batch process control, the basic intelligence functions and the principle of increasing precision with decreasing intelligence for intelligent systems, to propose the intelligent multiagent system for supervision and control (iMASSC). Hence, iMASSC creates intelligent power plants when specifically applied to either conventional or renewable power generation units.

The proposed structure of a hybrid power system as a community of intelligent systems can be realized once the power plants in the system are made intelligent through iMASSC. Each intelligent power plant has its own abilities and expertise to participate, either cooperating, negotiating or competing with the other plants in the community, using the guidelines set for those aims. A key guideline is that the hybrid power system must provide the required power demanded by the loads in an optimal way at any moment. With such guidelines the community of intelligent power plants will show a coherent and goal oriented behavior. Also, the structure is flexible, in the sense that the intelligent power plants can decide whether or not to participate in the activities of the community depending on a variety of reasons, such as environmental conditions, financial issues, physical health circumstances, maintenance and repair programs, etc. Henceforth, to proceed in an orderly manner to ensure the availability, reliability and profitability of the hybrid system, the need for intelligent multiagent systems for energy management and load control was also pointed out, and will be complementary reported after further elaboration.

Acknowledgements. Mónica Borunda wish to thank Consejo Nacional de Ciencia y Tecnologa (CONACYT) for funding her Catedra Research Position (ID 71557), and Instituto Nacional de Electricidad y Energas Limpias (INEEL) as host institution.

References

1. Galloway, B.: Introduction to industrial control networks. IEEE Commun. Surv. Tutor. **15**(2), 860–880 (2012)
2. Luger, G., Stubblefield, W.: Artificial intelligence: structures and strategies for complex problem solving (2004)
3. Van Tan, V., Yoo, D.-S., Yi, M.-J.: A multiagent-system framework for hierarchical control and monitoring of complex process control systems. In: Bui, T.D., Ho, T.V., Ha, Q.T. (eds.) PRIMA 2008. LNCS, vol. 5357, pp. 381–388. Springer, Heidelberg (2008). doi:10.1007/978-3-540-89674-6_42
4. Ward, P.T., Mellor, S.J.: Structured Development for Real-Time Systems, vol. 1–3. Yourdon Press (1985)
5. Gomma, A.: A software design method for real-time systems. Comm. ACM. **27**(9), 938 (1984)
6. Jennings, N.: Controlling cooperative problem solving in industrial multiagent systems using joint intention. Artif. Intell. **75**(2), 195 (1995)
7. Wooldridge, M.: Agent-based software engineering. IIE Proc. Soft. Eng. **144**, 26 (1997)
8. Knapik, M., Johnson, J.: Developing Intelligent Agents for Distributed Systems: Exploring Architecture Technologies, and Applications. McGraw-Hill, New York (1998)
9. Wooldridge, M., Weiss, G.: Multi-Agent Systems. The MIT Press, Cambridge (1999)
10. Ferber, J.: Multi-agent Systems: An Introduction to Artificial Intelligence. Addison-Wesley, Boston (1999)
11. Sycara, K.P.: Multiagent systems. AI Mag. **19**, 79 (1998). Summer
12. Durfee, E.H., Lesser, V.: Negotiating task decomposition and allocation using partial global planning. Distrib. Artif. Intell. **2**, 229 (1989). Morgan Kaufmann
13. Decker, K.S., Sycara, K.: Intelligent adaptive information agents. J. Intell. Inf. Syst. **9**(3), 239 (1997)
14. Cossentino, M., El Fallah Seghrouchni, A., Winikoff, M. (eds.): EMAS 2013. LNCS (LNAI), vol. 8245. Springer, Heidelberg (2013). doi:10.1007/978-3-642-45343-4
15. Jennings, N., Sycara, K., Wooldridge, M.: A roadmap for agent research and development. Auton. Agents Multiagent Syst. **1**(1), 7–38 (1998)
16. McArthur, S., Davidson, E., Catterson, V., Dimeas, A., Hatziargyriou, N., Ponci, F., Funabashi, T.: Multi-agent systems for power engineering applications, part i: concepts, approaches and technical challenge. IEEE Trans. Power Systems **22**(4), 1743–1752 (2007)
17. Velasco, J.R., Gonzalez, J.C., Magdalena, L., Iglesias, C.A.: Multiagent-based control systems: a hybrid approach to distributed process control. Control Eng. Pract. **4**(6), 839 (1996)
18. Chakraborty, S., Simões, M.G., Kramer, W.E.: Power Electronics for Renewable and Distributed Energy Systems: A sourcebook of Topologies, Control and Integration. Springer, London (2013). doi:10.1007/978-1-4471-5104-3
19. Lee, K.Y., Head, J.D., Gomes, J.R., Williams C.S.: Multi-agent system based intelligent distributed control system for power plants. In: IEEE Power and Energy Society General Meeting, pp. 1–7 (2011)

20. Tolbert, L., Qi, H. and Peng, F., Scalable multi-agent system for real-time electric, power management. In: Power Engineering Society Summer Meeting IEE, vol. 3, pp. 1676–1679 (2001)
21. Lagorse, J., Paire, D., Miraoui, A.: A multi-agent system for energy management of distributed power sources. Renew. Energy **35**(1), 174–182 (2010)
22. Roche, R., Blunier, B., Miraoui, A., Hilaire, V., Koukam, A.: Multi-agent systems for grid energy management: a short review. In: IECON 2010 36th Annual Conference on IEEE Industrial Electronics Society, pp. 3341–3346. IEEE (2010)
23. Narkhede, M.S., Chatterji, S., Ghosh, S.: Multi-agent Systems (MAS) controlled smart grid a review. Int. J. Comput. Appl., 0975–8887 (2013)
24. Khare, A.R., Kumar, B.Y.: Multiagent structures in hybrid renewable power system: a review. J. Renew. Sustain. Energy **7**, 063101 (2015)
25. Ling, Y.: Computational Intelligence in Industrial Application. CRC Press/Balkema, Leiden (2015)
26. Dimeas, A.L., Hatziargyriou, N.D.: Operation of a multiagent system for microgrid control. IEEE Trans. Power Syst. **20**(3), 1447–1455 (2005)
27. McArthur, S., Davidson, E., Catterson, V., Dimeas, A., Hatziargyriou, N., Ponci, F., Funabashi, T.: Multi-agent systems for power engineering applications part ii: technologies, standards, and tools for building multi-agent systems. IEEE Trans. Power Syst. **22**(4), 1753–1759 (2007)
28. Dimeas, A.L., Hatziargyriou, N.D.: Agent based control for microgrids. In: IEEE Power Engineering Society General Meeting, Tampa, FL, USA, pp. 1–5 (2007)
29. Chatzivasiliadis, S.J., Hatziargyriou, N.D., Dimeas, A.L.: Development of an agent based intelligent control system for microgrids. In: IEEE Power and Energy Society General Meeting-Conversion and Delivery of Electrical Energy in the 21st Century, Pittsburgh, PA, USA, pp. 1–6 (2008)
30. Jian, Z., Qian, A., Chuanwen, J., Xingang, W, Zhanghua, Z., Chenghong, G.: The application of multi agent system in microgrid coordination control. In: International Conference on Sustainable Power Generation and Supply, Nanjing, pp. 1–6 (2009)
31. Zheng, W., Cai, J.: A multi-agent system for distributed energy resources control in microgrid. In: 5th International Conference on Critical Infrastructure (CRIS), Beijing, China, pp. 1–5 (2010)
32. Cai, N., Mitras, J.: A decentralized control architecture for a microgrid with power electronic interfaces. In: North American Power Symposium, Arlington, TX, USA, pp. 1–8 (2010)
33. Kuo, M.T., Lu, S.D.: Design and implementation of real-time intelligent control and structure based on multi-agent systems in microgrids. Energies **6**, 6045–6059 (2013)
34. Kuznetsova, Y., Li, Y., Ruiz, C., Rio, E.: An integrated framework of agent-based modelling and robust optimization for microgrid energy management. Appl. Energy **129**, 70–88 (2014)
35. Wu, Z., Gu, W.: Active power and frequency control of islanded microgrid based on multi-agent technology. Electr. Power Automob. Equip. **11**, 57–61 (2009)
36. Velik, R., Nicolay, P.: A cognitive decision agent architecture for optimal energy management of microgrids. Energy Convers. Manag. **86**, 831–847 (2014)
37. Kantamneni, A., Brown, L.E., Parker, G., Weaver, W.W.: Survey of multi-agent systems for microgrid controls. Eng. Appl. Artif. Intell. **45**, 192–203 (2015)
38. Zambonelli, F., Jennings, N., Wooldridge, M.: Developing multiagent systems: the Gaia methodology. ACM Trans. Softw. Eng. Methodol. (TOSEM) **12**(3), 370 (2003)
39. Philips, L., Link, H., Smith, R., Welland, L.: Agent-based control of distributed infrastructure resources. Technical report, Sandia National Laboratories (2006)
40. Jimeno, J., Anduaga, J., Oyarzabal, J., de Muro, A.G.: Architecture of a microgrid energy management system. Eur. Trans. Electr. Power **21**(2), 1142–1158 (2011)

41. Rumley, S., Kaegi, E., Rudnick, H., Germond, A.: Multi-agent approach to electrical distribution networks control. In: 32nd Annual IEEE International Computer Software and Applications, CPMPSAC 2008, pp. 575–580, 28 July 2008

42. James, G., Cohen, D., Dodier R., Platt, G., Palmer, D.: A deployed multi-agent framework for distributed energy applications. In: AAMAS 2006: Proceedings of the Fifth International Joint Conference on Autonomous Agents and Multiagent Systems, pp. 676–678. ACM, New York (2006)

43. Rahman, S., Pippattanasomporn, M., Teklu, Y.: Intelligent distributed autonomous power systems (IDAPS). In: Power Engineering Society General Meeting, pp. 1–8. IEEE (2007)

44. Kok, J.K., Scheepers, M.J.J., Kamphuis, I.G.: Intelligence in electricity networks for embedding renewables and distributed generation. In: Negenborn, R., Lukszo, Z., Hellendoorn, H. (eds.) Intelligent Infrastructures. Intelligent Systems, Control and Automation: Science and Engineering, vol. 42, pp. 179–209. Springer, Dordrecht (2010). doi:10. 1007/978-90-481-3598-1_8

45. Momoh, J.: Smart Grid, Fundamentals of Design and Analysis. John Wiley & Sons, Inc., Hoboken, New Jersey (2012). El-Hawary, M.E., IEEE Press Series on Power Engineering

46. Garduno-Ramirez, R., Lee, K.Y.: Intelligent multiagent control for power plants. In: Leondes, C.T. (ed.) Intelligent Systems: Technology and Applications. Control and Electric Power Systems, vol. 6, pp. 181–209. CRC Press, Boca Raton (2002)

47. Rosenof, H.P., Ghosh, A.: Batch Process Automation: Theory and Practice. Van Nostrand Reinhold, New York (1987)

48. Albus, J.S.: Outline for a theory of intelligence. IEEE Trans. Syst. Man Cybern. **21**(3), 473–509 (1991)

49. Saridis, G.N.: Analytic formulation of the principle of increasing precision with decreasing intelligence for intelligent machines. Automatica **25**(3), 461–467 (1989)

50. Garduno-Ramirez, R.: Fossil-Fuel Power Plant Control: An Intelligent Hybrid Approach. Lambert Academic Publishing, Saarbrücken (2010)

Neural Networks and Deep Learning

Author Profiling with Doc2vec Neural Network-Based Document Embeddings

Ilia Markov[1(✉)], Helena Gómez-Adorno[1], Juan-Pablo Posadas-Durán[2],
Grigori Sidorov[1], and Alexander Gelbukh[1]

[1] CIC, Instituto Politécnico Nacional (IPN), Mexico City, Mexico
markovilya@yahoo.com, helena.adorno@gmail.com, sidorov@cic.ipn.mx
[2] ESIME-Zacatenco, Instituto Politécnico Nacional (IPN), Mexico City, Mexico
jpposadas@gmail.com
http://www.gelbukh.com

Abstract. To determine author demographics of texts in social media such as Twitter, blogs, and reviews, we use doc2vec document embeddings to train a logistic regression classifier. We experimented with age and gender identification on the PAN author profiling 2014–2016 corpora under both single- and cross-genre conditions. We show that under certain settings the neural network-based features outperform the traditional features when using the same classifier. Our method outperforms existing state of the art under some settings, though the current state-of-the-art results on those tasks have been quite weak.

Keywords: Document embeddings · doc2vec · Neural networks · Machine learning · Author profiling

1 Introduction

The author profiling (AP) task aims at identifying author demographics, such as age, gender, personality traits, or native language, basing on the analysis of text samples. This research area has experienced an explosive increase in interest in recent years. It contributes to marketing, security, terrorism prevention, and forensic applications, among other.

The approaches that tackle the task of AP from the machine-learning perspective view the task as a multi-class, single-label classification problem, when the set of class labels is known *a priori*. Thus, AP is modeled as a classification task, in which automatic methods have to assign class labels (e.g., male, female) to objects (texts).

Machine-learning algorithms require input data to be represented in the form of a fixed-length feature vector. Various approaches that have been used to obtain such a vector include bag-of-words, bag-of-n-grams, and bag-of-concepts [1–6] models, among others. Recently, deep-learning techniques have been extensively used for text analysis [7–12]. Accordingly, in this work we apply the doc2vec algorithm [13] to obtain the fixed-length feature vector, i.e., we learn neural

© Springer International Publishing AG 2017
O. Pichardo-Lagunas and S. Miranda-Jiménez (Eds.): MICAI 2016, Part II, LNAI 10062, pp. 117–131, 2017.
DOI: 10.1007/978-3-319-62428-0_9

network-based document embeddings (also known as document distributed representations or paragraph vectors) in an unsupervised manner from texts. This type of document embeddings allows representing texts as dense vectors, taking into account their semantic and syntactic structure. Furthermore, this representation has been shown to be efficient when dealing with high-dimensional and sparse data [13,14].

Our motivation was two-fold: first, to suggest an author profiling method better than existing ones; second, to compare the doc2vec features with traditional features when used with the same classifier. We show that using neural network-based document embeddings for the AP task improves the classifier performance in some settings; we conducted experiments not only under single-genre conditions but also under cross-genre AP conditions, when the training and test datasets are from significantly different sources, such as Twitter vs. reviews. Namely, the neural network-based features outperform the baseline features in many cases when used with the same classifier (logistic regression in our case), as well as outperform the state-of-the-art approaches under some AP conditions.

The rest of this paper is organized as follows. Section 2 presents related work. Section 3 describes the proposed methodology. Section 4 provides some characteristics of the corpora used. Section 5 describes the conducted experiments. Section 6 presents the obtained results and their evaluation. Section 7 draws the conclusions and points to the possible directions of future work.

2   Related Work

A wide range of approaches have been proposed to tackle the AP task, with a variety of feature types and feature representations used. In order to promote studies on author profiling (AP) and other authorship identification-related tasks, the PAN evaluation campaign,[1] which is held as part of the CLEF conference, has been organized annually since 2013. It is constantly gaining much attention of researchers from around the world. In this section, we will focus on the winning approaches of each edition of the PAN evaluation campaign.

In the first edition of PAN in 2013 [15], the task consisted in identifying the author's age and gender based on blog posts written in the English and Spanish languages. The work by López-Monroy et al. [16] is the overall winner of this year competition, even though their system was ranked second in the individual evaluation on both the English and Spanish datasets. Their approach consisted in using the second order representation based on relationships between documents and profiles. The best approach on the English dataset [17] used ensemble-based classification on a large feature set, including structural, part-of-speech (POS), and text difficulty features, when for Spanish, the best performing approach relied on content-based, style-based, and topic-based features [18].

---

[1] http://pan.webis.de [last access: 17.07.2016]. All other URLs in this document were also verified on this date.

The second PAN edition in 2014 [19] also focused on determining the author's age and gender. The provided dataset was composed of blog posts, tweets, and social media texts written in both English and Spanish, as well as hotel reviews written in English. As in the previous year, the approach that used the second order representation [20] outperformed other submitted systems.

In 2015 [21], the task aimed at predicting age, gender, and five personality traits: extroversion, stability, agreeableness, conscientiousness, and openness. This year task was limited to tweets, but was extended to four different languages: English, Spanish, Dutch, and Italian. Álvarez-Carmona et al. [22] who approached the task using second order profiles and latent semantic analysis (LSA) achieved the best results on the English, Spanish, and Dutch datasets. The best results on the Italian dataset were obtained using stylistic features represented by character and POS n-grams [23].

The focus of the recent 2016 shared task [24] has shifted towards cross-genre age and gender identification covering the English, Spanish, and Dutch languages, that is, the training corpus was on one genre (tweets), while the test set was on another genre (blog posts for English and Spanish, and reviews for Dutch). The best performing system [25] used combinations of stylistic features such as function words, POS, emoticons, punctuations marks, along with the second order representation.

As one can see, feature representation plays a crucial role in achieving high performance in this task. The second order representation based on relationships between documents and profiles led to the best results in all PAN editions. Taking it into account, we focus on an alternative feature representation based on a neural network, which we explain in detail in the next section.

The only work in all PAN editions that used distributed representations of words, namely, word2vec embeddings [26,27], to tackle the AP task is that by Bayot and Gonçalves [28]. They used the word2vec model trained only on Wikipedia dumps without using the training corpus; this may be the cause for their modest results.

The doc2vec algorithm for learning neural network-based document embeddings is widely used in natural language processing (NLP) tasks, e.g., in text classification, sentiment analysis, information retrieval, etc. [13,14]. However, to the best of our knowledge, the only work that has been done on AP using document embeddings is our previous research [29]. While the primary goal of that work was to evaluate the effect of pre-processing on learning document embeddings, in this work we focus on evaluating different parameters of the doc2vec algorithm itself, on comparing the doc2vec method with the state of the art, and on comparing the neural network-based features with the traditional features when using the same classifier. In addition, in this paper we address both single- and cross-genre AP settings.

Here, we learn the doc2vec model for author profile identification of anonymous texts; however, this approach can be also used for author demographics identification from other types of textual data, such as source codes [30,31]. Identification of author's personality from his/her source code is gaining much interest nowadays in automatic source code analysis, which led to the organisation of the first shared task in this filed.[2]

3   Methodolody

The pre-processing performed in this work include standardizing non-standard language expressions, that is, replacing slang words, contractions, abbreviations, and emoticons by their corresponding normalized language expressions. In our previous research [29], we showed that this pre-processing strategy improves the quality of a neural network-based feature representation when used for the AP task.

In order to obtain neural network-based document embeddings, we use the doc2vec algorithm introduced in [13]. It learns features from the corpus in an unsupervised manner and provides a fixed-length feature vector as output. Then, the output is fed into a machine-learning classifier. A framework for learning document vectors is shown in Fig. 1.

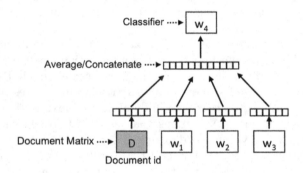

Fig. 1. Framework for learning document vectors. Adapted from [13].

Document vectors are asked to contribute to the prediction task of the next word given many contexts sampled from the document. Each document is mapped to a unique vector represented by a column in a document matrix D. Typically, the document vectors are initialized randomly and in the process of training capture semantics as a side effect of the prediction task.

It is usually recommended to train the doc2vec model several times with unlabeled data while exchanging the input order of the documents. Each iteration of the algorithm is called an epoch, and its purpose is to increase the quality of the output vectors. The selection of the input order of the documents is usually done by a random number generator.

In this work, instead of initializing the vectors randomly, we use a fixed number generator (fixed seed). Moreover, we apply the Fisher-Yates shuffle

---

[2] http://www.autoritas.es/prsoco/.

algorithm [32] with a fixed seed for exchanging the order the documents are input in each epoch of the training process. In this way, we ensure the reproducibility of the experiments.

4 Datasets

For the evaluation of neural network-based document embeddings in single-genre author profiling (AP), first, we conducted experiments on the PAN AP 2015 training corpus [21] under 10-fold cross-validation. The corpus is composed of Twitter messages in English, Spanish, Dutch, and Italian.

The English and Spanish training datasets are labeled with age and gender, whereas the Dutch and Italian datasets are labeled only with gender. The following age classes are considered: 18–24, 25–34, 35–49, and 50+. The distribution of age and gender over the number of authors can be seen in Table 1.

Table 1. Age and gender distribution over the PAN AP 2015 training corpus.

		English	Spanish	Dutch	Italian
Total		152	100*	34	38
Age	18–24	58	22	–	–
	25–34	60	46	–	–
	35–49	22	22	–	–
	50+	12	10	–	–
Gender	Male	76	50	17	19
	Female	76	50	17	19

* PAN AP 2015 overview [21] mentions 110; however, in fact the corpus contains 100 documents, and other papers in PAN AP 2015 proceedings, such as [22,23,33,34], report 100 as well.

Then, the experiments were conducted on the PAN AP 2016 training corpus [24] under single-genre setting (with 10-fold cross-validation). The PAN AP 2016 corpus consists of Twitter messages in English, Spanish, and Dutch. The PAN 2016 English and Spanish training datasets are labeled with age and gender, when the Dutch dataset is labeled only with gender. The distribution of age and gender over the number of authors in the PAN AP 2016 corpus can be seen in Table 2.

As one can see comparing Tables 1 and 2, the PAN AP 2016 corpus contains more documents, and there are more age classes than in the PAN AP 2015 corpus. Both corpora are perfectly balanced in terms of represented gender classes; however, they are highly unbalanced in terms of age classes. Figure 2 presents the alternative view of age distribution over the PAN AP 2015 and 2016 training corpora.

Finally, we carried out experiments under cross-genre AP conditions, that is, we used a training corpus on one genre, while the test set was on another

Table 2. Age and gender distribution over the PAN AP 2016 training corpus.

		English	Spanish	Dutch
Total		426*	250	384
Age	18–24	26	16	–
	25–34	135	64	–
	35–49	181	126	–
	50–64	78	38	–
	65+	6	6	–
Gender	Male	213	125	192
	Female	213	125	192

* PAN AP 2016 overview [24] mentions 428; however, the corpus contains two empty documents.

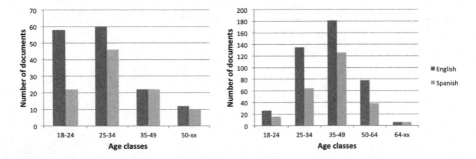

Fig. 2. Age distribution over the PAN AP 2015 (left) and 2016 (right) training corpora.

genre. As training corpus we used the PAN AP 2016 corpus and a subset of the PAN AP 2014 training corpus as test dataset, since the PAN 2016 test corpus is currently not available due to the policies of the PAN organizers. The used subset of the PAN AP 2014 corpus is composed of English and Spanish blog posts and social media, as well as of English reviews. The distribution of age and gender over the number of authors in the used subset of the PAN AP 2014 corpus is shown in Table 3. As one can see, this corpus is also highly unbalanced in terms of age classes.

5   Experimental Settings

In order to standardize non-standard language expressions mentioned in Sect. 3, we used the dictionaries of shortened vocabulary introduced in [35]. Moreover, we converted all characters to lowercase and separated each document with a new line.

In the case of cross-gender setting, we learned the doc2vec model from the training corpus (PAN AP 2016) and obtained a neural network-based distributed

Table 3. Age and gender distribution over the PAN AP 2014 training corpus.

		Blog posts		Social media		Reviews
		English	Spanish	English	Spanish	English
Total		147	88	7,746	1,272	4,160
Age	18–24	6	4	1,550	330	360
	25–34	60	26	2,098	426	1,000
	35–49	54	42	2,246	324	1,000
	50–64	23	12	1,838	160	1,000
	65+	4	4	14	32	800
Gender	Male	74	44	3,873	636	2,080
	Female	73	44	3,873	636	2,080

representation for each training text sample with the doc2vec algorithm [13]. In run-time, we inferred a vector for each previously unseen text sample in the test corpus (PAN AP 2014) using the doc2vec model previously learned from the training data.

However, for the single-genre setting, instead of using disjoint test and training corpora, we used one corpus (PAN AP 2015 or 2016) with 10-fold cross-validation experimental design. In this case we learned the doc2vec model from the whole corpus (not from the 90% of the corpus used for training in each fold of the 10-fold cross-validation setting) and obtained a neural network-based distributed representation for each text sample. We realize that this is not a clean experimental design, but we believe that other systems conducted their experiments in this way (given that typically WEKA [36] was used in those works for 10-fold cross-validation [37,38]), and replicated this experimental design to be able to compare our results with the previous work.

Then, these distributed vector representations were used to train a classifier. We conducted experiments using the Scikit-learn [39] implementation of the LR classifier. This classifier with default parameters has previously given good performance on high-dimensional data [40,41]. We generated different classification models for each of the aspects of an author profile, i.e., one model for the age profile and another one for the gender profile. For the 10-fold cross-validation experiments, we used the function from the Scikit-learn Python module that returns the accuracy for each of the 10 folds. The overall accuracy was calculated as the average of the 10 scores.

As we have mentioned in Sect. 3, the doc2vec method implements a neural network-based unsupervised learning algorithm that builds distributed representations of fixed length from texts [13]. In this work, we used a freely available implementation of the doc2vec algorithm included in the GENSIM[3] Python module. The implementation of the doc2vec algorithm requires the following three parameters: the number of features to be returned (length of the vector), the

---

[3] https://radimrehurek.com/gensim/.

size of the window that capture the adjacent words, and the minimum frequency of words to be included into the model. The values of these parameters depend on the corpus.

In order to narrow down the search of the parameters of the algorithm, similarly to [27,29], we performed a grid search over the following fixed ranges: vector length from 100 to 300 with step 100, window size from 3 to 15 with step 1, and minimum frequency from 3 to 4 with step 1. The optimal parameters for the PAN 2015 and 2016 corpora are shown in Table 4. The optimal parameters for age do not always correspond to the optimal parameters for gender. For a given corpus, we selected a single set of parameters that provided the best average accuracy between age and gender, i.e., we did not optimize the parameters for age and gender separately. When evaluating the document embeddings performance on the test dataset—the PAN AP 2014 training corpus, we used the parameters selected by 10-fold cross-validation on the training data—the PAN AP 2016 training corpus.

Table 4. Optimal parameters of the doc2vec algorithm for the PAN AP 2015 and 2016 corpora.

Parameter	Vector length	Window size	Minimum frequency
PAN AP 2015 corpus			
English	100	14	4
Spanish	100	5	3
Dutch	100	4	3
Italian	100	12	3
PAN AP 2016 corpus			
English	100	10	3
Spanish	100	9	4
Dutch	100	5	4

6 Experimental Results

In order to evaluate the efficiency of the doc2vec model on the AP task, we compared it with existing state-of-the-art approaches. Since there is no official competition of AP approaches with the settings considered in our work, and since undertaking an exhaustive literary research to identify the top-performing approaches was infeasible, we considered several top-performing systems of the PAN 2015 or 2016 AP competition and examined the corresponding papers to see whether, in addition to the official PAN AP task results, they reported results with the settings addressed in our work. Some of them did; of these, we selected those that reported the highest results:

– For the single-genre AP task on the PAN AP 2015 corpus: the work by Sulea and Dichiu [42], the fifth top system at PAN 2015, which used the author type/token ratio (verbosity rate) and tf-idf weighting scheme.
– For the single-genre AP task on the PAN AP 2016 corpus: the work by Busger *et al.* [25], the winning system at PAN 2016, which used stylistic features and second order feature representation.
– For the cross-genre AP task trained on the PAN AP 2016 corpus and tested on the PAN AP 2014 corpus: the work by Modaresi *et al.* [43], the second top system at PAN 2016, which used logistic regression classifier with stylistic and lexical features.

As baselines, we considered word unigram-based (bag-of-words model) and character 3-gram-based (bag-of-cn-grams model, $n = 3$) approaches, which are commonly believed to be highly predicative for the AP task, independently of language [21,44]. We used our own implementation of the bag-of-words and bag-of-c3-grams approaches, using a logistic regression (LR) classifier.

Table 5 compares our results with the state-of-the-art approaches on the PAN AP 2015 training corpus under single-genre setting (with 10-fold cross-validation) in terms of accuracy for age and gender classification for each language. Here, our method in all but one cases outperformed bag-of-words and bag-of-c3-grams baselines. However, it was below the state of the art [42].

Table 5. Single-genre results (accuracy, %) for age and gender classification on the PAN AP 2015 training corpus. LR stands for logistic regression classifier. The best results for age and gender for each language are in bold.

Approach	English		Spanish		Dutch	Italian
	Age	Gender	Age	Gender	Gender	Gender
Sulea and Dichiu [42]	**75.65**	**78.94**	**73.00**	**88.00**	**76.47**	**78.94**
LR on bag of words	57.71	61.96	47.00	66.00	44.17	63.33
LR on bag of c3-grams	63.00	58.75	52.00	70.00	49.17	65.83
LR on doc2vec (our)	65.00	69.08	56.00	62.00	56.67	70.00

Table 6 shows comparison of the results on the PAN AP 2016 corpus under single-genre setting. In this experiment, our method outperformed both the baseline and the state-of-the-art approaches for all considered cases; note that the state-of-the-art approach here performed very weakly in comparison with the baselines for gender classification, while we achieved higher improvement for gender than for age.

Tables 7 and 8 show cross-genre results, for the English and Spanish languages, respectively. Unlike under single-genre conditions, in cross-genre setting improvement in accuracy was mostly achieved for age and not for gender, regardless of the language or genre of documents. However, in this setting the state-of-the-art method performed weakly for age classification.

Table 6. Single-genre results (accuracy, %) for age and gender classification on the PAN AP 2016 training corpus.

Approach	English		Spanish		Dutch
	Age	Gender	Age	Gender	Gender
Busger *et al.* [25]	45.73	70.67	48.99	70.85	72.13
LR on bag of words	41.55	72.56	47.63	72.00	71.56
LR on bag of c3-grams	39.20	72.80	48.82	66.40	74.97
LR on doc2vec (our)	**46.01**	**76.98**	**50.44**	**77.20**	**75.54**

Table 7. Cross-genre results (accuracy, %) for English age and gender classification trained on the PAN AP 2016 corpus and tested on the PAN AP 2014 corpus.

Approach	Blog posts		Social media		Reviews	
	Age	Gender	Age	Gender	Age	Gender
Modaresi *et al.* [43]	38.78	**84.35**	20.00	**60.00**	15.24	**60.67**
LR on bag of words	35.37	65.31	26.61	50.50	23.85	55.34
LR on bag of c3-grams	**46.26**	55.10	27.49	50.81	22.57	58.49
LR on doc2vec (our)	35.37	54.42	**29.80**	49.85	**23.92**	51.75

Table 8. Cross-genre results (accuracy, %) for Spanish age and gender classification trained on the PAN AP 2016 corpus and tested on the PAN AP 2014 corpus.

Approach	Blog posts		Social media	
	Age	Gender	Age	Gender
Modaresi *et al.* [43]	40.91	**77.27**	16.27	**59.51**
LR on bag of words	29.55	70.45	32.23	55.66
LR on bag of c3-grams	30.68	61.36	**32.39**	56.84
LR on doc2vec (our)	**42.20**	64.77	31.29	55.90

Table 9 summarizes the comparison with the state of the art and the baselines. As we have stated in the introduction, our contribution is two-fold: on the one hand, we suggest a new method meant to outperform the state of the art; on the other hand, we suggest the features meant to improve the performance of a given classifier. Accordingly, in this table, *Method* refers to the comparison of our results with the state of the art; *Features* refers to the comparison of our results with the baseline features using the same classifier (LR). *Extraction* refers to whether the feature extraction was performed on the entire corpus, before splitting it into training and test corpora, or only on the training portion of the corpus. *Size* refers to the size of the training corpus. The value of '+' indicates that our results were better, '−' that they were worse, and '±' indicates varying comparison results. As we have mentioned above, in some cases the published state-of-the-art results are below our experiments with the baseline features; for those cases, when our doc2vec method outperformed the baseline features, it automatically outperformed those state-of-the-art results. Such trivial success cases are marked as '(+)'.

Table 9. Summary of the comparison.

Extraction	Setting	Size	Corpus	Method Age	Gender	Features Age	Gender
entire {	single {	small	2015	–	–	+	+
		large {	2016	(+)	(+)	+	+
training	cross		2016/2014	(+)	–	±	–

From this table one can observe that the doc2vec features outperformed the baseline features in single-genre setting, for which the experiment design included feature extraction from the entire corpus, both training and test portions, and gave varying results in cross-genre setting with feature extraction from the training corpus only.

As to the state of the art, our method outperformed only very weak methods, which, still, are the best ones reported in the literature so far. This is not surprising because we did not optimize our method but mainly aimed only at a clear comparison of the neural network-based features with the traditional ones, applying a commonly-used classifier.

7   Conclusions and Future Work

Author profiling (AP) is the task of identifying author demographics based on his or her writings. This is useful for security, marketing, and forensics applications. Recently, the interest in the task of AP has increased steadily, which to a large extent is caused by the annual organization of the PAN AP shared task with a high number of participating teams.

Machine-learning methods are commonly used to identify common stylistic patterns of the authors that share the same profiling aspects. In this work, we applied an approach based on neural network-based document embeddings for the identification of author's age and gender. We used the doc2vec algorithm to learn neural network-based document embeddings and evaluated their performance on the PAN AP 2014–2016 corpora under both single- and cross-genre AP conditions. Our method in certain settings outperformed the state-of-the-art approaches for the AP task.

The contribution of this work is two-fold:

– First, we compare the document-embedding features with traditional features, using the same machine-learning algorithm, and show that the former ones are better in some settings;
– Second, we compare our method with the state-of-the-art approaches and show that it outperforms those approaches under some AP conditions.

The obtained results, in line with the previous work in the field, indicate that feature representation is important for obtaining high performance in this task. Given the same learning algorithm (logistic regression), neural network-based document embeddings used as feature representation in many cases improved the results as compared with the baseline features. Namely, our features outperformed the baseline features in single-genre settings; in those experiments, features were extracted form the entire corpus, including the training and test portions. Moreover, our method outperformed state of the art in those cases when that state of the art was weaker than our baselines.

One of the directions for future work will be to examine the robustness of neural network-based document embeddings on other AP corpora. We will also evaluate the doc2vec-based AP methods using other types of feature as input data representation for the doc2vec method, such as n-grams of words, semantic relations of different types [45,46], syntactic dependency-based n-grams of various types [47–49], part-of-speech tags [50], and different categories of character n-grams [51,52].

Acknowledgments. This work was partially supported by the Mexican Government (CONACYT projects 240844 and 20161958, SNI, COFAA-IPN, SIP-IPN 20151406, 20161947, 20161958, 20151589, 20162204, and 20162064).

References

1. Cambria, E., Poria, S., Gelbukh, A., Kwok, K.: Sentic API: a common-sense based API for concept-level sentiment analysis. In: Proceedings of the 4th Workshop on Making Sense of Microposts, co-located with WWW 2014, 23rd International World Wide Web Conference. Number 1141 in CEUR Workshop Proceedings (2014)
2. Poria, S., Gelbukh, A., Agarwal, B., Cambria, E., Howard, N.: Common sense knowledge based personality recognition from text. In: Castro, F., Gelbukh, A., González, M. (eds.) MICAI 2013. LNCS, vol. 8266, pp. 484–496. Springer, Heidelberg (2013). doi:10.1007/978-3-642-45111-9_42
3. Poria, S., Gelbukh, A., Hussain, A., Howard, N., Das, D., Bandyopadhyay, S.: Enhanced SenticNet with affective labels for concept-based opinion mining. IEEE Intell. Syst. **28**, 31–38 (2013)
4. Cambria, E., Poria, S., Bajpai, R., Schuller, B.: SenticNet 4: a semantic resource for sentiment analysis based on conceptual primitives. In: COLING 2016, 26th International Conference on Computational Linguistics, Osaka, Japan (2016)
5. Poria, S., Cambria, E., Hazarika, D., Vij, P.: A deeper look into sarcastic tweets using deep convolutional neural networks. In: 26th International Conference on Computational Linguistics, COLING 2016, Osaka, Japan, pp. 1601–1612 (2016)
6. Poria, S., Cambria, E., Gelbukh, A., Bisio, F., Hussain, A.: Sentiment data flow analysis by means of dynamic linguistic patterns. IEEE Comput. Intell. Mag. **10**, 26–36 (2015)
7. Majumder, N., Poria, S., Gelbukh, A., Cambria, E.: Deep learning based document modeling for personality detection from text. IEEE Intell. Syst. **32**, 74–79 (2017)
8. Poria, S., Cambria, E., Bajpai, R., Hussain, A.: A review of affective computing: from unimodal analysis to multimodal fusion. Inf. Fus. **37**, 98–125 (2017)

9. Poria, S., Peng, H., Hussain, A., Howard, N., Cambria, E.: Ensemble application of convolutional neural networks and multiple kernel learning for multimodal sentiment analysis. Neurocomputing (2017, in press)

10. Chikersal, P., Poria, S., Cambria, E., Gelbukh, A., Siong, C.E.: Modelling public sentiment in twitter: using linguistic patterns to enhance supervised learning. In: Gelbukh, A. (ed.) CICLing 2015. LNCS, vol. 9042, pp. 49–65. Springer, Cham (2015). doi:10.1007/978-3-319-18117-2_4

11. Poria, S., Cambria, E., Gelbukh, A.: Aspect extraction for opinion mining with a deep convolutional neural network. Knowl.-Based Syst. **108**, 42–49 (2016)

12. Poria, S., Chaturvedi, I., Cambria, E., Hussain, A.: Convolutional MKL based multimodal emotion recognition and sentiment analysis. In: 16th International Conference on Data Mining, ICDM 2016, pp. 439–448. IEEE (2016)

13. Le, Q., Mikolov, T.: Distributed representations of sentences and documents. In: Proceedings of the 31st International Conference on Machine Learning. ICML 2014, pp. 1188–1196 (2014)

14. Dai, A., Olah, C., Le, Q.: Document embedding with paragraph vectors. CoRR abs/1507.07998 (2015)

15. Rangel, F., Rosso, P., Koppel, M., Stamatatos, E., Inches, G.: Overview of the author profiling task at PAN 2013. In: CLEF 2013 Labs and Workshops, Notebook Papers, vol. 1179 (2013)

16. López-Monroy, A.P., Montes-y-Gómez, M., Escalante, H.J., Villaseñor-Pineda, L., Villatoro-Tello, E.: INAOE's participation at PAN 2013: author profiling task. In: Working Notes Papers of the CLEF 2013 Evaluation Labs. CLEF 2013, CEUR (2013)

17. Meina, M., Brodzińska, K., Celmer, B., Czoków, M., Patera, M., Pezacki, J., Wilk, M.: Ensemble-based classification for author profiling using various features. In: Working Notes Papers of the CLEF 2013 Evaluation Labs. CLEF 2013, CEUR (2013)

18. Santosh, K., Bansal, R., Shekhar, M., Varma, V.: Author profiling: predicting age and gender from blogs. In: Working Notes Papers of the CLEF 2013 Evaluation Labs. CLEF 2013, CEUR (2013)

19. Rangel, F., Rosso, P., Chugur, I., Potthast, M., Trenkmann, M., Stein, B., Verhoeven, B., Daelemans, W.: Overview of the 2nd author profiling task at PAN 2014. In: CLEF 2014 Labs and Workshops, Notebook Papers. vol. 1180. 898–927 (2014)

20. López-Monroy, A.P., Montes-y-Gómez, M., Escalante, H.J., Villaseñor-Pineda, L.: Using intra-profile information for author profiling. In: Working Notes Papers of the CLEF 2014 Evaluation Labs. CLEF 2014, CEUR (2014)

21. Rangel, F., Celli, F., Rosso, P., Pottast, M., Stein, B., Daelemans, W.: Overview of the 3rd author profiling task at PAN 2015. In: CLEF 2015 Labs and Workshops, Notebook Papers, vol. 1391. CEUR (2015)

22. Álvarez-Carmona, M.A., López-Monroy, A.P., Montes-y-Gómez, M., Villaseor-Pineda, L., Jair-Escalante, H.: INAOE's participation at PAN 2015: author profiling task. In: Working Notes Papers of the CLEF 2015 Evaluation Labs, CLEF 2015, vol. 1391. CEUR (2015)

23. González-Gallardo, C.E., Montes, A., Sierra, G., Núñez-Juárez, J.A., Salinas-López, A.J., Ek, J.: Tweets classification using corpus dependent tags, character and POS n-grams. In: Working Notes Papers of the CLEF 2015 Evaluation Labs, CLEF 2015, vol. 1391. CEUR (2015)

24. Rangel, F., Rosso, P., Verhoeven, B., Daelemans, W., Potthast, M., Stein, B.: Overview of the 4th author profiling task at PAN 2016: cross-genre evaluations.

In: Working Notes Papers of the CLEF 2016 Evaluation Labs. CEUR Workshop Proceedings, CLEF and CEUR-WS.org (2016)

25. Busger Op Vollenbroek, M., Carlotto, T., Kreutz, T., Medvedeva, M., Pool, C., Bjerva, J., Haagsma, H., Nissim, M.: GronUP: groningen user profiling. In: CEUR Workshop Proceedings Working Notes Papers of the CLEF 2016 Evaluation Labs, vol. 1609, pp. 846–857. CLEF and CEUR-WS.org (2016)

26. Mikolov, T., Chen, K., Corrado, G.S., Dean, J.: Efficient estimation of word representations in vector space. Computing Research Repository abs/1301.3781 (2013)

27. Mikolov, T., Sutskever, I., Chen, K., Corrado, G.S., Dean, J.: Distributed representations of words and phrases and their compositionality. In: Proceedings of the 27th Annual Conference on Neural Information Processing Systems: Advances in Neural Information Processing Systems, vol. 26, pp. 3111–3119 (2013)

28. Bayot, R., Gonçalves, T.: Author profiling using SVMs and word embedding averages. In: CEUR Workshop Proceedings of the Working Notes Papers of the CLEF 2016 Evaluation Labs, vol. 1609, pp. 815–823. CLEF and CEUR-WS.org (2016)

29. Gómez-Adorno, H., Markov, I., Sidorov, G., Posadas-Durán, J.-P., Sanchez-Perez, M.A., Chanona-Hernandez, L.: Improving feature representation based on a neural network for author profiling in social media texts. Comput. Intell. Neurosci. **2016**, 13 p. (2016). doi:10.1155/2016/1638936. Article ID 1638936

30. Sidorov, G., Ibarra Romero, M., Markov, I., Guzman-Cabrera, R., Chanona-Hernández, L., Velásquez, F.: Detección automática de similitud entre programas del lenguaje de programación Karel basada en técnicas de procesamiento de lenguaje natural [Automatic detection of similarity of programs in Karel programming language based on natural language processing techniques (in Spanish, abstract in English)]. Computación y Sistemas, vol. 20, pp. 279–288 (2016)

31. Sidorov, G., Ibarra Romero, M., Markov, I., Guzman-Cabrera, R., Chanona-Hernández, L., Velásquez, F.: Measuring similarity between Karel programs using character and word n-grams. Programming and Computer Software 43 (2017, in press)

32. Ronald, F., Frank, Y.: Statistical Tables for Biological, Agricultural and Medical Research, 3rd edn. Oliver and Boyd, London (1948)

33. Kocher, M.: UniNE at CLEF 2015: author profiling. In: Working Notes Papers of the CLEF 2015 Evaluation Labs, CLEF 2015, vol. 1391. CEUR (2015)

34. Nowson, S., Perez, J., Brun, C., Mirkin, S., Roux, C.: XRCE personal language analytics engine for multilingual author profiling. In: Working Notes Papers of the CLEF 2015 Evaluation Labs, CLEF 2015, vol. 1391. CEUR (2015)

35. Gómez-Adorno, H., Markov, I., Sidorov, G., Posadas-Durán, J., Fócil-Arias, C.: Compilación de un lexicón de redes sociales para la identificación de perfiles de autor [Compiling a lexicon of social media for the author profiling task] (in Spanish, abstract in English), vol. 115, Research in Computing Science (2016)

36. Hall, M., Frank, E., Holmes, G., Pfahringer, B., Reutemann, P., Witten, I.H.: The WEKA data mining software: an update. SIGKDD Explor. **11**, 10–18 (2009)

37. Villena Román, J., González Cristóbal, J.C.: DAEDALUS at pan 2014: Guessing tweet author's gender and age. In: CLEF 2014 Labs and Workshops, Notebook Papers, CLEF 2014, vol. 1180, pp. 1157–1163 (2014)

38. De-Arteaga, M., Jimenez, S., Duenas, G., Mancera, S., Baquero, J.: Author profiling using corpus statistics, lexicons and stylistic features. In: CLEF 2013 Labs and Workshops, Notebook Papers. CLEF 2013, vol. 1179 (2013)

39. Buitinck, L., Louppe, G., Blondel, M., Pedregosa, F., Mueller, A., Grisel, O., Niculae, V., Prettenhofer, P., Gramfort, A., Grobler, J., Layton, R., VanderPlas, J.,

Joly, A., Holt, B., Varoquaux, G.: API design for machine learning software: experiences from the scikit-learn project. In: ECML PKDD Workshop: Languages for Data Mining and Machine Learning, pp. 108–122 (2013)

40. Nguyen, D., Gravel, R., Trieschnigg, D., Meder, T.: "How old do you think i am?"; A study of language and age in Twitter. In: Proceedings of the 7th International AAAI Conference on Weblogs and Social Media, AAAI Press (2013)

41. Maharjan, S., Solorio, T.: Using wide range of features for author profiling. In: Working Notes Papers of the CLEF 2015 Evaluation Labs, CEUR Workshop Proceedings, vol. 1391. CEUR (2015)

42. Sulea, O.M., Dichiu, D.: Automatic profiling of Twitter users based on their tweets. In: Working Notes Papers of the CLEF 2015 Evaluation Labs, CEUR Workshop Proceedings, vol. 1391. CEUR (2015)

43. Modaresi, P., Liebeck, M., Conrad, S.: Exploring the effects of cross-genre machine learning for author profiling in PAN 2016. In: Working Notes Papers of the CLEF 2016 Evaluation Labs, CEUR Workshop Proceedings, vol. 1609, pp. 970–977. CLEF and CEUR-WS.org (2016)

44. Schler, J., Koppel, M., Argamon, S., Pennebaker, J.: Effects of age and gender on blogging. In: AAAI Spring Symposium: Computational Approaches to Analyzing Weblogs, pp. 199–205. AAAI (2006)

45. Markov, I., Mamede, N., Baptista, J.: A rule-based meronymy extraction module for Portuguese. Computación Sistemas **19**, 661–683 (2015)

46. Markov, I., Mamede, N., Baptista, J.: Automatic identification of whole-part relations in Portuguese. In: Proceedings of the 3rd Symposium on Languages, Applications and Technologies, vol. 38, pp. 225–232. Schloss Dagstuhl - Leibniz-Zentrum fuer Informatik (2014)

47. Posadas-Durán, J., Markov, I., Gómez-Adorno, H., Sidorov, G., Batyrshin, I., Gelbukh, A., Pichardo-Lagunas, O.: Syntactic n-grams as features for the author profiling task. In: Working Notes Papers of the CLEF 2015 Evaluation Labs, CEUR Workshop Proceedings, vol. 1391. CEUR (2015)

48. Gómez-Adorno, H., Sidorov, G., Pinto, D., Markov, I.: A graph based authorship identification approach. In: Working Notes Papers of the CLEF 2015 Evaluation Labs, CEUR Workshop Proceedings, vol. 1391. CEUR (2015)

49. Sidorov, G., Gómez-Adorno, H., Markov, I., Pinto, D., Loya, N.: Computing text similarity using tree edit distance. In: Proceedings of the Annual Conference of the North American Fuzzy Information processing Society and 5th World Conference on Soft Computing, NAFIPS 2015, pp. 1–4 (2015)

50. Gómez-Adorno, H., Pinto, D., Montes, M., Sidorov, G., Alfaro, R.: Content and style features for automatic detection of users' intentions in tweets. In: Bazzan, A.L.C., Pichara, K. (eds.) IBERAMIA 2014. LNCS, vol. 8864, pp. 120–128. Springer, Cham (2014). doi:10.1007/978-3-319-12027-0_10

51. Sapkota, U., Bethard, S., Montes-y-Gómez, M., Solorio, T.: Not all character n-grams are created equal: a study in authorship attribution. In: Proceedings of the 2015 Annual Conference of the North American Chapter of the ACL: Human Language Technologies, NAACL-HLT 2015, Association for Computational Linguistics, pp. 93–102 (2015)

52. Markov, I., Gómez-Adorno, H., Sidorov, G., Gelbukh, A.: Adapting cross-genre author profiling to language and corpus. In: Working Notes Papers of the CLEF 2016 Evaluation Labs, CEUR Workshop Proceedings, vol. 1609, pp. 947–955. CLEF and CEUR-WS.org (2016)

Neural Network Modelling for Dissolved Oxygen Effects in Extensive Litopenaeus Vannamei Culture

José Juan Carbajal-Hernández[(⊠)] and Luis Pastor Sánchez-Fernández

Centro de Investigación en Computación – Instituto Politécnico Nacional,
Av. Juan de Dios Bátiz s/n, Nueva Industrial Vallejo, Gustavo A. Madero,
07738 Mexico, Mexico
{jcarbajalh, lsanchez}@cic.ipn.mx

Abstract. Shrimp aquaculture is an important activity currently practiced worldwide. Dissolved oxygen can be lethal in organisms when low concentrations are present in an extensive cultured pond. According to this, a new computational model for dissolved oxygen assessment using artificial neural networks is proposed. Measurements from environmental parameters related with dissolved oxygen were used, classifying those negative situations that can affect the environmental stability of the ecosystem. As a result, an indicator concerning the good or bad water quality condition is obtained. Finally, comparisons against models reported in literature show the good performance of the proposed model.

Keywords: Neural networks · Shrimp · Dissolved oxygen · Aquaculture

1 Introduction

Shrimp culture is an important activity that is mainly practiced in coastal zones where extensive areas are used for farming different type of species. The *Litopenaeus vannamei* is highly cultured due to their benefits in feeding and breeding facilities. Extensive ponds are the most common system used for culturing this specie; however, these systems have several problems whenever environmental parameters usually present concentrations out of the recommended limits [1, 2]. Water management is an important factor in shrimp aquaculture where the ecosystem must be under control in order to have good growing and reproduction rates. In extensive systems, controlling water quality parameters is a hard task; for this reason, monitoring systems are needed to avoid negative situations that can be harmful for the organism [3–5]. In this sense, several organizations have gathered efforts to create standards for water management in order to measure or evaluate environmental parameters such as the U.S. National Sanitation Foundation [6], the Canadian Council of Environmental Ministers [7], the Spanish Catalan Water Agency [8], the Mexican Ministry of Environment and Natural Resources [9] and the National Ecology Institute of México [10]. They have defined criteria about some water considerations in order to have a controlled ecosystem.

© Springer International Publishing AG 2017
O. Pichardo-Lagunas and S. Miranda-Jiménez (Eds.): MICAI 2016, Part II, LNAI 10062, pp. 132–140, 2017.
DOI: 10.1007/978-3-319-62428-0_10

In literature, different works have been developed to study the water quality behavior in various scenarios such as different species analysis, water bodies, using bio-indicators, for waste or drinking water [11–17]. Alternative works based on Fuzzy Logic [18], Analytical Hierarchy Processes [19, 20], Artificial Neural Networks [21] and Support Vector Machine [22] have been developed in order to provide different solutions on water management. Those models have been developed for other types of problems, making them incompatible for assessing dissolved oxygen interactions in shrimp culture; nevertheless, they represent a good antecedent, providing relevant information in water modelling.

The main contribution of this work is the development of a new computational model for assessing the dissolved oxygen impact in the *Litopenaeus vannamei* extensive ponds, using artificial intelligence technics such as Artificial Neural Networks (ANNs). Analyzing the main dissolved oxygen requirements of the ecosystem and those parameters that affects its stability, the neural model will provide an [0–1] ranged indicator that reflects the water quality condition from an uncontrolled habitat.

2 Dissolved Oxygen Requirements

In shrimp culture, a good water quality is important for healthy farming. Several parameters are involved in an aquatic ecosystem; furthermore, some of them take more importance because they have a bigger impact on the habitat than others such as dissolved oxygen. Fluctuation of dissolved oxygen are events that can be normally presented in aquaculture systems. Dissolved oxygen is considered the most critical quality parameter for shrimps, where in low concentrations they are more susceptible to disease; therefore, anoxia and hypoxia events must be avoided [3, 4, 23]. On the other hand, the demand of dissolved oxygen increases when temperatures are high due to control solubility of gases and chemical reactions [19, 23–25]. Likewise, high salinity concentrations reduce dissolved oxygen in water, whenever salt molecules displace oxygen [26]. Table 1 shows the permissible limits defined for the water quality parameters.

Table 1. Permissible limits defined for water quality parameters.

Parameters	Units	Hypoxia	Low	Normal	High
Temp	°C	——	0–23	23–30	30–∞
Sal	mg/L	——	0–15	15–25	25–∞
DO	mg/L	0–2	2–6	6–∞	——

Data Collection

Water quality parameters were measured in order to create a database that can be used for testing our model. In this case, the proposed parameters (Table 1) were monitored using sensor devices in a testing pond of the Rancho Chapo farm, located in Sonora, Mexico. The monitoring period was of 15 min. The data set contains three months of measurements; it means, a register of 8736 values per parameter (June, July and

August, 2007). However, sensor failures generated spurious registers and they were
erased from the testing database, having 5952 registers in this work. Individual
behaviors can be observed in Fig. 1, where the permissible limits are overpassed by all
the parameters, generating poor water quality conditions. It is important to remark that
dissolved oxygen reported hypoxia concentrations, which is known to be an extremely
dangerous problem in any kind of fishing culture system.

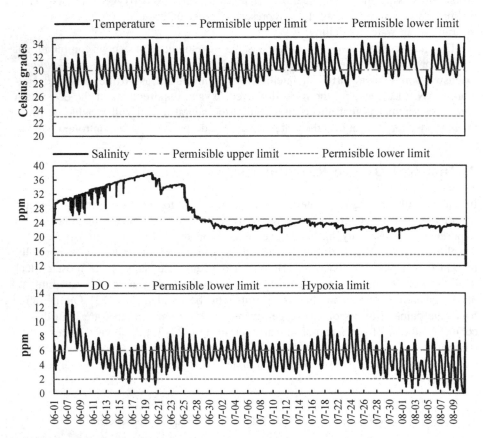

Fig. 1. Water quality parameters during one farming period in 2007 year (courtesy of the
CIBNOR, Sonora, Mexico).

3   Artificial Neural Network Modelling

In this work, Artificial Neural Networks (ANNs) are used for assessing dissolved
oxygen level risk in extensive shrimp ponds, due to them having been proved a very
effective learning model with high rates of effectiveness. Thus, the construction of an
ANN is not an easy task; for this reason, several architectures and a preprocessing
phase have been performed, establishing a better selection of the ANN parameters.

Salinity and temperature parameters directly affect dissolved oxygen concentrations because they control solubility in water. According to this, an ANN based model has been proposed, due to its capacity for capturing intrinsic relations between those defined environmental parameters.

Training Database

According to dissolved oxygen effects in the *Litopenaeus vannamei* ecosystem, a set of real and simulated measurements were used for creating water quality patterns. Simulated patterns guarantee having a complete set of different negative situations into the pond, whereas real measured patterns only provide a small part of them. A database of 9000 patterns was created to be used in the learning phase of the ANN, having the following order: 500 patterns for *excellent* conditions, 3000 for *regular* conditions and 5500 for *poor* water quality. As a target, a pattern with a numerical score provides the output response according to water quality considerations: *excellent* (1), *regular* (0.5) and *poor* (0). The data set was randomly divided into training and testing subsets. Three-fourths of the data was used for training, and one-fourth was used for testing and validating the learning performance.

Data Processing

A neural network training can be made more efficient if certain preprocessing steps are made in the data collected. They were applied to each input parameter (temperature, dissolved oxygen and salinity) and for each database (training and testing).

Water quality parameters have different range values. This information is not convenient to be used in its present form, because data with bigger values have more impact in the final result [27, 28]. First, a standardization transforms data to achieve zero mean, with unity standard deviation as follows:

$$y^k = \frac{y_i - \bar{y}}{\sigma} \tag{1}$$

Then, standardized parameters were scaled to a [0, 1] range according to:

$$y^\omega = \frac{y_i^k - \min(y^k)}{\max(y^k) - \min(y^k)} \tag{2}$$

where y^ω is the normalized pattern.

Structure of the Artificial Neural Network

The neural model for assessing dissolved oxygen interactions was built using a feed-forward artificial neural network (backpropagation). In this case, the defined training database was used as input in the learning process of the ANN. They were processed as the model input, using a hidden layer and computing three water quality conditions in the net output. In ANN building, there are no rules for defining the number of hidden layers, neither neurons by layer. The ANN topology was determined proving different configurations (number of hidden layers and neurons); nevertheless, an ANN architecture of 3 layers and [1, 3, 22] neurons, presented the best evaluation results such as time processing and classifying response (Fig. 2).

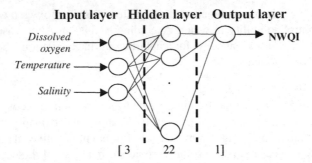

Fig. 2. ANN architecture used for assessing water quality in the *Litopenaeus vannamei* aquaculture.

Determining the type of transfer functions used in the ANN building process is important, due to they define the output characteristics of the entire neural model. In this case, a sigmoid transfer function was used in the first and second layer. It can be defined as the following function:

$$f(n) = \frac{1}{1+e^{-n}} \tag{3}$$

The output layer was built using a linear-sigmoid transfer functions as follows:

$$f(n) = max\{min\{1, n\}, 0\} \tag{4}$$

In this case, there was not a significant difference of an ANN with most number of neurons or hidden layers. The input layer processed the normalized and standardized patterns of parameter measurements. The output layer classified the dissolved oxygen effects in the pond (*excellent, regular* or *poor*). Tested architectures with lower number of neurons did not classify correctly. During the training process, 421 iterations were required for having a good mean square error (MSE) convergence with a 0.001% error. The MSE was used as the target error goal. The smaller values of MSE ensure the better performance and can be expressed as follows:

$$MSE = \frac{1}{N} \sum_{i=1}^{N} \left(x_{measured} - x_{computed}\right)^2 \tag{5}$$

where N is the number of observations.

4   Results and Discussions

An experimental phase was performed in order to show the ANN operation. Real measurements stored in the testing database were used as input of the neural model (see Sect. 2), computing the water quality assessment as output. In this case, June and July months were measured correctly; furthermore, the August month was partially measured because of a sensor failure.

Assessments using the proposed Neural Water Quality Index (NWQI) were compared with the Canadian Council Minister of Environment Index (CCME) [7], which allows evaluating any kind of water body if the corresponding parameter limits are known (Fig. 3). The rest of the models were not available to be used in this comparative because they were made for other types of applications, involving different water quality parameters or other types of species. According to this, the assessed CCME index scored in June and July months showed in general, *good* and *excellent* water quality evaluations (above 0.8 score). In August, CMME index presented the lowest evaluations; thus, it never decreases the 0.47 score. Analyses using the NWQI index showed evaluations below 0.6 value with a minimum of 0.067 in the farming period.

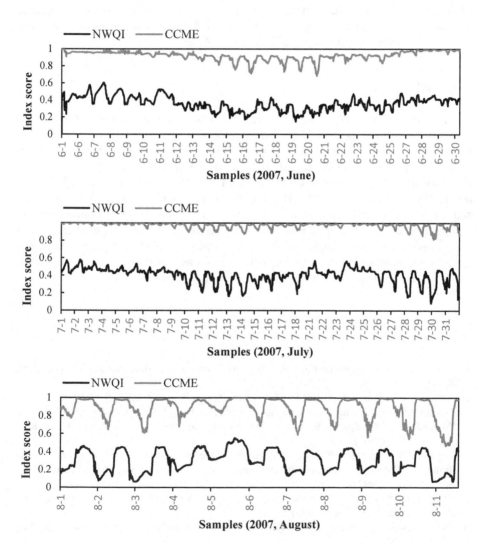

Fig. 3. Comparison between assessments using the CCME and the NWQI indexes.

This means, a *regular* to *poor* water quality assessed (Fig. 3). This behavior can be explained due to dissolved oxygen concentrations and temperature values usually presenting oscillatory values, were high or very low values measured during the experimental phase.

In June and July, dissolved oxygen presented good concentrations, but temperature and salinity showed the highest levels. In August, salinity presented concentrations in the optimal range; furthermore, dissolved oxygen showed the lowest concentrations, which means a poor water quality. Behavior differences between results is caused because the CCME index is based on calculating the frequency of the parameter values that are outside the optimal range and their deviation average, compensating those low or high concentrations with optimal values of other evaluated parameters. In this case, the ANN was trained with patterns that were chosen according to an undesirable situation (*excellent*, *good* or *poor*), where a negative or good water quality condition was carefully selected and classified in the training set.

5   Conclusions

In this work, we presented a neural model for assessing water quality according to dissolved oxygen effects in the *Litopenaeus vannamei* extensive culture. Temperature and salinity parameters are known to interact with the dissolved oxygen solubility in water. The proposed neural model is able to detect negative dissolved oxygen behaviors when the combination of the set of parameters represent an undesirable situation for a good water quality. The ANN's theory provides a good alternative to be used in environmental assessment, whenever they generate a non-linear relation between parameters and where a mathematical formulation can be a hard task. As a future direction, a more complete neural model will be studied, using a more detailed water quality analysis, where more negative situations can be defined, or a different parameter can be involved in the dissolved oxygen dynamic.

References

1. Boyd, C.: Water composition and shrimp pond management. Glob. Aquac. Advocate **3**(5), 40–41 (2000)
2. Arredondo, J., Ponce, J.: Calidad Del Agua en Acuacultura, Ed. AGT S.A (1998)
3. Chien, Y.: Water quality requirements and management for marine shrimp culture. In: Proceedings of the Special Session on Shrimp Farming, pp. 144–156. World Aquaculture Society, USA (1992)
4. Boyd, C.: Shrimp pond effluents: observations of the nature of the problem on commercial farms. In: Proceedings of the Special Session on Shrimp Farming. World Aquaculture Society, USA (1992)
5. Clifford, H.: Semi-intensive sensation: a case study in marine shrimp pond management. World Aquac. **25**(3), 6–12 (1994)
6. [NSF] National Sanitation Foundation International. http://www.nfsc.org. Accessed Aug 2016

7. [CCME] Canadian Council of Ministers of the Environment (Canada). An assessment of the application and testing of the Water Quality Index of the Canadian Council of Ministers of the Environment for selected water bodies in Atlantic Canada. National indicators and reporting office (2004). http://www.ccme.ca. Accessed Aug 2016

8. [ACA] Agencia Catalana del Agua (Catalonia, Spain) (2016). http://aca-web.gencat.cat/aca/appmanager/aca/aca/. Accessed Aug 2016

9. [SEMARNAT] Mexican Ministry of Environment and Natural Resources (Secretaría de Medio Ambiente y Recursos Naturales, in Spanish). http://www.semarnat.gob.mx. Accessed Aug 2016

10. [INE] Instituto Nacional de Ecología. La calidad del agua en los ecosistemas costeros de México (2000)

11. Ocampo, W., Ferré, N., Domingo, J., Schuhmacher, M.: Assessing water quality in rivers with fuzzy inference systems: a case of study. Environ. Int. **32**, 733–742 (2006). Elsevier

12. Lermontov, A., Yokoyama, L., Lermontov, M., Soares, M.: River quality analysis using fuzzy water quality index: Ribeira do Iguape river watershed, Brazil. Ecol. Indic. **9**(6), 1188–1197 (2009). Elsevier

13. Gharibi, H., Sowlat, M., Mahvi, A., Mahmoudzadeh, H., Arabalibeik, H., Keshavarz, M., Karimzadeh, N., Hassani, G.: Development of a dairy cattle drinking water quality index (DCWQI) based on fuzzy inference systems. Ecol. Indic. **20**, 228–237 (2012). Elsevier

14. Gutiérrez, J., Riss, W., Ospina, R.: Bioindicación de la calidad del agua en la Sabana de Bogota – Colombia, mediante la utilización de la lógica difusa neuroadaptativa como herramienta. Caldasia **28**(1), 45–46 (2006). Limnología

15. Romero, C., Shan, J.: Development of an artificial neural network-based software for prediction of power plant canal water discharge temperature. Expert Syst. Appl. **29**, 831–838 (2005). Elsevier

16. Ramesh, S., Sukumaran, N., Murugesan, A., Rajan, M.: An innovative approach of drinking water quality index—a case study from Southern Tamil Nadu, India. Ecol. Indic. **10**(4), 857–868 (2010). Elsevier

17. Simões, F., Moreira, A., Bisinoti, M., Nobre, S., Santos, M.: Water quality index as a simple indicator of aquaculture effects on aquatic bodies. Ecol. indic. **8**, 476–484 (2008). Elsevier

18. Gutiérrez, J.: Lógica difusa como herramienta para la bioindicación de la calidad del agua con macroinvertebrados acuáticos en la Sabana de Bogotá – Colombia. Caldasia **26**(1), 161–172 (2004)

19. Carbajal, J., Sánchez, L., Carrasco, A., Martínez, J.: Immediate water quality assessment in shrimp culture using fuzzy inference systems. Expert Syst. Appl. **40**, 5148–5159 (2012). Elsevier

20. Carbajal, J., Sánchez, L., Villa, L., Carrasco, A., Martínez, F.: Water quality assessment in shrimp culture using an analytical hierarchical process. Ecol. Indic. **29**, 148–158 (2013). Elsevier

21. Shen, X., Chen, M., YU, J.: Water environment monitoring system based on neural networks for shrimp cultivation. In: International Conference on Artificial Intelligence and Computational Intelligence, vol. 3, pp. 427–431 (2009)

22. Liu, S., Xu, L., Li, D., Zeng, L.: Online prediction for dissolved oxygen of water quality based on support vector machine with time series similar data. Trans. Chin. Soc. Agric. Eng. **30**(3), 155–162 (2014)

23. Martínez, L.: Cultivo de Camarones Pendidos, Principios y Prácticas, Ed. AGT Editor S.A (1994)

24. Hirono, Y.: Current practices of water quality management in shrimp farming and their limitations. In: Proceedings of the Special Session on Shrimp Farming. World Aquaculture Society, USA (1992)

25. Boyd, C.: Water quality standards: pH. Glob. Aquac. Advocate **4**(1), 42–44 (2001)
26. Páez, F.: Camaronicultura y Medio Ambiente. Instituto de Ciencias del mar y Limnología. UNAM, pp. 271–298, México (2001)
27. Chow, M.: Methodologies of Using Neural Network and Fuzzy Logic Technologies for Motor Incipient Fault Detection. World Scientific, Singapore (1997)
28. Principe, J., Luliano, N., Lefebvre, W.: Neural and Adaptative Systems: Fundamentals Through Simulations. Wiley, Hoboken (2000)

Neural-Network Based Algorithm for Algae Detection in Automatic Inspection of Underwater Pipelines

Edgar Medina[(⊠)], Mariane Rembold Petraglia,
and José Gabriel Rodriguez Carneiro Gomes

Department of Electronics Engineering,
Federal University of Rio de Janeiro, Rio de Janeiro, Brazil
{emedina,mariane,gabriel}@pads.ufrj.br

Abstract. Automatic inspection of underwater pipelines has been a growing challenge for the detection and classification of events, most often performed by Remotely Operated Vehicles (ROVs) and Autonomous Underwater Vehicles (AUVs). This article describes an algorithm for algae detection in underwater pipelines. The algorithm comprises a neural network and a wavelet-based feature extractor. Statistical parameters of the wavelet coefficients that take into account an appropriate algae texture description, as well as the neural network architecture that results in the optimal classifier performance, are selected. A post-processing algorithm, based on clustering of neighboring detection positions, was implemented to enhance the system response. The success rate of the resulting neural network classifier is 93.60%. When compared to support-vector machines (SVMs), the proposed classifier presents similar performance with the advantage of running significantly faster.

Keywords: Feature extraction · Wavelet transform · Algae detection · SVM · Neural networks

1 Introduction

Underwater inspection of pipelines and equipment has become increasingly challenging with the growth of the exploitation of submarine oil and gas fields. Most often such inspections are carried out by using Remote Operated Vehicles (ROVs), which carry sensors and cameras and are operated either through cable connections from the vehicle to the operators or through radio control [1]. In contrast to ROVs, Autonomous Underwater Vehicles (AUVs) are able to automatically detect and track automatically underwater pipelines. Visual inspection by humans is a tedious task under typical operating conditions, which include very long inspections, low quality images, and search for multiple targets, among others [2]. This work has been developed with the purpose of automatically detecting and classifying different types of events on pipelines, such as inner coating exposure and presence of algae, for maintenance purposes.

Subsea pipelines often have sand or algae on their surfaces, which should be signaled by the automatic inspection system. In particular, the algae present diverse

O. Pichardo-Lagunas and S. Miranda-Jiménez (Eds.): MICAI 2016, Part II, LNAI 10062, pp. 141–148, 2017.
DOI: 10.1007/978-3-319-62428-0_11

shapes, colors and textures [3], which vary with their constant movements due to water flow caused by sea current and turbulence generated by the ROV. Related algorithms for underwater algae detection include texture description, feature extraction and machine learning techniques. Ales et al. [4] presented a mathematical method for texture representation through wavelet and statistical parameters. Muwei et al. [5] combined perceptual features and Gabor wavelet features for texture classification. Moreover, Bin and Fen [6] proposed rotation-invariant features based on wavelet and PCA. Also Ishrat et al. [7] presented a comparison between wavelet feature extractor modeled by generalized Gaussian density and Curvelet texture features. Other works related to classification are [8, 9], which employ support-vector machine (SVM) and artificial neural networks (ANN), while a method related to underwater target was proposed by Donghui et al. [10].

The remainder of this paper is organized as follows. Section 2 gives an overview of the pre-processing and feature extraction stages. In Sect. 3, the classification stage is described, while in Sect. 4 the experimental results are presented. In Sect. 5, the main conclusions and a brief discussion of future work are given.

2 Image Pre-processing and Feature Extraction

2.1 Image Pre-processing

In the system employed in this work, each video frame had a size of 1280×720 pixels. To reduce the computational cost, image resizing was necessary, resulting in images of 317×638 pixels. Besides, segmentation techniques were applied to the image in order to reduce the action field of the classification system just to the pipeline surface. In this way, the segmentation algorithm contributes with the reduction of the computational cost, which will be smaller than that of a classifier applied along the complete image. It will also reduce the likelihood of false positives. The proposed pipeline segmentation algorithm is composed by a Gaussian filter (to remove noise), Canny edge detector and Hough transform, followed by an analysis algorithm for the selection of the lines corresponding to the pipeline borders based on the geometry, and temporal location of the pipeline [11–13]. Before obtaining the features from the image, it is convenient to select a window on the surface of the pipeline. Window size was tuned to 61×61. Each pixel of the selected window is then converted to gray scale (in order to eliminate the color dependence), the mean grayscale value over the window is subtracted from each pixel (to obtain zero-mean image), and the wavelet decomposition is applied. Since underwater algae have several color combinations, the problem becomes more complicated when it is analyzed using color characteristics.

Considering the high computational requirements of the image processing system and the fact that neighboring windows are similar, employing windows shifted by 1-pixel step in horizontal or vertical direction would not be appropriate. To find the range of appropriate step-size values for sliding the window along the image, we carried out a similarity analysis based on first and second order statistics of the pixels, that is, mean, standard deviation and Haralick matrix features [14–16]. The step-size range resulting from this analysis was between 8 and 16 pixels. In this work we adopted windows shifted by 8 pixels along both horizontal and vertical directions.

2.2   Feature Extraction

Each gray-scale zero-mean window is decomposed by Daubechies 2 (db2) Wavelet [17]. Denoting the corresponding analysis filters as H_1 and H_2 such that filters resulting from their combinations decompose the image as shown in Eqs. (1) and (2), where $H_k(u, v)$ are formed by H_1 and H_2 combined separately along the horizontal and vertical directions, represented by H_x and H_y (x and y could be 1 or 2 depending on the sub-band) to obtain the sub-bands S_{k+1} from 1 to 3 where k = 0, 1, 2. Additionally $S_k = 0$ is the resized grayscale input window.

$$H_k(u, v) = H_x(2u, 2v) * H_y(u, v) \qquad (1)$$

$$S_{k+1}(u, v) = H_k(u, v) * S_0(u, v); k = 0, \ldots, 2 \qquad (2)$$

Finally the features are extracted from first and second order statistical parameters, such as mean and standard deviation, from each subband image [14, 15]. The pre-processing and feature extraction algorithms are presented in Algorithm 1.

Algorithm 1.

Input: Window ; H_i , i=1,2

Output: y_i , i= 1, ... ,23

    Convert Window to grayscale

    Subtract the mean from Window

    FilterSequence = [1,1 ; 1,2 ; 2,1 ; 2,2]

    For n from 1 to 4

        S_n = Filter Window with $H_{FilterSequence(n)}$

    For n from 5 to 8

        S_n = Filter S_1 with $H_{FilterSequence(n)}$

    For n from 9 to 12

        S_n = Filter S_5 with $H_{FilterSequence(n)}$

    y_1 = StandardDeviation(S_1)

    For n from 1 to 11

        y_{2n} = Mean(S_n)

        y_{2n+1} = StandardDeviation(S_n)

---

3   Classification Based on Neural Network

3.1   Dataset

The dataset consists of manually selected annotated windows, obtained from 153 frames extracted from videos of underwater pipeline inspection tasks. The complete database contains more than 20 h of video in AVI format, and the video frame rate is 30 frames/s. Video segments with different types of plants and marine life were sought, and the most representative events were extracted from short video passages with a total length equal to 394 s. The positive and negative samples are presented in Figs. 1 and 2 respectively. The pipelines sometimes have textures similar to algae, and the algae textures are influenced by the brightness and movement in some scenarios. As the feature extractor is not rotation-invariant, seven extra samples of each original images were included: three images rotated by 90° increments and the corresponding mirrored images (also one mirrored image for 0° rotation). The database contains 19,921 samples, of which 44.58% are positive and 55.42% are negative.

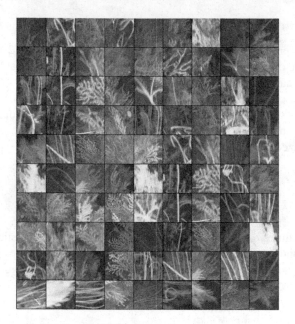

Fig. 1. Positive samples from algae dataset.

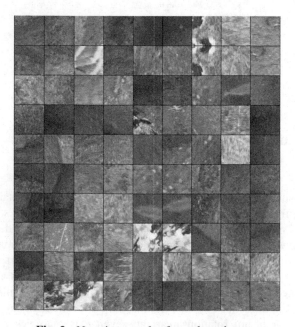

Fig. 2. Negative samples from algae dataset.

3.2   Neural-Network-Based Classifier

Before applying the feature vectors to the neural network input, the data is normalized as shown in Eq. (3), where m and σ are the mean and standard deviation vectors of the database. The neural network consists of a multilayer perceptron with 23 neurons in the input layer, 12 in the hidden layer and 1 output. Every neuron uses hyperbolic tangent as activation function as described in Eq. (4).

$$x_{in}(n) = (x(n) - m)/\sigma \tag{3}$$

$$o(n) = tanh\left(W_2\,x\,tanh\left(W_1\,x_{in}(n) + b_1\right) + b_2\right) \tag{4}$$

To avoid a large false positive rate, a large threshold was chosen. If the output $o(n)$ is above 0.9, then the sample is considered positive. The design procedure used 80% of the dataset for training and 20% for testing. The learning rate was set to 0.85×10^{-5}, the learning rate decay factor was set to 1 (constant learning rate), the mean squared error relative variation required for stopping was set to 10^{-10}, the number of full-batch training epochs was set to 8000, and the momentum constant was set to 0.6. To avoid outlier effects, data samples was discarded if they corresponded to neural network outputs with absolute error above 2. Outlier removal led to 1% improvement in neural network performance. The final performance achieved by the neural network was 93.60%.

3.3   False Positive Reduction Based on Clustering

To improve the system performance with respect to its false-positive rate, an algorithm for eliminating false positives is proposed in this section. In this algorithm, eight possible shifts of a 3 × 3 evaluation window are considered at any particular time step. Each one of the eight shifts occurs along each of the possible horizontal, vertical or diagonal directions: up, down, left, right, down-left, down-right, up-left or up-right. The size of each shift is eight pixels, i.e. the evaluation window is shifted by eight pixels along each direction. The algorithm operation is divided into two passes. In the first pass, the algorithm creates labels. To do that, it sets the pixel value to an arbitrary integer if the classification around it leads to a positive (algae) result. If the arbitrary integers are assigned to pixels located within the same above-defined eight-pixel neighborhood, then all pixels are set to the same integer value. In the second pass, the minimum and maximum coordinates within every cluster having the same integer classification are used to draw a rectangle around the cluster. If the overlap between clusters is below 20%, the algorithm keeps the clusters separate. Otherwise, the clusters are merged into a single one. Implementation details are presented in Algorithm 2. If a cluster has less than eight positive results, then that cluster is eliminated.

Algorithm 2.

Input: Detection, I (Image), Δ (step)

Output:

    Search labels into pixels: I(x-Δ, y) ; I(x-Δ, y-Δ) ;   I(x, y-Δ) ;   I(x+Δ, y-Δ)

    Case labels number found

        0: Current pixel I(x, y) is assigned a new label

        1: Current pixel I(x, y) is assigned the one label found

        2, 3, 4:   Current pixel I(x, y) is assigned one of the labels found

            Assign equality between the labels

    Replace every assigned equality label.

    Ignore groups with a pixels number lesser than 8.

    Calculate the maximum and minimum pixels I(x, y) per label group.

    Establish a squared region per group.

    Calculate regions intersection.

    Remain with region less of 20%- intersection through Non-maximum suppression.

---

4   Results and Comparison

Results for algae detection in different scenes are shown in Fig. 3. These results were obtained using specific features and neural networks as described in Algorithm 1. Figure 4. shows the system response obtained according to the post-processing method described in the Algorithm 2. As indicated in Sect. 3.3, an eight-pixel shift exists between each pair of evaluation windows.

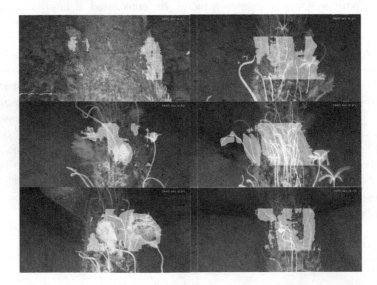

Fig. 3. Algae detection system using one-pixel step sliding window.

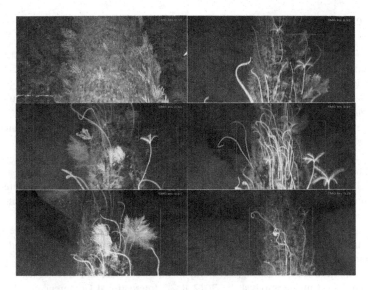

Fig. 4. Algae detection system with post-processing stage using eight-pixel step sliding window.

All images shown in this section were obtained from the test database. The proposed algorithm was applied to all frames of the available videos, corresponding to a great variety of conditions. The subjective evaluation of the classifier performance was carried out based on the size and quantity of plants, such that if they covered a large surface of the pipeline it should indicate the presence of algae, while if a small surface was covered by plants, such as in the middle of the pipeline of the first image of Fig. 4, it should not indicate as positive. For comparison purposes an SVM (support-vector machine) [18, 19] was trained on the same database from which the neural networks were obtained. The SVM training was repeated several times with different parameters. The best SVM result was 94.38% success rate, after using a Sequential Minimal Optimization (SMO) solver and Gaussian kernel. The architecture is based on 4562 support vectors. The best neural network and the best SVM were executed for video processing in MATLAB, achieving 1.01 s/frame and 3.73 s/frame respectively. This result suggests that the neural network works well in conditions handled by the SVM, while running considerably faster than the SVM. The neural network system was implemented partially in C++ using a MEX gateway, and the code execution timing improved to 0.45 s/frame. The CPU used in this test is a 7th-generation i5 processor with 3.5 GHz clock frequency.

5   Conclusions

A neural network trained with properly computed wavelet-based features was shown to efficiently solve algae detection problems in an automatic video processing context. The neural network performance is comparable to the performance achieved by an SVM (around 94%), while video processing based on the neural network is considerably faster.

References

1. Antich, J., Ortiz, A.: Underwater cable tracking by visual feedback. In: Perales, F.J., Campilho, A.J.C., Blanca, N.P., Sanfeliu, A. (eds.) IbPRIA 2003. LNCS, vol. 2652, pp. 53–61. Springer, Heidelberg (2003). doi:10.1007/978-3-540-44871-6_7
2. Jacobi, M., Karimanzira, D.: Underwater pipeline and cable inspection using autonomous underwater vehicles. MTS/IEEE, Germany (2013)
3. Mariângela, M., et al.: Update of the Brazilian floristic list of algae and cyanobacteria. Rodriguésia 66(4), 1047–1062 (2015). Rio de Janeiro, Brazil
4. Ales, P., Andrea, G., Karel, V.: Wavelet transform in image recognition. In: 47th International Symposium ELMAR, Czech Republic (2005)
5. Muwei, J., Lei, L., Feng, G.: Texture image classification using perceptual texture features and Gabor wavelet features. In: Asia-Pacific Conference on Information Processing APCIP 2009, China (2009)
6. Bin, L., Fen, P.: Rotation-invariant texture features extraction using dual-tree complex wavelet transform. In: International Conference on Information, Networking and Automation, China (2010)
7. Ishrat, J., Guojun, L., Dengsheng, Z.: Comparison of curvelet and wavelet texture features for content based image retrieval. In: 2012 IEEE International Conference on Multimedia and Expo, Australia (2012)
8. Buddhiraju, K.M., Rizvi, I.A.: Comparison of CBF, ANN and SVM classifiers for object based classification of high resolution satellite images. In: 2010 IEEE International Geoscience and Remote Sensing Symposium (IGARSS) (2010)
9. Mounir, E., Mohammed, R.: Improving pedestrian detection using support vector regression. In: 13th International Conference Computer Graphics, Imaging and Visualization (2016)
10. Donghui, L., Mahmood, A., Marc, R.: Comparison of different classification algorithms for underwater target discrimination. IEEE Trans. Neural Netw. 15, 189–194 (2004)
11. Asif, M., Rizal, M.: An active contour and kalman filter for underwater target tracking and navigation. In: Proceedings of International Conference on Man-Machine System (2006)
12. Ortiz, A., Antich, J., Oliver, G.: A particle filter-based approach for tracking narrow telecommunications cables. Mach. Vis. Appl. 22, 283–302 (2011)
13. Ortiz, A., Simó, M., Oliver, G.: A vision system for an underwater cable tracker. Mach. Vis. Appl. 13, 129–140 (2002)
14. Namita, A., Agrawal, R.K.: First and second order statistics features for classification of magnetic resonance brain images. J. Signal Inf. Process. 3, 146–153 (2012)
15. Majid, M., Xianghua, X., Jasjit, S.: Handbook of Texture Analysis. Imperial College Press, London (2009)
16. Haralick, R.M., Shanmugan, K., Dinstein, I.: Textural features for image classification. IEEE Trans. Syst.: Man Cybern. SMC 3, 610–621 (1973). doi:10.1109/TSMC.1973.4309314
17. Nixon, M., Aquado, A.S.: Feature Extraction & Image Processing for Computer Vision, 3rd edn. Academic Press, Cambridge (2012)
18. Madhogaria, S., Schikora, M., Koch, W., Cremers, D.: Pixel-based classification method for detecting unhealthy regions in leaf images. In: 6th IEEE ISIF Workshop on Sensor Data Fusion: Trends, Solutions, Applications (SDF), Germany (2011)
19. Heisele, B., Ho, P., Poggio, T.: Face recognition with support vector machines: global versus component-based approach. In: 8th IEEE International Conference on Computer Vision (ICCV), Canada (2001)

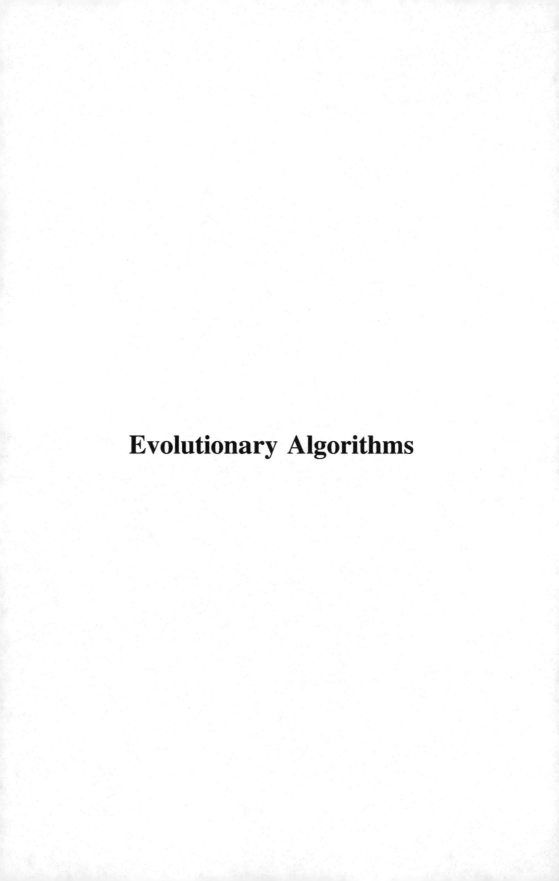

Evolutionary Algorithms

Study on the Development of Complex Network for Evolutionary and Swarm Based Algorithms

Roman Senkerik[1]([⊠]), Ivan Zelinka[2], Michal Pluhacek[1],
and Adam Viktorin[1]

[1] Faculty of Applied Informatics, Tomas Bata University in Zlin,
Nam T.G. Masaryka 5555, 760 01 Zlin, Czech Republic
{senkerik,pluhacek,aviktorin}@fai.utb.cz
[2] Faculty of Electrical Engineering and Computer Science,
Technical University of Ostrava, 17. listopadu 15,
708 33 Ostrava-Poruba, Czech Republic
ivan.zelinka@vsb.cz

Abstract. This contribution deals with the hybridization of complex network frameworks and metaheuristic algorithms. The population is visualized as an evolving complex network that exhibits non-trivial features. It briefly investigates the time and structure development of a complex network within a run of selected metaheuristic algorithms – i.e. PSO and Differential Evolution (DE). Two different approaches for the construction of complex networks are presented herein. It also briefly discusses the possible utilization of complex network attributes. These attributes include an adjacency graph that depicts interconnectivity, while centralities provide an overview of convergence and stagnation, and clustering encapsulates the diversity of the population, whereas other attributes show the efficiency of the network. The experiments were performed for one selected DE/PSO strategy and one simple test function.

Keywords: Complex networks · Graphs · Analysis · Differential Evolution · PSO

1 Introduction

Currently, the utilization of complex networks as a visualization tool for the analysis of population dynamics for evolutionary and swarm-based algorithms is becoming an interesting open research task. The population is visualized as an evolving complex network that exhibits non-trivial features – e.g. degree distribution, clustering, and centralities and in between. These features offer a clear description of the population under evaluation and can be utilized for adaptive population as well as parameter control during the metaheuristic run. The initial studies [1–3] describing the possibilities of transforming population dynamics into complex networks, were followed by the successful adaptation and control of the metaheuristic algorithm during the run through the given complex networks' frameworks [4–6].

O. Pichardo-Lagunas and S. Miranda-Jiménez (Eds.): MICAI 2016, Part II, LNAI 10062, pp. 151–161, 2017.
DOI: 10.1007/978-3-319-62428-0_12

This research represents the hybridization of complex network frameworks using the Differential Evolution (DE) [7] and Particle Swarm Optimization (PSO) algorithms [8].

Currently, both aforementioned algorithms are known as powerful metaheuristic tools for many difficult and complex optimization problems. A number of modern DE [9, 10] and PSO [11, 12] variants have also recently been developed.

The organization of this paper is as follows: Firstly, the motivation and the concept of DE and PSO algorithms with a complex network are briefly described; followed by the experiment's design. This is followed by graphical visualizations and the conclusions afterwards.

2 Motivation

This research is an extension and continuation of the previous successful initial experiment with the transfer of the population dynamics of the several DE variants being applied - e.g. to the flowshop scheduling problem [2] and the permutative flowshop scheduling problem [3]. This paper also extends the preliminary research [13] focused on capturing the inner dynamics of swarm algorithms in sufficient detail and in a network of appropriate size for further processing. The motivation for the research presented herein can be summarized as follows:

- To show the different approaches in building complex networks in order to capture the dynamics of evolutionary or swarm based algorithms.
- To investigate the time development of the influence of either individual selections inside a DE or communication inside a swarm transferred into the complex network.
- To briefly discuss the possible utilisation of complex network attributes – e.g. adjacency graphs, centralities, clustering, etc for adaptive population and parameter control during the metaheuristic run.

3 Complex Networks

A complex network is a graph which has unique properties - usually in the real-world graph domain. A complex network contains features which are unique to the assigned problem. These features are important markers for population used in Evolutionary/ Swarm based algorithms [2]. The following features are important for a quick analysis of the network thus created.

3.1 Degree Centrality

Degree Centrality is defined as the number of edges connected to a specific node. Degree Centrality is an important distribution hub in the network since it connects - and thereby, distributes most of the information flowing through the network. Together with the hybridization of metaheuristic and complex network analysis, this is one of the most important features under consideration. Using Degree Centrality, one can actually analyze if stagnation or premature convergence is occurring within the population. By analyzing the graphs, it can be seen that the multiple nodes are increasing (distinguished by their size), thereby emphasizing their prominence in the population - and, their effect in generating better individuals.

3.2 Clustering Coefficient

The average Clustering Coefficient for the entire network is calculated from every single local clustering coefficient for each node. The Clustering Coefficient of a node shows how concentrated the neighbourhood of that node is. Mathematically, it is defined as the ratio of the number of actual edges between neighbours to the number of potential edges between neighbours. For their utilization in Computational Intelligence, it is also very important to analyze the distribution of a clustering coefficient within an entire network, since we can assume that it can show the population diversity, its compactness or tendency to form heterogeneous subgroups (subpopulations).

4 Metaheuristic Methods

This section contains the background of the metaheuristic algorithms PSO and DE that were used, as well as the main principles of capturing their dynamics in an evolving complex network.

4.1 Differential Evolution

DE is a population-based optimization method that works on real-number-coded individuals [6]. DE is quite robust, fast, and effective, with global optimization ability. There are essentially five inputs to the heuristic [14]. D is the size of the problem, G_{max} is the maximum number of generations, NP is the total number of solutions, F is the scaling factor of the solution and CR is the factor for crossover. F and CR together make the internal tuning parameters for the heuristic.

The initialization of the heuristic is following: each solution $x_{i,j,G=0}$ is created randomly between the two bounds $x^{(lo)}$ and $x^{(hi)}$. The parameter j represents the index to the values within the solution and parameter i indexes the solutions within the population. So, to illustrate, $x_{4,2,0}$ represents the fourth value of the second solution at the initial generation. After initialization, the population is subjected to repeated iterations.

Within each iteration and for particular individual (solution), three random numbers r_1, r_2, r_3 are selected, unique to each other and to the current indexed solution i in the population. Two solutions, $x_{j,r1,G}$ and $x_{j,r2,G}$ are selected through the index r_1 and r_2 and their values subtracted. This value is then multiplied by F, the predefined scaling factor. This is added to the value indexed by r_3.

However, this solution is not arbitrarily accepted in the solution. A new random number is generated, and if this random number is less than the value of CR, then the new value replaces the old value in the current solution. The fitness of the resulting solution, referred to as a perturbed (or trial) vector $u_{j,i,G}$, is then compared with the fitness of $x_{j,i,G}$. If the fitness of $u_{j,i,G}$ is better than the fitness of $x_{j,i,G}$, then $x_{j,i,G}$, is replaced with $u_{j,i,G}$; otherwise, $x_{j,i,G}$, remains in the population as $x_{j,i,G+1}$. Hence the competition is only between the new *child* solution and its *parent* solution. This strategy is denoted as DE/Rand/1/bin. Trial vector for this strategy is given in (1).

$$u_{i,G+1} = x_{r1,G} + F \cdot \left(x_{r2,G} - x_{r3,G} \right)$$ (1)

4.2 PSO Algorithm

Original PSO algorithms take their inspiration from behaviour of fish and birds [8]. The knowledge of the global best-found solution (typically denoted as *gBest*) is shared among the particles in the swarm. Furthermore, each particle has the knowledge of its own (personal) best-found solution (designated *pBest*). The last important part of the algorithm is the velocity of each particle, which is taken into account during the calculation of the particle's movement. The new position of each particle is then given by (2), where x_i^{t+1} is the new particle position; x_i^t refers to the current particle position and v_i^{t+1} is the new velocity of the particle.

$$x_i^{t+1} = x_i^t + v_i^{t+1}$$ (2)

To calculate the new velocity, the distance from *pBest* and *gBest* is taken into account along with its current velocity (3).

$$v_{ij}^{t+1} = v_{ij}^t + c_1 \cdot Rand \cdot (pBest_{ij} - x_{ij}^t) + c_2 \cdot Rand \cdot (gBest_j - x_{ij}^t)$$ (3)

Where:

v_{ij}^{t+1} - New velocity of the ith particle in iteration $t + 1$; (component j of the dimension D).
v_{ij}^t - Current velocity of the ith particle in iteration t; (component j of the dimension D).
c_1, $c_2 = 2$ - Acceleration constants.
$pBest_{ij}$ - Local (personal) best solution found by the ith particle; (component j of the dimension D).
$gBest_j$ - Best solution found in a population; (component j of the dimension D).
x_{ij}^t - Current position of the ith particle; (component j of the dimension D) in iteration t.
Rand - Pseudo-random number, interval (0, 1).

4.3   DE and PSO with a Complex Network Framework

In this research, the complex network approach is utilised to show the linkage between different individuals in the population. Each individual in the population can be taken as a node in the complex network graph, where its links specify the successful exchange of information in the population.

Since the internal dynamics and principles are different for evolutionary (DE) and swarm based (PSO) algorithms, two different approaches for capturing the population dynamics have been developed and tested.

In the case of the DE algorithm, an *Adjacency Graph* was used. In each generation, the node is only active for the successful transfer of information, i.e. if the individual is successful in generating a new better individual which is accepted for the next generation of the population. If the trial vector created from three randomly selected individuals (*DE/Rand/1/Bin*) is better than the active individual, one establishes the connections between the new created individual and the three sources; otherwise, no connections are recorded in the Adjacency Matrix.

For the PSO algorithm, the main interest is in the communications that lead to population quality improvement. Therefore, only communication leading to improvement of the particles personal best (*pBest*) was tracked. The link was created between the particle that was improved and the particle that triggered the current *gBest*'s update. This approach creates a complex network with clusters - and can be used for particle performance evaluations. Of course, it is also possible to build an Adjacency Graph (see Sect. 7).

5   Experiment Design

A simple Schwefel's Test function (4) was used in this experimental research for the purpose of the generation of a complex network. Due to the limited space and focus of this paper, only one test function is used. The influences of different test functions for complex network frameworks are discussed in the Conclusion.

$$f(x) = \sum_{i=1}^{Dim} -x_i \sin\left(\sqrt{|x_i|}\right) \tag{4}$$

Function minimum:

Position for E_n: $(x_1, x_2...x_n) = (420.969, 420.969,..., 420.969)$.
Value for E_n: $y = -418.983 \cdot Dim$; Function interval: $<-512, 512>$.

Experiments were also performed in the *C language* environment, the data from the DE algorithm was analysed and visualised using *Cytoscape* software, while data from the PSO algorithm was analysed in the *Wolfram Mathematica SW* suite.

Within the ambits of this research, only one type of experiment was performed. It utilises the maximum number of generations fixed at 100 with a population size of $NP = 50$. Two DE control parameters for mutation and crossover were set as $F = 0.5$ and $CR = 0.8$. Two acceleration constants for PSO were set as $c_1, c_2 = 2$.

Since only one run of DE or PSO algorithms were executed for this particular case-study, no statistical results related to the cost function values and no comparisons are given here, since it is not possible to compare metaheuristic algorithms only from one run.

6   Visualizations for DE

The visualisations of complex networks are depicted in Figs. 1 and 2 containing Adjacency Graphs for this selected case-study.

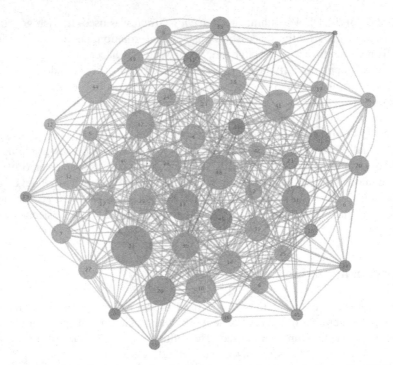

Fig. 1. Complex network representation for DE dynamics – case study 1: the first 10 iterations. (Color figure online)

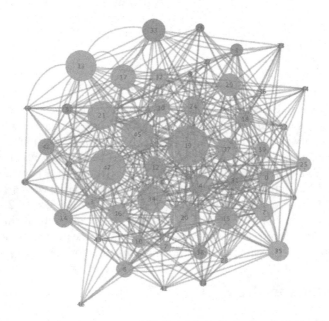

Fig. 2. Complex network representation for DE dynamics – case study 2: the last 10 iterations. (Color figure online)

The *Degree Centrality* value is highlighted by the size of the node, and the colouring of the node is related to the *Clustering Coefficient* distribution (light coloured-lower values ranging up to the red colours – higher values).

Simple analyses of the networks are given in Table 1; furthermore, it also contains the values of the total number of edges in the graph; the success rate of the evolution process in percentage, showing the ratio between the maximum possible edges in the graphs and the actual one. The theoretical maximum number of edges in the graph is given by $3*NP*10 = 1500$, i.e. the situation where every active individual in the population is replaced by a newly created one from three another individuals across the limited number of 10 generations as observed.

Table 1. Simple analysis of the networks for two case studies.

Case	No. of edges	Success rate (%)	Clustering coefficient	Network centralization	Avg. number of neighbours	Network density
First 10 gen.	558	37.20	0.390	0.117	18.48	0.377
Last 10 gen.	435	29.00	0.334	0.216	14.84	0.303

7   Visualizations for PSO

The complex network for all iterations of the PSO algorithm that was created is depicted in Fig. 3. Nodes of a similar colour represent particles with the same ID, and throughout different iterations. All links are from a particle that triggered the *gBest* update to a particle that has improved - based on that *gBest*. The nodes' code numbers represent a particle ID and its current iteration. This way, it is possible to precisely track the development of the network and the communication that occurs within the swarm. To be more precise, from particular cluster, it can be observed that a single *gBest* update led to the improvement of multiple particles in different iterations. Due to the complexity of the Fig. 3, it is not possible to clearly see the density of the network and links of various lengths.

Alternatively, it is possible to construct an Adjacency Graph and to benefit from its statistical features - as with the DE case. The link is created between the particle that triggered the last *gBest* update and the particle that triggers a new *gBest* update. The self-loops (when a new *gBest* is found by exactly the same particle as the previous *gBest*), are omitted. The simplified example is depicted in Fig. 4. Here, for a lower level of complexity and illustration purposes, the population size was limited to 20.

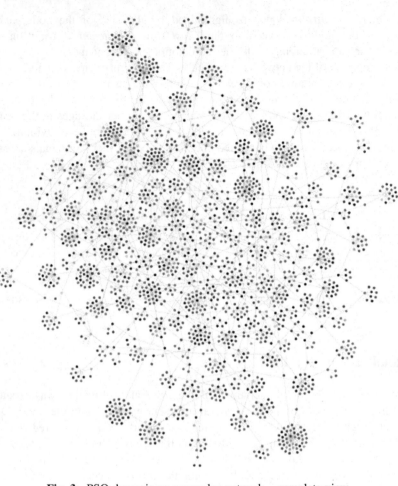

Fig. 3. PSO dynamic as a complex network – complete view.

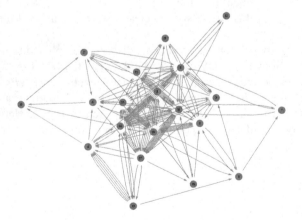

Fig. 4. PSO dynamic as an Adjacency Graph.

8 Conclusion

This work was aimed at the experimental investigation of the hybridization of a complex network framework using DE and PSO algorithms. The population was visualized as an evolving complex network, which exhibits non-trivial features. These features provided a clear description of the population during evaluation and can be used for adaptive population and parameter control during the metaheuristic run.

The graphical and numerical data presented herein has fully manifested the influence of either time frame selection, or type of construction to the features of the complex network. These features can be used in various adaptive or learning processes. The findings can be summarized as follows:

- Building of the Network: Since there is a direct link between parent solutions and offspring in the evolutionary algorithms, this information is used to build a complex network. In the case of swarm algorithms, the situation is a bit more difficult. It depends on the inner swarm mechanisms, but mostly, it is possible to capture the communications within the swarm during the updating of the information - based on the points of attraction. Two possible approaches are described herein, resulting in different graph visualizations and possible analyses (see Figs. 3, 4 and Sect. 7).
- Complex Network Features: A complex network created for evolutionary algorithms contains direct information about the selection of individuals and their success; therefore, many network features can be used for controlling a population during an EA run. At the beginning of the optimization process, intensive communication occurs (Fig. 1). Later, hubs (centralities) and clusters are created (Fig. 2), and it is possible to use such information either for the injection or replacement of individuals or to modify/alternate the evolutionary strategy (see Sects. 3.1 and 3.2). In the case of swarm algorithms, the communication dynamics are captured - thus the level of particle performance (usefulness) can be calculated; or alternatively, some sub-clusters and centralities of such a communication can also be identified - depending on the technique used for the transformation of swarm dynamics into the network.
- Other Features – Randomization, Fitness Landscape: Numerous previous experiments showed that there are no significant changes in complex network features for different test functions in the case of evolutionary algorithms. Nevertheless, the different randomization (distribution) used directly influences the network development through the selection of individuals. Thus, through the preferences of some clusters of individuals, it is possible to temporarily simulate the different randomization inside a metaheuristic for an entire/sub-population. Complex network construction for swarm algorithms is not distinctively sensitive to randomization, but the capturing of communications (swarm dynamics) is sensitive to the fitness landscape. Thus, network features can be used for the raw estimation of a fitness landscape (i.e. multimodal/uni-modal, or the identification of particular benchmark function) directly.

This novel topic has brought up many new open tasks, which will be resolved in future research. Another advantage is that this complex network framework can be used almost on any metaheuristic. Moreover, especially for swarm algorithms there exist many possible ways regarding how to build a complex network.

Acknowledgements. This work was supported by Grant Agency of the Czech Republic - GACR P103/15/06700S, further by the Ministry of Education, Youth and Sports of the Czech Republic within the National Sustainability Programme project No. LO1303 (MSMT-7778/ 2014) and also by the European Regional Development Fund under the project CEBIA-Tech No. CZ.1.05/2.1.00/03.0089., partially supported by Grant of SGS No. SP2016/175 of VSB - Technical University of Ostrava, Czech Republic and by Internal Grant Agency of Tomas Bata University under the project No. IGA/CebiaTech/2016/007.

References

1. Zelinka, I., Davendra, D., Lampinen, J., Senkerik, R., Pluhacek, M.: Evolutionary algorithms dynamics and its hidden complex network structures. In: 2014 IEEE Congress on Evolutionary Computation (CEC), pp. 3246–3251 (2014)
2. Davendra, D., Zelinka, I., Metlicka, M., Senkerik, R., Pluhacek, M.: Complex network analysis of differential evolution algorithm applied to flowshop with no-wait problem. In: 2014 IEEE Symposium on Differential Evolution (SDE), pp. 1–8 (2014)
3. Davendra, D., Zelinka, I., Senkerik, R., Pluhacek, M.: Complex network analysis of evolutionary algorithms applied to combinatorial optimisation problem. In: Körner, P., Abraham, A., Snášel, V. (eds.) Proceedings of the Fifth International Conference on Innovations in Bio-Inspired Computing and Applications IBICA 2014. AISC, vol. 303, pp. 141–150. Springer, Cham (2014). doi:10.1007/978-3-319-08156-4_15
4. Skanderova, L., Fabian, T.: Differential evolution dynamics analysis by complex networks. Soft. Comput. **21**, 1–15 (2015)
5. Metlicka, M., Davendra, D.: Ensemble centralities based adaptive Artificial Bee algorithm. In: 2015 IEEE Congress on Evolutionary Computation (CEC), pp. 3370–3376 (2015)
6. Gajdos, P., Kromer, P., Zelinka, I.: Network visualization of population dynamics in the differential evolution. In: 2015 IEEE Symposium Series on Computational Intelligence, pp. 1522–1528 (2015)
7. Price, K.V.: An introduction to differential evolution. In: Corne, D., Dorigo, M., Glover, F. (eds.) New Ideas in Optimization, pp. 79–108. McGraw-Hill Ltd. (1999)
8. Kennedy, J., Eberhart, R.: Particle swarm optimization. In: IEEE International Conference on Neural Networks, Nov/Dec 1995, pp. 1942–1948 (1995)
9. Qin, A.K., Huang, V.L., Suganthan, P.N.: Differential evolution algorithm with strategy adaptation for global numerical optimization. IEEE Trans. Evol. Comput. **13**(2), 398–417 (2009)
10. Mallipeddi, R., Suganthan, P.N., Pan, Q.K., Tasgetiren, M.F.: Differential evolution algorithm with ensemble of parameters and mutation strategies. Appl. Soft Comput. **11**(2), 1679–1696 (2011)
11. Jabeen, H., Jalil, Z., Baig, A.R.: Opposition based initialization in particle swarm optimization (O-PSO). Paper Presented at the Proceedings of the 11th Annual Conference Companion on Genetic and Evolutionary Computation Conference (2009)
12. Engelbrecht, A.P.: Heterogeneous particle swarm optimization. In: Dorigo, M., et al. (eds.) ANTS 2010. LNCS, vol. 6234, pp. 191–202. Springer, Heidelberg (2010). doi:10.1007/978-3-642-15461-4_17

13. Janostik, J., Pluhacek, M., Senkerik, R., Zelinka, I.: Particle swarm optimizer with diversity measure based on swarm representation in complex network. In: Abraham, A., Wegrzyn-Wolska, K., Hassanien, A.E., Snasel, V., Alimi, A.M. (eds.) Proceedings of the Second International Afro-European Conference for Industrial Advancement AECIA 2015. AISC, vol. 427, pp. 561–569. Springer, Cham (2016). doi:10.1007/978-3-319-29504-6_52
14. Das, S., Mullick, S.S., Suganthan, P.: Recent advances in differential evolution – an updated survey. Swarm Evol. Comput. **27**, 1–30 (2016)

Estimation of Distribution Algorithms Based on the Beta Distribution for Bounded Search Spaces

Rogelio Salinas-Gutiérrez[1(✉)], Ángel Eduardo Muñoz-Zavala[1],
José Antonio Guerrero-Díaz de León[1], and Arturo Hernández-Aguirre[2]

[1] Universidad Autónoma de Aguascalientes, Aguascalientes, Mexico
{rsalinas,aemz,jaguerrero}@correo.uaa.mx
[2] Centro de Investigación en Matemáticas, Guanajuato, Mexico
artha@cimat.mx

Abstract. This work presents a metaheuristic based on the use of the beta distribution as a search distribution for solving numerical optimization problems in search spaces defined on two sided intervals. The innovation of this work lies on the efficiency of the proposed method to estimate the parameters of the beta distribution with a minimal cost for each decision variable by using the method of moments. The numerical experiments provided evidence that applying the method of moments for parameter estimation and the beta distribution as a search distribution generates competitive results.

Keywords: Method of moments · Numerical optimization · Beta distribution

1 Introduction

Estimation of Distribution Algorithms (EDAs) [9] are considered as a novel proposal for solving optimization problems. This kind of algorithms belong to the field of Evolutionary Computation (EC) [15] and they are distinguished by the use of probabilistic models. Similar to other metaheuristics of EC, EDAs are iterative algorithms based on populations. Thus, an important characteristic of EDAs is the incorporation of probabilistic models in order to represent the statistical properties of the promising solutions. Such properties are taken into account by means of the decision variables from the selected individuals.

The research in EDAs has been performed for discrete domains as well for continuous domains. Some of the first contributions in discrete domains have been based in a predefined probabilistic graphical model and have been reported in [2,8,12]. Other EDAs have included the learning of sophisticated graphical models such as Bayesian networks and Markov networks [4,11,16]. On the other hand the Gaussian distribution and its related distributions, such as Gaussian kernels and Gaussian mixture models, have been employed and studied extensively as the main probabilistic models for continuous domains [1,5,6].

O. Pichardo-Lagunas and S. Miranda-Jiménez (Eds.): MICAI 2016, Part II, LNAI 10062, pp. 162–172, 2017.
DOI: 10.1007/978-3-319-62428-0_13

Algorithm 1 shows a pseudocode for EDAs. According to step 4, the statistical behavior of decision variables is taken into account by means of the probabilistic distribution $\mathcal{M}_t$. Step 5 shows how the statistical properties of the selected individuals are transferred to the new population, which greatly modifies the performance of an EDA.

Algorithm 1. Pseudocode for EDAs

1: Initialize the generation counter $t \longleftarrow 0$
  Generate the initial population $\mathcal{P}_0$ with N individuals at random.
2: Evaluate population $\mathcal{P}_t$ using the cost function.
3: Select a subset $\mathcal{S}_t$ from $\mathcal{P}_t$ according to the selection method.
4: Estimate a probabilistic model $\mathcal{M}_t$ from $\mathcal{S}_t$.
5: Generate the new population $\mathcal{P}_{t+1}$ by sampling from the model $\mathcal{M}_t$
  Assign $t \longleftarrow t + 1$.
6: If stopping criteria are not reached go to step 2.

As shown in Algorithm 1, step 4 involves an important and critical procedure in EDAs. Thus, much of the research in EDAs has been focused on proposing and enhancing new probabilistic models with many contributions in discrete and continuous domains. The interested reader is referred to [7] for knowing more about the probabilistic models used in EDAs.

Although the current research in EDAs for continuous decision variables has been mainly directed toward the Gaussian distribution, there is a lack of studies for the use of appropiate probabilistic models for bounded search spaces. This work shows how a non Gaussian distribution can be included and adapted for searching promising solutions in continuous search spaces with decision variables defined on limited intervals. Moreover, the proposed algorithm in this paper can be used for search spaces with different lower and upper bounds.

The structure of the paper is the following: Sect. 2 shows the theoretical characteristics and the practical implementation of the beta distribution as a search model in numerical optimization with bounded decision variables, Sect. 3 shows some preliminary results of the implementation of the beta distribution according to the method for estimating its parameters, Sect. 4 presents the experimental setting to solve five test global optimization problems, and Sect. 5 resumes the conclusions.

2 The Beta Distribution

In EDAs, the main approach for solving continuous optimization problems has been the use of Gaussian distribution. This distribution is also named normal distribution and is well known for its symmetry around its mean and for its bell shaped curve. Besides, a random variable that follows a Gaussian distribution has infinite support, i.e., its density function is non zero over the entire real line. Though practical, the Gaussian distribution could not fit very well in non symmetric cases or over limited intervals.

For continuous optimization problems defined on bounded search spaces, the decision variables are limited by a lower and upper bound. Therefore, for modeling purposes, it is desirable that the search distribution be consistent with the constraint of limited intervals. In this situation, the beta distribution is an appropriate choice given that it is defined on a two sided interval. Moreover, different from the Gaussian distribution, the beta is able to model skewed random variables. Figure 1 illustrates the versatility of the beta distribution for modeling symmetric and non-symmetric distributions over a two sided interval.

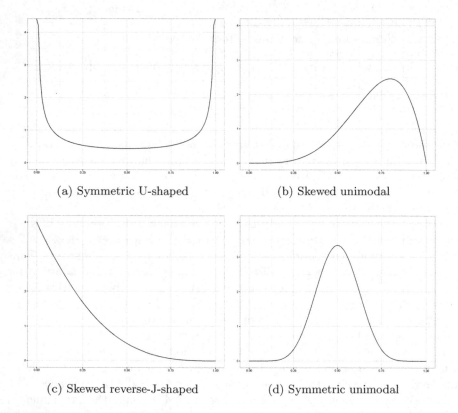

(a) Symmetric U-shaped   (b) Skewed unimodal

(c) Skewed reverse-J-shaped   (d) Symmetric unimodal

Fig. 1. Some graphical shapes of the standard beta distribution according to the values of its parameters. (a) $(\alpha, \beta) = (0.3, 0.3)$. (b) $(\alpha, \beta) = (5, 2)$. (c) $(\alpha, \beta) = (1, 4)$. (d) $(\alpha, \beta) = (9, 9)$.

As shown in Fig. 1, the shape of the beta distribution depends on the values of its parameters α and β. The probability density function of the standard beta distribution is given by the following expression

$$f(x; \alpha, \beta) = \frac{\Gamma(\alpha + \beta)}{\Gamma(\alpha)\Gamma(\beta)} x^{\alpha-1}(1-x)^{\beta-1}, \text{with } \alpha, \beta > 0 \text{ and } x \in [0, 1]. \quad (1)$$

Equation 1 refers to a beta distribution defined on the unit interval. However, a generalization of the beta distribution is possible through a linear transformation. For example, if a decision variable Y is defined over the interval $[a, b]$, then the variable

$$X = \frac{Y - a}{b - a},$$ (2)

is defined over the unit interval.

2.1   The Proposed Algorithm

According to Algorithm 1, the initial population is generated at random. This means that the first population is generated by sampling from the uniform distribution. However, it is worth noting that the uniform distribution is a special case of the standard beta distribution when both parameters are equal to one.

Once the steps 2 and 3 of the Algorithm 1 have been done, the following step requires the learning of the probabilistic model for each decision variable. In [13,14] and later in [3] the beta distribution was implemented as probabilistic model in an EDA based on copula functions. The implementation of the beta distribution in those publications employs the maximum likelihood method for estimating the shape parameters (α_i, β_i) of each decision variable Y_i. However, the maximum likelihood method does not provide closed formulas for getting the estimators and also it requires the additional application of an optimization procedure. In this work we propose the use of the method of moments for estimating the parameters of the beta distribution. This procedure of estimation does not requires an additional optimization and it does provide closed formulas.

According to the method of moments [10,17], the formulas for estimating the shape parameters of a standard beta distribution are the following

$$\hat{\alpha} = \bar{x} \left(\frac{\bar{x}(1 - \bar{x})}{s^2} - 1 \right), \text{ if } s^2 < \bar{x}(1 - \bar{x}),$$ (3)

$$\hat{\beta} = (1 - \bar{x}) \left(\frac{\bar{x}(1 - \bar{x})}{s^2} - 1 \right), \text{ if } s^2 < \bar{x}(1 - \bar{x}),$$ (4)

where $\hat{\alpha}$ and $\hat{\beta}$ are the point estimators of the population parameters α and β, $\bar{x}$ is the sample mean estimate and s^2 is the sample variance estimate.

For a general $d-$dimensional bounded search space where each decision variable Y_i is defined on a limited interval $[a_i, b_i]$, with $i = 1, \ldots, d$, Eq. 2 can be used for getting a standarized variable X_i and then its shape parameters (α_i, β_i) are calculated with Eqs. 3 and 4.

The proposed EDA in this paper is described in Algorithm 2.

3   Preliminary Results

In order to assess the performance of the beta distribution with the implementation of the method of moments, we compare two EDA approaches in five test

Algorithm 2. Pseudocode for EDA based on the beta distribution

---

1: Initialize the generation counter $t \longleftarrow 0$
   Generate the initial population $\mathcal{P}_0$ with N individuals at random.
2: Evaluate population $\mathcal{P}_t$ using the cost function.
3: Select a subset $\mathcal{S}_t$ from $\mathcal{P}_t$ according to the selection method.
4: **for** $i = 1 \rightarrow d$ **do**
5:     Obtain the transformed variable X_i according to Eq. 2
6:     Calculate the sample mean $\bar{x}$ and the sample variance s^2 from X_i.
7:     Estimate the shape parameters by using Eqs. 3 and 4.
8:     Generate the new values for the corresponding transformed variable by sampling
       from the beta distribution with parameters (α_i, β_i).
9:     Obtain the new values for the corresponding decision variable by using the inverse
       transformation of Eq. 2.
10: **end for**
11: Assign $t \longleftarrow t + 1$.
12: If stopping criteria are not reached go to step 2.

---

problems. The comparison is done between an EDA with beta distribution and the maximum likelihood method (EDA-BL) and an EDA with beta distribution and the method of moments (EDA-BM). These test functions are described in Fig. 2. The aim of this study is to attempt to answer the following research question: Is the EDA-BM performance similar or better than the EDA-BL?

The benchmark test suite includes separable functions and non-separable functions, from which there are unimodal and multimodal functions. In addition, the search domain is asymmetric. All test functions are scalable. We use test problems in 4, 6, 8 and 10 dimensions.

A graphical comparison between EDA-BL and EDA-BM is shown in Fig. 3. According to these graphical results, the performance of the EDA-BM is similar to the performance of the EDA-BL in the first 100 generations. However, more experiments and statistical comparisons are presented in Sect. 4 for the test functions described in Fig. 2 with different dimension.

4   Experiments

Five test problems are used to compare the following three EDAs.

1. The EDA which employs the maximum likelihood method for estimating the beta parameters (EDA-BL).
2. The EDA which employs the method of moments for estimating the beta parameters (EDA-BM).
3. The EDA which employs the Gaussian distribution and its parameters are estimated by closed formulas of the maximum likelihood method (EDA-G).

The test problems used in the experiments are the Ackley, Griewangk, Rastrigin, Rosenbrock, and Sphere functions. Figure 2 describe the test functions. The algorithms are tested in different dimensions with asymmetric bounded search

Description

Ackley

$$-20 \cdot \exp\left(-0.2\sqrt{\frac{1}{d} \cdot \sum_{i=1}^{d} x_i^2}\right) - \exp\left(\frac{1}{d} \cdot \sum_{i=1}^{d} \cos(2\pi x_i)\right) + 20 + \exp(1)$$

$$\boldsymbol{x} \in [-10, 30]^d$$

Properties: Multimodal, Non-separable	Global Minimum: $f(\boldsymbol{0}) = 0$

Griewangk

$$1 + \sum_{i=1}^{d} \frac{x_i^2}{4000} - \prod_{i=1}^{d} \cos\left(\frac{x_i}{\sqrt{i}}\right) \quad ; \quad \boldsymbol{x} \in [-10, 30]^d$$

Properties: Multimodal, Non-separable	Global Minimum: $f(\boldsymbol{0}) = 0$

Rastrigin

$$\sum_{i=1}^{d} (x_i^2 - 10\cos(2\pi x_i) + 10) \quad ; \quad \boldsymbol{x} \in [-10, 30]^d$$

Properties: Multimodal, Separable	Global Minimum: $f(\boldsymbol{0}) = 0$

Rosenbrock

$$\sum_{i=1}^{d-1} [100 \cdot (x_{i+1} - x_i^2)^2 + (1 - x_i)^2] \quad ; \quad \boldsymbol{x} \in [-10, 30]^d$$

Properties: Unimodal, Non-separable	Global Minimum: $f(\boldsymbol{1}) = 0$

Sphere Model

$$\sum_{i=1}^{d} x_i^2 \quad ; \quad \boldsymbol{x} \in [-10, 30]^d$$

Properties: Unimodal, Separable	Global Minimum: $f(\boldsymbol{0}) = 0$

Fig. 2. Names, mathematical definition, search domains, global minimum and properties of the test functions.

domain. The population size is ten times the dimension $(10 * d)$. Each algorithm is run 30 times for each problem. The maximum number of generations evaluations is 1,000. However, when convergence to a local minimum is detected the run is stopped. Any improvement less than 1×10^{-6} in 25 iterations is considered as convergence. The goal is to assess and compare the performance among the algorithms.

The results in dimensions 4, 6, 8, and 10 for non-separable functions are reported in Table 1, whereas the results for separable functions are reported in Table 2. Both tables report descriptive statistics for the fitness values reached in the all runs. The fitness value corresponds to the value of a test problem. For each algorithm and dimension, the minimum, mean, median, maximum and standard deviation are shown. The minimum (maximum) value reached is considered the best (worst).

Besides the descriptive results shown in Tables 1 and 2, a hypothesis test is conducted to properly compare the performance of the three EDAs. The statistical comparisons are for the algorithms with the same test problem and the same dimension. The Kruskal-Wallis test is employed to compare the median fitness

Rosenbrock   Sphere

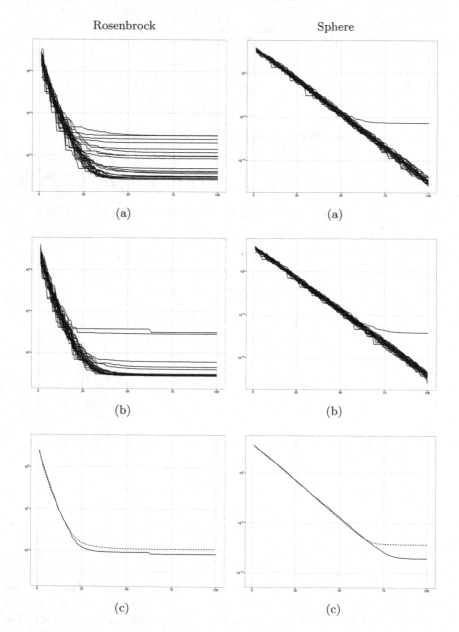

Fig. 3. The horizontal axis represents the generation and the vertical axis represents the fitness in logarithmic scale. (a) The fitness performance of EDA-BL. (b) The fitness performance of EDA-BM. (c) The dashed line is used for the average performance of EDA-BL and the solid line is used for the average performance of EDA-BM.

among EDA-BL, EDA-BM and EDA-G. When the null hypothesis is rejected, i.e., there is a significant difference among the performance of the algorithms and the corresponding median fitness in Tables 1 and 2 is marked with an asterix (*).

Table 1. Descriptive results of the fitness for non-separable functions.

Algorithm	d	Minimum	Mean	Median	Maximum	Standard deviation
Ackley						
EDA-BL	4	1.50E−09	6.14E−02	4.96E−09**	1.84E+00	3.36E−01
	6	1.18E−08	1.26E−04	2.22E−08**	3.47E−03	6.34E−04
	8	2.72E−08	5.42E−07	4.82E−08**	1.10E−05	2.10E−06
	10	4.91E−08	7.62E−05	8.07E−08**	2.28E−03	4.17E−04
EDA-BM	4	2.99E−09	6.13E−02	6.43E−09**	1.84E+00	3.36E−01
	6	1.45E−08	2.57E−08	2.51E−08**	4.03E−08	6.76E−09
	8	3.68E−08	7.74E−06	5.24E−08**	2.31E−04	4.21E−05
	10	6.85E−08	9.03E−08	8.95E−08**	1.30E−07	1.41E−08
EDA-G	4	2.24E−10	8.69E−09	5.96E−10**	2.40E−07	4.36E−08
	6	1.25E−09	2.82E−06	3.25E−09**	8.46E−05	1.54E−05
	8	5.06E−09	8.87E−09	7.77E−09**	2.47E−08	4.02E−09
	10	1.06E−08	1.57E−08	1.49E−08**	2.48E−08	3.43E−09
Griewangk						
EDA-BL	4	7.40E−03	7.64E−02	6.67E−02	1.87E−01	5.17E−02
	6	9.63E−13	1.66E−01	1.76E−01	4.21E−01	1.49E−01
	8	1.66E−11	7.17E−02	1.18E−10	7.17E−01	1.88E−01
	10	5.22E−11	6.53E−04	1.34E−10**	1.96E−02	3.58E−03
EDA-BM	4	7.40E−03	7.10E−02	7.26E−02	2.35E−01	5.78E−02
	6	2.17E−12	1.56E−01	1.46E−01	5.21E−01	1.59E−01
	8	1.91E−11	1.01E−01	7.10E−11	6.64E−01	2.04E−01
	10	8.26E−11	1.85E−04	1.96E−10**	4.60E−03	8.52E−04
EDA-G	4	7.40E−03	7.90E−02	6.39E−02	1.94E−01	5.78E−02
	6	4.79E−12	1.59E−01	1.29E−01	4.69E−01	1.58E−01
	8	9.63E−12	3.50E−02	1.18E−10	4.13E−01	1.03E−01
	10	1.22E−10	9.97E−06	2.11E−10**	2.99E−04	5.46E−05
Rosenbrock						
EDA-BL	4	2.34E−02	2.17E+01	2.32E+00	5.43E+02	9.87E+01
	6	3.32E+00	1.11E+02	5.51E+00	2.10E+03	3.88E+02
	8	4.74E+00	1.02E+02	6.63E+00	1.62E+03	3.02E+02
	10	8.05E+00	8.43E+01	9.53E+00*	1.06E+03	2.11E+02
EDA-BM	4	4.08E−02	2.69E+00	2.14E+00	1.75E+01	3.04E+00
	6	3.75E+00	1.60E+01	4.36E+00	1.61E+02	3.11E+01
	8	5.64E+00	8.51E+01	6.29E+00	1.75E+03	3.18E+02
	10	7.22E+00	2.72E+01	8.32E+00*	1.80E+02	4.20E+01
EDA-G	4	2.81E−01	2.96E+00	2.06E+00	1.18E+01	2.64E+00
	6	1.43E+00	1.72E+01	4.40E+00	7.85E+01	2.16E+01
	8	1.63E+00	5.06E+01	1.34E+01	5.12E+02	9.48E+01
	10	5.51E+00	7.54E+01	3.82E+01*	8.21E+02	1.46E+02

*Denotes a significant difference among the algorithms, at significance level 0.05
**Denotes a significant difference among the algorithms, at significance level 0.01

Table 2. Descriptive results of the fitness for separable functions.

Algorithm	d	Minimum	Mean	Median	Maximum	Standard deviation
Rastrigin						
EDA-BL	4	9.77E$-$14	1.11E+00	9.95E$-$01	3.98E+00	1.06E+00
	6	4.78E$-$12	3.24E+00	1.99E+00	1.85E+01	4.04E+00
	8	2.64E$-$11	3.84E+00	1.99E+00	2.73E+01	5.78E+00
	10	2.16E$-$10	6.83E+00	1.99E+00	3.97E+01	1.15E+01
EDA-BM	4	7.64E$-$14	1.03E+00	9.95E$-$01	4.03E+00	1.06E+00
	6	4.00E$-$12	2.56E+00	1.80E+00	1.54E+01	3.78E+00
	8	3.65E$-$11	5.70E+00	1.99E+00	2.63E+01	7.56E+00
	10	1.65E$-$10	6.84E+00	1.99E+00	4.25E+01	1.18E+01
EDA-G	4	2.08E$-$13	1.34E+00	9.95E$-$01	7.26E+00	1.62E+00
	6	5.48E$-$12	2.02E+00	9.95E$-$01	1.37E+01	2.97E+00
	8	1.08E$-$10	4.18E+00	1.58E+00	2.19E+01	6.13E+00
	10	1.61E$-$10	1.25E+01	1.99E+00	4.37E+01	1.53E+01
Sphere						
EDA-BL	4	3.33E$-$15	3.19E$-$04	2.22E$-$13*	7.01E$-$03	1.34E$-$03
	6	7.21E$-$13	9.78E$-$04	5.32E$-$12**	2.93E$-$02	5.35E$-$03
	8	7.74E$-$12	2.88E$-$06	4.34E$-$11*	4.56E$-$05	1.10E$-$05
	10	2.83E$-$11	8.75E$-$06	1.50E$-$10	2.62E$-$04	4.79E$-$05
EDA-BM	4	3.19E$-$14	3.54E$-$13	2.46E$-$13*	1.54E$-$12	3.36E$-$13
	6	9.75E$-$13	2.22E$-$07	1.06E$-$11**	6.67E$-$06	1.22E$-$06
	8	1.50E$-$11	8.63E$-$11	5.95E$-$11*	3.82E$-$10	8.49E$-$11
	10	6.33E$-$11	2.32E$-$10	1.93E$-$10	9.59E$-$10	1.75E$-$10
EDA-G	4	4.88E$-$14	2.89E$-$03	6.65E$-$13*	7.87E$-$02	1.44E$-$02
	6	2.25E$-$12	1.13E$-$05	1.20E$-$11**	3.38E$-$04	6.17E$-$05
	8	2.34E$-$11	1.79E$-$03	7.16E$-$11*	5.38E$-$02	9.83E$-$03
	10	4.38E$-$11	2.35E$-$10	2.19E$-$10	4.63E$-$10	1.06E$-$10

*Denotes a significant difference among the algorithms, at significance level 0.05
**Denotes a significant difference among the algorithms, at significance level 0.01

As shown in Table 1, there are 12 comparisons (3 test functions for each dimension) for non-separable functions in which 6 comparisons present significant differences among the algorithms. For the separable functions, see Table 2, there are 8 comparisons in which 3 comparisons indicate significant differences among the performance of the assessed algorithms. When a difference is considered significant, a post-hoc test (Nemenyi test) is applied for doing pairwise multiple comparisons.

For the Ackley function, all comparisons among the three EDAs are significant different. In all dimensions, the post-hoc test indicates that the best performance is gotten by the EDA-G. For the Griewangk function, there is no significant differences among the three algorithms in dimension 4, 6 and 8. The only difference is detected in dimension 10, where the EDA-BL has the best performance. The Rosenbrock function is solved by the three EDAs with similar results in dimension 4, 6 and 8. However, in dimension 10, the EDA-BM outperformed significantly to the algorithm EDA-G.

For the Rastrigin function the three EDAs provide solutions without significant differences in all dimensions. This means that the EDA-BM is able to find similar solutions to those found by the EDA-BL and the EDA-G. The Sphere function was solved similarly by the algorithms in dimension 10. For dimensions 4 and 8, the EDA-G was outperformed by the EDA-BL and the EDA-BM. In dimension 6 the best performance is achieved by the EDA-BL.

5   Conclusions

The statistical tests show no differences among the EDAs in almost the half of all comparisons. In particular, in these cases, it can be stated that the EDA-BM has a similar performance that the EDA-BL with the advantage of estimating their parameters with no additional cost. When a different performance has been detected, 7 out of 9 comparisons the post hoc test indicates similar results for the EDA-BL and the EDA-BM, i.e., the found difference comes from the EDA-G and the EDAs based on the beta distribution. This evidence confirms that the EDA-BM has a similar performance that the EDA-BL.

This work has proposed the use of the beta distribution as a search distribution in EDAs. In particular, the numerical estimation of the shape parameters has been done with minimal cost for each decision variable. According to the numerical experiments, the numerical procedure for estimating the shape parameters by using the likelihood function can be avoided and replaced by the method of moments.

An important contribution of this paper is to introduce the method of moments as an important tool for estimating the statistical parameters of the search distribution in EDAs.

References

1. Bosman, P.: Design and application of iterated density-estimation evolutionary algorithms. Ph.D. thesis, University of Utrecht, Utrecht, The Netherlands (2003)
2. De Bonet, J., Isbell, C., Viola, P.: MIMIC: finding optima by estimating probability densities. In: Advances in Neural Information Processing Systems, vol. 9, pp. 424–430. The MIT Press, Cambridge (1997)
3. Gonzalez-Fernandez, Y., Soto, M.: Copulaedas: an R package for estimation of distribution algorithms based on copulas. J. Stat. Softw. 58(9), 1–34 (2014)
4. Larrañaga, P., Etxeberria, R., Lozano, J., Peña, J.: Combinatorial optimization by learning and simulation of Bayesian networks. In: Proceedings of the Sixteenth Conference on Uncertainty in Artificial Intelligence, pp. 343–352 (2000)
5. Larrañaga, P., Etxeberria, R., Lozano, J., Peña, J.: Optimization in continuous domains by learning and simulation of Gaussian networks. In: Proceedings of the Optimization by Building and Using Probabilistic Models OBUPM Workshop at the Genetic and Evolutionary Computation Conference GECCO-2000, pp. 201–204 (2000)

6. Larrañaga, P., Lozano, J., Bengoetxea, E.: Estimation of distribution algorithm based on multivariate normal and gaussian networks. Technical report EHU-KZAA-IK-1/01, Department of Computer Science and Artificial Intelligence, University of the Basque Country (2001)
7. Larrañaga, P., Lozano, J. (eds.): Estimation of Distribution Algorithms: A New Tool for Evolutionary Computation. Genetic Algorithms and Evolutionary Computation. Kluwer Academic Publishers, Norwell (2002)
8. Mühlenbein, H.: The equation for response to selection and its use for prediction. Evol. Comput. **5**(3), 303–346 (1998)
9. Mühlenbein, H., Paaß, G.: From recombination of genes to the estimation of distributions I. Binary parameters. In: Voigt, H.-M., Ebeling, W., Rechenberg, I., Schwefel, H.-P. (eds.) PPSN 1996. LNCS, vol. 1141, pp. 178–187. Springer, Heidelberg (1996). doi:10.1007/3-540-61723-X_982
10. Olive, D.: Statistical Theory and Inference. Springer, Heidelberg (2014)
11. Pelikan, M., Goldberg, D., Cantú-Paz, E.: BOA: the Bayesian optimization algorithm. In: Banzhaf, W., Daida, J., Eiben, A., Garzon, M., Honavar, V., Jakiela, M., Smith, R. (eds.) Proceedings of the Genetic and Evolutionary Computation Conference GECCO-99, vol. 1, pp. 525–532. Morgan Kaufmann Publishers, Orlando (1999)
12. Pelikan, M., Mühlenbein, H.: The Bivariate Marginal Distribution Algorithm. In: Roy, R., Furuhashi, T., Chawdhry, P. (eds.) Advances in Soft Computing - Engineering Design and Manufacturing, pp. 521–535. Springer, London (1999). doi:10.1007/978-1-4471-0819-1_39
13. Salinas-Gutiérrez, R., Hernández-Aguirre, A., Villa-Diharce, E.R.: Using copulas in estimation of distribution algorithms. In: Aguirre, A.H., Borja, R.M., Garciá, C.A.R. (eds.) MICAI 2009. LNCS, vol. 5845, pp. 658–668. Springer, Heidelberg (2009). doi:10.1007/978-3-642-05258-3_58
14. Salinas-Gutiérrez, R., Hernández-Aguirre, A., Villa-Diharce, E.: D-vine EDA: a new estimation of distribution algorithm based on regular vines. In: GECCO 2010: Proceedings of the 12th Annual Conference on Genetic and Evolutionary Computation, pp. 359–366. ACM, New York (2010)
15. Simon, D.: Evolutionary Optimization Algorithms: Biologically Inspired and Population-Based Approaches to Computer Intelligence. Wiley, Hoboken (2013)
16. Soto, M., Ochoa, A., Acid, S., de Campos, L.: Introducing the polytree approximation of distribution algorithm. In: Ochoa, A., Soto, M., Santana, R. (eds.) Second International Symposium on Artificial Intelligence, Adaptive Systems, CIMAF 1999, pp. 360–367. Academia, La Habana (1999)
17. Wasserman, L.: All of Statistics. Springer Texts in Statistics. Springer, Heidelberg (2004)

Automated Analog Synthesis with an Estimation of the Distribution Algorithm

Aurora Torres$^{(\boxtimes)}$, María Dolores Torres$^{(\boxtimes)}$, and Eunice Ponce de León

Universidad Autónoma de Aguascalientes, Av. Universidad # 940,
Ciudad Universitaria, 20100 Aguascalientes, AGS, Mexico
{atorres,mdtorres,eponce}@correo.uaa.mx

Abstract. This paper presents a set of evolutionary mechanisms embedded on an estimation of distribution algorithm (MITEDA-AC) that performs the synthesis of an analog low pass filter. Analog circuits are modeled with linked lists in order to represent and evolve both, topology and sizing. The developed representation mechanism ensures that generated circuits be feasible, and in order to reduce the gap between real circuits and those evolvable, the concept of preferred values was included on representation and generation mechanisms. The algorithm interacts with SPICE to performance evaluation of each individual in the population. MITEDA-AC was inspired by the COMIT because like this, it uses bivariate probability distributions to generate the optimal dependency tree, but without local optimizers. Features integrated in the learning mechanism of this evolvable algorithm, were the number of capacitors, resistors and inductors included in each circuit of the population. This paper describes the algorithm and discusses its results.

Keywords: Automated analog circuit synthesis · Estimation of distribution algorithm · Spice simulation · Mutual information · Dependency tree

1 Introduction

Nowadays the use of computational intelligence techniques is becoming very popular for solving real-world problems automatically, and the area of circuit design is not the exception. The increasing complexity of real-world systems, combined with the constraints of time and resources, makes the construction of mixed circuits a very challenging task.

Although the analog part of current electronic devices is usually a small fraction of the entire circuit, it is much more difficult to design, due to the complex and knowledge-intensive nature of analog circuits.

According to Goh and Li, circuit synthesis is the process of designing and constructing a network to provide a prescribed response to a specified excitation [1]. Analog design is also described by Das [2], as traditionally less systematic, and more heuristic and knowledge intensive than the digital one. This task is usually described as two steps process: the selection of a suitable topology and the sizing of all its

© Springer International Publishing AG 2017
O. Pichardo-Lagunas and S. Miranda-Jiménez (Eds.): MICAI 2016, Part II, LNAI 10062, pp. 173–184, 2017.
DOI: 10.1007/978-3-319-62428-0_14

components. While topology consists of the determination of the type of components and its connections; sizing refers to the selection of the components values [3].

Although there are several research that have addressed this problem, analog synthesis has not reached an acceptable level [4].

Among the techniques that have been used for solving this problem, are simulated annealing (SA) [5], genetic algorithms (GA) [6, 7], ant colony optimization (ACO) [8], and even univariate marginal distribution algorithms (UMDA) [9]. Some researchers have proposed to establish a fixed structure and then optimize the values of its elements, however; this approach limits the search space; so the trend is to optimize both topology and dimension.

This paper, presents an algorithm MITEDA-AC, which performs the synthesis of topology and sizing of a classic analog filter, making use of a robust group of mechanisms designed for the evolutionary handling of circuits. They include representation, generation and sampling of electrical networks.

MITEDA-AC was inspired by the work of Baluja [10] because like this, it uses bivariate probability distributions to generate the optimal dependency tree.

Next sections have been organized in the following way; Sect. 2 presents the general approach. In Sect. 3 the algorithm, evolutionary mechanisms and target circuit are described. Section 4 describes the performed experiments, the results and a preliminary comparison of it against a genetic algorithm and a univariate marginal distribution algorithms; conclusions and future work are discussed in Sect. 5.

2   General Approach

The use of evolutionary computation techniques responds to the heuristic nature of circuit synthesis, the huge search space that has to be explored, the high consumption of computing resources and the high level of complexity of this problem.

Evolutionary computation algorithms mimic the biological mechanisms of evolution to approximate global optimal point of a problem. The idea of solving problems based on Darwinian principles, "survival of the fittest" appeared around the sixties, proposed by Holland and his collaborators [11]. The solution to search and optimization problems using evolutionary computation involves the establishment of mechanisms for representing solutions that can be manipulated, generated, evaluated and transformed algorithmically.

In order to integrate all these elements in the analog circuit synthesis, we use the framework proposed in [12], and presented in Fig. 1.

From Fig. 1, it can be seen that to artificially evolve a population, the first step is to generate it. Evolutionary metaheuristics are a group of evolvable algorithms whose goal is to find a good solution (could not be the best) to a complex problem. They have two ways to generate solutions; randomly or guided. For some problems, the way solutions are generated is not very relevant, but in the case of analog circuits, the best way to do it is guided; because of the huge amount of computational resources and time need to fix a non-valid circuit.

One of the most important aspects of solving problems with evolutionary algorithms is how to encode a solution. The representation of a circuit as a chromosome,

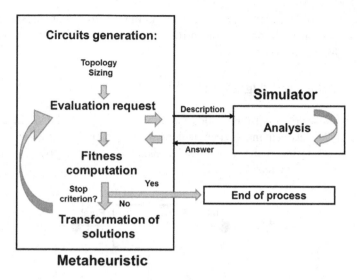

Fig. 1. General framework [12]

directly affects the success or failure of the used metaheuristic. There are two kinds of encoding systems: direct and developmental [13]; ours belongs to the last class, since the genotype leads the construction of the electrical networks.

Some benefits of our proposal are: most circuit are valid, the maximum number of elements in the circuit is a variable parameter, it allows handling both topology and sizing, it is flexible and uses preferred values.

With regard to the fitness computation, checking the operation of a circuit requires careful analysis, physical implementation or simulation. All alternatives are time and resources consuming, but perhaps the most widely used is the simulation. From Fig. 1, it can be seen that metaheuristic makes a request for specific simulation to the simulator, and it returns the analysis results. Subsequently, based on the behavior exhibited by the circuit, it receives an evaluation. The simulator used was SPICE (Simulation Program with Integrated Circuits Emphasis) because this and its variations are the most used simulation tools in this area according to Das and Vemuri [14]. Fitness computation depends on the difference between the expected behavior and the actual circuit. As smaller this difference is, better the circuit score will be.

The stopping criterion of a metaheuristic depends among other things, of knowledge about optimal solution. In the problem we are addressing, we do not know the optimal solution, even could be not one but many solutions to the same design problem; for this reason we chose to use the number of iterations.

Finally, the transformation of solutions (see Fig. 1), refers to the mechanism or group of them, responsible for creating new solutions from those previously obtained and selected. This is a very interesting part of each metaheuristic. In a genetic algorithm for example, it is performed by selection, crossover and mutation, and it is well known that of an adequate implementation of them depends the balance between exploration and exploitation; in the case of estimation of distribution algorithms, this step rely on probability theory. As in genetic algorithms, Estimation of Distribution Algorithms

(EDAs) are based on populations; but they are sampled from a probabilistic graphical model. In the case of UMDAs, the transformation depends on the implementation of selection and the probability vector.

3   The Evolutionary Algorithm

To understand how the algorithm builds circuits, see Fig. 2. All individuals in the population evolve between initial and final nodes. V_s and Rs represent a practical voltage source while R_L is the circuit load resistance. Other important part of this template is the ground node.

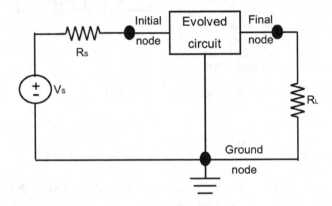

Fig. 2. Circuit template

3.1   Representation Mechanism

Linked lists of genes represent each individual in a population. They store both: circuit topology and its sizing. Figure 3 shows how topology and sizing of each circuit element (gene) are coded. This representation mechanism ensures that electrical networks are feasible.

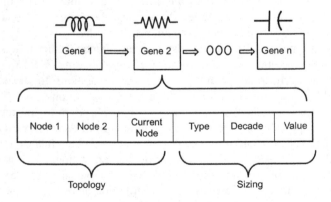

Fig. 3. Representation mechanism.

Considering that passive analog circuits are those constructed using only passive elements (two-terminal electric elements), the representation mechanism (Fig. 3) operates according to the following description. The first three nodes encode the topology; that is, the way the circuit is connected. "Node 1" and "Node 2" are nodes to which each terminal of the current element must be connected. "Current Node" is a pointer whose function is to drive the construction of the circuits. This pointer ensures electrical networks are feasible. On the other hand, "Type" values can vary between zero and two and its meaning is capacitor, resistor and inductor respectively; for "Decade" are considered values from zero to three encoding multipliers ranging from 10^6 to 10^9 for capacitors, from 10^3 to 10^6 for resistance and from 10^{-3} to 10^{-6} for inductors. Finally, "Value" can go from zero to five for capacitors and from zero to eleven for resistors and inductors. These values represent the commercial values of the E6 and E12 series of electronic devices.

Table 1 summarizes the values used in the sizing of a circuit.

Table 1. Sizing encoding system

Type	Decade	Value
C(0)	$10^{-6} - 10^{-9}$ (0–3)	E6 (0–5)
R(1)	$10^{+3} - 10^{+6}$ (0–3)	E12 (0–11)
L(2)	$10^{-3} - 10^{-6}$ (0–3)	E12 (0–11)

3.2 Generation Mechanism

The generation mechanism works by means of a randomly generated operation code. In order to manage the growth of circuits, we used a parameter named growth index. The UMDA-AC also uses a maximum circuit size parameter. When circuits reach this parameter value, the circuit construction ends. During circuit built each instruction connects the actual node pointer to an existed or new node. The operation codes and their meaning are presented in Table 2.

Table 2. The operation code of the generation mechanism

Opcode	Instruction
0	Connect to grown
1	Connect to final node
2	Connect to x node
3	Connect to new node

The first population uses a set of probabilities for each possible connection and the circuit element is selected randomly. From second generation onwards, the likelihood of generating each type of device depends on the optimal dependency tree. This tree is obtained from the mutual information of each pair of variables. Variables x_i, x_j and x_k represent the number of capacitors, resistors and inductors respectively. Each cell in the contingency table represents the likelihood given by the tree according to the next equation:

$$P(X_i, X_j, X_k) = \frac{P(X_i = a, X_j = b)P(X_j = b, X_k = c)}{P(X_j = b)}$$ (1)

Equation 1 represents the likelihood that a circuit has to present "a" capacitors, "b" resistors and "c" inductors; assuming that mutual information was highest between capacitors-resistors and resistors-inductors.

3.3 Low-Pass Filter

A passive low-pass filter is an analog circuit built with resistors, inductors and capacitors, which aim to allow the passage of low frequency signals and attenuate the amplitude of those whose frequency is greater. Figure 4 shows the frequency response of the filter designed by the MITEDA-AC.

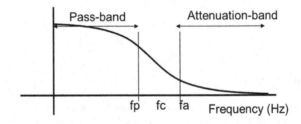

Fig. 4. Frequency response of a low-pass filter

A low-pass filter allows all signals below fc (cutoff frequency) to pass through and blocks those above it. Due to practical filter circuits, deploy variation of amplitude rejection with frequency (at the lowest frequency, the signal passes without effect; but as frequency grows up, the signal is effectively blocked), we left one "don't care band" located between the higher limit of the pass-band (fp) and the lower limit of the attenuation one (fa). The attenuation of the filter is defined in terms of the maximum signal in its pass and attenuation bands.

3.4 The MITEDA-AC Algorithm

The MITEDA_AC algorithm (Mutual Information Tree EDA for Analog Circuits) was inspired by the COMIT (Combining Optimizers With Mutual Information Trees), one of the most recognized algorithms that consider dependencies between pairs of variables created by Baluja and Davies [10]. The implemented system interacts with SPICE in the circuit evaluation and it has embedded the generation and encoding mechanisms previously discussed. The next pseudo code describes the general behavior of the MITEDA_AC.

Algorithm 1. MITEDA_AC pseudo code

```
1. Begin
2.   Do
                a) Generate an individual
                b) Compute fitness
        While (population size is not reached).
3.     Sort Population by fitness
4.     While (stop criterion is not reached) do
                a) Apply elitism to NewPopulation
                b) Select a set of individuals of Popula-
                   tion
                c) Estimated distribution function using
                   the optimal dependency tree
                   pG(x)=p(x|PopulationSE)
                d) While (the size of the population is not
                   reached)
                        • Samples from pG(x) a new member of
                          NewPopulation
                        • Computes its fitness
                   End_While
                e) Order NewPopulation by fitness
                f) Population=NewPopulation
        End_While
5.   End.
```

The above pseudo code outlines the behavior of all estimation of distribution algorithms except for the step 4.c, in which our algorithm calculates the relationship between each pair of variables through mutual information, to identify the optimal dependency tree and then use it to sample new-population individuals. Computation of mutual information between each pair of variables $I(X_i, X_j)$, is performed by the next equation.

$$I(X_i, X_j) = \sum_{a,b} P(X_i = a, X_j = b) * log \frac{P(X_i = a, X_j = b)}{P(X_i = a) * P(X_j = b)} \tag{2}$$

Where Xi and Xj are the variables that describe the circuit in terms of the number of capacitors, resistors and inductors, and "a", "b" are numbers that can take any value between zero and the size of the circuit (L), which represents the limit of elements that a circuit can have. For example in the case of L = 15 the contingency table would have $L^3 = 3375$ cells.

In each iteration, the algorithm calculates mutual information, selects optimal dependency tree and then samples new individuals from it.

3.5   Fitness Function

The low-pass filter problem was extracted from [15] and it is also discussed on [16, 17] thus, the frequency response performance for a candidate filter is similar to those defined by Koza and other researchers. As we mentioned before, the fitness function is a function of the sum of errors between the ideal frequency response and the actual over N sampling points. The normalized version of the fitness function taken from [12] is shown in Eq. 3.

$$F = \frac{1}{1 + \xi} \tag{3}$$

In the above equation ξ represents the total error function between the ideal and the current filter for N frequency points (see Eq. 4).

$$\xi = \sum_{i=1}^{N} \lambda(\varepsilon_i) * \varepsilon_i \tag{4}$$

The sampling points range from 1 Hz to 100 kHz, logarithmically distributed. If the deviation from target magnitude is inacceptable according to the frequency band, then a penalty factor "λ" has to be assigned to error function. In Eq. 4, "ε_i" give us the absolute deviation between the actual output response and the target response over the "i-th" sampling point. In the experiments described in this work λ was fixed in 10.

4   Experiments and Results

As we mentioned in the previous section, the target circuit is a low-pass filter. This filters was selected because of its wide range of possible applications and because it has been used with several approaches like genetic programming, genetic algorithm and estimation of distribution algorithms among others. Figure 5 shows the general target circuit behavior. As reader can see, the designed circuit has to let pass electrical signals which frequency is lower than 1 kHz and it has to block (attenuate) those which frequency is upper than 2 kHz.

Between 1 kHz and 2 kHz, was defined a "don't care" band. In this frequency band, there are not penalties in the fitness calculation. In the pass band, the allowable variation in the voltage magnitude is ±30 mV (ripple voltage) whereas, in the attenuation band, this specification was fixed at ±10 mV.

In order to evaluate the whole system in its best conditions, a factorial experiment was performed. Table 3 presents the used parameters. Each combination of parameters was executed 10 times.

The generation and subsequent circuit simulation involve a high consumption of computing resources. Twenty individuals per population and thirty generations are appropriate values according to the experiments conducted by Torres [3].

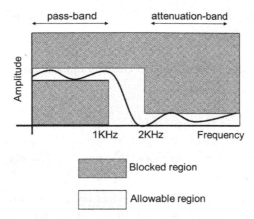

Fig. 5. Specifications of the target circuit

Table 3. Set of parameter-values used on the experiments

Parameter	Tested values
Population size	20
Number of generations	30
Growth index	X, Y, Z
Maximum size	10, 15, 20

Growth index refers to how the likelihood of each possible connection is distributed. The operation code performs the connection according to values shown in Table 4. The type of element that will be connected is randomly selected for the first generation; because as mentioned above, from the second generation onwards it depends on the optimal dependency tree.

Table 4. Growth index values

Growth index		
	Ground	Final	New
X	30%	20%	50%
Y	20%	20%	60%
Z	10%	10%	80%

Maximum size (see Table 3), refers to the maximum number of elements a circuit could have. This parameter is took by the generation mechanism and it forces the circuit termination if its size has reached this value. This parameter can be easily modified to design circuits that are more complex.

To calibrate our system, we took into account the fitness evaluation, the runtime, the size of the designed circuits and the number of circuits that spice was not able to simulate.

Table 5 shows the best results concerning fitness and time as well as the average values of each output variable.

Table 5. Best parameter combinations and results

Input parameters		Obtained results			
Growth	Maximum size	Fitness	Time (s)	Circuit size	Non SPICE simulations
Y	10	3.138×10^{-3}	83.016	2	0.0%
X	15	2.570×10^{-3}	76.469	5	0.18%
Average		2.612×10^{-3}	83.318	2	0.26%

Because data did not follow a normal behavior, a Kruskal-Wallis test was performed. Statistical results suggest that "growth = x" and "maximum size" = 15 are the parameter values that most rebounds on time. With respect to fitness and circuit size, there is not statistical evidence to suggest that results change according to values of input variables. Finally, the number of non-SPICE simulations is affected with the changes of both inputs according to Kruskal-Wallis test (p = 0.001). The combination that produced the least amount of non-SPICE simulated circuits was "growth = x" and "maximum size" = 5.

The percentage of truncation used for the selection of individuals in each population was 50%. We also retain two individuals per generation by elitism.

Once the algorithm was tuned, its performance was compared against a GA and a UMDA reported on [6]; all of them running on the framework described on Sect. 2. This time "growth" and "maximum size" were set in X and 5, respectively and the algorithms executed 200 generations of 50 individuals each. Table 6 shows average results of 10 executions.

Table 6. Empirical comparison results

Algorithm	Fitness	Time (s)	Circuit size	Non SPICE simulations	Fitness evaluations(#)
GA	3.26×10^{-3}	1834.6	4.4	1.59%	10051
UMDA	3.19×10^{-3}	1799.7	4.0	10.35%	9606
MITEDA	2.84×10^{-3}	1386.9	1.6	0.02%	9604

In summary, these results allow us to conclude that MITEDA-AC together with mechanisms that constitute the system described, are very efficient to generate and reproduce SPICE simulate circuits.

5 Conclusions and Future Work

The Kruskal-Wallis test applied to each of the parameters independently, revealed that the differences in the time of execution of the MITEDA-AC are due to the growth factor and that the differences regarding the number of non simulated circuit are consequence of the circuit size factor. When growth takes the value of "X" the time it takes to perform the evolutionary process is lower and when maximum size has a value of 5, the algorithm produces the least amount of circuits that will not be simulated. On the other hand, the presented framework demonstrated strength and flexibility; since it worked well with three different metaheuristics. Learning the structure that best represents the probabilistic model by using mutual information proved to be efficient in the problem of analog circuit design. Especially generating simulated circuits and minimizing the number of evaluations of the objective function.

Although the MITEDA-AC induces the tree structure that best fits the data in each iteration of the algorithm, tests suggests so far that MITEDA-AC is the fastest among the three compared algorithms. Besides, although apparently MITEDA-AC exhibits the lowest fitness of the three algorithms, the generated circuits are very good.

As future work, we intend to study the interaction of other characteristics of the circuits in addition to the number of elements of each type.

References

1. Goh, C., Li, Y.: GA automated design and synthesis of analog circuits with practical constraints. In: vol. 1, pp. 170–177 (2001)
2. Das, A.: Algorithms for topology synthesis of analog circuits. Ph.D. Electrical Engineering, University of Cincinnati, Ann Arbor, 304670077 (2008)
3. Soto, A.T., de León Sentí, E.E.P., Aguirre, A.H., Soto, M.D.T., Díaz, E.D.: A robust evolvable system for the synthesis of analog circuits. Computación y Sistemas 13(4), 409–421 (2010)
4. Meissner, M., Hedrich, L.: FEATS: framework for explorative analog topology synthesis. IEEE Trans. Comput.-Aided Des. Integr. Circ. Syst. 34(2), 213–226 (2015)
5. Krasnicki, M.J., Phelps, R., Hellums, J.R., McClung, M., Rutenbar, R.A., Carley, L.R.: ASF: a practical simulation-based methodology for the synthesis of custom analog circuits. In: pp. 350–357 (2001)
6. Torres, A., Ponce, E.E., Torres, M.D., Díaz, E., Padilla, F.: Comparison of two evolvable systems in the automated analog circuit synthesis. In: pp. 3–8 (2009)
7. Khalifa, Y.M.A., Khan, B.K., Taha, F.: Multi-objective optimization tool for a free structure analog circuits design using genetic algorithms and incorporating parasitics. In: Bosman, P.A.N., Yu, T., Ek, Rt, A. (eds.) GECCO 2007, pp. 2527–2534. ACM, (2007)
8. Zhong, J., Zhang, J.: A robust estimation of distribution algorithm for power electronic circuits design. In: Pelikan, M., Branke, J. (eds.) GECCO 2010, pp. 319–326. ACM (2010)
9. Zinchenko, L., Radecker, M., Bisogno, F.: Multi-objective univariate marginal distribution optimisation of mixed analogue-digital signal circuits. In: Lipson, H. (ed.) GECCO 2007, pp. 2242–2251. ACM (2007)
10. Baluja, S., Davies, S.: Combining multiple optimization runs with optimal dependency trees. DTIC Document (1997)
11. Goldberg, D.: Genetic Algorithms in Search, Optimization, and Machine Learning. Addison-Wesley Professional, Boston (1989)
12. Torres Soto, A.: Metaheurísticas evolutivas en el diseño de circuitos analógicos. Tesis (doctorado en ciencias de la computación) – Universidad Autónoma de Aguascalientes. Centro de Ciencias Básicas, Aguascalientes, Ags., Mexico (2010)

13. Mattiussi, C., Floreano, D.: Analog genetic encoding for the evolution of circuits and networks. IEEE Trans. Evol. Comput. **11**(5), 596–607 (2007)
14. Das, A., Vemuri, R.: An automated passive analog circuit synthesis framework using genetic algorithms. In: pp. 145–152 (2007)
15. Koza, J.R., Bennett, F.H., Andre, D., Keane, M.A., Dunlap, F.: Automated synthesis of analog electrical circuits by means of genetic programming. IEEE Trans. Evol. Comput. **1** (2), 109–128 (1997)
16. Hilder, J.A., Tyrrell, A.M.: An evolutionary platform for developing next-generation electronic circuits. Presented at the GECCO 2007 Proceedings of the 9th Annual Conference Companion on Genetic and Evolutionary Computation, London, United Kingdom (2007)
17. Hu, J., Zhong, X., Goodman, E.D.: Open-ended robust design of analog filters using genetic programming. Presented at the 7th Annual Conference on Genetic and Evolutionary Computation, Washington DC, USA (2005)

Mathematical Model of Glucose Metabolism by Symbolic Regression α β

Luis M. Torres-Treviño[✉]

CIIDIT-FIME, Universidad Autónoma de Nuevo León,
San Nicolás de los Garza, Mexico
luis.torres.ciidit@gmail.com

Abstract. A mathematical model of glucose process is generated using symbolic regression. Considering a record of data of glucose and insulin of a patient with type II diabetes, a data driven model is generated. Neural networks are black boxes and symbolic regression can generate equations that express explicit a relationship between input variables with respect to the output response. This model is a personalized version of the metabolism of the patient and different treatments can be considered using this model.

Keywords: Symbolic regression · Glucose metabolism systems · Modeling processes

1 Introduction

Diabetes mellitus type II has been considered a pandemia in several countries inclusive Mexico, some cases requires the pump of insulin depending of sensing of blood glucose. This procedure can be made automatically using different devices; however, calculation of insulin pump is made usually by trial and error and could take months to be determined properly. Modeling of glucose metabolism is a hard task because involves approximate functions using only information extracted from the process. Considering the complexity of the metabolism, linear regression can not be used because non linear relationship and correlation between variables is strong. Neural networks can be used for this purpose, but they are black boxes making unreadable any interpretation that can be made of the relationship between input and output variables. Symbolic regression has the best of two words because it can generate explicit equations (the are not black boxes) and has a good adjustment with real data.

There is an interest in the generation of personal mathematical models of patients to schedule a plan for insulin pump trying to reduce side effects due the excess or scarce of insulin. This mathematical model can be useful for a self management of insulin pump. Mathematical models of glucose metabolism has been study intensively in recent decades [1]. These models are useful to

© Springer International Publishing AG 2017
O. Pichardo-Lagunas and S. Miranda-Jiménez (Eds.): MICAI 2016, Part II, LNAI 10062, pp. 185–190, 2017.
DOI: 10.1007/978-3-319-62428-0_15

understand the glucose metabolism and disease. This work is focus in generation a mathematical model that provides predictions considerings actual conditions of blood glucose and an insulin dose.

A complex model can represent several aspects and interactions of glucose metabolism process; however, requires the setting of several parameters, making difficult for identification [2,4,5]. On the other hand, a simple model has the advantage that can be used easily because has a small number of identifiable parameters but its responses must be taken with care because a very simple model could be inappropriate.

2   Modeling Glucose Metabolism System

Prediction of blood glucose can be made using a relationship between insulin pumped and actual and delayed states of blood glucose. Architecture proposed is shown in Fig. 1.

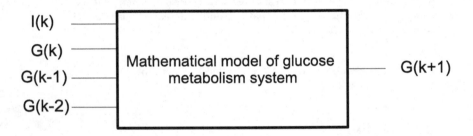

Fig. 1. Architecture proposed for modeling glucose metabolism system.

2.1   Symbolic Regression Alpha Beta

In place of propose a mathematical model, an evolutionary algorithm is used to determines the most suitable models and parameters to fit the performance of the proposed model with experimental data. Selection of variables are made automatically and some variables can be eliminated from the model to generate models with low complexity and low error. Symbolic regression α β uses a combination of unary and binary functions (α and *beta* operations respectively). Every functions is represented as an integer and depending of this number a specific operation is executed. Table 1 shows the functions used for alpha operators [6].

An alpha operator is defined in Eq. 1, otherwise, β operator has four basic arithmetics operations that requires two arguments 2.

$$Opr_\alpha(x, k_1, k_2) = \alpha(k_1 * x + k_2) \tag{1}$$

$$Opr_\beta(x_1, x_2) = \beta(x_1, x_2) \tag{2}$$

A model is represented considering a fixed structure or configuration determined by the number of alpha operators used per input variables, beta operators

Table 1. α operator parameters and its related unary functions.

α operator	Mathematical operation
1	$(k_1x + k_2)$
2	$(k_1x + k_2)^2$
3	$(k_1x + k_2)^3$
4	$(k_1x + k_2)^{-1}$
5	$(k_1x + k_2)^{-2}$
6	$(k_1x + k_2)^{-3}$
7	$(k_1x + k_2)^{1/2}$
8	$(k_1x + k_2)^{1/3}$
9	$\exp(k1x + k_2)$
10	$\log(k1x + k_2)$
11	$\sin(k1x + k_2)$
12	$\cos(k1x + k_2)$
13	$\tan(k1x + k_2)$

are used to connect alpha operators. A basic configuration uses only one α operator per input variable (3) but in this work a configuration with three alpha operators per input variable is used. Connectivity is established using a binary vector B that connects every alpha operator. If a variable with its respectively alpha operator is not required, then connectivity has a zero value.

$$y = \beta_{n-1}(\ldots\beta_2(\beta_1(B_1\alpha_1(x_1), B_2\alpha_2(x_2)),)),\ldots B_n\alpha_n(x_n)) \qquad (3)$$

2.2 Evolutionary Algorithm Evonorm

Evonorm is an easy implementation of estimation of distribution algorithm that includes an heuristic for implicit elitism to improve exploration and exploitation capabilities of the algorithm. A population of solutions are evaluated, then they are deterministically selected, then crossover and mutation are substituted by an estimation of parameters of a normal distribution function (Eqs. 4 and 5). Then a new population is generated where 50% of times uses the best found individuals and the other 50% is used the calculated mean 6.

$$\mu_{pr} = \sum_{k=1}^{I_s}(Ps_{pr,k})/I_s \qquad (4)$$

$$\sigma_{pr} = \sqrt{(\sum_{k=1}^{I_s}(Ps_{pr,k} - \mu_{pr})^2)/I_s} \qquad (5)$$

where $pr = 1..D_r$

$$P_{i,pr} = \begin{cases} N(\mu_{pr}, \sigma_{pr}) & U() > 0.5 \\ N(Ix_{pr}, \sigma_{pr}) & otherwise \end{cases} \qquad (6)$$

where random variable $U()$ has a uniform distribution function, $N()$ is a random variable with a normal distribution function.

2.3   Validation of Models

Models are validated using residual analysis involving new experimental data. A 80% percentage of experimental data was used to build the mathematical model, the rest was used for validation. Mean square error is the principal indicator used for validation calculated as shown in Eq. 9, it is expected a minimization of this indicator. PRESS is calculated by Eq. 7, R^2_{prec} is calculated by Eq. 8 [3].

$$PRESS = \sum_{i=1}^{n}(y(i) - \hat{y}(i))^2 \tag{7}$$

$$R^2_{prec} = 1 - \frac{\sum_{i=1}^{n}(y(i) - \hat{y}(i))}{y(i)^2 - (\sum_{i=1}^{n} y(i))^2} \tag{8}$$

3   Experimentation

A set of experimental data was extracted from a continuous glucose monitoring and continuous subcutaneous insulin infusion under medical advice. A female patient of 31 years old, 1.58 m, 55 kg, 22.2 Body Mass Index and 23 years since type 1 diabetes mellitus diagnosis. By private health institution in San Luis Potosí, México. A record of blood glucose and insulin pumped is taken every five minutes. Evaluation of every individual is made decoding the representation vector of 48 elements to establish an mathematical equation $\hat{y}$ that could fit to a specific set of data.

$$MSE = E_k = \sqrt{(\sum_{d=1}^{D}(y_d - \hat{y}(x_d))^2/D)} \tag{9}$$

where k is an individual of the population, D is total records of experimental data and x_d are inputs and y_d are outputs extracted from every record d of experimental data. The configuration model is shown in 10 and 11.

$$
\begin{aligned}
r_1 &= B_1\alpha_1(I(k), k_{11}, k_{21}) \\
r_2 &= B_2\alpha_2(I(k), k_{12}, k_{22}) \\
r_3 &= B_3\alpha_3(I(k), k_{13}, k_{23}) \\
r_4 &= B_4\alpha_4(G(k), k_{14}, k_{24}) \\
r_5 &= B_5\alpha_5(G(k), k_{15}, k_{25}) \\
r_6 &= B_6\alpha_6(G(k), k_{16}, k_{26}) \\
r_7 &= B_7\alpha_7(G(k-1), k_{17}, k_{27}) \\
r_8 &= B_8\alpha_8(G(k-1), k_{18}, k_{28}) \\
r_9 &= B_9\alpha_9(G(k-1), k_{19}, k_{29}) \\
r_{10} &= B_{10}\alpha_10(G(k-2), k_{110}, k_{210}) \\
r_{11} &= B_{11}\alpha_11(G(k-2), k_{111}, k_{211}) \\
r_{12} &= B_{12}\alpha_12(G(k-2), k_{112}, k_{212})
\end{aligned}
\tag{10}
$$

$$G(k+1) = \beta_{11}(\beta_{10}(\beta_9(\beta_8(\beta_7(\beta_6(\beta_5(\beta_4(\beta_3(\beta_2(\beta_1(r_1, r_2) \\ , r_3), r_4), r_5), r_6), r_7), r_8), r_9), r_{10}), r_{11}), r_{12}) \tag{11}$$

A percentage of 20% are selected from the population to estimate normal distribution function parameters. Representation vector has a size of 48 elements considering the number of alpha operators, beta operators, k's parameters and connectivity. A population of 100 individuals are used during 100 generations.

4 Results

Several models can be generated both satisfying criteria of minimum error and low complexity. In ten runs, the model of Eq. 12 was selected which statistics for validation msres is 0.0024578, PRESS is 0.4915608, and R2pred is 0.9865163.

Figure 2 show performance of the model considering 200 new records.

$$\begin{aligned} G(k+1) &= y(I(k), G(k), G(k-1), G(k-2))) \\ &= (((((((0.5279429I(k) + 0.503934)^3 - sin(0.2178475G(k) + 0.8269915)) \\ &\quad -(0.9998281G(k) + 0.5531444)^{-1}) + (0.5059958G(k-1) + 0.5806388)^2) \\ &\quad -(0.9998283G(k-1) + 0.8625242)^{-3}) + tanh(0.5716669G(k-2) \\ &\quad +0.5545745)) \end{aligned} \tag{12}$$

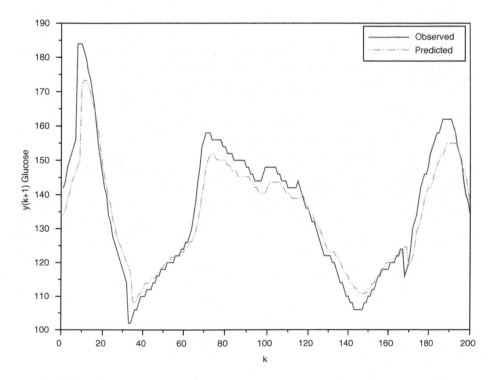

Fig. 2. Performance of the model to predict the following 200 records of blood glucose.

5   Conclusion

Generation of a mathematical model of this process is a complex task, evolutionary computation generate several alternatives, some of them consider elimination of insulin variable but thats no possible because it is necessary to generate models that includes Insulin for planning treatments for the patient. The model is personal for patient, so results according to the statistic are valid only for the actual patient and under conditions. More must be developed for validation and to consider Type 2 diabetes mellitus patients but this is part of a future work.

Acknowledgments. I thank to Griselda Quiroz from Universidad Autónoma de Nuevo León, and Instituto Potosino de Investigaciones Científicas y Tecnológicas (IPICYT) a by its contribution and experimental data provided for this paper.

References

1. Boutayeb, A., Chetouani, A.: A critical review of mathematical models and data used in diabetology. BioMed. Eng. OnLine **5**, 43 (2006). Singh, P.K., ed. PLoS ONE
2. Chauhan, A., Weiss, H., Koch, F., et al.: Dissecting long-term glucose metabolism identifies new susceptibility period for metabolic dysfunction in aged mice. BioMed. Eng. OnLine **10**, e0140858 (2015). Singh, P.K., ed. PLoS ONE
3. Montgomery, D.C., Peck, E.A., Vining, G.G.: Introduction to Linear Regression Analysis. Wiley, Hoboken (2012)
4. Liu, S.W., Huang, H.P., Lin, C.H., Chien, I.L.: Modified control algorithms for patients with type 1 diabetes mellitus undergoing exercise. J. Taiwan Inst. Chem. Eng. **45**(5), 2081–2095 (2014). http://www.sciencedirect.com/science/article/pii/S1876107014001795
5. Lunze, K., Woitok, A., Walter, M., Brendel, M.D., Afify, M., Tolba, R., Leonhardt, S.: Analysis and modelling of glucose metabolism in diabetic gottingen minipigs. Biomed. Signal Process. Control **13**, 132–141 (2014). http://www.sciencedirect.com/science/article/pii/S1746809414000603
6. Torres-Treviño, L.M.: Identification and prediction using symbolic regression alpha-beta: preliminary results. In: Proceedings of the Companion Publication of the 2014 Annual Conference on Genetic and Evolutionary Computation, GECCO Comp 2014, pp. 1367–1372. ACM, New York (2014). http://doi.acm.org/10.1145/2598394.2609859

Machine Learning

Jensen Inequality with Subdifferential for Sugeno Integral

Anikó Szakál[1,2,3,4]([✉]), Endre Pap[1,2,3,4], Sadegh Abbaszadeh[1,2,3,4],
and Madjid Eshaghi Gordji[5]

[1] Óbuda University, Becsi út 96/B, Budapest H-1034, Hungary
szakal@uni-obuda.hu
[2] Singidunum University, Danijelova 29, 11000 Belgrade, Serbia
epap@singidunum.ac.rs
[3] Department of Mathematics, Faculty of Mathematics,
Statistics and Computer Sciences, Semnan University, 35195-363 Semnan, Iran
abbaszadeh@semnan.ac.ir
[4] Intelligent Systems and Perception Recognition Laboratory,
CS Group of Mathematics Department, Shahid Beheshti University, Tehran, Iran
[5] Institute for Cognitive and Brain Science, Shahid Beheshti University, Tehran, Iran
meshaghi@semnan.ac.ir

Abstract. The classical Jensen inequality for concave function φ is adapted for the Sugeno integral using the notion of the subdifferential. Some examples in the framework of the Lebesgue measure to illustrate the results are presented.

Keywords: Sugeno integral · The Jensen inequality · Concave function · Supergradient · Superdifferential

1 Introduction

One of the basic operation in the science is the aggregation function, which combines several numerical values into a single one. We mention only few disciplines (see [12]), such as image processing [33], pattern recognition [32] and decision making [17,18]. To obtain a consensus quantifiable judgment, some synthesizing functions have been proposed. For obtaining a representation of interaction between criteria, fuzzy measures and fuzzy integrals have been introduced [34]. Two basic fuzzy integrals are Choquet and Sugeno integrals, which are idempotent, continuous and monotone operators. The properties and applications of the fuzzy measures and fuzzy integrals have been studied by many authors, see [14]. It was introduced a general integral covering previous two, see [15]. Among many applications of the Sugeno integral we shall mention only few. Chen *et al.* [9] proposed a fusion recognition scheme based on nonlinear decision fusion, Seyedzadeh *et al.* [31] presented a new RGB color image encryption using keystream generator, Zhang and Zheng [37] generalized Ying's model of linguistic quantifiers, Nemmour and Chibani [19] proposed a new support vector

© Springer International Publishing AG 2017
O. Pichardo-Lagunas and S. Miranda-Jiménez (Eds.): MICAI 2016, Part II, LNAI 10062, pp. 193–199, 2017.
DOI: 10.1007/978-3-319-62428-0_16

mixture, used to evaluate the interaction of scale factors and to compare the energy performance of buildings in different scale factors [16]. Wang and Klir [35] and Pap [20] have given a general overview on fuzzy measures and fuzzy integration theory. Very recently, many researchers have studied the most well-known integral inequalities for Sugeno integral, see [21]. The authors in the papers [1,2] obtained some Hadamard integral inequalities for Sugeno integral. Agahi *et al.* [4–6] proved general Minkowski type inequalities, general extensions of Chebyshev type inequalities and general Barnes-Godunova-Levin type inequalities for Sugeno integrals. Caballero and Sadarangani [7,8] proved Chebyshev type inequalities and Cauchy-Schwarz type inequalities for Sugeno integral. Kaluszka *et al.* [13] gave the necessary and sufficient conditions guaranteeing the validity of Chebyshev type inequalities for the generalized Sugeno integral in the case of functions belonging to a much wider class than the comonotone functions. Wu *et al.* [36] proved two inequalities for the Sugeno integral on abstract spaces generalizing all previous Chebyshev's inequalities. Flores-Franulič *et al.* [11] studied some fuzzy Markov type inequalities. Román-Flores *et al.* [10], [26–29] investigated the level-continuity of Sugeno integral. The classical Jensen's inequality (see [30]) is the following mathematical property of convex functions

$$\varphi\left(\int f(x)\,\mathrm{d}\lambda\right) \leqslant \int \varphi(f)\,\mathrm{d}\lambda, \tag{1}$$

where f is λ-measurable and $\varphi : [0,\infty[\longrightarrow [0,\infty[$ is a convex function. The above inequality should be reversed if φ is concave, i.e.,

$$\varphi\left(\int f(x)\,\mathrm{d}\lambda\right) \geqslant \int \varphi(f)\,\mathrm{d}\lambda, \tag{2}$$

where λ is the Lebesgue measure. Most of the integral inequalities obtained for the Sugeno integral are under conditions such as monotonicity or comonotonicity. The main purpose of this paper is to consider the Jensen-type inequalities for Sugeno integral under the condition of convexity (concavity).

The paper is organized as follows: Some necessary preliminaries are given in Sect. 2. In Sect. 3 new Jensen-type inequalities for Sugeno integral with the notion of the subdifferential are obtained and some examples are given. For the proofs an further results see [3]. A conclusion is given in Sect. 4.

2 Preliminaries

Let X be a non-empty set and $\mathcal{A}$ be a σ-algebra of subsets of X.

Definition 1. *A set function $\mu\colon \mathcal{A} \to [0,\infty]$ is called fuzzy measure if it satisfies*

1. *$\mu(\emptyset) = 0$;*
2. *$E, F \in \mathcal{A}$ and $E \subset F$ imply $\mu(E) \leqslant \mu(F)$;*
3. *$E_n \in \mathcal{A}$ $(n \in \mathbb{N})$, $E_1 \subset E_2 \subset \ldots$, imply $\lim_{n\to\infty} \mu(E_n) = \mu(\bigcup_{n=1}^{\infty} E_n)$;*

4. $E_n \in \mathcal{A}$ $(n \in \mathbb{N})$, $E_1 \supset E_2 \supset \ldots$, $\mu(E_1) < \infty$, imply $\lim_{n \to \infty} \mu(E_n) = \mu(\bigcap_{n=1}^{\infty} E_n)$.

The triple $(X, \mathcal{A}, \mu)$ is called a fuzzy measure space.

Let f be a non-negative real-valued function defined on X. We denote by

$$L_\alpha f = \{x \in X \mid f(x) \geqslant \alpha\} = \{f \geqslant \alpha\}$$

the α-level of f, for $\alpha > 0$. Note that if $\alpha \leqslant \beta$ then $L_\beta f \subset L_\alpha f$. We introduce the following notation

$$\mathcal{F}^\mu(X) = \{f : X \to [0, \infty] \mid f \text{ is } \mu\text{-measurable}\}.$$

Definition 2 *(Sugeno [34]). Let $(X, \mathcal{A}, \mu)$ be a fuzzy measure space, $f \in \mathcal{F}^\mu(X)$ and $A \in \mathcal{A}$, then the Sugeno integral of f on A with respect to the fuzzy measure μ is given by*

$$(S) \int_A f \, \mathrm{d}\mu = \bigvee_{\alpha \geqslant 0} \left(\alpha \wedge \mu(A \cap L_\alpha f) \right),$$

where $\vee$ and $\wedge$ denote the operations sup and inf on $[0, \infty[$, respectively.

The following properties of the Sugeno integral are well-known, see [20, 35]. Let $(X, \mathcal{A}, \mu)$ be a fuzzy measure space, $A, B \in \mathcal{A}$ and $f, g \in \mathcal{F}^\mu(X)$ then

(i) $(S) \int_A f \, \mathrm{d}\mu \leqslant \mu(A)$;
(ii) $(S) \int_A k \, \mathrm{d}\mu = k \wedge \mu(A)$, k non-negative constant;
(iii) If $f \leqslant g$ on A, then $(S) \int_A f \, \mathrm{d}\mu \leqslant (S) \int_A g \, \mathrm{d}\mu$;
(iv) If $A \subset B$, then $(S) \int_A f \, \mathrm{d}\mu \leqslant (S) \int_B f \, \mathrm{d}\mu$;
(v) $\mu(A \cap L_\alpha f) \leqslant \alpha \Rightarrow (S) \int_A f \, \mathrm{d}\mu \leqslant \alpha$;
(vi) If $\mu(A) < \infty$, then $\mu(A \cap L_\alpha f) \geqslant \alpha \Leftrightarrow (S) \int_A f \, \mathrm{d}\mu \geqslant \alpha$.

3   General Jensen Inequality for Sugeno Integral

With the aim to obtain a Jensen-type inequality for the Sugeno integral, it is clear that the classical conditions must be changed (see [22]). In this direction, and in connection with the order structure in $\mathbb{R}^+$, Román-Flores *et al.* [28] have replaced the convexity (concavity) condition of φ in (1) by a monotonic condition, obtaining the following new Jensen-type inequality in the context of Sugeno integral.

Theorem 1. *Let $(X, \mathcal{A}, \mu)$ be a fuzzy measure space and let $f \in \mathcal{F}^\mu(X)$ be such that $(S) \int f \, \mathrm{d}\mu = p$. If $\varphi \colon [0, \infty[\to [0, \infty[$ is a strictly increasing function such that $\varphi(x) \leqslant x$, for every $x \in [0, p]$, then*

$$\varphi\left((S) \int f(x) \, \mathrm{d}\mu \right) \leqslant (S) \int \varphi(f) \, \mathrm{d}\mu.$$

We shall prove Jensen type inequalities for Sugeno integral of concave and convex functions. Before that we shall need some notions.

To simplify the calculation of the Sugeno integral, for a given $f \in \mathcal{F}^\mu(X)$ and $A \in \mathcal{A}$ we define

$$\Gamma = \{\alpha \mid \alpha \geqslant 0, \mu(A \cap L_\alpha f) > \mu(A \cap L_\beta f) \text{ for } \beta > \alpha\}.$$

Then we have

$$(S) \int_A f \, d\mu = \bigvee_{\alpha \in \Gamma} (\alpha \wedge \mu(A \cap L_\alpha f)).$$

The following example shows that the classical Jensen inequality (2) can not be simply transferred for Sugeno integral.

Example 1. Let λ be the classical Lebesgue measure on $\mathbb{R}$. The function f: $[0,1] \to [0,\infty[$ is given by $f(x) = x^2$, and consider the non-negative and concave function $\varphi(x) = \sqrt{x}/2$. We easily obtain

$$(S) \int_{[0,1]} f \, d\lambda = \bigvee_{0 \leqslant \alpha < 1} (\alpha \wedge (1 - \sqrt{\alpha})) = \frac{3 - \sqrt{5}}{2}$$

and

$$(S) \int_{[0,1]} \varphi(f) \, d\lambda = \bigvee_{0 \leqslant \alpha < 1/2} (\alpha \wedge (1 - 2\alpha)) = 1/3.$$

On the other side we have

$$\varphi \left((S) \int f \, d\lambda \right) = \sqrt{\left(\frac{3 - \sqrt{5}}{2} \right)} \Big/ 2 \approx 0.309.$$

Therefore the inequality (2) is not satisfied by the Sugeno integral.

To obtain a Jensen type inequality for a concave function we shall need the notion of supergradient of a function, see [25].

Definition 3. *A function $f: [a,b] \to \mathbb{R}$ has a supergradient m, $f'_-(x_0) \leqslant m \leqslant f'_+(x_0)$, at $x_0 \in [a,b]$ if*

$$f(x) \leqslant f(x_0) + m(x - x_0) \tag{3}$$

for all $x \in [a,b]$, where $f'_+(x_0)$ and $f'_-(x_0)$ are respectively the right and left derivatives of f at x_0.

A function $f: [a,b] \to \mathbb{R}$ has a subgradient m $(f'_-(x_0) \leqslant m \leqslant f'_+(x_0))$ at $x_0 \in [a,b]$ if

$$f(x) \geqslant f(x_0) + m(x - x_0)$$

for all $x \in [a,b]$.

The set of all supergradient (subgradient) of f at x_0 is called the superdifferential (subdifferential) of f at x_0 and is denoted by $\partial f(x_0)$, i.e.,

$$\partial f(x_0) = \{m \in \mathbb{R} \mid f'_-(x_0) \leqslant m \leqslant f'_+(x_0)\}.$$

The following theorem gives a characterization of the differentiability by sub-differential, see [25].

Theorem 2. *Let $f \colon \,]a, b[\subseteq \mathbb{R} \to \mathbb{R}$ be a concave (convex) function. Then f is differentiable at x_0 if and only if $f'(x_0)$ is the unique supergradient (subgradient) of f at x_0.*

Now, we shall give a new Jensen integral inequality for Sugeno integral based on the notion of supergradient of functions (for the proof see [3]).

Theorem 3. *Let $(X, \mathcal{A}, \mu)$ be a fuzzy measure space, $A \subseteq X$ and let $f \in \mathcal{F}^\mu(A)$ be such that $f(A) = [a, b]$ and $p = (S) \int_A f \, d\mu$. If $\varphi : [0, \infty[\to [0, \infty[$ is a concave function, then*

$$(S) \int_A \varphi(f) \, d\mu \leqslant \begin{cases} \bigvee_{\psi(a) \leqslant \alpha < \psi(b)} \left(\alpha \wedge \right. \\ \quad \left. \mu \left(\left\{ x \mid f(x) \geqslant \frac{\alpha - \varphi(p)}{m} + p \right\} \right) \right), \ m > 0, \\ \\ \mu(A) \wedge \varphi(p), \hspace{2cm} m = 0, \\ \\ \bigvee_{\psi(b) \leqslant \alpha < \psi(a)} \left(\alpha \wedge \right. \\ \quad \left. \mu \left(\left\{ x \mid f(x) \leqslant \frac{\alpha - \varphi(p)}{m} + p \right\} \right) \right), \ m < 0, \end{cases}$$

where $m \in \partial\varphi(p)$ and $\psi(t) = \varphi(p) + m(t - p)$.

In a special case, when μ is the Lebesgue measure λ, we obtain the following result.

Corollary 1. *Let $\mathcal{B}$ be the Borel field and λ be the Lebesgue measure on $\mathbb{R}$. Let $A \in \mathcal{B}$ and $f \in \mathcal{F}^\lambda(A)$ be such that $f(A) = [a, b]$ and $p = (S) \int_A f \, d\lambda$. If $\varphi : [0, \infty[\to [0, \infty[$ is a concave function and $m \in \partial\varphi(p)$, then*

$$(S) \int_A \varphi(f) \, d\lambda \leqslant \begin{cases} \frac{m}{m+1}(b - p) + \frac{1}{m+1}\varphi(p), \ m > 0, \\ \\ \mu(A) \wedge \varphi(p), \hspace{1.5cm} m = 0, \\ \\ \frac{m}{m-1}(p - a) - \frac{1}{m-1}\varphi(p), \ m < 0. \end{cases}$$

Example 2. Let $\mathcal{B}$ be the Borel field and λ be the Lebesgue measure on $\mathbb{R}$. We take the concave function $\varphi(x) = \arctan(x)$ on $[0, \infty[$ and λ-measurable function $f(x) = \tan(x)$ on $[0, 1]$. We have $[a, b] = f([0, 1]) = [\tan(0), \tan(1)]$ and

$$(S) \int_{[0,1]} f \, d\lambda = \bigvee_{0 \leqslant \alpha < \tan(1)} (\alpha \wedge (1 - \arctan\alpha)) \approx 0.520.$$

By Theorem 2, we obtain $m = \varphi'(p) \approx 0.787 > 0$. It is obvious that $\psi(t) = \varphi(p) + m(t - p)$ is the only support function of φ at p. We have

$$(S) \int_{[0,1]} \varphi(f) \, d\lambda = \bigvee_{0 \leqslant \alpha < 1} (\alpha \wedge (1 - \alpha)) = 1/2.$$

Thus

$$0.500 = (S) \int_{[0,1]} \varphi(f) \, d\lambda \leqslant \frac{m}{m+1}(b-p) + \frac{1}{m+1}\varphi(p) \approx 0.777.$$

4   Conclusion

The importance of Sugeno integral toward applications is in its capability to express the possible interaction among single parts of a universe in a global representation of a function by means of a single value. This phenomenon cannot be captured by the standard Lebesgue integral. The classical Jensen inequality is one of the basic results for concave (convex) functions. In this paper, the Jensen type inequality for Sugeno integral is extended to the concept of concavity (convexity). There are numerous applications of Sugeno integral, and thus the study of Jensen-type and similar inequalities for the Sugeno integral is an important and interesting topic for the further research.

Acknowledgement. This research for the second author was supported by the grant MNPRS174009.

References

1. Abbaszadeh, S., Eshaghi, M., de la Sen, M.: The Sugeno fuzzy integral of log-convex functions. J. Inequal. Appl. **2015**(1), 1–12 (2015)
2. Abbaszadeh, S., Eshaghi, M.: A Hadamard type inequality for fuzzy integrals based on r-convex functions. Soft. Comput. **20**(8), 3117–3124 (2016)
3. Abbaszadeh, S., Eshaghi, M., Pap, E., Szakál, A.: Jensen-type inequalities for Sugeno integral. Inf. Sci. (submitted)
4. Agahi, H., Mesiar, R., Ouyang, Y.: General Minkowski type inequalities for Sugeno integrals. Fuzzy Sets Syst. **161**, 708–715 (2010)
5. Agahi, H., Mesiar, R., Ouyang, Y., Pap, E., Štrboja, M.: General Chebyshev type inequalities for universal integral. Inf. Sci. **187**, 171–178 (2012)
6. Agahi, H., Román-Flores, H., Flores-Franulič, A.: General Barnes-Godunova-Levin type inequalities for Sugeno integral. Inf. Sci. **181**, 1072–1079 (2011)
7. Caballero, J., Sadarangani, K.: A Cauchy-Schwarz type inequality for fuzzy integrals. Nonlinear Anal. **73**, 3329–3335 (2010)
8. Caballero, J., Sadarangani, K.: Chebyshev inequality for Sugeno integrals. Fuzzy Sets Syst. **161**, 1480–1487 (2010)
9. Chen, X., Jing, Z., Xiao, G.: Nonlinear fusion for face recognition using fuzzy integral. Commun. Nonlinear Sci. Numer. Simul. **12**, 823–831 (2007)
10. Flores-Franulič, A., Román-Flores, H.: A Chebyshev type inequality for fuzzy integrals. Appl. Math. Comput. **190**, 1178–1184 (2007)
11. Flores-Franulič, A., Román-Flores, H., Chalco-Cano, Y.: Markov type inequalities for fuzzy integrals. Appl. Math. Comput. **207**, 242–247 (2009)
12. Grabisch, M., Marichal, J.L., Mesiar, R., Pap, E.: Aggregation Functions. Encyclopedia of Mathematics and Its Applications, vol. 127. Cambridge University Press, Cambridge (2009)
13. Kaluszka, M., Okolewski, A., Boczek, M.: On Chebyshev type inequalities for generalized Sugeno integrals. Fuzzy Sets Syst. **244**, 51–62 (2014)

14. Klement, E.P., Li, J., Mesiar, R., Pap, E.: Integrals based on monotone set functions. Fuzzy Sets Syst. **281**, 88–102 (2015)
15. Klement, E.P., Mesiar, R., Pap, E.: A universal integral as common frame for Choquet and Sugeno integral. IEEE Trans. Fuzzy Syst. **18**(1), 178–187 (2010)
16. Lee, W.-S.: Evaluating and ranking energy performance of office buildings using fuzzy measure and fuzzy integral. Energy Convers. Manag. **51**, 197–203 (2010)
17. Merigó, J.M., Casanovas, M.: Decision-making with distance measures and induced aggregation operators. Comput. Ind. Eng. **60**, 66–76 (2011)
18. Merigó, J.M., Casanovas, M.: Induced aggregation operators in the Euclidean distance and its application in financial decision making. Expert Syst. Appl. **38**, 7603–7608 (2011)
19. Nemmour, H., Chibani, Y.: Fuzzy integral to speed up support vector machines training for pattern classification. Int. J. Knowl.-Based Intell. Eng. Syst. **14**, 127–138 (2010)
20. Pap, E.: Null-Additive Set Functions. Mathematics and Its Applications, vol. 337. Kluwer Academic Publishers, Dordrecht (1995)
21. Pap, E., Štrboja, M.: Generalizations of integral inequalities for integrals based on nonadditive measures. In: Pap, E. (ed.) Intelligent Systems: Models and Applications. Topics in Intelligent Engineering and Informatics, vol. 3, pp. 3–22. Springer, Heidelberg (2013). doi:10.1007/978-3-642-33959-2_1
22. Pap, E., Štrboja, M.: Generalization of the Jensen inequality for pseudo-integral. Inf. Sci. **180**, 543–548 (2010)
23. Ralescu, D., Adams, G.: The fuzzy integral. J. Math. Anal. Appl. **75**, 562–570 (1980)
24. Roberts, A.W., Varberg, D.E.: Convex Functions. Academic Press, New York (1973)
25. Rockafellar, R.T.: Convex Analysis. Princeton University Press, Princeton (1970)
26. Román-Flores, H., Chalco-Cano, Y.: H-continuity of fuzzy measures and set defuzzifincation. Fuzzy Sets Syst. **157**, 230–242 (2006)
27. Román-Flores, H., Chalco-Cano, Y.: Sugeno integral and geometric inequalities. Int. J. Uncertain. Fuzz. Knowl.-Based Syst. **15**, 1–11 (2007)
28. Román-Flores, H., Flores-Franulič, A., Chalco-Cano, Y.: A Jensen type inequality for fuzzy integrals. Inf. Sci. **177**, 3192–3201 (2007)
29. Román-Flores, H., Flores-Franulič, A., Chalco-Cano, Y.: The fuzzy integral for monotone functions. Appl. Math. Comput. **185**, 492–498 (2007)
30. Royden, H.L.: Real Analysis. Macmillan, New York (1988)
31. Seyedzadeh, S.M., Norouzi, B., Mirzakuchaki, S.: RGB color image encryption based on Choquet fuzzy integral. J. Syst. Softw. **97**, 128–139 (2014)
32. Soda, P., Iannello, G.: Aggregation of classifiers for staining pattern recognition in antinuclear autoantibodies analysis. IEEE Trans. Inf Technol. Biomed. **13**, 322–329 (2009)
33. Soria-Frisch, A.: A new paradigm for fuzzy aggregation in multisensorial image processing. In: Reusch, B. (ed.) Fuzzy Days 2001. LNCS, vol. 2206, pp. 59–67. Springer, Heidelberg (2001). doi:10.1007/3-540-45493-4_10
34. Sugeno, M.: Theory of fuzzy integrals and its applications. Ph.D. Dissertation, Tokyo Institute of Technology (1974)
35. Wang, Z., Klir, G.: Fuzzy Measure Theory. Plenum, New York (1992)
36. Wu, L., Sun, J., Ye, X., Zhu, L.: Hölder type inequality for Sugeno integral. Fuzzy Sets Syst. **161**, 2337–2347 (2010)
37. Zhang, X., Zheng, Y.: Linguistic quantifiers modeled by interval-valued intuitionistic Sugeno integrals. J. Intell. Fuzzy Syst. Preprint

Towards a More General XCS:
Classifier Fusion and Don't Cares in Actions

Alejandro Garza-Cuéllar, Manuel Valenzuela-Rendón[✉],
and Ricardo-Javier Parra-Álvarez

Escuela de Ingeniería y Ciencias, Tecnológico de Monterrey,
Monterrey, NL, Mexico
{lex.garza,ricardo.parra}@jara-ai.com, valenzuela@itesm.mx

Abstract. Wilson's XCS represents and stores the knowledge it has
acquired from an environment as a set of classifiers. In the XCS, *don't
cares* (#) may be used in the conditions of classifiers to express generalization. This paper is focused on the representation of knowledge
with the minimal number of classifiers. For this purpose, a new process
called *fusion* is implemented. Fusion promotes the emergence of more
generalized yet accurate classifiers and the reduction of the number of
macroclassifiers. Furthermore, to get even more compact rules sets, the
implementation of the # symbol in the action of the classifiers is proposed; this allows generalization when possible, and the existence non-
competing classifiers in the population if a state has multiple equally
correct actions that can be performed. The proposed modified generalized extended XCS (gXCS) was compared with the XCS on the *Woods2*
environment and a modification of this environment, *modified-Woods2*,
that has locations where there are multiple equally good actions. The
performances of XCS and gXCS are very similar; yet, gXCS obtains
more parsimonious rule sets. Furthermore, gXCS can find good rule sets
even when the probability of # is set zero, contrary to the XCS.

Keywords: XCS · gXCS · # symbol · Don't cares · Learning classifier
systems · Generalization · Fusion

1 Introduction

Classifiers systems [5] have come a long way since their first appearance. In
the last years, classifiers systems have gained increasing attention of researchers
across the globe. The learning classifier system (LCS) [4] maintains a population of rules called *classifiers*, of the form if-*condition*-then-*action*. Conditions
and actions are coded as strings on the alphabet {0, 1, #}. A classifier's condition specifies the input generated by the environment to which the classifier
is applicable. In response to that condition (or input), the system executes an
action on the environment. This population keeps evolving and searching for
classifiers that have a better performance as measured by their *strength* [8].

© Springer International Publishing AG 2017
O. Pichardo-Lagunas and S. Miranda-Jiménez (Eds.): MICAI 2016, Part II, LNAI 10062, pp. 200–210, 2017.
DOI: 10.1007/978-3-319-62428-0_17

Holland's work on LCSs has been used as a basis for many other developments. The LCS breakthrough gave path for Stewart Wilson's XCS system. XCS keeps the condition-action structure, but introduces rules that are evaluated based on their *accuracy*, or their ability to predict their reward, and not their strength. Traditionally, a classifier's strength served both to predict its reward if fired and as its fitness when a genetic algorithm (GA) is applied to create new, and possibly improved, classifiers. Nevertheless, the reward itself may inadequately represent the classifier fitness. This difference lets the XCS keep classifiers in the population that correctly predict their reward, even if they produce a low payoff from the environment, and eliminate those that may have on average receive large rewards, but cannot correctly predict it [12]. Another difference is that the genetic algorithm is applied to classifiers in the *action set*, a not on the whole population. With these changes and other adjustments, the classifier sets found can better solve problems [7,10,13].

In this paper an increase on the XCS's power of generalization through the implementation of two new features is proposed. First, the creation of general classifiers from more specific ones, called *fusion*. Second, the use of don't cares (# symbols) in the action. These modification allow the system to converge on the same result as the classical XCS but expressed with a smaller number of classifiers. We call this modified XCS, the *generalized extended classifier system* (gXCS). In order to test the capabilities of the gXCS, experiments were conducted on different environments comparing the performance of our gXCS with the XCS. The classical *Woods2* problem defined by Wilson [12] was tested using two different sets of parameters. Also, a modified version of *Woods2*, *modified-Woods2*, was also used for testing.

2   XCS

The XCS is based on the learning classifier system (LCS) [4], yet it differs from traditional LCSs on several processes [7,10]. XCS implements condition-action classifier rules, uses a genetic algorithm to create new classifiers, and modifies properties of the classifiers every time they are used. Neverthelss, XCS unlike LCS has no message list, and fitness (reproductive capacity for the genetic algorithm) is based on the accuracy of the prediction rather than the prediction itself [12].

In 1996, Wilson [10] proposed changes to the XCS to increase the accuracy on its generalization ability. His changes involved the application of the genetic algorithm on the action set rather than the match set, the use of *macroclassifiers*, and the use of *subsumption*.

The variables relevant to this research are the following:

- The *prediction p* of a classifier is the estimated pay of a classifier. Although higher values can yield better classifiers, the prediction alone is not enough to correctly measure the quality of a classifier.

- The *error* ε_{cl} of a classifier tells how good it is at predicting its payoff. A classifier with a very small error is more exact and more likely to survive in the population.
- Classifiers have an individual counter called *numerosity* num. This value is incremented when a new classifier is created with condition and action equal to an existing classifier in the population. The existing classifier has its numerosity increased by one, and the new classifier is not added to the population. When this situation occurs, the classifiers are labeled as *macro-classifiers*. If the new classifier does not exist, the classifier is added into the population and its numerosity value is set to one. The numerosity could also be seen as the number of copies of the classifier that exists on the population.
- The experience exp value is the number of times a classifier has been an element of the action set. The higher the value, the more reliable it becomes.

Some of the relevant operations done by the XCS in this research are the following:

- *Covering* is used when the matching set generated is empty and when the minimal number of actions on the matching set is below a threshold value. Covering creates a new classifier with a condition that matches the current input from the environment. With a given probability $P_\#$, don't cares (#) are introduced in the condition. The classifier's action is chosen randomly among those that are not present in the match set. Its prediction, prediction error, and fitness are initialized with default values.
- *Subsumption* in the XCS is applied in the GA on the action set. When an offspring is created, it is compared with its parents. If the offspring is a subset of one of its parents, the numerosity of that parent is incremented by one, and the new classifier is not inserted into the population. If it is not a subset, it is compared with the rest of the population. Moreover, subsumption is used over the action set after the action has been fired.

For a complete understanding on how the XCS works, the reader is referred to the algorithmic description of the XCS by Wilson and Butz [2]. This report also provide the system's parameters as well as a modular pseudo-code with the required methods and a deep explanation of the XCS.

3   Proposed Generalized Extended Classifier System

The proposed generalized extended classifier system (gXCS) is mostly based on Wilson's XCS. The gXCS adds two new ideas to the XCS: the use of don't cares in the actions of the classifiers and a new operation called *fusion*. In this section we will discuss both ideas.

3.1   Don't Cares in the Action of Classifiers

The don't care symbol # was introduced by Holland in the first descriptions of the LCS [5]. In the LCS, a don't care # in the condition of a classifier means that the value of the bit in that specific position could be either 0 or 1. In the LCS, a # character in the action of a classifier acts as a *pass-through* symbol, copying a position of the message that satisfies a condition of the classifier to its action [6].

In this paper we propose the use of don't cares in the action part of classifier that have the same semantic value as in the condition part. Don't cares in the action of classifiers can be advantageous in problems where for a given state there are multiply equally good actions that can be executed. For example, in the *Woods2* environment, most of the initial positions that are two steps away from the food have several actions that are equally as good; this is shown in Fig. 2. In the figure, there are three different types of cells: rocks O and Q, food F, and empty spaces (indicated by a period). Rocks represent obstacles that cannot be occupied by an agent, food is the main goal to be reached, and empty spaces represent cells an agent can occupy. As shown in the figure, there are many cells on which an agent has more than one equally good actions it can make. Being able to represent all those correct actions, with only one classifier, would reduce the number of classifiers needed to express the entirety of the problem at hand. This constitutes an intrinsic advantage of the use of don't cares in the action for the system. For example, the *Woods2* environment needs a minimum of 24 classifiers to express the problem, but only has 16 different states.

Yet there are environments in which the use of don't cares in the action can acquire further meaning. When dealing with artificial animals, or *animats* [11], multiple correct actions for a given state could model a non-deterministic being more accurately than with rules with only one possible outcome.

XCS uses Q-learning [9] in order to learn the condition-action relation with estimated rewards in a given environment. When using Q-learning, this relation is represented via a table known as the *Q-table*. Yet, by using don't care symbols to represent learned rules, the XCS is capable of obtaining a more compact representation than the Q-table [3]. Instead of individually representing all possible state-action combinations in a table, don't cares allow to search for multiple states and a same action, as long as they have similar predictions. In this paper we also propose obtaining even smaller rule sets by searching not only multiple states that indicate a given action, but several actions that have similar predictions. Table 1 shows a possible Q-table that could be obtained by the gXCS and compares it with one that would be obtained with the classic XCS.

Table 1. Q-tables that would be found by XCS and by a system where generalization not only on the columns but also on rows is allowed.

(a) XCS

State/Action	A	B	C
1	Rule1	Rule2	Rule5
2	Rule1	Rule2	Rule3
3	Rule4	Rule6	Rule7

(b) A more compact table

State/Action	A	B	C
1	Rule1	Rule1	Rule4
2	Rule1	Rule1	Rule2
3	Rule3	Rule5	Rule5

The gXCS introduces don't cares in the action of classifiers in two different operations: covering and fusion. During covering, once a classifier is created, the gXCS introduces don't care symbols in the action part with a given probability $P_{\#A}$. Don't cares in the action part of classifier can also appear through *fusion*. Don't cares in the action can express situations were two actions are equally rewarded when answering to the same input. For example consider a problem where the rules 100110/101 and 100110/100 are equally correct. Within the XCS, classifiers like $C_1 = 100110/101$ and $C_2 = 100110/100$ should be found, but a more general third classifier $C_3 = 100110/10\#$ can express the same knowledge.

3.2 Fusion Operator

We introduce the *fusion* operator to allow more general classifiers and more parsimonious rule sets. When this operator is called, it is applied on the condition and action of every classifier in the population. The following three conditions must be met when applying fusion to classifiers C_1 and C_2:

1. The error of the classifiers C_1 and C_2 must be less than the base error value (ε_0, the error below which classifiers are considered to be exact), or in other words, $\varepsilon_{C_1} < \varepsilon_0$ and $\varepsilon_{C_2} < \varepsilon_0$.
2. Classifier must be mature enough (their ages should exceed the subsumption threshold), i.e., $\exp_{C_1} > \theta_{\text{sub}}$ and $\exp_{C_2} > \theta_{\text{sub}}$.
3. The absolute value of the difference of the prediction from the classifiers must be lower than the error threshold, so that $|p_{C_1} - p_{C_2}| < \varepsilon_0$.

If these conditions are met, fusion of the classifiers is viable and this process is made.

Classifiers are coded in a ternary alphabet $\{0, 1, \#\}$. When applying fusion, pairs of classifiers are compared. If they differ in no more than one position being 0 in one and 1 in the other, they can be fused. The process involves changing that position into a # symbol. The numerosity (num) of the new classifier is the sum of the numerosities of the two classifiers being fused. Notice that fusion operates both on the condition and the action parts of classifiers.

For example, consider the $C_1 = 100110/101$ with numerosity of 4 and $C_2 = 100010/101$ with numerosity of 5. Moreover, assume both of these classifiers satisfy the three requirements to be fused. These are equal classifiers except for bit 4 in the condition part. Fusion creates a new classifier inserting the # symbol, generating the classifier 100#10/101 with a numerosity of 9. Once the classifiers are fused, the newly created classifier is inserted into the population and the original classifiers are deleted.

4 Experiments and Discussion

As previously noted, the main intention of this research is to present modifications to the XCS that will solve problems with a performance or expected payoff as good as the XCS, but arriving at more parsimonious rule sets. In order

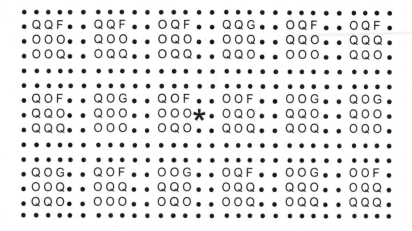

Fig. 1. *Woods2* environment [12].

to assess the performance of the XCS and the gXCS, both systems were tested on two different environments. *Woods2* is used in two different experiments, first as a benchmark using known parameters for solving the problem. Then, with no probability to generalize. The second environment, *modified-Woods2*, is a modified version of the *Woods2* environment, where most positions in the environment have several possible actions that are valid.

4.1 The Traditional Test Environment: *Woods2*

In our first experiments, we used the *Woods2* environment shown in Fig. 1. The parameters used where $\mu = 0.01$ (mutation probability), and $P_\# = 0.5$ for the XCS, and the same but additionally $P_{\#A} = 0.01$ for the gXCS. Out of the 4,000 problems, half where exploration problems, where the action selected for a given condition is chosen at random from the action set, while the other half were exploitation problems, where the best action among the action set is selected.

Figures 3(a) and (b) show the results for the XCS and gXCS, respectively. As shown by the plots, both algorithms yield practically the same results. With only minor differences in the number of best classifiers obtained. Finally, Fig. 4 shows the average steps to reach the food in the *Woods2* environment, where both the XCS and gXCS obtain similar results.

As shown in Fig. 2, the *Woods2* environment has locations where different actions can produce the same reward. It is for this type of environment that the gXCS can solve the problem with less number of best macroclassifiers without losing its ability to correctly solve the problem.

4.2 The Traditional Test Environment Again: *Woods2-0*

One of the difficulties that arises when using the XCS is setting the value of $P_\#$, the probability with which a bit 0 or 1 in the condition is changed to a

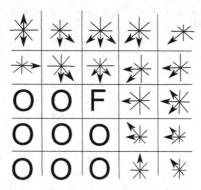

Fig. 2. Example of system predictions learned in *Woods2*. Line length is proportional to the prediction in that direction.

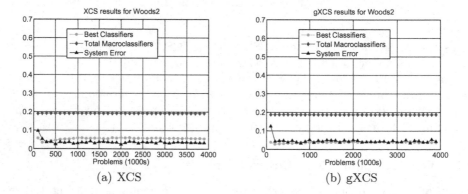

(a) XCS

(b) gXCS

Fig. 3. Results in a *Woods2* environment for the classic XCS and gXCS. Dotted curve: Number of best macroclassifiers (classifiers with $\varepsilon_{cl} < \varepsilon_0$) (divided by 1,000). Diamond curve: Current number of macroclassifiers (divided by 1,000). Triangle curve: System error as a fraction of external reward. Parameters are $\mu = 0.01$, and $P_\# = 0.5$. Curves are averages of 10 runs.

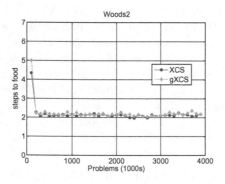

Fig. 4. Results in a *Woods2* environment for the XCS and gXCS. Average steps to food in last 50 exploit problems. Curves are averages of 10 runs.

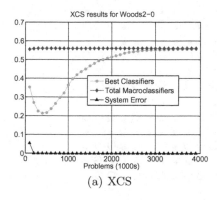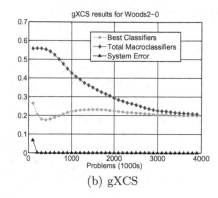

(a) XCS   (b) gXCS

Fig. 5. Results in a *Woods2* environment for the classic XCS with $P_\# = 0$, and the gXCS with $P_\# = 0$, $P_{\#A} = 0$. Dotted curve: Number of best macroclassifiers (classifiers with $\varepsilon_{cl} < \varepsilon_0$) (divided by 1,000). Diamond curve: Current number of macroclassifiers (divided by 1,000). Triangle curve: System error as a fraction of external reward. Curves are averages of 10 runs.

don't care # when a new classifier is created either by covering or by the genetic algorithm. The value of this parameter, as well as others, impacts on the generalization pressure [1]. A high value will conduce to finding classifiers as general as possible, maybe even too general for the problem at hand. If the value is too low, the problem may be solved (as shown on this experiment), but with the trade-off of having too many rules. If the value is too high, the XCS will not be able to correctly solve the problem, over-generalization will dominate in the population. Even with a small change, for example an increase of 0.1 to $P_\#$, the XCS would have a harder time solving the *Woods2* environment. gXCS is capable of generalizing even when $P_\#$ is low if it is unknown beforehand how high the parameter needs to be. This is achieved by the use of the fusion operator.

For this experiment, the *Woods2* environment was used once more. Nevertheless, the parameters used where $\mu = 0.01$, and $P_\# = 0$ for the XCS, and the same but additionally $P_{\#A} = 0$ for the gXCS. Out of the 4,000 problems, half where exploration problems, and the other half exploitation ones. Figures 5(a) and (b) show the results for the XCS and gXCS, respectively. As can be seen, both algorithms yield practically the same results. As in the previous experiment, the number of good classifiers, those considered to have no error ($\varepsilon_{cl} < \varepsilon_0$), found by gXCS are less than have than those found by XCS, proving that gXCS can find more parsimonious yet correct rule sets. Figure 8 shows the average steps to reach the food in this experiment, where both the XCS and gXCS obtain virtually the same results.

4.3   The New Test Environment: *modified-Woods2*

The behavior of the gXCS showed in the previously discussed experiments, is the one we can expect on the most common experimental environments usually used to test classifier systems.

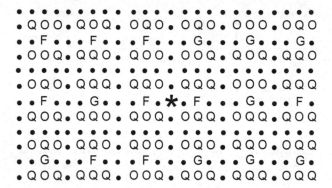

Fig. 6. *modified-Woods2*: a wood-like environment.

To further test the gXCS, we designed a harder environment which (a) requires rules that can be expressed with don't cares in the action, and (b) has inputs which have only one best decision. The proposed environment is shown in Fig. 6. This environment is similar to *Woods2*, with the difference that the food is now placed farther away from the possible starting positions. The *Woods2* problem can be solved with 1.68 steps at best, the *modified-Woods2* needs at least 2.33 steps. Additionally, in this environment some starting positions need 3 and 4 movements to find the food. These factors make this problem harder to solve than *Woods2* in the same 4,000 problems.

For this experiment, the parameters used where $\mu = 0.01$, and $P_\# = 0$ for the XCS and the same but $P_{\#A} = 0$ for the gXCS. Out of the 4,000 problems, half were exploration problems while the other half were exploitation problems. Figures 9(a) and (b) show the results for the XCS and gXCS, respectively. As can be seen from these figures, both systems yield similar results. As in previous experiments, the gXCS solves the problem with a smaller number of classifiers. Figure 10 shows the average steps to reach the food in this experiment. One more time, the XCS and gXCS obtain very similar results (Fig. 7).

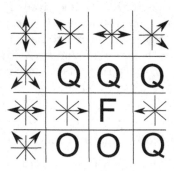

Fig. 7. Example of system prediction learned in *modified-Woods2*.

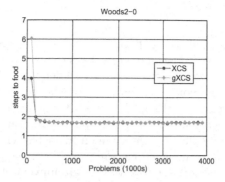

Fig. 8. Results in a *Woods2* environment for the XCS and gXCS. Average steps to food in last 50 exploit problems. Curves are averages of 10 runs.

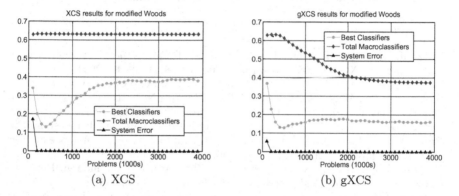

(a) XCS   (b) gXCS

Fig. 9. Results in the *modified-Woods2* environment for the classic XCS with $P_{\#} = 0$, and the gXCS with $P_{\#} = 0$, $P_{\#A} = 0$. Dotted curve: Number of best macroclassifiers (classifiers with $\varepsilon_{cl} < \varepsilon_0$) (divided by 1,000). Diamond curve: Current number of macroclassifiers (divided by 1,000). Triangle curve: System error as a fraction of external reward. Curves are averages of 10 runs.

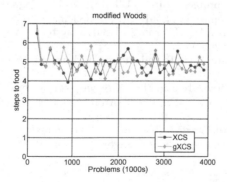

Fig. 10. Results in the *modified-Woods2* environment for the XCS and gXCS. Average steps to food in last 50 exploit problems (divided by 10). Curves are averages of 10 runs.

5 Conclusions

As demonstrated by the all the experiments presented, gXCS and XCS have similar performance in regard to number of steps to achieve payoff. Nevertheless, gXCS has the innate power to generalize even when the value of $P_\#$ is too low for the problem. Furthermore, the addition of the don't care symbol in the action part of classifier gives the gXCS two advantages over XCS. First, the ability to simplify rules when possible for better interpretation. And second, the elimination of competing rules in environmental states where different actions can lead to the same outcome when learning.

Even though this research shows a way to circumvent the lower limit of the value of $P_\#$, there still remains a problem with the upper bound. Future work includes dealing with this bound, as well as the application of the gXCS to multiagent behavior and content generation in video games.

References

1. Butz, M.V., Kovacs, T., Lanzi, P.L., Wilson, S.: Toward a theory of generalization and learning in XCS. IEEE Trans. Evol. Comput. **8**(1), 28–46 (2004)
2. Butz, M.V., Wilson, S.W.: An algorithmic description of XCS. In: Luca Lanzi, P., Stolzmann, W., Wilson, S.W. (eds.) IWLCS 2000. LNCS (LNAI), vol. 1996, pp. 253–272. Springer, Heidelberg (2001). doi:10.1007/3-540-44640-0_15
3. Dorigo, M., Bersini, H.: A comparison of Q-learning and classifier systems. In: Proceedings of From Animals to Animats, Third International Conference on Simulation of Adaptive Behavior, pp. 248–255. MIT Press (1994)
4. Holland, J.H., Holyoak, K.J., Nisbett, R.E., Thagard, P.R.: Induction: Processes of Inference, Learning, and Discovery. MIT Press, Cambridge (1986)
5. Holland, J.H., Reitman, J.S.: Cognitive systems based on adaptive algorithms. SIGART Bull. **63**, 49 (1977)
6. Holland, J.H.: Escaping brittleness: the possibilities of general purpose learning algorithms applied to parallel rule-bases systems. In: Machine Learning: An Artificial Intelligence Approach, pp. 129–138. Morgan Kauffman (1986)
7. Nakata, M., Sato, F., Takadama, K.: Towards generalization by identification-based XCS in multi-steps problem. In: 2011 Third World Congress on Nature and Biologically Inspired Computing (NaBIC), pp. 389–394 (2011)
8. Sigaud, O., Wilson, S.W.: Learning classifier systems: a survey. Soft. Comput. **11**(11), 1065–1078 (2007)
9. Watkins, C.C.H., Dayan, P.: Technical note: Q-learning. Mach. Learn. **8**(3–4), 279–292 (1992)
10. Wilson, S.W.: Generalization in the XCS classifier system. In: Genetic Programming 1998: Proceedings of the Third Annual Conference, pp. 665–674. Morgan Kauffman (1998)
11. Wilson, S.W.: Knowledge growth in an artificial animal. In: Proceedings of the 1st International Conference on Genetic Algorithms, pp. 16–23. L. Erlbaum Associates Inc., Hillsdale (1985)
12. Wilson, S.W.: Classifier fitness based on accuracy. Evol. Comput. **3**(2), 149–175 (1995)
13. Wilson, S.W.: State of XCS classifier system research. In: Lanzi, P.L., Stolzmann, W., Wilson, S.W. (eds.) IWLCS 1999. LNCS (LNAI), vol. 1813, pp. 63–81. Springer, Heidelberg (2000). doi:10.1007/3-540-45027-0_3

A Novel Artificial Hydrocarbon Networks Based Value Function Approximation in Hierarchical Reinforcement Learning

Hiram Ponce[✉]

Faculty of Engineering, Universidad Panamericana, 03920 Mexico City, Mexico
hponce@up.edu.mx

Abstract. Reinforcement learning aims to solve the problem of learning optimal or near-optimal decision-making policies for a given domain problem. However, it is known that increasing the dimensionality of the input space (i.e. environment) will increase the complexity for the learning algorithms, falling into the curse of dimensionality. Value function approximation and hierarchical reinforcement learning have been two different approaches proposed to alleviate reinforcement learning from this illness. In that sense, this paper proposes a new value function approximation using artificial hydrocarbon networks –a supervised learning method inspired on chemical carbon networks– with regularization at each subtask in a hierarchical reinforcement learning framework. Comparative results using a greedy sparse value function approximation over the MAXQ hierarchical method was computed, proving that artificial hydrocarbon networks improves accuracy and efficiency on the value function approximation.

Keywords: Reinforcement learning · Machine learning · Artificial organic networks · Regularization

1 Introduction

Reinforcement learning (RL) aims to solve the problem of learning optimal or near-optimal decision-making policies for a given domain problem [3]. In fact, the input space (i.e. environment) is represented using states that are also composed by a set of features. Depending on the domain problem, the state space can be continuous or discrete; but in any case, the number of features (dimensions) that represents the environment will impact in the dimensionality of the overall domain. However, it is known that increasing the dimensionality of the state space will increase the complexity for the learning algorithms, falling into the curse of dimensionality [8]. To this end, due to table structures of states or state-action pairs, and large state spaces, reinforcement learning becomes inefficient and impractical to be applied successfully in complex domains [7].

In that sense, hierarchical reinforcement learning (HRL) deals with large domains dividing the global goal into smaller subgoals with related subtasks,

© Springer International Publishing AG 2017
O. Pichardo-Lagunas and S. Miranda-Jiménez (Eds.): MICAI 2016, Part II, LNAI 10062, pp. 211–225, 2017.
DOI: 10.1007/978-3-319-62428-0_18

and attempts to tackle each subgoal separately [7,10]. Several hierarchical strategies have been proposed in the literature, for example: the options method [21] defines each subtask in terms of a fixed policy provided, the hierarchy of abstract machines (HAM) method [10] defines each subtask in terms of a nonlinear deterministic finite-state machine, or the MAXQ method [3] that defines each subtask in terms of a terminal predicate (i.e. terminal state of the subtask) and a local reward function. Focusing on the latter, there are three key factors that the MAXQ method supports and provides better learning performance in high dimensional spaces [3]: (i) *temporal abstraction* that assumes a certain task might take several steps to accomplish, modeled as a semi-Markov decision process, (ii) *state abstraction* that defines a relevant subset of features to represent the state space for each subtask, and (iii) *task sharing* that means certain task can be shared by other subtasks if needed.

In particular, Dietterich [3] proved that optimal or near-optimal state abstraction, i.e. safe state abstraction, improves the efficiency of the MAXQ method when dealing with high dimensional spaces. Looking closely, it means that the minimum subset of features will optimize value (or state-action) functions. In fact, value function approximation [11,18] tends to reduce the complexity of reinforcement learning algorithms due to its compact form representation, instead of tables. It allows to generalize over the state space so that the learning complexity is reduced much better [3]. Different approaches have been proposed for value function approximation in non-hierarchical reinforcement learning, such as: linear function approximators [4,18], greedy algorithms [9], machine learning approaches [11,19], sparse approximators [5,9], non-parametric approximators [9], and others.

From the above, this paper proposes a new value function approximation based on artificial hydrocarbon networks at each subtask in the hierarchy of the MAXQ method to improve accuracy and efficiency on that type of knowledge representation. In fact, the artificial hydrocarbon networks (AHN) method has been proved to be efficient in other function approximation approaches [13–16]. Currently, the present work is part of an ongoing research in hierarchical reinforcement learning and the automation of the safe state abstraction in a given problem domain. To this end, two key contributions are present in this paper. First, it is an alternative way of value function approximation using the notion of molecular packaging information through the AHN method, which also exploits the machine learning paradigm for modeling nonlinear and sparse spaces. Secondly, it presents a modified version of the AHN method using L_1 regularization to improve the efficiency of the approximator in terms of generalization and avoiding overfitting.

The rest of the paper is organized as follows. Section 2 presents the related work of value function approximation in RL and trends related to the HRL framework. Section 3 presents the description of the proposal including a brief overview of artificial hydrocarbon networks and the modified version based on L_1 regularization. Section 4 describes the experimentation based on the well-known Dietterich's taxi problem domain and the comparative results obtained so far, and Sect. 5 concludes the paper.

2   Fundamentals and Related Work

Value (state-action) function approximation has been widely studied in reinforcement learning. In this section, the fundamentals of RL and value function are considered. Then, the state-of-the-art in terms of value function approximation is described. Lastly, the MAXQ method is briefly introduced.

2.1   Preliminaries

A Markov decision process (MDP) provides a model M in which an agent interacts with its fully-observable environment, denoted as $M = \langle S, A, P, R, P_0 \rangle$; where, S is a finite set of states of the environment, A is a finite set of actions that the agent can perform, $P(s'|s, a)$ is the probabilistic transition of the environment from its current state s and the resulting state s' when an action $a \in A$ is performed, $R(s'|s, a)$ is the reward that the agent receives when it performs an action a and the environment makes a transition from s to s', and $P_0(s)$ is the starting probability when the MDP is initialized in a state s [3,4].

Then, the aim of the reinforcement learning is to produce (i.e. learn) a policy π that is a mapping from states to actions that tells the agent what action a to perform when it is in state s, such that $a = \pi(s)$. In that sense, the value function V^π provides a mechanism to find a policy π, which it is defined as the expected cumulative reward that an agent will obtain by executing π starting in state s. The value function is expressed as (1); where, r_t is the reward that an agent receives at time t, and γ a discount factor [3]. In fact, the value function satisfies the Bellman equation [1] for a fixed policy as (2).

$$V^\pi(s) = E\left\{ \sum_{i=0}^{\infty} \gamma^i r_{t+i} | s_t = s, \pi \right\} \tag{1}$$

$$V^\pi(s) = \sum_{s}^{\prime} P(s'|s, \pi(s)) \left\{ R(s'|s, \pi(s)) + \gamma V^\pi(s') \right\} \tag{2}$$

In addition, there is the state-action function, Q^π, or Q-function (3) that computes the expected cumulative reward of performing an action a in state s by following the policy π.

$$Q^\pi(s, a) = \sum_{s'} P(s'|s, a) \left\{ R(s'|s, a) + \gamma Q^\pi(s', \pi(s')) \right\} \tag{3}$$

2.2   Overview of MAXQ Method

Formally, MAXQ decomposes a given problem M modeled as an MDP into a finite set of subtasks. Each subtask M_i is defined as a semi-Markov decision process (SMDP) tuple $M_i = \langle T_i, A_i, \hat{R}_i \rangle$ that is completed in N time steps; where, T_i is a termination state of the current subtask, A_i is a set of actions that can be performed to achieve that subtask, and $\hat{R}_i$ is the pseudo-reward function that specifies a pseudo-reward for each transition to a terminal state. Associated to each subtask, there is a policy π_i, and the set of all policies in the problem $\pi = \{\pi_0, \ldots, \pi_n\}$ is called the hierarchical policy [3].

In order to find an optimal or near-optimal hierarchical policy, the MAXQ method decomposes the hierarchical value function V^π (i.e. the expected cumulative reward of following π starting in state s) into a subset of so-called projected value functions, $V^\pi(i, s)$, denoted as (4), or alternatively as (5) if the first action a chosen from π_i is a subroutine and it terminates in N steps. Notice that the expected cumulative reward after executing a is $V^\pi(\pi_i(s), s) = V^\pi(a, s)$.

$$V^\pi(i, s) = E\left\{\sum_{u=0}^{\infty} \gamma^u r_{t+u} | s_t = s, \pi\right\} \tag{4}$$

$$V^\pi(i, s) = E\left\{\sum_{u=0}^{N-1} \gamma^u r_{t+u} + \sum_{u=N}^{\infty} \gamma^u r_{t+u} | s_t = s, \pi\right\}$$
$$= V^\pi(\pi_i(s), s) + \sum_{s', N} P_i^\pi(s', N | s, \pi_i(s)) \gamma^N V^\pi(i, s') \tag{5}$$

Moreover, Dietterich [3] proved that the related projected state-action function can be expressed as (6) with C^π as the completion function (7); resulting in a re-expression of $V^\pi(i, s)$ as (8)[1].

$$Q^\pi(i, s, a) = V^\pi(a, s) + C^\pi(i, s, a) \tag{6}$$

$$C^\pi(i, s, a) = \sum_{s', N} P_i^\pi(s', N | s, a) \gamma^N Q^\pi(i, s', \pi(s')) \tag{7}$$

$$V^\pi(i, s) = \begin{cases} Q^\pi(i, s, \pi_i(s)) & \text{if } i \text{ is composite} \\ \sum_{s'} P(s', | s, i) R(s' | s, i) & \text{if } i \text{ is primitive} \end{cases} \tag{8}$$

To this end, MAXQ requires a hierarchy of the problem defined with a set of nodes [3]: Max nodes (representing primitive actions or subtasks), and Q nodes (actions of subtasks). In particular, Max nodes store $V^\pi(i, s)$ values, and Q nodes store completion functions $C^\pi(i, s, a)$ that represent the cumulative reward of completing subtask i after invoking action $a \in A_i$ in state s. The MaxQ-Q algorithm [3] implements the MAXQ method that works with arbitrary $\hat{R}_i$ functions. In [3], it is shown that $\hat{R}_i$ functions contaminate completion functions C^π. To solve this problem, MaxQ-Q uses two completion functions: the contaminated $\hat{C}_i$ function using $\hat{R}_i$, and the clean C_i function without using $\hat{R}_i$.

---

[1] Primitive subtasks are those that are performed and terminated by actions, while composite subtasks are those that performe other subtasks.

2.3   Value Function Approximation in Reinforcement Learning

Value or state-action function approximation has been proposed in reinforcement learning to relax the curse of dimensionality, to avoid table structures of knowledge representation, and to compute continuous state spaces [9,11,18]. In that sense, value function approximation considers to define states $s \in S$ using a finite number of features $f_i, \forall i = 1, ..., k$ where k is the number of features in state s, and to approximate the value function as a function of a finite-dimensional parameter vector like (9).

$$V^\pi(s) \simeq V^\pi(f_1, \ldots, f_k) \tag{9}$$

Different approaches have been proposed for value function approximation in non-hierarchical reinforcement learning, as described above. In fact, linear approximation is the most used technique, for example: least-squares temporal difference (LSTD) [2] or the gradient-based temporal difference (TD) learning [20]. Since linear mappings of nonlinear features have been considered [4], it does not offer well accuracy in discrete domains as well as it overfits data.

As an alternative, machine learning based approaches for value function approximation have been proposed in the literature. For example, Riedmiller [19] proposed the neural fitted Q (NFQ) algorithm that is based on multilayer perceptrons that stores and reuse experiences at each step of the retraining process. However, artificial neural networks and linear approaches tend to smooth the value function globally [11]. This behavior is not suitable for the expected cumulative reward function because it contaminates the overall performance of the RL algorithm. Thus, authors in [11] proposed to use model trees for state-action function approximators in a hierarchical reinforcement learning framework allowing an agent learns strategies for the Settlers of Catan game. They proved that value function approximation in combination with HRL improves the performance of the reinforcement learning in complex games.

Kolter and Ng [5] proposed to learn a sparse representation of the value function in order to improve generalization and reduce overfitting by adapting supervised learning models with regularization. In this way, Painter-Wakefield and Parr [9] proposed a sparse value function approximation to overcome overfitting in some approaches. They considered a regularization term in the optimization process, obtaining sparse, compact and more understandable value function approximations. Two different algorithms were proposed by them using the orthogonal matching pursuit (OMP), and both the Bellman residual minimization (BRM) and the temporal difference (TD) approaches.

Currently in this work, machine learning and sparse approximation techniques are used together in order to inherit the advantages of both in terms of the value function approximation. In addition, it is also proposed to be used in the MAXQ hierarchical reinforcement learning framework.

3   Description of the Proposal

In this section, a brief overview of artificial hydrocarbon networks is presented. Then, a modified version of this method using L_1 regularization is proposed, and lastly it describes how to use this proposal for value function approximation.

3.1   Artificial Hydrocarbon Networks

Artificial hydrocarbon networks technique is a supervised learning method inspired on chemical hydrocarbon compounds [14,16], and it belongs to the class of learning algorithms called artificial organic networks [14]. Similarly to chemical compounds, artificial hydrocarbon networks packages information in modules called *molecules* that can be related between them with similar chemical mechanisms, i.e. heuristic rules, resulting in graph models that are organized and optimized in terms of chemical energy. In [16], it is proved that the AHN method preserves chemical-based characteristics like: modularity, inheritance, organization and structural stability. For readability, Table 1 summarizes the relationship between chemical-based terms of the artificial organic networks framework and their computational meanings in the AHN technique [16].

Table 1. Description of the chemical terms used in artificial hydrocarbon networks.

Chemical terminology	Symbols	Meaning
Environment	x	(Features) data inputs
Behavior	y	(Target) data output, solution of mixtures
Atoms	h_i, v_C	(Parameters) basic structural units or properties
Molecules	$\varphi(x)$	(Functions) basic units of information
Compounds	$\psi(x)$	(Composite functions) complex units of information
Mixtures	$AHN(x)$	(Linear combinations) combination of compounds
Stoichiometric coefficients	α_i	(Weights) definite ratios in mixtures
Bounds	L_0, L_t	(Parameters) boundaries in the inputs
Energy	E_0, E_t	(Loss function) error between target and estimated values

In AHN, the basic unit of information is the CH-molecule. It is made of two or more atoms related among them in order to define a behavioral function $\varphi(x)$ due to the input vector $x = \{x_1, \ldots, x_k\}$. This molecule is made of a carbon atom with value v_C and surrounded with hydrogen atoms with values $h_i \in \mathbb{C}$, as expressed in (10); where, $1 \leq d \leq 4$ represents the number of hydrogen atoms in the molecule.

$$\varphi(x) = v_C \sum_{r=1}^{k} \prod_{i=1}^{d} (x_r - h_{i,r}) \tag{10}$$

Unsaturated CH-molecules, i.e. $d < 4$, can be joined together with other CH-molecules forming chains of molecules, so-called artificial hydrocarbon compounds. In this work, saturated and linear chains of molecules will be used as compounds like in (11) in which a compound is made of n molecules: $(n-2)$ CH_2 molecules and two CH_3 molecules to the sides. CH_d-symbol represents a molecule with d hydrogens [16]. A compound behavior function ψ is also defined. The simplest compound behavior is a piecewise function denoted as (12); where, $L_t = \{L_{t,1}, \ldots, L_{t,k}\}$ for all $t = 0, \ldots, n$ is a set of boundaries at which an CH-molecule can act over the input space.

$$CH_3 - CH_2 - \cdots - CH_2 - CH_3 \tag{11}$$

$$\psi(x) = \begin{cases} \varphi_1(x) & L_{0,r} \leq x_r < L_{1,r} \\ \cdots & \cdots \\ \varphi_n(x) & L_{n-1,r} \leq x_r \leq L_{n,r} \end{cases}, \forall r = 1, \ldots, k \tag{12}$$

To obtain the boundaries L_t, a distance δ between two adjacent bounds, i.e. $\{L_{t-1}, L_t\}$, is computed as in (13). In addition, $\Delta\delta$ is computed using a gradient descent method based on the energy of the adjacent molecules (E_{t-1} and E_t) like in (14), where $0 < \eta < 1$ is a learning rate parameter. For implementability, energy of molecules can be computed using the least squares error (LSE) as the loss function [16].

$$\delta = \delta + \Delta\delta \tag{13}$$

$$\Delta\delta = -\eta(E_{t-1} - E_t) , \quad E_0 \leftarrow 0 \tag{14}$$

Also, the AHN method defines a mixture AHN that is a linear combination of c compounds in definite ratios so-called stoichiometric coefficients $\{\alpha_1, \ldots, \alpha_c\}$ as shown in (15).

$$AHN(x) = \sum_{i=1}^{c} \alpha_i \psi_i(x) \tag{15}$$

The simplest training algorithm is so-called AHN-algorithm [17]. For this work, an artificial hydrocarbon network will be considered to be a single hydrocarbon compound, thus the simple AHN-algorithm was adapted for a unique hydrocarbon compound as shown in Algorithm 1. For a detailed description of this machine learning technique, see [14, 16, 17].

3.2   Modified AHN-Algorithm Using L_1 Regularization

As noted in Algorithm 1, the AHN-algorithm computes hydrogen $h_{i,r}$ and carbon v_C values using the least squares estimates method. Instead of this method

Algorithm 1. Simple AHN-Algorithm for a saturated and linear compound.

Input: a training data set $\Sigma = (x, y)$, the number of molecules in the compound $n \geq 2$, the learning rate parameter $0 < \eta < 1$, and a tolerance value $\epsilon > 0$.

Output: the saturated and linear hydrocarbon compound AHN.

Initialize an empty compound $AHN = \{\}$.
Create a new saturated linear compound C like (11).
Randomly initialize intermolecular distances δ.
while $|y - \psi| > \epsilon$ **do**
   Determine all bounds L_t of C using δ.
   for each j-th molecule in C **do**
      Determine all molecular parameters of φ_j in (10) using LSE.
   end-for
   Build the compound behavior ψ of C using (12).
   Update intermolecular distances using (13) and (14) with η.
end-while
Update AHN with C and ψ.
return AHN

is the most used in regression, several drawbacks have to be considered. Actually, LSE method does not guarantee generalization of the training model when dealing with new and unobserved data, and it easily falls into overfitting [9]. For instance, a modified version of the AHN-algorithm using natural computing such as simulated annealing and particle swarm optimization can be found in [12]. Some improvements in stability and generalization were found, but computational time was increased. In that sense, this work proposes to use an L_1 regularization in the LSE-based optimization process to find suitable molecular parameters in AHN providing generalization, interpretability and sparseness in the regression solution [9].

Let (10) be rewritten in its polynomial form as (16), where the set of coefficients a_i are computed from the hydrogen values $h_{i,r}$, i.e. the root values of the polynomials.

$$\varphi(x) = v_C \sum_{r=1}^{k} \sum_{i=0}^{d} a_i x_r^i$$
$$= v_C \left\{ \sum_{i=0}^{d} a_i x_1^i + \cdots + \sum_{i=0}^{d} a_i x_k^i \right\} \tag{16}$$

Assuming that the input vector x is composed of independent and indentically distributed features, then (16) can be restated as (17),

$$\varphi(x) = \sum_{i=1}^{\sigma} w_i \phi_i(x) \tag{17}$$

where the set of coefficients w_i are computed from a_i and v_C, the limit is calculated as $\sigma = k(d+1)$, and the set of basis functions ϕ_i is defined as:

$$\phi_i(x) = x_s^{\mathrm{mod}(i-1,d+1)} \, , \, s = \mathrm{quotient}((d+i)/(d+1))$$

Then, the set of molecular parameters w_i can be found in terms of the L_1 regularization that stands for minimizing the least squares error subject to a L_1-norm constraining w_i, as expressed in (18), where y_j is the jth response observation, q is the number of samples in the data, and T_w is a positive tuning parameter. In fact, the least absolute shrinkage and selection operator (LASSO) method [22] solves this optimization process by proposing the alternative problem (19) with some positive value β (actually related to T_w).

$$w_i = \arg\min \left\{ \sum_{j=1}^{q} (y_j - \varphi(x))^2 \right\}, \text{ s.t. } \sum_{i} |w_i| \leq T_w \qquad (18)$$

$$w_i = \arg\min \left\{ \sum_{j=1}^{q} (y_j - \varphi(x))^2 + \beta \|w\|_1 \right\} \qquad (19)$$

3.3   Value Function Approximation Using the AHN-Algorithm

From the above, this work proposes to use the modified version of the AHN-algorithm with L_1 regularization into the value function approximation approach in the hierarchy of the MAXQ method.

Let w_j be the set of all molecular parameters v_C and $h_{i,r}$ for each CH-molecule $\varphi_j(x)$ for all $j = 1, \ldots, n$ of the form as (10). Then, consider the projected value function $V^\pi(u,s)$ of (8) for the state u. It is easy to see that when the state u is primitive or when the subtask terminates after executing an action a, the value function is a cumulative reward, $V^\pi(a,s)$. Then, the projected value function approximation can be reduced to the completion function approximation. Thus, it can be represented as an artificial hydrocarbon network model AHN subject to L_1 regularization in its molecular parameters w_j, of a finite set of features $F_u = \{f_{1,u}, \ldots, f_{k,u}\}$ that characterizes state u, as expressed in (20).

$$C^\pi(u,s,a) \simeq AHN(F_u) \, , \, \text{ s.t.} \|w_j\|_1 \leq T_w, \forall j = 1, \ldots, n \qquad (20)$$

In [6], authors applied the LASSO to the Bellman residual minimization (BRM), stated as the minimum $R + \gamma V^\pi(s') - V^\pi(s)$, obtaining (21) when $V^\pi(s)$ is represented as a linear combination of a finite set of features F_u in definite ratios w_u.

$$w_u = \arg\min \left\{ \sum_{j=1}^{q} \left(R_j + \gamma \sum_{u} w_u F_u' - \sum_{u} w_u F_u \right)^2 + \beta \|w\|_1 \right\} \qquad (21)$$

Algorithm 2. AHN-based value function appromixation in MAXQ.

Input: the set of features F_u, the set of expected cumulative rewards $V^\pi(a,s)$, the discount factor γ, the regularization term $\beta > 0$, the number of molecules in the compound $n \geq 2$, the learning rate parameter $0 < \eta < 1$, and a tolerance value $\epsilon > 0$.
Output: the value function approximation using AHN.

Set $x = F_u - \gamma F'_u$ and $y = V^\pi(a,s)$.
Initialize an empty compound $AHN = \{\}$.
Create a new saturated linear compound C like (11).
Randomly initialize intermolecular distances δ.
while $|y - \psi| > \epsilon$ **do**
    Determine all bounds L_t of C using r_t.
    for each j-th molecule in C **do**
        Determine all molecular parameters w_j of φ_j in (10) using (19) with β.
    end-for
    Build the compound behavior ψ of C using (12).
    Update intermolecular distances using (13) and (14) with η.
end-while
Update AHN with C and ψ.
return AHN

Thus, the completion function approximation problem (20) can be solved using (19) with an equivalent solution to $C^\pi(u,s,a)$ as in (21) for a positive value β, if $x = F_u - \gamma F'_u$ and $y = V^\pi(u,s)$ when state u is primitive. Algorithm 2 summarizes the proposed AHN-based value function approximation in the MAXQ method.

4   Performance Evaluation

In order to prove the accuracy and efficiency of the value function approximation based on artificial hydrocarbon networks with L_1 regularization, the well-known Dieterich's taxi domain was used as case study. In particular, this experimentation considers a comparative analysis evaluating the proposed method, the simple AHN-algorithm without regularization and the OMP-BRM approach of [9]. In this section, a brief description of the taxi domain is presented. Then, some practical issues in the implementation of the proposal are described. Lastly, comparative results are summarized and discussed.

4.1   Description of the Taxi Domain

The taxi domain was formulated by Dieterich [3]. It consists on a 5-by-5 grid environment in which there is a taxi agent. The world has four locations marked as red (R), blue (B), green (G) and yellow (Y). In particular, this domain is episodic which starts when the taxi requires to pick up a passenger and stops when the passenger is put down after a trip. At each episode, the taxi starts in a random square into the world. Then, a passenger placed in one of the four specific

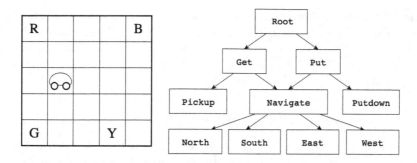

Fig. 1. Taxi domain and its hierarchical decomposition, based on [3].

locations wishes to be transported to another specific location. Both the starting and goal locations are randomly chosen at the beginning of the episode. In that sense, the taxi must travel to the passenger's location, pick up the passenger, go to the goal location, and put down the passenger. Figure 1 shows the taxi domain and its hierarchical decomposition based on [3].

4.2 Implementation of the AHN-Based Value Function Approximation

The taxi domain was used to evaluate the performance of the proposed value function approximation. The experiment consisted on running $30,000$ episodes using the MAXQ method. During the execution, the clean C values were collected which are equal to $V^\pi(u, s)$. Also, a set of features F_u was identified as: $f_{1,u}$ the current cab position, $f_{2,u}$ the source position, $f_{3,u}$ the goal position, and $f_{4,u}$ the current subtask's goal position. Five repetitions of this experiment were done, and the collected data was partitioned into training (70%) and testing (30%) sets. At last, these data sets were standardized.

Using the above information, the AHN-based value function approximation with L_1 regularization (Algorithm 2) was run. A cross-validation approach (only using the training dataset) was used to set the free parameters in the model, obtaining: the number of molecules $n = 4$ and the learning rate $\eta = 0.1$. The remaining parameters were set manually: the discount factor $\gamma = 0.95$ (as used in the MAXQ method) and the regularization parameter $\beta = 1 \times 10^{-10}$. To this end, the AHN-based approximator was evaluated using the testing set (i.e. unobserved data from the learner). Also, the comparative analysis considered the simple AHN-algorithm without regularization as another value function approximator with the same parameter values. In addition, the proposal was compared with the OMP-BRM based approximator. In fact, this is a recent approach that represents the value function in RL as a linear approximation with weight parameters obtained from the Bellman residual minimization (21) and computing it as a regression problem at the orthogonal matching pursuit algorithm [9]. In that sense, the training and testing sets were also used in the OMP-BRM method. The free parameters were also set manually: $\gamma = 0.95$ and $\beta = 1 \times 10^{-10}$.

The root-mean square error (RMSE) metric was employed to evaluate the performance of both approximators. In fact, since the Bellman residual is computed using the L_2-norm between the predicted value $\hat{V}$ function and the true value V function, $\|\hat{V} - V\|$, the RMSE metric gives an explicit and sensitive evaluation of the accuracy approximation.

4.3   Comparative Results and Discussion

The clean C value functions and their approximations from seven nodes in the hierarchy of the taxi domain were analyzed. Particularly, the approximations were performed in four primitive nodes (North, South, East, West) and three composite nodes (Get, NavigateForGet, NavigateForPut). Actually, the Put node was not evaluated since it always has a zero cumulative reward value [3]. Table 2 summarizes the RMSE performance evaluation for the proposed AHN-L_1, simple AHN and the OMP-BRM based value function approximators. In addition, Table 3 summarizes the RMSE performance of the three approximators using the training dataset.

Table 2. RMSE performance in the value function approximators (testing set).

Node	AHN-L_1	Simple AHN	OMP-BRM
North	0.719	0.726	0.989
South	0.759	0.765	0.995
East	0.768	0.835	0.991
West	0.824	0.884	0.994
Get	0.947	9.768	0.991
NavigateForGet	1.133	0.991	1.000
NavigateForPut	0.974	1.012	0.975

From Table 2, it can be seen that the AHN-L_1 based method obtained the lowest RMSE values (except for the NavigateForGet node) in comparison with the simple AHN and OMP-BRM based approximators, when validating the performance with the testing data set. Also, the simple AHN based method was able to approximate the clean C value functions better than the OMP-BRM method, except in the composite nodes Get and NavigateForPut. However, results show that composite nodes could be more difficult to approximate in any of these approaches.

On the other hand, Table 3 shows that RMSE values from the simple AHN approximator are better than those from the AHN-L_1 based method, when validating the performance with the training data set. It can be explained because regularization tends to generalize more than to overfit the response of the approximator. In that sense, it is evident that the AHN-L_1 based method tends to perform larger RMSE values than the simple AHN based method. It can also

Table 3. RMSE performance in the value function approximators (training set).

Node	AHN-L_1	Simple AHN	OMP-BRM
North	0.783	0.750	0.989
South	0.749	0.744	0.993
East	0.813	0.780	0.995
West	0.823	0.740	0.993
Get	0.931	0.840	0.995
NavigateForGet	1.087	0.947	0.976
NavigateForPut	0.988	0.779	0.987

be confirmed when comparing results between the simple AHN approximator and the OMP-BRM based method. RMSE values are larger from the OMP-BRM method, based on regularization, than those from the simple AHN based method. Nevertheless, it can be seen in Tables 2 and 3 that L_1 regularization offers better accuracy and efficiency after the training procedure, because the RMSE values are smaller in both AHN-L_1 and OMP-BRM methods based on regularization, when using the testing set (i.e. unobserved data), in contrast with the simple AHN approximator. At last, it is noted that the AHN-L_1 based method obtained better results when testing than training. This behavior might be explained because L_1 regularization tends to avoid overfitting, and underfitting is then a possibility.

To this end, in Fig. 2 is shown the function approximation of the clean C values in the East node using the AHN-L_1, simple AHN and the OMP-BRM based methods. As noticed, the OMP-BRM approximator is not well tuned; but it can make a distinction between negative and positive standardized C values. In addition, the proposed AHN-L_1 aproximator can deal with the nonlinearities of the true C values better than the simple AHN approximator.

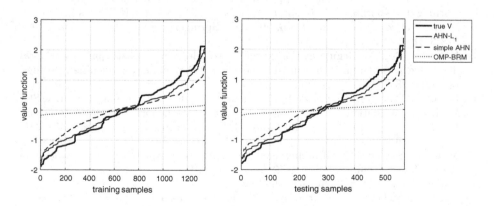

Fig. 2. Value function approximation in the East node.

5 Conclusions and Future Work

This paper presents a new value function approximation based on artificial hydrocarbon networks algorithm with L_1 regularization for hierarchical reinforcement learning. In particular, the proposed approach was implemented in the hierarchy of the MAXQ method.

The methodology of the proposed approximator consisted on using machine learning and regularization approaches in order to inherit characteristics from them, such as: defining nonlinear models to prevent overfitting, get interpretability and exploit sparseness. However, this work limited its attention to nonlinear models preventing overfitting.

In order to validate the proposal, the Dietterich's taxi domain was used as case study. The proposed AHN-L_1, the simple AHN and the OMP-BRM based methods were compared. In fact, the proposed AHN-L_1 based method was proved to be accurate and efficient in terms of the RMSE metric. Results confirm that the proposal obtains a nonlinear model for value function approximation in the hierarchy of the MAXQ method, preventing overfitting.

For future work, this proposal will be analyzed in terms of interpretability and sparseness, and it also be mathematically formalized. Additionally, underfitting on the AHN-L_1 based method will be analyzed in order to determine its influence in the value function approximation. As mentioned, this work is part of an ongoing research, so its implementation for automatic state abstraction will be considered too.

References

1. Bellman, R.: Dynamic Programming. Princeton University Press, Princeton (1957)
2. Brandtke, S., Barto, A.: Linear least-squares algorithms for temporal difference learning. Mach. Learn. **22**(1), 33–57 (1996)
3. Dietterich, T.: Hierarchical reinforcement learning with MAXQ value function decomposition. J. Artif. Intell. Rese. **13**, 227–303 (2000)
4. Jakab, H.S., Csató, L.: Sparse approximations to value functions in reinforcement learning. In: Koprinkova-Hristova, P., Mladenov, V., Kasabov, N.K. (eds.) Artificial Neural Networks. SSB, vol. 4, pp. 295–314. Springer, Cham (2015). doi:10.1007/978-3-319-09903-3_14
5. Kolter, J., Ng, A.: Regularization and feature selection in least-squares temporal difference learning. In: 26th Annual International Conference on Machine Learning, pp. 521–528 (2009)
6. Loth, M., Davy, M., Preux, P.: Sparse temporal difference learning using LASSO. In: IEEE International Symposium on Approximate Dynamic Programming and Reinforcement Learning, Honolulu, Hawaii, United States of America, pp. 352–359. IEEE, April 2007
7. Mahajan, S.: Hierarchical reinforcement learning in complex learning problems: a survey. Int. J. Comput. Sci. Eng. **2**(5), 72–78 (2014)
8. Mitchell, T.: Machine Learning. McGraw Hill, New York City (1997)
9. Painter-Wakefield, C., Parrm, R.: Greedy algorithms for sparse reinforcement learning. In: 29th International Conference on Machine Learning, pp. 1391–1398 (2012)

10. Parr, R., Russell, S.: Reinforcement learning with hierarchies of machines. In: Conference on Advances in Neural Information Processing Systems, pp. 1043–1049. MIT Press (1997)
11. Pfeiffer, M.: Reinforcement learning of strategies for Settlers of Catan. In: International Conference on Computer Games: Artificial Intelligence (2004)
12. Ponce, H.: Bio-inspired training algorithms for artificial hydrocarbon networks: a comparative study. In: 13th Mexican International Conference on Artificial Intelligence (MICAI), Tuxtla Gutierrez, Chiapas, Mexico, pp. 162–166. IEEE, November 2014
13. Ponce, H., Miralles-Pechúan, L., de Lourdes Martínez-Villaseñor, M.: Artificial hydrocarbon networks for online sales prediction. In: Lagunas, O.P., Alcántara, O.H., Figueroa, G.A. (eds.) MICAI 2015. LNCS, vol. 9414, pp. 498–508. Springer, Cham (2015). doi:10.1007/978-3-319-27101-9_38
14. Ponce, H., Ponce, P.: Artificial organic networks. In: 2011 IEEE Conference on Electronics, Robotics and Automotive Mechanics, Cuernavaca, Morelos, Mexico, pp. 29–34. IEEE (2011)
15. Ponce, H., Ponce, P., Molina, A.: Adaptive noise filtering based on artificial hydrocarbon networks: an application to audio signals. Expert Syst. Appl. **41**(14), 6512–6523 (2014)
16. Ponce-Espinosa, H., Ponce-Cruz, P., Molina, A.: Artificial Organic Networks. SCI, vol. 521. Springer, Cham (2014)
17. Ponce, H., Ponce, P., Molina, A.: The development of an artificial organic networks toolkit for LabVIEW. J. Comput. Chem. **36**(7), 478–492 (2015)
18. Qin, Z., Li, W., Janoos, F.: Sparse reinforcement learning via convex optimization. In: 31st International Conference on Machine Learning, vol. 32, pp. 424–432 (2014)
19. Riedmiller, M.: Neural fitted Q iteration – first experiences with a data efficient neural reinforcement learning method. In: Gama, J., Camacho, R., Brazdil, P.B., Jorge, A.M., Torgo, L. (eds.) ECML 2005. LNCS, vol. 3720, pp. 317–328. Springer, Heidelberg (2005). doi:10.1007/11564096_32
20. Sutton, R., Maei, H., Precup, D., Bhatnagar, S., Silver, D., Szepesvari, C., Wiewiora, E.: Fast gradient-descenet methods for temporal-difference learning with linear function approximation. In: 26th Annual International Conference on Machine Learning, pp. 993–1000. ACM (2009)
21. Sutton, R., Singh, S., Precup, D., Ravindran, B.: Improved switching among temporally abstract actions. In: Conference on Advances in Neural Information Processing Systems, vol. 11, pp. 1066–1072. MIT Press (1999)
22. Tibshirani, R.: Regression shrinkage and selection via the lasso. J. Royal Stat. Soc. Ser. B **58**(1), 267–288 (1996)

Wind Power Forecasting for the Villonaco Wind Farm Using AI Techniques

Alberto Reyes[1(✉)], Pablo H. Ibargüengoytia[1], J. Diego Jijón[2],
Tania Guerrero[2], Uriel A. García[1], and Mónica Borunda[1]

[1] Instituto Nacional de Electricidad y Energías Limpias, Cuernavaca, Mexico
{areyes,pibar,uriel.garcia,monica.borunda}@iie.org.mx
[2] Instituto Nacional de Eficiencia Energética y Energías Renovables, Quito, Ecuador
{juan.jijon,tania.guerrero}@iner.gob.ec

Abstract. Forecasting represents a very important task for planning, control and decision making in many fields. Forecasting the dollar price is important for global companies to plan their investments. Forecasting the weather is determinant to make the decision of either giving a party outdoors or indoors. Forecasting the behaviour of a process represents the key factor in predictive control. In this paper, we present a methodology to build wind power forecasting models from data using a combination of artificial intelligence techniques such as artificial neural networks and dynamic Bayesian nets. These techniques allow obtaining forecast models with different characteristics. Finally, a model recalibration function is applied to raw discrete models in order to gain an extra accuracy. The experiments ran for the unit 1 of the Villonaco wind farm in Ecuador demonstrated that the selection of the best predictor can be more useful than selecting a single high-efficiency approach.

1 Introduction

Power forecasting of renewable resources for short and very short terms horizons allows planning the electric power dispatch. The impact of a good dispatch results in significant economic savings and better profitness of renewable resources for electricity suppliers [11]. When the user's demand and the provider's dispatch is estimated synchronically the benefits are even higher.

A typical prediction of the electric power produced by a wind farm is computed using a fixed weighted measure of the wind farm nominal power [7], with the weight computed using historical data of atmospheric conditions. As a result, this approximation will not match with the actual farm production curves [1]. These (inaccurate) predictions will become a potential point of failure when scheduling the generation units on/off cycles (i.e. what wind turbines to switch on/off and at what time) to satisfy the demand of energy.

The current wind forecasting models that are based on the predictions of atmospheric changes coming from certain numerical models [5], do not have enough precision to forecast wind speed for horizons of more than 5 h. In the

© Springer International Publishing AG 2017
O. Pichardo-Lagunas and S. Miranda-Jiménez (Eds.): MICAI 2016, Part II, LNAI 10062, pp. 226–236, 2017.
DOI: 10.1007/978-3-319-62428-0_19

case of wind power forecasting [1] for short and very short time horizons (terms of days and hours respectively), literature reports that the most popular techniques are concentrated around ARIMA time series [15], Artificial Neural Networks [3,10] and Support Vector Machines [14]. The alternative techniques based on statistical models or neural networks, usually do not take into account other relevant variables and produce single value predictions.

In this paper, we present a methodology to build wind power forecasting models from data using artificial intelligence techniques. After collecting and pre-processing a set of historical data, the resulting dataset is then used to approximate two forecasting models, one using the dynamic Bayesian network approach and other using a multi-layer perceptron. These two wind power forecasting models for each wind profile is finally evaluated and compared in order to select the one with the highest performance. Finally, a model recalibration function is finally applied to raw discrete models in order to gain an extra accuracy. The novelty of the method consists in that comparing several high-efficiency approaches and selecting the best one is more useful than using a single approach straightforward. Furthermore, the results show improvement through calibration with the hybrid technique. The experiments were run using two-year historical data for the Villonaco wind farm, which is located at the Andean region in Ecuador.

This paper is organized as follows. The next section provides a brief summary about the main characteristics of the Villonaco wind farm. Section 3 describes the fundamentals of clustering, dynamic Bayesian networks and artificial neural networks. Section 4 presents our proposed methodology to obtain efficient forecasting models. In Sect. 5, we show some experiments performed and preliminary results. Finally, Sect. 6 concludes the paper and suggests future work.

2   Villonaco Wind Farm

Villonaco has 11 wind turbines installed at 2700 m high, approximately. Each turbine has a maximum hub height of 65 m and 1.5 MW of rated power, achieving a total of 16.5 MW of installed capacity. The farm is operating commercially since July 2013, contributing with an average of 74 GW-h per year, according to the data registered in 2014. The electric power is delivered by direct connection to the electricity grid, which has a similar operation as an infinite bus. This farm is subject to special conditions since it is built in the Andean region of Ecuador, with high average wind speed over 11 m/s, low air density of 0.89 kg/m^3 and turbulence intensity of 0.15.

The wind speed behavior in Villonaco wind farm follows a well defined pattern during a typical year. Figure 1 shows a monthly historical comparison between the wind speed pattern from 2013 to 2015. Figure 2 shows the wind rose for Villonaco using data directly collected from the SCADA of the Wind Farm. Predominantly, the richest distribution of wind speed flows to the east with a slightly trend of 20° to the north. The power and speed data were provided by CELEC EP (Electric Corporation of Ecuador) from its Business Unity of GENSUR.

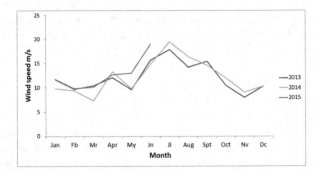

Fig. 1. A monthly historical comparison between the wind speed pattern from 2013 to 2015 in Villonaco. Notice that the dataset for 2015 covers information from January to June.

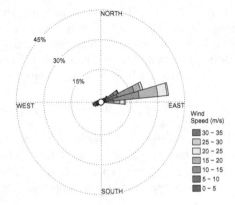

Fig. 2. Wind rose for Villonaco using data directly collected from the SCADA of the wind farm.

3   Fundamentals

3.1   Dynamic Bayesian Networks

Dynamic Bayesian Networks (DBN) [12] represent temporal relations by replicating each variable for every time instant in the temporal range of interest, including dependency relations within and between temporal intervals. In general, DBNs follow two basic assumptions:

- Markovian process: Each variable only depends on variables from the previous and current time steps,
- Stationary process: The structure and parameters of the model remain the same for all time steps.

According to these assumptions, a typical DBN is inspired on the definition presented by Murphy [12]. The DBN is formed by certain initial conditions and

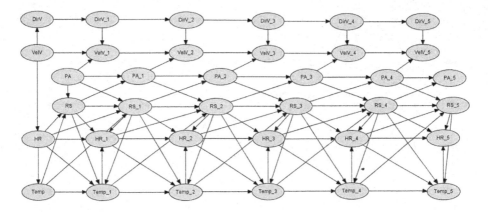

Fig. 3. DBN developed with the methodology established in textbooks for DBNs, and the model developed in [8].

by a two-slice temporal Bayes net which defines $P(X_t \mid X_{t-1})$ for all t in the process. This is called the transition model. The complete model is obtained by *unrolling* the two slice transition model in the number of time slices that are required in the forecast. For example, if we define an hourly time slice and we need five hours in advance, then the DBN is unrolled to complete six slices. Figure 3 shows the resultant six slices dynamic model.

3.2 Artificial Neural Networks

The Artificial Neural Networks (ANN) model is inspired by neurons and their connections in the brain, neural network is a representation used in machine learning. After running the back-propagation learning algorithm [13] on a given set of examples, the neural network can be used to predict outcomes for any set of input values.

A neural network consists of a network whose nodes are arranged in layers. The arcs resemble the interconnection between neurons (the nodes) in the brain. Figure 4 left exemplifies this method. The first layer is the input layer with the number of nodes as the number of input variables. The output layer produces the output of the network. In the figure there is only one output: the predicted signal. There can be none or several hidden layers. Figure 4 right represents the jth neuron of the p layer. This neuron receives n inputs from layer $p-1$ and produces one output that will be connected to neurons in layer $p+1$. The output level will be the sum of all the inputs multiplied by a weight w_{ij}^p, and modified by a sigmoidal function[1]. These weights are learned during a training phase. To train the network, several examples of a learned concept are presented and several examples of what is not the concept are also presented. Consequently,

---

[1] A sigmoidal is an S-shaped function equivalent to $1/(1 + e^{-x})$.

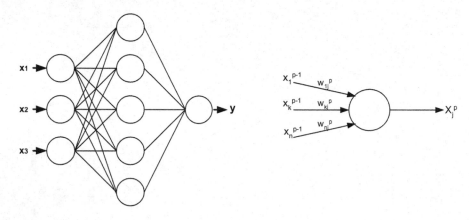

Fig. 4. A basic neural network. Left: a typical network. Right: a *Perceptron* or basic neuron.

the weights are defined so that future examples receive a similar conclusion. This is a typical method for parameter estimation.

4 Methodology

As a first step, it is important to count with historical data from a set of wind turbine units or from a whole wind farm. The estimation should be achieved characterizing the power energy production directly, so that the set of main variables at least should consider the day, month, wind speed and wind power for a period of at least one year (a time cycle). The data collected should then be cleaned and filtered in such a way that no noise or missing data are included in the preprocessed data set.

After collecting and pre-processing a set of historical data, the resulting dataset is then used to approximate two forecasting models, one using a tool for learning dynamic Bayesian networks and other using a tool for learning artificial neural networks.

The construction of dynamic Bayesian models might be performed through the K2 algorithm [4], greedy and search methods or others. Among the main advantages of the use of machine learning techniques is that it filters irrelevant attributes. In general, a Bayesian model shows good accuracy and the forecasting values obtained with this approach are probability distributions and not fixed point values.

The usage of an artificial neural network (ANN) allows approximating a deterministic function of the wind power behavior given the remaining variables in the form of a time series. The back propagation algorithm might be used as it is enough to construct models with the highest correlation when compared predicted values with respect to actual values.

The two resulting forecasting models for each wind profile are evaluated in order to select the best ones. At the end, an assembly of AI techniques is performed in such a way that only the best models might be selected and collected in a set of hybrid forecasting models. Algorithm 1 shows a summarized version of the methodology for selecting the best forecasting model.

As an ANN returns a fixed point value and a DBN returns a probability distribution, the most probable value in the Bayesian model is used for comparison.

In the case of discrete models, a recalibration is required in order to refine the resulting forcast values. In order to do this, the forecast values produced by the DBN model should be postprocessed. In a DBN, the statistical weights for the intervals (value discretization) to predict power depends on the historical data. The empirical relationship function, showed in Eq. 1, is used to find the forecast in the nonlinear power curve behavior. This procedure must be applied recursively until a convergence criterion to be achieved.

$$forecast = b + m(Ln(x)) \tag{1}$$

Where, b and m are the constants obtained in the multivariate interpolation between forecast and real data, x is the predict value by DBN and $forecast$ is the forecasting.

Algorithm 1. Model selection algorithm

1: **procedure** MAIN(historicalData) returns forecastingModels
2:     $phd \leftarrow preprocess(historical Data)$
3:     $dbn \leftarrow learnRBD(phd)$
4:     $dbn* \leftarrow postprocess((dbn)$
5:     $ann \leftarrow learnANN(phd)$
6:     **if** $correlation(ann) <= correlation(dbn*)$ **then return** $dbn*$
       return ann

---

5   Experimental Results

In order to evaluate the methodology, the tests were performed using historical data from the Villonaco wind farm unit 1 (WT1). The experiments were run for a forecasting time-horizon of three hours. Historical data from 2013 to 2014 were also used.

Initially, the wind speed and power data were filtered according to an outlier identification criterion across the power curve. Given the preprocessed dataset, a Bayesian and a neural model were learned. The data in the year 2014 was used as training set while the data in 2013 was used as test set.

The dynamic Bayesian model was built using OpenMarkov [2], Hugin Expert and other proprietary tools [9]. The best linear correlation coefficient obtained using this approach after several tests was 0.84. The linear correlation coefficient (also known as Pearson product moment correlation coefficient) measures the strength and the direction of a linear relationship between two variables, in this case the real value (of power) versus the expected (predicted) value. A correlation greater than 0.8 is generally described as strong, whereas a correlation less than 0.5 is generally described as weak. These values can vary based upon the "type" of data being examined. Table 1 shows the structural and parametric characteristics of the Dynamic Bayesian network model used in this work.

The neural network model was built using Weka [6]. The best correlation coefficient obtained after several tests was 0.8949 and its corresponding relative error obtained was 18.96%. The relative error is the absolute error (difference of the true value of a quantity and a measured or inferred value of the same quantity) with respect to the true value. The relative error of the quotient or product of a number of quantities is less than or equal to the sum of their relative errors. Table 2 shows the structural and parametric characteristics of the neural model and Table 3 shows the correlation coefficient and relative error obtained for the neural model.

Table 1. Structural and parametric characteristics of the dynamic Bayesian network model

DBN	
Horizon:	3 h
Time step:	1 h
Attributes: 4	Month
	Hour
	Speed
	Power
Learning algorithm:	K2 + Greedy and search
Instances:	7543
Test set:	5877
AI tool:	Hugin expert + OpenMarkov
Number of nodes:	16

The scatter plot of Fig. 5A shows a nonlinear behavior of the predicted values using a DBN approach with respect to real values. The correlation coefficient under this scenario is 0.84. A post processing stage based on the interpolation Eq. 1 was then used to provide better forecasts (with higher probabilities) for the DBN model. The *DBN* output is then optimized to obtain the prediction values *DBN** showed in Fig. 5B. After the post processing stage, the correlation coefficient improved to a value of 0.9782.

Table 2. Structural and parametric characteristics of the artificial neural network model

ANN	
Scheme:	MultilayerPerceptron -L 0.3 -M 0.2 -N 500 -V 0 -S 0 -E 20 -H a -G -R
Attributes: 4	Month
	Hour
	Speed
	Power
Epochs:	667
Instances:	7543
Test set:	5877
Learning rate:	0.3
Momentum:	0.2
Hidden layers:	2
Output layers:	1
Input layers:	3

Table 3. Correlation coefficients and relative errors for the ANN model and the DBN model with output improvements (DBN*)

	Correlation coefficient	Relative error (%)	successful coincidences (%)
DBN*	0.9782	23.10	87.71
ANN	0.8949	18.96	-

The evaluation of the DBN forecasting model was performed considering a length of the interval of 121.3 kW for the variable *power* (13 equidistant partitions). Hence, the count of success values predicted are the percentage of forecasting to be improved by Eq. 1. This equation is a recurrent learning function that converged to a relative error of 23.10 %. This error value is a bit higher than the ANN's, which means that apparently the ANN showed a better performance. However, when comparing the correlation coefficients for the ANN model and the DBN model with output improvements (DBN*) (Fig. 3), the DBN* model results the best option. One possible reason for the difference in performance for DBN and ANN is the size of discrete intervals in the DBN nodel. This variable partition introduces an implicit error which is proportional to the size of intervals. The ANN model does not have this problem because of the continuous nature of its variables. In consequence, the role of the recalibration must be enhanced because using this post-processing feature the performance of the DBN was finally increased considerably.

A) DBN forecast

B)DBN with post processing stage

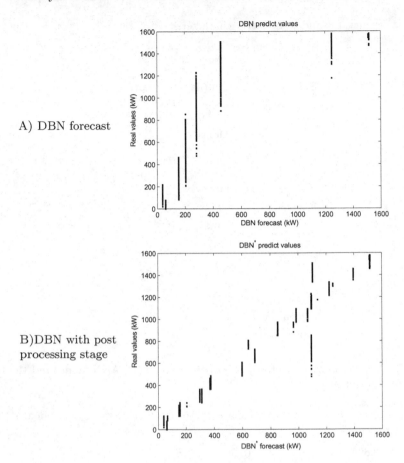

Fig. 5. Relation between the real (true) value of wind power versus the inferred value of wind power at WT1 (DBN forecast). (A) Relation for the DBN model before the post-processing stage (raw DBN model). (B) Relation for the DBN model after the post-processing stage.

Finally, a comparison between the real data and the forecasting values of the winner model (Fig. 6) shows graphically that the predicted values of wind power using a test dataset are very accurate when using this methodology. The experiments have demonstrated that a combination of predictors could be more useful than a single high-efficiency approach.

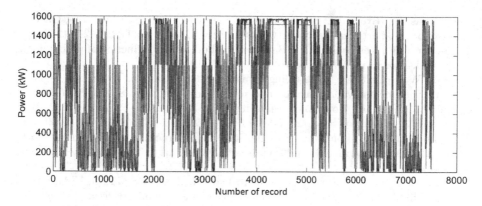

Fig. 6. Real (blue dots) and forecast values (green dots) using the DBN^* approach. The sampling frequency in this dataset is 10 min. (Color figure online)

6   Conclusions and Future Work

In this paper, we presented a methodology to build wind power forecasting models from data using a combination of artificial intelligence techniques such as artificial neural networks and dynamic Bayesian nets. In this work, the ANN and DBN approaches were applied alone and combinationally. The experiments demonstrated that (i) a combination of predictors could be more useful than a single high-efficiency approach, and (ii) that a recalibrated Bayesian model (DBN*) resulted to be more efficient than an Artificial Neural Network model (ANN). In the future, comparative results with other techniques in the literature, such as support vector machines, will be reported.

As another future work a set of wind profiles will be clustered to obtain different wind behavior profiles. The usage of wind profiles might warranty that a model of maximum persistence can be obtained.

The optimal way of obtaining the size of discrete intervals of variables is determinant for future work so that it is an open research topic. The time-horizon was set for showing the methodology only and it has to be extended in order to obtain more useful wind forecasts. This work will be also extended to cover the whole wind farm in order to have local and global predictions in Villonaco, Loja Ecuador. Authors claim that the results of this work might have general significance for wind prediction in any geographical location.

References

1. Ackermann, T.: Wind power in power systems. Wiley, West Sussex, England (2005)
2. Bermejo, I., Oliva, J., Díez, F.J., Arias, M.: Interactive learning of Bayesian networks using OpenMarkov, Madrid, Spain, CISIAD, UNED (2012)

3. Cadenas, E., Rivera, W.: Short term wind speed forecasting in La Venta, Oaxaca, México, using artificial neural networks. Renew. Energy **34**(1), 274–278 (2009)
4. Cooper, G.F., Herskovits, E.: A Bayesian method for the induction of probabilistic networks from data. Mach. Learn. **9**, 309–347 (1992)
5. Enke, W., Spekat, A.: Downscaling climate model outputs into local and regional weather elements by classification and regression. Clim. Res. **8**, 195–207 (1997)
6. Hall, M., Frank, E., Holmes, G., Pfahringer, B., Reutemann, P., Witten, I.H.: The weka data mining software: an update. SIGKDD Explor. **11**(1), 10–18 (2009)
7. Hollingsworth, A., Lönnberg, P.: The Statistical Structure of Short-range Forecast Errors as Determined from Radiosonde Data. Part I: The Wind Field. Wiley, Hoboken (1986)
8. Ibargüengoytia, P.H., Reyes, A., Romero-Leon, I., Pech, D., García, U.A., Sucar, L.E., Morales, E.F.: Wind power forecasting using dynamic Bayesian models. In: Gelbukh, A., Espinoza, F.C., Galicia-Haro, S.N. (eds.) MICAI 2014. LNCS (LNAI), vol. 8857, pp. 184–197. Springer, Cham (2014). doi:10.1007/978-3-319-13650-9_17
9. Ibargüengoytia, P.H., Reyes, A., Romero, I., Pech, D., García, U.A., Borunda, M.: A tool for learning dynamic Bayesian networks for forecasting. In: Lagunas, O.P., Alcántara, O.H., Figueroa, G.A. (eds.) MICAI 2015. LNCS, vol. 9414, pp. 520–530. Springer, Cham (2015). doi:10.1007/978-3-319-27101-9_40
10. Catalo, J.P.S., Pousinho, H.M.I., Mendes, V.M.F.: Short-term wind power forecasting in Portugal by neural networks and wavelet transform. Renew. Ener. **36**(4), 1245–1251 (2011)
11. Lew, D., Milligan, M., Jordan, G., Piwko, R.: The value of wind power forecasting. In: Proceedings of the 91th American Meteorological Society Annual Meeting, Washington, DC, USA (2011)
12. Murphy, K.P.: Dynamic Bayesian networks: representation, inference and learning. Ph.D. thesis. University of California, Berkeley, CA, USA (2002)
13. Rumelhart, D.E., Hinton, G.E., McClelland, J.L.: A general framework for parallel distributed processing, vol. 1. MIT Press, Cambridge (1986). chapter 2, pp. 45–76
14. Santamaría-Bonfil, G., Reyes-Ballesteros, A., Gershenson, C.: Wind speed forecasting for wind farms: a method based on support vector regression. Renew. Ener. **85**, 790–809 (2016)
15. Di Wang, M., Qiu, Q.R., Cui, B.W.: Short-term wind speed forecasting combined time series method and arch model. In: International Conference on Machine Learning and Cybernetics, vol. 3, pp. 924–927 (2012)

Predicting the Need of Mechanical Ventilation in Guillain-Barré Patients Using Machine Learning Algorithms with Relevant Features

José Hernández-Torruco, Juana Canul-Reich$^{(\boxtimes)}$, and Oscar Chávez-Bosquez

División Académica de Informática y Sistemas,
Universidad Juárez Autónoma de Tabasco, Cunduacan, Tabasco, Mexico
{jose.hernandezt,juana.canul,oscar.chavez}@ujat.mx

Abstract. Guillain-Barré Syndrome (GBS) is an autoimmune neurological disorder characterized by a fast evolution. Almost a third of patients with this condition presents breathing difficulty and need a mechanical device to assist them. We aim at creating a diagnostic model of the need for mechanical ventilation in GBS. We use for experimentation a real dataset that contains clinical, serological, and nerve conduction tests data. In this dataset, 41 patients out of a total of 122 required mechanical ventilation. JRip, SVM (Support Vector Machines) with linear kernel and C4.5 are used to create the predictive models. We examine whether selecting the relevant variables in the dataset through filter methods makes possible to increase the accuracy of the model. The methods analyzed are: symmetrical uncertainty, chi squared and information gain. An accurate predictive model was obtained after experimentation.

Keywords: Predictive model · Classification · Performance evaluation · Balanced accuracy

1   Introduction

Guillain-Barré Syndrome (GBS) is an autoimmune neurological disorder characterized by a fast evolution; usually it goes from a few days up to four weeks. GBS is an autoimmune disease, preceded by a respiratory or gastrointestinal acute infection. Rapidly progressive symmetric weakness, distal beginning and proximal advancement with loss of tendon reflexes (muscle stretch reflexes), with few symptoms and varying sensory autonomic dysfunction characterize it. The prodromal interval between infection and the onset of symptoms varies from one to three weeks.

Approximately a third of patients with this condition presents breathing difficulty and need a mechanical device to assist them [8]. Respiratory failure represents up to 50% of causes of admission to pediatric intensive care units. Mechanical ventilation is a breathing advanced support that artificially introduces gas in the patient's respiratory system, through an external mechanical

---

All three authors equally contributed to this paper.

© Springer International Publishing AG 2017
O. Pichardo-Lagunas and S. Miranda-Jiménez (Eds.): MICAI 2016, Part II, LNAI 10062, pp. 237–247, 2017.
DOI: 10.1007/978-3-319-62428-0_20

device or fan bracket. Fortunately, this need can be predicted by means of a diagnostic model. Knowing in advance the presence of this need can help doctors to be prepared to address this problem and reduce risks to patients.

There are computational techniques in the area of machine learning that create predictive models for the problem described above, same that have been used successfully in similar cases [1–3]. In this work, JRip, SVM (Support Vector Machines) with linear kernel and C4.5 are used to create the predictive models. We examine whether selecting the relevant variables in the dataset through filter methods makes possible to increase the accuracy of the model. The methods analyzed are symmetrical uncertainty, chi squared and information gain.

2   Materials and Methods

2.1   Data

The dataset used in this work comprises 122 cases of patients seen at Instituto Nacional de Neurología y Neurocirugía located in Mexico City. Data were collected from 1993 through 2002. In this dataset, 41 patients required MV and 81 did not. The original dataset consisted of 156 attributes corresponding to clinical data, results from two Nerve Conduction Studies (NCS), and results from two Cerebrospinal Fluid (CSF) analyses. In this study, we analyze 21 clinical, four CSF and 25 NCS variables. This selection was made according to the findings in the specialized literature. Variables V10 (Days from the onset of breathing difficulty) and V34 (Breathing difficulty) were excluded, since in this study our interest is to investigate whether clinical variables explored by physicians before the onset of the breathing difficulty, if any, allows to accurately predict the necessity of mechanical ventilation. The variable V8 (Date of the onset of the previous event) was excluded and a new variable named *season* was created from it. *Season* takes the values 1 = spring, 2 = summer, 3 = autumn and 4 = winter. The complete lists of each type of variable are shown in Tables 1, 2 and 3.

2.2   Classifiers

Support Vector Machines (SVM). SVM was first introduced by Vapnik and colleagues [11]. Given a set of training instances (input space), where each instance belongs to class A or class B, SVM uses a mapping function (kernel) to transform the input space into a higher dimension space (feature space), that is, if input space is 2-D, then it is mapped into a 3-D space. In the feature space, SVM finds a hyperplane that gives the largest separation between classes, named maximum marginal hyperplane. The maximum margin hyperplane has the largest distance from the hyperplane to the closest training instances. The instances located in the boundaries of the hyperplane are called support vectors. However, the largest margin is not always the best solution since it can compromise the generalization of the model to new instances. For the sake of flexibility, SVM introduces a parameter C that creates a soft margin that allows

Table 1. List of clinical features

Feature label	Feature name
V4	Age
V5	Sex
V6	Previous event pathology
V7	Days from the onset of muscle strength diminishing or cranial nerve compromise to the previous event
V8 (Season)	Date (Season of the year) of the onset of the previous event
V9	Days from the onset of symptoms to seek medical advice
V21	Weakness
V22	Symmetry
V23	Paresthesia
V24	Upper limb muscle strength
V25	Lower limb muscle strength
V26	Location of symptom onset
V27	Reflexes
V29	Affectation of extraocular muscles
V30	Ptosis
V31	Cerebellar affectation
V32	Ataxic gait
V33	Cranial nerve involved
V37	Complications
V38	Involvement of sphincters
Dysautonomia	Disorder of the autonomic nervous system

for some errors in classification but at the same time, it penalizes them. A tuning procedure is necessary for finding the best value of C.

In this study, we use the linear kernel (SVMLin) for experiments given its good performance and implementation simplicity. This kernel requires the optimization of only one parameter, the aforementioned C penalty parameter.

Table 2. List of serological features

Feature label	Feature name
V43	Albuminocytologic dissociation
V44	Cell count
V45	Proteins
V46	Glucose

Table 3. List of NCS features

Feature label	Feature name
V54	Decreased nerve conduction velocity in two or more motor nerve
V55	Nerve conduction block or dispersion
V56	Prolonged distal latency in two or more motor nerve
V57	Absence or extension of F wave in two or more motor nerve
V58	How many Asbury criteria are present?
V59	Which Asbury criteria is not present?
V60	Affectation of motor nerve conduction velocity
V79	Side-to-side difference in left median motor nerve F wave
V98	Side-to-side difference in right median motor nerve F wave
V99	F wave disturbance
V100	Number of disturbed F waves
V101	Motor nerve conduction velocity < 80%
V102	Number of disturbed F waves
V113	Side-to-side difference in left ulnar motor nerve F wave
V124	Side-to-side difference in right ulnar motor nerve F wave
V135	Side-to-side difference in left tibial motor nerve F wave
V146	Side-to-side difference in right tibial motor nerve F wave
V157	Side-to-side difference in left peroneal motor nerve F wave
V168	Side-to-side difference in right peroneal motor nerve F wave
V169	Abnormal sensory conduction velocity in left median nerve
V174	Abnormal sensory conduction velocity in right median nerve
V179	Abnormal sensory conduction velocity in left ulnar nerve
V184	Abnormal sensory conduction velocity in right ulnar nerve
V189	Abnormal sensory conduction velocity in left sural nerve
V194	Abnormal sensory conduction velocity in right sural nerve

C4.5. C4.5 [9] builds a decision tree from training data using recursive partitions. In each iteration, C4.5 selects the attribute with the highest gain ratio as the attribute from which the tree branching (splitting attribute) is performed. This results in a more simplified tree (fewer subtrees). C4.5 is widely used in classification problems of diverse nature.

JRip. JRip is an implementation of the RIPPER (Repeated Incremental Pruning to Produce Error Reduction) algorithm [5]. It belongs to the rule induction learning methods. JRip builds a set of rules that identify the classes while minimizing the amount of error. A rule has the form:

    if attribute1 <relational operator> value1 <logical operator> attribute2 <relational operator> value2 < ... > **then** decision-value.

2.3   Filter Methods

We selected filter methods for feature selection in this study, as they are in computational terms the fastest and simplest methods available in the literature for this task. Filters work independently from any classification algorithm and base their decision solely on characteristics of data. All filter methods used in this study deliver a ranking according to the goodness of each feature.

Chi-Square. This method evaluates the chi-square statistic of each feature taken individually with respect to the class [12].

Information Gain. Information gain measures the goodness of a feature to predict the class given that the presence or absence of the feature in the dataset is known [10].

Symmetrical Uncertainty. This method measures the correlation between pairs of attributes using normalization of information gain. The normalization is performed to compensate for the bias of information gain to benefit attributes with more values and to ensure that they are comparable [6].

2.4   Performance Measures

Balanced Accuracy. The balanced accuracy is a better estimate of a classifier performance when a unequal distribution of two classes is present in a dataset. This metric was used as our based metric along all the experiments. Balanced accuracy is defined as:

$$BalancedAccuracy = \left(\frac{TP}{TP + FN} + \frac{TN}{FP + TN} \right) /2 \qquad (1)$$

where TP = True Positive, TN = True Negative, FP = False Positive and FN = False Negative.

Sensitivity. Sensitivity measures the proportion of true positives, which were correctly identified by a predictive model. For a diagnostic test, sensitivity measures the ability of a test to detect ill subjects.

Specificity. Specificity measures the proportion of true negatives, which were correctly identified by a predictive model. For a diagnostic test, specificity measures the ability of a test to detect healthy subjects.

Kappa Statistic. Kappa statistic, introduced by Cohen [4], measures the agreement between the classifier itself and the ground truth corrected by the effect of the agreement between them by chance. Formally:

$$kappa = \frac{P(A) - P(E)}{1 - P(E)} \tag{2}$$

where $P(A)$ is the proportion of agreement between the classifier and the ground truth, $P(E)$ is the proportion of agreement expected between the classifier and the ground truth by chance.

2.5 Model Evaluation Scheme

Cross Validation. Cross-validation divides the original complete dataset into k independent new datasets (k folds). Then, it performs k loops in which $k - 1$ partitions of the original dataset is used for training and the rest for testing. For each fold, the measure of evaluation of the model obtained from the confusion matrix is calculated and summed. When all the k loops have ended, the cross-validation accuracy is obtained. In this study, we use a 10-fold cross-validation (10-FCV).

3   Experimental Design

We performed two types of experiments. In the first case, we used the 50-feature subset, described in Sect. 2.1, for experiments. We added the class variable to this subset, which is mechanical ventilation. Finally, we created a dataset containing the 122 instances and 51 features. As mentioned in Sect. 2.1, our dataset has 2 classes, identified with numbers 1 and 2, where 1 means mechanical ventilation was required and 2 means mechanical ventilation was not required.

In the second case, each of the filter methods investigated in this work was applied to the 50-feature dataset. New datasets were created with the resultant most relevant features selected using each filter. Along with these features, the class attribute was included in the datasets during this new classification process.

We used 10-FCV evaluation scheme, described above. For this scheme, we performed 30 runs where we applied each of the classifiers described earlier. In each run, we set a different seed. The same seeds were used for each kernel. These seeds were generated using Mersenne-Twister pseudo-random number generator [7]. The use of a different seed for each run ensures producing different splits of train and test sets. For each run, we computed accuracy, balanced accuracy, sensitivity, specificity, and Kappa statistic. Finally, we averaged each of these quantities across the 30 runs.

A baseline balanced accuracy using all the 50 features included in the dataset was computed. This value was compared to that of the balanced accuracy obtained using only the relevant features as determined by each filter method. Such comparison would allow for a clear view of the benefits of the feature selection process over using the entire dataset, in terms of balanced accuracy.

3.1   SVMLin Parameter Optimization

For tuning C, we tried values 0.01, 0.1, 1, 10, 50, 80 and 100. For each of these values, we performed 30 SVM runs of 10-FCV process with different seeds each. We calculated the balanced accuracy of each run and the average over 30 runs. We selected the value of C that obtained the highest balanced accuracy averaged over 30 runs.

4   Results and Discussion

All the filter methods investigated in this work, that is, chi-squared, information gain and symmetrical uncertainty, selected the same relevant features from the original dataset. These features were V24, V25, V37 and V59. The first three features are clinical and the last one is from the NCS. As described before, we performed experiments using all features and using only these relevant features. Below, we describe the results of these experiments.

As mentioned before, SVMLin requires a tuning procedure. The results of this optimization using all features and using only relevant features are shown in Table 4. With this classifier, the highest balanced accuracy was obtained using only the relevant features. This value was 0.8908. We can observe that a slight improvement in balanced accuracy was obtained using a feature selection procedure.

Table 4. SVMLin optimization. The units of the results are shown in balanced accuracy over 30 runs. The highest value appears in bold.

C	All features	Relevant features
0.01	0.8327	**0.8908**
0.1	**0.8777**	0.8852
1	0.7777	0.8840
10	0.7479	0.8840
50	0.7465	0.8840
80	0.7465	0.8840
100	0.7465	0.8835

Table 5 shows the results of the experiments by each classifier. The highest balanced accuracy was obtained by C4.5 using all the 50 features. In C4.5 and JRip classifications, results decreased with feature selection. Only in SVMLin classifier, feature selection had a positive effect over balanced accuracy.

Tables 6 and 7 show the classification results using all features and only the relevant features respectively. The remaining metrics investigated in this work were computed in these classifications. The standard deviation (sd) of each measure is also shown. The best classification result was obtained by C4.5

Table 5. Balanced accuracy using all features and only the relevant features found by filter methods. The units of the results are shown in balanced accuracy over 30 runs. The highest value appears in bold.

Classifier	All features	Relevant features
C4.5	**0.8925**	0.8731
JRip	0.8908	0.8777
SVMLin	0.8777	**0.8908**

using all the 50 features. JRip and SVMLin obtained a slightly lower balanced accuracy, JRip using all features and SVM using only four relevant features. All models resulted to be more specific than sensitive, meaning that they are better predicting the lack of mechanical ventilation necessity. This could be a result of the imbalance characteristic of the dataset used in this study. Further investigation is recommended.

The feature selection process selected three clinical variables and one from NCS. Clinical features are obtained earlier and more easily than those of CFS and NCS. We investigated the effect of eliminating the NCS variable from the predictors in the classification task. With this aim, we performed new

Table 6. Classification results using all features. The results are shown in average over 30 runs. The highest value appears in bold.

Classifier	Balanced accuracy	Accuracy	Sensitivity	Specificity	Kappa
C4.5	**0.8925**	0.9141	0.8275	0.9575	0.8027
	(0.0163)	(0.0151)	(0.0310)	(0.0212)	(0.0340)
JRip	0.8908	0.9153	0.8175	0.9642	0.8041
	(0.0169)	(0.0161)	(0.0287)	(0.0207)	(0.0363)
SVMLin	0.8777	0.9011	0.8075	0.9479	0.7723
	(0.0209)	(0.0173)	(0.0354)	(0.0147)	(0.0405)

Table 7. Classification results using only the relevant features. The results are shown in average over 30 runs. The highest value appears in bold.

Classifier	Balanced accuracy	Accuracy	Sensitivity	Specificity	Kappa
SVMLin	**0.8908**	0.9272	0.7817	1	0.8267
	(0.0056)	(0.0037)	(0.0112)	(0)	(0.0094)
JRip	0.8777	0.9075	0.7883	0.9671	0.7843
	(0.0113)	(0.0136)	(0.0157)	(0.0209)	(0.0296)
C4.5	0.8731	0.9017	0.7875	0.9588	0.7715
	(0.0082)	(0.0108)	(0.0143)	(0.0189)	(0.0229)

experiments where our dataset consisted of V24, V25 and V37 variables (clinical) and the outcome variable, which is mechanical ventilation. Experiments with all classifiers were performed.

The result of SVM optimization using these features are shown in Table 8. The highest balanced accuracy obtained was 0.8829. As we can observe, the effect of eliminating variable V59 is minimal, therefore the original SVMLin predictive model is practically not affected.

Table 8. SVMLin optimization in three different experiments. The units of the results are shown in balanced accuracy over 30 runs. The highest value appears in bold.

C	All features	Relevant features	Clinical relevant features
0.01	0.8327	**0.8908**	**0.8829**
0.1	**0.8777**	0.8852	0.8819
1	0.7777	0.8840	0.8819
10	0.7479	0.8840	0.8810
50	0.7465	0.8840	0.8825
80	0.7465	0.8840	0.8825
100	0.7465	0.8835	0.8815

Table 9 shows the results of three different experiments: using all features, only relevant features and clinical relevant features. Again, the effect of eliminating V59 variable from the relevant predictors was practically null. The balanced accuracy in two predictive models using relevant features and using only clinical relevant features is almost the same. This metric did not vary in JRip from one case to another.

Table 9. Balanced accuracy in three different experiments. The units of the results are shown in balanced accuracy over 30 runs. The highest value appears in bold.

Classifier	All features	Relevant features	Clinical relevant features
C4.5	**0.8925**	0.8731	0.8729
JRip	0.8908	0.8777	0.8777
SVMLin	0.8777	**0.8908**	**0.8829**

Table 10 show the classification results using only the clinical relevant features. The standard deviation (sd) of each measure is also shown. SVMLin obtained the best classification result. JRip and C4.5 obtained similar results.

SVMLin using only three clinical predictors obtained the best prediction model. This is concluded by two reasons. First, there is no major difference in balanced accuracy among the three best models. Secondly, in addition to the

Table 10. Classification results using only the clinical relevant features. The results are shown in average over 30 runs. The highest value appears in bold.

Classifier	Balanced accuracy	Accuracy	Sensitivity	Specificity	Kappa
SVMLin	**0.8829**	0.9219	0.7658	1	0.8133
	(0.0129)	(0.0086)	(0.0258)	(0)	(0.0200)
JRip	0.8777	0.908	0.7867	0.9688	0.7852
	(0.0086)	(0.0103)	(0.0157)	(0.0176)	(0.0225)
C4.5	0.8729	0.9008	0.7892	0.9566	0.7699
	(0.0077)	(0.0093)	(0.0142)	(0.0160)	(0.0200)

previous finding, the simplest model of them will be more effective since it allows a fast, yet accurate prediction of the mechanical ventilation necessity in GBS patients. Finally, a diagnostic model using only clinical variables is even better since these variables are obtained earlier and more easily than those of CFS and NCS.

5   Conclusions

In this study, we aimed at building and comparing predictive models for the mechanical ventilation necessity in GBS patients. We applied machine learning techniques, specifically classification algorithms and feature selection. We analyzed the effect of feature selection in the performance of the predictive models. We performed experiments using a real dataset containing clinical, NCS and CFS data.

Filter methods allowed identifying a reduced set of relevant features. However, the feature selection process had a slight effect in the prediction models. This effect was negative in C4.5 and JRip and positive in SVM.

After an analysis of different predictive models, a model using only three clinical predictors was found to perform the best. From the medical point of view, this finding could help physicians to promptly and accurately identify GBS patients with mechanical necessity. Therefore, the adequate medical procedures may be timely carried out.

References

1. Arisi, I., D'Onofrio, M., Brandi, R., Felsani, A., Capsoni, S., Drovandi, G., Felici, G., Weitschek, E., Bertolazzi, P., Cattaneo, A.: Gene expression biomarkers in the brain of a mouse model for alzheimer's disease: mining of microarray data by logic classification and feature selection. J. Alzheimers Dis. **24**, 721–738 (2011)
2. Asha, T., Natarajan, S., Murthy, K.N.B.: Data mining techniques in the diagnosis of tuberculosis. In: Cardona, P.J. (ed.) Understanding Tuberculosis - Global Experiences and Innovative Approaches to the Diagnosis. InTech, Rijeka, Croacia (2012)

3. Barati, E., Saraee, M., Mohammadi, A., Adibi, N., Ahamadzadeh, M.R.: A survey on utilization of data mining approaches for dermatological (skin) diseases prediction. J. Sel. Areas Health Inf. **2**(3), 1–11 (2011)
4. Cohen, J.: A coefficient of agreement for nominal scales. Educat. Psychol. Meas. **20**(1), 37–46 (1960)
5. Cohen,W.W.: Fast effective rule induction. In: Proceedings of the Twelfth International Conference on Machine Learning, pp. 115–123. Morgan Kaufmann (1995)
6. Liu, Y., Schumann, M.: Data mining feature selection for credit scoring models. J. Oper. Res. Soc. **56**(9), 1099–1108 (2005)
7. Matsumoto, M., Nishimura, T.: Mersenne twister: a 623-dimensionally equidistributed uniform pseudo-random number generator. ACM Trans. Model. Comput. Simul. **8**(1), 3–30 (1998)
8. Paul, B.S., Bhatia, R., Prasad, K., Padma, M.V., Tripathi, M., Singh, M.B.: Clinical predictors of mechanical ventilation in Guillain-Barre syndrome. Neurol. India **60**(2), 150–153 (2012)
9. Quinlan, J.R.: C4.5: Programs for Machine Learning. Morgan Kaufmann Publishers Inc., San Francisco (1993)
10. Sebastiani, F.: Machine learning in automated text categorization. ACM Comput. Surv. **34**(1), 1–47 (2002)
11. Vapnik, V.: Statistical Learning Theory. Wiley, New York (1998)
12. Zheng, Z., Wu, X., Srihari, R.: Feature selection for text categorization on imbalanced data. ACM SIGKDD Explor. Newslett. **6**(1), 80–89 (2004)

A Robust Machine Learning Approach to Microprocessor Instructions Identification

Hippolyte Djonon Tsague[1(✉)] and Bheki Twala[2]

[1] Smart Token Research Group, Modelling and Digital Science (MDS),
Council for Scientific and Industrial Research (CSIR), Pretoria, South Africa
hdjonontsague@csir.co.za
[2] Department of Electrical and Electronic Engineering Science,
Faculty of Engineering, Institute for Intelligent Systems,
University of Johannesburg (UJ), Johannesburg, South Africa

Abstract. Since the first publication, side channel leakage has been widely used for the purposes of extracting secret information, such as cryptographic keys, from embedded devices. However, in a few instances it has been utilised for extracting other information about the internal state of a computing device. In this paper, we show how to create a robust instruction-level side channel leakage profile of an embedded processor. Using the profile we show how to extract executed instructions from the device's leakage with good accuracy. In addition, we provide a comparison between several performance and recognition enhancement tools.

Keywords: Side channel leakage · Templates · Principal Components Analysis · Linear Discriminant Analysis · Multivariate gaussian distribution · k-Nearest Neighbours Algorithm · Reverse engineering

1 Introduction

The microelectronics industry has improved enormously over the last few decades; it has steadily moved to occupy a central position in modern electronic system design. It has grown in a large part because of its ability to continually improve performance while reducing costs. There is a constant drive to make devices that occupy less space, consume less power and have shorter delays. This improvement has resulted in device smaller feature size and the increase in clock-speed as predicted by Moore's law, which states that the transistor density on integrated circuits doubles every 18 months. A large part of the success of the Complementary Metal Oxide Silicon (CMOS) transistor is due to the fact that it can be scaled to increasingly smaller size. The ability to improve performance while decreasing power consumption has made the CMOS the dominant technology for Very Large Scale Integration (VLSI) circuits.

As a direct result of the CMOS improvement, an increasing number of embedded systems have gained entrance to our everyday life. According to [4], more than 14 billion micro-controller units were sold in 2010. The unit shipments are forecast to double by 2017, while at the same time the average selling price per unit is expected to drop by about half of the current value. Besides the everyday use of µCs in non-critical

© Springer International Publishing AG 2017
O. Pichardo-Lagunas and S. Miranda-Jiménez (Eds.): MICAI 2016, Part II, LNAI 10062, pp. 248–258, 2017.
DOI: 10.1007/978-3-319-62428-0_21

applications, a steadily increasing number is assigned to manage security-critical tasks. Examples include contactless and traditional smart cards used in banking and access control applications, electronic control units (ECUs) in cars, industrial machine controllers (for services such as software download or feature activation) and medical implants in the healthcare sector. The continuing trend to get everything networked and linked will only increase the need for embedded applications with strong security features. It is thus of great interest for design engineers and users to assess the feasibility of μCs as security devices. The use of microprocessor devices is said to make fraud related attacks more difficult, however, available literature has found them susceptible to side-channel attacks. When a microprocessor executes a program, its power consumption can be used to reveal the content of program and/or data memory of the microprocessor. The application of correlation between power consumption and microprocessor activity has found many uses including recovering cryptographic keys, revealing hidden hardware faults, creating a covert channel or reverse engineering the code executed by the processor. This is concerning, considering the increasing demand for and dependability upon microprocessors in secure applications.

Embedded devices need security and privacy mechanisms to be built-in to ensure that data are handled securely. In general, cryptographic protocols are designed with the chief aim of providing such security. However, it has now become known that attacks based on the utilisation of device's emitted physical measures can be used to breach their actual security. These attacks named side channel attacks consist in retrieving stored or secret data by observing physical properties of the device during data processing. Each observed trace is characterised by a matrix of real values and each component of this matrix is seen as a variable. In a side channel attack scenario, the attacker eavesdrops on the device's side channel emissions while the device is being used to encrypt data. This small amount of information recorded can then be used to successfully duplicate the key. Even better an attacker can use the technique to reverse engineer contents of CMOS devices without the user being aware of such attacks. That is probably the reason why security experts believe that such attacks are among the most dangerous in cryptanalysis.

This work intends to present a methodology for recovering the instruction flow of smartcard based on side channel information only. Further steps will be taken in explaining the use of statistical analysis of power consumption data by taking advantage of machine learning techniques. The role of machine learning in cryptanalysis has been discussed in many publications. In our work, the main focus will be on two aspects of power consumption analysis which have been neglected thus far in the literature: the issue of dimension reduction and the one of model selection. These two aspects will further help in increasing the identification rate of the template process.

2   Related Work

Side-channel analysis (SCA) has now been scientifically studied for almost 20 years. Due to this long period, it is perhaps somewhat surprising that the vast majority of SCA research has been restricted to methods for extracting secret keys and corresponding countermeasures. There are only very few contributions reported in the literature that consider other uses of SCA, such as reverse-engineering of code by means of side-channel leakages.

According to our findings, there are two research topics relating to side-channel reverse-engineering. They are Side-Channel Analysis for Reverse-Engineering (SCARE) and Side-Channel-based Disassembler (SCANDAL). SCARE is mainly concerned with recovering individual values of a (partially) known algorithm. For instance, in 2003 Novak described how to recover the contents of one (out of two) S-box tables of the A3/A8 algorithm [1]. The research revealed that equal intermediate results have similar side-channel leakage. In a follow-up paper, Clavier presented an improved attack on A3/A8 that recovers the contents of both S-box tables including the secret key used by the cipher [2]. A number of subsequent publications dealt with revealing secret S-box entries or with reverse-engineering a substitution-permutation network or a Feistel scheme [3–5]. In contrast, SCANDAL attempts to extract code from side-channel information. In particular, by measuring and analysing the side-channel leakage of a μC. In this scenario, the chief goal is to extract the executed instructions. In 2002, [6] presented a correlation attack that uses a generated dictionary for each instruction, which is compared with an unknown observation. Additionally, neuronal networks were used to automate the process. A recognition rate "better than 87%" for a complex instruction set computing (CISC) processor was reported. However, the authors do not give any detailed results for a reduced instruction set computer (RISC) processor. Instead, they state that they were not able to extract the executed code on a RISC processor. In 2008, [7] first described the analysis of an 8-bit RISC processor, the Microchip PIC16F687. Follow-up work was performed by [8]. In the latter contribution different linear feature extraction algorithms were tested. A recognition rate of 70.1% on test data and 40.7% on real code were achieved. By further applying a hidden Markov model, the result on the real code could be improved to 58%. In a recent paper, Msgna et al. report a 100% recognition rate for a side-channel disassembler for an ATXmega163 μC [9]. While Fisher's LDA for the dimensionality reduction in combination with k nearest neighbours (kNN) achieved a recognition rate of only 48.74% and means-PCA with kNN a slightly better recognition rate of 56.88%, plain PCA with kNN surprisingly outperforms all other techniques with reported results of 100%. Even though impressive, we see several limitations to these findings. First, only 39 of the 130 instructions of the μC were supported, which limits the practical applicability. Second, the approach was not tested on real code, e.g., an implementation of the AES. As findings by others and us show, there is often quite a difference between recognition rates on test data versus real data.

3   Template Construction

The first step in profiling an embedded processor is the collection of training (template) data. Here we make the assumptions that all legitimately manufactured devices of the same model have similar leakage characteristics. The training traces are collected by recording the power intake of a reference device while executing the selected instructions repeatedly. This can be achieved by running simple training programs on a batch of reference devices. Now let us consider N L-dimensional observations of the device's power consumption $\{x_n\}$. Where, $1 \leq n \leq N$. Each of these N L-dimensional observations belongs to one of the K instructions I_k where $1 \leq k \leq K$. The template for each recorded instruction would now be made up of computed mean and covariance matrix of the N L-dimensional observations. The mean μ_k and covariance σ_k are calculated as follows:

$$\mu_k = \frac{1}{N} \sum_{\{x_n \in I_k\}} x_n \tag{1}$$

$$\sigma_k = \sum_{\{x_n \in I_k\}} (x_n - \mu_k)(x_n - \mu_k)^T \tag{2}$$

Therefore the template for each instruction is defined by the tuplets of (μ_k, σ_k). However, in practice the observations $\{x_n\}$ may have too many closely correlated points which in turn may force the template construction exercise to become very expensive as far as time is concerned. Therefore, in order to obtain a statistically sound and reliable result we have to employ dimensionality reduction techniques.

4   Linear Feature Extction

Dimension reduction processes are feature selection algorithms used to compress data while preserving as much variance of the original data as possible. In the literature, several dimensionality reduction methods have been proposed [10, 11]. In this paper we have implemented three of the most common techniques, the Principal Components Analysis (PCA), Fisher's Linear Discriminant Analysis (LDA) and Class-Mean-PCA.

Among feature extraction techniques, PCA and LDA are very common dimensionality reduction algorithms that have successfully been applied in many classification problems like face recognition, character recognition, speech recognition, etc. [12] with the chief objective being to eliminate insignificant data (without losing too much information) during the pre-processing step.

4.1   Principal Component Analysis

A captured side-channel trace often carries a certain amount of redundancies. For instance, a good amount of information is embedded in the amplitude of a clock peak. However, the digital sample points forming the whole shape of the peak only adds little useful information. The idea behind PCA is to minimize superfluous correlated data by transforming the coordinate system. PCA attempts to minimize these correlations by transforming the data into a subspace with a new basis. The axes of the new basis are selected such that the first axis points to the direction of the largest variance and the second one to the largest variance under the constraint that the two axes are orthogonal, and so on. The reduction takes place by choosing only axes that are based on the highest variances.

One major disadvantage of the standard PCA is that it does not assimilate any information about the different classes, i.e., computing the PCA from a data set representing features of one class leads to the same result as using a data set being composed of many different classes. A workaround is the so-called Class-Mean-PCA. Here, instead of computing the PCA for all data, it is only applied on the class means to maximize the variances between these classes. Still, the distance between the class means does not take the standard deviation within the classes into account.

4.2   Linear Discriminant Analysis

Fisher's LDA solves this problem of PCA and Class-Mean-PCA by maximizing the distance between two class means while simultaneously minimizing the variances inside the classes.

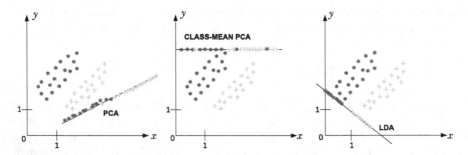

Fig. 1. Comparison between PCA, Class-Mean-PCA, and LDA

Figure 1 shows a comparison between LDA, Class-Mean-PCA and LDA. In this example, there is a high overlap on the new axis of PCA and Class-Mean-PCA. However, LDA clearly separates the classes. Although in this figure LDA seems to be the best solution for classification tasks, there is no general rule that one algorithm is always outperforming the others. There are certain situations where PCA yields better results than LDA. In its original form, LDA was introduced for two classes. The idea is to transform a given set of observations X with a weight vector $\vec{w}$ to a new one-dimensional set Y in a new basis:

$$Y = \vec{w}^T X \tag{3}$$

5   Experimental Setup

In this section, we describe our approach to acquire side-channel traces usable for the classification of the executed instructions. To this end, two problems have to be solved: (i) programming the target device with suitable code to obtain the training data and (ii) the actual measurement of the side-channel signal.

5.1   Target Device

To implement the techniques discussed above we have selected an ATMega163 24C256 based smart card. The ATMega163 is an 8-bit microcontroller based on AVR architecture, and it has 130 instructions. According to the Atmel datasheet most of the 130 instructions supported by the μC are processed in one clock cycle. Other instructions such as multiply (Mul) are performed in 2 clock cycles. Other instructions such as "JMP" are performed in 3 clock cycles. During the instruction study process we discovered two important features of the Atmel microprocessors namely redundancy and usage of instructions. The redundancy refers to more than one instruction performing the same operation; for example in ATMega163 the instructions LD Rd, Z and LDD Rd, perform indirect load operation. Besides the redundancy we also studied the instruction usage frequency by analysing several source codes. We created a source code base by using publicly available source codes from various web sites [13, 14]. For the classification task, we have taken all instructions into account. We have also included our own implementation of cryptographic algorithms and general purpose applications in the analysis. The power traces are captured via a voltage drop across a tiny resistor connected between the ground pin of the smart card and the ground pin of the supply voltage. The smart card is set to run at a clock frequency of 4 MHz and is powered by a +5 V supply from the reader. The measurements are recorded using a Picoscope digital oscilloscope 6403.

5.2   Template Construction

To generate the number of traces we needed for the templates construction we created a number of separate assembly files for each target instruction to be profiled. After the initialization of the μC, all general purpose registers are filled with random values. The subsequent part of the code is used for the actual profiling and testing. First, a rising edge on a pin of the μC is generated to trigger the acquisition of measurements. Then, a three-instruction pattern is repeated until the end of the flash of the μC has been reached:

(a) A preceding random instruction with random operand(s),
(b) The instruction for which the assembler file was created (again with random operand(s)),
(c) A subsequent random instruction with random operand(s).

It is important to note at this stage that the term "random" simply makes reference to a value that is uniformly generated when creating the assembly file; such value is kept constant throughout program execution.

To decrease the influence of the source and destination registers and memory cells we carefully selected a random source and destination before executing the selected instructions and we initialised them with random values sent from the terminal over the Application Protocol Data Unit (APDU) channel. For the data processed, we have generated random data for each execution of the target instruction. To minimise the influence of the ambient noise introduced in the measurement, all equipment is properly warmed up beforehand so that it is all running at a uniform temperature throughout the trace collection stage. This requires running a few test measurements to be discarded before the actual power trace collection begins. To minimise the effect of measurement noise introduced by the reference card on the power traces we used 10 of the same model reference cards throughout the experiment. To reduce the influence of other random noise from our measurement we collected 5000 traces for each of the selected instructions (i.e. 500 traces from each of the reference cards). Out of these 5000 traces, we used 4500 of them to construct the templates.

6 Results

Before starting the classification, we normalized the traces by subtracting the mean and dividing by the standard deviation. The tests were accomplished using a 10-fold cross validation: The measurements were split into 10 parts where 90% of the data is used as training data and 10% as test data. Each experiment was conducted 10 times with each part of the data being used one time as test data and the remaining nine times as subset of the training data. The results shown in the following are the average values of all 10 classification runs.

  To decrease the computing time, we first tried to scale the measurement traces. However, due to this scaling much information was lost, resulting in a reduced recognition rate. For this reason, we followed another approach. While the peaks at the rising edge of each clock cycle seem to contain most of the information, we assumed the space between to be irrelevant noise. Thus, as a first quick dimensionality reduction we removed these areas of the traces by ignoring all dimensions with a low variance between analysed classes. It turned out that this reduction preserves most of the necessary information for the forthcoming classification.

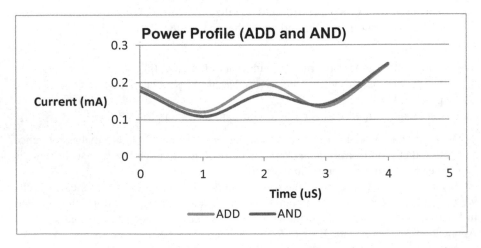

Fig. 2. AND vs ADD power profile

For multiple clock cycle instructions like Move or even Multiply (MUL), the clock cycles are regarded as consecutive instructions. Therefore, more than one template was generated for them. For conditional branching instructions like Jump (JMP), templates are generated for both conditions. Should the condition of interest be evaluated to false the branching instruction only need one clock cycle; however, whenever such condition was evaluated to true they needed two clock cycles. In short, for every conditional branching type of instruction we created three templates.

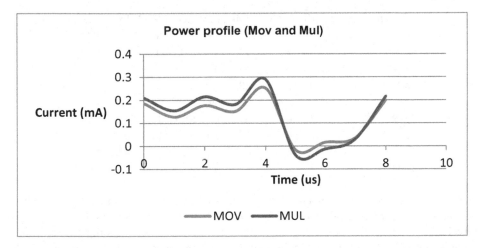

Fig. 3. Mul vs Mov power profile

Figures 2 and 3 show the power consumed by selected instruction. In this case "ADD" and "MOV" instructions which are single clock cycle instructions and "MOV" and "MUL" which are two clock cycle instructions, some instructions generate sufficiently different power profiles to identify them easily. However, others (Figs. 2 and 3) generate almost identical power profiles which make it harder to recognise them from their power profiles. Therefore, in order to successfully identify each instruction, there was a need to create well-conditioned templates and this required several training traces.

6.1   Dimensionality Reduction

When using the Linear Discriminant Analysis to reduce the dimensionality we computed 3850 vector subtractions and additions. Linear Discriminant Analysis is a straight forward method and involves the computation of variance for 125 column vectors. When using PCA, the new dimensionality has to be chosen carefully. If the dimensionality is too small, too much of variance of the original data may be lost and with it important information about the observations. On the other hand, if the dimensionality is too large, the templates cross-correlation increases and the classification become less reliable.

6.2   Instruction Classification

As stated earlier, we have profiled 130 instructions from an Atmega163 smart card. In the process we have collected 5000 power consumption traces for each of the instructions. Out of these 5000 traces we used 4500 of them to train the templates. Now we discuss the classification result for the remaining 500 traces as shown in Table 1 below

Table 1. Percentage of true (bold) and false positive recognition rate for a selected instructions using LDA.

Instruction	ADD	SUB	MULT	JMP	LD	XOR	NOP	INC	DEC
ADD	**31.2**	2	0	0	3.6	13	0	1.7	1.23
SUB	9.12	**55.6**	1.2	2.3	5	9	0.4	0	0.3
MULT	5.3	0	**61.32**	1.6	0	2.3	2.1	3.1	0
JMP	0.3	3.1	0.8	**48.9**	0.7	3.1	0	06	0
LD	0	0.2	2.1	0	**66**	0	3.7	0.9	1.3
XOR	0.4	1.6	0	4	0	**51.3**	1.2	4.2	2.2
NOP	0.1	0	0.6	3.2	2.1	0	**77.8**	0	0.7
INC	2.4	0.3	8	0	2	1.3	0.2	**43.4**	1.3
DEC	11	0.5	0	0.5	0	3	0	5.1	**54.8**

During our tests, we compared two different dimensionality reductions in combination with the kNN classifier. The combination using a multiclass LDA has the advantage of being very efficient as reported in the literature, as the computation of the weight matrix, and hence, the eigenvectors and eigenvalues, has to be accomplished only once. However, our results show that the multiclass LDA did not yield very good results. We took a measurement near the centre of the chip and tested both techniques on the same training and test data. The average recognition rate was about 57% for the multiclass LDA.

k-Nearest Neighbours Algorithm (kNN): In kNN there are two major design decisions that need to be made. One is the number of neighbours, k, participating in the decision making. The other is the distance function used to compute the closeness between the template data and the signal that need to be classified. We started our investigation testing with k = 1, Euclidean distance function and full dimension of the traces. In order to see the effect of changing k on the recognition rate, we repeated the experiment for k = {5, 10, 15, 20} and the result was the same. The average recognition rate for all the templates rose to about 78.31%. The recognition rate for a selected 9 instructions is presented in Table 2.

This sharp improvement in recognition rate could be attributed to both the removal of inter-class correlated points using PCA and the fact that the traces are not generalised during the learning process of the algorithm. Finally, it is worth mentioning that beside the two classification techniques reported on in this document, we have also experimented with several others. These algorithms include Self-Organizing Maps, Support Vector Machines, Linear Vector Quantization and Naive Bayes Classifiers. However, their results were not satisfactory enough and so there was not enough motivation to continue experimenting with them.

Table 2. Percentage of true (bold) and false positive recognition rate for a selected instructions using kNN

Instruction	ADD	SUB	MULT	JMP	LD	XOR	NOP	INC	DEC
ADD	**71.6**	0.2	0	0	5.1	0.7	0.9	6.1	0
SUB	4.2	**87.4**	0.2	6.3	0	6	0.1	0.1	0.9
MULT	0.3	0	**71.82**	1.6	0	2.3	2.1	3.1	0
JMP	1.3	0.1	0.8	89	0.7	3.1	0	4	0.9
LD	0	0.1	2.1	0	**86**	0	3.7	0.5	1.3
XOR	0.7	1.9	0	4	0	**65.8**	1.2	0.2	2.2
NOP	0.8	0.7	0.6	3.2	0.1	0	**75.8**	0	0.7
INC	2.1	4.3	8	0	2	1.3	0.2	**58.4**	1.3
DEC	11	0.5	0	0.5	0	3	0	5.1	**54.8**

7 Conclusion

This paper has explored the idea of side channel profiling of a processor down to its instruction-level properties. The maximum classification success rate achieved prior to our work was 51.1% when profiling all 130 instruction set of an Atmel Atmega63 microcontroller. In our experiment we discussed a four stage classification process; trace collection, pre-processing, template construction and classification. We tested several dimensionality reduction and classification algorithms some of which were not investigated previously in the context of side channel analysis. We experimented on the algorithms using traces collected from five AVR processors, ATMega163. We improved the previous classification success rate to a 78.31% using a specific combination of dimensionality reduction and classification algorithm. These are PCA and k-NN algorithm.

References

1. Novak, R.: Side-channel attack on substitution blocks. In: Zhou, J., Yung, M., Han, Y. (eds.) ACNS 2003. LNCS, vol. 2846, pp. 307–318. Springer, Heidelberg (2003). doi:10.1007/978-3-540-45203-4_24
2. Clavier, C.: Side channel analysis for reverse engineering (SCARE) -an improved attack against a secret A3/A8 GSM algorithm. In: 2004 IACR Cryptology ePrint Archive, vol. 49 (2004)
3. Réal, D., Dubois, V., Guilloux, A.-M., Valette, F., Drissi, M.: SCARE of an unknown hardware feistel implementation. In: Grimaud, G., Standaert, F.-X. (eds.) CARDIS 2008. LNCS, vol. 5189, pp. 218–227. Springer, Heidelberg (2008). doi:10.1007/978-3-540-85893-5_16
4. Rivain, M., Roche, T.: SCARE of secret ciphers with SPN structures. In: Sako, K., Sarkar, P. (eds.) ASIACRYPT 2013. LNCS, vol. 8269, pp. 526–544. Springer, Heidelberg (2013). doi:10.1007/978-3-642-42033-7_27
5. Clavier, C., Isorez, Q., Wurcker, A.: Complete SCARE of AES-like block ciphers by chosen plaintext collision power analysis. In: Paul, G., Vaudenay, S. (eds.) INDOCRYPT 2013. LNCS, vol. 8250, pp. 116–135. Springer, Cham (2013). doi:10.1007/978-3-319-03515-4_8

6. Quisquater, J.-J., Samyde, D.: Electromagnetic analysis (EMA): measures and counter-measures for smart cards. In: Attali, I., Jensen, T. (eds.) E-smart 2001. LNCS, vol. 2140, pp. 200–210. Springer, Heidelberg (2001). doi:10.1007/3-540-45418-7_17

7. Goldack, M.: Side-channel based reverse engineering for microcontrollers. Diploma Thesis, Ruhr-University Bochum (2008). https://www.emsec.rub.de/media/attachments/files/2012/10/da_goldack.pdf

8. Eisenbarth, T., Kasper, T., Moradi, A., Paar, C., Salmasizadeh, M., Shalmani, M.T.M.: on the power of power analysis in the real world: a complete break of the KeeLoq code hopping scheme. In: Wagner, D. (ed.) CRYPTO 2008. LNCS, vol. 5157, pp. 203–220. Springer, Heidelberg (2008). doi:10.1007/978-3-540-85174-5_12

9. Msgna, M., Markantonakis, K., Mayes, K.: Precise instruction-level side channel profiling of embedded processors. In: Huang, X., Zhou, J. (eds.) ISPEC 2014. LNCS, vol. 8434, pp. 129–143. Springer, Cham (2014). doi:10.1007/978-3-319-06320-1_11

10. Standaert, F.-X., Archambeau, C.: Using subspace-based template attacks to compare and combine power and electromagnetic information leakages. In: Oswald, E., Rohatgi, P. (eds.) CHES 2008. LNCS, vol. 5154, pp. 411–425. Springer, Heidelberg (2008)

11. Bishop, C.M., Nasrabadi, N.M.: Pattern recognition and machine learning. J. Electron. Imaging 16(4), 33–46 (2007)

12. Bishop, C.M.: Pattern Recognition and Machine Learning (Information Science and Statistics). Springer, New York (2006)

13. Rechberger, C., Oswald, E.: Practical template attacks. In: Lim, C.H., Yung, M. (eds.) WISA 2004. LNCS, vol. 3325, pp. 440–456. Springer, Heidelberg (2005). doi:10.1007/978-3-540-31815-6_35

14. Mousa, A., Hamad, A.: Evaluation of the RC4 algorithm for data encryption. IJCSA 3(2), 44–56 (2006)

Classification and Clustering

Stochastic Semantic-Based Multi-objective Genetic Programming Optimisation for Classification of Imbalanced Data

Edgar Galván-López[1(✉)], Lucia Vázquez-Mendoza[2], and Leonardo Trujillo[3]

[1] Department of Computer Science,
National University of Ireland Maynooth, Maynooth, Ireland
edgar.galvan@nuim.ie
[2] School of Social Sciences and Philosophy,
Trinity College Dublin, Dublin, Ireland
lucyvaz@gmail.com
[3] Posgrado en Ciencias de la Ingeniería,
Instituto Tecnológico de Tijuana, Tijuana, Mexico
leonardo.trujillo@tectijuana.edu.mx

Abstract. Data sets with imbalanced class distribution pose serious challenges to well-established classifiers. In this work, we propose a stochastic multi-objective genetic programming based on semantics. We tested this approach on imbalanced binary classification data sets, where the proposed approach is able to achieve, in some cases, higher recall, precision and F-measure values on the minority class compared to C4.5, Naive Bayes and Support Vector Machine, without significantly decreasing these values on the majority class.

1 Introduction

Classification is one of the most studied and challenging problems in machine learning and data mining. The task consists in predicting a value of an attribute, so-called class, based on the values of other attributes. The importance of this research problem can be understood by the fact that many real-world problems have been stated as classification problems, including image recognition [24] and medical diagnosis [1].

Multiple classification algorithms have been proposed and successfully used on classifications tasks, including decision trees, neural networks, support vector machines, Bayesian networks and nearest neighbour classifiers. However, data sets with an imbalanced class distribution (i.e., when the learning examples from at least one class are very uncommon) have posed challenges to well-established classifiers that work under the assumption of a relatively well-balanced class distribution [3,20].

E. Galván-López—Research conducted during Galván's stay at TAO, INRIA and LRI, CNRS & U. Paris-Sud, Université Paris-Saclay, France.

© Springer International Publishing AG 2017
O. Pichardo-Lagunas and S. Miranda-Jiménez (Eds.): MICAI 2016, Part II, LNAI 10062, pp. 261–272, 2017.
DOI: 10.1007/978-3-319-62428-0_22

In binary classification, the class with the smaller number of examples is called the positive or minority class, whereas the other class is referred as the negative or majority class. Good accuracy on the positive class can in many cases be more important than the accuracy on the negative class. However, it has been reported that very often when trying to increase the accuracy on one class, the accuracy on the other tends to decrease [2]. This is because these two objectives are usually in conflict.

A natural form to deal with this scenario is to use evolutionary multi-objective optimisation [5]. Evolutionary Algorithms (EAs) [8], also known as Evolutionary Computation systems, are influenced by the theory of evolution by natural selection. These algorithms have been with us for some decades and are very popular because they have proven competitive in the face of challenging problem features, such as deceptiveness and multiple local optima, among other characteristics [7]. They are also popular because EAs have been successfully used in many different problems, ranging from the automated optimisation of game controllers [12,19] to the automated design of circuits [10,17].

The idea behind EAs is to automatically generate (nearly) optimal solutions by "evolving" potential solutions (individuals forming a population) over time (generations) by using bio-inspired operators (e.g., crossover, mutation). Briefly, the evolutionary process includes the initialisation of the population $P(0)$ at generation $g = 0$. The population consists of a number of individuals which represent potential solutions to the problem. At each iteration or generation (g), every individual within the population ($P(g)$) is evaluated using a *fitness function* that determines its fitness (i.e., how good or bad an individual is). Then, a selection mechanism takes place to stochastically pick the fittest individuals from the population. Some of the selected individuals are modified by genetic operators and the new population $P(g + 1)$ at generation $g + 1$ is created. The process stops when some halting condition is satisfied. Further details on how these stochastic optimisation algorithms work can be found in [8].

The goal of this work is to use a Evolutionary Multi-objective Optimisation (EMO) method [4], in specific a MO Genetic Programming (MOGP) paradigm to *automatically* design classifiers that can correctly classify imbalanced data. Moreover, MOGP has the potential to yield programs (classifiers) that are readable to a human expert. It also has the advantage that from a single run, the approach is able to produce multiple results allowing the user to select the most convenient for the final application (e.g., a high accuracy on the positive class regardless of the accuracy achieved on the negative class). The novelty of this work is the use of semantics in the proposed MOGP. The motivation for doing so is because the specialised EA literature indicates that the adoption of semantics in a canonical Genetic Programming (GP) [22] system yields better results compared to a GP system without semantics. We apply the proposed approach, described in detail in Sect. 2, on a number of imbalanced classification problems of different nature and complexity, and we used these problems as 'they are', that is, we do not try to balance the classes with a sampling method.

The rest of this paper is organised as follows. In Sect. 2, we introduce our proposed approach. Section 3 provides details on the experimental setup used in this research. Section 4 shows and discusses the results found in this study, and finally, conclusions are drawn in Sect. 5.

2   Proposed Approach

2.1   Evolutionary Multi-objective Optimisation

Multi-objective optimisation (MO) aims to simultaneously optimise several objectives. No single solution exists when these objectives are in conflict and the optimal trade-offs between these must be sought. This idea is captured in the Pareto dominance relation: a solution will dominate another one if it is at least as good as the other solution on all the objectives and better on at least one. Similarly, solutions are non-dominated if they are not dominated by any solution in the set of candidate solutions.

Evolutionary multi-objective optimisation (EMO) [5] is based on the following: by replacing the single-objective selection steps, based on the comparison of fitness values, by some Pareto-based comparison, one turns a single-objective evolutionary optimisation algorithm into a multi-objective evolutionary optimisation algorithm, but because Pareto dominance is not a total order, some additional criterion must be used so as to allow the comparison of any pair of points of the search space.

In NSGA-II [6], the Pareto-based comparison uses the non-dominated sorting procedure: all non-dominated individuals in the population are assigned Rank 1 and removed from the population, the remaining non-dominated individuals are assigned Rank 2, and so on. The secondary criterion is the *crowding distance* that promotes diversity among the individuals having the same Pareto rank: in objective space, for each objective, the individuals in the population are ordered, and the partial crowding distance for each of them is the difference in fitness between its two immediate neighbours. The crowding distance is the sum over all objectives of these partial crowding distances. Intuitively, it can be seen as the Manhattan distance between the extremal vertices of the largest hypercube containing the point at hand and no other point of the population. Selecting points with the largest crowding distance amounts to favour the low-density regions of the objective space, thus favouring diversity.

In general, NSGA-II proceeds as follows. From a given population of size N, N offspring are created using standard variation operators (crossover and mutation). Parents and offspring are merged and the resulting population, of size $2N$, is ordered using non-dominated sorting and the crowding distance as a secondary criterion. The best N individuals according to this ranking are selected to survive at the next generation.

2.2   Semantics in Genetic Programming

GP has been successfully used in various different challenging problems (see Koza's article on human competitive results for a comprehensive review [23]).

Despite its proven success, it also suffers from some limitations and researchers have been interested in making GP more robust or reliable by studying various elements of the search process (e.g., neutrality [16,18,25], locality [13,14]). One of these elements that has relatively recently attracted the attention of researchers is the study of semantics in GP, resulting in a dramatic increase in the number of related publications (e.g., [11,15,26,27]).

Semantics is a broad concept that has been studied in different fields (e.g., natural language, psychology), making it hard to give a precise definition of the concept. Moreover, the way semantics have been adopted in canonical GP varies significantly (see [27] for a summary of works carried out on semantics in GP).

In this work we adopted the popular use of semantics in GP from recent related works [26], where researchers have defined it as the output a program produces when it is evaluated on the complete set of training instances, as adopted in various previous works [11,26].

Thus, two individuals (in this case, two expressions/classifiers) are regarded as semantically different if their output vectors are different, they are considered semantically similar, otherwise. Similarly, a semantic distance is defined as the number of different outputs between two individuals. Commonly, when computing the semantic distance, two outputs are considered different if their absolute difference is greater than a given threshold [11,26]. In this work, we set the threshold at 0.5. The speciliased literature indicates that promoting semantically different individuals tends to yield better results.

2.3 Incorporating Semantics into MOGP

In this work, we incorporated semantics into the core of the NSGA-II algorithm. This algorithm, as briefly described before, relies on two main elements: a ranking system and a crowding distance.

We incorporated semantics by replacing this last element, the crowing distance, with a semantic-based indicator called Semantic-based Crowding Distance (SCD). This is computed the following way: a *pivot* is chosen, being the individual from the first Pareto front (Rank 1) that is the furthest away from the other individuals of this front using the crowding distance. For each point, its semantic distance with the pivot is computed. Similarly to the crowding distance, the SCD is computed as the average of the semantic distance differences with its closest neighbours in each direction. The higher values of this SCD are favored during the selection step of NSGA-II. This allows us to have a set of individuals that are spread in semantic space, thereby promoting semantic diversity, the same way NSGA-II promotes diversity ('spreadness') in objective space. Hereafter, this variant of NSGA-II will be called Distance based on Semantics (DBS).

3   Experimental Design

We used binary imbalanced classification problems taken from the well-known UCI Machine Learning Repository [1]. These problems are of different nature

Table 1. Binary imbalanced classification data sets used in our research. Table adapted from [2].

Data set	Classes	Number of examples			Imb.	Features	
	Positive/negative (brief description)	Total	Positive	Negative	Ratio	No.	Type
Ion	Good/bad (ionsphere radar signal)	351	126 (35.8%)	225 (64.2%)	1:3	34	Real
Spect	Abnormal/normal (cardiac tom. scan)	267	55 (20.6%)	212 (79.4%)	1:4	22	Binary
Yeast$_1$	mit/other (protein sequence)	1482	244 (16.5%)	1238 (83.5%)	1:6	8	Real
Yeast$_2$	me3/other (protein sequence)	1482	163 (10.9%)	1319 (89.1%)	1:9	8	Real
Derma	Pityriasis/other (dermatology diseases)	358	20 (5.5%)	338 (94.5%)	1:17	34	Integer
Balanced	Balanced/unbalanced (balance scale)	625	49 (7.8%)	576 (92.2%)	1:12	4	Integer
Abalone$_1$	9/18 (biology of abalone)	731	42 (5.75%)	689 (94.25%)	1:17	8	Real
Abalone$_2$	19/other (biology of abalone)	4177	32 (0.77%)	4145 (99.23%)	1:130	8	Real

Table 2. Confusion matrix.

	Predicted object	Predicted non-object
Actual object	True Positive (TP)	False Negative (FN)
Actual non-object	False Positive (FP)	True Negative (TN)

and complexity (e.g., from a few number of features up to dozens of them, and these include real, binary and integer-value features, from low to relatively high imbalanced data). Table 1 shows the sizes of both negative (majority) and positive (minority) classes for each of the problems used in this work along with some details[1]. We used the data 'as is' (e.g., we did not try to balance the classes with sampling techniques). For each data set, half of the data (with the same class balance than in the whole dataset) was used as a training set and the rest as a test set. All reported results, discussed in the following section, are on the latter.

To automatically generate classifiers via MOGP, we defined our terminal and function in the same manner as in [2]. The terminal set consists of problem features from each data set. The function set consists of a conditional IF function and the typical four standard arithmetic operators, and so, the function set is defined by $F = \{if, +, -, *, /\}$, where the latter operator is protected division, which returns the numerator if the denominator is zero. The IF function takes three arguments: if the first is negative, the second argument is returned, otherwise the last argument is returned. These functions are used to build a classifier (e.g., mathematical expression) that returns a single value for a given input (data example to be classified). This number is mapped onto a set of class labels using zero as the class threshold. In our studies, an example is assigned to the positive class if the output of the classifier is greater or equal to zero. It is assigned to the negative class, otherwise.

The most common way to measure fitness in classification is the overall classification accuracy: using the four outcomes for binary classification shown in Table 2 and the minority class being the positive class, we have that the accuracy

---

[1] For the abalone data sets, we substituted F, M and I by 1, 2 and 3, respectively.

Table 3. Total number of independent runs executed for our experiments.

Description	Value
Number of independent runs	50
Number of data sets	8
Number of algorithms (NSGA-II and NSGA-II DBS)	2
Total number of runs	800*

*800 = 50 * 8 * 2.

is given by $Acc = \frac{TP+TN}{TP+TN+FP+FN}$. The drawback with Acc is that it can bias the evolutionary search towards the majority class as pointed out in [28] via [2]. Also, as pointed out in [2], a better approach is to treat each objective (class) 'separately' using MOGP. To this end, we used in the fitness function of our MOGP the true positive rate ($TPR = \frac{TP}{TP+FN}$) and the true negative rate ($TNR = \frac{TN}{TN+FP}$) to measure the accuracy for the positive and negative class, respectively.

The experiments were conducted using a steady state approach with tournament selection of size 7. To initialise our population, we used the ramped half-and-half method (initial and final depth set at 1 and 5, respectively). To control bloat (a dramatic increase of programs' length without observing a corresponding improvement in fitness) a maximum depth of 8 was specified (where root was considered of depth 0) or a maximum number of 800 nodes was used. Crossover and mutation rates were 60% and 40%, respectively. Elitism for NSGA-II is not required given the nature of the algorithm. We compare our proposed approached, NSGA-II DBS with canonical NSGA-II, as well with three well-known machine learning algorithms (i.e., Naive Bayes, C4.5 and SVMs).

Because of the stochasticity associated to MOGP, we performed extensive independent runs (we executed 800 runs in total, see Table 3 for details). Runs were stopped when the maximum number of generations was reached.

4   Experimental Results

4.1   Precision, Recall and F-Measure

We compared our results against three very popular machine learning algorithms: Naive Bayes (NB), C4.5 and SVMs. To this end, we use the well-known weka tool [21]. The comparison of results is conducted by computing the F-measure which reflects the performance on both precision and recall. Recall is defined by

$$R = TP_{rate} = \frac{TP}{TP + FN} \tag{1}$$

and precision is defined by

$$P = \frac{TP}{TP + FP}. \tag{2}$$

Table 4. F-measure comparison on the positive (minority) class.

Data set	NSGA-II		NSGA-II DBS		NB		C4.5		SVM	
	Positive	Negative	Positive	Negative	Positive	Negative	Positive	Negative	Positive	Negative
				Precision						
Ion	0.838 ± 0.097	0.645 ± 0.025	0.873 ± 0.075	0.657 ± 0.018	0.689	0.881	0.939	0.865	0.930	0.826
Spect	0.560 ± 0.021	0.491 ± 0.052	0.563 ± 0.020	0.496 ± 0.052	0.614	0.763	0.63	0.759	0.644	0.797
Yeast$_1$	0.452 ± 0.055	0.832 ± 0.016	0.455 ± 0.055	0.833 ± 0.019	0.685	0.918	0.685	0.888	0.737	0.845
Yeast$_2$	0.546 ± 0.064	0.879 ± 0.006	0.541 ± 0.047	0.879 ± 0.006	0.827	0.964	0.817	0.951	0.917	0.890
Derma	0.963 ± 0.073	0.955 ± 0.002	0.970 ± 0.060	0.955 ± 0.002	1	0.917	1	0.917	1	1
Balanced	0.636 ± 0.346	0.893 ± 0.021	0.643 ± 0.322	0.899 ± 0.020	0	0.917	0	0.917	0	0.917
Abalone$_1$	0.199 ± 0.097	0.941 ± 0.018	0.29 ± 0.074	0.945 ± 0.012	0.186	0.974	0.333	0.953	0	0.948
Abalone$_2$	0.017 ± 0.006	0.992 ± 0.004	0.014 ± 0.005	0.979 ± 0.084	0.019	0.995	0	0.993	0	0.993
				Recall						
Ion	0.832 ± 0.045	0.896 ± 0.076	0.818 ± 0.052	0.926 ± 0.050	0.81	0.795	0.730	0.973	0.635	0.973
Spect	0.716 ± 0.077	0.550 ± 0.062	0.711 ± 0.078	0.558 ± 0.060	0.66	0.725	0.642	0.750	0.717	0.738
Yeast$_1$	0.753 ± 0.033	0.799 ± 0.057	0.750 ± 0.039	0.801 ± 0.061	0.587	0.945	0.49	0.956	0.111	0.992
Yeast$_2$	0.925 ± 0.036	0.894 ± 0.027	0.928 ± 0.033	0.893 ± 0.024	0.736	0.978	0.637	0.980	0.121	0.998
Derma	0.995 ± 0.035	0.998 ± 0.005	0.995 ± 0.035	0.998 ± 0.003	1	0.994	1	0.994	1	1
Balanced	0.922 ± 0.940	0.868 ± 0.156	0.893 ± 0.177	0.889 ± 0.127	0	1	0	1	0	1
Abalone$_1$	0.835 ± 0.900	0.760 ± 0.910	0.836 ± 0.111	0.800 ± 0.096	0.579	0.861	0.105	0.988	0	1
Abalone$_2$	0.688 ± 0.186	0.660 ± 0.156	0.692 ± 0.150	0.69 ± 0.154	0.333	0.873	0	1	0	1
				F-measure						
Ion	0.831 ± 0.053	0.749 ± 0.043	**0.843 ± 0.050**	0.768 ± 0.027	0.745	0.836	0.821	0.916	0.755	0.893
Spect	0.627 ± 0.032	0.518 ± 0.056	0.626 ± 0.034	0.525 ± 0.055	0.636	0.744	0.636	0.755	**0.679**	0.766
Yeast$_1$	0.562 ± 0.037	0.815 ± 0.038	0.562 ± 0.037	0.816 ± 0.042	**0.632**	0.931	0.507	0.921	0.193	0.913
Yeast$_2$	0.684 ± 0.048	0.887 ± 0.016	0.681 ± 0.037	0.886 ± 0.014	**0.779**	0.971	0.716	0.965	0.214	0.941
Derma	0.977 ± 0.049	0.976 ± 0.002	0.981 ± 0.041	0.976 ± 0.002	0.957	0.997	0.957	0.997	1	1
Balanced	**0.703 ± 0.285**	0.873 ± 0.095	0.700 ± 0.271	0.890 ± 0.074	0	0.957	0	0.957	0	0.957
Abalone$_1$	0.303 ± 0.099	0.835 ± 0.093	**0.330 ± 0.089**	0.863 ± 0.063	0.282	0.914	0.160	0.970	0	0.973
Abalone$_2$	0.032 ± 0.011	0.782 ± 0.118	0.028 ± 0.009	0.744 ± 0.146	**0.035**	0.930	0	0.996	0	0.996

The F-measure represents a harmonic mean between these two elements. Hence, a high value on the F-measure denotes that both recall and precision are high. The F-measure is defined by

$$F - measure = \frac{2}{1/R + 1/P}. \tag{3}$$

We compare precision, recall and F-measure results on the five different learning methods (NSGA-II, NSGA-II DBS, NB, C4.5 and SVM) for each of the eight data sets used (Table 1). For the Pareto front (PF) found by every independent run of the NSGA-II and NSGA-II DBS, we took the best pair of true positive rate and true negative rate measured in terms of the Euclidean distance between a point in the PF against the optimal solution (100% accuracy). These results are shown in Table 4.

Due to space constraints, we focus our attention on the F-measure values on the positive (minority) class. The best (higher) values are highlighted in boldface. The MOGP approaches (NSGA-II and NSGA-II DBS) are better compared to the other three algorithms in three problems (Ion, Balanced and Abalone$_1$). In two of these problems (Ion and Abalone$_1$), NSGA-II DBS is better than NSGA-II (Balanced). When comparing these two algorithms on the latter problem, we can see that they are very close to each other (the difference is only 0.003) but NSGA-II DBS is better when one takes into account also the negative (majority) class.

When we focus our attention on the results of the other learning algorithms we can see that the worst performance is achieved by C4.5. On the other hand,

MOGP Approach Evolved Classifier	
NSGA-II	IF + IF IF * f3 f1 / f1 f2 * f4 f1 * * f2 f2 IF f4 f2 f1 / - f1 f3 * f2 f4 - IF IF f1 f1 f2 * * f2 f2 IF f4 f2 f1 / f3 f2 * / f4 f2 * f3 f2 - * * / f3 f2 * f1 f4 - * / f3 f2 - f1 f1 IF * f1 f1 / f2 f3 * f1 f4 / IF IF f1 f1 f2 * / f4 f2 * f3 f2 / f3 f2 f2 IF + / * f2 * f2 f3 - f1 f4 / / - f1 f3 - f2 f1 + f4 f2 * / f2 f2 / f1 f4 + * IF * f1 f1 / f2 f3 * f1 f4 / / - f1 * f2 f3 - f2 f1 + f4 f2 * * f2 f3 - f1 f1
NSGA-II DBS	IF - * - / f1 IF f2 f2 f2 f3 * - f3 f3 / / + - f3 f3 - f1 f3 IF - f2 f4 - f3 f3 + f1 f1 f1 - / + f2 f4 f2 / + f3 f1 IF f2 f3 f1 - IF IF f4 f1 f1 - - f2 f4 + f2 f1 - - f4 f2 / + f2 f4 f2 / + f3 f1 IF f4 f1 f1 * - + + f3 f4 / + f2 f4 f2 IF + f4 f4 * f1 f2 / f1 f1 - / + f2 f4 f2 / + f3 f1 IF f4 f1 f1

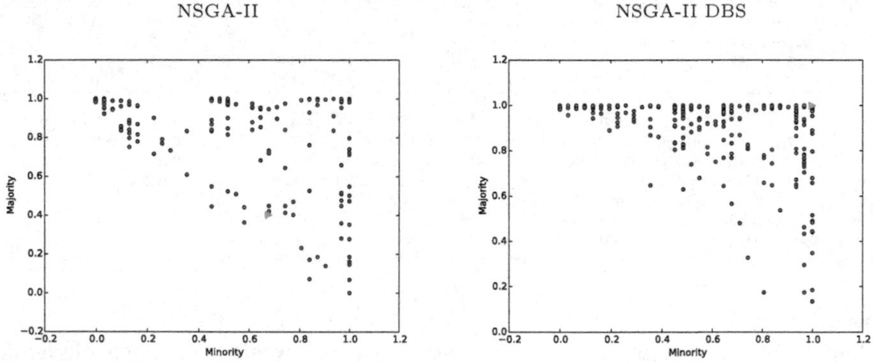

NSGA-II	NSGA-II DBS

Fig. 1. Accuracy of all unique evolved solutions on the balanced data set found by NSGA-II and NSGA-II DBS shown in the left and right-hand side of the figure, respectively. The red triangles indicate the evolved classifiers found by these approaches, shown at the top of the figure. f denotes a feature, where f1 denotes the first feature of the data set. (Color figure online)

Naive Bayes achive good results on the Yeast and Abalone$_2$ problems, and SVMs achive good results on the Spect and Derma problems.

Overall, our MOGP approaches are very competitive to well-established machine learning classifiers. In fact, they show excellent performance on a specific problem, discussed next.

4.2 MOGP Classifiers

We now focus our attention on the results produced by NSGA-II and NSGA-II DBS. To do so, we analyse the balanced data set, where the results obtained by these two approaches on the positive (minority) are impressive without decreasing significantly their precision, recall, F-measure on the negative (majority) call. F-measure values on the positive class are 0.703 ± 0.285 and 0.700 ± 0.271, when using NSGA-II and NSGA-II DBS, respectively, against the other algorithms where they failed completely (i.e., F-measure on the positive class is 0).

Figure 1 shows all the unique solutions found by NSGA-II and NSGA-II DBS on this data set over all 50 independent runs (notice that a single run yields

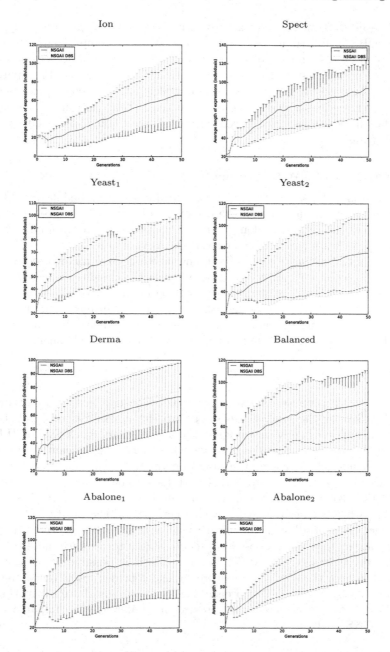

Fig. 2. Average length of evolved solutions, indicated in the y-axis, over 50 generations, indicated in the x-axis, over 50 independent runs using NSGA-II (blue line) and NSGA-II DSB (cyan line). (Color figure online)

multiple results). Some elements are worth mentioning. Our proposed approach, NSGA-II DBS, is able to produce more unique solutions compared to the NSGA-II as noticed by the number of scatter points in the figure. Furthermore, there are more solutions close to the optimal solutions (100% accuracy) compared to NSGA-II. The evolved classifiers, shown at the top of Fig. 1, correspond to those marked by the red triangles shown in the scatter plots (bottom of the figure). These classifiers were selected based on the shortest solutions found by these two algorithms.

4.3   Length of Evolved Classifiers

Very often it is necessary to account for a classifier that can be interpreted. One element that helps towards this is the size of the classifier [9]. Figure 2 shows the average size of the classifier, along with the standard deviation, found by both MOGP approaches for each of eight data sets used in this work.

There are two elements worth discussing: the length of the evolved classifier gets larger as evolution continues (i.e., in all cases the classifiers are significantly larger at the end of the evolutionary search compare to when search starts). The other element is that both algorithms tend to produce evolved classifier of similar length. This means that there is no extra cost when using our proposed approach, NSGA-II DBS, in terms of analysing the evolved classifer.

5   Conclusions

In this work, we proposed a stochastic multi-objective genetic programming approach based on the semantics of programs, for classification of imbalanced data. The results are highly encouraging: the proposed approach (NSGA-II DBS) is able to classify data from the positive class without significantly decreasing the recall, precision and F-measure values on the negative class.

The MOGP approaches used in this work have some advantages: a single run offers multiple solutions and the final user could decide which is the best suited according to his/her needs (e.g., a 100% accuracy on the positive class could be good enough regardless of the accuracy obtained on the negative class). We have also learnt that the proposed approach is able to produce more solutions compared to the traditional NSGA-II. Morever, it is possible to interpret the evolved classifiers thanks to the nature of the representation (encoding of a solution) used by the MOGP approaches. Finally, we also have learnt that the NSGA-II DBS produces classifiers that are of similar length compared to the well-known NSGA-II.

Acknowledgements. EGL's research is funded by an ELEVATE Fellowship, the Irish Research Council's Career Development Fellowship co-funded by Marie Curie Actions. EGL would like to thank the TAO group at INRIA Saclay France for hosting him during the outgoing phase of the fellowship. LVM thanks the SSSP for hosting her during her research visit at TCD. The authors would like to thank the reviewers for their comments that helped us to improve our work. EGL would also like to thank E. Mezura-Montes, O. Ait Elhara and M. Schoenauer for their earlier involvement in this work.

References

1. Asuncion, A., Newman, D.: UCI machine learning repository (2007)
2. Bhowan, U., Johnston, M., Zhang, M., Yao, X.: Reusing genetic programming for ensemble selection in classification of unbalanced data. IEEE Trans. Evol. Comput. **18**(6), 893–908 (2014)
3. Chawla, N.V., Japkowicz, N., Kotcz, A.: Editorial: special issue on learning from imbalanced data sets. SIGKDD Explor. Newsl. **6**(1), 1–6 (2004)
4. Coello, C.A.C.: Evolutionary multi-objective optimization: a historical view of the field. IEEE Comput. Intell. Mag. **1**(1), 28–36 (2006)
5. Deb, K., Kalyanmoy, D.: Multi-Objective Optimization Using Evolutionary Algorithms. Wiley, New York (2001)
6. Deb, K., Pratap, A., Agarwal, S., Meyarivan, T.: A fast and elitist multiobjective genetic algorithm: NSGA-II. IEEE Trans. Evol. Comput. **6**, 182–197 (2002)
7. Eiben, A.E., Smith, J.: From evolutionary computation to the evolution of things. Nature **521**, 476–482 (2015)
8. Eiben, A.E., Smith, J.E.: Introduction to Evolutionary Computing. Springer, Berlin (2003). doi:10.1007/978-3-662-05094-1
9. Freitas, A.A.: Data Mining and Knowledge Discovery with Evolutionary Algorithms, 1st edn. Springer, Berlin (2002). doi:10.1007/978-3-662-04923-5
10. Galván-López, E.: Efficient graph-based genetic programming representation with multiple outputs. Int. J. Autom. Comput. **5**(1), 81–89 (2008)
11. Galván-López, E., Cody-Kenny, B., Trujillo, L., Kattan, A.: Using semantics in the selection mechanism in genetic programming: a simple method for promoting semantic diversity. In: 2013 IEEE Congress on Evolutionary Computation, pp. 2972–2979, June 2013
12. Galván-López, E., Fagan, D., Murphy, E., Swafford, J., Agapitos, A., O'Neill, M., Brabazon, A.: Comparing the performance of the evolvable π grammatical evolution genotype-phenotype map to grammatical evolution in the dynamic Ms. Pac-Man environment. In: 2010 IEEE Congress on Evolutionary Computation (CEC), pp. 1–8, July 2010
13. Galván-López, E., McDermott, J., O'Neill, M., Brabazon, A.: Defining locality in genetic programming to predict performance. In: IEEE Congress on Evolutionary Computation, pp. 1–8. IEEE (2010)
14. Galván-López, E., McDermott, J., O'Neill, M., Brabazon, A.: Towards an understanding of locality in genetic programming. In: Proceedings of the 12th Annual Conference on Genetic and Evolutionary Computation, GECCO 2010, NY, USA, pp. 901–908. ACM (2010)
15. Galván-López, E., Mezura-Montes, E., Ait ElHara, O., Schoenauer, M.: On the use of semantics in multi-objective genetic programming. In: Handl, J., Hart, E., Lewis, P.R., López-Ibáñez, M., Ochoa, G., Paechter, B. (eds.) PPSN 2016. LNCS, vol. 9921, pp. 353–363. Springer, Cham (2016). doi:10.1007/978-3-319-45823-6_33
16. Galván-López, E., Poli, R.: Some steps towards understanding how neutrality affects evolutionary search. In: Runarsson, T.P., Beyer, H.-G., Burke, E., Merelo-Guervós, J.J., Whitley, L.D., Yao, X. (eds.) PPSN 2006. LNCS, vol. 4193, pp. 778–787. Springer, Heidelberg (2006). doi:10.1007/11844297_79
17. López, E.G., Poli, R., Coello, C.A.C.: Reusing code in genetic programming. In: Keijzer, M., O'Reilly, U.-M., Lucas, S., Costa, E., Soule, T. (eds.) EuroGP 2004. LNCS, vol. 3003, pp. 359–368. Springer, Heidelberg (2004). doi:10.1007/978-3-540-24650-3_34

18. Galván-López, E., Poli, R., Kattan, A., O'Neill, M., Brabazon, A.: Neutrality in evolutionary algorithms.. What do we know? Evol. Syst. **2**(3), 145–163 (2011)
19. Galván-López, E., Swafford, J.M., O'Neill, M., Brabazon, A.: Evolving a Ms. Pac-Man controller using grammatical evolution. In: Di Chio, C., et al. (eds.) EvoApplications 2010. LNCS, vol. 6024, pp. 161–170. Springer, Heidelberg (2010). doi:10.1007/978-3-642-12239-2_17
20. Guo, X., Yin, Y., Dong, C., Yang, G., Zhou, G.: On the class imbalance problem. In: 2008 Fourth International Conference on Natural Computation, vol. 4, pp. 192–201, October 2008
21. Hall, M., Frank, E., Holmes, G., Pfahringer, B., Reutemann, P., Witten, I.H.: The weka data mining software: an update. SIGKDD Explor. Newsl. **11**(1), 10–18 (2009)
22. Koza, J.R.: Genetic Programming: On the Programming of Computers by Means of Natural Selection. The MIT Press, Cambridge (1992)
23. Koza, J.R.: Human-competitive results produced by genetic programming. Genet. Program. Evolvable Mach. **11**(3–4), 251–284 (2010)
24. Kubat, M., Holte, R.C., Matwin, S.: Machine learning for the detection of oil spills in satellite radar images. Mach. Learn. **30**(2), 195–215 (1998)
25. Poli, R., Galván-López, E.: The effects of constant and bit-wise neutrality on problem hardness, fitness distance correlation and phenotypic mutation rates. IEEE Trans. Evol. Comput. **16**(2), 279–300 (2012)
26. Uy, N.Q., Hoai, N.X., O'Neill, M., McKay, R.I., Galván-López, E.: Semantically-based crossover in genetic programming: application to real-valued symbolic regression. Genet. Program. Evolvable Mach. **12**(2), 91–119 (2011)
27. Vanneschi, L., Castelli, M., Silva, S.: A survey of semantic methods in genetic programming. Genet. Program. Evolvable Mach. **15**(2), 195–214 (2014)
28. Weiss, G.M., Provost, F.: Learning when training data are costly: The effect of class distribution on tree induction. J. Artif. Int. Res. **19**(1), 315–354 (2003)

Consensus Clustering for Binning Metagenome Sequences

Isis Bonet[1(✉)], Adriana Escobar[1], Andrea Mesa-Múnera[1],
and Juan Fernando Alzate[2]

[1] Universidad Escuela de Ingeniería de Antioquia, Envigado,
Antioquia, Colombia
ibonetc@gmail.com, adriana.escobarv@gmail.com,
amesamu@gmail.com
[2] Centro Nacional de Secuenciación Genómica-CNSG, Facultad de Medicina,
Universidad de Antioquia, Medellín, Colombia
jfernando.alzate@udea.edu.co

Abstract. The advances in next-generation sequencing technologies allow researchers to sequence in parallel millions of microbial organisms directly from environmental samples. The result of this "shotgun" sequencing are many short DNA fragments of different organisms, which constitute the basis for the field of metagenomics. Although there are big databases with known microbial DNA that allow us classify some fragments, these databases only represent around 1% of all the species existing in the entire world. For this reason, it is important to use unsupervised methods to group the fragments with the same taxonomic levels. In this paper we focus on the binning step in metagenomics in an unsupervised way. We propose a consensus clustering method based on an iterative clustering process using different lengths of sequences in the databases and a mixture of distance as approach to finding the consensus clustering. The final performance clustering is evaluated according with the purity of clusters. The results achieved by the proposed method outperforms results obtained by simple methods and iterative methods.

Keywords: Metagenomics · Consensus clustering · Sequences binning · *K*-means

1 Introduction

During the last years, the development of next-generation sequencing technologies allows researchers to sequence multiple genomes of different organisms within an environmental sample. These sequencing methods have the capacity to sequence uncultivable organisms, which have lead a revolution in genetics, taking into account, in many environments, as many as 99% of the microorganisms cannot be cultured by standard techniques [1]. Shotgun sequence, as is also called this kind of sequencing, enable researchers to analyze several types of ecosystems, including extreme environments, with known and unknown microorganism. Moreover, the sequenced genomes provide valuable insights about the microbial community and answers to a wide

© Springer International Publishing AG 2017
O. Pichardo-Lagunas and S. Miranda-Jiménez (Eds.): MICAI 2016, Part II, LNAI 10062, pp. 273–284, 2017.
DOI: 10.1007/978-3-319-62428-0_23

range of questions [2]. A Sequencing run using such technologies generates hundreds of thousands or millions of DNA fragments, also known as reads. The handling of this result has driven the development of new computational methods and technologies, which rises big and new challenges. To deal with these challenges, emerge metagenomics as a new science. Metagenomics aims to study genomes of many microbial organisms from a specific environment, without a prior need for isolation and cultivation of individual genome in a lab [3].

The objective of metagenomics, based on shotgun sequencing results, is to reconstruct and identify the whole genomes of species within an environmental community under study. In a single genome sequencing, the subsequent processes are assembly of sequence reads, gene prediction, functional annotation and metabolic pathway construction. Additionally, a binning process is required in metagenomics [4].

Usually, the first process, before binning, is an assembly of overlapping shorter reads obtained from the sequencing, in order to provide a consensus sequence (contigs and scaffolds) [2].

Binning methods has the task to group (bin) reads or contigs into their corresponding phylogenetic group. It is can divided into two categories based on the information to group the sequences: composition-based and similarity-based methods. Similarity- or homology-based binning use alignment tools as BLAST [5], MEGAN [6]. From the point of view of machine learning, similarity-based binning is a supervised method supported by a database of known species genome. On the other hand, composition-based binning made analyzes of genomes features, such as GC content, codon usage or oligonucleotide frequencies to describe the sequences. There are supervised algorithms based on composition features as Phylopythia [7], TACOA [8] and NBC classifier [9] which based the classification in a similarity. Another kind of binning algorithm is referred to as unsupervised methods based on composition features. Unlike the previous algorithms, unsupervised binning is taxonomy independent [10].

Although supervised methods are more accurate than unsupervised methods, the limitation of unknown the majority of the species leads the use of unsupervised methods or the combination of both methods.

There are some unsupervised binning reported in the literature, differing in the clustering method, distance measure and the features. For example, TETRA [11] and MetaCAA [12] use the k-mers feature, with $k = 4$ also known as tetranucleotide frequencies. In [13] a Self-Organizing Maps (SOM) method was used for efficiently cluster complex data using the oligonucleotide frequencies calculation, while in [14] Growing Self-organizing maps was used. In [15] the authors use a fuzzy k-means based on GC percentage and oligonucleotides frequencies. MetaCluster is another method that use k-median algorithm and k-mers to represent the features [16, 17]. Others researchers use clustering methods based on expectation maximization (EM) [18, 19].

Also, some authors are reported hybrid algorithms that combine the composition-based methodology along with an alignment-based methods as PhymmBL [20] and new versions of MetaCluster [17]. In [21] a comparison of some clustering methods is done.

Different problematics can arise with a binning process: (1) fragments cover a great range of possible lengths, (2) the amount of fragments which belong to each specie is very different, resulting in an unbalanced database, (3) very large amount of data, and (4) unknown number of organisms, as a classical unsupervised problem. These issues are the cause of the complexity of the unsupervised binning, and lead to a search of good features to represent the DNA fragments and complex algorithms that can hand complex and big data.

In this paper we show an ensemble of cluster based on k-means and sequence-based measures, such as GC content and k-mers frequencies. As comparison, we compare with simple clustering algorithm and evaluate according with the sensitivity of clusters.

2 Methods and Data

2.1 Data

Assembled genomic sequences at contig level of different organisms including viruses, bacteria and eukaryotes were downloaded from the FTP site of the Sanger institute.

Table 1 has the description of each organism including in the database. It illustrate the number of contigs representing the organism and the range of minimum and maximum lengths for each one.

Table 1. Organisms in the database

Organism	Contigs	Min length	Max length
Ascaris	137650	50	30000
Aspergillus_fumigatus	295	1001	29660
Bacteroides_dorei	1928	500	29906
Bifidobacterium_longum	18	540	26797
Bos_taurus	315841	101	5000
Candida_parasilopsis	1540	1003	29956
Chikung	1	11826	11826
Dengue	64	10392	10785
Ebola	1	18957	18957
Glossina_morsitans	20334	101	29996
HIV	1	9181	9181
Influenza	8	853	2309
Malus_domestica	66739	102	5000
Manihot_esculenta	7192	1998	4998
Pantholops_hodgsonii	159729	50	5000
Zea_mays	161235	102	5000
	872576	**50**	**30000**

In order to have representation of different groups of domains, but also a variety in each group, database consists of 9 eukaryotes, 2 bacteria and 5 virus.

2.2   Features

Considering that the sequences have very different length ranging from 50 to 30000 nucleotides bases (Table 1), it is clear how important is the use of composition-based feature to represent the DNA fragments.

Based on good results obtained by previous authors, we select k-mer ($k = 4$) as the features to represent the DNA fragments, that means 256 possible tetranucleotides (256 features). It was compute as the number of each tetranucleotide and normalized with the total of tetranucleotides in the sequence.

The features and the amount of instances in the database are the basis to perform the bases clustering methods for the ensemble clustering.

We use another representative and supervised database with an information gain measure to select the more representative features. The features with highest score are: TCGA, TTCG, CGAA, CGAT, and ATCG.

2.3   Clustering Methods

We test different clustering algorithms as SOM, EM and k-means, but we report the results obtained by k-means because it get the best performance. We also proposed a consensus of clustering with k-means as the base clustering method.

Despite the problem to estimate the parameter k (number of cluster), k-means is one of the most popular clustering methods. This algorithm finds a set of k centroids, and associates each instance in the data to the nearest centroid, based on a distance function [22]. Here we used a variant of k-means, called k-means ++ [23]. As distance functions to compare the contigs we used Euclidean and Cosine distance (Eq. 1).

$$Cosine(X, Y) = 1 - \frac{\sum_{i=1}^{n} (x_i \times y_i)}{\sqrt{\sum_{i=1}^{n} (x_i)^2} \times \sqrt{\sum_{i=1}^{n} (y_i)^2}} \qquad (1)$$

Where X and Y are the instance to compare, with dimension N (features number), and x_i and y_i denote the ith feature of X and Y respectively.

For the implementation of the clustering methods, we used Weka 3.9 [24], which is a free machine learning package that has implemented k-means ++. Furthermore, it has the advantage that it is easy to add a new clustering method.

3   Consensus Clustering Method

One of the problematics in the binning process is the different length of fragments. Some binning algorithms have been built for a specific range of lengths. Based on the variability of the clustering algorithms according with the length of contigs we propose train clustering methods with different range of length.

Figure 1 describes the steps of our algorithm, including the initial pre-processing data. The input is a fasta file with contigs information which is convert in a weka file (arff). The representation of sequences is based on GC and k-mers as we explain before. Here, the selection of feature is based on the scores obtained with the gain information algorithm. After data pre-processing, the data is ready to be used.

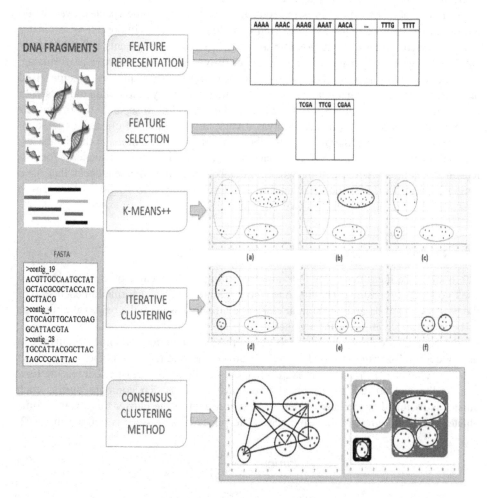

Fig. 1. Consensus clustering method.

The first part of the proposed approach is focused on an iterative clustering where each run process is based on the error of previous run [25]. This means that, a first clustering methods is trained and the results clusters are evaluated based the distance within each cluster and between the centroids of clusters. From this run the best clusters are separated and the rest are used as the new database to train the new cluster method. This process is repeated over several iteration until a number N of run or all resulting clusters achieve a good evaluation value, selecting the compactness clusters for each iteration.

Once the iterative clustering is performed we can obtain a large number of clusters. The consensus clustering approach is based on compute the distance between the centroids with Euclidean and Cosine distance. The average of these distances are the measure to join closest clusters and decrease the number of them.

In that problem the priority is to group fragments of the same species, even when the organism is represented by more than one cluster. What is important is to cluster groups, which, at least, make possible assembly groups of fragments to build longer DNA sequences. Longer sequences, as will be shown below, can improve performance in a new clustering process. On the other hand, using longer sequences in supervised databases may be more likely to succeed. That means, the key is to obtain clusters with high value of purity. In that spirit, we focused the algorithm to separate the organisms as much as possible, even if this involves a very large number of clusters generated.

Taking into account the problematic about the diversity of lengths in the databases, the idea in this method is to split the database based on length of sequences, for this reason the database is divided in two. One database contains the sequences that have length superior to 10000 and the other one with length inferior to 10000. The algorithm describe above is applied to this two database.

3.1 Performance Measures

There are some measures in the literature to evaluate performance of clusters. Here we use two kind of measures. The first one is to evaluate the cluster formed in each step of the proposed method and join similar clusters evaluate, based on the pairwise difference of between and within-cluster distances.

As explained before, our aim is to obtain pure clusters despite some organism can be divided in different clusters. For this reason, the second measure is the purity of the clusters. The aim of this measure is quantify the purity of each cluster, computing how similar the clusters are to the benchmark classifications. To compute purity, each cluster is assigned to the class which is most frequent in the cluster that means, some cluster can be assigned to the same class. The purity of a cluster j is defined in Eq. 2.

$$Purity = \frac{max(n_{ij})}{n_j} \qquad (2)$$

where n_j is the number of organisms in cluster j and n_{ij} is the number of organisms of class i in cluster j.

High purity is easy to achieve when the number of clusters is large.

4 Results and Discussion

Firstly we train an iterative k-means ++ as described above, with Cosine distance and different number of clusters, k between 15 to 2500, keeping the clusters with higher distance inter-cluster, that is the distance between the centroids.

A metagenome database built from 16 different organisms is used to evaluate the method. GC content and tetranucleotides are the attributes used to describe the sequences. Euclidean and Cosine distances were used for the k-means algorithms.

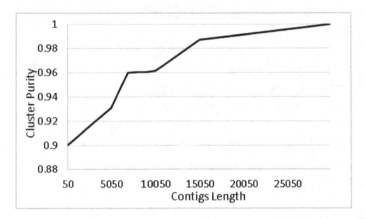

Fig. 2. Cluster Purity with different min of contigs lengths.

We test simple k-means ++ algorithms with different size of data. We decrease the database on the lengths of the organisms, in order to know the influence of diversity in contigs lengths. Figure 2 illustrates the average of purity with respect to the minimum length of the organisms included, showing a significant increase in the purity of cluster obtained when larger sequences are used.

The first step was to select the best features to describe the data, in order to reduce dimensionality. We use internationals database to adjust the best features, using the algorithm based on gain information measure. We select the 17 features best ranked.

Hence, we divided the database in two: one based on the sequences with lengths lower than 10000 and another with lengths greater than or equal to 10000. For each partition of database, we build the clustering method proposed. Afterward, we use Cosine and Euclidean distance to measure the distance between the centroids and regroup the cluster with lowest distances, i.e. those whose average of distances is lower than a threshold (here we use 0.5).

The best result was obtained with the increment of number of clusters. For example the Fig. 3 shows the results with $k_1 = 15$, $k_2 = 30$ for the iterative clustering of two iteration, where k_i is the number of cluster of iteration i. The left part of the figure represents the number of clusters, the organisms assigned and the number of fragments associated with each organism. It can be seen most of clusters have a percentage relative to the predominant organism superior of 90%. The average of purity was 92.85 the clusters only represent 8 organisms.

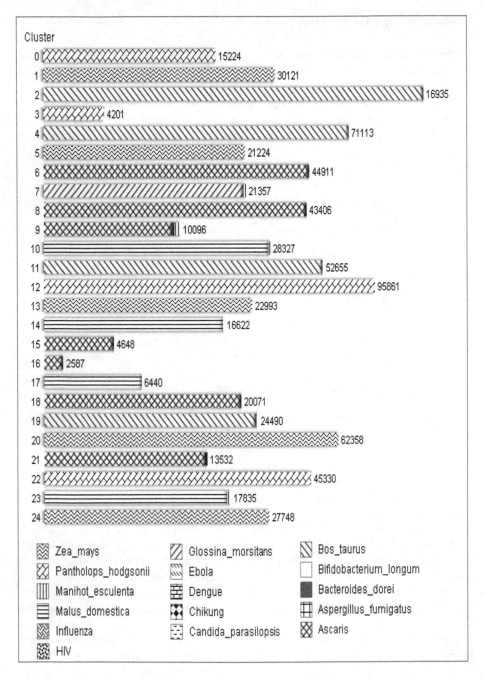

Fig. 3. Results of proposed clustering methods with $k_1 = 15$, $k_2 = 20$

With a more deep analysis of the results, we can see that *bifidobacterium_longum* and the all virus are distributed into all clusters. On the other hand, *Ascaris, Pantholops, Malus, Bos Taurus, Bacteroides dorei and Zea mays* are the organisms grouped in clusters with high purity.

We increase the number of cluster in order to separate the more difficult organisms, in that case the virus because of the low number of contigs.

Figure 4 shows two results of clustering, with $k_1 = 15$ for both runs, $k_2 = 2500$ for sequences with max length of 10000 (at the left of figure) and k = 250 for lengths superior to 10000 (at the right of figure). In second database, the half of species are not considerate because all genomic fragments of them are smaller than 10000 bases. Bars represent the number of cluster that represent each organism. Although the organisms are very scattered, we obtain a high purity and we can separated the virus in independent clusters. Using lengths larger than 10000, the algorithm achieves 100% of purity for all clusters, and 98.11% when the lengths are shorter than 10000.

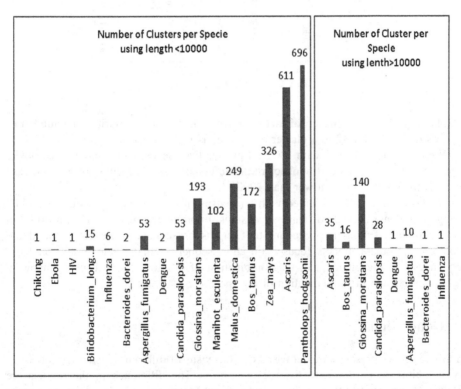

Fig. 4. Results of proposed clustering methods with $k_1 = 15$, $k_2 = 2500$ and lengths superior to 10000

The average between Euclidean and Cosine distance was used to compare the distance between the centroids of clusters obtained. The closest clusters were grouped together based on a threshold of 0.5. The number of clusters is reduce from 2715 to

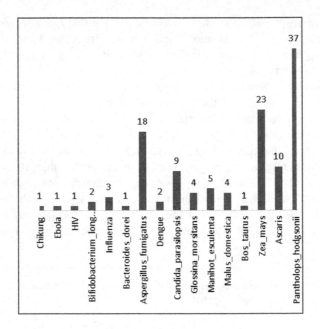

Fig. 5. Consensus clustering

122, having a least one cluster for each specie, yielding a 99% of purity. The number of clusters oscillate into 37 to 1 cluster by specie, as it is shown in Fig. 5.

We obtain 117 clusters with 100% of purity. The species with cannot be complete separate from the rest are Bifidobacterium, Influenza and Aspergilus. In most of case are sequence with lengths lower than 10000.

In short, the results presented with consensus of clusters based on iterative clustering and consensus of distances measures improve the results of clustering in metagenomics. Taking into account the lengths of sequences we can divided the problem and create models focused on short sequences and model based on large sequences. On the other hand, the combination of different distance can generate a significant change in the separation of the space.

5 Conclusions

In this paper we present a model based on consensus of different clustering models by the combination of different distances measures. The difference in the models are referred to the data use to train them. The data are reconstructed using different lengths of sequences.

The proposed method is applied to a metagenome dataset composed of 16 different organisms. The result achieved by the proposed method, in line with the objective of obtaining clusters with high purity, outperforms result obtained with a simple k-means and also compared with an iterative k-means. Taking into account the purity, even the number of cluster, the proposed method provide pure clusters by organisms, reaching

100% of purity in all cluster when the lengths of contigs is greater than 10000, and 99% for all possible lengths.

This paper is not intended to show the best clustering method for metagenomics, but rather to show a promising method to bear in mind in order to build larger sequences or as a prior step in the binning process. Longer DNA fragments can improve performance in a new binning process.

This consensus clustering can be used with other base clustering method such as SOM or Expectation Maximization. In future work we expect compare the proposed method with other base methods and other metagenome databases.

References

1. Riesenfeld, C.S., Schloss, P.D., Handelsman, J.: Metagenomics: genomic analysis of microbial communities. Annu. Rev. Genet. **38**, 525–552 (2004)
2. Oulas, A., et al.: Metagenomics: tools and insights for analyzing next-generation sequencing data derived from biodiversity studies. In: Bioinform. Biol. Insights. pp. 75–88 (2015)
3. Council, N.R.: The New Science of Metagenomics: Revealing the Secrets of Our Microbial Planet. The National Academies Press, Washington (2007)
4. Chan, C.-K., et al.: Binning sequences using very sparse labels within a metagenome. BMC Bioinf. **9**(1), 215 (2008)
5. Camacho, C., et al.: BLAST + : architecture and applications. BMC Bioinf. **10**(1), 421 (2009)
6. Huson, D.H., et al.: MEGAN analysis of metagenomic data. Genome Res. **17**(3), 377–386 (2007)
7. McHardy, A.C., et al.: Accurate phylogenetic classification of variable-length DNA fragments. Nat. Methods **4**(1), 63–72 (2007)
8. Diaz, N.N., et al.: TACOA – Taxonomic classification of environmental genomic fragments using a kernelized nearest neighbor approach. BMC Bioinf. **10**, 56 (2009)
9. Rosen, G.L., Reichenberger, E., Rosenfeld, A.: NBC: The Naïve Bayes classification tool webserver for taxonomic classification of metagenomic reads. Bioinf. **27**(1), 127–129 (2010)
10. Mande, S.S., Mohammed, M.H., Ghosh, T.S.: Classification of metagenomic sequences: methods and challenges. Brief Bioinf. **13**(6), 669–681 (2012)
11. Teeling, H., et al.: TETRA: a web-service and a stand-alone program for the analysis and comparison of tetranucleotide usage patterns in DNA sequences. BMC Bioinf. **5**(1), 163 (2004)
12. Reddy, R.M., Mohammed, M.H., Mande, S.S.: MetaCAA: A clustering-aided methodology for efficient assembly of metagenomic datasets. Genomics **103**(2–3), 161–168 (2014)
13. Abe, T., et al.: Informatics for unveiling hidden genome signatures. Genome Res. **13**(4), 693–702 (2003)
14. Chan, C.K.K., et al.: Using growing self-organising maps to improve the binning process in environmental whole-genome shotgun sequencing. J. Biomed. Biotechnol. **2008** (2008)
15. Nasser, S., Breland, A., Harris Jr., F.C., Nicolescu, M.: University of Nevada Reno. A Fuzzy Classifier to Taxonomically Group DNA Fragments within a Metagenome (2016). http://www.cse.unr.edu/~monica/Research/Publications/nafips2008.pdf
16. Leung, H.C., et al.: A robust and accurate binning algorithm for metagenomic sequences with arbitrary species abundance ratio. Bioinformatics **27**(11), 1489–1495 (2011)

17. Wang, Y., et al.: MetaCluster-TA: taxonomic annotation for metagenomic data based on assembly-assisted binning. BMC Genom. **15**(1), 1–9 (2014)
18. Siegel, K., et al.: Puzzlecluster: a novel unsupervised clustering algorithm for binning DNA fragments in metagenomics (2016)
19. Wu, Y.W., Ye, Y.: A novel abundance-based algorithm for binning metagenomic sequences using l-tuples. J. Comput. Biol. **18**(3), 523–534 (2011)
20. Brady, A., Salzberg, S.L.: Phymm and PhymmBL: metagenomic phylogenetic classification with interpolated Markov models. Nat. Methods **6**(9), 673–676 (2009)
21. Li, W., et al.: Ultrafast clustering algorithms for metagenomic sequence analysis. Brief. Bioinf. **13**(6), 656–668 (2012)
22. MacQueen, J.: Some methods for classification and analysis of multivariate observations. In: Proceedings of the Fifth Berkeley Symposium on Mathematical Statistics and Probability. Statistics, Vol. 1, pp. 281–297. University of California Press: Berkeley, California (1967)
23. Arthur, D., Vassilvitskii, S.: K-Means ++: The Advantages of Careful Seeding. In: 8th Annual ACM-SIAM Symposium on Discrete Algorithms. New Orleans (2007)
24. Witten, I., Frank, E.: Data Mining: Practical Machine Learning Tools and Techniques, 2nd Edition. In: Jim Gray, M.R. (ed). . Morgan Kaufmann, San Francisco, 525 (2005)
25. Bonet, I., Montoya, W., Mesa-Múnera, A., Alzate, J.F.: Iterative clustering method for metagenomic sequences. In: Prasath, R., O'Reilly, P., Kathirvalavakumar, T. (eds.) MIKE 2014. LNCS, vol. 8891, pp. 145–154. Springer, Cham (2014). doi:10.1007/978-3-319-13817-6_15

Algorithm for Clustering of Web Search Results from a Hyper-heuristic Approach

Carlos Cobos[1(✉)], Andrea Duque[1], Jamith Bolaños[1],
Martha Mendoza[1], and Elizabeth León[2]

[1] Universidad del Cauca, Popayán, Colombia
{ccobos,aduque,jbvidal,mmendoza}@unicauca.edu.co
[2] Universidad Nacional de Colombia, Bogotá D.C., Colombia
eleonguz@unal.edu.co

Abstract. The clustering of web search results - or web document clustering (WDC) - has become a very interesting research area among academic and scientific communities involved in information retrieval. Systems for the clustering of web search results, also called Web Clustering Engines, seek to increase the coverage of documents presented for the user to review, while reducing the time spent reviewing them. Several algorithms for clustering of web results already exist, but results show there is room for more to be done. This paper introduces a hyper-heuristic framework called WDC-HH, which allows the defining of the best algorithm for WDC. The hyper-heuristic framework uses four high-level-heuristics (performance-based rank selection, tabu selection, random selection and performance-based roulette wheel selection) for selecting low-level heuristics (used to solve the specific problem of WDC). As a low level heuristics the framework considers: harmony search, improved harmony search, novel global harmony search, global-best harmony search, eighteen genetic algorithm variations, particle swarm optimization, artificial bee colony, and differential evolution. The framework uses the k-means algorithm as a local solution improvement strategy and based on the Balanced Bayesian Information Criterion it is able to automatically define the appropriate number of clusters. The framework also uses four acceptance/replacement strategies (replacement heuristics): Replace the worst, Restricted Competition Replacement, Stochastic Replacement and Rank Replacement. WDC-HH was tested with four data sets using a total of 447 queries with their ideal solutions. As a main result of the framework assessment, a new algorithm based on global-best harmony search and rank replacement strategy obtained the best results in WDC problem. This new algorithm was called WDC-HH-BHRK and was also compared against other established WDC algorithms, among them: Suffix Tree Clustering (STC) and Lingo. Results show a considerable improvement -measured by recall, F-measure, fall-out, accuracy and SSL_k- over the other algorithms.

Keywords: Hyper-heuristics · Clustering of web results · Web document clustering · Balanced Bayesian Information Criterion · K-means

© Springer International Publishing AG 2017
O. Pichardo-Lagunas and S. Miranda-Jiménez (Eds.): MICAI 2016, Part II, LNAI 10062, pp. 285–316, 2017.
DOI: 10.1007/978-3-319-62428-0_24

1   Introduction

In recent years, web document clustering (WDC) results has become a very interesting research area among academic and scientific communities involved in information retrieval (IR) and web search [1] since it is very likely that the results relevant to the user are close to each other in the document space, thus tending to fall into a relatively small number of clusters [2] and thereby achieve a significant reduction of search time. In IR, these clustering of web result systems are called web clustering engines and the main exponents in the field are Carrot^2 (http://www.carrot2.org), Yippy (http://yippy. com, originally known as Vivisimo and later as Clusty), iBoogie (http://www.iboogie. com), and KeySRC [3]. Such systems usually consist of four main components, namely: search results acquisition, processing of input, cluster construction and labeling, and visualization of resulting clusters [1] (see Fig. 1).

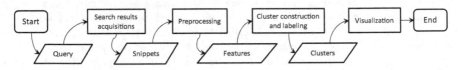

Fig. 1. The components of a web clustering engine (adapted from [1])

The **search results acquisition** component begins with a query defined by the user. Based on this query, a document search is conducted in diverse data sources, for example Google, Yahoo!, Bing and Ask. Web clustering engines work as meta-search engines and collect between 50 and 200 results from traditional web search engines. These results contain as a minimum a URL, a snippet and a title. The **preprocessing** of search results comes next. This component converts each of the search results (as snippets) into a sequence of words, phrases, strings, attributes or features, which are then used by the clustering algorithm. Once the preprocessing is finished, **cluster construction and labeling** is begun. This stage makes use of three types of algorithm: data-centric, description-aware and description-centric. Each of these builds clusters of documents and assigns a label to the groups. Finally, in the **visualization** step, the system displays the results to the user in folders organized hierarchically (or other display schemes based on graphs). Each folder seeks to have a label or title that represents well the documents it contains and that is easily identified by the user. As such, the user simply scans the folders that are actually related to their specific needs [1].

To obtain good results in WDC the algorithms must meet the following specific requirements [1]: automatically define the number of clusters that are going to be created; generate relevant clusters for the user and assign the documents to appropriate clusters; define labels or names for the clusters that are easily understood for users; handle overlapping clusters (documents can belong to more than one cluster); reduce the high dimension of document collections; handle the processing time i.e. less than or equal to 2.0 s; and handle the noise frequently found in documents.

The two predominant problems with existing web clustering engines are inconsistencies in cluster content and inconsistencies in cluster description [1]. The first problem refers to the content of a cluster that does not always correspond to the label. In addition, navigation through the cluster hierarchies does not necessarily lead to more specific results. The second problem refers to the need for more expressive descriptions of the clusters (cluster labels are confusing). These two problems are the main motivation of the present work, in which a new algorithm that obtains better results for clustering of web results is put forward. This algorithm was obtained from a hyper-heuristic framework, which is based on four high-level heuristics, a further twenty five low-level heuristics used to solve the specific problem of WDC, four replacement heuristics, the k-means algorithm as a local improvement strategy of solutions and balanced Bayesian information criterion as fitness function.

The remainder of the paper is organized as follows. Section 2 presents some related work on WDC and hyper-heuristics. The proposed hyper-heuristic framework is described in detail in Sect. 3. Section 4 shows the experimental results. Finally, some concluding remarks and suggestions for future work are presented.

2   Related Work

2.1   Web Document Clustering

As mentioned earlier, there are three types of web document clustering algorithms [1]: data-centric, description-aware and description-centric.

Data-centric algorithms are the algorithms traditionally used for data clustering (partitional, hierarchical, fuzzy, density-based, etc.) [1, 4, 5]. They seek the best solution in data clustering, but are not so strong on the presentation of the labels or in the explanation of the groups obtained. The algorithms most commonly used for clustering of web results have been the hierarchical and the partitional ones [4]. Best proposal with this approach include the following. UPGMA (Unweighted Pair-Group Method using Arithmetic averages) proposed in 1990 [6] using an average link hierarchical algorithm based on cosine distance. In partitional clustering the most representative algorithms are: k-means, k-medoids, and Expectation Maximization. Bisecting k-means [4, 6] algorithm (2000) that combines the strengths of the hierarchical and partitional methods and reporting better results than the UPGMA and k-means. A hybridization method between the Harmony Search (HS) and k-means algorithms (2007) [7, 8] that converges to the global optimum. A new algorithm based on k-means and neural networks was also proposed in 2009 [9]. ArteCM algorithm (2009) [10] uses an incremental approach for clustering documents, offering the ability to grow the number of clusters adaptively. A link-based algorithm [11] (2009) has the advantages of creating clusters in various shapes (with high accuracy) and removing noisy data. A fuzzy transduction-based clustering algorithm called FTCA [12] (2010). The RElational Document clustering (RED-clustering) algorithm (2010) [13] that outperforms k-means and Expectation Maximization both in terms of effectiveness, purity and agreement between classes and partitions. METIS (2011), an algorithm that performs spectral bisecting and merge operations over web documents [14]. And a method based on multiclass spectral clustering for grouping of documents - including web pages in English and Chinese [15] (2011).

Description-aware algorithms give greater weight to one specific feature of the clustering process than to the rest. For example, they make as their priority the quality of the labeling of groups and as such achieve results that are more easily interpreted by the user. Their quality drops, however, in the cluster creation process. An example of this type of algorithm is Suffix Tree Clustering (STC) [6] proposed in 1998, which incrementally creates labels easily understood by users, based on common phrases that appear in the documents. STC uses a phrase-based-model for document representation.

Description-centric algorithms [1, 6, 16–20] are designed specifically for WDC, seeking a balance between the quality of clusters and the description (labeling) of them. In 2001, the SHOC (Semantic, Hierarchical, Online Clustering) algorithm was introduced [17]. SHOC improves STC and is based on LSI and frequent phrases. FTC (Frequent Term-Based Text Clustering) and HFTC (Hierarchical Frequent Term-Based Text Clustering) algorithms (2002) [20]. These algorithms use combinations of frequent words (association rules approach) shared in the documents to measure their proximity in the text clustering process. Then in 2003, FIHC (Frequent Itemset-based Hierarchical Clustering) was introduced [18], which measures the cohesion of a cluster using frequent word sets, so that the documents in the same cluster share more frequent word sets than those in other groups. These algorithms provide accuracy similar to that reported for Bisection k-means, with the advantage that they assign descriptive labels to clusters. Also in 2003, the Lingo algorithm [16, 21] was devised. This algorithm is used by the Carrot^2 web clustering engine and it is based on complete phrases and LSI with Singular Value Decomposition (SVD). Lingo is an improvement of SHOC and STC and unlike most algorithms first tries to discover descriptive names for the clusters and only then organizes the documents into appropriate clusters. NMF (2003) is another example of these algorithms. It is based on the non-negative matrix factorization of the term-document matrix of the given document corpus [22]. This algorithm surpasses LSI and the spectral clustering methods in document clustering accuracy but does not care about cluster labels. In 2007, the Dynamic SVD clustering (DSC) [19] algorithm was made available. This algorithm uses SVD and minimum spanning tree (MST). This algorithm outperforms Lingo but they use a small sample of data sets. Another approach was proposed by the Pairwise Constraints guided Non-negative Matrix Factorization (PCNMF) algorithm [23] (2007). This algorithm transforms the document clustering problem from an un-supervised problem to a semi-supervised problem, using must-link and cannot-link relations between documents. Full-Subtopic Retrieval with Keyphrase-Based Search Results Clustering (KeySRC) [24] (2009) comprises an algorithm based on key phrases. The key phrases are extracted from a generalized suffix tree built from the search results. Documents are then clustered based on a hierarchical agglomerative clustering algorithm. Also in 2009, a method based on granular computing (WDCGrc) was presented [25]. This algorithm transforms the term-by-document matrix (TF-IDF) to a document-by-binary granules matrix, then, using an association rules algorithm obtains frequent word sets between documents. These frequent word sets are pruned and finally used to create clusters. WDCGrc takes the number of the same words shared by documents as a similarity measure. A novel approach based on the automatic discovery of word senses from raw text, a task referred to as Word Sense Induction (WSI) [26] was presented in 2010. Experiments show better results than STC, Lingo and KeySRC algorithms over AMBIENT and MORESQUE data sets. Also in 2010 OPTIMSRC (OPTImal Meta Search Results Clustering) [27] algorithm was proposed, OPTIMSRC outperforms the results shown by KeySRC, Lingo, Lingo3G and the original order of results reported by the Yahoo! search engine. Additionally in 2010, two new algorithms based on heuristics, partitional clustering and different strategies for labeling were put forward. The first algorithm, called IGBHSK [28] was based on global-best harmony search, k-means and frequent term sets and the second, called WDC-NMA [29] was based on memetic algorithms with niching techniques and frequent phrases. These researches outperform results obtained with STC and Lingo, evaluate two different document representation models (term-document matrix and frequent term-document matrix) and use the Bayesian Information Criterion (BIC) for evaluating quality of solutions. In 2012, a new algorithm called Topical was put forward [30]. It models the problem of clustering of web results as the problem of labeling clustering nodes of a graph of topics. Topics are Wikipedia pages identified by a topic annotator and edges of the graph denote the relatedness of these topics. The new graph it is based on the annotation by Tagme that replaces the traditional bag of words paradigm. Finally, in 2014, a new algorithm for clustering of web search results based on the cuckoo search algorithm and Balanced Bayesian Information Criterion was presented [31]. In this work, the cuckoo search meta-heuristic provides a combined global and local search strategy in the solution space. Split and merge methods replace the original Lévy flights operation and improve existing solutions (nests), as a local search strategy. The algorithm also includes an abandon operation that provides diversity and prevents early convergence of the population. Balanced Bayesian Information Criterion is used as a fitness function and allows defining the number of clusters automatically. The algorithm was compared against other established WDC algorithms, including STC, Lingo, and Bisecting k-means. The results show a considerable improvement upon the other algorithms as measured by recall, F-measure, fall-out, accuracy and SSL_k.

2.2 Hyper-heuristics (HH)

The hyper-heuristics (HH) include a set of approaches in order to automate the design and optimization of heuristic methods to solve complex computational search problems. The HH operate on a search space of heuristics rather than directly on the given problem, that is trying to find a heuristic method or sequence in a given situation instead of trying to solve the problem directly, it aims to produce generic methods, solutions that produce acceptable quality, based on a set of heuristics low level easy implements [32, 33].

A detailed state of the art about Hyper-heuristics (HH) is available online in [32], where Burke *et al.* initially define HH as "heuristics to choose heuristics" and they show recently this definition as having changed to "… HH attempts to automatically generate new heuristics suited to a given problem or class of problems, by combining, mainly through the use of genetic programming, components or building-blocks of human designed heuristics". This last approach is different to the "traditional" meta-heuristics strategy of searching directly through a search space of candidate solutions.

Burke *et al.* [32] also provide a classification of HH research. HH are classified according to the nature of the heuristic search space and the source of feedback during learning (see Fig. 2). In relation to the nature of the heuristic search space, there are two approaches: heuristic selection and heuristic generation. In relation to the learning, there are three options: Online learning, Offline learning and No learning.

Heuristic selection focuses on combining pre-existing heuristics in one higher-level search strategy (our approach in the current research). Heuristic generation is concerned with generating completely new heuristics consisting of basic components or building blocks of existing heuristics.

On the next level there are two options: construction heuristics and perturbation heuristics. Construction heuristics attempts to construct a single good candidate solution through the intelligent application of different low-level heuristics. Perturbation heuristics uses one low-level heuristic to construct a complete solution, but repetitively applies low-level heuristics in a local search approach to obtain better candidate solutions in each one of the iterations (also our approach in the current research).

A hyper-heuristic is classified as online learning when the algorithm learns to adaptively solve a single instance of the optimization problem (our approach in the current research), offline learning when a training set of problems is used to develop a method that may generalize to unseen problem instances, and no learning when the algorithm does not learn from previously selected low-level heuristics.

Research on hyper-heuristics include for example: In 2005 [34] a hyper-heuristic approach was presented using tabu search as high-level heuristic and as low-level heuristics: SD (least saturation degree first), CD (Largest color degree first), LD (Largest degree first), LE (Largest enrollment first), LWD (Largest weighted degree first), RO (random ordering), applied to the scheduling problem. The research offers the conclusion that the HH performance is better when using a larger number of low level heuristics. In [35] it is proposed that in hyper heuristic approaches heuristic combinations usually take the form of a list of low-level heuristics that are applied sequentially, therefore, a hierarchical display form for the combination of heuristics is proposed, which is evaluated in scheduling problems review.

In 2008 [36] a HH approach is presented that seeks to determine the data mining technique to be used for a specific situation based on the performance of low-level heuristics. In particular, it seeks to answer questions like: what learning algorithm can derive knowledge that could guide the search in order to produce good solutions? To achieve the goal, three associative classification techniques are compared - CBA (classification based on association), MCAR (multi-class classification based on association rule), MMAC (Multi-class, multi-label associative classification) - as well as two traditional classification techniques PART and Ripper (Repeated incremental pruning to produce Error reduction algorithm) on data sets generated using a hybrid HH called Peckish combining greedy and random approaches to the problem of programming trainer. As a result of the tests shows better performance in associative classification techniques MCAR, MMAC, CBA on C4.5 decision trees, rule induction RIPPER and PART algorithm, with reference to the accuracy of predicting the appropriate set low-level heuristics.

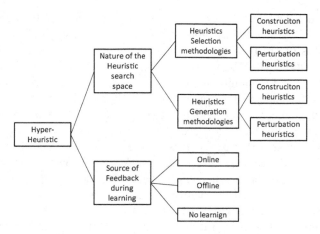

Fig. 2. Classification of HH (adapted from [37])

In 2010 [38] was proposed two types of HH approaches, the first based on construction heuristics and the second using improvement methods (heuristics Greedy), these methods are tested on a scheduling problem known as the problem of time variability response. Research shows that better results are obtained when using sophisticated low-level algorithms as meta heuristics, with the drawback of increasing the calculation time, to solve this arises using selection strategies based on performance.

In 2010 [39], arises HH approach meta-heuristics based optimization applied to air launch of a satellite vehicle (ASLV), so it is proposed without learning a random function that controls low level meta-heuristics. The low-level heuristics are genetic algorithms (GA), Particle Swarm Optimization (PSO) and Simulated Annealing (SA). The methodology proposed shows a better performance in terms of convergence and diversity, which can be applied to various optimization problems. One of the drawbacks of the investigation is only used as heuristic high random selection.

In 2010 [40] arises replace selection tasks of low-level heuristic and evaluation of the objective function by applying data mining techniques, specifically with neural networks and binary logistic regression. With this change, proposed a more efficient HH about processing time. Furthermore, the above techniques are able to find global patterns hidden in large data sets in order to properly classify the data. Finally, with the training of the classification rules or estimated parameters, the performance of the resulting solution can be predicted without the need to undertake computational tasks implicit in traditional HH approaches. Focus evaluation is performed by generating a graph based on the HH proposed for exam timetabling problems, the results show that the neural network and logistic regression may accelerate the search process significantly.

In 2011 [41] HHWDC algorithm was proposed, which applies a HH approach that uses seven low-level heuristics: harmony search, improved harmony search, new best harmony search, global-better harmony search, memetic algorithm with restrictive matching, memetic algorithm with roulette wheel selection and particle swarm optimization. HHWDC uses the k-means algorithm as a strategy for improving local solutions and the Bayesian Information Criterion to automatically define the number of clusters. It makes use of two replacement strategies which are replace the worst and restricted competition. This HH work is the first in the field of web documents clustering and it shows the feasibility of the approach. This work is exploratory and it has the following disadvantages: the limited use of high-level, low-level and replacement heuristics. Further experiments were performed on a small set of test data and no experiments were conducted with users.

In 2014 [42] an unified hyper-heuristic framework for solving bin packing problems (one and two dimensions) was presented. Authors show an alternative way to solve the bin packing problem with competitive results, and sometimes even better, but without the cost of trying all the heuristics. Also in this year, [43] a new learning selection choice function based hyper-heuristic to solve multi-objective optimization problems was proposed. This high level approach controls and combines the strengths of three well-known multi-objective evolutionary algorithms (i.e. NSGAII, SPEA2 and MOGA), utilizing them as the low level heuristics. Results over the Walking Fish Group test suite are competitive over other methods in the state of the art.

In 2015 [44] a new approach for solving high school timetabling problems worldwide using selection hyper-heuristics was proposed. Authors evaluate the performance of a range of selection hyper-heuristics combining different reusable components for high school timetabling and results show the success of the approach which embeds an adaptive great-deluge move acceptance method on the third International Timetabling Competition (ITC 2011) benchmark instances. Also in this year, in [45] a Monte Carlo tree search hyper-heuristic framework for combinatorial optimization problems was proposed. Authors model the search space of the low level heuristics as a tree and use Monte Carlo tree search to search through the tree in order to identify the best sequence of low level heuristics to be applied to the current state of the population in the evolutionary process. They apply the framework to solve different problems, including: Boolean satisfiability (MAX-SAT), one dimensional bin packing, permutation flow shop, personnel scheduling, traveling salesman and vehicle routing with time windows. The results are competitive over all six problems when compared to the best known results in the scientific literature.

3   The Proposed Hyper-heuristic Framework

WDC-HH is a hyper heuristic framework with online learning that combines pre-existing heuristics in an iterative way to search for better solutions in the search space. WDC-HH uses a high-level search strategy to intelligently control the use of a set of low-level sub-algorithms over a single optimization run of a real problem, in this case, WDC.

In WDC-HH, the algorithm executes several islands (each of one of them can evolve separately) and selects the best solution for them. In each island, a population or set of solutions is first Randomly Generated (RG), then, each of the solutions is optimized by the k-means algorithm. Next, WDC-HH tries to select based on high-level heuristics the appropriate low-level heuristic in each of the iterations to generate a new vector solution (chromosome, harmony solution, vector, particle, food source or agent), optimizes the current solution using the k-means algorithm, decides if the current solution should replace one vector solution in the population based on the fitness value of the solutions, and finally records the success or failure of the specific low-level and replacement heuristics.

Figure 3 shows different components of the algorithm and explains the flow of information between these components. Four (4) high-level selection heuristics: Performance-based Rank (Rank), Tabu (Tabu), Random, and Performance-based Roulette Wheel (Roulette). Twenty five (25) low level heuristics are used in WDC-HH, namely: Harmony Search (HS), an Improved Harmony Search algorithm (IH), Novel Global Harmony Search (NH), Global-Best Harmony Search (BH), Particle Swarm Optimization (PS), Differential Evolution (ED), Artificial Bee Colony (CA), and eighteen (18) genetic algorithms generated from several selection, crossover and mutation micro heuristics. The selection micro heuristics are: Restrictive Mating (RM), Roulette Wheel Selection (RW) and Rank (RK). The crossover micro heuristics are: One point crossover (UP), Uniform crossover (CU) and Multi-point crossover (CM). And the micro level heuristics for Mutation are: one bit uniform mutation (MO) and multi-bit uniform mutation (MM). At the same time each heuristic with the exception of CA is combined with four replacement methods: Rank (RR), Replace Worst (WR), Restricted Competition Replacement (RC), and Stochastic Replacement (SR), resulting in a total of 97 combined low-level and replacement heuristics (24 * 4 + 1).

Figure 4 shows the relationship between the problem domain and the control domain for the hyper-heuristic environments [46]. In this case, the problem domain focuses on the creation of solutions for the problem of WDC, the optimization of such solutions using K-means and their evaluation based on Balanced Bayesian Information Criterion (BBIC). The solutions are created with the set of low-level heuristics that are in the control domain. These low-level heuristics are selected by high-level heuristics based on the number of successes of each low level heuristic. A low-level heuristics records a success when it achieves that the solution created enters the population based on a specific replacement heuristic.

3.1   The Fitness Function

In the literature of partitional clustering, various criteria have been used to compare two or more solutions and decide which is better [47]. The most popular criteria are based on the within-cluster and between-cluster scatter matrices. In this research, the Balanced Bayesian Information Criterion (BBIC) [48] was used to define one solution as better than another one and to automatically define the number of clusters. BBIC is expressed by (1).

$$BBIC = n * Ln\left(\frac{SSE}{n \times ADBC}\right) + k * Ln(n) \tag{1}$$

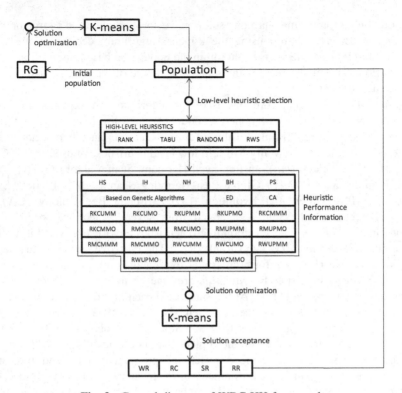

Fig. 3. General diagram of WDC-HH framework

Where n is the total number of documents, k is the number of clusters, SSE is the sum of squared error expressed by formula (4), and ADBC is the average distance between centroids expressed by formula (2).

$$ADBC = \frac{2}{k \times (k-1)} \sum_{i=1}^{k-1} \sum_{j=i+1}^{K} \left(1 - SimCos\left(C_i, C_j\right)\right) \qquad (2)$$

Where SimCos is the cosine similarity expressed by formula (3).

$$SimCos(d, q) = \frac{\sum_{i=1}^{D} W_{i,d} \times W_{i,q}}{\sqrt{\sum_{i=1}^{D} W_{i,d}^2}\sqrt{\sum_{i=1}^{D} W_{i,q}^2}} \qquad (3)$$

Where d is a document represented in a multidimensional space of D dimensions (in this case terms or pre-processed words), q is a query also represented in a multi-dimensional space of D dimensions, $W_{i,d}$ is the weight of the term i in the document, and $W_{i,q}$ is the weight of the term i in the query.

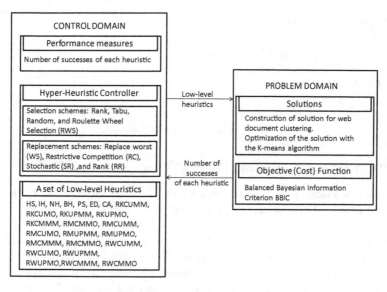

Fig. 4. Classification of HH (adapted from [37])

3.2   The K-Means Algorithm

The k-means algorithm (Fig. 5) is the simplest and most commonly used algorithm for clustering employing a Sum of Squared Error (SSE) criterion based on (4).

$$SSE = \sum_{j=1}^{k} \sum_{i=1}^{n} P_{i,j} \left\| x_i - c_j \right\|^2 \tag{4}$$

Where x_i is a data set object (point or record), c_j is the centroid of the cluster j and $P_{i,j}$ is equal to one (1) if the object x_i belongs to cluster j or cero (0) in other case.

This algorithm is popular because it finds the local minimum (or maximum) in a search space, it is easy to implement, and its time complexity is O(n). Unfortunately, the quality of the result is dependent on the initial points and may converge to a local minimum of the criterion function value if the initial partition is not properly chosen [49, 50]. k-means inputs are: The number of clusters (K value) and a set (table, array or collection) containing n objects (or registers) in a D-dimensionality feature space, formality defined by $X = \{x_1, x_2, \ldots, x_n\}$ (In our case, xi is a row vector, for implementation reasons). k-means outputs are a set containing K centers. The steps in the procedure of k-means can be summarized as shown in Fig. 5.

In step 01, there are several approaches for selecting K initial centers [51], for example Forgy suggested selecting K instances randomly from the data set and McQueen suggested selecting the first K points in the data set as the preliminary seeds and then using an incremental strategy to update and select the real K centers of the initial solution [51]. In step 02, it is necessary to recompute membership according to the current solution. Several similarity or distance measurements can be used. In this paper, we used Cosine similarity formality defined as (3).

01	Select an Initial Partition (k centers)
	Repeat
02	Re-compute Membership
03	Update Centers
04	**Until** (Stop Criterion)
05	Return Solution

Fig. 5. The k-means algorithm

3.3 WDC-HH from an Algorithm Point of View

Figure 7 shows a description of each process executed by de WDC-HH framework. Next, some details of this process are presented.

01: **Initialize algorithm parameters:** In this research, the optimization problem lies in minimizing the BBIC criterion, called fitness function. WDC-HH needs the following parameters: the Best Memory Results Size (BMRS), Population Size (PS), the Number of Iterations (NI) or Maximum Execution Time (MET), and other specific parameters from all low-level heuristics (Typical values for each parameter are shown in parenthesis): Harmony Memory Considering Rate (HMCR, 0.95), Pitch Adjusting Rate (PAR, between 0.3 and 0.99), Selection Group Size (SGS, 25% of population size) for restricted mating, Replacement Group Size (RGS, 25% of population size) for restricted competition replacement, Mutation Rate (MR, between 0.2% and 0.5%), Minimum Bandwidth (MinB, 0.0005), Maximum Bandwidth (MaxB, 005) for mutation operation. Two parameters for ABC heuristic: Probability Employed Bee (PEB, 10%) and Exploitation Probability Random (EPR, 40%). Mutation Factor (F, 50%) and Recombination Probability (RC, 20%) in differential evolution heuristic. And three parameters for PSO heuristic: Social scaling parameter (C2, 1.49445) and Particle Inertia Minimum and Maximum (Wmax and Wmin) [8, 52, 53].

02: **Document preprocessing:** Initially, Lucene (http://lucene.apache.org) is used at a document pre-processing stage. The pre-processing stage includes: tokenize, lower case filtering, stop word removal, text stemming based on Porter's algorithm, delete documents with empty preprocessed content (snippet) and the building of the Term-Document Matrix (TDM). The TDM matrix is the most widely-used structure for document representation in IR, and is based on the vector space model [4]. In this model, the documents are designed as bags of words; the document collection is represented by a matrix of N-documents (as rows) by D-terms (as columns). Each document is represented by a vector of normalized frequency term (tf_i) by the document inverse frequency for that term, in what is known as TF-IDF value (expressed by Eq. (5)), and the cosine similarity (see Eq. (3)) is used for measuring the degree of similarity between two documents, between a document and the user's query, or between a document and a cluster centroid.

$$w_{i,j} = \frac{freq_{i,j}}{\max(freq_i)} \times \log\left(\frac{N}{n_j}\right) \tag{5}$$

Where $freq_{i,j}$ is the observed frequency of the term j in document i, $\max(freq_i)$ is the maximum observed frequency in the document i, N is the total number of documents in collection, and n_j is the number of documents where term j is presented.

03: **Initialize the best memory results and call the HHK routine:** The Best Memory Results (BMR) is a memory structure where the best solution vectors of each island are stored (see Fig. 6). Each row in BMR stores the result of one call to the Hyper-Heuristic k-means (HHK) routine, in a basic cycle. Each row vector in BMR has four parts: The Centroids, the low-level heuristic used to generate it, the replace heuristic used to enter in population, and the Fitness value of that vector. The number of centroids in each row vector in BMR can be different.

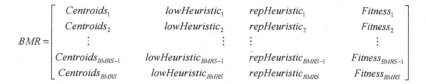

Fig. 6. Best Memory Results

04: **Select the best result:** Find and select the best result from the Best Memory Results (BMR). The best result is the row with the lowest fitness value (minimize f(x)). Then return this row as the best clustering solution (centroids and fitness).

05: **Assign labels to clusters:** the WDC-HH framework uses a frequent phrases approach for labeling each cluster. This step corresponds with step 2 called "Frequent Phrase Extraction" in Lingo [16] (with some modifications). See Sect. 3.7 for more details.

06: **Overlap clusters:** Finally, each cluster includes documents that fall into other clusters too, if these documents are at a distance less than or equal to the average distance of the cluster.

In HHK routine, each solution vector used has a different number of clusters (centroids), and the objective function (BBIC) depends on the centroid location in each vector solution and the number of centroids (K value).

In step 01: **Initialize Population** of HHK routine, the population is a memory structure where all the solution vectors are stored. The general structure of the population is similar to BMR in Fig. 7. Each vector solution is created with a random number of centroids (k < Kmax), a random initial location for each centroid, a value of RG for describing that this solution was generated with a random generation strategy, a value of NR for describing that this solution entered the population without any specific replacement strategy, and the fitness value for this solution. The cluster centers in the

WDC-HH algorithm:

01	Initialize algorithm parameters
02	Document preprocessing: Tokenize, stop word removal, text stemming based on Porter's algorithm, delete documents with empty preprocessed content, and Term-Document matrix (TDM) building
03	Initialize the BMR and call the HHK routine For each i ∈ [1, BMRS] do BMR[i] = HHK (TDM) Next-for
04	Select the best result
05	Assign labels to clusters
06	Overlap clusters

HHK routine:

01	Initialize Population: Define centroids (forgy strategy), Execute k-means (Steps 02-06, See **Fig. 5**) and Calculate fitness (BBIC) for each solution vector generated in population. A total set of PS vector solutions is created.
02	Repeat
03	Generate a new vector solution: Using performance-based rank selection tabu selection, random selection, or performance-based roulette wheel selection to select the low-level heuristics from HS, IH, NH, BH, PS, ED, CA or the other 18 genetic-based low-level heuristics.
04	Execute k-means (Steps 02-06, See **Fig. 5**) and Calculate fitness (BBIC) for the new vector solution
05	Update population: The solution competes to one solution in population for entering in the population. There are four alternative acceptance (replace) strategies: Replace the worst, stochastic replacement, rank replacement and restricted competition replacement. ABC is the unique low-level heuristic that does not use these replace strategies, because ABD has its own replace strategy.
06	Until stopping conditions are satisfied: for example, the maximum number of iterations (NI) is satisfied or the maximum execution time (MET) is reached.
07	Select the best solution in population and return to WDC-HH

Fig. 7. The WDC-HH algorithm and the HHK routine

solution consist of $k_i \times D$ real numbers, where k_i is the number of clusters and D is the total number of terms (words in vocabulary). The Initial centroids are selected randomly from the original data set. Next, the **k-means algorithm** (Fig. 5 steps 02 to 06) is executed and then fitness value for this solution calculated.

In summary, PS vector solutions are generated and then the fitness value for each vector is calculated. Initially, each centroid corresponds to a different document randomly selected in the TDM matrix (Forgy strategy in the K-means algorithm). The initial number of clusters k_i, K value, is randomly calculated from 2 to kmax (inclusive), where K is a natural number and kmax is the upper limit of the number of clusters and is taken to be $\sqrt{N} + 1$, (where N is the total number of documents in the TDM matrix, but this value cannot be less than eight), which is an adapted rule of thumb used in the clustering literature by many researchers.

In the evolution process, vector solutions change all or most of the original vector solutions in the population. Therefore, it is normal to find vectors with different values of low-level and replacement heuristics. For example, a solution could be <[0.4|0.2| 0.7], [0.2|0.3|0.1], [0.1|0.4|0.5], [0.7|0.7|0.7], BH, RK, 0.193> . This sample solution encodes centers of four (K value) clusters in a three dimensional space with a fitness value of 0.193, generated using Global-best Harmony Search low level-heuristic (BH) and finally, this solution uses rank replacement strategy (RK) to enter the population.

3.4   High-Level Heuristics

In step 03: **Generate a new vector solution** of the HHK routine, a new vector solution (centroids) is generated based on low-level heuristics using one of the high-level heuristics, namely: Performance-based Rank selection, Tabu selection, Random selection or Performance-based Roulette Wheel selection.

Performance-Based Rank Selection: Rank selection was initially proposed by Baker to eliminate the high convergence presented by proportional selection methods. The selection strategy selects a new low-level heuristic based on a ranking, and this ranking is based on past heuristic success. The heuristics are organized based on number of successes in descending order, and then the table of rankings is created. The table of rankings contains different probability values for each low-level heuristic. Probability values are calculated based on formula (6) [54, 55].

$$(0.25 - 1.5 * (i*1.0/n - 1))/n \qquad (6)$$

Where n is the total number of low-level heuristics and i (between 0 and n − 1) is the order number of each specific low-level heuristic.

Tabu Selection: The original version of this heuristic avoids exploring previously visited areas using a tabu list [56]. In this research the tabu list has a maximum length of 18% (approximating the largest integer value) of all the low-level heuristics being run. In this way, if only two combined low and replacement heuristics are being run, this selection heuristic behaves as an alternator, selecting first one and then the other. Low level heuristics enter the tabu list when a maximum number of executions have been run. Figure 8 shows a general description of tabu selection in the framework.

Random Selection: The random selection strategy randomly uses a low-level heuristic to generate a new vector solution. No memory of previous good performance is retained and no learning is attempted.

Performance-Based Roulette Wheel Selection: This strategy was inspired by "Roulette Wheel" and "Stochastic Universal" Sampling. The selection strategy selects a new low-level heuristic based on past heuristic success. This is achieved using a roulette wheel-based selection operator which ensures that low-level heuristics that have previously performed well (high success rate) have a higher probability of being selected again. The probability $P_{i,j}$ of selecting low-level heuristic i for creating a new solution at iteration j can be calculated based on Laplace estimator [57], as in formula (7).

$$P_{i,j} = \frac{NSH_i + 1}{TE + NH} \tag{7}$$

Where NSH_i is the number of times when the heuristic i has been successfully, TE is the total number of times when all heuristics have been successful, and NH is the total number of heuristics being tested.

```
Initialize tabu parameters: Define the tabu list size and the maximum number of executions.
Repeat
        index ~ U (1...number of heuristics)        //Select one of the heuristics
                                                    // that is not in the tabu list
Until tabu list does not contain the heuristic index
Heuristic[index].NumberOfExecutions++
if (tabulist is full) then
        Tabulist[0].delete //Delete the first heuristic in tabu list based on a FIFO behavior.
End if
//If exceed the number of visits
If (Heuristic[index]. NumberOfExecutions > Maximum Number of Executions) then
        Tabulist.Add(index) //Add the heuristic index to tabu list
End if
```

Fig. 8. Tabu selection

3.5   Low-Level Heuristics

In step 03: **Generate a new vector solution** of the HHK routine, a new vector solution (centroids) is generated based on the low-level heuristic selected. There are 25 low-level heuristics: harmony search, improved harmony search, novel global harmony search, global-best harmony search, eighteen genetic algorithm variations, particle swarm optimization, artificial bee colony, and differential evolution.

Harmony Search (HS): HS is a meta-heuristic algorithm mimicking the improvisation process of musicians (where music players improvise the pitches of their instruments to obtain better harmony) [8, 53]. HS has been successfully applied to many optimization problems: travelling salesman problem [4], power economic dispatch [29], and for WDC [53], among others. Figure 9 shows a general description of the improvisation step of HS used in the HHK routine as a low-level heuristic.

The HMCR and PAR parameters of HS help the method in searching for globally and locally improved solutions, respectively. PAR has a profound effect on the performance of the HS algorithm. Thus, the fine tuning of this parameter is very important (see [52] for details).

An Improved Harmony Search Algorithm (IH): IH uses in general the same logic as the HS algorithm, see Fig. 9. The key difference between IHS and the traditional HS method is in the method of adjusting the PAR (Pitch Adjustment Rate) and BW (Bandwidth) parameters in each iteration. PAR is defined based on (8) and BW based on (9).

$$PAR(iteration) = PAR_{min} + ((PAR_{max} - PAR_{min}) \times iteration)/NI \qquad (8)$$

Where PAR is the pitch adjustment rate for each iteration, PAR_{min} is the minimum pitch adjustment rate, PAR_{max} is the maximum pitch adjustment rate, NI is the maximum number of iterations, and iteration is the current iteration number.

$$bw(iteration) = bw_{max} \exp(c \times iteration) \text{ and } c = \frac{Ln\left(\frac{bw_{min}}{bw_{max}}\right)}{NI} \qquad (9)$$

Where bw(iteration) is the bandwidth for each iteration, bw_{min} is the minimum bandwidth, and bw_{max} is the maximum bandwidth.

A Novel Global Harmony Search Algorithm (NH): NH is inspired by the swarm intelligence of a particle swarm. NH includes two important operations: position updating and genetic mutation with a small probability. Figure 10 shows a general description of the improvisation step of NH used in HHK routine as a low-level heuristic.

```
For i=1 to K (number of centroids) do
    If U (0, 1) ≤ HMCR then
    Begin /*memory consideration*/
        j ~ U (1... PS);
        p ~ U (1... Population [j].K) //selection of centroid
        New [i] = Population [j].Centroid[p]
        If U(0,1) ≤ PAR then
        Begin /*pitch adjustment*/
            For j=1 to D (number of dimensions) do
                New [i] = New[i] ± BW
            Next-For
        End-if
    Else /*random selection − forgy strategy*/
        j ~ U (1... N);
        New [i] = TDM[j]
    End-if
Next-for
```

Fig. 9. Improvisation steps of HS algorithm in HHK routine

```
For i=1 to K (number of centroids) do
    Best ~ U (1 ... Population [BestSolution].k);
    Worst ~ U (1 ... Population [WorstSolution].k);
    For j=1 to D (number of dimensions) do
        high = Population[BestSolution].Centroid[Best][j]
        low = Population[WorstSolution].Centroid[Worst][j]
        X = 2 * high - low
        If X < 0 then X =0
        r ~ U (0, 1)
        New [i][j] = low +    r * (X - low)
        If U(0,1) ≤ PM then
            p ~ U (1... N);
            New [i][j] = TDM[j][p]
        End-if
    Next-for
Next-for
```

Fig. 10. Improvisation steps of NH algorithm in HHK routine

Global-Best Harmony Search Algorithm (BH): Global-Best Harmony Search [52] is a new variant of HS. BH is inspired by the concept of swarm intelligence as proposed in Particle Swarm Optimization. Figure 11 shows a general description of the improvisation step of BH used in HHK routine as a low-level heuristic.

```
For i=1 to K (number of centroids) do
    If U (0, 1) ≤ HMCR then
    Begin /*memory consideration*/
        j ~ U (1... PS);
        p ~ U (1... Population [j].K) //selection of centroide
        New [i] = Population [j].Centroid[p]
        If U(0,1) ≤ PAR then
        Begin /*Particle Swarm Optimization*/
            p ~ U (1... Population [Best].k); // Best is the position of the best vector solution in
            population
            New [i] = Population [Best].Centroid[p]
        End-if
    Else /*random selection – forgy strategy*/
        j ~ U (1... N);
        New [i] = TDM[j]
    End-if
Next-for
```

Fig. 11. Improvisation steps of BH algorithm in HHK routine

Particle Swarm Optimization (PS): PS is a population-based, co-operative search meta-heuristic. In PS, a potential solution to an optimization problem is treated as a bird in a flock, without quality and volume, and referred to as a particle, coexisting and evolving simultaneously based on knowledge shared with neighboring particles. While flying through the problem search space, each particle modifies its velocity to find a better solution (position) by applying its own flying experience and the experience of neighboring particles. Particles update their positions and velocities based on (10) and (11), respectively.

$$v_{t+1}^i = \omega_t * v_t^i + c_1 * R_1 * \left(p_t^i - x_t^i\right) + c_2 * R_2 * \left(p_t^g - x_t^i\right) \tag{10}$$

$$x_{t+1}^i = x_t^i + v_{t+1}^i \tag{11}$$

Where x_t^i represents the current position of particle i in solution space and subscript t indicates an iteration count, p_t^i is the best-found position of particle i up to iteration count t and represents the cognitive contribution to the search velocity v_t^i. p_t^g is the global best-found position among all particles in the swarm up to iteration count t and forms the social contribution to the velocity vector, R_1 and R_2 are random numbers uniformly distributed in the interval (0, 1), and c_1 and c_2 are the cognitive and social scaling parameters, respectively. ω_t is the particle inertia, which is reduced dynamically to decrease the search area in a gradual fashion [15]. The variable ω_t is updated by (12).

$$\omega_t = (\omega_{max} - \omega_{min}) * (NI - in)/NI + \omega_{min} \tag{12}$$

Where ω_{max} and ω_{min} denote the maximum and minimum of ω_t respectively, NI is the maximum number of iterations, and in is the current iteration number.

In this research, c_1 is equal to zero because vector solutions do not evolve. They are replaced by new, better solutions, and each one of them has the best possible value in its neighbourhood. The new solution is based on one vector solution from current population. Figure 12 shows a general description of the PS algorithm used in HHK routine as a low-level heuristic.

```
/* select particle */
i ~ U (1... PS);
New = Population [i]
For i=1 to K (number of centroids) do
    p ~ U (1... Population [Best].k);
    For j=1 to D (number of dimensions) do
        r ~ U (0... 1)
        velocity = wt * velocity + C2 * r *
        ( Population[Best].Centroid[p][j] - New[i][j])
        New [i][j] = New[i][j] + velocity
    Next-for
Next-for
```

Fig. 12. PS algorithm in HHR routine

Differential Evolution (ED): In ED [58], three different parents are initially randomly selected from the population. The calculation of the number of centroids to be generated in the new solution is dened by formula (13), where Xri with i = 1, 2 and 3 is the number of centroids of each parent and F is a real constant for mutation between [0, 2], which controls the amplification in the differential variation (Xr2 − Xr3). Next, it is ensured that the number of groups is greater than or equal to 2.

$$|Xr1 + F(Xr2 - Xr3)| \tag{13}$$

A fourth vector solution (different to the parents) is then selected from the population, called the base vector. Next, to define each one of the centroids, a random number between 0 and 1 is generated. If the number is less than the probability of reproduction or recombination (CR parameter) the centroid is taken from a vector randomly selected from the centroid base. Otherwise, a random centroid is taken from each of the parents and the attributes of the centroid are calculated based on formula (13).

Artificial Bee Colony (CA): Inspired by [59], a new random number is generated between 0 and 1. If this value is less than or equal to 0.1, a new individual is created using random centroids, similar to the work carried out by an employed bee. If the performance of the new individual is better than the performance of the worst individual in the population, the new individual replaces the worst in the population.

If the random number generated is between (0.1, 0.4], an individual (vector solution) is chosen randomly from the population. A perturbation is applied to this individual, creating some centroids at random, if the new individual has a better performance than the original individual, the new individual replaces the original.

If the randomly generated number is greater than 0.4, one of the best individual is chosen from the population, based on the roulette wheel method. An exploitation is applied to this individual, creating some centroids at random. If the performance of the new individual is better than the performance of the original individual, the new one replaces the original one.

Heuristics Based on Genetic Algorithms: Genetic heuristics result from the combination of different selection, crossover and mutation schemes widely used in the literature. The selection schemes were: Restrictive mating (RM), Roulette wheel selection (RW) and Rank selection (RK). The crossover schemes were: One point crossover (UP), Multi-point crossover (CM) and Uniform crossover (CU). During crossover, the cluster centers (centroids) are considered to be indivisible, so, crossover points can only lie in between two cluster centers. After crossover, with a low probability (Mutation Rate, MR) a mutation operation is applied to the offspring. The mutation schemes were: one bit uniform mutation (MO) and multi-bit uniform mutation (MM). Mutation between Minimum Bandwidth (MinB) and Maximum Bandwidth (MaxB) (similar to Harmony Search Algorithm [8]) is applied to the chosen cluster dimension/attribute/term [x = x ± Random (MinB, MaxB)]. When the mutation operation generates a value that reaches data boundaries, the mutation value is applied in the opposite way (mirror). Figure 13 shows the eighteen low-level genetic heuristics created.

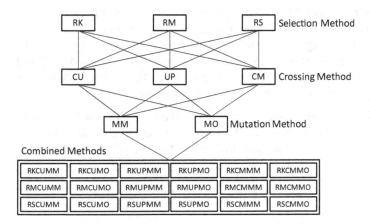

Fig. 13. Heuristics based on genetic algorithms

Rank Selection (RK): Applies the same process explained in 0 to select the two parents of the new individual, but performance is based on the fitness value of the individuals from the population rather than the number of successes of the heuristics.

Restrictive Mating Selection (RM): One parent p1 is randomly selected from the population. Its mate p2 is chosen from a selection group (SGS solution vectors randomly selected from current population) with the most similar number of clusters as for p1. If this results in a group with more than one candidate solution, the similarity of cluster centers (based on cosine similarity) is further used to select the most similar one.

Roulette Wheel Selection (RW): Applies the same process explained in 0 to select the two parents of the new individual, but performance is based on the fitness value of the individuals from the population rather than the number of successes of the heuristics.

Traditional crossover schemes produce two offspring, but in the proposed framework just one is generated. The framework generates a random number between 0 and 1 and selects the left offspring if the generated number is less than 0.5 otherwise the framework generates the right offspring.

One-Point Crossover: First a random cutting point is chosen for both parents. The left offspring will be comprised of the centroids to the left of the first parent and the centroids to the right of second parent using the cutting point as reference, and the right offspring is built with the centroids to the left of the second parent and the right centroids of the first parent using as reference the cutting point [55].

Multi-point Crossover: The total crossing points between 1 and the smallest number of the centroid of the two parents are defined. A segment is defined as a set of centroids between two adjacent crossing points. The left offspring is formed by centroids in the left segments of the first parent (p1) and centroids in the right segments of the second parent (p2). The right offspring is formed by centroids in the right segments of p1 and in the left segments of p2.

Uniform Crossover: The size of the new offspring is calculated generating a random value between the size of the lesser parent (smaller number of centroids) and the size of the greater parent (greater number of centroids). Subsequently, to build each new centroid the framework generates a random number between 0 and 1. When the number is 0 the centroid is taken from parent 1 and if it is 1 the centroid is taken from parent 2, checking at all times that the centroids are not repeated [55].

One-Bit Uniform Mutation: A centroid of the new individual is randomly selected and one of its attributes modified by adding or subtracting a value that is calculated by formula (14), taking into account that the probability of mutation of the attributes is 0.5%

$$(BWmax - BWmin) * RandomDouble + BWmin \qquad (14)$$

where $BW_{max} = 0.005$ and $BW_{min} = 0.0005$.

Multi-bit Uniform Mutation: For each of the centroids of the new individual, a modification of the attributes takes place by adding or subtracting a value resulting from formula (14). The probability of an attribute change is 0.5%.

3.6 Replacement Heuristics

In step 05: **Update population** of the HHK routine. The solution competes with one solution in the population in order to gain entry to the population. There are four alternative replacement (acceptance) strategies: Replace worst, Restricted competition replacement, Stochastic Replacement and Rank Replacement.

Replace Worst (WR): In this case, the new solution competes with the worst solution in the population. If the fitness of the new solution is better than its paired solution, then the paired solution is replaced by the new one.

Restricted Competition Replacement (RC): The new solution is compared with each solution that has the same number of clusters as the new solution in a competition group (RGS vector solutions randomly selected from the current population), and paired with the one with the most similar cluster centers (cosine distance) if such exists; otherwise, it is paired with a solution with the lowest fitness. If the fitness of the new solution is better than its paired solution, the latter is replaced [29].

The extended restricted competition replacement is mostly used to balance competition during replacement among solutions with different numbers of clusters. An appropriate value for RGS should be set to allow both thorough exploration of the search space with the same number of clusters and competition among solutions with different numbers of clusters.

Stochastic Replacement (SR): It selects the best individual from the population based on performance and compares it with the new individual generated. If the new individual has a better fitness than the best it replaces the best in the population. Otherwise formula (15) is applied to decide whether or not the new individual enters the population [37]. In this method, a new random number is generated between 0 and 1. If it is less than the result of applying formula (15), the new individual replaces the worst individual in the population.

$$e^{-\frac{10*ActualIteration}{NI}} \qquad (15)$$

Rank Replacement (RR): The same process explained in section 0 is applied, but here it works on the fitness of individuals in the population rather than the number of successes of the heuristics. It selects the individual to replace; if the performance of the new individual is better than the performance of the selected individual, the new individual replaces the selected individual in the population.

3.7 Frequent Phrases for Labeling

This step corresponds to step 2 "Frequent Phrase Extraction" in Lingo [60], but in WDC-HH-BHRK this method is used for each cluster generated in the previous steps. By the above method, some changes were made to the original algorithm, so that it works using the following steps: (1) Conversion of the representation, (2) Document concatenation, (3) Complete phrase discovery, (4) Final selection, (5) Building of the "Others" label and cluster, and (6) Cluster label induction (more details in [31]).

4 Experimentation

4.1 Data Sets for Assessment

The proposed framework was used for clustering of web results on four traditional benchmarking data sets, namely: **DMOZ-50** (50 queries derived from Open Directory Project. It is available at http://artemisa.unicauca.edu.co/~ccobos/wdc/wdc.htm), **AMBIENT** (AMBIguous ENTries, 44 queries extracted from *ambiguous* Wikipedia entries and results collected from Yahoo! It is available at http://credo.fub.it/ambient), **MORESQUE** (MORE Sense-tagged QUEry results, 114 ambiguous queries which were conducted as a complement to AMBIENT data set. It is available at http://lcl.uniroma1.it/moresque) and **ODP-239** (239 queries derived from Open Directory Project with a comparatively large set of classes, as opposed to having one large collection of documents with a small number of classes. It is available for download at http://credo.fub.it/odp239).

4.2   Metrics for Assessment

The assessment included two points of view: Ground-truth validation and Assessment of user behavior. Ground-truth validation is aimed at assessing how good a clustering method is at recovering known clusters (referred to as classes) from a gold standard partition. Several evaluation measures are available for this task, including precision, recall, F-measure, Fall-out, and Accuracy (Rand index) [7]. In this research, weighted Precision, weighted Recall, weighted F-measure (harmonic means of precision and recall), weighted Fall-out and weighted Accuracy measures are used to evaluate the quality of the solution.

In relation to the Assessment of user behavior, the Subtopic Search Length under the k document sufficiency (SSL_k) metric was used for assessing the ease in which users can use clustering results [24, 27, 30]. This measure is defined as the average number of items (cluster labels or search results) that must be examined before finding a sufficient number (k) of documents relevant to any of the query subtopics, assuming that both cluster labels and search results are read sequentially from top to bottom, and that only clusters with labels relevant to the subtopic at hand are opened. SSL_k allows an evaluation of full-subtopic retrieval (i.e. retrieval of multiple documents relevant to any subtopic) rather than focusing on subtopic coverage (i.e. retrieving at least one relevant document for some subtopics). SSL_k also allows a realistic modelization of the user search behavior because the role played by cluster labels is taken into account.

4.3   Compared Systems

The best heuristics obtained from the **WDC-HH** framework were compared with STC and Lingo from two perspectives - the quality of the clustering results and the ease in which users can use clustering results.

Results from **WDC-HH-BHRK** – as the best heuristic obtained above - were also compared to previously reported results from Lingo3G, KeySRC, OPTIMSRC and Yahoo! **Lingo3G** is a commercial web clustering algorithm also available on Carrot^2. This algorithm is very different to Lingo. It uses a custom-built meta-heuristic to select well-defined and diverse cluster labels. **KeySRC** [24] is a web clustering engine built on top of STC with part-of-speech pruning and dynamic selection of the clustering dendrogram cut-off level. **OPTIMSRC** [27] is a WDC algorithm based on generation of the meta partition with stochastic hill climbing followed by meta labeling based on Lingo, STC, KeySRC labels, while **Yahoo!** results are the original search results returned by the Yahoo! search engine.

4.4   Results and Discussion

In order to select the best WDC heuristic several tests were executed using the WDC-HH framework. All individual heuristics and several combinations of best heuristics (pairs, thirds, quartets, quintets, groups of eleven, and groups of fifteen) were evaluated using the datasets DMOZ, AMBIENT, MORESQUE and ODP239 during one (1) second of executions time. For all tests, the assessment metrics were calculated and the results of the best heuristics were summarized in Table 1. The best results were reported by BHRK heuristic (Global-best Harmony Search as low-level heuristic and Rank replacement heuristic) (see Table 1).

Table 1. Consolidated results of best heuristics

Heuristic	Estimated K	Precision	Recall	F-measure	Accuracy	Fall-out	SSL$_1$	SSL$_2$	SSL$_3$	SSL$_4$	Sum of SSL
BHRK	7.37	69.27	49.18	52.40	0.78	0.05	16.55	25.41	32.92	40.89	115.8
Tabu: BHRK-BHWR	7.39	69.28	49.16	52.38	0.78	0.05	16.71	25.57	33.11	41.02	124.3
BHWR	7.36	69.26	49.16	52.37	0.78	0.05	16.71	25.64	33.09	41	116.4
Rank: BHRK BHWR	7.39	69.29	49.10	52.33	0.78	0.05	16.58	25.49	33.05	41.06	124.3
Tabu: BHRK BHWR HSRK	7.69	70.09	48.66	52.27	0.78	0.05	16.67	25.61	33.13	41.1	124.3
Rank: BHRK BHWR HSRK	7.71	70.15	48.66	52.24	0.78	0.05	16.71	25.56	33.06	40.99	124.3
Rank: BHRK BHWR HSWR	7.74	70.26	48.59	52.23	0.78	0.05	16.8	25.64	33.08	40.98	124.3
Tabu: BHRK-BHWR-HSWR	7.70	70.12	48.63	52.22	0.78	0.05	16.61	25.48	32.99	40.94	124.3
BHSR	7.50	69.55	48.81	52.19	0.78	0.05	16.63	25.58	33.13	41.11	116.4
Tabu: BHWR-HSRK	7.83	70.46	48.44	52.19	0.77	0.05	16.79	25.65	33.13	40.99	124.3
Tabu: BHRK-HSRK	7.83	70.48	48.42	52.17	0.77	0.05	16.79	25.73	33.19	41.08	124.3
Tabu: BHWR-HSWR	7.86	70.50	48.40	52.16	0.77	0.05	16.78	25.64	33.15	41.11	124.3
Tabu: BHRK-HSWR	7.85	70.48	48.36	52.15	0.77	0.05	16.65	25.52	33.13	41.09	124.3
Tabu: BHRK BHWR HSWR HSRK	7.85	70.43	48.39	52.13	0.77	0.05	16.74	25.67	33.14	41.09	124.3
BHRC	7.39	69.07	48.89	52.13	0.78	0.05	16.55	25.49	33	40.97	116
Rank: BHRK BHWR HSWR HSRK	7.87	70.52	48.32	52.10	0.77	0.05	16.74	25.69	33.2	41.18	124.3
Tabu: BHWR HSWR HSRK	8.02	70.95	48.15	52.09	0.77	0.05	16.83	25.75	33.26	41.1	124.3
Tabu: BHRK BHWR RWCUMMRK	7.84	70.65	48.32	52.08	0.77	0.05	16.77	25.65	33.11	41.02	124.3
Tabu: BHRK BHWR HSWR RWCUMMRK	7.94	70.89	48.20	52.08	0.77	0.05	16.76	25.63	33.11	40.99	124.3
Rank: BHRK BHWR HSRK RWCUMMRK	8.00	71.11	48.07	52.05	0.77	0.05	16.85	25.75	33.27	41.22	124.3
Tabu: BHRK BHWR HSRK RWCUMMRK	7.93	70.86	48.16	52.04	0.77	0.05	16.74	25.59	33.08	41.03	124.3
Rank: BHWR HSWR	8.11	71.08	48.01	52.04	0.77	0.05	16.83	25.64	33.15	41.11	124.3
Rank: BHWR HSWR HSRK	8.07	71.00	48.07	52.03	0.77	0.05	16.8	25.64	33.11	41.14	124.3
Rank: BHRK BHWR HSWR RWCUMMRK	8.00	71.07	48.04	52.01	0.77	0.05	16.79	25.6	33.1	41.07	124.3

The successful WDC-HH-BHRK also was compared with state of the art algorithms based on F-measure and SSL (see Tables 2 and 4). On the DMOZ-50 dataset, WDC-HH-BHRK outperforms all other algorithms in all evaluation measures with the sole exception of precision when measured against Lingo. On the AMBIENT dataset, WDC-HH-BHRK outperforms Lingo and STC in recall, F-measure, and accuracy. On this dataset, fall-out is also competitive, but Lingo shows better precision. Results on the MORESQUE dataset favor STC but precision favors Lingo. WDC-HH-BHRK performs best on fall-out. On the ODP-239 dataset, WDC-HH-BHRK outperforms all other algorithms in recall, F-measure, accuracy, and fall-out.

Table 2. Ground-truth validation results

Dataset	Algorithm	Estimated K	Difference to ideal K	Precision	Recall	F-measure	Accuracy	Fall-out
DMOZ-50 Ideal K 6.02	WDC-HH-BHRK	**8.19**	**2.17**	84.03	**70.00**	**74.25**	**91.65**	**0.03**
	Lingo	34.29	28.27	83.85	37.88	48.23	83.41	0.05
	STC	16.00	9.98	**84.82**	57.85	65.12	88.81	**0.03**
AMBIENT Ideal K 7.91	WDC-HH-BHRK	**5.82**	**2.09**	74.11	**62.36**	**63.21**	**84.30**	0.04
	Lingo	20.86	12.95	**86.75**	50.21	58.68	80.43	**0.03**
	STC	11.00	3.09	72.40	53.14	55.38	81.89	0.06
MORESQUE Ideal K 3.81	WDC-HH-BHRK	**6.09**	**2.27**	86.81	43.30	52.43	60.22	**0.05**
	Lingo	20.16	16.34	**90.50**	39.35	50.55	59.18	0.06
	STC	11.17	7.35	82.83	**49.96**	**57.18**	**65.45**	0.13
ODP-239 Ideal K 9.56	WDC-HH-BHRK	**8.09**	**1.47**	56.93	**45.21**	**45.83**	**81.92**	**0.06**
	Lingo	31.39	21.83	**71.56**	32.93	41.01	79.15	0.07
	STC	15.98	6.42	57.33	39.74	41.80	80.65	0.10
Average Ideal K 7.54	WDC-HH-BHRK	**7.37**	**0.17**	69.27	**49.18**	**52.40**	**77.71**	**0.05**
	Lingo	27.81	20.28	**79.26**	36.82	45.99	74.66	0.06
	STC	14.27	6.73	68.39	45.69	49.67	**77.81**	0.09

WDC-HH-BHRK obtains a better number of clusters on all datasets, and the difference is very significant compared to Lingo and STC. On average, WDC-HH-BHRK differs from the ideal number of cluster (7.54) by only 0.17 groups, while STC differs by 6.73 and Lingo by 20.28. WDC-HH-BHRK also outperforms Lingo and STC in recall, f-measure, and fall-out, with accuracy very similar to STC.

Average rankings of precision using the Friedman test show Lingo to be the best algorithm, with a statistic (distributed according to chi-square with 2 degrees of freedom) equal to 163.356823 and p-value of 9.398559708273524E-11 (see Table 3). Additionally, Lingo improves all algorithms and STC improves WDC-HH-BHRK with a level of significance equal to 0.95 in the Wilcoxon test.

Average rankings of recall using Friedman testing show WDC-HH-BHRK to be the best algorithm, with a statistic equal to 346.53132 and p-value 1.4228018763162709E-10 (see Table 3). Additionally, WDC-HH-BHRK improves all algorithms with a Wilcoxon level of significance equal to 0.95. STC improves Lingo with a level of significance equal to 0.9 in the same test.

Average rankings of f-measure show that WDC-HH-BHRK is the best algorithm with a Friedman statistic of 104.209172 and p-value equal to 7.932499102025758E-11 (see Table 3). Additionally, WDC-HH-BHRK improves all algorithms with a level of significance equal to 0.95 in the Wilcoxon test, in which STC also improves Lingo with a level of significance equal to 0.9.

Average rankings of accuracy using the Friedman test show that WDC-HH-BHRK is the best algorithm with a statistic equal to 131.802013 and p-value of 6.079925451 984991E-11 (see Table 3). WDC-HH-BHRK also improves all algorithms with a level of significance equal to 0.95 in Wilcoxon test. STC improves Lingo with a level of significance equal to 0.9 in the same test.

Average rankings of fall-out using the Friedman test show that Lingo is the best algorithm with a statistic equal to 51.309843 and p-value of 6.3349658852011882 E-11 (see Table 3). Additionally, Lingo and WDC-HH-BHRK improve STC with a level of significance equal to 0.95 in the Wilcoxon test but Lingo does not improve WDC-HH-BHRK in this test.

Table 3. Ground-truth Friedman test rankings

Algorithm	Precision		Recall		F-measure		Accuracy		Fall-out	
	Ranking	Position	Ranking	Position	Ranking	Position	Ranking	Position	Ranking	Position
WDC-HH-BHRK	2.340	3	**1.415**	**1**	**1.635**	**1**	**1.598**	**1**	1.988	2
Lingo	**1.520**	**1**	2.654	3	2.312	3	2.363	3	**1.766**	**1**
STC	2.139	2	1.930	2	2.052	2	2.038	2	2.245	3

In Fig. 14, curves of precision, recall and F-measure through different numbers of iterations are shown. All values increase with the number of iterations. Therefore, when users can wait longer for results, WDC-HH-BHRK organized clusters of documents better and proved the best option. BBIC with cosine similarity is a good option for clustering of web results because precision, recall, and F-measure all increase when WDC-HH-BHRK evolves (F-measure = 2.0306 * ln (iteration) + 53.654 with R^2 = 0.9739), but in some iterations (e.g. 50 to 55 iterations) this positive relation fails. Thus, the research group plans to define a better fitness function for evolutionary algorithms in the clustering of web results based on genetic programming. Further analysis showed that in general WDC-HH-BHRK increases the cluster quality (based on precision, recall, and F-measure) when it uses more iterations, regardless of the number of documents, number of topics, or number of attributes in the data set. Only MORESQUE data set does not comply with this rule.

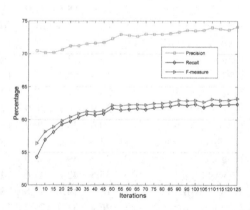

Fig. 14. Precision, Recall and F-Measure for WDC-HH-BHRK through different iterations on AMBIENT data set

New vector solutions generated using the BHRK combined heuristic increase its effectiveness over iterations. Figure 15 shows 64% of effectiveness of the new solution in the first five iterations, i.e. the new solution is better than other solutions in population 64% of the time. Effectiveness increases to 81% in the next five iterations. It then increases to 89% in iteration 15, and finally it is around 98% over the sixtieth iteration (the vector solution generated is almost always better than the other vector solution selected from the population). The behavior in Fig. 15 is for the AMBIENT dataset, but it is similar for other datasets.

Table 4 shows results on the SSL_k (with k = 1, 2, 3, 4) metric for WDC-HH-BHRK, Lingo and STC over all datasets. On DMOZ, AMBIENT, MORESQUE and

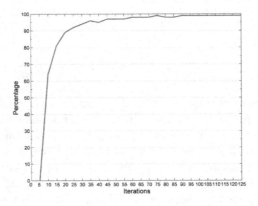

Fig. 15. Effectiveness of new vector solutions generated at different number of iterations on AMBIENT data set

Table 4. User behavior evaluation

Dataset	Algorithm	SSL_1	SSL_2	SSL_3	SSL_4	Sum of SSL_k
DMOZ-50	WDC-HH-BHRK	15.1	19.1	22.1	24.6	80.9
	Lingo	14.2	16.6	**18.5**	21.9	71.2
	STC	**12.1**	**16.4**	18.6	**21.3**	**68.4**
AMBIENT	WDC-HH-BHRK	**14.6**	**26.0**	**32.5**	**37.1**	**110.2**
	Lingo	22.4	36.5	47.2	54.3	160.4
	STC	27.2	44.9	54.8	60.4	187.3
	Best combination*	21.7	29.3	33.2	37.3	121.5
	OPTIMSRC*	20.6	28.9	34.1	38.9	122.5
	Lingo*	24.4	30.6	36.6	40.7	132.3
	KeySRC*	24.1	32.4	38.2	42.1	136.8
	Lingo3G*	24.0	32.4	39.6	43.0	139.0
	Yahoo!*	21.6	35.5	42.0	47.6	146.7
MORESQUE	WDC-HH-BHRK	**11.1**	**18.6**	**24.1**	**27.8**	**81.6**
	Lingo	16.5	26.4	33.9	39.2	116.0
	STC	19.6	32.3	40.2	45.2	137.3
ODP-239	WDC-HH-BHRK	**19.8**	**29.9**	**39.5**	**51.2**	**140.4**
	Lingo	25.6	38.1	51.4	66.4	181.5
	STC	26.3	43.1	60.7	78.4	208.5
	Lingo**	22.0	35.0	48.3	63.8	169.1
	Lingo3G**	21.5	34.4	48.2	63.3	167.4
	KeySRC**	22.8	40.1	57.3	75	195.2

*Taken from [27] and **Taken from [3]

ODP-239 datasets, WDC-HH-BHRK outperforms Lingo and STC in SSL_1, SSL_2, SSL_3, SSL_4 and Sum of SSL_k. DMOZ dataset gives poor results for WDC-HH-BHRK because this dataset has no keywords, meanwhile MORESQUE uses 2, 3 or 4 keywords to describe the query and therefore WDC-HH-BHRK improves results of SSL_k by a greater amount. The keywords in the queries are very important for the labeling step on WDC-HH-BHRK (the traditional scenario in web result clustering).

5 Conclusions and Future Work

The successful modeling, implementation and evaluation of a hyper heuristic framework specifically for the problems related to WDC were achieved. The HH framework can be run directly for WDC and it works in the same way as description-centered algorithms. It uses four high-level selection strategies: random selection, tabu selection, rank selection and roulette wheel selection based on the performance of low-level heuristics. It also employs a wide set of low-level heuristics: harmony search, improved harmony search, new global harmony search, global-best harmony search, particle swarm optimization, artificial bee colony, differential evolution, and a further eighteen heuristics based on genetic algorithms, each a product of the combination of micro-heuristics: restricted pairing selection (RM), roulette wheel selection (RW), rank selection, one-point crossover (UP), uniform crossover (CU), multi-point crossover (CM), one-bit uniform mutation (MU) and multi-bit uniform mutation (MM). It also uses the k-means algorithm as a strategy for improving the solution at the local level and, based on the Balanced Bayesian Information Criterion, it is able to automatically define the number of groups. Finally it uses four replacement strategies: replace worst, restricted competition replacement, stochastic replacement and rank replacement.

From the results obtained in the tests applied to the datasets DMOZ, AMBIENT, MORESQUE and ODP239, the best low-level heuristic BHRK was found. This comprises global-best harmony search and rank replacement. It gave the best performance based on the measures of recall, F-measure, accuracy, and SSL_k compared with various framework heuristics as well as with the Lingo and STC algorithms.

As can be seen from the results of the best individual heuristics and their combinations, making use of heuristics that work together to obtain the best solution gives good results (position 2 of the table) so that it is possible that if all heuristic combinations are tried, improvements can be achieved in WDC results, surpassing the results of the best individual heuristic, in this case BHRK. In order to perform an exhaustive evaluation of the hyper heuristic framework it would be necessary to carry out a total of $1.58456E + 29 \left(\sum_{i=1}^{97} (97!/(i! \times (97 - i)!)) \right)$ evaluations. In recognizing that such a number of evaluations are not feasible, the use of covering arrays is recommended in order to significantly reduce the number of evaluations required and obtain results with a greater coverage of the total possible evaluations.

Other tasks await future work. Among these are (1) Use of WordNet or other semantic tools to work with concepts instead of terms and compare results with other state of the art algorithms, (2) Use of disambiguation techniques in order to improve the quality of cluster results and compare the results with other algorithms, and (3) Design of other high, low and replacement heuristics in the framework proposed and compare the results with other state of the art algorithms in WDC.

References

1. Carpineto, C., et al.: A survey of web clustering engines. ACM Comput. Surv. **41**(3), 1–38 (2009)
2. Manning, C., Raghavan, P., Schütze, H.: Introduction to Information Retrieval. Cambridge University Press, Cambridge (2008)
3. Carpineto, C., D'Amico, M., Romano, G.: Evaluating subtopic retrieval methods: clustering versus diversification of search results. Inf. Process. Manage. **48**(2), 358–373 (2012)
4. Hammouda, K.M.: Web mining: clustering web documents a preliminary review, 1–13 (2001). http://citeseerx.ist.psu.edu/viewdoc/summary?doi=10.1.1.86.4076
5. Berkhin, P.: A survey of clustering data mining techniques. In: Kogan, J., Nicholas, C., Teboulle, M. (eds.) Grouping Multidimensional Data, pp. 25–71. Springer, Heidelberg (2006). doi:10.1007/3-540-28349-8_2
6. Li, Y., Chung, S.M., Holt, J.D.: Text document clustering based on frequent word meaning sequences. Data Knowl. Eng. **64**(1), 381–404 (2008)
7. Mahdavi, M., Abolhassani, H.: Harmony K-means algorithm for document clustering. Data Min. Knowl. Disc. **18**(3), 370–391 (2009)
8. Geem, Z., Kim, J., Loganathan, G.V.: A new heuristic optimization algorithm: harmony search. Simulation **76**(2), 60–68 (2001)
9. Hemalatha, M., Sathyasrinivas, D.: Hybrid neural network model for web document clustering. In: Second International Conference on the Applications of Digital Information and Web Technologies, ICADIWT 2009 (2009)
10. Carullo, M., Binaghi, E., Gallo, I.: An online document clustering technique for short web contents. Pattern Recogn. Lett. **30**(10), 870–876 (2009)
11. Chehreghani, M.H., Abolhassani, H., Chehreghani, M.H.: Density link-based methods for clustering web pages. Decis. Support Syst. **47**(4), 374–382 (2009)
12. Matsumoto, T., Hung, E.: Fuzzy clustering and relevance ranking of web search results with differentiating cluster label generation. In: 2010 IEEE International Conference on Fuzzy Systems (FUZZ) (2010)
13. Fersini, E., Messina, E., Archetti, F.: A probabilistic relational approach for web document clustering. Inf. Process. Manage. **46**(2), 117–130 (2010)
14. Lee, I., On, B.-W.: An effective web document clustering algorithm based on bisection and merge. Artif. Intell. Rev. **36**(1), 69–85 (2011)
15. He, X., et al.: Clustering web documents based on multiclass spectral clustering. In: 2011 International Conference on Machine Learning and Cybernetics (ICMLC) (2011)
16. Osiński, S., Weiss, D.: A concept-driven algorithm for clustering search results. IEEE Intell. Syst. **20**(3), 48–54 (2005)
17. Zhang, D., Dong, Y.: Semantic, hierarchical, online clustering of web search results. In: Yu, J.X., Lin, X., Lu, H., Zhang, Y. (eds.) APWeb 2004. LNCS, vol. 3007, pp. 69–78. Springer, Heidelberg (2004). doi:10.1007/978-3-540-24655-8_8
18. Fung, B., Wang, K., Ester, M.: Hierarchical document clustering using frequent itemsets. In: Proceedings of the SIAM International Conference on Data Mining (2003)
19. Mecca, G., Raunich, S., Pappalardo, A.: A new algorithm for clustering search results. Data Knowl. Eng. **62**(3), 504–522 (2007)

20. Beil, F., Ester, M., Xu, X.: Frequent term-based text clustering. In: KDD 2002: International Conference on Knowledge Discovery and Data Mining (ACM SIGKDD). ACM, Edmonton (2002)
21. Osiński, S.: Improving quality of search results clustering with approximate matrix factorizations. In: 28th European Conference on IR Research (ECIR 2006), London, UK (2006)
22. Wei, X., Xin, L., Yihong, G.: Document clustering based on non-negative matrix factorization. In: Proceedings of the 26th Annual International ACM SIGIR Conference on Research and Development in Information Retrieval 2003, pp. 267–273. ACM, Toronto (2003)
23. Zhong-Yuan, Z., Zhang, J.: Survey on the variations and applications of nonnegative matrix factorization. In: ISORA 2010: The Ninth International Symposium on Operations Research and Its Applications. ORSC & APORC, Chengdu-Jiuzhaigou (2010)
24. Bernardini, A., Carpineto, C., D'Amico, M.: Full-subtopic retrieval with keyphrase-based search results clustering. In: WI-IAT 2009: IEEE/WIC/ACM International Joint Conferences on Web Intelligence and Intelligent Agent Technologies (2009)
25. Zheng, S., et al.: Web document clustering research based on granular computing. In: Second International Symposium on Electronic Commerce and Security, ISECS 2009 (2009)
26. Navigli, R., Crisafulli, G.: Inducing word senses to improve web search result clustering. In: Proceedings of the 2010 Conference on Empirical Methods in Natural Language Processing, pp. 116–126. Association for Computational Linguistics, Cambridge (2010)
27. Carpineto, C., Romano, G.: Optimal meta search results clustering. In: Proceedings of the 33rd International ACM SIGIR Conference on Research and Development in Information Retrieval, pp. 170–177. ACM, Geneva (2010)
28. Cobos, C., et al.: Web document clustering based on global-best harmony search, k-means, frequent term sets and Bayesian information criterion. In: 2010 IEEE Congress on Evolutionary Computation (CEC). IEEE, Barcelona (2010)
29. Cobos, C., et al.: Web document clustering based on a new niching memetic algorithm, term-document matrix and Bayesian information criterion. In: 2010 IEEE Congress on Evolutionary Computation (CEC). IEEE, Barcelona (2010)
30. Scaiella, U., et al.: Topical clustering of search results. In: Proceedings of the Fifth ACM International Conference on Web Search and Data Mining, pp. 223–232. ACM, Seattle (2012)
31. Cobos, C., et al.: Clustering of web search results based on the cuckoo search algorithm and balanced Bayesian information criterion. Inf. Sci. 281, 248–264 (2014)
32. Burke, E.K., et al.: A Survey of Hyper-heuristics, p. 43. University of Nottingham, Nottingham (2009)
33. Mısır, M., et al.: An investigation on the generality level of selection hyper-heuristics under different empirical conditions. Appl. Soft Comput. 13(7), 3335–3353 (2013)
34. Burke, E.K., et al.: A graph-based hyper-heuristic for educational timetabling problems. Eur. J. Oper. Res. 176(1), 177–192 (2007)
35. Pillay, N., Banzhaf, W.: A study of heuristic combinations for hyper-heuristic systems for the uncapacitated examination timetabling problem. Eur. J. Oper. Res. 197(2), 482–491 (2009)
36. Thabtah, F., Cowling, P.: Mining the data from a hyperheuristic approach using associative classification. Expert Syst. Appl. 34(2), 1093–1101 (2008)
37. Grobler, J., et al.: Alternative hyper-heuristic strategies for multi-method global optimization. In: 2010 IEEE Congress on Evolutionary Computation (CEC). IEEE, Barcelona (2010)
38. Villoria García, A., et al.: Hyper-heuristic approaches for the response time variability problem (2010)
39. Rafique, A.F., et al.: Hyper heuristic approach for design and optimization of satellite launch vehicle. Chin. J. Aeronaut. 24(2), 150–163 (2011)

40. Li, J., Burke, E.K., Qu, R.: Integrating neural networks and logistic regression to underpin hyper-heuristic search. Knowl.-Based Syst. **24**(2), 322–330 (2011)
41. Cobos, C., Mendoza, M., Leon, E.: A hyper-heuristic approach to design and tuning heuristic methods for web document clustering. In: 2011 IEEE Congress on Evolutionary Computation (CEC). IEEE, New Orleans (2011)
42. López-Camacho, E., et al.: A unified hyper-heuristic framework for solving bin packing problems. Expert Syst. Appl. **41**(15), 6876–6889 (2014)
43. Maashi, M., Özcan, E., Kendall, G.: A multi-objective hyper-heuristic based on choice function. Expert Syst. Appl. **41**(9), 4475–4493 (2014)
44. Ahmed, L.N., Özcan, E., Kheiri, A.: Solving high school timetabling problems worldwide using selection hyper-heuristics. Expert Syst. Appl. **42**(13), 5463–5471 (2015)
45. Sabar, N.R., Kendall, G.: Population based Monte Carlo tree search hyper-heuristic for combinatorial optimization problems. Inf. Sci. **314**, 225–239 (2015)
46. Rattadilok, P.: An investigation and extension of a hyper-heuristic framework. Informatica **34**(4), 523–534 (2010)
47. Webb, A.: Statistical Pattern Recognition, 2nd edn. Wiley, Hoboken (2002)
48. Cobos, C., Muñoz, L., Mendoza, M., León, E., Herrera-Viedma, E.: Fitness function obtained from a genetic programming approach for web document clustering using evolutionary algorithms. In: Pavón, J., Duque-Méndez, N.D., Fuentes-Fernández, R. (eds.) IBERAMIA 2012. LNCS, vol. 7637, pp. 179–188. Springer, Heidelberg (2012). doi:10.1007/978-3-642-34654-5_19
49. Berkhin, P.: Survey of Clustering Data Mining Techniques. Accrue Software, Inc., San Jose (2002)
50. Mahamed, G.H.O., Andries, P.E., Ayed, S.: An overview of clustering methods. Intell. Data Anal. **11**(6), 583–605 (2007)
51. Redmond, S.J., Heneghan, C.: A method for initialising the K-means clustering algorithm using kd-trees. Pattern Recogn. Lett. **28**(8), 965–973 (2007)
52. Omran, M.G.H., Mahdavi, M.: Global-best harmony search. Appl. Math. Comput. **198**(2), 643–656 (2008)
53. Mahdavi, M., et al.: Novel meta-heuristic algorithms for clustering web documents. Appl. Math. Comput. **201**(1–2), 441–451 (2008)
54. Jiang, H., Liu, Y., Zheng, L.: Design and simulation of simulated annealing algorithm with harmony search. In: Tan, Y., Shi, Y., Tan, K.C. (eds.) ICSI 2010. LNCS, vol. 6146, pp. 454–460. Springer, Heidelberg (2010). doi:10.1007/978-3-642-13498-2_59
55. Kuri, A., Galaviz, J.: Algoritmos Genéticos. Fondo de Cultura Económica/UNAM/IPM, México (2002)
56. Bianchi, L., et al.: A survey on metaheuristics for stochastic combinatorial optimization. Nat. Comput.: Int. J. **8**(2), 239–287 (2009)
57. Witten, I., Frank, E.: Data Mining: Practical Machine Learning Tools and Techniques. Morgan Kaufmann, San Francisco (2005)
58. Omran, M.G.H., Engelbrecht, A.P., Salman, A.: Bare bones differential evolution. Eur. J. Oper. Res. **196**(1), 128–139 (2009)
59. Panigrahi, B.K., et al.: Population variance harmony search algorithm to solve optimal power flow with non-smooth cost function. In: Geem, Z.W. (ed.) Recent Advances in Harmony Search Algorithm. Studies in Computational Intelligence, vol. 270, pp. 65–75. Springer, Heidelberg (2010). doi:10.1007/978-3-642-04317-8_6
60. Osiński, S., Stefanowski, J., Weiss, D.: Lingo: search results clustering algorithm based on singular value decomposition. In: Kłopotek, M.A., Wierzchoń, S.T., Trojanowski, K. (eds.) Intelligent Information Processing and Web Mining. Advances in Soft Computing, vol. 25, pp. 359–368. Springer, Heidelberg (2004). doi:10.1007/978-3-540-39985-8_37

Clustering Business Process Models Based on Multimodal Search and Covering Arrays

Hugo Ordoñez[1]([⊠]), Jose Torres-Jimenez[2], Armando Ordoñez[3],
and Carlos Cobos[4]

[1] Research Laboratory in Development of Software Engineering,
Universidad San Buenaventura, Cali, Colombia
haordonez@usbcali.edu.co
[2] Information Technology Laboratory, CINVESTAV-Tamaulipas,
Victoria, Tamps, Mexico
jtj@cinvestav.mx
[3] Intelligent Management Systems, Fundación Universitaria de Popayán,
Popayán, Colombia
jaordonez@unicauca.edu.co
[4] Information Technology Research Group (GTI), Universidad del Cauca,
Popayán, Colombia
ccobos@unicauca.edu.co

Abstract. Due to the large volume of business process repositories, manually finding a particular process or a subset of them based on similarities in functionality or activities may become a difficult task. This paper presents a search method and a cluster method for business processes models. The search method considers linguistic and behavior information. The cluster method is based on covering arrays (a combinatorial object used to minimize the set of trials to find a particular structure). The cluster method avoids overlapping and improves the homogeneity of the groups created using a covering array. Obtained results outperform the precision, recall and F-Measure of previously reported approaches.

Keywords: Clustering · Business process models · Multimodal search · Covering arrays

1 Introduction

In order to get an overall overview of the activities carried out in an organization, it is relevant to present formally these activities as business process models (BPs). In these models, the information of the activities is sequentially represented. This information may include the instructions for each task, responsible for each task, messages between participants and interfaces with other systems [1].

Modeling BPs helps organizations to focus on improving the management of operational resources. This improvement leads to more mature and repeatable processes, highly scalable operations and improvement of the overall organization performance [2].

In order to design or model a new BP, it is necessary to know the existing processes of an organization. The knowing of existing processes enables to reuse functionalities and integrate the new process with the processes currently in operation.

© Springer International Publishing AG 2017
O. Pichardo-Lagunas and S. Miranda-Jiménez (Eds.): MICAI 2016, Part II, LNAI 10062, pp. 317–328, 2017.
DOI: 10.1007/978-3-319-62428-0_25

To knowing of existing processes of the organization involves reviewing manually vast amounts of information about existing BPs in some repositories. This search aims at finding particular BP or a set of them based on multiple similarities or shared activities (Common Tasks). Due to the size of the repositories, this manual search may become a cumbersome task [3].

For example, there may be a BP for product purchases and the repository can contain multiple variants of the same BP that apply to different products, customers, markets or versions of the products. Consequently, for the continuous administration of these BPs models, analysts may need to associate multiple variants or versions of the same BP [4], in order to manage these BPs models, the analysts must compare multiple versions of the same BP. This task may be very time-consuming.

Various research approaches have been presented for BP clustering. These are based on measures such as linguistics, structure, and behavior. However, other techniques from the field of Information Retrieval (IR) may be applied to improve existing results. Among these IR techniques, the multimodal search reports good results; this is in part because multimodal search combines different information types to increase the accuracy of the results [5]. Moreover, clustering techniques have been used in BP search to improve the results display. Clustering techniques create groups or families of the BPs: that share similarities in functionality or may contain common tasks. The clustering process may contribute to a better display of results and consequently may help to save time during results analysis [6].

This paper presents an approach for clustering of BPs models based on multimodal search and the use of Covering Array (CA). Multimodal approach unifies linguistic and behavioral information of BP in one search space and uses clustering techniques for improving results display.

The present approach is based on a multimodal mechanism previously described in [7]. Additionally, the present approach introduces improvements in the grouping phase by incorporating a CA (to minimize the number of trials to maximize the possibility of finding good results) and an algorithm that determines the best grouping based on the lower value of the intra-cluster minimal Sum of Square Error (*SSE*). The evaluation of the proposed approach was done using a BPs repository created collaboratively by experts [8]. The results obtained using the present approach, were compared with the results of other state-of-the-art algorithms. This comparison was performed using measures from information retrieval domain, and our results outperformed them.

The remainder of this paper is organized as follows: Sect. 2 presents the related work. Section 3 describes CA related concepts. Section 4 presents the proposed approach as well as an example of its use. Section 5 presents the experimental evaluation. Finally, Sect. 6 depicts conclusions and future works.

2 Related Works

The present approach is focused on clustering of BPs models. This section presents the most relevant related works.

Some approaches are based on hierarchical clustering algorithms [9, 10]. These methods build a hierarchy of groups based on the similarity of the structural characteristics and behavior of the BPs. Then, users review the hierarchy and select the group with the greater similarity to the needs they have.

Sequential clustering of BP is another option. Here, file logs containing data from previous executions of the BP are used as input. These approaches groups BPs with the same type of behavior based on the execution, and data flow [6, 11].

Despite the contributions of the approaches described above, the quality of results may be improved if additional BP characteristics are considered. Some of these characteristics are activity description, task type, Gates type, structure, and behavior. In other words, if only the textual component is considered, so the grouping is performed using the names and description of the BP elements. This textual based grouping may leave aside many other relevant components such as the structure, tasks and behavior.

The present approach presents a BP clustering algorithm that uses a unified representation of BPs including structural units of behavior and textual characteristics of BP. This unification is known as multimodal search representation. The present approach also uses a Covering Array (CA) and an algorithm that creates an optimal grouping by reducing the lower minimal intra-cluster *SSE*.

3 Covering Array Definition

A CA is a combinatorial structures that can be used for representing search spaces. CAs have been used successfully to automate a variety of processes such as software testing. The CAs have the characteristics of minimum cardinality (i.e. they minimize the number of test cases or rows) and maximize coverage (i.e. they guarantees that all combinations of a certain size between the input parameters are analyzed) [12].

A *CA* with k parameters (attributes or columns), with v possible values for each parameter j $(0 \leq j < k)$, an interaction size t and cardinality N, is defined with the following notation: *CA(N; t, k, v)* [13]. Therefore, a *CA* is represented by a matrix M of size $N \times k$, where each element $m_{i,j}$ takes a single element of the set $S = \{0, 1,..., v - 1\}$. v is called the alphabet of the *CA,* and the parameter t is called the strength of the *CA*. A *CA* with strength 2 $(t = 2)$ complies with the following property: any subset of 2 columns j, l $(0 \leq j < l < k)$ contains all the elements of $\{0, 1 ... v - 1\}$ at least once.

Table 1. Example of a CA (9; 2, 4, 3)

0	0	0	0
0	1	2	1
0	2	1	2
1	0	2	2
1	1	1	0
1	2	0	1
2	0	1	1
2	1	0	2
2	2	2	0

The CA presented in Table 1 has 9 tests ($N = 9$), 4 columns ($k = 4$), strength 2 ($t = 2$) and alphabet 3 ($v = 3$). In this CA each of the sub-matrices of size 9×2 has at least once the combinations of three different values belonging to the alphabet v, namely: {(0 0), (0 1), (0 2), (1 0), (1 1), (1 2), (2 0), (2 1), (2 2)}.

4   Proposed Method

The proposed method follows the model of multiple layers: the input layer, the search layer, and the storage layer (See Fig. 1).

4.1   Input Layer

This layer provides interfaces to interact with users. It receives a BP-Input modeled in BPMN (Business Process Management Notation). This layer provides users a graphical user interface (GUI) to enter the BP-Input to be stored in the repository. Additionally, the search Interface allows users to enter the request BP-Input, which is used as a model for searching similar BPs in the repository. The results of the search are grouped for a better display.

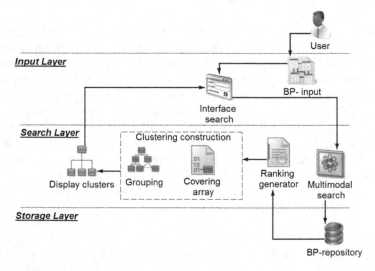

Fig. 1. Architecture of the multimodal search and grouping approach for BP

4.2   Search Layer

In this layer, a BP-input is used as a query for searching similar BP. It is worth noting that not only a complete BP is allowed as input but also BP fragments or even a list of activities. In this layer, a multimodal search algorithm was implemented to rank BP from the repository according to its similarity with the input BP. Equally, it was implemented an algorithm for grouping BPs and for displaying the results in a categorized and organized way. This layer is made up of four modules: Multimodal search, Ranking generator, Clustering construction and Display clusters.

- **Multimodal search:** The present approach uses the multimodal algorithm described in [14, 15]. This algorithm searches BP based on textual and structure features of the BPs. This module is composed of the following components: (i) *Textual Analyzer,* in this procedure, a matrix *MC* is generated by extracting labels (e.g., names, types, and descriptions) from activities of *BP* stored in the repository. (ii) *Structural Analyzer,* this procedure creates a matrix named *MCd,* which is composed of codebooks formed by the union of *n* structural components ruled by the sequential control-flow for each *BP* stored in the repository. (iii) *Search Index:* this module creates an index composed of two search spaces: (1) a textual indexing of business functions and (2) a structural indexing (characterization between types of tasks, events, and links). These two search spaces are unified in a multimodal structure to create a broader index to have an accurate representation of *BP* regarding their category set. Search index efficiently stores a conceptual structure named term-index matrix $MI = \{MC_{i,j} \cup MCd_{i,j}\}$.
- **Ranking Generator:** This component sorts and filters the BPs returned from the search. The ordering is done using an adaptation of the equation of conceptual score (used by Lucene library) [16].

4.2.1 Clustering Construction

In this component, the recovered BPs are used to create groups based on the similarity (linguistic and structural) between the BP models. For the grouping process, the CAClusterBP algorithm was implemented. A CA contains some possible groupings (the alphabet v of the CA defines the upper bound of the number of groups, and the number of parameters k of the CA defines the upper bound of the number of BPs that the CA can handle), and the algorithm is used to find the best grouping present in a CA. This component is divided into two modules which are described below.

- **Covering array:** This mathematical object is interpreted as some possible combinations of the formation of groups with strength *t*. The groups are formed with the BPs retrieved during the search process. The CA is defined by the parameters: CA $(41; 2,20,5)^1$. Where N = 41, is the number of rows of the CA, each row represents a grouping that contains some possible groups formed with a maximum of k BPs retrieved during the multimodal process search (20 for the present approach), the $m_{i,j}$ value represents the location (index) of each item (BP) in a group. v is the upper bound of the number of possible groups to be formed. For this experimentation v = 5 (the number of groups to form for each line of the CA), that is to say, that the groups are formed with the CA (41; 2, 20, 5). The latter means that in each pair of columns there exist at least once all the combinations of the values of the alphabet v.
- **Grouping:** This module uses the algorithm *CAclusterBP*. The algorithm takes as input a CA. This CA was created off-line and then stored in the repository. This CA contains some possible groupings of results. The algorithm takes each line of the CA (N_i) to form the grouping. From each N_i, it is taken sequentially an element v_j of

---

[1] This CA was constructed using a generalization of cover starters [20] proposed by Jose Torres-Jimenez and Charles Colbourn.

the alphabet of the CA to form the groups. For example, the group 0, $v_j = 0$ consists of the BPs referenced by the column of the CA with value 0. As explained above, the index of the reference column (is equal) to the index of the item in the results list. Once each BP is assigned to its respective group v_j, the algorithm repeats the process until the best grouping is found based on the lower value of *Sum of Square error* (SSE, calculated using Eq. 4), the algorithm uses the parameters of Table 2. Below, a step by step sample is presented.

Table 2. Parameters for refining the grouping

Symbol	Description
x	BP (score value in the result list)
C_i	The ith cluster
c_i	The centroid of cluster C_i
c	The average of all points
m_i	The number of objects in the ith cluster
m	The number of objects in the data set
K	The number of clusters

The steps of the *CAClusterBP* algorithm are described below:

- *Step 1*: The algorithm takes each line of the *CA*, which represents a possible grouping and forms the groups using the elements of the alphabet of the *CA*.
- *Step 2*: Once the groups are formed, the algorithm calculates the centroid of each group using Eq. 1.

$$c_i = \frac{1}{m_i} \sum_{x \in C_i} x \tag{1}$$

- *Step 3:* Once c_i is calculated, The SSE_i is calculated for each grouping C_i, using Eq. 2.

$$SSE_i = \sum_{x \in C_i} dist(c_i, x)^2 \tag{2}$$

- In this equation, *dist* is calculated using Eq. 3.

$$dist = \sqrt{\sum_{j=1}^{A} (c_{i,j} - x_j)^2} \tag{3}$$

A is the total number of characteristics of a BP

- *Step 4*: Calculated SSE for the whole grouping using Eq. 4.

$$SSE = \sum_{i=1}^{k} \sum_{x \in C_i} dist(c_i, x)^2 \tag{4}$$

- *Step 5*: While the CA has more lines to be processed repeat steps 1 to 4, otherwise return the best grouping which has the lower SSE.

- **Clusters display:** This component displays the created groups in organized and categorized way. This structure enables users to review and select the group with higher similarity with the query.

4.3   Storage Layer

This layer stores BPs in a repository. The repository was developed containing physical files of BPs. Furthermore, the BPs are extracted from the repository to be ranked according to the search algorithm.

4.4   Example of Clustering Execution

The Fig. 2 shows an example BP called "Activate services." To execute a query in the repository, the model of multimodal search retrieves the BPs with the greatest

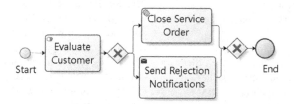

Fig. 2. BP query

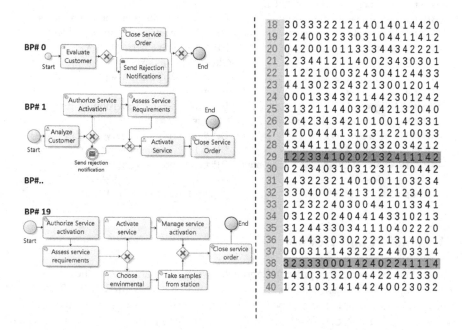

Fig. 3. a. List of results, b. CA(41; 2, 20,5) used

similarity with the user query and generates a list of results filtered and sorted in descending order (Fig. 3a). After that, the *CAClusterBP* algorithm takes each of the lines of the CA (Fig. 3b) to group the results (following the steps previously described). This process continues until all the lines of the CA are analyzed. Finally, the algorithm returns the grouping with the lower value of SEE (the selected grouping is highlighted in Fig. 3b). In Fig. 3b, highlighted lines correspond to the groupings formed for the lines 38 and 29 of the CA (which are shown in Table 3).

Table 3. Groupings created using *CAClusterBP*

Examples of created groupings	
Groupings for row 38	Groupings for row 29
-Cluster:0 #bps :4	**-Cluster:0 #bps :2**
–BP # 5 - service delivery process	–BP # 7 - pre-sales
–BP # 6 - telecom service delivery	–BP # 9 - service activation process
–BP # 7 - pre-sales	**-Cluster:1 #bps :6**
–BP # 12 - service provisioning process	–BP # 0 - activate services
-Cluster:1 #bps :4	–BP # 6 - telecom service delivery
–BP # 8 - service flow	–BP # 11 - request service
–BP # 16 - installation service order	–BP # 15 - market a new product
–BP # 17 - promote new product	–BP # 16 - installation service order
–BP # 18 - provisioning process	–BP # 17 - promote new product
-Cluster:2 #bps :4	**-Cluster:2 #bps :6**
–BP # 1 - activate service	–BP # 1 - activate service
–BP # 10 - handling customer problems	–BP # 2 - sell a service
–BP # 13 - manage customer problem	–BP # 8 - service flow
–BP # 14 - customer credit check	–BP # 10 - handling customer problems
-Cluster:3 #bps :4	–BP # 13 - manage customer problem
–BP # 0 - activate services	–BP # 19 - solve network service problem
–BP # 2 - sell a service	**-Cluster:3 #bps :3**
–BP # 3 - implement a service	–BP # 3 - implement a service
–BP # 4 - enable service	–BP # 4 - enable service
-Cluster:4 #bps :4	–BP # 12 - service provisioning process
–BP # 9 - service activation process	**-Cluster:4 #bps :3**
–BP # 11 - request service	–BP # 5 - service delivery process
–BP # 15 - market a new product	–BP # 14 - customer credit check
–BP # 19 - solve network service problem	–BP # 18 - provisioning process
- Group SSE: 2.112869554	- Group SSE: 2.78644319

5 Evaluation and Results

Results obtained using the present approach, were compared with the results of a manual evaluation performed on a closed test set, which is presented in [8]. This closed test set was created collaboratively by 59 experts in business process management. Also, the results of the *CAClusterBP* approach were also compared with the results of two state-of-art approaches **Lingo** [14] and *BPClustering* for grouping [17] (from now on **HC**). *Lingo* uses two components; firstly a multimodal search based on bigrams (n = 2) and the clustering is based on the Lingo algorithm. HC uses cosine coefficient to measure the similarity between two process models and implements a hierarchical agglomerative algorithm for clustering.

The evaluation was conducted in two phases: (1) internal assessment and (2) external assessment. The first phase involves the application of some internal metrics for clustering analysis that do not require human intervention. These metrics are used to identify how close or distant BPs are from each other in the formed groups. The used metrics are described below.

Sum of squares Between clusters (*SSB*): This measures the separation between clusters (high values are desired). In Eq. 5, k is the number of clusters, n_j is the number of elements in the cluster j, c_j is the centroid of cluster j, *and* x is the mean of the data set [18].

$$SSB = \sum\nolimits_{i=1}^{k} n_j dist^2 \left(c_j - \bar{x} \right) \tag{5}$$

Davis Building index: This measures the relation of the dispersion within the cluster and the separation between clusters. A lower value means that the group is right. This measure is useful to evaluate the formation of unique groups Eq. 6 [19].

$$DB = \frac{1}{k} \sum\nolimits_{i=1, i \neq j}^{k} max \left(\frac{\sigma_i + \sigma_j}{d\left(c_i, c_j \right)} \right) \tag{6}$$

Where k is the number of clusters, σ_i is the average distance between each point in the cluster i and the centroid, σ_j is the average distance between each point in the cluster j and the centroid of the cluster, and $(c_{i,})$ is the distance between the centroids of the two clusters.

Table 4 shows the results of the internal evaluation in each one of the metrics used.

Regarding SSB, the high average of 0.380 reached by *CAClusterBP* shows that the separation of groups created is good since the elements are assigned to the cluster having higher similarity, and intermediate elements are avoided. The latter result is due to the fact that BP in each group is very similar to each other in the group. This situation can be evidenced by the lower value of *SSE_i*. *CAClusterBP* exceeds Lingo and HC in 290%. On the other hand, the low value of *Davis Building* index expresses that elements are well placed within each cluster, in other words, they are not dispersed based on information shared between them.

Table 4. Results of internal assessment of the grouping

Algorithm	SSB	Davis building
CAClusterBP	**0.380**	**0.137**
Lingo	0.129	0.527
HC	0.128	0.582

The second phase, external assessment is focused on the quality of clustering by comparing groups created using automatic grouping techniques with groups generated manually by domain experts [8].

In the second phase, common BPs between pairs of clusters (M generated manually and A generated automatically) are analyzed. Metrics such as precision, recall, and F-measure were used. These metrics were calculated in a standard way using True positives tp (are the number of common BPs in M and A), false positives fp (the number of BPs in A, but not in M), and false negatives fn (the number of BPs in M, but not A).

$$P = \frac{tp}{fp + tp} \tag{7}$$

$$R = \frac{tp}{fn + tp} \tag{8}$$

$$Fmeasure = \frac{2(p * r)}{p + r} \tag{9}$$

Figure 4 shows the results of the second evaluation phase. Regarding P, best results were achieved by *CAClusterBP* with 71%, exceeding Lingo in 6% and HC in 11%. These results allow to see that the algorithm performs the grouping process correctly using the data from the CA. As a result, the selection of the best grouping using the lower SSE increases the number of tp shared between the groups created manually and groups created automatically. This situation demonstrates that the groups created using CAClusterBP have a high similarity with the groups created manually by the expert evaluators (i.e. "ideal grouping"). The results obtained by Lingo can be explained by the fact that Lingo contains shared BPs, i.e. BPs belonging to various groups which Increase the number of fn (BPs Placed in groups different to the one that was expected) and consequently the P is reduced. Regarding HC, the values are explained by the fact that only structural information was used during the formation of groups. Besides, this creation of groups is done statically, which means that one BP is assigned to one group and cannot be assigned to another group with higher similarity.

Regarding Recall, *CAClusterBP* increases Recall by 21% in comparison to Lingo and 20% in comparison to HC (*CAClusterBP* with 65%, Lingo 44% and HC with 45%). The recall value reached shows that more items in the groups created with *CAClusterBP* appeared in the same groups created manually. The latter can be explained by the absence of overlap (BPs existing in many groups simultaneously), i.e. each BP is assigned to only one group. As a result, *CAClusterBP* reduces false negatives (FN). Conversely, Lingo and HC allow overlapping (BPs existing in several groups simultaneously), thus making that the number of items per group decreases the value of true positives (TP) (BPs in the same group that was created manually).

Regarding F- measure, *CAClusterBP* (68%) reaches 16% more than Lingo and HC. The latter allows us to infer that the grouping by *CAClusterBP* has higher harmony between Precision and Recall; for this reason, the groups created are more relevant and similar to the groups created manually by experts.

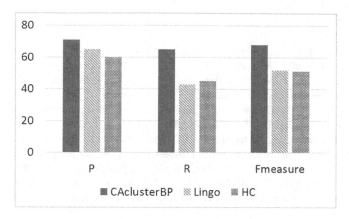

Fig. 4. Results in the external clustering evaluation

6 Conclusions and Future Works

This paper presents a novel approach for improving the clustering quality of business processes (BP) presented in [14]. The presented approach relies on the use of a CA. The present approach implements an algorithm called *CAClusterBP* to find the best grouping. The algorithm is based on the Sum of Square Error (SEE) which allows optimizing the grouping due to the set of ordered pairs of BPs represented in the Covering array.

The use of a CA for creating BPs groups contributes to makes the algorithm faster and simpler. This improvement results from the fact that a CA is built offline, and subsequently used online to find the best grouping among the possible combinations recorded in a CA.

The results of the internal evaluation show that the use of SEE allows generating more compact groups of BP. This result is achieved because the elements in the same group share several characteristics. Moreover, by eliminating overlapping (BPs which can exist in several groups at the same time), *CAClusterBP* creates groups with more similar elements and also provides greater separation between the created groups.

The grouping process using *CAClusterBP* showed a high similarity (71% of precision) with the grouping performed by experts. This similarity is higher that the similarity achieved by Lingo (65%) and HC (60%). This result can be explained by the absence of overlapping (elements in many groups simultaneously) and high refinement of groups using *CAClusterBP* (by identifying the grouping with the lower intra-cluster SEE).

Future work includes adding specific domain ontologies to the proposed model; this will make possible including semantics to the search process, achieving more precise results. Equally, future work will be focused on the assessment of labeling method to determine if created labels help users to identify more easily information and functionality in the created groups. Equally, it is envisaged to evaluate the use of CAs with strength 3, 4 or more to determine the best value of strength for the clustering of BPs. Finally, the future work will involve using towers of CAs or incremental or mixed CA as an additional option to determine which CA achieves higher precision during the grouping process.

References

1. Rajnoha, R., Sujová, A., Dobrovič, J.: Management and economics of business processes added value. Procedia - Soc. Behav. Sci. **62**, 1292–1296 (2012)
2. Gröner, G., Bošković, M., Silva Parreiras, F., Gašević, D.: Modeling and validation of business process families. Inf. Syst. **38**(5), 709–726 (2013)
3. Yan, Z., Dijkman, R., Grefen, P.: Business process model repositories – framework and survey. Inf. Softw. Technol. **54**, 380–395 (2012)
4. La Rosa, M., Dumas, M., Ekanayake, C.C., García-Bañuelos, L., Recker, J., ter Hofstede, A. H.M.: Detecting approximate clones in business process model repositories. Inf. Syst. **49**, 102–125 (2015). http://www.sciencedirect.com/science/article/pii/S0306437914001860
5. Caicedo, J.C., BenAbdallah, J., González, F.A., Nasraoui, O.: Multimodal representation, indexing, automated annotation and retrieval of image collections via non-negative matrix factorization. Neurocomputing **76**(1), 50–60 (2012)
6. Melcher, J., Seese, D., Aifb, I.: Visualization and clustering of business process collections based on process metric values. Measurement **8**, 9 (2008)
7. Ordoñez, H., Corrales, J.C., Cobos, C.: Business processes retrieval based on multimodal search and lingo clustering algorithm. IEEE Latin Am. Trans. **13**(3), 769–776 (2015). doi:10. 1109/TLA.2015.7069103
8. Ordonez, H., Corrales, J.C., Cobos, C., Wives, L.K.: Collaborative grouping of business process models. In: Proceedings of the 7th Euro American Conference on Telematics and Information Systems, p. 35. ACM (2014). doi:10.1145/2590651.2590686
9. Information Systems Engineering and United States: Hierarchical clustering of business process models, Computer (Long. Beach. Calif), vol. 5, pp. 613–616 (2009)
10. Aiolli, F., Burattin, A., Sperduti, A.: A business process metric based on the alpha algorithm relations. In: Daniel, F., Barkaoui, K., Dustdar, S. (eds.) BPM 2011 Workshops, Part I. LNBIP, vol. 99, pp. 141–146. Springer, Heidelberg (2012). doi:10.1007/978-3-642-28108-2_13
11. Diamantini, C., Potena, D., Storti, E.: Clustering of process schemas by graph mining techniques (extended abstract). Methodology **4**, 7 (2011)
12. Torres-Jimenez, J., Izquierdo-Marquez, I.: Survey of Covering Arrays. Symb. Numer. Algorithms Sci. Comput. **1**(1), 20–27 (2013)
13. Hartman, A., Raskin, L.: Problems and algorithms for covering arrays. Discrete Math. **284**, 149–156 (2004)
14. Ordoñez, H., Corrales, J.C., Cobos, C.: Business processes retrieval based on multimodal search and lingo clustering algorithm. IEEE Lat. Am. Trans. **13**(9), 40–48 (2015)
15. Ordoñez, H., Ordoñez, A., Cobos, C., Merchan, L.: Multimodal indexing and search of business processes based on cumulative and continuous N-grams. In: Bridge, D., Stuckenschmidt, H. (eds.) EC-Web 2016. LNBIP, vol. 278, pp. 129–141. Springer, Cham (2017). doi:10.1007/978-3-319-53676-7_10
16. Hu, Y.-C., Su, B.-H., Tsou, C.-C.: Fast VQ codebook search algorithm for grayscale image coding. Image Vis. Comput. **26**(5), 657–666 (2008)
17. Jung, J.Y., Bae, J., Liu, L.: Hierarchical clustering of business process models. Int. J. Innovative Comput. Inf. Control **5**(12(A)), 4501–4511 (2009). http://www.ijicic.org/isii08-123-1.pdf
18. Zhao, Q., Fränti, P.: WB-index: a sum-of-squares based index for cluster validity. Data Knowl. Eng. **92**, 77–89 (2014)
19. Handhayani, T., Hiryanto, L.: Intelligent kernel K-means for clustering gene expression. Procedia Comput. Sci. **59**, 171–177 (2015)
20. Lobb, J.R., Colbourn, C.J., Danziger, P., Stevens, B., Torres-Jimenez, J.: Cover starters for covering arrays of strength two. Discrete Math. **312**(5), 943–956 (2012). http://www. sciencedirect.com/science/article/pii/S0012365X11004833

Optimization

A New Method to Optimize Dynamic Environments with Global Changes Using the Chickens-Hen' Algorithm

Mostafa Zarei, Hamid Parvin$^{(\boxtimes)}$, and Marzieh Dadvar

Department of Computer Engineering, Boushehr Branch,
Islamic Azad University, Boushehr, Iran
parvin@alumni.iust.ac.ir

Abstract. Many different methods for optimization have been proposed and they are swarm-based intelligence algorithms. By these types of algorithms optimized solutions can be found that almost close global solution. Optimization algorithms both maximize and minimize issues to cover. Optimization problems can be divided into two general categories: static and dynamic optimization. Most of the problems in the real world are dynamic in nature. Solving dynamic optimization problems due to the change in the optimal location would be very difficult. To solve dynamic optimization problems we should use an appropriate algorithm. Division algorithm chickens species and collective intelligence algorithms derived from nature is presented in this paper. This is a technically efficient algorithm for solving dynamic optimization based on the laws of probability and on the basis of the working population. This algorithm is an example of behaviorism in artificial intelligence. In this way, each member of the population who are called chickens with the implementation of individual and group behaviors are behaviors that proposed algorithm, they move towards the final answer. The algorithm for estimating the efficiency of a memory density with Euclidean clustering is used. Suitable solutions have been used to preserve the memory of the past. To test the efficiency of the proposed method of moving peaks benchmark famous simulator is used. Experimental results show that the proposed revision on moving peaks benchmark in dynamic performance is acceptable solve optimization problems.

Keywords: Collective intelligence · Dynamic optimization problems · Moving peaks benchmark

1 Introduction

In the real world often face complex issues that need to be optimized and important [1–5]. In fact, these issues can optimize time, costs and optimize our many other useful things [6–16]. In general, optimization problems can be put into two basic groups: (1) static optimization problems (2) dynamic optimization problems [17–31].

Static optimization problems, optimization problem is fixed and does not change, so the optimal tracking this stuff is somewhat easy task [32–42]. Given that most of the problems in the real world are dynamic, so in these environments requires that in

© Springer International Publishing AG 2017
O. Pichardo-Lagunas and S. Miranda-Jiménez (Eds.): MICAI 2016, Part II, LNAI 10062, pp. 331–340, 2017.
DOI: 10.1007/978-3-319-62428-0_26

addition to finding the optimal variable algorithms, optimal variable to follow desirable manner. So in these areas will be optimal algorithms, with an average error found the best solution in every moment of time is lowest. Whenever a change in the target optimization, sample issue or restriction of an optimization problem to occur some changes, it may change its optimum. If this happens it is necessary to adapt the solution to old solution. A standard way to face with these dynamics, dealing with each new change as an optimization problem must be solved first. This method is sometimes impractical because of this that solving a problem from the beginning, without reuse of the information is very time consuming. In the optimization of complex issues, using careful optimization is impossible, so the random search methods used to achieve a near-optimal response. In fact, in this type of algorithms appropriate response can be taken in an acceptable timeframe, but there is no guarantee to obtain the best response. Among the random search methods evolutionary algorithms that are derived from nature have a special place. Given the complexity of many optimization problems with a dynamic, developing ways to improve the efficiency of the algorithms for solving dynamic optimization has been done. Since evolutionary algorithms have traditionally been evolving, a perfect candidate for solving optimization problems seems to come.

Most species of animals have been seen in group behaviors. Perhaps that some of these species are also guided by a top member groups. For example, lions, monkeys and deer-quite seen it. There's more interesting is that there are species of animals that live in groups, but not tips. Each member has a self-organizing behavior without the use of a guide can-can in the environment and their natural needs to iron out such as birds, fish and flocks of sheep. These animals do not have any knowledge about the general behavior of the entire group or even no knowledge of the environment in which they are not. Instead, members are able to exchange the information with your neighbors move in. This simple interaction between particles caused more complex treatment group. Find a particle-like environment.

Division algorithm eggs and chicks of collective intelligence algorithms are based on population and random search work. HCSA of chickens is based on social behavior and on the basis of random searches, works the crowd and behaviorism. This algorithm has features such as high convergence speed, flexibility and fault tolerance is that it is acceptable for solving optimization problems. This algorithm is a method in this article to solve dynamic optimization problems are presented and detailed in the following sections will be described.

As stated, there are three main problems in dynamic environments: The first problem is to identify the changes in the environment could algorithm timely to show an appropriate response to these changes. The third problem, the basic problem in dynamic environments problem is the loss of diversity, because diversification is optimized for mobile and converged a group then it is optimized convergence algorithms to dramatically reduce efficiency.

2   Related Works

Regarding dynamic environment, a variety of techniques have been suggested recently. In following you can find some of them.

Yazdani et al. [43] proposed a novel multi-swarm algorithm for optimization based on particle swarm optimization. They try to maximize diversity in the environment. A collaborative model for tracking optima in dynamic environments [43] has been proposed [44]. CESO, their method, employs two subpopulations with the same volume to recognize and follow the movable optimal solutions in dynamic environments.

In 2015, Ozoydan and Baykasoglu [45] presented a multi-population algorithm based on the fireflies algorithm to solve dynamic optimization problems. In that method, the chaos mapping was used to generate the initial population. The multi-population method in the fireflies algorithm was used to maintain the diversity at an appropriate level.

Hu and Ebrehart provided a method based on collective optimization of particles, namely RPSO, for dynamic environments in which the random movement of particles will occur whenever the necessary diversity is lost [46].

Sadeghi et al. [47] presented an algorithm based on particle crowding for solving dynamic optimization problems. In this method, a clear memory is used for fast track of the changed optimum. Also an appropriate strategy is used to update the memory. In this algorithm the best past solutions that are not too old are used in the memory to track the optimum in the future.

In [48] the SPSO method has been provided for dynamic environments. The SPSO algorithm is capable of dynamic distribution of the particles to some groups. SPSO has been designed based on the concept of "species". The center of a species which is called the species core is a particle that has always the best fitness in the species. All particles that are located within a predefined radius of the species core are in the same species. The algorithm converges the groups to several local optimums instead of converging them to a single global optimum. Hence, several sub-populations are developed in parallel.

The idea of using several populations, especially in multimodal environments, is very useful. Here, the idea of multi-groups to divide the total search space into several subspaces has been used in order to converge each of group on one of the possible peaks.

In FMSO [49] a parent group has been used as a base class for identifying promising areas, and a swarm of children groups has been also used for the local search in their own related sub-space. Each children group has its own search area which is considered as a sphere with the radius r and the center of the best particle in that group. Hence, a particle $\vec{x}$ with a distance less than r from the best particle of that group $(\vec{s})$ is considered. Therefore, a particle $\vec{x}$ with a distance less than r from $\vec{s}$ belongs to the children group.

In [50] an algorithm named EA-KDTree has been suggested. In this method, the explorative and non-explorative areas are separated by adaptation. The algorithm divides the search areas into several regions. In this method the areas are covered to detect the changing optimum. A simple solution has been used. According to this approach, each area is estimated to find the optimum, and a special data structure called the KD-Tree has been used to memorize the search areas in order for the convergence speed to increase.

In [51] a particle crowd algorithm based on clustering has been proposed. In this algorithm the particles are divided into some clusters of. Each particle does a local search in its own cluster. The k-means clustering has been used. Also a parameter named the crowd factor has been used in this method. The crowd factor has been used for more diversity. The crowd factor states that if the particle crowd occurs in some area of the search space, some particles crowded in that area will randomly migrate to a less crowded area of the search space. This model is a strategy to encourage the simulated tracking for multi-peak functions that prevents the accumulation of particles in the peaks. In this algorithm, instead of using a group that has s particles and aims at finding the optimal solution of the n-dimensional vector, a group of particles is chosen per dimension. So, n particle groups are used, each with s particles.

In [52] a collective optimization of particles based on the cellular automata, called CellularPSO, has been suggested. The main idea of this approach is to utilize local interactions in the cellular automaton (CA) and divide the population of particles within the CA cells. Each group tries to find a local optimum and this leads to finding the global optimum. In this method, a cellular automaton with cd equal cells in a d-dimensional environment has been used. Therefore, a particle in the search space can be assigned to a cell of the cellular automaton. This concept is used to maintain the diversity in the search space. In addition, a concept known as particle density is used for each cell. According to that, a threshold for the maximum number of particles that can be placed in a cell has been determined. This causes all the particles not to be converging on a cell; so only a portion of the particles can search in a single area of the search space and other particles do the search in other areas of the search space.

In [53], Blackwell et al. offered the adaptive algorithm Adaptive mQSO for dynamic environments. In the Adaptive mQSO algorithm, the number of groups is not specified in the beginning, and it increases with the changes in the environment and finding new peaks so that whenever all groups get converged, an anti-convergence operator will create a new free group that helps to find new local optimums.

A special kind of particle swarm algorithms proposed for dynamic environments is the mQSO algorithm [54]. In this algorithm, the particles are divided into two categories:

1. Neutral particles: neutral particles particle were first presented in the standard particle swarm algorithm. Neutral particles, the particles are responsible for rapid convergence of the particles to the intended optimum.
2. Quantum particles: quantum particles were presented in [54] as a tool to maintain a certain level of diversity within a group. They are affected by atomic models. Quantum particles are placed in random positions to maintain group diversity.

The mQSO algorithm is known as the particle swarm algorithm based on quantum particles, and the total population in this algorithm is divided into several groups. It includes three diversity operators namely quantum particles, disposal and anti-convergence. The disposal operator uses a mechanism to prevent premature convergence and create diversity. If the disposal operator finds two overlapping groups, it will give initial values to the worse one again. When all groups are convergent, the anti-convergence operator will give initial values to the worse one again [54].

Kamoosi et al. provided an optimization method for multi-population particle which is suitable for dynamic environments and has been much better than the conventional methods. The algorithm is based on the standard algorithm of particle swarm [55]. In the method provided by Kamoosi et al., the algorithm begins its work by creating a group. Then each child group will update their position and speed equations if they are active. After updating the position and speed equations, a group is checked. In case the convergence radius (the maximum distance between two particles in a group determines its convergence radius) is less than the total convergence radius and the fitness of the group is less than the fitness of the best position found among all groups, the group will become inactive and instead of that, among all inactive groups whose convergence radiuses are more than the total convergence radius, the one with the highest level of fitness will become active. Also in this method if two groups are within each other's within radiuses, the one with less fitness will be removed from the search space [56].

3 Method and Results

The quasi-code of the hen and chicken algorithm is shown in Fig. 1.

$POP_{::} = rand(h, d)$
$\quad \forall i \in \{1, ..., m\} : \ M_{i:} = H_{i:}$
$\quad \forall i \in \{1, ..., ch\} : \ ch_{i:} = POP_{i:}$
$\quad \forall i \in \{ch + 1, ..., N\} : \ H_{(i-ch):} = POP_{i:}$
$\quad \forall i \in \{1, ..., m\} : \ B_i = false$
$B_i = false \ \ \forall i \in \{1 ..... m\}$
$Change - flag = false$
$For \ i=1 \ to \ cycle$
$\quad For \ j=1 \ to \ h$
$\quad \forall \ q \in ((j-1) * k + 1, ..., min \ (jk, ch)) \Rightarrow \vec{r}_{q:} = \vec{ch}_{q:} - \vec{H}_{j:}$

$$\vec{T} = \sum_{q=((j-1) \cdot k+1)}^{min \ (jk,ch)} \vec{r}_{q:}$$

$if \ (|\vec{T}| < threshold \ \&\& \ B_j)$
$\{$

$$Best\_ind = arg \begin{pmatrix} min(jk, ch) \\ min(F(ch_{r:})) \\ r = (j-1) * k + 1 \end{pmatrix}$$

$\quad If \ (F(H_{j:}) < F(ch_{Best\_ind,:}))$
$\quad\quad Best\_ind = j + ch$
$\quad\quad Save(POP_{Best\_ind,:})$
$\quad\quad POP_{ch+j:=rand}$
$\quad\quad \forall \ r \in \{(j-1) * k + 1, ... min(jk, ch)\} : POP_{r:} = ch_{r:} = rand$
$\}$
$Else \ \ if(B_j)$
$\{$
$\quad$ //child nears to hen & nears to best & far from worst
$\quad if \ f(H) > f(ch) \Rightarrow ch = \dfrac{(ch - w)r_1 + (B - ch)r_2 + (H - ch)r_3}{|(ch - w) + (B - ch) + (H - ch)|} \times strp + ch$
$\}$
$Else \ \ if \ |\vec{T}| < threshold$
$\{$
$B_i = true$
$\}$
$Else \ \{$
$\quad Wander \ \}$

Fig. 1. The quasi-code of the proposed algorithm.

The default setting for moving peaks benchmark [57] is indicated in Table 1.

Table 1. Standard setting for moving peaks benchmark [57].

Parameter	Value
m (Number of peaks)	10
f	Every 5000 evaluations
Height severity	7.0
Width severity	1.0
Peak shape	Cone
Basic function	No
Shift length s	1.0
Number of dimensions	5
A	[0, 100]
H	[30.0, 70.0]
W	[1, 12]
I	50.0

The default setting for proposed algorithm is indicated in Table 2.

Table 2. Standard setting for proposed algorithm.

Parameter	Value
Hen visual	5
Chicken visual	1
Memory size	10
Total population	100
Number of swarm	5

The proposed algorithm was compared to mQSO [54], FMSO, CellularPSO [52] and Multi-Swarm [56] algorithms. Here, for mQSO the 10 (5 + 5 q) configurations were used in which 10 groups were created and each group had 5 neutral particles as well as 5 quantum particles. In addition, the quantum radius for this algorithm was considered 5/0 while the disposal radius and the convergence radius were equal to 5/31. For the FMSO algorithm, the maximum number of child groups is 10 while the disposal radius between the children groups, the number of particles in the parental group and in the child groups were 25, 100 and 10, respectively. For CellularPSO a 5-dimensional cellular automata with105 cells and Moore neighborhood 1 with the cell radius 2 has been used in the search space. The maximum particle speed equaled the neighborhood radius and the maximum number of particles per cell equaled 10 and also the local search radius was set 5/0. Besides, all particles do the local search for a stage after observing some change in the environment. For the Multi-Swarm methods, the number of particles for the parent group and the number of particles for the children groups were 5 and 10, respectively. The disposal radius between the groups of children and the radius of the quantum particles were respectively 30 and 5/0.

In this section the experiments conducted on the proposed model at frequencies of 500 to 10,000 as well as the number of peaks equal to 1 to 200 were explained. The default setting for the moving peak function is shown in Table 2. The result of the experiments for all algorithms is the mean offline error with 95% in 100 runs. Hereby, the proposed algorithm was compared with mQSO10 (5 + 5q), FMSO, CellularPSO and Multi-SwarmPSO, AmQSO [53], HdPSO [58], FTMPSO [39], CDEPSO [59] and DPSABC [60] algorithms.

The offline error and the standard error obtained from the experiments are shown in Table 3 from the environments with different dynamics. Better results are shown in bold. As can be seen, the difference between the offline error of the proposed algorithm and other algorithms increases with the increase of the environment frequency as well as the increase of the space complexity (an increase in the number of peaks). The reason for this is that the proposed algorithm can obtain better solutions faster after seeing the changes in the environment. In the proposed method, due to the wide variety, almost all peaks are covered by the particles.

Table 3. A comparison between the offline error and the standard error of the proposed method with other methods for f = 500.

m	mQSO (5,5q)	Adaptive mQSO	CellularPSO	FMSO	Multi Swarm PSO	FTMPSO	DPSABC	HCSA
1	33.67 (3.42)	3.02 (0.32)	13.46 (0.73)	7.58 (0.9)	5.46 (0.30)	**1.76 (0.09)**	2.77 (0.00)	4.01 (0.21)
5	11.91 (0.76)	5.77 (0.56)	9.63 (0.49)	9.45 (0.4)	5.48 (0.19)	**2.93 (0.18)**	–	3.78 (0.24)
10	9.62 (0.34)	5.37 (0.42)	9.35 (0.37)	18.2 6(0.3)	5.95 (0.09)	3.91 (0.19)	**3.42 (0.00)**	3.54 (0.12)
20	9.07 (0.25)	6.82 (0.34)	8.84 (0.28)	17.34 (0.3)	6.45 (0.16)	4.83 (0.19)	**3.12 (0.00)**	3.27 (0.16)
30	8.80 (0.21)	7.10 (0.39)	8.81 (0.24)	16.39 (0.4)	6.60 (0.14)	5.05 (0.21)	3.69 (0.00)	**3.19 (0.11)**
40	8.55 (0.21)	7.05 (0.41)	8.94 (0.24)	15.34 (0.4)	6.85 (0.13)	–	–	**3.14 (0.13)**
50	8.72 (0.20)	8.97 (0.32)	8.62 (0.23)	5.54 (0.2)	7.04 (0.10)	4.98 (0.15)	3.22 (0.00)	**3.10 (0.10)**
100	8.54 (0.16)	7.34 (0.31)	8.54 (0.21)	2.87 (0.6)	7.39 (0.13)	5.31 (0.11)	3.01 (0.00)	**3.06 (0.13)**
200	8.19 (0.17)	7.48 (0.19)	8.28 (0.18)	11.52 (0.6)	7.52 (0.12)	5.52 (0.21)	3.16 (0.00)	**3.01 (0.12)**

4 Conclusion

In this paper a new approach has been proposed for dynamic optimization. This method is based on a behavior from nature. This method has been completely evaluated on moving peak problem. In all conditions of moving peak problem, the proposed method has been effective.

Through experimental results it is concluded that this method is effective amongst the best recent dynamic optimizers.

References

1. Kim, M.: Sparse inverse covariance learning of conditional Gaussian mixtures for multiple-output regression. Appl. Intell. **44**(1), 17–29 (2016)

2. Tanveer, M., Shubham, K., Aldhaifallah, M., Nisar, K.S.: An efficient implicit regularized Lagrangian twin support vector regression. Appl. Intell. **44**(4), 831–848 (2016)
3. Balasundaram, S., Meena, Y.: Training primal twin support vector regression via unconstrained convex minimization. Appl. Intell. **44**(4), 931–955 (2016)
4. Yang, L., Qian, Y.: A sparse logistic regression framework by difference of convex functions programming. Appl. Intell. **45**(2), 241–254 (2016)
5. Bang, S., Cho, H., Jhun, M.: Adaptive lasso penalised censored composite quantile regression. IJDMB **15**(1), 22–46 (2016)
6. Yaghoobi, T., Esmaeili, E.: An improved artificial bee colony algorithm for global numerical optimisation. IJBIC **9**(4), 251–258 (2017)
7. Ding, J., Liu, Y., Zhang, L., Wang, J., Liu, Y.: An anomaly detection approach for multiple monitoring data series based on latent correlation probabilistic model. Appl. Intell. **44**(2), 340–361 (2016)
8. Cai, Q., Ma, L., Gong, M., Tian, D.: A survey on network community detection based on evolutionary computation. IJBIC **8**(2), 84–98 (2016)
9. Alishavandi, H., Gouraki, G.H., Parvin, H.: An enhanced dynamic detection of possible invariants based on best permutation of test cases. Comput. Syst. Sci. Eng. **31**(1), 53–61 (2016)
10. Parvin, H., Minaei-Bidgoli, B., Alinejad-Rokny, H.: A new imbalanced learning and dictions tree method for breast cancer diagnosis. J. Bionanosci. **7**(6), 673–678 (2013)
11. Parvin, H., Alinejad-Rokny, H., Minaei-Bidgoli, B., Parvin, S.: A new classifier ensemble methodology based on subspace learning. J. Exp. Theor. Artif. Intell. **25**(2), 227–250 (2013)
12. Parvin, H., Minaei-Bidgoli, B., Alinejad-Rokny, H., Punch, W.F.: Data weighing mechanisms for clustering ensembles. Comput. Electr. Eng. **39**(5), 1433–1450 (2013)
13. Parvin, H., Minaei-Bidgoli, B.: A clustering ensemble framework based on elite selection of weighted clusters. Adv. Data Anal. Classif. **7**(2), 181–208 (2013)
14. Alizadeh, H., Minaei-Bidgoli, B., Parvin, H.: Optimizing fuzzy cluster ensemble in string representation. IJPRAI **27**(2), 1350005 (2013)
15. Parvin, H., Beigi, A., Mozayani, N.: A clustering ensemble learning method based on the ant colony clustering algorithm. Int J Appl Comput Math **11**(2), 286–302 (2012)
16. Parvin, H., Minaei-Bidgoli, B.: A clustering ensemble framework based on selection of fuzzy weighted clusters in a locally adaptive clustering algorithm. Pattern Anal. Appl. **18**(1), 87–112 (2015)
17. Novoa-Hernández, P., Corona, C.C., Pelta, D.A.: Self-adaptation in dynamic environments - a survey and open issues. IJBIC **8**(1), 1–13 (2016)
18. Adewumi, A.O., Akugbe, M.A.: On the performance of particle swarm optimisation with (out) some control parameters for global optimisation. IJBIC **8**(1), 14–32 (2016)
19. Wang, H., Wang, W., Sun, H., Rahnamayan, S.: Firefly algorithm with random attraction. IJBIC **8**(1), 33–41 (2016)
20. Castelli, M., Vanneschi, L., Popovic, A.: Parameter evaluation of geometric semantic genetic programming in pharmacokinetics. IJBIC **8**(1), 42–50 (2016)
21. Srinivasa Rao, B., Vaisakh, K.: Multi-objective adaptive clonal selection algorithm for solving optimal power flow problem with load uncertainty. IJBIC **8**(2), 67–83 (2016)
22. Rio de Souza e Silva Jr., L.D., Nedjah, N.: Distributed strategy for robots recruitment in swarm-based systems. IJBIC **8**(2), 99–108 (2016)
23. Jia, Z., Duan, H., Shi, Y.: Hybrid brain storm optimisation and simulated annealing algorithm for continuous optimisation problems. IJBIC **8**(2), 109–121 (2016)
24. Srivastava, P.R.: Test case optimisation a nature inspired approach using bacteriologic algorithm. IJBIC **8**(2), 122–131 (2016)

25. Xu, Z., Ünveren, A., Acan, A.: Probability collectives hybridised with differential evolution for global optimisation. IJBIC **8**(3), 133–153 (2016)
26. Osuna-Enciso, V., Cuevas, E., Oliva, D., Sossa, H., Pérez Cisneros, M.A.: A bio-inspired evolutionary algorithm: allostatic optimisation. IJBIC **8**(3), 154–169 (2016)
27. Ahirwal, M.K., Kumar, A., Singh, G.K.: Study of ABC and PSO algorithms as optimised adaptive noise canceller for EEG/ERP. IJBIC **8**(3), 170–183 (2016)
28. Niknam, T., Kavousi-Fard, A.: Optimal energy management of smart renewable micro-grids in the reconfigurable systems using adaptive harmony search algorithm. IJBIC **8**(3), 184–194 (2016)
29. Khan, M.A., Shahzad, W., Baig, A.R.: Protein classification via an ant-inspired association rules-based classifier. IJBIC **8**(1), 51–65 (2016)
30. Lee, C.-P., Lin, W.-S.: Using the two-population genetic algorithm with distance-based k-nearest neighbour voting classifier for high-dimensional data. IJDMB **14**(4), 315–331 (2016)
31. Zhu, M., Liu, S., Jiang, J.: A hybrid method for learning multi-dimensional Bayesian network classifiers based on an optimization model. Appl. Intell. **44**(1), 123–148 (2016)
32. Cerrada, M., Sanchez, R.-V., Pacheco, F., Cabrera, D., Zurita, G., Li, C.: Hierarchical feature selection based on relative dependency for gear fault diagnosis. Appl. Intell. **44**(3), 687–703 (2016)
33. Parvin, H., Alizadeh, H., Minaei-Bidgoli, B.: A new method for constructing classifier ensembles. JDCTA **3**(2), 62–66 (2009)
34. Parvin, H., Alinejad-Rokny, H., Asadi, M.: An ensemble based approach for feature selection. J. Appl. Sci. Res. **7**(9), 33–43 (2011)
35. Parvin, H., Alizadeh, H., Minaei-Bidgoli, B., Analoui, M.: CCHR: combination of classifiers using heuristic retraining. In: International Conference on Networked Computing and Advanced Information Management (NCM 2008) (2008)
36. Parvin, H., Alizadeh, H., Fathy, M., Minaei-Bidgoli, B.: Improved face detection using spatial histogram features. In: IPCV, pp. 381–386 (2008)
37. Parvin, H., Alinejad-Rokny, H., Parvin, S.: A classifier ensemble of binary classifier ensembles. Int. J. Learn. Manag. Syst. **1**(2), 37–47 (2013)
38. Alizadeh, H., Minaei-Bidgoli, B., Parvin, H.: To improve the quality of cluster ensembles by selecting a subset of base clusters. J. Exp. Theor. Artif. Intell. **26**(1), 127–150 (2014)
39. Alizadeh, H., Minaei-Bidgoli, B., Parvin, H.: Cluster ensemble selection based on a new cluster stability measure. Intell. Data Anal. **18**(3), 389–408 (2014)
40. Minaei-Bidgoli, B., Parvin, H., Alinejad-Rokny, H., Alizadeh, H., Punch, W.F.: Effects of resampling method and adaptation on clustering ensemble efficacy. Artif. Intell. Rev. **41**(1), 27–48 (2014)
41. Parvin, H., Mirnabibaboli, M., Alinejad-Rokny, H.: Proposing a classifier ensemble framework based on classifier selection and decision tree. Eng. Appl. of AI **37**, 34–42 (2015)
42. Parvin, H., Mohammadi, M., Rezaei, Z.: Face identification based on Gabor-wavelet features. Int. J. Digital Content Technol. Appl. **6**(1), 247–255 (2012)
43. Yazdani, D., Nasiri, B., Sepas-Moghaddam, A., Meybodi, M.R.: A novel multi-swarm algorithm for optimization in dynamic environments based on particle swarm optimization. Appl. Soft Comput. **13**, 2144–2158 (2013)
44. Lung, R.I., Dumitrescu, D.: A collaborative model for tracking optima in dynamic environments. In: IEEE Congress on Evolutionary Computation, pp. 564–567 (2007)
45. Ozsoydan, F.B., Baykasoglu, A.: A multi-population firefly algorithm for dynamic optimization problems. In: IEEE International Conference on Evolving and Adaptive Intelligent Systems (EAIS), pp. 1–7 (2015). doi:10.1109/EAIS.2015.7368777

46. Hu, X., Eberhart, R.C.: Adaptive particle swarm optimization: detection and response to dynamic systems. In: IEEE Congress on Evolutionary Computation, vol. 2, pp. 1666–1670, Honolulu, HI, USA (2002)

47. Sadeghi, S., Parvin, H., Rad, F.: Particle swarm optimization algorithm for dynamic environments. In: Sidorov, G., Galicia-Haro, S.N. (eds.) MICAI 2015. LNCS, vol. 9413, pp. 260–269. Springer, Cham (2015). doi:10.1007/978-3-319-27060-9_21

48. Petrowski, A.: A clearing procedure as a niching method for genetic algorithms. In: Proceedings of the 2003 Conference on Evolutionary Computation, pp. 798–803. IEEE Press (2003)

49. Yang, S., Li, C.: Fast multi-swarm optimization for dynamic optimization problems. In: Proceedings of International Conference on Natural Computation, vol. 7, no. 3, pp. 624–628 (2008)

50. Nguyen, T.T.: Solving dynamic optimization problems by combining evolutionary algorithms with KD-Tree. In: International Conference on Soft Computing and Pattern Recognition (SoCPaR), pp. 247–252 (2013)

51. Yang, S., Li, C.: A clustering particle swarm optimizer for dynamic optimization. In: Proceedings of Congress on Evolutionary Computation, pp. 439–446 (2009)

52. Hashemi, Ali B., Meybodi, M.R.: Cellular PSO: a PSO for dynamic environments. In: Cai, Z., Li, Z., Kang, Z., Liu, Y. (eds.) ISICA 2009. LNCS, vol. 5821, pp. 422–433. Springer, Heidelberg (2009). doi:10.1007/978-3-642-04843-2_45

53. Blackwell, T., Branke, J., Li, X.: Particle swarms for dynamic optimization problems. In: Blum, C., Merkle, D. (eds.) Swarm Intelligence. Natural Computing Series, pp. 193–217. Springer, Heidelberg (2008)

54. Blackwell, T.M., Branke, J.: Multi-swarms, exclusion and anti-convergence in dynamic environments. IEEE Trans. Evol. Comput. **10**, 459–472 (2006)

55. Kennedy, J., Eberhart, R.C.: Particle swarm optimization. In: Proceedings of IEEE International Conference on Neural Networks, pp. 1942–1948, Piscataway, NJ (1995)

56. Kamosi, M., Hashemi, A.B., Meybodi, M.R.: A new particle swarm optimization algorithm for dynamic environments. In: SEMCCO, pp. 129–138 (2010)

57. http://www.aifb.unikarlsruhe.de/~jbr/MovPeaks/

58. Kamosi, M., Hashemi, A.B., Meybodi, M.R.: A hibernating multi-swarm optimization algorithm for dynamic environments. In: Proceedings of World Congress on Nature and Biologically Inspired Computing, pp. 370–376, NaBIC, Kitakyushu, Japan (2010)

59. Kordestani, J.K., Rezvanian, A., Meybodi, M.R.: CDEPSO: a bi-population hybrid approach for dynamic optimization problems. Appl. Intell. **40**, 682–694 (2014)

60. Baktash, N., Meybodi, M.R.: A new hybrid model of PSO and ABC algorithms for optimization in dynamic environment. Int. J. Comput. Theory Eng. **4**, 362–364 (2012)

Transit Network Frequencies-Setting Problem Solved Using a New Multi-Objective Global-Best Harmony Search Algorithm and Discrete Event Simulation

Edgar Ruano[1], Carlos Cobos[1(✉)], and Jose Torres-Jimenez[2]

[1] Universidad del Cauca, Popayán, Colombia
{eruano, ccobos}@unicauca.edu.co
[2] CINVESTAV, Ciudad Victoria, Mexico
jtj@cinvestav.mx

Abstract. The rise of Bus Rapid Transit Systems (BRTS) in urban centers involves complex problems of design and scheduling including the scheduling of route intervals across the bus network. The difficulty stems from the fact that transport systems keep to established routes and must set frequencies for each route to minimize costs (measured in terms of transport capacity wasted) and maximize the quality of service (minimizing the total time of users in the system). All this depends on the maximum number of buses available in the system. In an effort to find an alternative solution to the Transit Network Frequencies Setting Problem (TNFSP) on BRTS, this paper proposes using Multi-Objective Global Best Harmony Search (MOGBHS), a multi-objective heuristic algorithm based on three main components: (1) Global-Best Harmony Search, as a heuristic optimization strategy, (2) Non-Dominated Sorting, as a multi-objective optimization strategy, and (3) Discrete Event Simulation, for obtaining quality measures in the solutions found. To test the proposed approach, a simulation model was implemented for Megabus, a BRTS located in Pereira (Colombia), for which the frequency of the buses assigned to routes previously defined in the system was optimized so that operating costs were reduced to a minimum, while user satisfaction was maximized. The MOGBHS algorithm was compared with NSGA-II. It was concluded that MOGBHS outperformed NSGA-II in the number of optimal solutions found (Pareto front points), from 175% in 3,000 fitness function evaluations to 488% in 27,000 evaluations.

Keywords: Bus Rapid Transit Systems · Transit Network Frequencies Setting Problem · Global-Best Harmony Search · Multi-objective optimization · Non-Dominated Sorting · Discrete Event Simulation

1 Introduction

Around the world, Bus Rapid Transit Systems (BRTS) have proven to be a viable alternative solution to growing transportation needs of the population [1]. However, to implement a BRTS several problems must be addressed: the design of the network, the design of routes, the definition of frequencies for each route, the assignment of buses to

© Springer International Publishing AG 2017
O. Pichardo-Lagunas and S. Miranda-Jiménez (Eds.): MICAI 2016, Part II, LNAI 10062, pp. 341–352, 2017.
DOI: 10.1007/978-3-319-62428-0_27

routes, and the assignment of personnel (drivers) to buses and routes. These problems are grouped into a global problem called "Transit Network Design and Scheduling Problem" (TNDSP) [2]. Solving them usually involves conflicting goals within them. For example, if the frequency of the routes is increased to improve quality service, the cost of operating the whole transportation system increases. In addition, each problem has it owns constraints that must be satisfied, such as the maximum availability of buses for the system.

Multi-objective optimization (MO) allows handling problems with multiple conflicting objectives, in order to find a set of non-dominated optimal solutions so that an end user is responsible for selecting the non-dominated solution that meets specific criteria [3]. This paper proposes an MO discrete optimization algorithm to be applied for solving a specific TNDSP problem, the Transport Network Frequencies Setting Problem (TNFSP). This approach of solving TNSFP using a MO discrete optimization algorithm was adopted based on the following observations: (1) major investigations have reported promising results using meta heuristics as a solution strategy, and (2) the hybridization of MO with Harmony Search Algorithm (HS) has shown good results in other areas of application, but this approach has not been used to solve the TNFSP [4, 5].

The proposed optimization algorithm, called MOGBHS has three main components: (a) Global Best Harmony Search (GBHS) [6] as a heuristic optimization strategy (global and local search in the solution space); (b) Non-Dominated Sorting for sorting solutions based on multiple objectives, and (c) Discrete Event Simulation for obtaining quality measures in the solutions found. The GBHS is a hybridization of Harmony Search Algorithm and Particle Swarm Optimization Algorithm, and is responsible for: (a) the generation of new individuals and, (b) the evolution of the individuals in each generation. The second component of MOGBHS carries out the sorting of solutions using the concept of non-dominated solutions to build a Pareto front. The third component of MOGBHS is a discrete event simulation implementation that is responsible for executing simulations in specific scenarios (controlled by the frequency of buses on each route, the specific defined routes and, the pattern of arrivals of the passengers, among others); and collecting the information for bus occupancy and time spent by customers in the system (these measures form the evaluation function to be used by the MOGBHS). In this paper, we have calculated the fitness of the generated solutions by MOGBHS based on the results from the simulation (BRTS) in a specific simulation tool called ARENA [7], in order to provide feedback to the algorithm to facilitate evolution.

MOGBHS was evaluated in a case study based on Megabus, an existing BRTS in Pereira (Risaralda, Colombia), and compared with NSGA-II [8]. In order to make this comparison, the activities involved were: (1) implementation of MOGBHS and NSGA-II; (2) review, selection and analysis of existing BRTS; (3) build a simulation model based on a simplification of selected BRTS; (4) test of MOGBHS and NSGA-II supported by the implemented simulation model; and (5) consolidation and analysis of results. On completing the test activities it was found that MOGBHS greatly improves the efficiency compared with the solutions generated by NSGA-II, from 175.12% in 3,000 fitness functions evaluations (FFE) to 488.68% in 27,000 FFEs.

The remainder of this paper comprises four more sections. In Sect. 2 a state of the art review about TNFSP solutions is presented. In Sect. 3 the multi-objective heuristic algorithm (MOGBHS) proposed is presented. Section 4 presents the results of the MOBGHS contrasted with the results of NSGA-II (a fast and elitist multi-objective genetic algorithm) for a specific case real-based used to make the comparison. Finally, Sect. 5 presents the conclusions of the work and some future activities the authors plan to undertake.

2 State of the Art

In the state of the art, many meta-heuristic approaches for solving the TNDSP are reported [4, 9–12]. Many of them have in common that they solve the problem one objective at a time and/or subdivide the problem in sub-problems and then solve each sub-problem separately. Examples of these meta heuristics are: (a) GRASP-TNDP that bases its operation on GRASP with the difference that instead of generating a single solution, it seeks a Pareto approximation [13]; and (b) the set of heuristics proposed in [14] that includes routines for generating routes and a genetic algorithm to find an optimal set of routes with corresponding frequencies for the implementation of a system of ZEV (Zero Emission Vehicles) public transport vehicles. Given that these algorithms do not use a multi-objective approach to solve the problem, the obtained solutions are in general not so useful (given that a predefined priority to solve each objective is implied). More recent works include: a genetic algorithm with elitism for transit network design [15], a bi-level modeling for the transit route and frequency design and a hybrid artificial bee colony algorithm in order to solve the entire problem [16], and a multi-objective approach with objectives alternation for transit network design and frequencies setting [17], among others.

In order to solve a multi objective problem, with two or more objectives generally in conflict with each other, an evolutionary approach was originally proposed. The algorithms that follow this approach are called Multi-Objective Evolutionary Algorithms (MOEA). Reported MOEA implementations have used three basic approaches to deal with the objectives: (a) Naive; (b) Non-Dominated Sorting; and (c) Pareto Strength [3]. The strategy of a non-dominated system basically consists in taking the solutions that are part of the Pareto front. The solutions of this front will be considered the best and therefore belong to the result of the optimization process. One of the best algorithms based on this strategy is the Non-dominated Sorting Genetic Algorithm II (NSGA-II), which to ensure good dispersion of the solutions on the Pareto front uses the Crowding Distance measure [8].

The non-dominated and strength Pareto based approaches deals with many objectives and have proven to be more successful in solving the TNDP [14, 18, 19]. A good review of the use of simulation models and multi-objective optimization to solve the TNDP can be found in [20]. The main differences between the proposal by Wang and the proposed approach of this paper (MOBGHS) are: (a) the problem to be solved is the TNFSP; (b) the objectives in conflict to be optimized are: minimize both the average time spent by passengers in the system and the average wasted bus capacity; (c) the algorithm used to solve the problem is based on Global-Best Harmony

Search (moreover as far as we know this is the first time that this algorithm has been applied to solve the TNFSP problem as a multi-objective problem); and (d) the model for carrying out the simulation is totally different: discrete event simulation.

The Harmony Search (HS) optimization algorithm was originally proposed in [21]. It is based on jazz musicians' improvisation process, performed in search of a perfect harmony, in short: HS randomly generates, evaluates and sorts a population in a place called Harmony Memory (HM). Then, for a determined number of improvisations it generates one element at a time where each variable of that harmony may be completely random or taken from the HM (probability defined by Harmony Memory Consideration Rate parameter, HMCR), and in case of it being taken from HM, may or may not (depending on the parameter Pitch Adjustment Rate, PAR) be altered by addition or subtraction of an arbitrary value called Bandwidth (BW) also defined in the configuration. Later some variants/improvements for the HS algorithm were proposed in: (a) improved harmony search (IHS) where the accuracy and convergence rate of HS was improved, arranging for PAR and BW parameters to depend on the current iteration number [22]; (b) global-best harmony search (GBHS) that introduces swarm intelligence, changing the pitch-adjustment by extraction of values from the best harmony in HM [6]; (c) others such as global-best harmony search using learnable evolution models (GHS + LEM) [23], improved global-best harmony search [24], parameter adaptive harmony search [25] and, global dynamic harmony search (GDHS) [26].

3 Details of the MOGBHS Applied to Solve the TNFSP

In an attempt to improve user satisfaction and reduce operating costs in BRTS, a multi-objective algorithm that searches configurations of bus output frequencies is proposed. The objectives are: (1) Minimize the average time spent by passengers on the system, and (2) Minimize the average wasted bus capacity. It additionally included the constraint of the maximum available fleet (maximum amount of buses) for the BRTS.

Given that; (1) HS, IHS and GBHS have in common that they have a small number of parameters to tune the performance of the algorithm (7 parameters for IHS and 5 for the other two); (2) HS, IHS and GHS have a fast convergence, demand a modest amount of computer resources, and have a low probability of getting trapped in a local optima; (3) GBHS improves IHS results (which in turn improves the accuracy and convergence rate of HS); (4) GBHS facilitates the parameter tuning; and (5) GBHS works efficiently in continuous and discrete problems; in this research it was decided to use GBHS as the core of the proposed MO algorithm.

GBHS was originally designed to work with a unique objective. Therefore, in this work it was adapted to work with more than one objective using non-dominated sorting, based on the concepts of ordering by Pareto front and Crowding distance [3, 8]. The proposed algorithm, called Multi-Objective Global Best Harmony Search (MOGBHS) generates a set of harmonies and stores them in harmony memory, evaluates all the objectives for each element in HM, and then sorts by Pareto front and Crowding Distance. Then improvisations (evolutionary iterations) are carried out, in each element of which a new harmony is generated by applying the logic of the GBHS algorithm. The New Harmony is evaluated, added (or inserted) to the existing HM, the HM then is sorted by Pareto fronts and Crowding distance, and the element that make the population exceed the maximum harmony memory size (HMS) is eliminated (the worst harmony in HM). Figure 1 shows the MOGBHS pseudo-code.

The algorithms require the following parameters

- NI: number of improvisations performed by the algorithm
- PARmin, PARmax: Pitch Adjusting Rate minimum and maximum respectively, used to calculate the PAR(γ) value for each iteration (see line 9 in Fig. 1)
- HMCR: Harmony Memory Consideration Rate, used to decide whether a variable from a new improvise is taken from harmony memory or randomly generated
- HMS: Harmony Memory Size defines the maximum length of solution vector that represents the harmony memory
- NR: number of routes/variables in the target system
- NO: number of objectives to evaluate and optimize
- Limits: integer array of size [NR, 2], where for each variable (that represents a route in the system), the maximum and minimum are defined for the value of the output interval for this route
- MNB: Maximum Number of Buses into the system, used to calculate the feasibility of a solution.

```
01   HM.PopulationRandomInitialize(Limits, MNB)
02   HM.NonDominatedOrderCalculate()
03   HM.CrowdingDistanceCalculate()
04   HM.Sort() /*Based on Pareto Front and Crowding Distance if solutions are in the same Pareto front */
05   for i = 1 to NI do
06           ActualHarmony = new Harmony() /* Create a new empty solution (improvisation or harmony) */
07           for j = 1 to NR do
08                   if Random(0,1) < HMCR then
09                           ActualHarmony.Intervals[j] = HM.Harmonies[Random(0,HMS)].Intervals[j]
10                           PAR = PARMin + (((PARMax - PARMin) *i) / NI)
11                           if Random(0,1) < PAR then
12                                   ActualHarmony.Intervals[j] = HM.FromBestHarmony(Random(0,NR))
13                           end if
14                   else
15                           ActualHarmony.Intervals[j] = HM.RandomSelection(j, Limits)
16                   end if
17           end for
18           if HM.InPopulation(ActualHarmony) == false and ActualHarmony.Viable(MNB) == true then
19                   HM.Evaluate() /* Set fitness values using results of ARENA simulation */
20                   HM.Add(ActualHarmony)
21                   HM.NonDominatedOrderCalculate()
22                   HM.CrowdingDistanceCalculate()
23                   HM.Sort()
24                   HM.RemoveTheWorst()
25           end if
26   end for
```

Fig. 1. Multi-Objective Global Best Harmony Search (MOGBHS).

Each harmony (solution) generated by MOGBHS includes:

- A vector of integers with NR positions called Intervals, where Intervals[α] $\forall$ $\alpha \in$ [1, NR] is the interval of time between the outputs of the buses that serve the route α
- A vector of doubles with NO positions called Evaluations, where Evaluations[β] $\forall$ $\beta \in$ [1, NO] is the fitness value of the current solution (harmony) for the objective β
- An integer variable called Front that stores the number of Pareto front points for this harmony compared to the members of the population at any given time
- A float variable called CrowdingDist that stores the crowding distance of the harmonies to other elements at the same Pareto front.

The *PopulationRandomInitialize* procedure is responsible for generating an initial population of size HMS, considering the restrictions defined in Maximum Number of Buses into the system (MNB) and Limits parameters. The *NonDominatedOrderCalculate* procedure set the Pareto front number for each element in the harmony memory. This procedure is adapted from [8]. The *CrowdingDistanceCalculate* procedure takes the existing population and provides for each element the crowding distance to harmonies at the same Pareto front. Finally, the *Sort* function, as the name implies, sorts the population according to the following criteria: (1) in ascending order based on the Pareto front number if the harmonies (solutions) have a different front number and, (2) in descending order based on crowding distance when the harmonies have the same Pareto front number.

In addition to the above functions the algorithm uses the following auxiliary functions:

- *InPopulation*: check if a harmony exists in the HM
- *IsViable*: check if a harmony is a feasible solution based on the size of the available fleet (MNB parameter). Returns true when the New Harmony can be implemented with this fleet size
- *Add*: This procedure adds a new item to the end of a specific list
- *Length*: Returns the length of a list
- *RemoveTheWorst*: removes the worst harmony from harmony memory (HM) based on Pareto front number and crowding distance.

Given the need to evaluate the fitness of each harmony generated by the algorithm against the selected objectives and considering some successful cases of algorithms supported by simulations, it was proposed to use discrete event simulation for this purpose. Therefore before the execution of the algorithm, a model of discrete event simulation was created to measure the time spent by passengers and wasted bus capacity in the system. Later, during the execution of MOGBHS, the *Evaluate* function uses the intervals values of the current harmony into the simulation model, executes the simulation, reads the assessment for each of the objectives and loads them in the Evaluations vector of the harmony.

4   Case Study

To test the solution approach to TNFSP on BRTS the following activities were performed:

- Implementation of the MOGBHS algorithm
- Review, Selection and Analysis of BRTS to model
- Implementation of a simplified version of the selected BRTS using the proposed meta-model as a concept test
- Testing of the algorithm with the simulation model.

1. **Implementation and Test Environment:** MOGBHS was implemented in C# programming language, chosen for its ability to manage files and character strings for information extraction from the output of the simulations, speed of language (being compiled) and experience of the research group (over 7 years).

   The experiments were run on an ASUS N56VZ computer with an Intel Core i7-3630QM Processor at 2.4 GHz and 8 GB of RAM. The following software was used: Windows 8 (64 bits), Microsoft Visual Studio 2010 (.Net Framework 3.5), and Arena 14.0.

2. **Review, Selection and Analysis of BRTS to Use:** In selecting a BRTS to model for MOGBHS testing, the whole range of such systems in Colombia was reviewed, including Transmilenio (Bogota D.C), Mio (Cali, Valle), Metrolinea (Bucaramanga, Santander) and Megabus (Pereira, Risaralda). Due to the amount of documentation available, the size and configuration, and simplicity of routes it was decided to take Megabus as a basis for BRTS.

   The Megabus system has 37 stations and 3 routes; however it was subsequently decided to create a simplified version that had the same number of routes with the same design and layout, but with fewer stations. This is because the aim is to look for a proof of concept of the solution strategy proposed in this investigation. The real test of the system will be made in a second phase, mainly involving additional time to implement the BRTS in ARENA and the achievement of real system parameters (for example, the real average arrival time of the passengers, their distribution and destinations).

   To simplify the model, stations with similar characteristics were grouped and only one station was selected for each group, causing the total number of stations to be modeled to be reduced to eleven (11). There was a similar reduction from two to a single Bus Central. Figure 2 presents the simplified model, in which the green color indicates the path traveled by vehicles with route number one (1), the red color route number two (2) and the blue color for the buses that make up route number three (3).

3. **Implementation of Simulation Model:** ARENA [7] was the modeling and implementation of discrete event simulation software selected to create the simulation model that MOGBHS requires for evaluation of the objectives to be minimized. The operation of ARENA is based on SIMAN, a general purpose simulation language that facilitates integration with programming languages with the ability to

manage files. Using the simplified BRTS, the research group proceeded with the generation of the simulation model. A screenshot of the BRTS simulation model is presented in Fig. 3. Once the model is completed, and using ARENA, SIMAN language source files were generated, these files serve as a resource for the MOGBHS algorithm implementation that generates, evaluates and improves specific harmonies using results of simulations associated with each harmony.

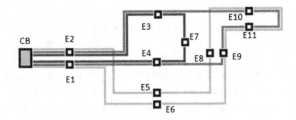

Fig. 2. Megabus simplified route design (Color figure online)

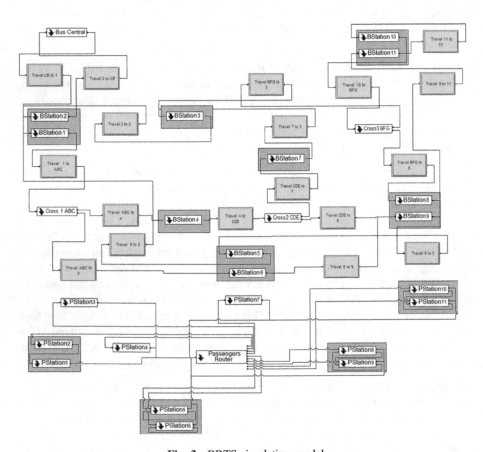

Fig. 3. BRTS simulation model

4. **Experimentation:** An NSGA-II algorithm implementation was also used in order to compare the results of MOGBHS algorithm. The results were obtained from the average of 30 runs of each algorithm (MOGBHS and NSGA-II), using its own setting and with different numbers of fitness function evaluations (FFE).

The configuration parameters for MOGBHS algorithm were: Number of Variables: 3, corresponds to the number of intervals to configure the three routes for operating the BRT system, equivalent to the number of routes in "real" system; Harmony Memory Size (HMS): 100; Harmony Consideration Rate (HMCR): 0.7; Pitch Adjustment Rate (PAR) minimum: 0.1; Pitch Adjustment Rate (PAR) maximum: 0.9; It was decided that a reasonable domain for intervals for output routes of buses would be between 1 min and 30 min, including limits; and Improvisation Number: 3,000 to 27,000.

Values for PAR and HMCR were set based on the values recommend in [6, 22]. The defined value for HMS is higher than recommended in state of the art because is unviable to obtain a good Pareto front with small values of HMS. The maximum improvisation number was calculated with the number of possible configurations for a single route (30) and with the number of considered routes (3), resulting in 27,000 possible configurations.

Given that in the state of art NSGA-II [3, 8] is reported as one of the best algorithms in the field of multi-objective optimization, it was decided to include it as a baseline and a point of comparison against the results obtained by MOGBHS. NSGA-II involves selecting parents by binary tournament, simulated binary crossover (SBX) and polynomial mutation. Since NSGA-II was created to solve continuous problems, it was necessary to adjust the simulation and exploration operations to limit results to valid solutions in the space of discrete values. The parameters for the test were based on those recommended in [8], namely: Probability of mutation: 1/3; Probability of crossing: 0.8; Population size: 100; Number of variables: 3; Allowed output intervals: 1 to 30 min; and Number of evaluations (fitness function evaluations): 3,000 to 27,000.

To obtain all the best solutions in order to be able to calculate the effectiveness of both algorithms, and considering relatively few variables and few possibilities, an exhaustive search was run. Given the number of options per route (30), and the number of routes in BRTS considered (3), the number of options amounted to 27,000. After implementing the exhaustive search, 99 solutions were found for the first Pareto front, considered as the best existing solutions.

In Fig. 4, the effectiveness of MOGBHS and NSGA-II are compared (optimal solutions number found divided by total number of optimal solutions in the Pareto front), every 3,000 FFE over the 30 tests in each algorithm. Similarly, Table 1 shows a comparison of the average effectiveness of the two algorithms (MOGBHS and NSGA-II), taking measurements every 3,000 evaluations of the objective functions.

MOGBHS found more optimal solutions than NSGA-II after 3,000 evaluations (FFEs), that is, it is more effective. The effectiveness is improved from 175.12% in 3,000 FFEs up to 488.68% in 27,000 FFEs. A Wilcoxon signed rank test shows with 95% confidence that MOGBHS results outperformed the NSGA-II results.

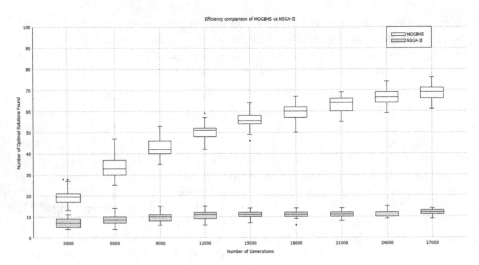

Fig. 4. Graphic effectiveness comparison of MOGBHS vs NSGA-II

Table 1. Effectiveness comparison of MOGBHS vs NSGA-II

FFE	MOGBHS		NSGA-II		
	Optimal solutions found (AVG)	Effectiveness (%)	Optimal solutions found (AVG)	Effectiveness (%)	Effectiveness improve (%)
3000	19.53	19.73	7.10	7.17	175.12
6000	33.93	34.28	8.73	8.82	288.55
9000	42.73	43.16	9.87	9.97	333.11
12000	50.40	50.91	10.80	10.91	366.67
15000	55.40	55.96	10.97	11.08	405.17
18000	59.60	60.20	10.80	10.91	451.85
21000	63.47	64.11	11.13	11.25	470.06
24000	66.30	66.97	11.60	11.72	471.55
27000	68.48	69.17	11.63	11.75	488.68

5   Conclusions and Future Work

The proposed algorithm (MOGBHS) is based on (a) Global-Best Harmony Search as a heuristic optimization strategy, (b) Non-Dominated Sorting as a multi-objective optimization strategy, and (c) Discrete Event Simulation (based on ARENA and SIMAN) for obtaining quality measures in the solutions (harmonies) found.

The MOGBHS was compared against an NSGA-II implementation using a real test case from the city of Pereira, and the comparison indicated that MOGBHS effectiveness is superior to NSGA-II, from 175.12% (in 3,000 FFEs) to 488.68% (in 27,000 FFEs).

MOGBHS can be used to solve various problems of multi-objective optimization. In this respect, the research team hopes to make a comprehensive evaluation of the discrete multi-objective benchmark problems and compare the performance of the algorithm against others in the state of the art, including NSGA-II and SPEA-2 [27].

Given that the evaluation of an individual requires to do a simulation (this is the most time-consuming part of the solution process) it appears promising to speed up the convergence, remembering some previous solutions to avoid resampling them (approach similar to the one followed in Tabu Search [28, 29]). Also, given the large number of possible combinations of the parameters of the algorithm, we plan to use Covering Arrays [30] and meta-algorithms in order to identify the best parameter settings for the algorithm in more complex scenarios.

References

1. Cervero, R., Bus Rapid Transit (BRT): An efficient and competitive mode of public transport. IURD Working Paper 2013–01 (2013)
2. Farahani, R.Z., et al.: A review of Urban transportation network design problems. Eur. J. Oper. Res. **229**(2), 281–302 (2013)
3. Luke, S.: Essentials of Metahuristics. Lulu, Raleigh (2010)
4. Mazloumi, E., et al.: Efficient transit schedule design of timing points: a comparison of ant colony and genetic algorithms. Transp. Res. Part B: Methodol. **46**(1), 217–234 (2012)
5. Sivasubramani, S., Swarup, K.: Environmental/economic dispatch using multi-objective harmony search algorithm. Electr. Power Syst. Res. **81**(9), 1778–1785 (2011)
6. Omran, M.G., Mahdavi, M.: Global-best harmony search. Appl. Math. Comput. **198**(2), 643–656 (2008)
7. Automation, R.: Arena simulation software, vol. 24, Accessed Nov 2013
8. Deb, K., et al.: A fast and elitist multiobjective genetic algorithm: NSGA-II. Evolutionary Computation, IEEE Trans. **6**(2), 17 (2002)
9. Ibarra-Rojas, O.J., et al.: Planning, operation, and control of bus transport systems: a literature review. Transp. Rese. Part B: Methodol. **77**, 38–75 (2015)
10. Kechagiopoulos, P.N., Beligiannis, G.N.: Solving the Urban transit routing problem using a particle swarm optimization based algorithm. Appl. Soft Comput. **21**, 654–676 (2014)
11. Nikolić, M., Teodorović, D.: Transit network design by bee colony optimization. Expert Syst. Appl. **40**(15), 5945–5955 (2013)
12. Yu, B., et al.: Transit route network design-maximizing direct and transfer demand density. Transp. Res. Part C: Emerg. Technol. **22**, 58–75 (2012)
13. Mauttone, A., Urquhart, M.E.: A route set construction algorithm for the transit network design problem. Comput. Oper. Res. **36**(8), 2440–2449 (2009)
14. Beltran, B., et al.: Transit network design with allocation of green vehicles: a genetic algorithm approach. Transp. Res. Part C: Emerg. Technol. **17**(5), 475–483 (2009)
15. Nayeem, M.A., Rahman, M.K., Rahman, M.S.: Transit network design by genetic algorithm with elitism. Transp. Res. Part C: Emerg. Technol. **46**, 30–45 (2014)
16. Szeto, W.Y., Jiang, Y.: Transit route and frequency design: bi-level modeling and hybrid artificial bee colony algorithm approach. Transp. Res. Part B: Methodol. **67**, 235–263 (2014)
17. Arbex, R.O., da Cunha, C.B.: Efficient transit network design and frequencies setting multi-objective optimization by alternating objective genetic algorithm. Transp. Res. Part B: Methodol. **81**, 355–376 (2015)

18. Cipriani, E., Gori, S., Petrelli, M.: Transit network design: a procedure and an application to a large Urban area. Transp. Res. Part C: Emerg. Technol. **20**(1), 3–14 (2012)
19. Mauttone, A., Urquhart, M.: A multi-objective metaheuristic approach for the transit network design problem. Publ. Transport **1**(4), 253–273 (2009)
20. Wang, J., Sun, G., Hu, X.: Optimization of transit operation strategies: a case study of Guangzhou, China Annual Meeting of the Transportation Research Board (2013)
21. Lee, K.S., Geem, Z.W.: A new meta-heuristic algorithm for continuous engineering optimization: harmony search theory and practice. Comput. Methods Appl. Mech. Eng. **194** (36–38), 3902–3933 (2005)
22. Mahdavi, M., Fesanghary, M., Damangir, E.: An improved harmony search algorithm for solving optimization problems. Appl. Math. Comput. **188**(2), 1567–1579 (2007)
23. Cobos, C., Estupiñán, D., Pérez, J.: GHS + LEM: Global-best Harmony Search using learnable evolution models. Appl. Math. Comput. **218**(6), 2558–2578 (2011)
24. El-Abd, M.: An improved global-best harmony search algorithm. Appl. Math. Comput. **222**, 94–106 (2013)
25. Kumar, V., Chhabra, J.K., Kumar, D.: Parameter adaptive harmony search algorithm for unimodal and multimodal optimization problems. J. Comput. Sci. **5**(2), 144–155 (2013)
26. Khalili, M., et al.: Global dynamic harmony search algorithm: GDHS. Appl. Math. Comput. **228**, 195–219 (2014)
27. Zitzler, E., Laumanns, M., Thiele, L.: SPEA2: improving the strength pareto evolutionary algorithm. TIK-report, vol. 103 (2001)
28. Glover, F.: Tabu search—Part I. ORSA J. Comput. **1**(3), 190–206 (1989)
29. Glover, F.: Tabu search—Part II. ORSA J. Comput. **2**(1), 4–32 (1990)
30. Torres-Jimenez, J., Izquierdo-Marquez, I.: Survey of covering arrays. In: 2013 15th International Symposium on Symbolic and Numeric Algorithms for Scientific Computing (SYNASC). IEEE (2013)

Optimal Pricing Model: Case of Study for Convenience Stores

Laura Hervert-Escobar[1,2(✉)], Jesus Fabian López-Pérez[2],
and Oscar Alejandro Esquivel-Flores[1]

[1] Instituto Tecnológico y de Estudios Superiores de Monterrey, Monterrey,
Nuevo León, Mexico
laura.hervert@itesm.mx
[2] SINTEC Customer and Operations Strategy, Monterrey, Nuevo León, Mexico

Abstract. Pricing is one of the most vital and highly demanded component in the mix of marketing along with the Product, Place and Promotion. An organization can adopt a number of pricing strategies, which usually will be based on corporate objectives. The purpose of this paper is to propose a methodology to define an optimal pricing strategy for convenience stores. The solution approach involves a multiple linear regression as well as a linear programming optimization model. To prove the value of the proposed methodology a pilot was performed for selected stores. Results show the value of the solution methodology. This model provides an innovative solution that allows the decision maker include business rules of their particular environment in order to define a price strategy that meet the objective business goals.

Keywords: Price strategy · Correlation · Multiple linear regression · Optimization

1 Introduction

A convenience store is a small retail business that stocks a range of everyday items such as groceries, snack foods, candy, toiletries, soft drinks, tobacco products, magazines and newspapers. Such stores may also offer money order and wire transfer services. In some jurisdictions, corner stores are licensed to sell alcohol, typically beer and wine. Typically, this type of stores open 24 h and operate in locations with surface less than $500\,\mathrm{m}^2$. According to data provided by marker research firm Euromonitor International, the most important growth of the market in Mexico is through these small formats. Currently there are approximately 20000 convenience stores located throughout the country. This type of stores has had a growth of 50.6% since 2009 [12]. Convenience stores usually charge significantly higher prices than conventional grocery stores or supermarkets, as convenience stores order smaller quantities of inventory at higher per-unit prices from wholesalers. However, convenience stores make up for this by having longer opening hours, serving more locations, and having shorter cashier lines. Custom

© Springer International Publishing AG 2017
O. Pichardo-Lagunas and S. Miranda-Jiménez (Eds.): MICAI 2016, Part II, LNAI 10062, pp. 353–364, 2017.
DOI: 10.1007/978-3-319-62428-0_28

research pricing methods fall into two main approaches: pricing the total product (pricing for a complete concept/product) and/or pricing elements of a variable concept/product offering such as branding or features. This research focus on pricing the total product. In different areas of science and applied research data analysis and forecasts have been treated using linear regression [9,15] considering multiple explanatory variables combined with other methods for selecting variables in order to reduce the dimensionality of the problem, for instance stepwise and genetic algorithms [2]. Currently the multiple linear regression (MLR) is a technique used in machine learning to refine decision making in finance and economics. Ismail et al. [6] use multiple linear regression as a tool to develop forecasting model for predicting gold prices based on economic factors. Shabri and Samsudin [14] propose a hybrid model which integrates wavelet and multiple linear regressions for crude oil price forecasting, it is important to highlight the use of principal component analysis to process subseries data in MLR to reduce the dimensions of sub-time components series. Various proposals have tried to use MLR and correlation analysis to calculate the optimal price in retail products considering the law of demand known or uncertain. Meijer et al. [10,11] address the problem of optimal price retailing considering law of demand. They use Cox regression to diagnose identity hazard rates for different products besides characteristics of spline regression is used to find the price elasticity parameter related to the markdown moment. The main concept in their work is to derive unbiased estimates to sell through curves used in retail based through the use of survival analysis. On the other had, Kwong et al. [8] consider demand as a Bayesian belief updated and cumulative demand as Brownian motion with unknown drift. Keskin et al. [7] consider dynamic pricing where the seller does not know the parameters of product's linear demand curve (incomplete learning). Chakravarty et al. [3] propose a simulation-based algorithm for computing the optimal pricing policy with a stochastic differential equation model for uncertain demand dynamics of the product. Close to our methodology is the proposal of Hu et al. [4] who use predictive modeling based in regression estimates for home value. They build multivariate regression model using maximum information coefficient (MIC) statistic [13] to the observed values and predictive values as an evaluation of the regression. The MIC propose a measure of dependence for two-variate relationships, this coefficient is used as a measure for selecting the "best subset" of predictor for building the regression model. Hu et al. divides the process in some steps, (a) select variables, (b) build linear regression models for selected variables, (c) analysis for residual errors and fix problems using Box-Cox transformation, (d) build the final model. The organization of the document is as follows, the introduction above served to set the business frame as well as the literature review. The definition of the problem is presented in Sect. 2. Then, the mathematical formulation is presented in Sect. 3. Section 4 describes the design and implementation of the pilot test, including results of the pilot. Finally the conclusion and future work in Sect. 4.

2   Case Study

The pricing strategy is by definition the efforts aimed at finding a product's optimum price, typically including overall marketing objectives, consumer demand, product attributes, competitors' pricing, and market and economic trends [5]. In this case of study, a company that operates several convenience stores desire to improve the current pricing strategy in order to maximize the business performance. The main goals are to obtain the optimum price of each product and to increase the gross margin.

In the current pricing strategy, the company use a simplistic process to define the prices of the products for all the stores. The process is based on salespeople information, pricing personnel and other customer-facing staff for pricing intelligence. Although the process considers marketing, competition and financial data, the company has failed to establish internal procedures to optimize prices. Consequently, the process is prone to error, in addition, it is hard to recognize opportunities to adjust the price to improve the business performance. The methodology proposed consist of a pricing model that considers the analysis of historical data. The information contains product attributes, customers behavior, marketing strategies, competitor's pricing, among others. The model is given in three stages given in Fig. 1. The first stage is the cleaning and organization of data, the main goal is to organize a cluster of products (categories) belonging to the same commercial hierarchy level and share attributes. The second stage is a regression model of the clusters obtained in previous stage. The regression model allows to establish product associations, as well as trend, likelihood and promotional effects. Finally, the third stage is an optimization model that incorporates business rules, objective goals as well as external factors in order to define the optimum price.

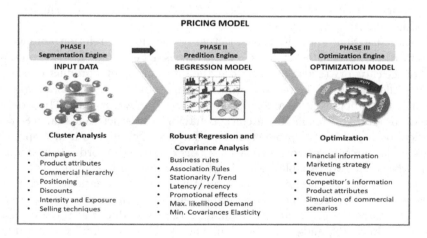

Fig. 1. Stages of the proposed pricing model

Following section explained in detail the mathematical formulation used in each stage of the pricing model.

3 Mathematical Formulation

In this case study, the pricing model proposed is based on three stages. The first stage is the cleaning and organization of data. The complexity of this stage lies in the purification and management of data in order to select the information that is most useful for the following models. Typically, historical data is used to provide insight as to how volume sales (V) is affected by changes in price and market variables such as seasonality, advertising, promotions, competitive product prices and other variables deemed appropriate. However, for a business based on convenience sales the measure of most interest is the gross margin given in Eq. (1). The gross margin (Y) is the total sales income (IS) minus the cost of goods $(COGS)$, divided by the total sales income (I), expressed as a percentage. The higher the percentage, the more the company retains on each monetary unit of sales, to service its other costs and debt obligations. The margin is computed for a set of products G.

$$\%y_i = \frac{is_i - cogs_i}{is_i}; \qquad \forall i \in G \tag{1}$$

Historical weekly data of this study case is given by product and includes income sales, cost, seasonality, competitors price, promotions, volume sales, commercial hierarchy, and other attributes of the product that allow to build groups of products with similarities features into categories, where the category C is a subset of G. Therefore, each category contains similar products and its size depend on the type of category. Some categories will contain a large number of different products e.g. a category of candies, and others will have a small group of products e.g. dairy products.

In the clustering analysis, the objective is to find the relation among the products of the same category $k \in C$. The analysis is performed for each product $i \in C$ of the category (cluster). Therefore, the information of a product is crossed with the information of the rest of products of the same category. Historical data is per product, then, records among products may o may not match. In order to compare products with similar purchase behavior, a product that shares 80% of historical records with the product under analysis is selected to next step.

Next, the sample Pearson correlation (ρ) is computed in order to define the relation between two variables: Margin of the product under analysis (Y) and Price (P) of other product of the category. Where historical data per each product have a size of T weeks and each record is denoted by index t (week), therefore $t \in T$. Consequently, $y_{i,t}$ represent the margin of the product i at the time t and analogously for $p_{j,t}$. $\bar{y}_i$ and $\bar{p}_i$ are the sample mean. Finally s_{y_i} and s_{p_j} are sample standard deviations. For this step, if the absolute value of the Pearson correlation (2) is moderate, then P_j is selected for next step. Consequently, we obtain a set of selected prices $PRi = \bigcup\limits_{j \in G} P_j \; \ni \; |\rho_{y_i p_j}| \geq 0.4$

$$\rho_{y_i p_j} = \frac{\sum\limits_{t=1}^{T} y_{it} p_{jt} - T \cdot \bar{y}_i \cdot \bar{p}_j}{(T-1)\, s_{y_i} s_{p_j}}; \qquad \forall i,j \in C_k \subset G; \qquad i \neq j \qquad (2)$$

Until this step, we have only cross information between Margin and Prices, where information of Margin comes from the product under analysis and information of Prices comes from the product under analysis and other products in the same category. However, there is more information in the historical data that can be useful in the understanding of the commercial behavior of the product. Therefore, final step in the cluster analysis is to cross information of tendency (E), seasonality (S), cost $(COGS)$, promotions (EC), competitive price (CP), weather conditions (W) and selected prices in the previous step (PR_i).

Lets have a set of information variables associated to a product i given by $Z^i = \{E_i \cup S_i \cup COGS_i \cup EC_i \cup CP_i \cup W_i \cup PR_i\}$. Where Z^i has a size H and each element is denoted by h. Then, a column vector of ratios r_i is computed using equation given in (3), where ρ^i_{yh} is the sample Pearson correlation between the margin and the information variable h and $\rho^i_{h,l}$ is the sample Pearson correlation between two different information variables. The ratio is computed for each variable of information. In this way, a high ratio means lower relation with other variables. This ratio is helpful to avoid multicollinearity issues.

$$ratio^i_h = \frac{H \cdot |\rho_{y_i, h_i}|}{\sum\limits_{l_i \in Z^i} |\rho_{h_i, l_i}|}; \qquad \forall i \in C_k \subset G; \qquad h, l \in Z^i; \qquad h \neq l \qquad (3)$$

Finally, the vector of ratios is order from higher to lower value, finally, a mix of nine explanatory variables X are selected to later perform the regression analysis. The mix of variables consist of 5 variables of prices $(X_1, X_2, X_3, X_4, X_5)$ including the price of the product under analysis, 2 variables of business metrics (cost, competitive prices, promotions) X_6, X_7, 1 variable of temporality (tendency, seasonality) and 1 variable of the weather conditions. An example of the selection is showed in Fig. 2. Phase 1 ends with the selection of variables, leading to Phase 2, the multiple linear regression analysis.

Multiple linear regression attempts to model the relationship between two or more explanatory variables and a response variable by fitting a linear equation to observed data. Multiple linear regression attempts to model the relationship between two or more explanatory variables and a response variable by fitting a linear equation to observed data. Every value of the independent variable x is associated with a value of the dependent variable y. The population regression line for p explanatory variables $x1, x2, \ldots, xp$ is defined to be $\mu_y = \beta_0 + \beta_1 x_1 + \beta_2 x_2 + \ldots + \beta_p x_p$. This line describes how the mean response y changes with the explanatory variables. The observed values for y vary about their means y and are assumed to have the same standard deviation. The fitted values $b_0, b_1, \ldots, b_p$

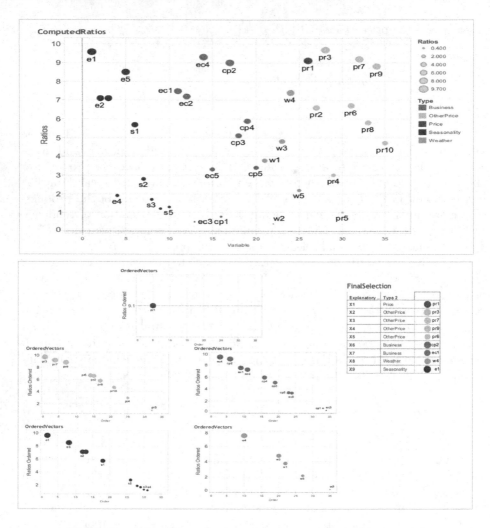

Fig. 2. Example of the selection of explanatory variables using (3)

estimate the parameters $\beta_0, \beta_1, \ldots, \beta_p$ of the population regression line. With the selection of the explanatory variables, formally, the model for multiple linear regression, given n observations, is given by (4).

$$y_i = \beta_0 + \sum_{p=1}^{9} \beta_{ip} x_{ip}; \qquad \forall i \in C_k \subset G \tag{4}$$

A stepwise procedure using Akaike information criterion was used in the regression analysis. The procedure start with all candidate variables, testing the deletion of each variable using a chosen model comparison criterion, deleting the variable (if any) that improves the model the most by being deleted, and repeating this process until no further improvement is possible. The price of the product is always included in the final econometric model. Details of the Akaike information criterion can be found in [1]. Second phase ends with the econometric models. The third and final phase is the optimization model. The optimization phase consider the econometric models obtained during the regression analysis. In order to enrich the proposal with features of the real operation of the convenience stores, a set of business rules are included. Business rules includes operational considerations of the business as well as the external factors of the market. The optimization model is performed per category. The mathematical formulation of the model is given in the following equations. The objective function is given in (5), which consist on maximizes the total gross margin per category. The objective function is subject to constraints given by (6) to (11).

$$\text{Maximize Z} = \sum_{i \in C_k \subset G} y_i; \tag{5}$$

Econometrics models obtain during the regression analysis are used as a constraint in (6), this equation is given by each product i belonging to the same category C.

$$y_i = \beta_0 + \sum_{p=1}^{9} \beta_{ip} x_{ip}; \qquad \forall i \in C_k \subset G \tag{6}$$

The primary business rule for a price is to overcome the net cost of the product for a 3% (7).

$$x_i \geq 1.03 * cogs_i; \qquad i = 1, 2, 3, 4, 5 \tag{7}$$

Upper and lower bound are given in (8) and (9). In these equations, the proposed price should be $\pm 15\%$ of the selected reference. The options are the competitor price cp or the reference price ref. The reference price is the last price used in the convenience store.

$$x_i \geq 0.85 * \min(cp_i, ref_i); \qquad \forall i \in C_k \subset G; \qquad i = 1, 2, 3, 4, 5 \tag{8}$$

$$x_i \leq 1.15 * \max(cp_i, ref_i); \qquad \forall i \in C_k \subset G; \qquad i = 1, 2, 3, 4, 5 \tag{9}$$

When category of products is under analysis, it is common to find products of the same brand and same content, they only differ in flavor. Therefore, those products should have the same price, unless a marketing strategy suggest differentiate one of the products. In this way, all products under the same features F and marketing strategy are constraint to have the same price (10).

$$x_i = x_j; \qquad \forall i \neq j; \qquad i, j \in C_k, F; \qquad i, j = 1, 2, 3, 4, 5 \tag{10}$$

Another characteristic to consider for a product is the different sizes available at the store. Then, (11) considers that the price of the product i should be less than the price of the product j if both are the same product under different size, where j is bigger than i. Such definition is given in SZ. This constraint also serve to differentiate one of the products under F in order to define a marketing strategy.

$$x_i \geq x_j; \qquad \forall i,j \in SZ, C_k; \qquad i,j = 1,2,3,4,5 \qquad (11)$$

Typically, convenience stores are free to set the price of the products as appropriate to the business, however, there are products that are controlled by the government or by special promotion of the supplier LG. Then, the products under this description are constrained to the controlled price kl_i (12).

$$x_i = kl_i; \qquad \forall i \in C_k, LG; \qquad i = 1,2,3,4,5 \qquad (12)$$

The optimization is always given for a period of time. In this way, explanatory variables for seasonality, business, and weather are set to a constant value k_{itp} where i is the product t is the period of time and p is the type of explanatory variable (13).

$$x_i = k_{itp}; \qquad \forall p = 6,7,8,9 \qquad (13)$$

Finally, non-negativity of the variables is given in (14). It is important to highlight that prices in a convenience store are usually rounded to cents. For this case study, the prices should be rounded to $0, 0.1\cent, 0.5\cent, 0.9\cent$, due to is the price to be label at the store.

$$x_i \geq 0 \qquad \forall i \in C_k \qquad i = 1,2,3,4,5 \qquad x_i \in \{a.b \,|\, a \in \mathbb{N}, b \in \{0,1,5,9\}\} \quad (14)$$

The details of the implementation of the models as well as instances and case study are describe in next section.

4   Test and Results

To test the performance of the proposed models, several instances were tested in a case study. The data for each instance correspond to a real life case from stores located in three cities. The stores were classified into two groups: mirror and pilot. The pilot stores use the price of the proposed methodology while mirror stores remain with the actual strategy. In this way, mirror stores are used to compare the value of the proposed methodology. The classification of the stores was defined by the company according to their business interest.

Table 1 shows the nomenclature used to identify instances. Due to data confidentiality, the nomenclature will not show compromised information of the actual places. Then, cities are identified as CT. Products are classified in different levels regarding its purpose. In this research, two levels of classification are used. The first level is named "Segment" and give information about the market segment of the product. The next level is the "Category", which grouped the products by specific similarities. Categories were built during phase 1 of the proposed methodology.

Then, for city CT1, the proposed methodology was tested in 31 stores. The price strategy includes 558 products classified in 27 categories. The performance of the store was compared with 164 mirror stores.

Table 1. Instances used for the test of the proposed methodology

Cities	Pilot stores	Mirror stores	Segment	Category	Products
CT1	31	101	S	26	527
CT2	25	96	G	46	407
CT3	31	104	S,G	71	1090

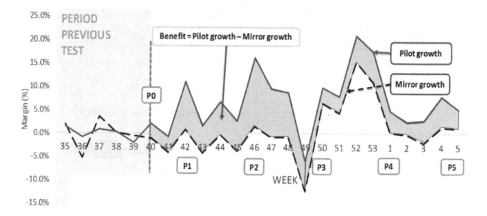

Fig. 3. Results for instances CT2- segment G during the test period

A weekly historical data of the total stores (Pilot + Mirror) from 2013 to 2015 was used for the regression analysis. Given the amount of data, a procedure to select, clean and organized data was implemented using Visual Fox Pro. The selection of explanatory variables as well as the regression analysis was implemented using a statistical software R. The linear optimization model was implemented in FICO Xpress 7.0.1, the optimization model runs until optimality.

As shown in the Table 1, and according to the objectives of the company, the variety of size is good enough to prove whether the proposal is efficient for a business plan. During the test, there were five proposals of price every four weeks for each city. The generation of the proposal includes the information generated until two week before implementation. The time available to generate new prices is one business day, then it is reviewed and authorized to be sent to the pilot stores for implementation. Meanwhile, the company generate the prices with the current price strategy for the mirror stores. Results of the methodology are given in terms of % margin for mirror and pilot stores. Also, the econometrics model are review in order to monitor the weight of the price in the strategy.

An example of the results obtained after the implementation of the price strategy is given in Fig. 3, where the x-axis is the period of time during the test, and y-axis shows the % margin. The figure shows highlights of the implementation of the new strategy.

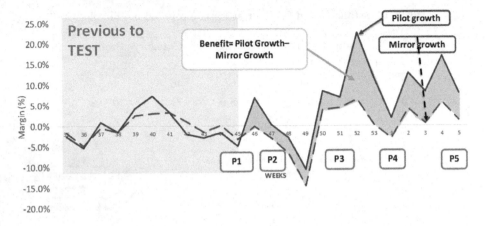

Fig. 4. Results for instances CT1- segment S during the test period

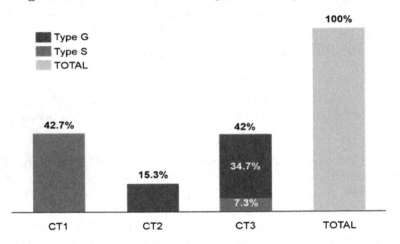

Fig. 5. Results for instances CT1- segment S during the test period

As Fig. 3 shows, the performance of pilot stores is better than mirror stores. Even with a decrease in the sales income, the margin still better. This can be explained with the proposal of prices, where the optimization model is focused in changing the prices of those products with higher % margin in the category. Also, the trend of the results are better in segment S as Fig. 4 shows. For this segment and city, both mirror and pilot stores increase their income sales in a similar rate, however, the price strategy allows to get a better margin in pilot stores.

Finally, Fig. 5 shows the benefits obtained for pilot stores. Due to confidentiality agreement, we are only able to present the % of benefits obtained after compared the actual strategy and the methodology proposed. It can be noted that in all cities and segments, the pilot stores were able to obtained benefits. Also, the strategy performed better for segment S, than for segment G.

5 Conclusion

Convenience stores serve the entire purchasing population of its geographical area but focuses on customers who need to purchase items outside of normal working hours such as swing shift employees and quick shoppers looking for snacks and related items. In order to capture attention and sales they use prominent signs at the store locations, billboards, media bites on local news, and radio advertisements to capture customers. These actions combined with a right price strategy will lead to the success of the business.

In this research we proposed a pricing strategy composed for three phases. The objective in the first phase was to understand and use the most appropriate variables for the business, in this way through a MLR we can obtained econometric model that will better focus in the major goal, the increase of the margin. Then, the optimization model will take additional business rules (internal and external) in order to obtain a price proposal that allowed to increase the margin under the most possible real scenario. The strategy was tested in a real case study, where the results proved the value of the methodology.

The proposed methodology is easy to understand and implement within most fields of business. Also, it produces information that can be used to create forecasting and planning models and it is relatively inexpensive research process if a firm has high quality data. Also, the use of business rules give an advantage over typical econometric models that only considers one price and not crossed information. However, risks during implementation are the lack of information or little variation of data, because it would produce a low quality regression analysis.

Future work in this research includes the exploration of new methodologies during the selection of explanatory variables, as well as improved the regression analysis. During the definition of the price strategy, the metric of most interest is the margin, however, future work considers the inclusion of other metrics, such as volume sales.

Acknowledgments. The authors are grateful to Sintec for financial and technical support during the development of this research. Sintec is the leading business consulting firm for Supply Chain, Customer and Operations Strategies with a consultative model in Developing Organizational Skills that enable their customers to generate unique capabilities based on processes, organization and IT. Also, we appreciate the financial support of CONACYT-SNI program in order to promote quality research.

References

1. Akaike, H.: Akaikes information criterion. In: Lovric, M. (ed.) International Encyclopedia of Statistical Science, p. 25. Springer, Heidelberg (2014). doi:10.1007/978-3-642-04898-2_110
2. Ganjali, M.R., Norouzi, P., Avval, Z.M., Pourbashir, E.: Application of genetic algorithm - multiple linear regressions to predict the activity of RSK inhibitors. J. Serb. Chem. Soc. **80**, 187–196 (2015)

3. Chakravarty, S., Padakandla, S., Bhatnagar, S.: A simulation-based algorithm for optimal pricing policy under demand uncertainty. Inte. Trans. Oper. Res. **21**(5), 737–760 (2014)
4. Hu, G., Wang, J., Feng, W.: Multivariate regression modeling for home value estimates with evaluation using maximum information coefficient. In: Lee, R. (ed.) Software Engineering, Artificial Intelligence, Networking and Parallel/Distributed Computing 2012. Studies in Computational Intelligence, vol. 443, pp. 69–81. Springer, Berlin (2013). doi:10.1007/978-3-642-32172-6_6
5. WebFinance Inc.: pricing strategy (2016)
6. Ismail, Z., Yahya, A., Shabri, A.: Forecasting gold prices using multiple linear regression method. Am. J. Appl. Sci. **6**, 1509–1514 (2009)
7. Bora Keskin, N., Zeevi, A.: Dynamic pricing with an unknown demand model: asymptotically optimal semi-myopic policies. Oper. Res. **62**(5), 1142–1167 (2014). doi:10.1287/opre.2014.1294
8. Kwon, H.D., Lippman, S.A., Tang, C.S.: Optimal markdown pricing strategy with demand learning. Probab. Eng. Inf. Sci. **26**(1), 77–104 (2012)
9. Chowdhury, B., Abuella, M.: Solar power probabilistic forecasting by using multiple linear regression analysis. In: SoutheastCon 2015, pp. 1–5, April 2015
10. Meijer, R., Bhulai, S.: Optimal pricing in retail: a Cox regression approach. Int. J. Retail Distrib. Manag. **41**(4), 311–320 (2013)
11. Meijer, R., Pieffers, M., Bhulai, S.: Markdown policies for optimizing revenue, towards optimal pricing in retail. J. Bus. Retail Manag. Res. **08**(1), 10 (2013)
12. Rivas, R.: Tiendas de conveniencia, un negocio a tomar en cuenta (2016)
13. Reshef, D.N., Reshef, Y.A., Finucane, H.K., Grossman, S.R., McVean, G., Turnbaugh, P.J., Lander, E.S., Mitzenmacher, M., Sabeti, P.C.: Detecting novel associations in large data sets. Science **334**(6062), 1518–1524 (2011)
14. Ani, S., Ruhaidah, S.: Crude oil price forecasting based on hybridizing wavelet multiple linear regression model, particle swarm optimization techniques, and principal component analysis. Sci. World J. **2014**, 1–8 (2014). doi:10.1155/2014/854520
15. Tong, W., Yan, X., Xie, H.: A multiple linear regression data predicting method using correlation analysis for wireless sensor networks. Cross Strait Quad-Regional Radio Science and Wireless Technology Conference (CSQRWC), 2011, vol. 2, pp. 960–963 (2011)

Method of Musical Composition
for the Portfolio Optimization Problem

Roman Anselmo Mora-Gutiérrez[1,2], Antonin Ponsich[1,2],
Eric Alfredo Rincón García[1,2(✉)], Sergio Gerardo de-los-Cobos-Silva[1,2],
Miguel Ángel Gutiérrez Andrade[1,2], and Pedro Lara-Velázquez[1,2]

[1] Dpto. de Sistemas, Universidad Autónoma Metropolitana,
Unidad Azcapotzalco, 02200 Mexico, D.F., Mexico
{mgra,aspo,rigaeral}@correo.azc.uam.mx,
{cobos,gamma,plara}@xanum.uam.mx
[2] Dpto. de Ing. Eléctrica, Universidad Autónoma Metropolitana,
Unidad Iztapalapa, 09340 Mexico, D.F., Mexico

Abstract. The constrained portfolio optimization problem with multi-objective functions cannot be efficiently solved using exact techniques. Thus, heuristics approaches seem to be the best option to find high quality solutions in a limited amount of time. For solving this problem, this paper proposes an algorithm based on the Method of Musical Composition (MMC), a metaheuristic that mimics an multi-agent based creativity system associated with musical composition. In order to prove its performance, the algorithm was tested over five well-known benchmark data sets and the obtained results prove to be highly competitive since they outperform those reported in the specialized literature in four out of the five tackled instances.

Keywords: Method of Musical Composition · Portfolio optimization · Markowitz model

1 Introduction

Selecting investment portfolios nowadays represents a very common practice and a difficult task, covering a wide range of applications. Because of its importance, the solution of this problem has attracted considerable attention in different research areas such as economics [4], finance [18], computer science [7], operation research [11] and mathematics [3]. The construction of an investment portfolio seeks to balance gains and losses, distributing and offsetting the risk and return of different assets.

One of the most popular methodologies used for solving portfolio optimization problems was formulated by Markowitz in 1952 [9] and includes the two main features considered by any investor: risk and return. Markowitz states that the investor searches for a portfolio that minimizes the risk of losses while simultaneously maximizing the return.

© Springer International Publishing AG 2017
O. Pichardo-Lagunas and S. Miranda-Jiménez (Eds.): MICAI 2016, Part II, LNAI 10062, pp. 365–376, 2017.
DOI: 10.1007/978-3-319-62428-0_29

In the Markowitz'mean-variance model, a portfolio is represented by a vector of real numbers, where each entry indicates the ratio or percentage of the total invested capital corresponding to each available asset. This way, the objective is to optimize a weighted sum of the assets'expected rate of return and the risk expressed as the variance of the portfolio's rate of return. The resulting model can be solved exactly using Quadratic Programming (QP) [10].

However, the problem becomes much more difficult when real-world requirements are imposed, such as cardinality, which forces the construction of a portfolio having a specific number of assets, or constraints on the ratios of capital to invest in a selected asset. When such constraints are included, a nonlinear mixed integer programming model must be solved and classical exact solution techniques become inadequate. This higher complexity has encouraged the development and application of more robust heuristic strategies, such as genetic algorithms, tabu search, simulated annealing, neural networks, evolutionary algorithms and multi-objective techniques [2,6,8,12].

In this paper, an algorithm based on the Method of Musical Composition (MMC) is introduced for solving the constrained portfolio optimization problem. The proposed method is used to solve five well-known benchmark instances and its performance levels are compared against other algorithms reported in the specialized literature. The numerical results show that this strategy is able to find better solutions than those reported by other state-of-the-art techniques for four out of the five instances, highlighting the fact that the MMC is appropriate for solving this kind of problems.

The remainder of this paper is organized as follows: in Sect. 2, an introduction to the Markowitz's model is presented. Section 3 describes the canonical Method of Musical Composition, while the relevant features of the algorithm adapted to the portfolio selection problem are explained in Sect. 4. Experimental methodology and numerical results are included in the Sect. 5 and, finally, conclusions and future research are drawn in Sect. 6.

2   Portfolio Optimization Problem

The classical Markowitz's mean-variance model addresses the simultaneous minimization of risk and maximization of return, according to the following mathematical formulation for an N-asset problem:

$$\text{Minimize } \lambda \sum_{i=1}^{N} \sum_{j=1}^{N} x_i \sigma_{ij} x_j - (1 - \lambda) \sum_{i=1}^{N} x_i \mu_i, \tag{1}$$

subject to:

$$\sum_{i=1}^{N} x_i = 1, \tag{2}$$

$$0 \leq x_i \leq 1, \quad i = 1, 2, \ldots, N, \tag{3}$$

where

N is the number of available assets,

x_i is the proportion of capital invested in asset i ($1 \leq i \leq N$),

σ_{ij} is the covariance between assets i and j ($1 \leq i, j \leq N$),

μ_i is the expected return of asset i ($1 \leq i \leq N$),

$\lambda \in [0, 1]$ is the risk aversion parameter.

Thus, the first term of the objective function represents the risk measured as the total variance of the return of the portfolio, that must be minimized. On the other hand, the second term of the objective function is the expected return and has to be maximized. When $\lambda = 0$, the objective function only accounts for the expected return maximization and the optimal portfolio is the single asset with the highest return whereas if $\lambda = 1$, only minimization of the risk is performed and the resulting optimal portfolio is constituted by the single asset having the lowest corresponding risk. This way, the objective function seeks for a balance between risk and return, a balance obviously biased by the λ parameter. Finally, constraint 2 ensures that all the available capital is invested.

As mentioned earlier, the simple initial Markowitz' model was modified and adapted to real-world requirements and different operating modes. In the framework of this paper, *cardinality* and *floor-ceiling* constraints are included. For a more detailed description of other constraints sometimes taken into account in the portfolio selection problem, we refer the reader to [19].

Cardinality constraints forces the number of assets selected in a portfolio to fulfill some conditions. This constraint has two versions: the first (exact) one imposes the number of selected securities to be equal to a given value K, while the second (soft) one only provides lower and upper bounds (Z_L, Z_U) on this number. The mathematical formulation typically involves new binary variables z_i, denoting the presence or absence of asset i in the considered portfolio: $z_i = 1$ if $x_i > 0$ and $z_i = 0$, otherwise. In this paper, the cardinality constraint is formulated as:

$$\sum_{i=1}^{N} z_i = K, \tag{4}$$

Besides, floor-ceiling constraints impose lower and upper bounds on the values of each asset weight, e.g. on the x_i variables. This means that an asset cannot represent less, or more, than some proportion of the total invested capital. This requirement is explained as follows: (i) regarding the lower bound, devoting very small percentages of the capital would involve too many securities, resulting in high transaction costs; (ii) for upper bounds, it provides from assigning too large ratios of the total invested capital to a single asset, thus allowing to minimize the risk by sharing it among several assets. The mathematical expression of the floor-ceiling constraint is:

$$\varepsilon_i z_i \leq x_i \leq \delta_i z_i, \quad 1 \leq i \leq N, \tag{5}$$

This constraint ensures that if any asset i is held ($z_i = 1$) its proportion x_i must lie between upper and upper bounds, ϵ_i and δ_i.

Finally the constrained portfolio optimization model used in this work is given by:

$$\text{Minimize } \lambda \sum_{i=1}^{N} \sum_{j=1}^{N} x_i x_j \sigma_{ij} - (1 - \lambda) \sum_{i=1}^{N} x_i \mu_i, \tag{6}$$

subject to:

$$\sum_{i=1}^{n} x_i = 1, \tag{7}$$

$$\sum_{i=1}^{n} z_i = K, \tag{8}$$

$$\varepsilon_i z_i \le x_i \le \delta_i z_i, \quad 1 \le i \le N, \tag{9}$$

$$z_i \in \{0, 1\}, \quad 1 \le i \le N, \tag{10}$$

As in the canonical model, constraint (7) ensures that the total available capital is invested, while rows (8) and (9) respectively enforce the cardinality and floor-ceiling constraints. Finally, the binary variables z_i (constraint (10)) are added to indicate the presence or absence of asset i in the portfolio.

As above-mentioned, it is important to note that, when cardinality constraints are not considered, the problem can solved exactly. However, when cardinality constraints are imposed, no exact solution method exists [20].

3   Method of Musical Composition

The Method of Musical Composition, denoted as MMC, is an algorithm that mimics a creativity system associated with musical composition. The MMC is based on a multi-agent model, with a specific social network. This latter is composed of a set of Nc vertices or agents (composers) and a set E of edges or links (which represent relationships between composers). In this model, a solution is called a "tune" or "melody" and it is represented by an n-dimensional vector, $tune = [x_1, x_2, \ldots, x_n]$, where x_i is value of the $i - th$ decision variable. Each composer has a personal knowledge, i.e. a set of tunes. Besides, a set of mechanisms and policies governs the possible interactions and information exchange between composers.

A brief description of the MMC is as follows. Initially, the MMC builds a social network with Nc composers and a set of randomly generated links between composers. For each composer i, an artwork is created randomly (an artwork is a set of solutions used as the previous knowledge of composers) and stored in a score matrix ($P_{\star,\star,i}$). Then, while a stopping criterion is not met, the following steps are performed: (a) the social network's links are updated, (b) each composer i ($i = 1, \ldots Nc$) establishes contact with composer j from i's neighborhood ($\forall j \in \mathcal{N}_i$) and examine his/her personal artwork ($P_{\star,\star,j}$), (c) each composer i ($i = 1, \ldots Nc$) greedily decides whether selecting information from composer j

($\forall j \in \mathcal{N}_i$): if the worst solution in $P_{\star,\star,j}$ ($tune_{j,worst}$) is better than the worst solution in $P_{\star,\star,i}$ ($tune_{i,worst}$), then composer i randomly selects one tune from j's artwork, *(d)* each composer i ($i = 1, \ldots Nc$) builds his/her acquired knowledge, composed of the tunes selected from other composers, and stores it the matrix ($ISC_{\star,\star,i}$), *(e)* each composer i ($i = 1, \ldots Nc$) builds his/her knowledge background, stored in matrix $KM_{\star,\star,i}$, as the concatenation of $P_{\star,\star,i}$ and $ISC_{\star,\star,i}$, *(f)* each composer i ($i = 1, \ldots Nc$) creates a new tune ($x_{i,new}$) based on his/her $KM_{\star,\star,i}$ matrix and finally, *(g)* each composer i ($i = 1, \ldots Nc$) greedily replaces, or not, his/her worst tune $tune_{i,worst}$ by $x_{i,new}$ in $P_{\star,\star,i}$, according to the respective quality of both tunes. Generally, the stopping criterion is the maximum number of arrangements ($max_{arrangement}$), i.e. the total number of composed tunes (equivalent to a maximum number of computed solutions). The basic structure of MMC is presented in Algorithm 1.

Algorithm 1. The basic MMC algorithm

Input: MMC parameters and data about the instance to solve.
Output: The best tunes generated by the composers society.
1 Create an artificial society with specific interaction rules between agents.
2 **for** *every agent-composer i in the society* **do**
3   **repeat**
4   Randomly generate tune q for composer i ($tune_{i,q}$).
5   Evaluate $tune_{i,q}$.
6   **until** *Ns tunes are created*;
7   Store the Ns created tunes in the score matrix ($P_{\star,\star,i}$) of composer i
8 **end**
9 **repeat**
10   Update the artificial society.
11   Exchange information between agents.
12   **for** *each agent-composer i in the society* **do**
13   Update the knowledge matrix $KM_{\star,\star,i}$.
14   Evaluate the fitness of every tune in the knowledge matrix.
15   Set $tune_{i,worst} \leftarrow$ tune in the knowledge matrix with the worst objective value.
16   Generate a new tune ($tune_{i,new}$).
17   Evaluate the new tune.
18   **if** *$tune_{i,new}$ is better than $tune_{i,worst}$ (in terms of the fitness function)* **then**
19   Replace $tune_{i,worst}$ by $tune_{i,new}$ in $P_{\star,\star,i}$.
20   **end**
21   **end**
22   Build the new set of solutions.
23 **until** *The termination criterion is satisfied*;

The parameters used within the MMC are: the maximum number of arrangements (max _$arrangement$), the number of composers (Nc) and number of tunes in each composer's artwork (Ns). Furthermore, the factor of genius over innovation (ifg) represents the probability that a composer generates a new tune without considering foreknowledge while cfg is the probability of generating a single decision variable without considering previous knowledge. Finally, parameter ($fcla$) (factor of exchange between agents) is the probability of creating/eliminating an edge in the social network. For more detailed information about the MMC algorithm, we refer the reader to [13–17].

4   Method of Musical Composition for the Portfolio Optimization Problem

In this section, the proposed adaptation of the MMC to the constrained portfolio optimization problem is presented. For this algorithm, the j-th solution is represented by a N-dimensional vector, see Eq. 11.

$$tune_j = [x_{j,1}, x_{j,2}, \ldots, x_{j,N}] \tag{11}$$

where N is the number of assets considered in each instance and $x_{j,i} \in [0,1]$.
The adaptation of the MMC method consists of six phases detailed next.

1. **Initialization.** In this phase, the information of the instance to be solved and the value of the working parameters of the algorithm are introduced. Then, a different weighting factor, λ_i, is assigned to each composer, $1 \leq i \leq Nc$. Composers will use their own λ_i value to compute the fitness of their solutions according to Eq. 6. In this work, these weighting factors must be uniformly distributed in $[0,1]$. Next, a set of Ns melodies, e.g. feasible solutions, is generated for each composer, thus a $Nc \times Ns$ solutions are created in this phase. Finally, each composer computes its initial score according to Algorithm 2.

2. **Information exchange among agents.** In this phase, composers exchange information using a specific interaction policy, defined in this work as: "composer i learns from composer k if there is a link between them and if the artwork of composer k has more desirable characteristics than the artwork of composer i". These desirable characteristics are evaluated in terms of the objective function.
   This operating mode involves the three following steps. First, each composer i finds his/her worst tune, called $x_{i-worst}$. Next, if there is a link between composers i and k, $x_{i-worst}$ and $x_{k-worst}$ are compared. Finally, composer i uses information from the composer k only if $x_{k-worst}$ is better that $x_{i-worst}$.

Algorithm 2. Initial score for composer i

Input:
Nc, number of composers
$P^{initial}$, set of $Ns \times Nc$ random solutions
$\{\lambda_1, \lambda_2, \ldots, \lambda_{Nc}\}$, set of weighting factors for composers
   Output: $P_{\star,\star,i}$
1   **for** $i = 1$ to $Ns \times Nc$ **do**
2 | $return_i \longleftarrow$ expected return of solution i in $P^{initial}$
3 | $risk_i \longleftarrow$ risk of solution i in $P^{initial}$
4   **end**
5   **for** $i = 1$ to Nc **do**
6 | **for** $j=1$ to Ns **do**
7 | | $aux \leftarrow$ solution wit the lowest cost in $P^{initial}$ according to Eq. 6, using λ_i
8 | | Include aux in $P_{\star,\star,i}$
9 | | Delete aux from $P^{initial}$
10 | **end**
11 **end**

---

3. **Generation of a new tune.** Each composer creates a new tune using his/her knowledge, $P_{i,\star,\star}$, and the knowledge acquired from other composers, ISC. This procedure is described in Algorithm 3. Note that the new solution, $x_{i,new}$, can be unfeasible, thus requiring a repair process. The following rules are considered in this case:

RP1. An asset is rejected if it does not satisfy the floor-ceiling constraint.

RP2. If the number of assets is higher than K, the assets with the lowest capital ratios are rejected.

RP3. If the number of acquired is lower than K, some randomly selected assets are included into the solution and are assigned a ratio equal to ϵ_i.

RP4. In order to satisfy constraint 7, the ratios of selected assets are normalized.

Algorithm 3. Building a new melody

```
Input: ifg, cfg, N
Pi,*,*, is the composer's knowledge matrix
ISC, is the matrix of acquired knowledge
Output: xi,new
```

$$1 \quad KM = P_{i,\star,\star} \cup ISC$$
2   **for** $i = 1\ to\ NC$ **do**
3   KM_1' is the best melody in KM according Eq. 6 and λ_i
4   KM_2' is a melody (stochastically) selected according to its costfrom KM
5   KM_3' is a melody randomly taken from KM
6   **for** $j = 1\ to\ N$ **do**
7          $HM_{1,j} \leftarrow \max\{KM_{1,j}', KM_{2,j}', KM_{3,j}'\}$
8          $HM_{2,j} \leftarrow \min\{KM_{1,j}', KM_{2,j}', KM_{3,j}'\}$
9          $KM_{1,j}'' \leftarrow average\{KM_{1,j}', KM_{2,j}', KM_{3,j}'\}$
10         $KM_{2,j}'' \leftarrow variance\{KM_{1,j}', KM_{2,j}', KM_{3,j}'\}$
11   **end**
12   **if** $rand(0,1) < 1 - cfg$ **then**
13   **for** $j = 1\ to\ N$ **do**
14   **if** $rand(0,1) < 1 - ifg$ **then**
15   Generate a random number b, using a standard normal distribution
16             $x_{i,j} \leftarrow KM_{1,j}'' + b * KM_{2,j}$
17   **else**
18   **if** $rand(0,1) < 0.5$ **then**
19              $x_{i,j} \leftarrow HM_{2,j} + rand(0,1) * (HM_{1,j} - HM_{2,j})$
20   **else**
21              $x_{i,j} \leftarrow rand(0,1)$
22   **end**
23   **end**
24   **end**
25   **else**
26   **if** $rand(0,1) < 0.5$ **then**
27            $x_{i,new} \leftarrow rand(0,1)$
28   **else**
29   **for** $j = 1\ to\ N$ **do**
30             $x_{i,j} \leftarrow HM_{2,j} + rand(0,1) * (HM_{1,j} - HM_{2,j})$
31   **end**
32   **end**
33   **end**
34        $x_{i,new} = (x_{i,1}, x_{i,2}, \ldots, x_{i,N})$
35   **end**
36   Make $x_{i,new}$ a feasible solution

---

4. **Updating $P_{\star,\star,i}$.** In this step, each composer replaces the worst tune in his/her score matrix $P_{\star,\star,i}$ with the new tune, $x_{i,new}$, if $x_{i,new}$ has a lower cost than $x_{i-worst}$.

5. **Use of discarded solutions.** Each composer can replace the worst tune in his/her score matrix $P_{\star,\star,i}$ with some melody discarded by other composer, $x_{j-discarded}$, if $x_{i-worst}$ has a higher cost than $x_{j-discarded}$.

6. **Building the set of solutions.** In this phase, the MMC based algorithm selects the melody that achieves the best objective function value in the artwork of every composer.

A brief description the MMC based algorithm for the portfolio optimization problem is shown in Algorithm 4.

Algorithm 4. Adaptation of MMC algorithm to solve portfolio selection problem

---

Input: MMC parameters and treated instance information.
Output: Best tunes generated by composers.
1 Create an artificial society with rules of interaction among Nc agents.
2 $a = \frac{1}{Nc}$
3 **for** *each composer i in society* **do**
4 $\quad$ $\lambda_i = i * a$
5 **end**
6 Randomly generate $Nc * Ns$ melodies ($P^{initial}$)
7 Determine the risk and the return associated with each melody in $P^{initial}$
8 Assign to each composer a set of Ns melodies using Algorithm 2
9 **repeat**
10 $\quad$ Update the artificial society of composers.
11 $\quad$ Exchange information between agents.
12 $\quad$ Discarded melodies$= \emptyset$
13 $\quad$ **for** *each composer i in the society* **do**
14 $\quad\quad$ Update the knowledge matrix
15 $\quad\quad$ Generate and evaluate a new tune ($x_{i,new}$)
16 $\quad\quad$ Determine risk ($risk_{x_{i,new}}$) and return ($return_{x_{i,new}}$) for $x_{i,new}$
17 $\quad\quad$ $f(x_{i,new}) \leftarrow \lambda_i * risk_{x_{i,new}} + (1 - \lambda_i) * return_{x_{i,new}}$
18 $\quad\quad$ **if** $f(x_{i,new})$ *is better than the worst tune of composer i ($f(x_{i,worst})$)* **then**
19 $\quad\quad\quad$ Replace $x_{i-worst}$ with $x_{i,new}$ in the artwork.
20 $\quad\quad\quad$ Discarded melodies $\leftarrow x_{i-worst}$
21 $\quad\quad$ **else**
22 $\quad\quad\quad$ Discarded melodies$\leftarrow x_{i,new}$
23 $\quad\quad$ **end**
24 $\quad$ **end**
25 $\quad$ **for** *each composer i in the society* **do**
26 $\quad\quad$ Evaluate all solutions in discarded melodies based on Eq. 6 and λ_i
27 $\quad\quad$ $x_{i,best\_discarded} \leftarrow$ lower cost solution
28 $\quad\quad$ **if** $f(x_{i,best\_discarded}) \leq f(x_{i-worst})$ **then**
29 $\quad\quad\quad$ $x_{i-worst} \longleftarrow x_{i,best\_discarded}$
30 $\quad\quad$ **end**
31 $\quad$ **end**
32 $\quad$ Build the solution set.
33 **until** *termination criterion is met*;

---

5   Computational Experiments and Numerical Results

In order to evaluate the performance of the proposed algorithm, five benchmark instances proposed in [2] were used. These instance were created using five different capital market indices, the Hang Seng (Hong Kong), DAX 100 (Germany), FTSE 100 (UK), S&P 100 (USA) and Nikkei 225 (Japan). The number of different assets, N, considered for each index is equal to 31, 85, 89, 98 and 225, respectively. The sets of mean return of each asset, covariance between these assets and an efficient frontier with 2000 points are available at http://people.brunel.ac.uk/mastjjb/jeb/orlib/portinfo.html. For the constrained version of the portfolio optimization problem the cardinality constraint establishes that exactly 10 assets must be included in the portfolio, e.g. $K = 10$, while the floor-ceiling constraints establish $\epsilon_i = 0.01$ and $\delta_i = 1$.

The performance of the proposed MMC based algorithm was quantified according to the quality of the generated solutions. This analysis measures a percentage deviation error of the risk of the solutions found by MMC to the risk of a point created through a linear interpolation in the standard efficient frontier. Similarly, a percentage deviation error of the return is calculated. Finally, the percentage deviation error metric is defined, for each solution, as the minimum between its risk and return percentage deviations. For a more detailed description of this specific metric, we refer the reader to [2].

In [2], the performances of three heuristics are reported: genetic algorithms (GA), tabu search (TS) and simulated annealing (SA). Additionally, in [5] the performances of different particle swarm optimization (PSO) based algorithms are also presented. These algorithms were used to compare the solutions obtained by the proposed MMC algorithm.

In order to provide a fair comparison basis, our algorithm uses 50 different λ values in each run, and was limited to $1000N$ evaluations of the objective function (eof) for each λ, since this is the number of eof reported in [2]. For the parameter tuning, a brute force strategy such as that described in [1] was used. The resulting parameter value selected for the following computational experiments are: $ifg = 0.15, cfg = 0.05, Nc_v = 50, Nsi = 5$, and $fcla = 0.15$.

Table 1 shows a comparison between the MMC algorithm and the heuristics proposed in [2] and [5]. In the first column the name of the instance and the number of assets are indicated. Columns 2 to 4 indicate the median and the mean percentage error reported for GA, TS, SA, and PSO respectively, see [2] and [5]. In column 5, the median and the mean percentage errors for MMC are presented.

Table 1. Error results for the constrained efficient frontier.

Instance/(N)		GA	TS	SA	PSO	MMC
Hang Seng (31)	Median percentage error	1.2181	1.2181	1.2181	–	**1.173722**
	Mean percentage error	1.0974	1.1217	1.0957	1.0953	**1.016957**
DAX (85)	Median percentage error	2.5466	2.638	2.5661	–	**2.513767**
	Mean percentage error	2.5424	3.3049	2.9297	2.5417	**2.397792**
FTSE (89)	Median percentage error	1.0841	1.0841	1.0841	–	**0.6141566**
	Mean percentage error	1.1076	1.608	1.4623	1.0628	**0.9992334**
S& P (98)	Median percentage error	1.2244	1.2882	1.1823	–	**1.111530**
	Mean percentage error	1.9328	3.3092	3.0696	1.6890	**1.646952**
Nikkei (225)	Median percentage error	0.6133	0.6093	**0.6066**	–	0.631646
	Mean percentage error	0.7961	0.8975	**0.6732**	0.6870	0.694443

The information showed in Table 1 highlights the fact that MMC has a good behavior to solve these classical portfolio optimization instances. For four instances (Hang Seng, DAX, FTSE and S&P), MMC was able to find solutions

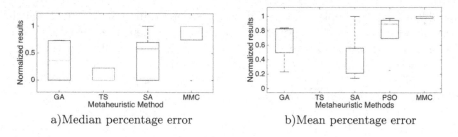

a)Median percentage error   b)Mean percentage error

Fig. 1. Comparison of the normalized errors obtained by each technique

Table 2. Results of Wilcoxon rank sum test

	GA	TS	SA	MMC
GA	FALSE	FALSE	FALSE	FALSE
TS	FALSE	FALSE	FALSE	TRUE
SA	FALSE	FALSE	FALSE	FALSE
MMC	FALSE	TRUE	FALSE	FALSE

	GA	TS	SA	PSO	MMC
GA	FALSE	TRUE	FALSE	FALSE	TRUE
TS	TRUE	FALSE	TRUE	TRUE	TRUE
SA	FALSE	TRUE	FALSE	FALSE	TRUE
PSO	FALSE	TRUE	FALSE	FALSE	TRUE
MMC	TRUE	TRUE	TRUE	TRUE	FALSE

a)Median percentage error   b)Mean percentage error

with median and mean percentage errors lower than those reported by GA, TS, SA and PSO. On the other hand, MMC obtains the worst median and the third lowest mean percentage errors for the Nikkei instance.

For further insights, the same results (median and mean percentage errors) were normalized through Eq. 12.

$$Norm\_error_i^\alpha = \frac{error_{worst}^\alpha - error_i}{error_{worst}^\alpha - error_{best}^\alpha} \tag{12}$$

where $Norm\_error_i^\alpha$ is the normalized error obtained by technique α for instance i. If $Norm\_error_i^\alpha = 1$, then the $\alpha - th$ method produces the best results in the $i - th$ instance. On the other hand, if $Norm\_error_i^\alpha = 0$, the $\alpha - th$ method generates the worst result in the $i - th$ instance. The median and average of these normalized results are shown in the box plots if Fig. 1. They clearly illustrate that the MMC is able produce highly competitive results, the atypical points are caused by Nikkei case. The results produced by MMC are best than those generated by other methods in four of five cases.

Finally, a Wilcoxon rank sum test was applied to the above-mentioned normalized errors and the corresponding results are presented in Table 2 (TRUE indicates that the produced solution samples are statistically different one from another, with a 5% significant level). This information proves that, even though the MMC produces results with a median percentage error similar with that of GA and SA, it is able to generate results with a significantly better mean percentage error with respect to all the other contenders.

Using this information, it can be concluded that MMC is able to find high quality solutions for the constrained portfolio optimization problem, even if some modifications might be considered in order to enable better performance levels for instances with a high asset number.

6   Conclusions

In this paper, an algorithm based on the Method of Musical Composition is introduced for solving the portfolio optimization problem. The performance of the proposed algorithm was tested over five benchmark data sets and the quality of the solutions was evaluated according to the median and mean percentage error, as proposed in [2]. These values, when compared against the errors reported for algorithms based on genetic algorithms, tabu search, simulated annealing and particle swarm optimization, highlight the fact that our algorithm outperforms the performance of its counterparts for four out of the five instances. However, MMC was unable to maintain this trend in and finally had the highest mean percentage error for one instance.

Nevertheless, the MMC seems to be a competitive strategy for the portfolio optimization problem and some modifications might improve its behavior. For example, a set of uniform distributed weighting factors, λ_i, could affect the convergence of the proposed algorithm, and a more detailed selection of these factors may improve the quality of the obtained solutions. In addition, the proposed algorithm used the same working parameters for all instances. Future work will include the implementation of a MMC variant with auto-adaptive control parameters. Hopefully, this auto-adaptive scheme could reduce the percentage errors. Finally, it is of common knowledge that the performance of an algorithm can be improved if appropriate search strategies are added, whence an hybridization with exact or different heuristic strategies is under consideration.

References

1. Birattari, M.: Tuning Metaheuristics: A Machine Learning Perspective. Springer, Heidelberg (2009). doi:10.1007/978-3-642-00483-4
2. Chang, T.J., Meade, N., Beasley, J.E., Sharaiha, Y.M.: Heuristics for cardinality constrained portfolio optimisation. Comput. Oper. Res. **27**(13), 1271–1302 (2000)
3. Chen, F.E.I., Weiyin, F.E.I.: Optimal control of markovian switching systems with applications to portfolio decisions under inflation. Acta Math. Sci. **35**(2), 439–458 (2015)
4. da Barrosa, M.R., Sallesa, A.V., Ribeiroa, C.D.O.: Portfolio optimization through Kriging methods. Appl. Econ. (2016). doi:10.1080/00036846.2016.1167827
5. Deng, G.F., Lin, W.T., Lo, C.C.: Markowitz-based portfolio selection with cardinality constraints using improved particle swarm optimization. Expert Syst. Appl. **39**, 4558–4566 (2012)
6. Fernandez, A., Gomez, S.: Portfolio selection using neural networks. Comput. Oper. Res. **34**(4), 1177–1191 (2007)
7. Jia, L., Zhiping, C.: Regime-dependent robust risk measures with application in portfolio selection. Procedia Comput. Sci. **31**, 344–350 (2014)
8. Lwin, K., Qu, R., Kendall, G.: A learning-guided multi-objective evolutionary algorithm for constrained portfolio optimization. Appl. Soft Comput. **24**, 757–772 (2014)
9. Markowitz, H.: Portfolio selection. J. Finance **7**(1), 77–91 (1952)

10. Markowitz, H.: Mean-Variance Analysis in Portfolio Choice and Capital Markets. Blackwell Publishers, Oxford (1987). isbn 0631153810
11. Min, J.K., Yongjae, L., Jang, H.K., Woo, C.K.: Sparse tangent portfolio selection via semi-definite relaxation. Oper. Res. Lett. **44**(4), 540–543 (2016)
12. Mishra, A.K., Panda, G., Majhi, B.: Prediction based mean-variance model for constrained portfolio assets selection using multiobjective evolutionary algorithms. Swarm Evol. Comput. **28**, 117–130 (2016)
13. Mora-Gutiérrez, R., Ramírez-Rodríguez, J., Rincón-García, E.A.: An optimization algorithm inspired by musical composition. Artif. Intell. Rev. **41**(3), 301–315 (2014a)
14. Mora-Gutiérrez, R.A., Ramírez-Rodríguez, J., Rincón-García, E.A., Ponsich, A., Herrera, O., Lara-Velázquez, P.: Adaptation of the musical composition method for solving constrained optimization problems. Soft Comput. **18**(10), 1931–1948 (2014b)
15. Mora-Gutiérrez, R.A., Ramírez-Rodríguez, J., Rincón-García, E.A., Ponsich, A., Herrera, O.: An optimization algorithm inspired by social creativity systems. Computing **94**(11), 887–914 (2012b)
16. Mora-Gutiérrez, R.A.: Diseño y desarrollo de un método heurístico basado en un sistema socio-cultural de creatividad para la resolución de problemas de optimización continuos no lineales y diseño de zonas electorales. Ph. D. Thesis. UNAM (2013)
17. Mora-Gutiérrez, R.A., Rincón-García, E.A., Ramírez-Rodríguez, J., Ponsich, A., Herrera-Alcántara, O., Lara-Velázquez, P.: An optimization algorithm inspired by musical composition in constrained optimization problems. Revista de Matemática: Teoría y Aplicaciones **20**(2), 183–202 (2013)
18. Meia, X., DeMiguel, V., Nogales, F.J.: Multiperiod portfolio optimization with multiple risky assets and general transaction costs. J. Banking Finan. **69**, 108–120 (2016)
19. Ponsich, A., Jaimes, A.L., Coello, C.A.C.: A survey on multiobjective evolutionary algorithms for the solution of the portfolio optimization problem and other finance and economics applications. IEEE Trans. Evol. Comput. **17**(3), 321–344 (2013)
20. Shaw, D.X., Shucheng, L., Kopman, L.: Lagrangian relaxation procedure for cardinality-constrained portfolio optimization. Optim. Methods Softw. **23**(3), 411–420 (2008)

Metaheuristic Hybridized Applied to Solve the Capacity Vehicle Routing Problem

Ernesto Liñán-García[1](✉), Linda Crystal Cruz Villegas[1],
Pascual Montes Dorantes[1], and Gerardo Maximiliano Méndez[2]

[1] Universidad Autónoma de Coahuila, Facultad de Sistemas,
Ciudad Universitaria, Carretera a México km 13, Arteaga, Coahuila, Mexico
{ernesto_linan_garcia, lindacruzvillegas}@uadec.edu.mx,
pascualresearch@gmail.com
[2] Instituto Tecnológico de Nuevo León, Monterrey, Nuevo León, Mexico

Abstract. In this paper, a metaheuristic hybridized for solving the Capacity Vehicle Routing Problem (CVRP) is proposed. The classical simulated annealing is combined with Saving's Algorithm (Clarke-Wright Algorithm) in order to obtain solution of CVRP with stochastic demand. This approach was tested with different solomon's instances of CVRP. Simulated Annealing is a simulation of heating and cooling of a metal to solve an optimization problem. Saving's algorithm is a deterministic heuristic for solving the Capacity Vehicle Routing Problem. In order to generate high quality solution of CVRP, our approach applies Saving's algorithm into Metropolis Cycle of Simulated Annealing. Initial solution of Simulated Annealing is also generated by Saving's Algorithm. This new approach has lead to increase the quality of the solution to CVRP with respect to the classical Simulated Annealing algorithm and classical Saving's Algorithm.

Keywords: Simulated Annealing · Saving's Algorithm · Vehicle Routing Problem · Metaheuristic

1 Introduction

The VRP was introduced by Dantzig and Ramser [1, 2], which is basic in distribution management. VRP has converted in one of the most extensively studied problems in combinatorial optimization area. The Vehicle Routing Problem (VRP) is an very important activity in many corporations. This task can generate important savings for companies. The planning optimal routes for the transport of goods to several business's customers can reduce the transportation's costs and distribution. Vehicle Routing Problem is a extension of the Traveling Salesman Problem (TSP). This last one is a classical challenge in combinatorial optimization area. VRP and its variants are classified as NP-Hard Problem [3–5] because there are many factors are considered and many possibilities of permutation and combinations. There are VRP's variations, e.g., capacity VRP (CVRP), multi-depot VRP (MDVRP), periodic VRP (PVRP), stochastic VRP (SVRP) [6], VRP with time windows (VRPTW) among others. Normally, this problem is solved by metaheuristic methods [7]. The main objective of VRP is to

© Springer International Publishing AG 2017
O. Pichardo-Lagunas and S. Miranda-Jiménez (Eds.): MICAI 2016, Part II, LNAI 10062, pp. 377–387, 2017.
DOI: 10.1007/978-3-319-62428-0_30

calculate the optimal route to serve many customers, using a set of vehicles to minimize the overall transportation cost.

Computational algorithms have been applied to solve the Vehicle Routing Problem, which are divided in exact and metaheuristic methods. Exact algorithms have been proposed for solving the VRP [8, 9]. The advantage of using exact algorithms is that they always obtain optimal solutions to a certain size of the problem, but they become inefficient for large instances of VRP. So, metaheuristic algorithms have been designed to obtain sub-optimal solution of a VRP variant, e.g., Ant Colony Algorithm [10], Simulated Annealing [11, 12], Genetic Algorithm [13, 14], Tabu Search [15, 16] among others. Metaheuristics can generate solutions very close to the optimal in a reasonable processing time, but they do not guarantee optimal solutions.

In this paper, a new algorithm is proposed. This combines the Simulated Annealing algorithm with the Saving's Algorithm. An initial solution required by Simulated Annealing algorithm is generated by Saving's Algorithm. Normally, the initial solution is high quality for this problem. In order to improve the initial solution, Simulated Annealing algorithm is applied. Simulated Annealing generates new solutions of VRP, in the metropolis cycle, new solutions are generated by Saving's Algorithm. Each solution generated can be accepted when it is better than previous one else it can be accepted by Boltzmann probability or likewise rejected. In order to generate CVRP solutions, the customers' demands are calculated for a stochastic way.

This paper is organized as follows: in Sect. 2, the CVRP is formally described, the classical Simulated Annealing algorithm is detailed at Sect. 2, in Sect. 3, Saving's algorithm is described, in Sect. 4, the algorithm proposed is explained in detail. Experimentation and results are shown in Sect. 5; and finally, in Sect. 6 the conclusions are discussed.

2   The Capacity Vehicle Routing Problem

The Capacity Vehicle Routing Problem is formally defined as follows:

Let $G(V, A)$ an undirected graph is given. V is defined as a set of $n + 1$ vertices. The set A denotes an arc set, which is defined as $A = \{(v_i, v_j) : v_i, v_j \in V, i \neq j\}$. V defines the set $V = \{0, 1, 2, \ldots, n\}$ where n represent the number of customers. The specific vertex number $\{0\}$ represents the depot. The remaining of vertices, $\{1, \ldots, n\}$, corresponds to n customers.

A route is defined as a least cost simple cycle of graph G passing through depot 0. The total demand of the vertices visited does not exceed the vehicle capacity. Each (v_i, v_j) of set A is related to nonnegative cost C_{ij}. Each customer of the set $\{1, \ldots, n\}$ has a non-negative demand q_i, which defines the units are supplied from depot 0 to customer i. A set of m identical vehicles of capacity Q must be used to supply goods to the $\{1, \ldots, n\}$ customers. The m vehicles must start and finish at depot. The demand of depot q_0 is equal to zero $(q_0 = 0)$.

The objective of VRP is to minimize the total travelled distance, time or cost by the m vehicles, subject to:

- Each route of a solution must to starts and ends at the depot.
- Each customer of a route is visited exactly once by exactly one vehicle.
- The total demand of each route does not exceed the capacity of vehicle.

The objective function (1) is the total cost of the solution. The constraints 1. The CVRP is formulated as follows:

$$\min \sum c_{ij} x_{ij} \tag{1}$$

where $(i, j) \in V$, the set V is defined by $\{0, 1, 2, ..., n\}$, $X_{ij} \in \{0,1\}$

This equation is subject to 5 constraints.

$$\sum x_{0j} = m \tag{1.1}$$

$$\sum x_{i0} = m \tag{1.2}$$

$$\sum_{j=1} x_{ij} = 1\,(i = 1, ..., n) \tag{1.3}$$

$$\sum_{i=1} x_{ij} = 1\,(j = 1, ..., n) \tag{1.4}$$

$$m \geq 1 \tag{1.5}$$

The objective function (1) is the total cost of the solution. The constraints 1.1 represents the m is the number of vehicles used in the solution. The constraints 1.2 indicate all vehicles that leave the deposit should be returned. The constraints 1.3 and 1.4 ensure that every client is an intermediate node of a route.

Monte Carlo method simulates the equilibrium state of a collection of atoms at any given temperature [19]. Nicholas Metropolis developed an algorithm for simulating the cooling of the material in a bath of heat, a process called annealing. The classical Simulated Annealing involves first heating and then slowly cooling some material. This algorithm simulates the gradual metal cooling for crystallization [17]. SA starts at high value of temperature, and then the temperature is decreased until a final one is reached.

The final temperature is typically very close to zero ($T_{final} \approx 0$) [17, 18]. The temperature value is decreased by a cooling function from the initial one to the final one.

There are different cooling functions, These have been applied in the SA algorithm [20–23]. The most common cooling function is defined by $T_{k+1} = \alpha * T_k$, where T_k is the value temperature at k time, T_{k+1} is the value temperature at k + 1 time, and α is the decrement factor of temperature. This function decreases the temperature value by an α factor, which does a range of $0.70 < \alpha < 1.0$. A gradual cooling is applied when α is very close to 1 ($\alpha \approx 1$), and a fast cooling is applied when α is very close to 0.70 ($\alpha \approx 0.70$).

The classical SA has two cycles; the first one is named Temperature Cycle where the temperature value is decreased by a cooling function. The second cycle is applied to generate, accept or reject solutions in order to optimize a problem. This last cycle is named Metropolis Cycle (MC).

Figure 1 shows the pseudo code of the classical SA. The initial and final temperature values are set. The initial temperature be as high as possible, and the final temperature be close to zero.

```
1:Setting initial and final temperatures
2:Create Scurrent from Initial solution Sinitial
3:T = Tinitial
4:While (T > Tfinal) do // Temperature Cycle
5:  While (stop criteria) // Metropolis Cycle
6:      Create Snew using a perturbation to Scurrent
7:      Obtain difference between Snew and Scurrent
8:      If (difference <= 0) then
9:          Accept Snew
10:     else
11:         Boltzmann probability  = exp(-difference/T)
12:         If (Boltzmann probability > random(0,1) then
13:     Accept Snew
14:         end if
15:     end if
16: end while
17: Decrease T by a cooling function   ·
19:end while
```

Fig. 1. Pseudo code of classical Simulated Annealing

The initial solution $S_{initial}$ of the problem to be optimized is created by a random way (see line 2). The current solution $S_{current}$ is set with $S_{initial}$. T is set to initial temperature (see line 3). The temperature cycle is executed from the initial temperature to the final temperature (see lines 4–19). The Metropolis Cycle gets started (see lines 5–16). This cycle takes a number of times specified in the stop criteria. A new solution S_{new} is generated within the Metropolis Cycle by creating a small perturbation to the current solution $S_{current}$ (see line 6). The difference between these two solutions (S_{new} and $S_{current}$) is obtained (see line 7).

In order to solve a minimization problem, if the difference is less or equal than zero (see line 8), the new solution is accepted (see line 9). If the difference is greater than zero, the Boltzmann probability is calculated (see line 11). If the Boltzmann probability is higher than a random value between 0 and 1 (see line 12) then the new solution is accepted (see line 13). After the Metropolis Cycle is completed, the temperature value is decreased (see line 17).

3 Saving's Algorithm

One of the most widely used algorithms for the VRP is the Savings Algorithm of Clarke and Wright [24]. In order to maximize the saving, two different routes (0, ..., i, 0) and (0, j, ..., 0) can be combined to form a new one. In the new route, the arcs (i, 0) and (0, j) will not be used and will be added the arc (i, j).

In this paper, a modified Saving's Algorithm is described, which the pseudo code is shown in the Fig. 2. The customer coordinates are read from a file instances. The

```
1:Read customer coordinates
2:Read customer demands
3:Calculate of distances between pair customer
4:Calculate the savings matrix
5:Sort the savings matrix
6:While (there are savings without to process) do
7:obtain customers i and j of the maximum savings not
processed
8:if customer i or custumer j has not been processed then
9:  obtain Ri or Rj (routes of i or j respectively)
10: if Ri=(0,i,..,0) then modify Ri to (0,j,i,..,0)
11: if Ri=(0,..,i,0) then modugy Ri to (0,..,i,j,0)
12: if Rj=(0,j,..,0) then modify Rj to (0,i,j,..,0)
13: if Rj=(0,..,j,0) then modify Rj to (0,..,j,i,0)
14: else // merge two routes
15:  obtain Ri and Rj (routes of i and j respectively)
16:  if Ri=(0,..,i,0) then
17:   if Rj=(0,..,j,0) or Rj=(0,j,..,0) then
18:    if it is factible
19:      create (0,..,i,j,..,0)and Rj is deleted
20:     end if
21:   else
22:    if Ri=(0,i,..,0) then
23:      if Rj=(0,j,..,0) or Rj=(0,..,j,0) then
24:       if it is factible
25:         create (0,..,j,i,..,0) and Rj is deleted
26:       end if
27:     end if
28:   end if
29: end if
30:end while
```

Fig. 2. Pseudo code of Saving's Algorithm

customer demands are read too. Distance Euclidean is calculated between pair of customers. The cost matrix is used in order to calculate the savings by the equation $s_{ij} = c_{i0} + c_{0j} - c_{ij}$ [24].

The values of savings are sorted. There is a cycle, which is done while there are savings without to process. Into this cycle, the savings are processed in order to add customers to route or merge two routes. Customer i and j are from savings matrix. If customer i or j have been processed, the other one can be added to customer processed route.

The route of customer i (R_i) or j (R_j) is obtained. If customer i is located in the route $(0, i, ..., 0)$ and customer j still has not been processed then the customer j can be added to the beginning of the route such that the restraint load is valid therefore, the route $(0, i, ..., 0)$ can be converted into $(0, j, i, ..., 0)$. If customer i is found into $(0, ..., i, 0)$ and the customer j is not in any route then it is possible to add the customer j at the end of route of customer i, so the route $(0, ..., i, 0)$ can be converted by $(0, ..., i, j, 0)$. If customer j is located in the route $(0, j, ..., 0)$ and customer i still has not been processed then the customer i can be added to the beginning of the route such that the restraint load is valid therefore, the route $(0, j, ..., 0)$ can be converted into $(0, i, j, ..., 0)$. If $R_j = (0, ..., j, 0)$ then it is possible to add the customer i at the end of route of customer j, so the route $(0, ..., j, 0)$ can be converted to $(0, ..., j, i, 0)$. If the customer i and j have been processed and these are at the beginning or end on different routes, it is possible merge R_i and R_j. If $R_i = (0, ..., i, 0)$ and $R_j = (0, ..., j, 0)$ or $R_j = (0, j, ..., 0)$ then merge R_i and R_j, so the R_i is defined by $(0, ..., i, j, ..., 0)$ and the route R_j is deleted. If $R_i = (0, i, ..., 0)$ and $R_j = (0, ..., j, 0)$ or $R_j = (0, j ,..., 0)$ then merge R_i and R_j, so the R_i is defined by $(0, ..., j, i, ..., 0)$ and the route R_j is deleted.

4 Metaheuristic Hybridized Proposed

In order to solve the Capacity Vehicle Routing Problem, a new hybridized algorithm has been designed and implemented. This new approach combines the classical Simulated Annealing with the Saving's algorithm. This last algorithm is applied to generate new CVRP solutions with customer stochastic demands. Saving's Algorithm is applied to generate both an initial as a new solution into Metropolis Cycle.

The Simulated Annealing is applied to reduce the temperature value and to accept or reject solutions. If a new CVRP solution is better than previous one, the new solution is accepted; on the other hand, the new solution can be accepted or rejected by applying the Boltzmann probability.

The pseudo code of metaheuristic proposed is shown in Fig. 3. This algorithm is divided in two sections, the first one is named setting section, where several setting are specified. The second one is named simulated annealing section, in which simulated annealing algorithm is specified. The initial and final temperatures ($T_{initial}$ and T_{final}) is set. The cooling factor alpha (α) is set. Demands of all customers are generated by a stochastic way. A feasible initial solution ($S_{initial}$) of CVRP is created, it can be created

```
// Setting section
1:Setting initial temperature (Tinitial)
2:Setting final temperatures (Tfinal)
3:Setting cooling factor (alpha)
4:Generate stochastic demands of all customer
5:Create a factible initial solution of CVRP
6:Calculate the cost of this initial solution of CVRP
7:Scurrent is initialized with the initial solution of CVRP
8:Sbest is initialized with initial solution of CVRP
9:T is equal to Tinitial
10:Lcm_max is initialized
// simulated annealig section
11:While (T > Tfinal) do // Temperature Cycle
12: lcm = 1
13: While (lcm < Lcm_max) // Metropolis Cycle
14:  Generate stochastic demand of a customer in random way
15:  Create new solution using saving's algorithm or random way
16:  Obtain difference of costs between Snew and Scurrent
17:  If (difference <= 0) then
18:    The new solution of CVRP is accepted
19:    If the new solution is best than the best solution then
20:       Sbest is equal to Snew
21:    End if
22:  Else
23:    Boltzmann probability  = exp(-difference/T)
24:    If (Boltzmann probability > random(0,1) then
25:      The new solution of CVRP is accepted
26:    else
27:      The new solution of CVRP is rejected
28:    End if
29:  End if
30:  lcm = lcm + 1
31: End while
32: Decrease T by cooling function T = alpha * T
33:End while
34:Show Sbest, which represents the best found solution of CVRP
```

Fig. 3. Pseudo code of metaheuristc proposed

by applying Saving's algorithm or a random way. The CVRP initial solution's cost ($C_{Sinitial}$) is calculated. The CVRP current solution ($S_{current}$) is set to initial solution. The best CVRP solution is set to initial solution. The variable T is set to initial temperature ($S_{initial}$). The maximal length of Metropolis Cycle is setting.

Into simulated annealing section, the two cycles of SA are described. The first one is named temperature cycle, which contains the metropolis cycle and it reduces the temperature values. While the variable T is greater than final temperature, this cycle is executed. The Metropolis Cycle length is started to 1, this length is increased until the maximal length is reached.

The metropolis is executed while the length is less than the maximal length of MC. Into MC, stochastic demand of a customer is generated in random way, this change of demand is used for generating a new CVRP solution (S_{new}) by applied alternatively the

Saving's Algorithm or random way. The cost's difference between S_{new} and $S_{current}$ is calculated. In order to solve a minimization problem, new CVRP solution is accepted if the difference is less or equal than zero. If the new CVRP solution is better than the best CVRP solution then the best solution is replaced by S_{new}.

If the difference between S_{new} and $S_{current}$ is greater than zero, Boltzmann probability is calculated by $e^{-Difference/T}$. If this probability is greater than a random number within range of [0, 1] then the new CVRP solution is accepted else this solution is rejected.

5 Experimentation and Results

The metaheuristic proposed is implemented using Powerbuilder software tool. The parameters of Simulated Annealing were established by an experimental way. The initial temperature is set at 1000, and final temperature is set at 1. The alpha factor is set to 0.85.

In this section, the results obtained are shown and analyzed. The algorithm proposed is tested with 20 CVRP instances (see Table 1), which were defined in solomon's instances. The information of each instance includes its name instance and the number of customers. The capacity of all instances is equal to 100.

Table 1. Solomon's instances

Number instance	Solomon's instance	Customers	Number instance	Solomon's instance	Customers
1	A-n32-k5	32	11	A-n44-k6	44
2	A-n33-k5	33	12	A-n45-k6	45
3	A-n33-k6	33	13	A-n45-k7	45
4	A-n34-k5	34	14	A-n46-k7	46
5	A-n36-k5	36	15	A-n48-k7	48
6	A-n37-k5	37	16	A-n53-k7	53
7	A-n37-k6	37	17	A-n54-k7	54
8	A-n38-k5	38	18	A-n55-k9	55
9	A-n39-k5	39	19	A-n61-k9	61
10	A-n39-k6	39	20	A-n65-k9	65

The comparison of results between optimal solution of solomon's instances and the results of metaheuristic proposed are shown on Table 2. In this table are shown the solomon's instance costs, number of routes of each one, the metaheuristic proposed minimum solution, the average cost and number of routes obtained by this approach.

Table 2. Comparison of results

Instance number	Solomon's cost	Routes Solomon's instance	Metaheuristic proposed minimum cost	Routes obtained	Metaheuristic proposed average cost
1	784	5	771.47	4	812.03
2	661	5	647.48	5	662.97
3	742	6	733.43	6	739.94
4	778	5	775.95	6	783.82
5	799	5	781.35	5	800.07
6	669	5	673.57	5	694.92
7	949	6	905.98	6	929.15
8	730	5	716.15	5	726.76
9	822	5	824.44	5	838.53
10	831	6	827.23	6	835.15
11	937	6	928.61	6	937.64
12	944	6	917.14	6	929.37
13	1146	7	1148.84	7	1168.68
14	914	7	892.51	7	913.42
15	1073	7	1064.61	7	1087.96
16	1010	7	1014.15	7	1025.87
17	1167	7	1162.11	7	1181.58
18	1073	9	1076.55	9	1083.63
19	1034	9	1033.58	9	1054.49
20	1174	9	1182.21	9	1210.00

In order to analyze the information on Table 2, the new proposed approach obtained better results than the optimal reported at all solomon's instances. The algorithm was executed 30 times by each solomon's instance.

An average cost was calculated. The proposed algorithm improved average cost of some instances.

On Table 3, the comparison between Saving's Algorithm and the metaheuristic proposed is shown. The new proposed approach obtained better results than the optimal reported by Saving's Algorithm.

The results obtained by the metaheuristic proposed were compared by other algorithms, e.g., the hybrid algorithm based on Ant Colony Optimization (ACO) and Particle Swarm Optimization (PSO) proposed by [25], an improved savings algorithm proposed by [26], and a multi-space sampling heuristic proposed by [27]. The quality solutions obtained by metaheuristic are better than the quality solutions of these algorithms.

Table 3. Comparison of results

Instance number	CW's average cost	Metaheuristic proposed minimum cost	Metaheuristic proposed average cost
1	857.66	771.47	812.03
2	706.57	647.48	662.97
3	781.96	733.43	739.94
4	824.77	775.95	783.82
5	870.92	781.35	800.07
6	714.23	673.57	694.92
7	1000.79	905.98	929.15
8	772.74	716.15	726.76
9	895.33	824.44	838.53
10	872.58	827.23	835.15
11	987.56	928.61	937.64
12	1005.34	917.14	929.37
13	1224.48	1148.84	1168.68
14	974.99	892.51	913.42
15	1153.90	1064.61	1087.96
16	1093.51	1014.15	1025.87
17	1246.41	1162.11	1181.58
18	1134.50	1076.55	1083.63
19	1119.53	1033.58	1054.49
20	1297.23	1182.21	1210.00

6 Conclusions

The new proposed approach to solve Capacity Vehicle Routing Problem with stochastic demands generates better high quality solutions at all of solomon's instances. The average cost of 30 runs was better than the optimum reported at solomon's instances. The metaheuristic proposed reduced the number of routes only one instance (instance number 1). In order to generate high quality solution of CVRP, Simulated Annealing and Saving's Algorithm combination works better than they by apart. As a future work, this new approach can be modified in order to generate high quality solution of CVRP. This algorithm can be hybridized with other heuristics or metaheuristics.

References

1. Dantzig, G., Fulkerson, R., Johnson, S.: Solution of a large-scale traveling-salesman problems. Oper. Res. **2**, 393–410 (1954)
2. Dantzig, G., Ramser, J.: The truck dispatching problem. Manag. Sci. **6**, 80–91 (1959)
3. Wen-Chyuan, C., Robert, R.: Simulated annealing metaheuristics for the vehicle routing problem with time windows. Ann. Oper. Res. **63**, 3–27 (1996)

4. Olli, B., Wout, D., Michel, G.: Evolutionary algorithms for the vehicle routing problem with time windows. J. Heuristics **10**, 587–611 (2004)
5. Gabor, N., Said, S.: Location-routing: issues, models and methods. Eur. J. Oper. Res. **177**, 649–672 (2007)
6. Flatberg, T.: Dynamic and Stochastic Aspects in Vehicle Routing: A Literature Survey. SINTEF rapport. SINTEF ICT (2005). ISBN 9788214028430
7. Olli, B., Michel, G.: Vehicle routing problem with time windows, part i: route construction and local search algorithms. Transp. Sci. **39**, 104–118 (2005)
8. Gilbert, L., Yves, N.: Exact algorithms for the vehicle routing problem. Surv. Comb. Optim. **31**, 147–184 (1987)
9. Gilbert, L.: The vehicle routing problem: an overview of exact and approximate algorithms. Eur. J. Oper. Res. **59**, 345–358 (1992)
10. Bell, J.E., McMullen, P.R.: Ant colony optimization techniques for the vehicle routing problem. Adv. Eng. Inform. **18**, 41–48 (2004)
11. Osman, I.H.: Metastrategy simulated annealing and tabu search algorithms for the vehicle routing problem. Ann. Oper. Res. **41**, 421–451 (1993)
12. Czech, Z.J., Czarnas, P.: Parallel simulated annealing for the vehicle routing problem with time windows. In: 10th Euromicro Workshop on Parallel, Distributed and Network-Based Processing, Canary Islands-Spain, pp. 376–383 (2002)
13. Thangiah, S.R.: Vehicle routing with time windows using genetic algorithms (1995)
14. Homberger, J.H.G.: A two-phase hybrid metaheuristic for the vehicle routing problem with time windows. Eur. J. Oper. Res. **162**, 220–238 (2005)
15. Bruno-Laurent, G., Jean-Yves, P., Jean-Marc, R.: A parallel implementation of the tabu search heuristic for vehicle routing problems with time window constraints. Comput. Oper. Res. **21**, 1025–1033 (1994)
16. Taş, D., Dellaert, N., Van Woensel, T., De Kok, T.: Vehicle routing problem with stochastic travel times including soft time windows and service costs. Comput. Oper. Res. **40**, 214–224 (2013)
17. Kirkpatrick, S., Gelatt, C., Vecchi, M.: Optimization by simulated annealing. Science **4598**, 671–680 (1983)
18. Cerny, V.: Thermodynamical approach to the traveling salesman problem: an eficient simulation algorithm. J. Optim. Theory Appl. **45**, 41–51 (1985)
19. Nicholas, M., Arianna, R., Marshall, R., Augusta, T., Edward, T.: Equation of state calculations by fast computing machines. J. Chem. Phys. **21**, 1087–1092 (1953)
20. Aarts, E., Korst, J.: Simulated Annealing and Boltzmann Machines: A Stochastic Approach to Combinatorial Optimization and Neural Computing. Wiley, Hoboken (1989)
21. Ingber, L.: Simulated annealing: practice versus theory. J. Math. Comput. Model. **18**, 29–57 (1993)
22. Kjaerul, U.: Optimal decomposition of probabilistic networks by simulated annealing. Stat. Comput. **2**, 7–17 (1991)
23. van Laarhoven, P.J., Aarts, E.H.: Simulated Annealing: Theory and Applications. Kluwer Academic Publishers, Berlin (1987)
24. Clarke, G., Wright, J.W.: Scheduling of vehicles from a central depot to a number of delivery points. Oper. Res. **12**, 568–581 (1964)
25. Tantikorn, P., Ruengsak, K.: An improved Clarke and Wright savings algorithm for the capacitated vehicle routing problem. ScienceAsia **38**, 307–318 (2012)
26. Kao, Y., Chen, M.-H., Huang, Y.-T.: A hybrid algorithm based on ACO and PSO for capacitated vehicle routing problems. Math. Prob. Eng. **2012**, 17 (2012)
27. Mendoza, J.E., Villegas, J.G.: A multi-space sampling heuristic for the vehicle routing problem with stochastic demands. Optim. Lett. **7**, 1–14 (2013)

ABC-PSO: An Efficient Bioinspired Metaheuristic for Parameter Estimation in Nonlinear Regression

Sergio Gerardo de-los-Cobos-Silva[1,2], Miguel Ángel Gutiérrez Andrade[1,2],
Pedro Lara-Velázquez[1,2], Eric Alfredo Rincón García[1,2(✉)],
Roman Anselmo Mora-Gutiérrez[1,2], and Antonin Ponsich[1,2]

[1] Dpto. de Ing. Eléctrica, Universidad Autónoma Metropolitana Unidad Iztapalapa,
09340 Mexico, D.F., Mexico
{cobos,gamma,plara}@xanum.uam.mx
[2] Dpto. de Sistemas, Universidad Autónoma Metropolitana Unidad Azcapotzalco,
02200 Mexico, D.F., Mexico
{rigaeral,mgra,aspo}@correo.azc.uam.mx

Abstract. Nonlinear regression is a statistical technique widely used in research which creates models that conceptualize the relation among many variables that are related in complex forms. These models are widely used in different areas such as economics, biology, finance, engineering, etc. These models are subsequently used for different processes, such as prediction, control or optimization. Many standard regression methods have been proved that produce misleading results in certain data sets; this is especially true in ordinary least squares. In this article three metaheuristic models for parameter estimation of nonlinear regression models are described: Artificial Bee Colony, Particle Swarm Optimization and a novel hybrid algorithm ABC-PSO. These techniques were tested on 27 databases of the NIST collection with different degrees of difficulty. The experimental results provide evidence that the proposed algorithm finds consistently good results.

Keywords: ABC · PSO · Nonlinear regression

1 Introduction

Non-linear least squares criterion, unlike linear regression under no collinearity, are very difficult problems, as a matter of fact for some instances an exact algorithm could not find optimal solutions. Even for some linear regression problems where the associated matrices have near zero elements, it is difficult to find optimal solutions using statistical packages, as can be seen in [4].

The National Institute for Standards and Technology (NIST) [14] states that: "nonlinear least squares regression problems are intrinsically hard, and it is generally possible to find a dataset that will defeat even the most robust codes", and continues: "The datasets provided here are particularly well suited for such

© Springer International Publishing AG 2017
O. Pichardo-Lagunas and S. Miranda-Jiménez (Eds.): MICAI 2016, Part II, LNAI 10062, pp. 388–400, 2017.
DOI: 10.1007/978-3-319-62428-0_31

testing of robustness and reliability". There are several challenges in nonlinear regression to ensure that certain methods such as Levenberg-Marquart, Gauss-Newton, etc. can find the optimal parameter values [5], these challenges consider: (1) increased functional complexity due to non-convexity of the search space, (2) unavailable derivative information, and (3) unfavourable initial solution.

Several statistical packages (SPSS, S-Plus, NCSS, SYSTAT) [18] were tested on higher-level-difficulty tasks collected by NIST [14]. Either failure or significant disagreement with certified values were found in about one half tasks. Iterative deterministic procedures can stop at a local minimum different from the global one in many tasks. Moreover, these algorithms need starting values of parameters and the choice of starting values has substantial influence on convergence of iteration process. This general theoretical argumentation is supported by the experimental results [12] where 14 regression functions have been considered. In [12] it was shown that the standard algorithms from the statistical packages NCSS, SYSTAT, S-PLUS, SPSS for the large percentage of random starting points failed to find the global minimum. In the specialized literature, different heuristic methods have been reported to deal with nonlinear regression problems, such as: Artificial Bee Colony (ABC) [2], Differential Evolution (DE), [2,18], Genetic Algorithm (GA), [5], Particle Swarm Optimization (PSO) [1,3,4,16].

In general, iterative procedures that use derivatives do not guarantee finding the optimal values in nonlinear regression problems, besides these strategies require differentiability of the functions involved, and in several instances it is not possible to find such condition. An alternative to solve this problem was proposed by Tvrdík [17], he considers the nonlinear regression problem as a global optimization problem. Tvrdík [17] proposes a metaheuristic method based on DE that finds the parameters of the nonlinear regression problems. The results were compared with those reported in NIST databases [14], which were calculated to 11 decimal places for each dataset. The performance of the proposed DE based algorithm was evaluated in terms of the number of decimal digits of the certified results that was able to duplicated, λ. It is noteworthy that in [17] a success rate of $\lambda > 4$ was reported. In [2] the same problem is solved using an ABC based algorithm and its results are reported, getting $\lambda - mean > 3$. In [3] the same problem is solved using an PSO based algorithm and its results are reported getting $\lambda - mean > 6$. In this paper we propose an hybrid algorithm ABC-PSO that produces excellent results, $\lambda - mean > 10$. The objective of this work is to compare numerically PSO, ABC and a hybrid method ABC-PSO on nonlinear regression functions that are well known [14]. These algorithms were tested on 27 databases, from which 8 are considered highly difficult, 11 with a medium difficulty level and 8 with a low difficulty level.

This article is presented as follows: Sect. 2 is an overview of the nonlinear regression problem; Sect. 3 provides general concepts of the ABC algorithm; Sect. 4 describes the PSO strategy; Sect. 5 shows the proposed ABC-PSO algorithm; Sect. 6 describes the comparative results of experimentation of the three algorithms related to the NIST reference functions. Finally, the conclusions are presented in Sect. 7.

2   Nonlinear Regression

Given two variables x and y, observed on n objects, where x is an explanatory variable and y is a variable to explain that depends on x, we want to describe the dependence of y with respect to x by a function f, i.e. we want to establish the functional relation $y = f(x) + \epsilon$ where ϵ is an error term that is a random variable with mean zero (in this work is not assumed that ϵ follows some particular distribution). The function f generally depends on certain parameters, which we denote by vector θ so the regression function can be written as:

$$y = f(x, \theta) + \epsilon \tag{1}$$

In the regression problem, we want to find the numeric values of the parameter $\theta = (\theta_1, \theta_2, \ldots, \theta_p)$ such that it optimize some criteria, in particular we want to minimize the least squares criterion, which measures the quality of the functional approximation proposed by minimizing the sum of squared differences:

$$S(\theta) = \|y - f(x, \theta)\|^2 = \sum_i [y_i - f(x_i, \theta)]^2 \tag{2}$$

where $x_i = (x_{1i}, x_{2i}, \ldots, x_{mi})^t$, for $i = 1, 2, \ldots, n$ and $y = (y_1, y_2, \ldots, y_n)^t$ are the vectors of observations of the variables, and $\| \cdot \|$ is the Euclidean norm.

Thus we can define a global optimization problem as follows. Given an objective function $S : D \longrightarrow \Re$, we wish to find [17]:

$$\theta^* = \operatorname{argmin}_{\theta \in D} S(\theta).$$

The point θ^* is called the global minimum, the search space D is defined as $D = \prod_i [\theta_{min_i}, \theta_{max_i}]$, where $\theta_{min_i} < \theta_{max_i}, i = 1, 2, \ldots, p$, this specification of S is known as box restriction.

Except when $f(x, \theta)$ is a linear function with respect to the parameter vector θ, there is no general solution to this problem. For the nonlinear case, there are deterministic iterative algorithms, Levenberg-Maquardt or Gauss-Newton for instance, that can be used in statistical packages, but they generally fail to find the optimal solution. Therefore, when we want to find a nonlinear regression model of best fit using the criterion of least squares we got a general continuous programming problem, which is a problem difficult to solve (c.f. [17]).

3   Artificial Bee Colony

The Artificial Bee Colony metaheuristic is a technique of the family of swarm intelligence, which emulates the behavior of finding food sources for foraging honey bees and the information that share bees for this purpose. ABC was initially proposed by Karaboga [6] and has been applied to diverse problems such as constrained optimization [8], neural networks [7] and clusters [9,15].

In ABC, the bees are classified into three classes: employed bees, onlooker bees and scout bees. A food source is a solution to the optimization problem and the amount of nectar of the food source is equivalent of the quality (fitness function) of the associated solution represented by the source.

In the initialization phase, S_N random food sources are generated, where S_N denotes the number of employed bees, which is the same as that of onlooker bees. Each solution $\theta_i (i = 1, 2, \ldots, S_N)$ is a p-dimensional vector, where p is the number of parameters to optimize, i.e., $\theta_i = (\theta_{i1}, \theta_{i2}, \ldots, \theta_{ip})$. Then we evaluate the amount of nectar fit_i, which is the value of the fitness function to optimize. In the phase when employed bees are used, each of them looks for a new food source in the neighbourhood v_i of θ_i using the following expression:

$$v_{ij} = \theta_{ij} + O_{ij}(\theta_{ij} - \theta_{kj}) \tag{3}$$

where $k \in \{1, 2, \ldots, SN\}$ and $j \in \{1, 2, \ldots, p\}$ are indexes that were chosen randomly, $k \neq i$, and O_{ij} is a random number in $[-1, 1]$. Then each employed bee compares the new solution against the current and memorizes the best by a greedy procedure.

In the phase of onlooker bees, each one chooses a food source with a certain probability, which is related to its amount of nectar. The probability associated with the i-th food source is calculated by the following expression:

$$P_i = fit_i / \sum_{j=1,\ldots,S_N} fit_j. \tag{4}$$

where fit_i is the fitness function evaluated in θ_i.

In the phase of scout bees, if a food source is not improved for a certain number of cycles, referred to as the Limits, that source is removed from the population, and the scout bee find a new food sources randomly using the following equation:

$$\theta_{ij} = \theta_{min_j} + \text{rand}[0, 1](\theta_{max_j} - \theta_{min_j}) \tag{5}$$

where θ_{min_j} and θ_{max_j} are the lower and upper bounds of the parameter j, respectively. These steps are repeated until a number of cycles (MCN) is reached or until the stop criterion is satisfied. The main steps of ABC are described in Algorithm 1.

4   Particle Swarm Optimization

The Particle Swarm Optimization heuristic is a subset of what is known as swarm intelligence and has its roots in artificial life, social psychology, engineering and computer science. PSO is based on the use of a set of particles or agents that correspond to states of an optimization problem, where each particle moves across the solution space in search of an optimal position or at least a good solution. In PSO there exist communication between agents, and the agent with a better position (measured according to an objective function) influences the others by attracting them to it.

The population is initialized assigning random position and speed to each particle. At each iteration the velocity of each particle is randomly accelerated

---

Algorithm 1. ABC Algorithm

1 Initialize and evaluate the population of solutions θ_i, $i = 1, 2 \ldots, SN$
2 **while** *number of cycles MCN is not reached* **do**
3   Generate and evaluate new solutions for employed bees v_i using Eq. 3.
4   Apply a greedy selection process for employed bees.
5   Calculate the probability values P_i for the solutions θ_i using Eq. 4.
6   Generate and evaluate new solutions v_i for onlookers bees from solutions selected depending from P_i.
7   Apply the greedy selection process for onlookers bees.
8   Determine the solutions abandoned by the scouts, if any, and generate a new randomly produced solution θ_i by Eq. 5.
9   Save in memory the best solution reached.
10 **end**

---

towards its best position (where the value of the fitness function or objective function improves) and also considering the best positions of their neighbours.

To solve a problem, PSO uses a dynamic management of particles; this approach allows breaking cycles and diversifies the search. For this article a swarm of r-particle solutions in time t is given in the form $\theta_{1t}, \theta_{2t}, \ldots, \theta_{rt}$ with $\theta_{jt} \in D, j = 1, 2, \ldots, r$. Then we define a movement of the swarm by:

$$\theta_{jt+1} = \theta_{jt} + V_{jt+1}, \tag{6}$$

where the velocity V_{jt+1} is given by:

$$V_{jt+1} = \alpha V_{jt} + rand(0, \varphi_1)[\theta'_{jt} - \theta_{jt}] + rand(0, \varphi_2)[\theta'_{gt} - \theta_{jt}], \tag{7}$$

where:

D: Space of feasible solutions,
V_{jt}: Speed at time t of the j-th particle,
V_{jt+1}: Speed at time $t + 1$ in the j-th particle,
θ_{jt}: j-th particle at time t,
θ'_{gt}: The particle with the best value for all time t,
θ'_{jt}: j-th particle with the best value to the time t,
rand$(0, \varphi)$: Random value uniformly distributed on the interval $[0, \varphi]$,
α: Parameters of scale.

The main steps of PSO are described in Algorithm 2.

5 Proposed ABC-PSO Algorithm

Crowding has a major effect in swarm-based algorithms. It causes a narrowing of the search space as well as premature convergence. Because of this, in [2,3] authors reported that ABC provides solutions that have a smaller standard deviation than those produced by PSO. On the other hand, in [3,4] it was observed

---

Algorithm 2. PSO Algorithm

---

1 Create a population of particles distributed throughout the feasible space.
2 **while** *termination criterion is not satisfied* **do**
3 | Evaluate each position of the particles according to the objective function (fitness function).
4 | If the current position of a particle is better than the previous, update it.
5 | Determine the best particle, according to the best previous positions.
6 | Update the particle velocities $j = 1, 2, \ldots, r$ according to Eq. 7
7 | Shift the particles to new positions according to Eq. 6
8 **end**

---

that PSO found the optimal solution more often than ABC. Based in this behaviour we proposed the following ABC-PSO hybrid algorithm. First a set of random food sources is generated, and these solutions are improved using an ABC strategy, as described in Sect. 3. After a number of iterations, the best food source is saved as a particle. This process is repeated until r particles are created. Finally, these particles explore the solution spaces using a PSO strategy, as described in Sect. 4, and the best found solution is returned. This hybrid method has the advantage that the solutions found are of better quality compared to ABC and PSO. The main steps of the proposed ABC-PSO are described in Algorithm 3.

Algorithm 3. ABC-PSO Algorithm

---

1 Create a population of particles θ_i where each θ_i is the best bee solution using ABC, for $i = 1, 2, \ldots, r$.
2 **while** *termination criterion is not satisfied* **do**
3 | Evaluate each position of the particles according to the objective function (fitness function).
4 | If the current position of a particle is better than the previous, update it.
5 | Determine the best particle, according to the best previous positions.
6 | Update the particle velocities $j = 1, 2, \ldots, r$ according to Eq. 7.
7 | Shift the particles to new positions according to Eq. 6.
8 **end**

---

6   Results

In order to compare the performance of the three algorithms previously described, 50 runs were performed considering a maximum of 100,000 evaluations of the objective function, given by Eq. 2, per run.

[14] specifies that the certified values are "best-available" solutions, obtained using 128-bit precision and confirmed by at least two different algorithms and software packages using analytic derivatives. [14] also affirms "The certified

results are reported to 11 decimal places for each dataset. Clearly, most of these digits are not statistically significant, and we are not advocating that results should be reported to this number of digits in a statistical context. We do believe, however, that this number of digits can be useful when testing the numerical properties of a procedure".

Therefore, [14] states that "Except in cases where the certified value is essentially zero (for example, as occurs for Lanczos3 problems), a good nonlinear least squares procedure should be able to duplicate the certified results to at least 4 or 5 digits." That is, it should be the case that:

$$- log_{10}[\|q - c\|/\|c\|] > 4,\tag{8}$$

where q denotes the estimated value from the code being tested and c denotes the certified value.

Table 1. Values obtained by PSO, ABC and ABC-PSO.

Date base (difficulty)	PSO		ABC		ABC-PSO	
	Std. dev	$\lambda - mean$	Std. dev	$\lambda - mean$	Std. dev	$\lambda - mean$
Misra1a (low)	1.34E+04	3.47	1.04E−02	1.51	1.68E−15	10.45
Lanczos3 (low)	2.39E−08	0.82	2.73E−09	0.78	4.94E−22	10.55
Chwirut (low)	3.45E−13	11.21	7.87E−02	4.28	3.45E−13	11.21
Chwirut1 (low)	9.19E−13	11.41	2.12E−01	4.53	9.19E−13	11.41
Gauss1 (low)	1.62E+01	3.77	3.12E−03	5.9	1.90E−04	8.81
Gauss2 (low)	1.39E+01	5.25	1.47E−01	3.71	2.68E−03	9.46
DanWood (low)	7.36E−18	11.68	1.34E−05	−4.28	7.36E−18	11.68
Misra1b (low)	1.52E−02	3.95	2.33E−03	1.69	5.10E−15	11.37
Kirby2 (medium)	3.61E−01	3.09	2.74E−01	1.05	1.73E−14	11.63
Hahn1 (medium)	5.96E−01	0.65	4.51E−02	1.44	4.59E−05	9.58
Nelson (medium)	2.17E−05	4.8	2.85E−07	7.57	1.35E−15	10.92
MGH17 (medium)	2.20E−05	3.69	2.37E−06	1.37	5.62E−09	9.41
Misra1c (medium)	3.24E−15	11.07	1.69E−04	3.23	4.13E−15	11.07
Misra1d (medium)	6.79E−16	11.19	4.38E−04	2.49	6.02E−16	11.19
Rozman1 (medium)	7.93E−06	5.85	3.36E−09	5.22	6.19E−19	12.19
Gauss3 (medium)	7.53E+01	2.85	6.20E−01	3.14	1.40E−03	9.11
ENZO (medium)	1.52E+00	3.24	5.96E−03	5.17	1.10E−05	9.92
Bennett5 (high)	1.80E−06	3.66	1.84E−05	1.66	3.75E−17	11.11
BoxBod (high)	9.19E−13	10.42	9.19E−13	10.42	9.19E−13	10.42
Thurber (high)	5.75E+03	1.58	2.94E+02	0.83	3.68E−01	8.24
Rat42 (high)	1.33E−14	11.86	8.83E−03	3.29	1.28E−14	11.86
MGH09 (high)	1.23E−05	9.76	2.97E−07	2.99	1.10E−19	11.6
Rat43 (high)	3.49E+01	5.66	5.19E+00	3.2	7.46E−12	11.38
Eckerle4 (high)	6.77E−03	10.24	9.51E−18	10.73	4.38E−19	10.73
MGH10 (high)	1.40E+02	3.43	7.84E+03	−1.63	4.10E−11	11.04

The goodness of the results of the proposed algorithms was estimated by the number of duplicated digits when compared to the certified results provided in [14], which were found using iterative deterministic algorithms (Levenberg-

Table 2. Parameter values obtained with ABC-PSO.

BASE (D, n) $[\lambda]$	Certified value	"ABC-PSO value"	$\lambda(\beta)$
Lanczos3 (6,24) [10.55]	0.086816415	0.086816349	6.12
	0.954981015	0.954980646	6.41
	s 0.844007775	0.844007612	6.72
	2.951595183	2.951594765	6.85
	1.58256859	1.582568818	6.84
	4.986356508	4.986356373	7.57
			6.75
Chwirut2 (3,54) [11.21]	0.166576665	0.166576664	8.01
	0.005165329	0.005165329	8.47
	0.012150007	0.012150007	8.32
			8.27
Chwirut1 (3,214) [11.41]	0.190278184	0.190278183	8.45
	0.0061314	0.0061314	9.44
	0.010530908	0.010530908	8.92
			8.94
Gauss1 (8,25)[11.59]	98.77821087	98.77821118	8.5
	0.010497277	0.010497277	8.45
	100.4899063	100.4899061	8.59
	67.48111128	67.4811113	9.47
	23.12977336	23.12977336	9.81
	71.994503	71.99450348	8.18
	178.9980502	178.9980503	9.3
	18.38938903	18.38938896	8.42
			8.84
Gauss2 (8,250)[10.6]	99.01832841	99.01832832	9.04
	0.010994945	0.010994945	8.33
	101.8802253	101.8802251	8.71
	107.0309552	107.0309552	10.48
	23.57858403	23.57858398	8.64
	72.04558947	72.04558916	8.37
	153.2701019	153.2701019	10.2
	19.52597264	19.52597267	8.75
			9.07

(*continued*)

Table 2. (*continued*)

BASE (D,n) $[\lambda]$	Certified value	"ABC-PSO value"	$\lambda(\beta)$
Kirby2 (5,151) [11.63]	1.674506306300E+00	1.674506332787E+00	7.8
	−1.392739786700E−01	−1.392739811356E−01	7.75
	2.596118119100E−03	2.596118146181E−03	7.98
	−1.724181187000E−03	−1.724181157276E−03	7.76
	2.166480257800E−05	2.166480272612E−05	8.17
			7.89
Hahn1 (7,236) [11.01]	1.077635173300E+00	1.077641980726E+00	5.2
	−1.226929692100E−01	−1.226935762542E−01	5.31
	4.086375061000E−03	4.086388725818E−03	5.48
	−1.426266251400E−06	−1.426282719575E−06	4.94
	−5.760994090100E−03	−5.760984024115E−03	5.76
	2.405373550300E−04	2.405379696874E−04	5.59
	−1.231445019900E−07	−1.231453051843E−07	5.19
			5.35
Nelson (3,128) [10.92]	2.590683602100E+00	2.590683602005E+00	10.44
	5.617771702600E−09	5.617771697533E−09	9.04
	−5.770101317400E−02	−5.770101318075E−02	9.93
			9.80
MGH17(5,33) [12.55]	3.754100521100E−01	3.754100393965E−01	7.47
	1.935846912700E+00	1.935846308394E+00	6.51
	−1.464687136600E+00	−1.464686522256E+00	6.38
	1.286753464000E−02	1.286753311826E−02	6.93
	2.212269966200E−02	2.212270166994E−02	7.04
			6.87

Maquardt and Gauss-Newton). The number of duplicate digits, denoted by λ, can be calculated via the *log* relative error [13], using the following expression:

$$\lambda = \begin{cases} 0 & \text{si } \frac{|w-c|}{|c|} \geq 1, \\ 1 & \text{si } \frac{|w-c|}{|c|} < 1 \times 10^{-11}, \\ -log_{10}(\frac{|w-c|}{|c|}) & \text{in other case.} \end{cases}$$

where $c \neq 0$ denotes the certified value and w denotes the value estimated by the proposed algorithm. According to [17], for the database given in [14], except for the case where the certified value is essentially zero, a good procedure for non-linear least squares allows duplicate at least 4 digits of the certified values. This paper presents the results considering the number of duplicate digits, denoted

Table 3. Parameters obtained from the best value achieved by ABC-PSO.

BASE (D, n) $[\lambda]$	Certified value	"ABC-PSO value"	$\lambda(\beta)$
Gauss3 (8,250) [10.98]	9.894036897000E+01	9.894036899152E+01	9.66
	1.094587933500E−02	1.094587933651E−02	9.86
	1.006955307800E+02	1.006955308137E+02	9.48
	1.116361945900E+02	1.116361946164E+02	9.63
	2.330050002900E+01	2.330050004869E+01	9.07
	7.370503141800E+01	7.370503138853E+01	9.4
	1.477616425100E+02	1.477616425402E+02	9.69
	1.966822123000E+01	1.966822120270E+01	8.86
			9.46
Misra1c (2,14) [11.08]	6.364272580900E+02	6.364272600415E+02	8.18
	2.081362725600E−04	2.081362718640E−04	8.51
			8.48
Rozman1 (4,25) [12.2]	2.019686639600E−01	2.019686618360E−01	7.98
	−6.195351625600E−06	−6.195351451332E−06	7.55
	1.204455670800E+03	1.204455683225E+03	7.99
	−1.813426953700E+02	−1.813426999517E+02	7.6
			7.78
Bennett5 (3,154) [2.68]	−5.235058043000E+02	−5.235061701934E+02	6.16
	4.673656464400E+01	4.673656618843E+01	7.48
	9.321848319300E−01	9.321848070204E−01	7.57
			7.07
Misra1a (2,14) [10.45]	2.389421291800E+02	2.389421291692E+02	10.35
	5.501564318100E−04	5.501564317648E−04	10.09
			10.22
ENZO (9,168) [11.43]	1.051074919300E+01	1.051074919969E+01	9.2
	3.076212808500E+00	3.076212806665E+00	9.22
	5.328013822700E−01	5.328013764909E−01	7.96
	4.431108870000E+01	4.431108855549E+01	8.49
	−1.623142858600E+00	−1.623142858277E+00	9.7
	5.255449375600E−01	5.255448689001E−01	6.88
	2.688761444000E+01	2.688761442506E+01	9.26
	2.123228848800E−01	2.123228612357E−01	6.95
	1.496687041800E+00	1.496687029378E+00	8.08
			8.42
Thurber (7,37) [11.23]	1.288139680000E+03	1.288139680308E+03	9.62
	1.491079253500E+03	1.491079258545E+03	8.47
	5.832383687700E+02	5.832383722019E+02	8.23
	7.541664429100E+01	7.541664497860E+01	8.04
	9.662950286400E−01	9.662950314096E−01	8.54
	3.979728579700E−01	3.979728598888E−01	8.32
	4.972729734900E−02	4.972729868648E−02	7.57
			8.4
Rat42(3,9) [11.86]	7.246223757600E+01	7.246223752371E+01	9.14
	2.618076840200E+00	2.618076841538E+00	9.29
	6.735920006600E−02	6.735920014515E−02	8.93
			9.12

(*continued*)

Table 3. (*continued*)

BASE (D, n) [λ]	Certified value	"ABC-PSO value"	$\lambda(\beta)$
MGH09 (4,11) [11.6]	1.928069345800E−01	1.928069349762E−01	8.69
	1.912823287300E−01	1.912823272940E−01	8.12
	1.230565069300E−01	1.230565106120E−01	7.52
	1.360623306800E−01	1.360623298635E−01	8.22
			8.14
Rat43(4,15) [11.38]	6.996415127000E+02	6.996415125217E+02	9.59
	5.277125302500E+00	5.277125283471E+00	8.44
	7.596293832900E−01	7.596293820090E−01	8.77
	1.279248385900E+00	1.279248379482E+00	8.3
			8.78
DanWood (2,6) [11.68]	0.768862262	0.768862264	8.6
	3.860405587	3.860405582	8.91
			8.76
Eckerle4 (3,35) [10.73]	1.554382718	1.554382719	9.35
	4.088832175	4.088832178	9.24
	451.5412184	451.5412184	11.32
			9.97
MGH10 (3,16) [11.1]	0.005609636	0.005609637	7.63
	6181.346346	6181.346326	8.49
	345.2236346	345.2236339	8.71
			8.28
Misra1b (2,14) [11.39]	337.9974616	337.9974643	8.1
	0.000390391	0.000390391	8.04
			8.07
Misra1d (2,14) [11.19]	437.3697075	437.3697086	8.63
	0.000302273	0.000302273	8.55
			8.59
BoxBod (2,6) [10.42]	213.8094089	213.8094087	8.98
	0.547237485	0.547237487	8.49
			8.74

by λ, which was obtained using the following expression:

$$\lambda = -log_{10}(\frac{|w - c|}{|c|})$$

Description of Table 1 is as follows: The first column provides the name of the database as well as its difficulty. Column 2 provides the standard deviation of the solutions obtained with PSO. The third column provides the average λ with respect to the obtained solutions with PSO. In the fourth and fifth columns are provided the correspondent results obtained with ABC and in columns 6 and 7 the results obtained with ABC-PSO.

In all cases the proposed ABC-PSO algorithm got an average value λ greater than or equal to 8.24. From Table 1 we see that in general, PSO finds better results for the sum of squares of the residue that ABC, but ABC is more robust than PSO in the sense that results have a smaller standard deviation. Using this information, we decide to design the ABC-PSO algorithm, that was applied to the same instances. As can be seen in Table 1 the proposed hybrid algorithm was able to find better solutions than those obtained by ABC and PSO.

In order to show a more detailed description of the performance of the proposed ABC-PSO algorithm, we include in Tables 2 and 3 the best solutions found. The first column provides the name of the database, the dimension (D), the number of data (n), and the best value achieved by ABC-PSO [λ]. The second column provides the certified values. In column 3 the best value achieved by ABC-PSO are presented. Finally column 4 provides the corresponding values of the parameter and the average for each database is provided in bold.

7   Conclusions

In this paper we proposed a hybrid ABC-PSO algorithm, combining two popular swarm intelligence heuristics, ABC and PSO, which finds estimated parameters of well known nonlinear regression problems. The results show that this algorithm found the global minimum in most tasks where gradient algorithm fails. The purpose of this study is to show that ABC-PSO can be used as an alternative solution tool.

According to [17] for the database given in [14], except for the case where the certified value is essentially zero, a good procedure for non-linear least squares allows duplicate at least 4 digits of the certified values. It was observed that the hybrid bioinspired method ABC-PSO provides very good results, since for all cases it gave a $\lambda > 8$ for the average values of the sum of squares obtained. This represents at least double digit accuracy with respect to solutions reported by other authors. In general, to find the values of the parameters in nonlinear regression problems, the use of ABC does not provide as good results as PSO. However, ABC provides solutions in more compact intervals. Moreover, PSO has the advantage that can leave suboptimal solutions regions easier than ABC. As can be seen in Table 1, the standard deviation obtained by ABC-PSO is significantly lower than those obtained by ABC and PSO, so the proposed hybrid is very robust.

In all cases the best value found by ABC-PSO, got at least one λ of 10 compared to the certified value of the residual sum of squares, and an average λ of 8.31, as can be seen in Tables 2 and 3.

We can suggest ABC-PSO algorithm approach as a tool for solving problems involving complex nonlinear relations, that is to say that the use of ABC-PSO is an alternative to find the values of the parameters that provides good results in nonlinear regression problems.

References

1. Cheng, S., Zhao, C., Wu, J., Shi, Y.: Particle swarm optimization in regression analysis: a case study. In: Tan, Y., Shi, Y., Mo, H. (eds.) ICSI 2013. LNCS, vol. 7928, pp. 55–63. Springer, Heidelberg (2013). doi:10.1007/978-3-642-38703-6_6

2. de-los-Cobos-Silva, S.G., Gutiérrez-Andrade, M.A., Rincón-García, E.A., Lara-Velázquez, P., Aguilar-Cornejo, M.: Estimación de parámetros de regresión no lineal mediante colonia de abejas artificiales. Revista de Matemática: Teoría y Aplicaciones **20**(1), 49–60 (2013)

3. de-los-Cobos-Silva, S.G., Gutiérrez-Andrade, M.A., Rincón-García, E.A., Lara-Velázquez, P., Aguilar-Cornejo, M.: Colonia de Abejas Artificiales y Optimización por Enjambre de Partículas para la Estimación de Parámetros de Regresión No Lineal. Revista de Matemática: Teoría y Aplicaciones **21**(1), 107–126 (2014)

4. de-los-Cobos-Silva, S.G., Terceño-Gómez, A., Gutiérrez-Andrade, M.A., Rincón-García, E.A., Lara-Velázquez, P., Aguilar-Cornejo, M.: Particle swarm optimization an alternative for parameter estimation in regression. Fuzzy Econ. Rev. **21**(1), 107–126 (2014)

5. Kapanoglu, M., Koc, I.O., Erdogmus, S.: Genetic algorithm in parameter estimation for nonlinear regression models: an experimental approach. J. Stat. Comput. Simul. **77**(10), 851–867 (2007)

6. Karaboga, D.: An idea based on honey bee swarm for numerical optimization. Technical report, Erciyes University, Engineering Faculty, Computer Engineering Department (2005)

7. Karaboga, D., Akay, B.: Artificial bee colony (ABC) algorithm on training artificial neural networks. In: Proceedings of 15th IEEE Signal Processing and Communications Applications (2007)

8. Karaboga, D., Akay, B.: A comparative study of artificial bee colony algorithm. Appl. Math. Comput. **214**, 108–132 (2009)

9. Karaboga, D., Osturk, C.: Fuzzy clustering with artificial bee colony algorithm. Sci. Res. Essays **5**(14), 1899–1902 (2010)

10. Kennedy, J., Eberhart, R.C., Shi, Y.: Swarm Intelligence. Morgan Kaufmann, San Francisco (2001)

11. Kennedy, J., Eberhart, R.C.: Intelligent Swarm Systems. Academic Press, New York (2000)

12. Kriv, I., Tvrdík, J., Krepec, R.: Stochastic algorithms in nonlinear regression. Comput. Stat. Data Anal. **33**, 277–290 (2000)

13. McCullough, B.D., Wilson, B.: On the accuracy of statistical procedures in Microsoft Excel 2003. Comput. Stat. Data Anal. **49**, 1244–1252 (2005)

14. National Institute of Standards and Technology. http://www.itl.nist.gov/div898/strd/index.html

15. Osturk, C., Karaboga, D.: Classifications by neural networks and clustering with artificial bee colony (ABC) algorithm. In: Proceedings of 6th International Symposium on Intelligent and Manufacturing Systems, Features, Strategies and Innovation (2008)

16. Schwaab, M., Biscaia, E.C., Monteiro, J.L., Pinto, J.C.: Nonlinear parameter estimation through particle swarm optimization. Chem. Eng. Sci. **63**, 1542–1552 (2008)

17. Tvrdík, J., Kriv, I.: Comparison of algorithms for nonlinear regression estimates. In: Antoch, J. (ed.) COMSTAT, pp. 1917–1924. Physica-Verlag, New York (2004)

18. Tvrdík, J.: Adaptation in differential evolution: a numerical comparison. Appl. Soft Comput. **9**(3), 1149–1155 (2009)

19. Zilinskas, A., Zilinskas, J.: Interval arithmetic based optimization in nonlinear regression. Informatica **21**(1), 149–158 (2010)

Data Mining

Data Mining in EEG Wave Trains in Early Stages of Parkinson's Disease

Olga S. Sushkova[1(✉)], Alexei A. Morozov[1,2], and Alexandra V. Gabova[3]

[1] Kotel'nikov Institute of Radio Engineering and Electronics of RAS,
Mokhovaya 11-7, Moscow 125009, Russia
o.sushkova@mail.ru, morozov@cplire.ru
[2] Moscow State University of Psychology and Education,
Sretenka 29, Moscow 107045, Russia
[3] Institute of Higher Nervous Activity and Neurophysiology of RAS,
Butlerova 5A, Moscow 117485, Russia

Abstract. A method of analysis and visualization of electroencephalograms (EEG) based on wave trains is developed. In this paper, we use the "wave train" term to denote a signal localized in time, frequency, and space. The wave train is a typical pattern in a background EEG and detecting/analyzing such signals gives useful information about the brain activity. Alpha spindles, beta spindles, and sleep spindles are the best known examples of the wave trains in EEG. The preliminary results of the research give evidence that EEG analysis and visualization method based on the wave trains is useful for looking for group statistical regularities in early stages of Parkinson's disease and searching EEG features that are prospective for early stages of Parkinson's disease diagnostics. The novelty of this work is in developing a new method to search parameters of wave trains useful for evaluating the group statistical regularities in EEG data.

1 Introduction

The method of analysis of electroencephalograms (EEG) based on wave trains that was described in [1] was extended and visualization of the data was added. In physics, a wave train (or a wave packet) is a short "burst" or "envelope" of localized wave action that travels as a unit. We use the "wave train" term to denote a signal localized in time, frequency, and space. The wave train is a typical pattern in a background EEG and detecting/analyzing such signals gives useful information about the brain electrical activity. Alpha spindles, beta spindles, and sleep spindles are the best known examples of the wave trains in EEG. Several methods based on Fourier spectra, wavelets, autoregressive models, adaptive filtering, etc. have been developed for detecting and analyzing these EEG patterns (see surveys in [2,3]).

The idea of the new method of EEG analysis consists of that the wave trains in a wide frequency band from 2 Hz to 30 Hz are detected and analyzed using ROC curves. The wave trains are detected as local maxima in a wavelet spectrogram of EEG record. Various attributes of these wave trains are computed.

© Springer International Publishing AG 2017
O. Pichardo-Lagunas and S. Miranda-Jiménez (Eds.): MICAI 2016, Part II, LNAI 10062, pp. 403–412, 2017.
DOI: 10.1007/978-3-319-62428-0_32

Then visualization and statistical analysis on the base of these attributes are implemented. In the paper [1], it was demonstrated that the investigation of wave train attributes reveals the new statistically significant regularities in a group of de novo Parkinson's disease patients. Namely, the Mann-Whitney statistical test indicates a significant decrease of the quantity of the wave trains in the C3 and C4 electrodes in the beta frequency range. In this paper, the problem of searching such wave train features that are appropriate for recognition/diagnosis of early stages of Parkinson's disease on the base of EEG data is considered. Thus, the main difference between this paper and the previous work [1] is in that earlier we have analyzed the wave train features in standard theta, alpha, beta, and gamma frequency ranges and in this paper we also determine frequency ranges that are prospective for the recognition/diagnosis using ROC curves.

The idea of the wave trains in EEG is described in Sect. 2. In the Sect. 3, the experimental setting used for the verification of the wave train analysis method is considered. The data mining method is introduced in Sect. 4. Examples of data visualization are considered in Sect. 5.

2   The Idea of the Wave Trains in EEG

Let M be a local maximum in a wavelet spectrogram (see Fig. 1). We estimate the full width at half maximum (FWHM) of M in the time plane $FWHM_{TIME}$ and in the frequency plane $FWHM_{FREQUENCY}$. Then we check whether there are no values in the rectangle area

$$FWHM_{TIME} \times FWHM_{FREQUENCY}$$

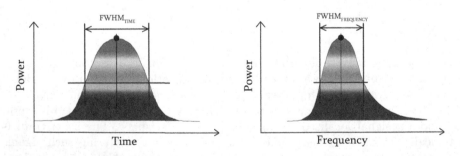

Fig. 1. An example of a spectrogram of a wave train in a time-frequency domain. The diagram on the left shows the spectrogram of the signal in the time plane. The abscissa indicates a time and the ordinate indicates a power. The diagram on the right shows the spectrogram of the signal in the frequency plane. The abscissa indicates a frequency and the ordinate indicates a power.

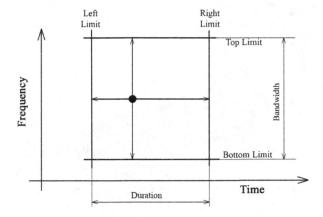

Fig. 2. Time and frequency bounds of the M wave train in the wavelet spectrogram. The abscissa indicates the time and the ordinate indicates the frequency.

that are bigger than the M value (see Fig. 2). We consider M as a case of a wave train if $FWHM_{TIME}$ of M is greater or equal to the T_D threshold (see Fig. 1). The T_D threshold is a function of the central frequency f of the maximum M:

$$FWHM_{TIME} \geq T_D = N_P/f,$$

where N_P is a constant given by an expert. In this paper, we apply the value: $N_P = 2$.

3   The Experimental Setting

In the paper, the analysis and visualization method is considered by an example of real data acquired in a neurophysiological examination. Let us consider a set of wave trains detected in a group of de novo Parkinson's disease patients and a healthy volunteers group (see Fig. 3). The group of patients includes 17 patients with right-hand tremor and 11 patients with left-hand tremor in the first stage of Parkinson's disease without Parkinson's disease treatment. The group of healthy volunteers includes 15 people.

The ages of patients were from 38 to 71 years old; the mean age was 60 years old. The ages of healthy volunteers were from 48 to 81 years old; the mean age was 58 years old. No statistically significant differences between the patients' ages and the volunteers' ages were detected. The amount of male patients was 11; the amount of female ones was 17. The amount of male healthy volunteers was 5; the amount of female ones was 10. The size of the groups is typical for a neurophysiological examination. It is difficult to collect more patients without any treatment in the early stage of Parkinson's disease.

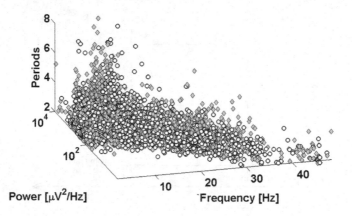

Fig. 3. The set of wave trains detected in the group of de novo Parkinson's disease and the healthy volunteers group. The abscissa indicates frequencies of the wave trains. The ordinate indicates squared amplitudes of the wave trains in a logarithmic scale. The applicate indicates durations of the wave trains. The patients are indicated by dark red diamonds and the healthy volunteers are indicated by light circles. The patients with right-hand tremor, background EEG, channel C4. (Color figure online)

The patients were diagnosed according to the standard Hoehn and Yahr scale. All patients and volunteers were right-handed. A standard 10×20 EEG acquisition schema was used. A background EEG was recorded in standard condition. Examined person sat in an armchair relaxing with arms disposing on the armrests and fingers dangling freely from the ends of armrests. Besides, EEG was recorded in a non-standard condition [4]. Namely, a subject was instructed to keep a special pose with the muscle tension that provokes a tremor: the arms were placed on armrests of the chair; the palms were straightened, placed in a vertical plane, and stretched a bit; the feet were stretched a bit and touched the floor by the heels only. The eyes were closed during the recordings. A 41-channel digital EEG system Neuron-Spectrum-5 (Neurosoft Ltd.) was used for the data acquisition. The sampling rate was 500 Hz. The 0.5 Hz high-pass filter and the 50 Hz supply-line filter were used. Three EEG records were acquired for every subject with interruptions for a rest and a relaxation. The duration of every record was about 2 min. Then the best of three records was selected that contains a minimal number of artifacts. The record was analyzed as is, without selection of areas in the signal.

Special software was developed for analyzing the data. The analysis includes the following EEG pre-processing operations:

1. The Huber's X84 method [5] for outlier rejection was used for removing EEG artifacts.
2. A set of notch filters was applied for removing a power-line noise at 50, 100, 150, and 200 Hz.

3. The eight order 2–240 Hz band pass Butterworth filter was applied. Signals were filtered in the forward and reverse directions to eliminate a phase distortion.
4. Signals were decimated with the decimation factor 4.

The spectrograms were created using the complex Morlet wavelet:

$$\Psi(x) = \frac{1}{\sqrt{\pi F_b}} exp\left(2i\pi F_c x\right) exp\left(-\frac{x^2}{F_b}\right)$$

In this paper, F_b equals 1 and F_c equals 1. The frequency step in the spectrograms equals 0.1 Hz.

In this paper, the C3 and C4 electrodes are considered only, because these electrodes approximately correspond to the motor cortex areas and are situated in the scalp area that produces a minimal number of muscle artifacts.

4   The Data Mining Method

Let $MinFreq$, $MaxFreq$ are frequency bounds of 3D area S (a parallelepiped S) in the space of the wave trains. Let $MinPower$, $MaxPower$ are power bounds of the area S; $MinDurat$, $MaxDurat$ are duration bounds of the area S; and $MinBandwidth$, $MaxBandwidth$ are bandwidth bounds of the area S. One can calculate a number of wave trains per second located in the area S in every individual patient and healthy volunteer and create histograms of the quantity of the wave trains per second (see an example in Fig. 4). A statistical difference between the diagrams may indicate that the area S contains wave trains that are typical for Parkinson's disease, but not for the control group, or vice versa. A second interesting issue is whether one can specify a threshold (a limit of the number of the wave trains in the area S) that separates adequately the histograms, because the presence of such threshold means that the quantity of the wave trains in the area S may be used for the clinical diagnosis of Parkinson's disease. For instance, there is a strong statistical difference between the histograms in the Fig. 4 (the Mann-Whitney test, $p < 0.009$). The diagram demonstrates that a typical number of the wave trains in the control group is about 0.13 per second in the given frequency band. At the same time, a typical number of the wave trains in the patients is about 0.06.

Let us consider a threshold Q of the wave trains quantity in the histograms. Let us utilize this threshold as an indicator of Parkinson's disease, that is, a quantity of the wave trains per second greater than Q in a person N in the given area S will indicate that the person N is probably ill. Thus, the True Positive Rate (TPR) indicates the number of the patients that were diagnosed properly using the threshold Q; and the False Positive Rate (FPR) indicates the number of the controls that were mistakenly diagnosed as Parkinson's patients. A ROC

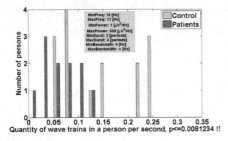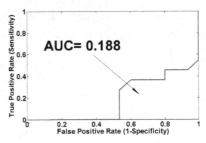

Fig. 4. On the left: histograms of the quantity of the wave trains per second in the patients and the control group. Left hand tremor patients, channel C3. The wave trains are considered in a parallelepiped S bounded by the following limits: a frequency range is 10–12 Hz, a power range is 1–500 $\mu V^2/Hz$, the duration range is 2–4 periods. The patient histogram is indicated by the dark magenta color; and the control histogram is indicated by the light cyan color. On the right: a ROC curve based on the histograms. The abscissa indicates the False Positive Rate. The ordinate indicates the True Positive Rate. The area under the ROC curve (AUC) indicates whether the area S is applicable for separation of the patients and the control group. $AUC < 0.5$ indicates that the wave trains quantity is greater in the control group than in the patients. (Color figure online)

curve can be created based on the histograms of the wave trains quantity, that is, a diagram that indicates a relation between the TPR and FPR for various values Q (see Fig. 4). The area under the ROC curve (AUC) is a standard indicator of the quality of the ROC curve; big values of AUC (that are much more than 0.5) and small values of AUC (that are much less than 0.5) indicate that the given area S may be prospective for making clinical diagnosis.

Thus, in mathematical terms, the goal of our investigation is searching such areas in the multidimensional space of the wave trains, where AUC differs sufficiently from 0.5 and is approached to 1 or to 0. $AUC > 0.5$ indicates that the wave trains quantity is greater in the patients than in the controls. Similarly, $AUC < 0.5$ indicates that the wave trains quantity is greater in the control group. An exhaustive search of the values $MinFreq$, $MaxFreq$, $MinPower$, $MaxPower$, $MinDurat$, $MaxDurat$, $MinBandwidth$, and $MaxBandwidth$ can be implemented to investigate the multidimensional space, but we prefer an accurate consideration of different slices of the space using various 2D and 3D diagrams not to miss any interesting regularities in the space of the wave trains. Several examples of this analysis are considered below.

Let us compute AUC values for various frequency ranges. In Fig. 5, the functional dependence of AUC is shown, where the arguments of the function are the $MinFreq$ and $MaxFreq$ bounds. The frequency values varied from 2 to 25 Hz (with the 0.5 Hz step); the $MinPower$, $MaxPower$, $MinDurat$, $MaxDurat$, $MinBandwidth$, and $MaxBandwidth$ were constant: $MinPower = 1$, $MaxPower = \infty$, $MinDurat = 0$, $MaxDurat = \infty$, $MinBandwidth = 0$,

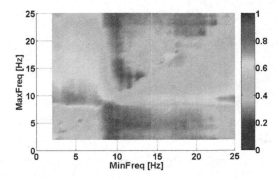

Fig. 5. A diagram of AUC values calculated for various frequency bands. In the upper left triangle of the diagram: the abscissa is the lower bound of the frequency band and the ordinate is the upper bound of the frequency band. In the lower right triangle of the diagram: the abscissa is the upper bound of the excluded frequency band and the ordinate is the lower bound of the excluded band. The frequency varied from 2 to 25 Hz with the 0.5 Hz step. The background EEG was analyzed, right hand tremor patients, the C3 electrode. (Color figure online)

$MaxBandwidth = \infty$. The upper left triangle of the diagram indicates the values of AUC corresponding to the $MinFreq \ldots MaxFreq$ frequency range. The lower right triangle of the diagram indicates the AUC values corresponding to the total frequency band $2 \ldots 25$ Hz except the $MaxFreq \ldots MinFreq$ band. Note that in the lower right triangle of the diagram the $MinFreq$ indicates the upper limit (but not the lower) of the excepted frequency band and the $MaxFreq$ indicates the lower bound of the excepted values. The diagram in Fig. 5 reveals three interesting frequency ranges that may be prospective for research. The first range is mu (a blue region, the $10.5 \ldots 13.5$ Hz frequency band approximately), the second is mu too (a red region, the $6 \ldots 9.5$ Hz frequency band approximately), and the third range is beta (a dark blue region, $18 \ldots 24$ Hz frequency band approximately). We suppose that the first and second regions in the diagram give a visual evidence for a shift of the mu rhythm to the lower frequency areas. The third region in the diagram is a visual confirmation of the regularity (a significant decrease of the wave train number in the beta band) discovered by a group statistical analysis and reported in [1]. Moreover, a "good" values $AUC = 0.22$ and $AUC = 0.75$ in the first and second colored spots indicate that the mu frequency range may be prospective for making clinical diagnostic.

5   Examples of Data Visualization

Let us consider several examples of AUC diagrams. In Fig. 6, diagrams for left hand tremor patients (the left column) and right hand tremor patients (the right column) are demonstrated. The first row corresponds to the C3 electrode and the

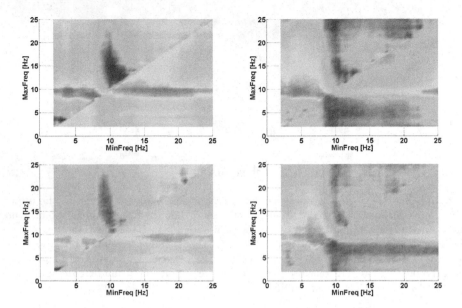

Fig. 6. Diagrams of AUC values calculated for various frequency bands. In the left column: left hand tremor patients; in the right column: right hand tremor patients. The first row corresponds to the C3 electrode and the second row corresponds to the C4 electrode. (Color figure online)

second row corresponds to the C4 electrode. One can see a blue area $10 \ldots 11\,\mathrm{Hz}$ in all the diagrams. The corresponding red areas exist in all the diagrams too. Thus, similar regularities are presented in both C3 and C4 electrodes, but the diagrams corresponding to the left tremor patients and the right tremor patients differ more than the diagrams corresponding to the C3 and C4 electrodes. This is evidence than the compensatory mechanisms in the cortex in these two groups of patients are not equal.

Let us compare these AUC diagrams corresponding to the background EEG with diagrams corresponding to the EEG records created in the special pose that provokes tremor. In the Fig. 7, the left column corresponds to the background EEG and the right column corresponds to the special pose EEG. Only the right tremor patient diagrams are demonstrated in both columns. The first row corresponds to the C3 electrode and the second row corresponds to the C4 electrode. Note that in the special pose the mu rhythm colored spots are less pronounced. This is the evidence that we observe a shift of the mu rhythm, but not of the alpha rhythm in the diagrams, because the special pose may suppress the mu rhythm. Note that the blue spot in the beta frequency range is more pronounced in the special pose diagrams. Probably the special pose increases the regularity [1] in the beta frequency range.

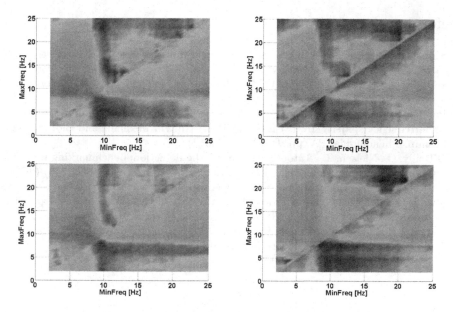

Fig. 7. Diagrams of AUC values calculated for various frequency bands. In the left column: background EEG records; in the right column: the special pose records. Only the right hand tremor patients are analyzed. The first row corresponds to the C3 electrode and the second row corresponds to the C4 electrode.

6   Conclusions

The method of a brain electrical activity investigation based on the EEG wave train analysis and visualization is developed. The preliminary results of the research give evidence that EEG analysis method based on the wave trains is prospective for:

- Looking for group statistical regularities in the early stages of Parkinson's disease that gives a basic knowledge about the disease and compensatory mechanisms in the cortex;
- Searching EEG features that are prospective for the early stages of Parkinson's disease diagnostics.

Acknowledgments. Authors are grateful to Alexei V. Karabanov for selection and medical examination of the patients, to Galina D. Kuznetsova and Alexander F. Polupanov for co-operation and a help in the research, and Yuriy V. Obukhov for a help in the statement of the problem. We acknowledge a partial financial support from the Russian Foundation for Basic Research, grants 16-37-00426 and 15-07-07846.

References

1. Sushkova, O., Morozov, A., Gabova, A.: A method of analysis of EEG wave trains in early stages of Parkinson's disease. In: International Conference on Bioinformatics and Systems Biology (BSB-2016), Allahabad, India, Indian Institute of Information Technology (2016)
2. Parekh, A., Selesnick, I., Rapoport, D., Ayappa, I.: Sleep spindle detection using time-frequency sparsity. In: IEEE Signal Processing in Medicine and Biology Symposium, Philadelphia, PA, pp. 1–6. IEEE (2014)
3. O'Reilly, C., Nielsen, T.: Automatic sleep spindle detection: benchmarking with fine temporal resolution using open science tools. Front. Hum. Neurosci. 9(353) (2015)
4. Andreeva, Y., Khutorskaya, O.: EMGs spectral analysis method for the objective diagnosis of different clinical forms of Parkinson's disease. J. Electromyogr. Clin. Neurophysiol. 36, 187–192 (1996)
5. Hampel, F.R., Ronchetti, E.M., Rousseeuw, P.J., Stahel, W.A.: Robust Statistics: The Approach Based on Influence Functions. Wiley, New York (1986)

Data Mining in the Analysis
of Ocean-Atmosphere Dynamics in Colombia's
Central Caribbean Ocean

Fran Ernesto Romero Alvarez[1(✉)] and Oswaldo E. Vélez-Langs[1,2]

[1] Engineering Department, Jorge Tadeo Lozano University,
Bogotá D.C, Colombia
{frane.romeroa,oswaldoe.velezl}@utadeo.edu.co
[2] Facultad de Ingeniería, Universidad de Córdoba, Montería, Colombia

Abstract. This document presents a proposal for the development of an ocean-atmosphere dynamic predictive model for the central Caribbean region of Colombia. The proposal is based on temporary data mining techniques and includes the development of a software tool that complements the model. The software tool uses Weka API to implement several algorithms, such as data mining association rules, decision trees, classifiers, artificial neural networks and time series forecasting. The research results demonstrate the predictive power and advantages of using temporary Data Mining, rather than the conventional methods used in climate modeling.

1 Introduction

Communities in the Caribbean region of Colombia must take measures to manage, control and safeguard socio-economic activities in the region. These activities largely depend on climatic conditions that result from, among other factors, ocean-atmosphere coupling, which determines evaporation, precipitation and ocean circulation, as well as physical, chemical and biological processes on the ocean surface. Some factors that make climate dynamics in this region very complex are: the Sierra Nevada de Santa Marta - SNSM, which alters and models wind fields in this region of the Caribbean; a narrow continental shelf; inland water from the Ciénaga Grande de Santa Marta, the Magdalena River and rivers of the SNSM which alter the heat load of the central Caribbean area of Colombia (Franco Herrera and Vélez Langs [1]); fluctuations in the Intertropical Convergence Zone; and the side effects of El Niño-Niña events. In order to make a forecast, information from the two components – atmosphere and ocean – are required.

Increased temperature and changes in the duration of the rainy or dry seasons have already demonstrated their potential effects on tropical marine and land ecosystems and have generated disturbances and irreversible impacts. Various research centers around the world have reported that cold oceans, which regulate and naturally control global climate, due to their capacity to absorb CO_2, are already saturated with this gas and are consequently losing their capacity to absorb any more of it. Thus, it remains in the atmosphere contributing to global warming. The effect is significant in tropical areas,

© Springer International Publishing AG 2017
O. Pichardo-Lagunas and S. Miranda-Jiménez (Eds.): MICAI 2016, Part II, LNAI 10062, pp. 413–424, 2017.
DOI: 10.1007/978-3-319-62428-0_33

where more light radiation is absorbed, and higher air temperature affects wind and air patterns and precipitation and evaporation rates, all of which have a serious impact on oceanographic dynamics.

Creating scientific tools to establish predictive models for climate dynamics in the continental shelf of the Colombian Caribbean is a priority. This is vital in order to properly develop common scientific, productive and cultural activities in this coastal area. In addition, the generation of rigorous scientific information for this global problem can help others reach reliable and consistent conclusions that may be truly useful in making local and global decisions.

This paper presents a scientific software tool that uses data mining to generate climate models applicable in the Caribbean region of Colombia. The database was established with information collected at a Davis Vantage Pro2 weather station located in Santa Marta city, since November 2009. This station generates atmospheric daily and monthly information from data sampled every 30 min.

Section 2 of this paper summarizes survey papers on various climate modeling investigations, especially those related to ocean-atmosphere dynamics and techniques developed for the study. Section 3 describes the methodologies used to collect data and the pre-processing activities for each one. Section 4 covers the scientific software tool used for data mining analysis as well as the main results from applying various models. The most relevant conclusions from the study are presented in Sect. 5.

2 Survey Papers

International organizations such as the IPCC (Intergovernmental Panel on Climate Change), which recently received Nobel Peace Prize, as well as national environmental organizations such as the Institute of Hydrology, Meteorology and Environmental Studies of Colombia (IDEAM), have agreed that climate change is intensifying and that its effects have been observed throughout this century. Increased temperature and changes in the duration of rainy and dry seasons show the potential effects they could have on tropical marine and terrestrial ecosystems and have already generated disturbances and irreversible impacts (i.e. water softening, increased siltation and coral choking, fish species migration). Since 2007 the University of East Anglia in the UK, CSIRO (Commonwealth Scientific and Industrial Research Organization) in Australia, and the Max Planck Institute in Germany have been reporting that cold oceans, which regulate and control global climate due to their ability to absorb CO_2, are already saturated with this gas and are consequently losing their potential to absorb any more of it (Environment News Service, 2007). Thus, it remains in the atmosphere accentuating global warming. In tropical areas, the effect is particularly important, since more light irradiation is absorbed, the increased air temperature affects the wind flow patterns as well as precipitation and evaporation rates, and this impacts on oceanographic dynamics, due to the fact that in these areas, energy comes from physical processes and not chemical ones. The Caribbean region of Colombia is not an exception to this situation.

Moreover, different contributions are found in literature, where predictive models are developed using meteorological and/or oceanographic data. Weather Data Mining finds patterns hidden in large volumes of meteorological data that can be transformed into usable knowledge. Using Data Mining processes for climate data is well documented. This focuses on Kalyankar and Alaspurkar clustering methods [4], where certain patterns can be found in large volumes of climate data and are extracted. This knowledge is useful to classify and predict weather conditions. An example of this is Data Mining Meteo (DMM) project which researches parametric models and detection methods, as well as predicts certain meteorological phenomena such as fog and low cloud cover (Bartok et al. [7]). In the same vein, Nandagopal et al. (2010) focus on the use of association rules. The study extends the approach of association rules by going beyond the intra-transaction approach to N-dimensional inter-transactions and presents a modified version of apriori algorithms to find these inter-transactional rules.

Meanwhile, the approach used by Kohail and Et-Halees [8] tries to extract useful knowledge of historical climate data (from 1985 to 1997) collected in the Gaza Strip. There, pre-processing is initially performed, to analyze outliers, and finally apply techniques related to typecasting, prediction, classification and association rules. Similar strategies are used in oceanography, where climate prediction indexes can also be included, such as those performed by Steinbach et al. (2002), who used the so-called "ocean climate indices" (OCIs) to try to predict the effect oceans have on the planet's weather. These time series OCIs summarize behavior of certain areas. The methodology attempts to overcome certain traditional drawbacks associated with OCI discoveries based on typecasting oceanic regions with homogeneous behavior.

3 Methodology

Data to begin the analysis were received in spreadsheets containing atmospheric information gathered from 2009 to 2014 using Vantage Pro2 equipment.

3.1 Data Pre-processing

To start data mining activities, data was pre-processed and a preliminary statistical approximation was established. Due to the effects of solar radiation, the 24-h day was divided into three groups: morning 6 a.m.–12:00 a.m., afternoon 12:00 p.m.–6:00 p.m., and night 6:00 p.m.–6:00 a.m. Considering the sun's influence during these different variables, these averages were determined: morning 6 a.m.–12:00 a.m., afternoon 12:00 p.m.–6:00 p.m. and night 6:00 p.m.–6:00 a.m. Figure 1 shows the time series that corresponds to the temperature variable. Three different ranges can be observed which correspond to morning, afternoon and evening.

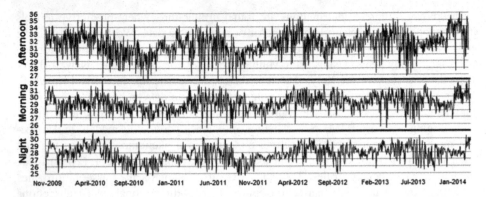

Fig. 1. Time series for the temperature variable

3.2   Class Balance

The problem of data imbalance results from the predominance of certain values in data as well as the lack or absence of other values, which makes it difficult to extract information. Figure 2 shows the frequency distribution of each one of the variables in the variable associated with rain rate. As you can see, there is a problem of unbalanced classes which needs to be resolved before proceeding with the analysis.

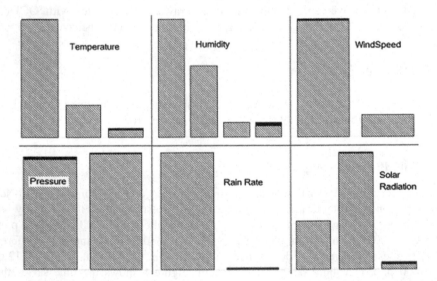

Fig. 2. Variable distribution (in crossed lines) compared with RAIN (in solid black). The imbalance problem of the latter is clearly seen in this variable.

There are different strategies to solve the problem of imbalanced classes. An often used algorithm, in this case, is Synthetic Minority Over Sampling Technique - *SMOTE*, which generates new instances of the minority class by interpolating the values of

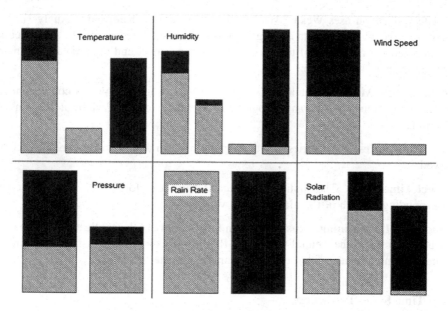

Fig. 3. Distribution of variables (in crossed lines) corresponding to the RAIN (in solid black) variable after class balance was performed.

minority instances that are closest to a given instance. Figure 3 shows the final result of applying the *SMOTE* algorithm to solve the problem of class imbalance.

4   Implementing a Data Mining Tool

To streamline visualization tasks, analysis, and data mining, an application in Java with MySQL as a database engine and Weka as a data mining library was developed. The application generates different data sets from the database for subsequent mining and analysis. Figure 4 shows the overall design of the application.

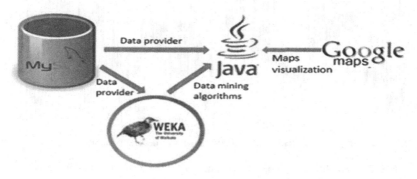

Fig. 4. Overall design of the application.

The application uses Weka - Waikato Environment for Knowledge Analysis as a library to execute various data mining algorithms. This is an ideal tool to use, since it has an extensive collection of techniques to process, model and mine data. The main characteristics of the tool are:

Use of Google Maps. This allows Google Maps to be used, which is convenient to quickly and simply access any geographic reference to the Caribbean Region of Colombia.

View Time Series. Time series that correspond to each main climate variable can be viewed.

Project Time Series. The application forecasts and views forecasts in the time series corresponding to each of the main climate variables.

Temporary Data Mining. This is the main functionality of the application, where rain can be predicted in the Central Caribbean Region of Colombia by using data mining techniques and a database that measures various climate variables.

4.1   Time Series Predictions

There are several strategies for forecasting climate time series: classical statistical methods, such as Autoregressive Integrated Moving Averages (ARIMA), Frequency Domain Analysis, and Harmonic Analysis, among others (Javier Aguado-Rodriguez et al. [3]).

Meanwhile, Weka uses learning-based algorithms for time series forecasting. First, it performs a data transformation that encodes dependence time while adding new variables. Later, multiple linear regression algorithms, and even nonlinear regression algorithms to forecast the time series are applied (Damle [9]). Figure 5 shows the forecast of the humidity variable classified with a Gaussian process.

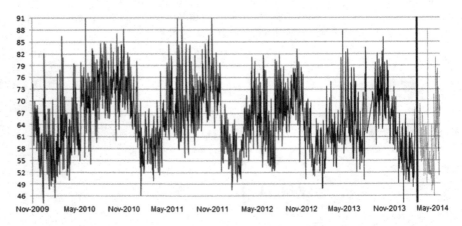

Fig. 5. Humidity prediction (dotted line) classified using a Gaussian process

4.2   Association Rules

Association rules are a data mining strategy used to discover common events that occur within a data set. Occurrences, or records, within the data set correspond to attribute/value type pairs and an association rule relates a particular conclusion with a set of conditions in a sentence like "If <Background> Then <Result>." This is not necessarily true in all cases, but it meets minimum acceptability metrics. Since algorithms used to find association rules can produce an abundance of rules, the focus is on so-called "interesting rules," which must meet certain precision and confidence standards and must apply to a sufficiently large number of instances – support (Petelin et al. [6]).

To find "interesting" association rules, or those that meet minimum confidence-support, a foundation of climate variables is determined, such as temperature, humidity, pressure, wind and solar radiation. From these, other variables such as evapotranspiration, which correspond to a linear combination of the first ones, are established. The next step is to bring the numeric value of each variable to discrete values, for which two strategies are applied: the range of each variable is partitioned in n equal-length intervals, or the range is partitioned into n subintervals according to distribution frequency. The partition based on frequencies only found rules with confidence values below 1%, so this strategy was discarded. Meanwhile, the partition based on intervals of equal length resulted in some interesting rules to predict the occurrence of rain, some of which are shown in Table 1. As can be seen, for values higher than 24 °C and 80% humidity and pressure greater than 1010, there is more than 75% probability of rainfall.

Table 1. Association rules found. Only the antecedent of each rule is listed, and in each case the consequent is {Rain = RAIN}

Antecedent	Sup	Conf
{Temp = [24.2,27.4), Hum = [80.2,92.8], Press = [1010,1013), SolarRad = [0,200)}	3.96%	76.17%
{Temp = [24.2,27.4), Hum = [80.2,92.8], Wind = [0.00,1.20), Press = [1010,1013), SolarRad = [0,200)}	3.90%	75.89%
{Temp = [24.2,27.4), Hum = [80.2,92.8], Pres = [1010,1013)}	4.40%	75.61%
{Temp = [24.2,27.4), Hum = [80.2,92.8], Wind = [0.00,1.20), Press = [1010,1013)}	4.34%	75.35%
{Temp = [24.2,27.4), Hum = [80.2,92.8], SolarRad = [0,200)}	5.62%	75.07%

4.3   Bayesian Classifiers

In its most general form, the problem of classifying consists of assigning a vector of observations $V = \{v_1, v_2, \ldots, v_N\}$ to one of the classes of a certain objective variable $C = \{c_1, c_2, \ldots, c_N\}$. The objective of a classifier is to minimize the total cost of errors produced in the assignment. Since the function of the set distribution $p(v_1, \ldots, v_N, c)$ is unknown, it can be estimated using a set of training examples, $D = \{(x^{(1)}, c^{(1)}), \ldots, (x^{(N)}, c^{(N)})\}$. Thus, learning can be seen as the process of finding the most probable hypothesis given a set of training examples D and apriori knowledge of the probability of each hypothesis.

A Bayesian network is a type of Bayesian classifier in the form of a directed graph in which the nodes represent variables and the arcs are the dependent relationships between these variables. The structure of the network provides the information about the dependencies – or independencies – conditional to a variable given other variables.

The software developed can generate Bayesian Networks from a set of data and an objective variable, which depends on the data. Table 2 shows an example.

Table 2. Bayesian network to classify rain occurrence.

Press	Humidity	Rain	No Rain
HIGH	VERY_HIGH	0.522	0.478
HIGH	HIGH	0.909	0.091
HIGH	MEDIUM	0.988	0.012
HIGH	LOW	0.977	0.023
LOW	VERY_HIGH	0.48	0.52
LOW	HIGH	0.894	0.106
LOW	MEDIUM	0.991	0.009
LOW	LOW	0.997	0.003

Example: The probability of RAIN, since pressure is HIGH and humidity is VERY_HIGH, is 0.478

Bayesian networks have several learning algorithms to find the network structure that best fits the data. Different algorithms generate different network structures; for example, when applying the Simulated Annealing method to the same data set used for Table 3, the result is the network structure of Table 3.

Table 3. Bayesian network to classify rain occurrence (simulated annealing method)

OutHum	Rain	No Rain
VERY_HIGH	0.51	0.49
HIGH	0.901	0.099
MEDIUM	0.991	0.009
LOW	0.998	0.002

Example:The probability of RAIN, since humidity is VERY_HIGH, is 0.49

4.4   Decision Tree

In essence, a decision tree is a set of rules organized in a hierarchical structure. A decision is made following the conditions that are met from the root of the tree to any one of its leaves. The application generates different types of decision trees such as Alternating Decision Trees - ADT, Logistic Model Trees - LMT and Nayve Bayes Trees - NBT. Figure 6 shows a decision tree generated by applying the J48 algorithm to classify the occurrence of rain; the J48 algorithm uses the "divide and conquer" inductive technique to generate a structure of rules in every learning step and to evaluate their effectiveness based on accuracy in qualifying.

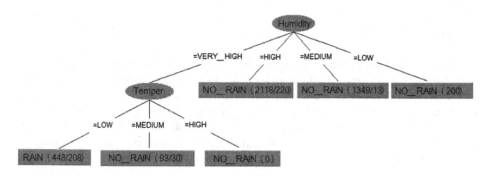

Fig. 6. Decision tree generated with algorithm J48

4.5   Neural Networks

Neural networks are a model to find a way to combine a set of parameters in order to predict an outcome. Finding the combination that best fits is done in the training phase of the neural network. Once trained, the network can be used to predict or classify, applying the combination of previously found parameters.

The problem of determining the occurrence of rain based on temperature, humidity, pressure, wind and solar radiation variables is not linearly separable, so it is appropriate to use the multilayer perceptron to address the problem from the perspective of artificial neural networks. Several different perceptrons were tested to perform the analysis, varying both the number of layers and of neurons, as well as testing different transfer functions and learning algorithms.

To use artificial neural networks, the software allows for the specification of a valid SQL query with the variables used as input to the network and the target variable. The application displays the selected data set and a list with predictions in the network along with the actual values. Figure 7 shows an example of a neural network generated with Weka to predict the occurrence of rain.

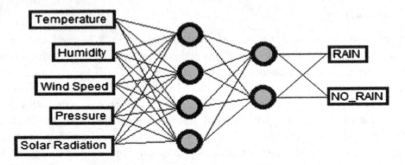

Fig. 7. Neural network to predict rain

5 Analysis of Results

To evaluate the effectiveness of different models obtained from using the tool, Receiver Operating Characteristic - ROC analysis was used, which provides tools to select potentially optimal models and discard other models independently from (and prior to specifying) the cost of distribution of the two classes. For example, using humidity, wind, temperature, pressure and solar radiation as prediction variables and the occurrence of rain as the target variable, different strategies can be compared, as shown in Table 4. Different classifiers can be compared using the ROC analysis of this software tool.

Table 4. Results of different models to predict rain

Classifier	Precision	ROCArea	False positives	True positives
AD tree	73.20%	0.866	0.50%	10.90%
J48 tree	56.30%	0.824	5%	48%
NB tree	56.30%	0.865	4.90%	47.30%
Bayesnet	54.90%	0.867	5.20%	47.80%
ANN	72.5%	0.944	2%	76%

Cost curves are another frequently used way to evaluate the performance of a classifier, allowing for the identification of confidence intervals relative to the performance of a classifier in a context, as well as its statistical significance in the performance of classifiers (Orallo [10]). Brier curves are particularly used to visualize the performance of a classifier and compare it to other classifiers, based on cost space, with the advantage that the area under the Brier curve corresponds to the Brier score, an indicator often used to compare probabilistic classifiers. Figure 8 shows graphs applying ROC analysis and Brier curves to two classifiers – AD Trees and Artificial Neural Networks – to predict rain.

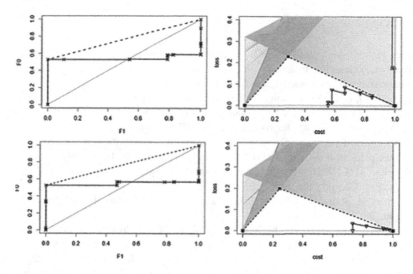

Fig. 8. ROC curve and Brier curve for two classifiers: AD tree and RNA tree. Upper left: ROC curve –AD tree, upper right: Brier curve –AD tree, bottom left: ROC– RNA curve, bottom right: Brier – RNA Curve.

6 Conclusions

Data mining techniques, applied to the study of climate behavior, provide a powerful tool, with confirmed results, previously obtained through classical statistical methods and, more importantly, they generate various models that provide a better description of behaviors associated with change climate.

Developing a software tool based on climate mining data that is specific to the Caribbean region of Colombia is useful, not only to effectively support scientific research on new dynamics due to climate change, but also to help communities in this region to adapt infrastructure, the economy and even customs related to climatic conditions in the region. In the future, it will be necessary to expand the functionality of this software and initiate an awareness campaign to make it available to different groups that may be interested in using it.

Using Weka, a mining tool that is highly developed, complete, free, and widely tested, has been essential in the development of this research. It is not just an end-user package but is also an API that uses all the benefits of Weka in a custom application. The software has combined the benefits of the Weka API with other very useful APIs such as Google Maps and JFreeChart to develop a scalable application with excellent performance. Using free software makes it possible to implement it at low cost, which is convenient, considering the economic constraints that communities in the Caribbean region of Colombia have when investing in software.

Acknowledgments. This research study has been financed by the OCEAN-ATMOSPHERE DYNAMICS IN THE CENTRAL CARRIBEAN REGION OF COLOMBIA. HISTORIC ASSESSMENT AND PREDICTION MODELS project, code 12201542 of *internal call 11-2014* of the Jorge Tadeo Lozano University.

References

1. Franco Herrera, A., Vélez Langs, O.: Dinámica océano-atmósfera en el mar caribe central de Colombia. Valoración histórica y modelos predictivos. Santa Marta: Universidad Jorge Tadeo Lozano. Convocatoria Interna No. 11 de 2014J (2014)
2. Goyal, M., Ojha, C.: Evaluation of rule and decision tree induction algorithms for generating climate change scenarios for temperature and pan evaporation on a lake basin. J. Hydrol. Eng. **19**, 828–835 (2014). doi:10.1061/(ASCE)HE.1943-5584.0000795
3. Javier Aguado-Rodriguez, G., Quevedo-Nolasco, A., Castro-Popoca, M.: Meteorological variables prediction through ARIMA models. Agrociencia **50**, 1–13 (2014)
4. Kalyankar, M.A., Alaspurkar, S.J.: Data mining technique to analyse the metrological data. J. Adv. Res. Comput. Sci. Softw. Eng. (2013)
5. Chaudhari, R., Rana, D.P., Mehta, R.G.: Data mining with meteorological data. Int. J. Adv. Comput. Res. **3**(3), 25 (2013)
6. Petelin, B., Kononenko, I., Malačič, V., Kukar, M.: Multi-level association rules and directed graphs for spatial data analysis. Expert Syst. Appl. **40**, 4957–4970 (2013)
7. Bartok, J., Habala, O., Bednar, P., Gazak, M., Hluchý, L.: Data mining and integration for predicting significant meteorological phenomena. In: International Conference on Computational Science, ICCS 2010 (2012)
8. Kohail, S.N., El-Haless, A.M.: Implementation of data mining techniques for meteorological data analysis (A case study for Gaza Strip). The Islamic University of Gaza, Faculty of Information Technology, Gaza (2011)
9. Damle, C.: Flood Forecasting Using Time Series Data Mining. University of South Florida, Department of Industrial and Management Systems Engineering, Florida (2005)
10. Orallo, J., Flach, P., Ferri, C.: Brier Curves: A New Cost-Based Visualisation of Classifier Performance. Departamento de Sistemas Informáticos y Computación, Universidad Politécnica de Valencia – España (2015)

Molecular Docking Based on *Ligand* by *Complexity LMC*

Mauricio Martínez Medina, Miguel González-Mendoza$^{(\boxtimes)}$,
and Neil Hernández Gress

Tecnológico de Monterrey - Estado de México, Atizapán de Zaragoza, Mexico
{A00964166,mgonza,ngress}@itesm.mx

Abstract. *Molecular Docking* faces problems related to *Curse of dimensionality*, due to the fact that it analyzes data with high dimensionality and few samples. (*Ligand-Based Virtual Screening*) conducts studies of docking among molecules using common attributes registered in data bases. This branch of *Molecular Docking*, uses *Optimization methods* and *Machine learning* algorithms in order to discover molecules similar to known drugs and can be proposed as drug candidates. Such algorithms are affected by effects of *Curse of dimensionality*. It this paper we propose to use *LMC complexity measure* (*Complexity of Lopez-Ruiz, Mancini, and Calbet*) [1] as similarity measurement among vectors in order to discover the best molecules to be drugs; and present an algorithm, which evaluates the similarity among vectors using this concept. The results suggest that application of this concept on *Drug Example* vectors; in order to classify other vectors as drugs candidates which is more informative than individually searching for vectors. Since the *Drug Examples* show a global similarity degree with drug candidate vectors. The aforementioned similarity degree makes it possible to deduce which elements of the *Drug Examples* show higher degree of similarity with drug candidates. Searching of vectors through individual comparison with *Drug Examples* was less efficient, because their classification is affected by the *Drug Examples* with a higher number of global discrepancies. Finally, the proposed algorithm avoids some of the *Curse of dimensionality* effects by using a ranking process where the best drug candidate vectors are those with the lowest complexity.

Keywords: Molecular docking · Active compound · Drug candidates · LMC Complexity · Curse of dimensionality

1 Introduction

Docking molecular techniques seek to find best matching among two o more molecules in such way that they have optimal affinity among them [2]. Such Methods are applied to discovery and design drugs, Computational chemistry, Molecular biology, and Environmental remediation. Modelling of bonds among

© Springer International Publishing AG 2017
O. Pichardo-Lagunas and S. Miranda-Jiménez (Eds.): MICAI 2016, Part II, LNAI 10062, pp. 425–436, 2017.
DOI: 10.1007/978-3-319-62428-0_34

molecules through geometrical characteristics as position, flexibility and rotation implies the use of Optimization algorithms [3]. Solution space's exploration of aforementioned characteristics and its evaluation have great defiances when number of molecules and attributes is increased [3].

Virtual screening in *Docking molecular* brings together a series of procedures based on computational algorithms that identify new molecules using similarity, activity and inactivity relations, physical properties, chemical, structural, functional, etc. Such properties are registered for millions of compounds in public and private databases [4–7]. Information contained in them is represented with higher dimensional vectors which are examined with *Optimization* and *Machine learning* algorithms [3, 8]. These algorithms under this kind of data causes that they be slow and have a poor performance.

Effects of high dimensionality in different algorithms is known as *Curse of dimensionality*. This phenomenon includes the next effects: *Empty space phenomenon, Hypervolume of cubes and spheres, Volume of thin hypersphere shell,* and *Concentration of norms and distances* [5, 9].

In *Virtual screening* there are two trends in molecular docking: *Structured Based Virtual Screening (SBVS)* and *Ligand Based Virtual Screening (LBVS)*. The last one is based on *Support Vector Machines, Decision Trees,* and *Neural Networks,* etc., which aims it is classifying compounds in accordance with their attributes and affinity to interact with a *Objective molecule* [10]. The challenges for these algorithms are large amounts of data for processing, and design new ways of classifying active and inactive compounds [11].

1.1 Previous Works

Major uses of *Machine Learning algorithms* in *LBVS* are classifying and searching similarity among compounds, as well as identify similarity patterns among them. The *Support Vector Machines (SVM)* are used on the first two activities; the basic idea in these algorithms is the identification of a hyperplane which separates nearest data vectors optimally. In order to classify compounds according to this plane. These methods have the disadvantages of a high computational cost, besides the need of an appropriate training data set. *SVMs* have a poor performance with the noise on data and overlap on classes [10].

Decision trees associate specific attributes of molecules with an activity or property related to docking. The construction of *Decision trees* uses information measurements as *Information gain Gain ratio*, and *Gini Index*. The number of branches and bifurcations in them are calculated using the measures aforementioned, and the approaches for its construction can be *Top-Down* and *Bottom-Up*. *Decision trees* are simple models, easy to interpret and validate. However, they suffer high variance since small changes in measures trigger a high number of bifurcations. Its design depends on size of training data sets and can be affected by overfitting [10].

Naïve Bayes classifiers determine the probability of an event B given that it has observed the event A what is the Bayes' theorem. This method is applied in *Molecular docking* when it is seeking the probability that a compound be active.

Given an active compound A; represented by a vector of attributes, and a set of inactive compounds Z, Eq. 1. These algorithms have a high computational cost when the dependence among variables is high [10].

$$p(C_A|Z) = \frac{p(C_A)p(Z|C_A)}{p(Z)} \tag{1}$$

K-nearest neighbors is applied in classification of compounds, ranking and forecasting under regression modality. This method is based on *Distance measures* as *Euclidean, Manhattan, Mahalanobis*, etc. and depends on training data sets [7].

1.2   Problem Statement and Research Questions

A problem of Molecular docking involves the design and implementation of *Optimization functions* and efficient searches that explore the solutions space, in order to match a set of molecules in a appropriate way or to discover similarity among them [5,12]. Such algorithms must be rapid and to find relevant attributes that satisfy restrictions imposed for required matchings among different molecules, as well as satisfying the proposed *Optimization functions* [2,13].

Nowadays, there exists databases that register millions of compounds according their physical properties, chemical, structural, functional, among others. Some problems in Molecular docking ask what compounds registered in them have appropriate structure to resemble with a Objective molecule known as drug. Then, it looks for those compounds that have a high degree of similarity with the molecule in order to discover candidates to drugs [10,14].

The algorithms aimed at these activities work under *Supervised learning*, they have large learning processes y require a number of specific instances for being trained and validated. *Curse of dimensionality (CoD)* affects these algorithms due to high dimensionality of data coming from the databases. On the other hand, *Unsupervised learning* methods are rapid since its implementation depends on *Relevance measurements* from data sets, but they are imprecise due its dependency on *parameters, Statistical distributions, Scale factors*, presence of *outliers*, incomplete data, etc.

Relevance measurements based on *Entropy information* give a degree of independence from problems above mentioned. They require only to identify the events or simple categories that comprise each one of instances of the data sets, along with its frequency [15]. One of the less explored concepts based on *Entropy information* is that of *Complexity*. This term calculates the *Disorder* or *Order* present in a dataset given the rate that exists among individual Entropy information from each event in it, and the *Maximum entropy* that they keep under a uniform distribution [16]. Several researchers have proposed different definitions for Complexity; among them are *Measurement of Complexity* introduced by Shiner et al., *Complexity LMC* raised by Ricardo López-Ruiz et al. and *Kolmogorov Complexity* among other definitions [1,17,18].

The first two concepts from the point of view of Relevance measurements can be implemented for distinct kind of data what it cannot with *Kolmogorov Complexity* [19]. *Measurement of Complexity* and *Complexity LMC* are defined by the *Disorder* and *Order* concepts [4]. *Measurement of Complexity* is a dimensionless measurement and describes behaviour of simple events present at a phenomenon, Eqs. 2, 3, 4, 5 and 6. This concept is expressed as product between *Disorder* and *Order* in its most simple expression [4]. Instances of data with low magnitudes of disorder and low complexity, imply a predictable phenomenon or invariant. But when it is achieved the maximum complexity, the phenomenon is unpredictable due to uniform distribution of the events. Finally, the *Measurement of Complexity* in its more high level of disorder acquire once again a low magnitude [20]. Hence association between *Measurement of Complexity*; defined by Shiner et al., and data sets is only useful inside a limited range of complexity's magnitudes.

$$S = \sum_{i=1}^{n} -P_i log_2 P_i \tag{2}$$

$$S_{max} = Log_2 N \tag{3}$$

$$\Delta \equiv S/S_{max} \tag{4}$$

$$\Omega \equiv 1 - \Delta \tag{5}$$

$$\Gamma_{\alpha\beta} \equiv \Delta^\alpha \Omega^\beta \tag{6}$$

Measurement of Complexity requires for its definition of the *Entropy information* expression; Eq. 2. The *Disorder*; denoted by Δ, is defined as the rate that exists between *Entropy information* and the *Maximum entropy*; Eqs. 4, 2 and 3 respectively. While *Order* or Ω is the difference between one and Δ; Eq. 5. *Order* and *Disorder* are complementary measures. Finally, the *Measurement of Complexity* or $\Gamma_{\alpha\beta}$; it is defined as product between *Order* and *Disorder* for $\alpha = 1$ and $\beta = 1$ in its most simple expression.

Complexity LMC is expressed in terms of *Entropy information* and *Disequilibrium*. This definition of complexity is the *Entropy information* weighting with the maintained distance among simple probability of each one events that composes an instance of data, respect to the inverse number of occurrences on it, Eq. 7. In this case, the minimum magnitude of Complexity occurs when There is only one event, or there are so many events as data there are in the dataset. In the case of a single event, the entropy becomes zero and is known as *Crystal state* due to the predictability of the event. When all data are distinct, the disequilibrium becomes zero and entropy acquires its maximum magnitude which is named *Gas state*. This characteristics are suited to compare compounds by similarity [17, 20].

$$C = H * D = -(K) * (\sum_{i=1}^{N} P_i * Log_2 P_i) * (\sum_{i=1}^{N} (P_i - \frac{1}{N})^2) \tag{7}$$

The following questions arise: Is it possible to posit a molecular docking problem according to Complexity concept? The ease of deployment of Complexity concept, can it be used to search for compounds or appropriate molecules for docking with a objective molecule? Can it be posited a Objective function through Complexity concept in order to evaluate similarity?

1.3   Hypothesis and Objectives

The high dimensionality of vectors and low number of instances in a problem of *LBVS* can be posed in matters of *Complexity LMC* which is simple and playable.

The objective of this work is designing an algorithm which emphasizes similarity among compounds through the *Complexity LMC* concept. Expressing the similarity among compounds through their attributes in terms of matched and unmatched attributes. All this avoiding an expensive exploration of solutions space and The design of complex *Optimization functions*.

What is proposed, therefore, is development an algorithm where the similarity between a compound and an objective molecule or active compound can be determined by *Complexity LMC* using matched and unmatched attributes as simple events. Each analysis between a set of instances of inactive and active compounds will have a value of Complexity, which will be ranking in ascending order. The degree of similarity expressed by complexity between a inactive compound and a drug (or active compound) will keep a value of relevance respect to the other comparisons. Low complexities will indicate a high degree of similarity between an inactive compound and active otherwise, they will have a low degree of similarity, in other words, a high complexity. Therefore, the classification of inactive vectors as candidates to drugs will be depend of this characteristic.

2   Materials and Methods

DuPont Pharmaceuticals released by KDD Cup 2001 competition a dataset composed of 1908 compounds[1] which match with Thrombin molecule. Each one vector are consisted of 139,351 attributes with binary representation [21]. Such attributes are active when they have a value of zero, and inactive when they have one.

These vectors are divided into two sets: 42 are classified as *Drugs* or *Active Compounds*, 1886 vectors to be postulated as *Candidates to drug*, given similarity that they have with the active compounds. The duty is to determine which inactive compounds are the best candidates to drug once they were compared with the active vectors. For it aforementioned, it will be employed the Algorithm 1 which adopts the *Complexity LMC* as measurement of similarity among vectors.

The algorithm are divided in two sections: a preprocessing section and one of Similarity calculation by *Complexity LMC*. The preprocessing seeks to identify those inactive and active vectors which components be zeros in all they. Subsequently, these vectors will be labelled in order to avoid additional comparisons. A searching process of ones and its positions is carried out on the rest of the

---

[1] We are grateful to DuPont Pharmaceuticals Research Laboratories and KDD Cup 2001 by provided this data set through UCI Machine Learning Repository.

Input: $Comp[1\ldots N][1\ldots M]$
Output: $TabMatchByHlmc[M][Row_{Inact}, Row_{Act}, Match, NoMatch, Hlmc]$
begin

    $i \leftarrow 0,\ j \leftarrow 0,\ k \leftarrow 0,\ V^{(0)}[N]$
    $RowListOnes[[N]] = RowListOnes[[1\ldots L_1]\ldots[1\ldots L_N]]\quad 1 \le L_i \le N$
    $Row_{Inact},\ Row_{Act},\ Match,\ NoMatch,\ Hlmc$
    $TabMatchByHlmc[M][Row_{Inact}, Row_{Act}, Match, NoMatch, Hlmc]$
    foreach $i \in N$ **do**

        if $Comp[i][1\ldots M] == \vec{0}$ **then**
            $V^{(0)}[j] \leftarrow i$
            $j \leftarrow j + 1$
        end

    end
    foreach $i \in N$ **do**

        if $i \in V^{(0)}$ **then**
            $AddUp(RowListOnes[[L_i]], 0)$
        else
            foreach $j \in M$ **do**
                if $Comp[i][j] == 1$ **then**
                    $AddUp(RowListOnes[[L_i]], j)$
                end
            end
        end

    end
    forall the $Row_{Inact} \in Indexes(Comp_i\ != \text{``Active''})$ **do**
        forall the $Row_{Act} \in Indexes(Comp_i == \text{``Active''})$ **do**
            if $Row_{Inact} \in V^{(0)} \lor Row_{Act} \in V^{(0)}$ **then**
                if $Row_{Inact} \in V^{(0)} \land Row_{Act} \in V^{(0)}$ **then**
                    $Match = N$
                else
                    if $Row_{Inact} \in V^{(0)}$ **then**
                        $Match \leftarrow (N - \mathbf{card}(S_{RowListOnes[[Row_{Inact}]]}))$
                        $NoMatch \leftarrow \mathbf{card}(S_{RowListOnes[[Row_{Inact}]]})$
                    else
                        $Match \leftarrow (N - \mathbf{card}(S_{RowListOnes[[Row_{Act}]]}))$
                        $NoMatch \leftarrow \mathbf{card}(S_{RowListOnes[[Row_{Act}]]})$
                  end
                end
            else
                $NoMatch \leftarrow \mathbf{card}(S_{RowListOnes[[Row_{Inact}]]} \vartriangle S_{RowListOnes[[Row_{Act}]]})$
                $Match \leftarrow (N - NoMatch)$
            end
            if $Match == N$ **then**
                $Hlmc \leftarrow 0$
            else
                $Hlmc \leftarrow \left. \left(\sum_{i=1}^{N} P_i * Log_2 P_i\right) * \left(\sum_{i=1}^{N} (P_i - \tfrac{1}{N})^2\right) \right|_{i \in \{Match, NoMatch\}}$
            end
            $TabMatchByHlmc_{k+1} \leftarrow c(Row_{Inact}, Row_{Act}, Match, NoMatch, Hlmc)$
        end

    end
    $return(TabMatchByHlmc)$
end

Algorithm 1. Complexity LMC H*D

vectors. A list of list holds these positions for each one of the vectors or a label which indicates if they are only composed by zeros. Therefore, there will be so many lists as vectors has the dataset.

Once the preprocessing stage was carried out, it calculates the similarity by *Complexity LMC* among the *Inactive* and *Active* vectors using the list of lists. This process will carry out so many comparisons as combinations there are between active and inactive vector sets. A simple comparison between a pair of vectors will take from their lists the indexes where they have ones; for indexes where the attributes coincide, the vectors will have so many coincidences as indexes have in common. While the vectors are different, where the indexes are mutually exclusive for both vectors. In the first case, the total of matches between the vectors will be calculated using the dimensionality of the vectors minus the number of indexes, where both vectors have ones; independently if these indexes are common or not, plus the number of common indexes to both vectors. Finally, the number of attributes where the vectors do not match, it is calculated using the dimensionality of vectors minus the number of matches among them.

The frequency of events above mentioned are the basis for calculating the *Complexity LMC*. An exception took in account in this stage, it is when both vectors are zero. In this case, the complexity receives a value of zero since both vectors are same. Once the calculation of complexity is carried out, the magnitudes of complexity for each comparison among active and inactive compounds is ranked in ascending order. Hence emerges the inactive compounds which can be postulated as drugs by having the lowest complexity magnitudes.

The first places in this ranking will have the highest degree of similarity due to their low magnitudes of complexity; on the contrary, the last places will have the lowest degree of similarity in correspondence with the highest magnitudes of complexity.

3   Results

First results showed the existence of 593 vectors in which all their components were zero. Two of them belong to *Active Compounds*, the rest of them to *Inactive Compounds*. This resulted in 1182 comparisons with *Complexity LMC* zero coming from combinations among active and inactive from these vectors. An analysis by *Complexity LMC* quartile of rest of vectors is showed in Fig. 1.

It is noted that *Inactive Compounds* with low complexity magnitudes, in its comparison with the *Active Compounds* hold a high scattering respect to them. In opposite way, when the complexity magnitude is high, the scattering of *Inactive Compounds* respect to the *Active Compounds* is low.

The individual identification of Candidates to drugs in *Inactive Compounds* through lowest magnitudes of complexity with their comparisons with the 42 *Active Compounds* showed wide ranges of complexity in their analysis by quartile. The ranking of *Inactive Compounds* in ascending order respect complexity range from 3.648×10^{-4} hasta 0.51. Table 1 shows the *Candidates to drug* with the lowest complexity along with their minimum and maximum magnitudes when they were individually compared with the *Active Compounds*, as well as the *Active compound*; identified by its number in dataset, with which they coincided under this consideration.

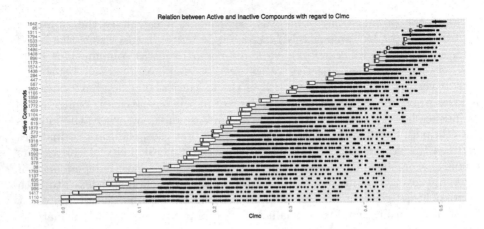

Fig. 1. Similarity of active compounds with Inactive vectors by *Complexity LMC*

Table 1. Inactive compounds with the lowest value of *Complexity LMC*

Inactive vector	Max. Clmc	Min. Clmc	Active vector
2	0.041	0.35	13
105	0.0003	0.0003	2
511	0.35	0.4	2
1060	0.18	0.41	3
1459	0.17	0.18	3

Likewise, it was identified the *Candidates to drug* with high magnitudes of complexity. Results are showed on Table 2. It is noted that the number of *Active Compounds* with which they coincide is higher than those shown low complexity, but the degree of similarity with them is the lowest.

Table 2. Inactive Compounds with the highest value of *Complexity LMC*

Inactive vector	Max. Clmc	Min. Clmc	Active vector
13	0.051	0.49	4
438	0.47	0.42	19
1024	0.5	0.43	4
1090	0.5	0.42	12
1210	0.5	0.45	3

The individual analysis by similarity; expressed through *Complexity LMC*, for the *Inactive Compounds* show a mixed behaviour. The range of complexities covered by *Inactive Compounds* with the lowest magnitudes was narrower than those *Inactive Compounds* with the highest complexity magnitudes, Fig. 2.

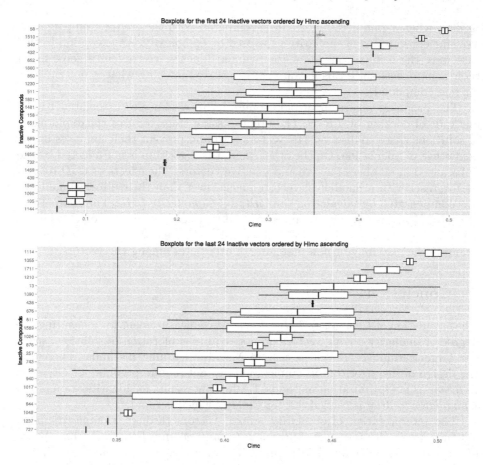

Fig. 2. Inactive vectors

In the first box of Fig. 2, It is noted that vectors 105, 1060 and 1546 coincide in the median of their boxplots. When proving the status of these vectors, it was found that very few of their attributes are inactive only three attributes for the vector 105, and 32 for the last two. A similar observation was carried out for the second box in Fig. 2, where It is noted that vectors 676, 811 and 1589 coincide in their median. In this case the number of inactive attributes is high with 12598, 10791 and 12147 attributes respectively.

4   Discussion

The coupling of compounds in *LBVS* using the *Complexity LMC* concept highlights the degree of overall similarity that *Active Compounds* hold with the *Inactive Compounds*. This characteristic show the best examples inside of *Active Compounds* to identify the best *Candidates to drug* when they hold with them low complexity magnitudes. However, the individual identification of *Candidates to drug* when a *Inactive Compound* is compared with the *Active Compounds* is less efficient in terms of similarity expressed by complexity. An exception to this case were the comparisons among active and inactive vectors with zeros in all their components since this meant that complete matching what is not the case for real compounds.

The proposed algorithm avoids some of the weaknesses associated to the methods of docking by *LBVS*. The preprocessing stage reduces the exploration of solutions space to discover the vectors zero and prevent their analyses in the next stage of calculation. On the other hand, the algorithm is not affected by the unbalanced in number of active and inactive vectors. The effects of *CoD* related to a dataset with a number of vectors much lower than their dimensionality, it was compensated by calculating similarity by *Complexity LMC*. The comparison of vectors by similarity can be implemented through the concept of *Complexity LMC* in an algorithm. Whenever it be possible to identify simple events as for example the matching or non matching of attributes among the vectors.

5   Conclusions

The calculation of *Complexity LMC* as relevance measurement for measuring the degree of similarity among vectors do not require exploration of solutions space nor large learning processes in case of Machine learning methods. Therefore, the design of the algorithm is simple and does not require planning of *Objective function* as in Optimization methods. Evaluating results for identification of the *Candidates to drug* is carried out for ranking which is rapid.

The interpretation of similarity among vectors through *Complexity LMC* depends upon the terms of *Entropy information* and *Disequilibrium*. A low entropy denotes a magnitude of complexity low due to the preponderance in frequency of some of the simple events (matching or non matching). If the frequency of the events is uniform, it is obtained the maximum entropy in consequence the maximum complexity. This implies that the similarity among vectors is the lowest due to existence of an equal number of coincidences than non-coincidences among their attributes.

A low complexity by disequilibrium did not show up for this analysis; due to the fact that the number of events is minimum with respect to the number of components in the vectors. The interpretation of the results, it is easy to deduce. High degree of similarity among vectors is related to low magnitudes of complexity, in consequence the textitCandidates to drug hold low magnitudes of complexity with the *Active Compounds* or drugs.

The effects of *CoD* on the proposed algorithm are minimum due to use of *Complexity LMC* as a relevance measurement for similarity among vectors. The ordering of the comparisons among Inactive and Active Compounds by this measurement for discovering *Candidates to drug* avoids high costs in computing times. The algorithm might be labelled as a unsupervised method and does not require a large training process, nor datasets of training and test, as required by the supervised methods. Although, the aspect of Accuracy and precision is difficult to establish [22]. Because *Complexity LMC* as relevance measurement is an indicator of how much *Order* or *Disorder* exists between two vectors with respect to their similarity [23]. We consider that the concept of *Complexity LMC* is a flexible option of analysis for *LBVS* in the case of matching of molecules by similarity of attributes [24, 25].

References

1. Shiner, J.S., Davison, M., Landsberg, P.T.: Simple measure for complexity. Phys. Rev. E **59**(2), 1459 (1999)
2. Halperin, I., Ma, B., Wolfson, H., Nussinov, R.: Principles of docking: an overview of search algorithms and a guide to scoring functions. Proteins: Struct. Funct. Bioinf. **47**(4), 409–443 (2002)
3. Teodoro, M.L., Phillips, G.N.: Molecular docking: a problem with thousands of degrees of freedom. In: IEEE International Conference on Robotics and Automation, pp. 960–966 (2001)
4. Kearsley, S.K., Sheridan, R.P.: Why do we need so many chemical similarity search methods? Drug Discov. Today **7**(17), 903–911 (2002)
5. Karthikeyan, M., Vyas, R.: Practical Chemoinformatics. Springer, New Delhi (2014). doi:10.1007/978-81-322-1780-0
6. Lavecchia, A., Di Giovanni, C.: Virtual screening strategies in drug discovery: a critical review. Curr. Med. Chem. **20**(23), 2839–2860 (2013)
7. Zheng, M., Liu, Z., Yan, X., Ding, Q., Gu, Q., Xu, J.: LBVS: an online platform for ligand-based virtual screening using publicly accessible databases. Mol. Divers. **18**(4), 829–840 (2014)
8. Nicolaou, C.A., Brown, N.: Multi-objective optimization methods in drug design. Drug Discov. Today, **30**(20) (2013)
9. Clarke, R., Ressom, H.W., et al.: The properties of high-dimensional data spaces: implications for exploring gene and protein expression data. Nat. Rev. Cancer **8**, 13 (2008)
10. Lavecchia, A.: Machine-learning approaches in drug discovery: methods and applications. Drug Discov. Today **20**(3), 318–331 (2015)
11. Danishuddin, M., Khan, A.U.: Virtual screening strategies: a state of art to combat with multiple drug resistance strains. MOJ Proteomics Bioinform
12. Shan, S., Wang, G.G.: Survey of modeling and optimization strategies to solve high-dimensional design problems with computationally-expensive black-box functions. Struct. Multidiscip. Optim. **41**(2), 219–241 (2010)
13. Sousa, S.F., Ribeiro, A.J.M., Coimbra, J.T.S., Neves, R.P.P., Martins, S.A., Moorthy, N.S.H.N., Fernandes, P.A., Ramos, M.J.: Protein-ligand docking in the new millennium-a retrospective of 10 years in the field. Curr. Med. Chem. **20**(18), 2296–2314 (2013)
14. Li, Q., Cheng, T., Wang, Y., Bryant, S.H.: PubChem as a public resource for drug discovery. Drug Discov. Today **15**(23), 1052–1057 (2010)
15. Shannon, C.E.: A mathematical theory of communication. Bell Syst. Tech. J. **27**, 10–12 (1948)
16. Crutchfield, J.P.: Between order and chaos. Nat. Phys. **8**(1), 17–24 (2012)
17. Lopez-Ruiz, R., Mancini, H., Calbet, X.: A statistical measure of complexity. arXiv preprint nlin/0205033 (2002)

18. Grünwald, P.D., Vitányi, P.M.B.: Kolmogorov complexity and information theory. With an interpretation in terms of questions and answers. J. Logic Lang. Inform. **12**(4), 497–529 (2003)
19. Seaward, L., Matwin, S.: Intrinsic plagiarism detection using complexity analysis. In: Proceedings of the SEPLN, pp. 56–61 (2009)
20. Feldman, D.P., Crutchfield, J.P.: Measures of statistical complexity: why? Phys. Lett. A **238**(4), 244–252 (1998)
21. DuPont Pharmaceuticals Research Laboratories. Dorothea data set
22. Zhang, W., Ji, L., Chen, Y., Tang, K., Wang, H., Zhu, R., Jia, W., Cao, Z., Liu, Q.: When drug discovery meets web search: learning to rank for ligand-based virtual screening. J. Cheminform. **7**, 5 (2015)
23. Kurczab, R., Smusz, S., Bojarski, A.J.: Evaluation of different machine learning methods for ligand-based virtual screening. J. Cheminform. **3**(S–1), 41 (2011)
24. Tanrikulu, Y., Krüger, B., Proschak, E.: The holistic integration of virtual screening in drug discovery. Drug Discov. Today **18**(7), 358–364 (2013)
25. Klebe, G.: Virtual ligand screening: strategies, perspectives and limitations. Drug Discov. Today **11**(13), 580–594 (2006)

Integrating Information of Films by a Multi-source Combining Framework

Elias Dasturian, Hamid Parvin$^{(\boxtimes)}$, and Samad Nejatian

Department of Computer Engineering, Yasouj Branch,
Islamic Azad University, Yasouj, Iran
parvin@iust.ac.ir

Abstract. The paper provides a methodology for the integration of film information from different sources. To identify films information validation algorithms are used. The background and methodology are clearly described. This method can fuse the identical films and complete its information. In order to detect two related film information (they describe the identical film), we proposed three film information validation algorithms. All of these methods can detect films' information which need integration processing. Our experiments show that method we proposed generally outperforms one-dimensional detection methods by different evaluation methods, i.e., precision, recall and F1.

Keywords: Information of films · Multi-source · Combining framework

1 Introduction

These days are artificial intelligence era. In this era artificial intelligence is much desired to be implemented in almost every application to mechanize every task [1–15]. A subfield in artificial intelligence is data mining. Knowledge extraction from a huge data is named data mining [16, 42]. Integrating information from multi-source is a subfield in data mining. Integrating information of films by a multi-source combining framework is a shared subfield of data mining and image processing. In general, the researchers found the topic very interesting and simple and effective.

With the Internet, information on the web has grown exponentially in recent years. This growth reflects an increase in wealth is a source of knowledge significantly. On the other hand it is also a challenge for the more complex organization of information like this site, for example, structural, semi-structural, non-structural has to offer. Therefore, more attention to combining web data in industry and in academic communities. The combination of information can effectively achieve the integration of multi-source information and a critical approach to the problem of diversity of information [43].

Suggesting system is an information tool. It is able to advice the products to potential clients by their needs and interests [44]. But it has huge totals of data support. A popular method of information integration are as follows: On average, weighted Bayesian method [45], the Kalman filter [46], DS rule, fuzzy logic, neural networks, rough set theory [47–49], Sugeno fuzzy integration mixed [50] and gray correlation analysis [51]. Current research combining Web information [52, 53] mainly on the

© Springer International Publishing AG 2017
O. Pichardo-Lagunas and S. Miranda-Jiménez (Eds.): MICAI 2016, Part II, LNAI 10062, pp. 437–446, 2017.
DOI: 10.1007/978-3-319-62428-0_35

Web with multi-source information integration recovery [52] and the document is a compilation of scientific focus. Any film is as an example.

Consequently, it is necessary to analyze the review of recent expansions in this field [47]. A method has been suggested, where it employs a flowchart to compute between-films likeness. The procedure of task is done once by evaluating likeness of films against a preset threshold value. This method is very effective and dominant. Simultaneously, it is superior to other methods in terms of many criteria.

2   The Film Information Integration Model

To fuse information of films there are some important steps such as information gain, information refinement, information evaluation and information integration. Among the mention steps, WWW information extraction is the foundation of machinery.

Information integration is a technique to efficiently employ a host of data from numerous supplies [55]. This subject deals with integrating the data about the identical nature by information validation. In fact, the mixing procedure is the filling out of each feature. Initially hidden semantic examination and normalization are done on films kind and location of construction. After that, blending is implemented on five features including: player director, kind, location of construction and URL. Lastly, film name, placard, plan sketch, time will be determined from the most popular providers which are decided during marketplace information investigation.

3   FIV Algorithms

The procedure of film information integration mostly concentrated on huge information from more than one source. The task of information validation is to discover information which explains the same films from dissimilar film sources. This step is vital in the entire procedure of integration and is the focus of the paper. We proposed the Film Information Validation (FIV) algorithms and the results of validation are evaluated and analyzed on three dissimilar forms.

According to our investigation of the web constructions of dissimilar film suppliers on the Internet in addition to the sensible need of clients, we employ nine features to represent film information.

We build 5-dimensional vectors by employing 5 attributes of title, actor, director, genre in addition to intro. This procedure is founded on the semi-structural and non-structural features [56], which is incorporated in film information. The resemblance between two films from dissimilar sources is given by the FIV algorithms and then is compared with the predefined threshold $Sim0$. If $Movie > Sim0$, then information integration has to be accomplished, or else do not any operation.

One significant feature of the algorithms is to set a suitable first threshold; another feature is the calculation of film resemblance in each feature of the 5-dimensional vectors. The resemblances of dissimilar features are computed based on (1).

$$Sim_{A,B} = \frac{V_A \cap V_B}{V_A \cup V_B} \qquad (1)$$

where A and B are two films from dissimilar sources; $Sim_{A,B}$ is the resemblance of the two films in actor, director and genre; V_A, V_B are the feature values of film A and B on the three features correspondingly.

1. A review over the favorites of a group of size 2000 from dissimilar sex and period collections for each film feature is conducted. The review demonstrates that almost half of the people place the most stress on the labels of the films while actors, directors, genres and plot explanations approximately is shared on the reminder of the concentration consistently. Figure 1 is a pie-diagram demonstrating the results of the review.

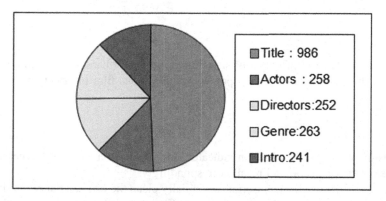

Fig. 1. Popularity of film features.

2. Usually the nearness among 2 points possessing numerous features is described by a mixture of the resemblance of each feature. So the resemblance of points containing only one feature is initially argued; here 2 points are believed that are explained by only a nominal feature. As nominal features just take information in relation to the divergence of the points, the 2 points have the same value either or vice versa. Consequently the resemblance is near to 1 when the feature is the same, or else as 0. Divergence is defined vice versa [58].
3. Accepting the linear regression approach in machine learning: numerous linear regressions are an important method and is extensively accepted in the research in many fields of sciences.

4 Experiential Results Section

The For assessing the sensibleness and efficiency of the proposed algorithm, film information of 1500 films from *Iqiyi* and 2700 films from *Xunleikankan* are gotten by using the *HTMLPaser* instrument and accepting depth based policy [43]. After that, the obtained data are employed as dataset.

This paper employs FIV algorithms to assess the efficiency of the information incorporation, consequently we employ precision, recall and F1 as assessment meters.

Precision is described as the relation of the amount of recovered points of superfluous film information to the amount of points of all the fused film information [59], which can be explained by Eq. (2).

$$P = \frac{N_{tp}}{L} \tag{2}$$

where, L is the extent of the list of film information in the test set, N_{tp} is the amount of recovered points of superfluous film information.

Precision is described as the relation of the amount of recovered points of redundant film information to the number of records of unnecessary film information in the whole test set [59], which can be explained by Eq. (3):

$$R = \frac{N_{tp}}{B} \tag{3}$$

where, B is the amount of points of superfluous film information in the entire test set and N_{tp} is the amount of recovered points of superfluous film information.

$$F1 = \frac{2 * P * R}{P + R} \tag{4}$$

$F1$ is the widespread evaluation indicator united precision and recall; where, P and R locate for the precision and recall correspondingly.

Within the trial of this manuscript, we initially clean the original dataset to discover and eliminate noise data, after that contract with idleness by affecting essential field equaling algorithms and eliminates superfluous information [61]. Finally a novel dataset of 3808 films is gained.

We employ 80% of the previously declared dataset which is clean and have information from 3038 films like training sets for the 3 FIV algorithms. The 2nd algorithm and the 3rd algorithm are explained by Eqs. (5) and (6). According to testing set (20 films are arbitrarily selected from each 2 suppliers, 10 films information is superfluous information by synthetic naming), the preliminary threshold of each algorithm is predefined, correspondingly. As shown in Figs. 2, 3 and 4, 200 points of resemblances among films are registered and the preliminary threshold of the 3 algorithms is set to 0.5, 1.5 and 0.4, correspondingly.

After that we build 3 test sets denoted by TeS1, TeS2 and TeS3. Those test sets consist 20%, 50% and 100% data of the dataset independently. Each of them consists 244 film information (the recurrence happens in pairwise), and the rest are arbitrarily chosen from 2 film websites as noise data (no recurrence). We assess the FIV algorithms on those 3 test sets independently. In addition, we furthermore assess each of the 5 aspects and evaluate its efficacy with FIV. The investigational results are depicted in Figs. 5, 6, 7 and 8, where the x-coordinate signifies different forms and y-coordinate represents the efficacy. The reasonableness and efficiency of our FIV algorithms are verified, particularly the 1st algorithm and the 2nd algorithm.

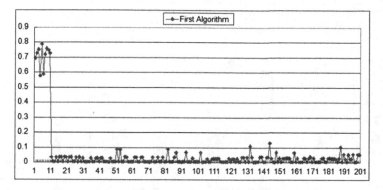

Fig. 2. The initial threshold of the first algorithm

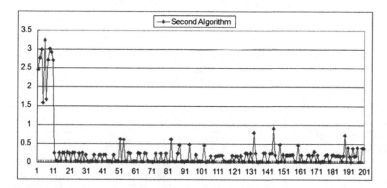

Fig. 3. The initial threshold of the second algorithm

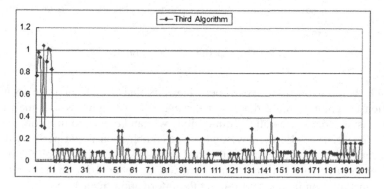

Fig. 4. The initial threshold of the third algorithm

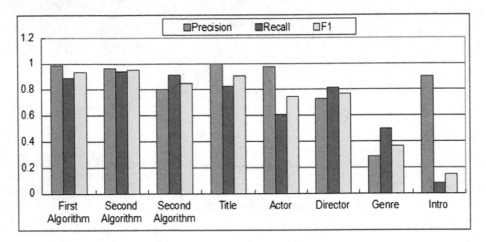

Fig. 5. The experimental result on TeS1

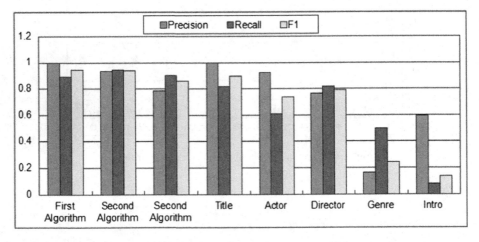

Fig. 6. The experimental result on TeS2

It could be seen from the experimental results that it is inadequate to use film information integrating on a 1-dimensional way, and its toughness is somewhat low. Only by sensibly considering all the dimensions we can be assured that combination is essentially required, or else the development of combination is not performed. In the end we employ the second FIV algorithm and employed it to confirm all the data. The last part of the FIV model incorporates formerly discovered information by accomplishing semantic examination and joining the information in each feature. Figure 9 is an assessment between the size of the dataset previous to and subsequent to the combination.

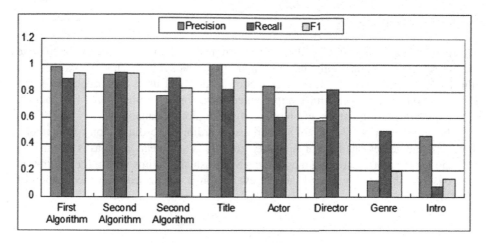

Fig. 7. The experimental result on TeS3

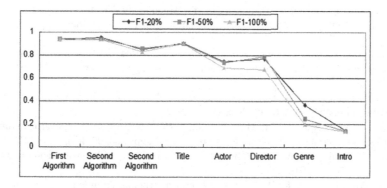

Fig. 8. The comparison of three TeS on F1

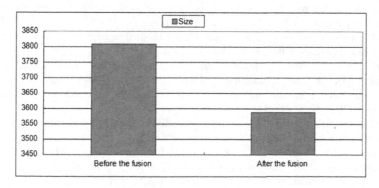

Fig. 9. The size of data set before and after integration

5 Conclusion

This paper suggests a model for film information incorporation, that is, a model to unite the information of a known film using as input dissimilar sources. The authors signify a film by 9 attributes to present the information to the final user. Nevertheless, for the incorporation model, each film is represented using only 5 dimensions: title, actors, director (or directors), genres and intro (that is the plot explanation).

The paper describes 3 types of similarities regarding the 5-dimensions: for authors, directors, and genres one type of similarity, for title is a boolean value as is de same or not, and for the plot description they use the SimHash algorithms. Then, for integration they describe three methods and then an evaluation is performed with a collection of 3808 films.

References

1. Ding, J., Liu, Y., Zhang, L., Wang, J., Liu, Y.: An anomaly detection approach for multiple monitoring data series based on latent correlation probabilistic model. Appl. Intell. **44**(2), 340–361 (2016)
2. Cerrada, M., Sánchez, R.V., Pacheco, F., Cabrera, D., Zurita, G., Li, C.: Hierarchical feature selection based on relative dependency for gear fault diagnosis. Appl. Intell. **44**(3), 687–703 (2016)
3. Novoa-Hernández, P., Corona, C.C., Pelta, D.A.: Self-adaptation in dynamic environments - a survey and open issues. IJBIC **8**(1), 1–13 (2016)
4. Adewumi, A.O., Arasomwan, M.A.: On the performance of particle swarm optimisation with(out) some control parameters for global optimisation. IJBIC **8**(1), 14–32 (2016)
5. Wang, H., Wang, W., Sun, H., Rahnamayan, S.: Firefly algorithm with random attraction. IJBIC **8**(1), 33–41 (2016)
6. Castelli, M., Vanneschi, L., Popovič, A.: Parameter evaluation of geometric semantic genetic programming in pharmacokinetics. IJBIC **8**(1), 42–50 (2016)
7. Rao, B.S., Vaisakh, K.: Multi-objective adaptive clonal selection algorithm for solving optimal power flow problem with load uncertainty. IJBIC **8**(2), 67–83 (2016)
8. Cai, Q., Ma, L., Gong, M., Tian, D.: A survey on network community detection based on evolutionary computation. IJBIC **8**(2), 84–98 (2016)
9. Rio de Souza e Silva Junior, L.D., Nedjah, N.: Distributed strategy for robots recruitment in swarm-based systems. IJBIC **8**(2), 99–108 (2016)
10. Jia, Z., Duan, H., Shi, Y.: Hybrid brain storm optimisation and simulated annealing algorithm for continuous optimisation problems. IJBIC **8**(2), 109–121 (2016)
11. Srivastava, P.R.: Test case optimisation a nature inspired approach using bacteriologic algorithm. IJBIC **8**(2), 122–131 (2016)
12. Xu, Z., Ünveren, A., Acan, A.: Probability collectives hybridised with differential evolution for global optimisation. IJBIC **8**(3), 133–153 (2016)
13. Osuna-Enciso, V., Cuevas, E., Oliva, D., Sossa, H., Pérez-Cisneros, M.A.: A bio-inspired evolutionary algorithm: allostatic optimisation. IJBIC **8**(3), 154–169 (2016)
14. Ahirwal, M.K., Kumar, A., Singh, G.K.: Study of ABC and PSO algorithms as optimised adaptive noise canceller for EEG/ERP. IJBIC **8**(3), 170–183 (2016)

15. Niknam, T., Kavousi-Fard, A.: Optimal energy management of smart renewable micro-grids in the reconfigurable systems using adaptive harmony search algorithm. IJBIC **8**(3), 184–194 (2016)
16. Alishvandi, H., Gouraki, G.H., Parvin, H.: An enhanced dynamic detection of possible invariants based on best permutation of test cases. Comput. Syst. Sci. Eng. **31**(1), 53–61 (2016)
17. Parvin, H., Minaei-Bidgoli, B., Alinejad-Rokny, H.: A new imbalanced learning and dictions tree method for breast cancer diagnosis. J Bionanosci. **7**(6), 673–678 (2013)
18. Parvin, H., Alinejad-Rokny, H., Minaei-Bidgoli, B., Parvin, S.: A new classifier ensemble methodology based on subspace learning. J. Exp. Theoret. Artif. Intell. **25**(2), 227–250 (2013)
19. Parvin, H., Minaei-Bidgoli, B., Alinejad-Rokny, H., Punch, W.F.: Data weighing mechanisms for clustering ensembles. Comput. Electr. Eng. **39**(5), 1433–1450 (2013)
20. Parvin, H., Alizadeh, H., Minaei-Bidgoli, B.: A new method for constructing classifier ensembles. JDCTA **3**(2), 62–66 (2009)
21. Parvin, H., Alinejad-Rokny, H., Asadi, M.: An ensemble based approach for feature selection. J. Appl. Sci. Res. **7**(9), 33–43 (2011)
22. Parvin, H., Alizadeh, H., Minaei-Bidgoli, B., Analoui, M.: CCHR: combination of classifiers using heuristic retraining. In: International Conference on Networked Computing and Advanced Information Management (NCM 2008) (2008)
23. Parvin, H., Alizadeh, H., Fathy, M., Minaei-Bidgoli, B.: Improved face detection using spatial histogram features. In: IPCV 2008, pp. 381–386 (2008)
24. Parvin, H., Alinejad-Rokny, H., Parvin, S.: A classifier ensemble of binary classifier ensembles. Int. J. Learn. Manag. Syst. **1**(2), 37–47 (2013)
25. Parvin, H., Minaei-Bidgoli, B.: A clustering ensemble framework based on elite selection of weighted clusters. Adv. Data Anal. Classif. **7**(2), 181–208 (2013)
26. Alizadeh, H., Minaei-Bidgoli, B., Parvin, H.: Optimizing fuzzy cluster ensemble in string representation. IJPRAI **27**(2), 1350005 (2013)
27. Parvin, H., Beigi, A., Mozayani, N.: A clustering ensemble learning method based on the ant colony clustering algorithm. Int. J. Appl. Comput. Math. **11**(2), 286–302 (2012)
28. Alizadeh, H., Minaei-Bidgoli, B., Parvin, H.: To improve the quality of cluster ensembles by selecting a subset of base clusters. J. Exp. Theoret. Artif. Intell. **26**(1), 127–150 (2014)
29. Alizadeh, H., Minaei-Bidgoli, B., Parvin, H.: Cluster ensemble selection based on a new cluster stability measure. Intell. Data Anal. **18**(3), 389–408 (2014)
30. Minaei-Bidgoli, B., Parvin, H., Alinejad-Rokny, H., Alizadeh, H., Punch, W.F.: Effects of resampling method and adaptation on clustering ensemble efficacy. Artif. Intell. Rev. **41**(1), 27–48 (2014)
31. Parvin, H., Minaei-Bidgoli, B.: A clustering ensemble framework based on selection of fuzzy weighted clusters in a locally adaptive clustering algorithm. Pattern Anal. Appl. **18**(1), 87–112 (2015)
32. Parvin, H., Mirnabibaboli, M., Alinejad-Rokny, H.: Proposing a classifier ensemble framework based on classifier selection and decision tree. Eng. Appl. AI **37**, 34–42 (2015)
33. Parvin, H., Mohammadi, M., Rezaei, Z.: Face identification based on Gabor-wavelet features. Int. J. Digit. Content Technol. Appl. **6**(1), 247–255 (2012)
34. Khan, M.A., Shahzad, W., Baig, A.R.: Protein classification via an ant-inspired association rules-based classifier. IJBIC **8**(1), 51–65 (2016)
35. Lee, C.-P., Lin, W.-S.: Using the two-population genetic algorithm with distance-based k-nearest neighbour voting classifier for high-dimensional data. IJDMB **14**(4), 315–331 (2016)
36. Zhu, M., Liu, S., Jiang, J.: A hybrid method for learning multi-dimensional Bayesian network classifiers based on an optimization model. Appl. Intell. **44**(1), 123–148 (2016)

37. Kim, M.: Sparse inverse covariance learning of conditional Gaussian mixtures for multiple-output regression. Appl. Intell. **44**(1), 17–29 (2016)
38. Tanveer, M., Shubham, K., Aldhaifallah, M., Nisar, K.S.: An efficient implicit regularized Lagrangian twin support vector regression. Appl. Intell. **44**(4), 831–848 (2016)
39. Balasundaram, S., Meena, Y.: Training primal twin support vector regression via unconstrained convex minimization. Appl. Intell. **44**(4), 931–955 (2016)
40. Yang, L., Qian, Y.: A sparse logistic regression framework by difference of convex functions programming. Appl. Intell. **45**(2), 241–254 (2016)
41. Bang, S., Cho, H., Jhun, M.: Adaptive lasso penalised censored composite quantile regression. IJDMB **15**(1), 22–46 (2016)
42. Chen, Y.-S., Cheng, C.-H., Chiu, C.-L., Huang, S.-T.: A study of ANFIS-based multi-factor time series models for forecasting stock index. Appl. Intell. **45**(2), 277–292 (2016)
43. Su, W.: Key Technologies Research On Personalized WEB Business Information Integration System. Zhejiang University (2010)
44. Su, X., Khoshgoftaar, T.M.: A survey of collaborative filtering techniques. Adv. Artif. Intell. **2009**, 4 (2009)
45. Dezert, J., Tchamova, A.: On the validity of Dempster's integration rule and its interpretation as a generalization of bayesian integration rule. Int. J. Intell. Syst. **29**(3), 223–252 (2014)
46. Tsanas, A., Zañartu, M., Little, M.A., et al.: Robust fundamental frequency estimation in sustained vowels: detailed algorithmic comparisons and information integration with adaptive Kalman filtering. J. Acoust. Soc. Am. **135**(5), 2885–2901 (2014)
47. Khaleghi, B., Khamis, A., Karray, F.O., et al.: Multisensor data integration: a review of the state-of-the-art. Inf. Integr. **14**(1), 28–44 (2013)
48. Jian, X., Jia, H., Shi, L.: Advances on multi-sensor information integration technologies. Chin. J. Constr. Mach. **7**(2), 227–232 (2009)
49. Zu-ping, C.K.Z., Jun, L.: Multisource information integration: key issues, research progress and new trends. Comput. Sci. **8**, 003 (2013)
50. Chunhui, S., Shengquan, M.A.: An information integration algorithm based on sugeno fuzzy complex-valued integral. J. Comput. Inf. Syst. **7**(6), 2166–2171 (2011)
51. Hongguang, L., Xiuyan, S., Kaili, Z., Li, Z.: Study on multi-target tracking algorithm based on multi-source information integration using gray correlation analysis. J. Comput. Inf. Syst. **8**(11), 4467–4474 (2012)
52. Keyhanipour, A.H., Moshiri, B., Kazemian, M., et al.: Aggregation of web search engines based on users' preferences in WebIntegration. Knowl.-Based Syst. **20**(4), 321–328 (2007)
53. Xie, N., Cao, C., Guo, H.Y.: A knowledge integration model for web information. In: Proceedings of the 2005 IEEE/WIC/ACM International Conference on Web Intelligence, pp. 67–72 IEEE, (2005)
54. Xu, Y., Xu, Z.M., Wang, X.L.: Multi-document automatic summarization technique based on information integration. Chin. J. Comput.-Chin. Ed. **30**(11), 2048 (2007)
55. Dong, J., Zhuang, D., Huang, Y., et al.: Advances in multi-sensor data integration: algorithms and applications. Sensors **9**(10), 7771–7784 (2009)
56. Chen, F., Steinbach, M., Kumar, V.: Introduction to Data Mining: Full Version, pp. 20–25. Posts & Telecom Press, Beijing (2011)
57. Song, L.: Research on Semantic Similarity Computation and Applications. Shandong University (2009)
58. Zhu, Y.X., Lu, L.Y.: Evaluation metrics for recommender systems. J. Univ. Electron. Sci. Technol. China **41**(2), 163–175 (2012)
59. Hao, Z.: Clustering and Classification of Data and Text Using such Technologies as Genetic Algorithm. Tianjin University (2006)

Graph-Based Algorit

Computing the Clique-Width of Polygonal Tree Graphs

J. Leonardo González-Ruiz[1]([✉]), J. Raymundo Marcial-Romero[1],
J.A. Hernández[1], and Guillermo De Ita[2]

[1] Facultad de Ingeniería, UAEM, Toluca, Mexico
leon.g.ruiz@gmail.com, jrmarcialr@uaemex.mx, xoseahernandez@gmail.com.mx
[2] Facultad de Ciencias de la Computación, BUAP, Puebla, Mexico
deita@cs.buap.mx

Abstract. Similar to the tree-width (*twd*), the clique-width (*cwd*) is
an invariant of graphs. There is a well-known relationship between the
tree-width and clique-width for any graph. The tree-width of a special
class of graphs called polygonal trees is 2, so the clique-width for those
graphs is smaller or equal than 6. In this paper we show that we can
improve this bound to 5 and we present a polynomial time algorithm
which computes the 5-expression.

1 Introduction

The clique-width has recently become an important graph invariant in parameterized complexity theory because measures the difficulty of decomposing a
graph in a kind of tree-structure, and thus efficiently solve certain graph problems if the graph has small clique-width. The computation of the clique-width
of a graph G consists on building a finite term which represents the graph,
Courcelle et al. [1] presents a set of four operations to build the term: (1) the
creation of labels for vertices, (2) disjoint union of graphs, (3) edge creation and
(4) re-labelling of vertices. The number of labels used to build the finite term
is commonly denoted by k. The minimum k used to built the term, called k-
expression, defines clique-width. Finding the best combination which minimize
the k-expression is a NP complete problem [2].

The clique-width, also called the corresponding decomposition of the graph
is measured by means of a k-expression [3]. As the clique-width increases the
complexity of the respective graph problem to solve increases too, in fact for
some automata that represent certain graph problems (according to the scheme
in Courcelle's main theorem), computation runs out-of-memory, see [4] for some
examples of graphs with the clique-width 3 or 4.

Tree decomposition and its tree-width parameter of a graph, are among the
most commonly used concepts [5]. Therefore, clique-width can be seen as a generalization of tree-width in a sense that every graph class of bounded tree-width
also have bounded clique-width [6].

In recent years, clique-width has been studied in different classes of graphs
showing the behavior of this invariant under certain operations; the importance

© Springer International Publishing AG 2017
O. Pichardo-Lagunas and S. Miranda-Jiménez (Eds.): MICAI 2016, Part II, LNAI 10062, pp. 449–459, 2017.
DOI: 10.1007/978-3-319-62428-0_36

of the clique-width is that if a problem on graphs is bounded by this invariant it can be solved in linear time. For example Golumbic and Rotics [7] show that for every distance hereditary graph G, the $cwd(G) \leq 3$, so the following problems have linear time solution on the class of distance-hereditary graphs: minimum dominating set, minimum connected dominating set, minimum Steiner tree, maximum weighted clique, maximum weighted stable set, diameter, domatic number for fixed k, vertex cover, and k−colorability for fixed k. On the other hand the following graph classes and their complements are not of bounded clique–width: interval graphs, circle graphs, circular arc graphs, unit circular arc graphs, proper circular arc graphs, directed path graphs, undirected path graphs, comparability graphs, chordal graphs, and strongly chordal graphs [7].

Another major issue in graphs of bounded clique-width is to decide whether or not a graph has clique-width of size k, for fixed k. For graphs of bounded clique-width, it was shown in [8] that a polynomial time algorithm ($O(n^2m)$) exists that recognize graphs of clique-width less than or equal to three. However, as the authors pointed out the problem remains open for $k \geq 4$. On the other hand, it is well known a classification of graphs of clique-width ≤ 2, since the graphs of clique-width 2 are precisely the cographs. There are, however, some results in general. In [9] the behaviour of various graph operations on the clique-width are presented. For instance, for an arbitrary simple graph with n vertices the clique-width is at most $n - r$ if $2^r < n - r$ where r is rank [10]. In [11], it is shown that every graph of clique-width k which does not contain the complete bipartite graph $K_{n,n}$ for some $n > 1$ as a subgraph has tree-width at most $3k(n - 1) - 1$, whereas in [9] is shown that the clique-width under binary operations on graphs behaves as follows, if k_1, k_2 are the clique-width of graphs G_1, G_2, respectively, then $cwd(G_1 \oplus G_2) = \max(k_1, k_2)$, $cwd(G_1[v/G_2]) = \max(k_1, k_2)$ where $G_1[v/G_2]$ means substitute vertex v in G_1 by G_2. Similar results are presented for the *joint, composition, substitution* and some other important graph operation such as *edge contraction*, among others.

Regarding our present work, we are interested in the class of graphs called *Polygonal trees*, array of polygons of l sides (also called l-gons) which follows the structure of a tree where instead of nodes we have l-gons, and any two consecutive l-gons share exactly one edge. Polygonal trees represent a great importance for theoretical chemistry because they have been used to study intrinsic properties of molecular graphs [12]. For example, *Hexagonal trees*, which are a subclass of polygonal trees, play an important role in mathematical chemistry as natural representation of benzenoid hydrocarbons. In particular, hexagonal chains have been treated in the literature [13]. Harary [14] realizes that hexagonal system and as a consequence hexagonal trees are very attractive objectives for graph theoretical studies and the first to initiate their mathematical investigations. A considerable amount of research in mathematical chemistry has been devoted to hexagonal chains. The structure of these graphs is apparently the simplest among all hexagonal systems and trees, therefore, mathematical and mathematico-chemical results known in the theory of hexagonal systems apply only to hexagonal chains [13].

Polygonal tree graphs have already a tree like structure, thus we can apply a well known result by Courcelle and Olariu [15], for any graph G, which is $cwd(G) \leq 2^{twd(G)+1} + 1$. Thus we can obtain a quote for the clique-width of *Polygonal tree graphs*. This result was further improved by Corneil and Rotics in [6] showing that $cwd(G) \leq 3 \cdot 2^{twd(G)-1}$. It is also known that the tree-width of an Polygonal tree graphs is 2, so by using the latter inequality, the bound clique-width smaller or equal to 6 is obtained. In this paper, our main result is to show that the clique-width of Polygonal tree graphs is smaller or equal to 5 improving the best known bound and also we present a polynomial time algorithm which computes the 5-expression.

2   Preliminaries

All graphs in this work are simple i.e. finite with no self-loops nor multiple edges and are undirected. A graph is a pair $G = (V, E)$ where V is a set of elements called vertices and E is a set of unordered pairs of vertices. As usual we let $|A|$ denote the cardinality of a set A. The *degree* of a vertex v in a graph G, is the number of edges of G incident with v. We denote by $\Delta(G)$ the maximum degree of the vertices of G.

An *abstract*graph is an isomorphism class of a graph. A path from v to w, denoted by $path(v, w)$, is a sequence of edges: $v_0v_1, v_1v_2, \ldots, v_{n-1}v_n$ such that $v = v_0$ and $v_n = w$ and v_k is adjacent to v_{k+1}, for $0 \leq k < n$. The length of the path is n. A simple path is a path where $v_0, v_1, \ldots, v_{n-1}, v_n$ are all distinct. A cycle is a non-empty path such that the first and last vertices are identical, and a simple cycle is a cycle in which no vertex is repeated, except the first and last that are identical. P_n, C_n denote respectively, a path graph, a simple cycle, all of those graphs have n vertices.

A spanning tree of a graph on n vertices is a subset of $n - 1$ edges that forms a tree. Given a graph G, let T_G be one of its spanning trees. The edges in T_G are called *tree edges*, whereas the edges in $E(G) \backslash E(T_G)$ are called *fronds*. Let $e \in E(G) \backslash E(T_G)$ be a frond edge, the union of the path in T_G between the endpoints of e with the edge e itself forms a simple cycle, such cycle is called a basic (or fundamental) cycle of G with respect to T_G. Each frond $e = \{x, y\}$ holds the maximum path contained in the basic cycle that it is part of. Let $\mathcal{C}$ be the set of fundamental cycles of G.

A regular polygon is the one that has all sides equal and all interior angles equal and are congruent if they have the same number of sides. A polygonal chain is a graph obtained by identifying a finite number of congruent regular polygons, and such that each basic polygon, except the first and the last one, is adjacent to exactly two basic polygons. When each polygon in a polygonal chain has the same number of l-sides, then we can say that is a linear array of l-gons. The way that two adjacent l-gons are joined, via a common vertex or via a common edge, defines different classes of polygonal chemical compounds.

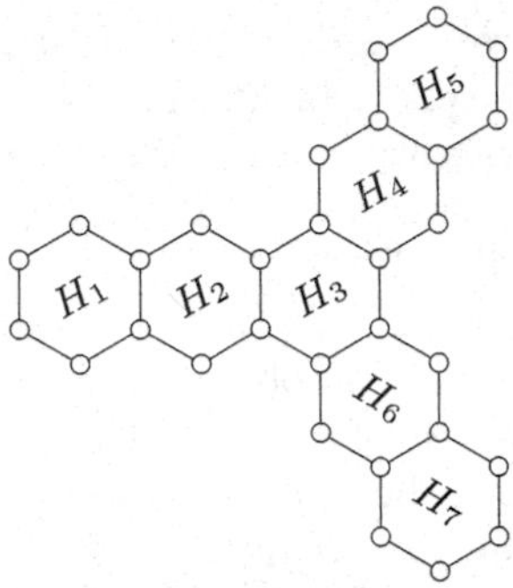

Fig. 1. Hexagonal tree

If the array of polygons follows the structure of a tree where instead of nodes we have polygons, and any two consecutive polygons share exactly one edge, then we call the resulting graph a polygonal tree. Figure 1 shows an example of a Hexagonal tree.

We now introduce the notion of clique-width (*cwd*, for short). Let $\mathscr{C}$ be a countable set of labels. A *labeled* graph is a pair (G, γ) where γ maps $V(G)$ into $\mathscr{C}$. A labeled graph can be defined as a triple $G = (V, E, \gamma)$ and its labeling function is denoted by $\gamma(G)$. We say that G is C-labeled if C is finite and $\gamma(G)(V) \subseteq C$. We denote by $\mathscr{G}(C)$ the set of undirected C-labeled graphs. A vertex with label a will be called an a-port.

We introduce the following symbols:

- a nullary symbol $a(v)$ for every $a \in \mathscr{C}$ and $v \in V$;
- a unary symbol $\rho_{a \to b}$ for all $a, b \in \mathscr{C}$, with $a \neq b$;
- a unary symbol $\eta_{a,b}$ for all $a, b \in \mathscr{C}$, with $a \neq b$;
- a binary symbol $\oplus$.

These symbols are used to denote operations on graphs as follows: $a(v)$ creates a vertex with label a corresponding to the vertex v, $\rho_{a \to b}$ renames the vertex a by b, $\eta_{a,b}$ creates an edge between a and b, and $\oplus$ is a disjoint union of graphs.

For $C \subseteq \mathscr{C}$ we denote by $T(C)$ the set of finite well-formed terms written with the symbols $\oplus, a, \rho_{a \to b}, \eta_{a,b}$ for all $a, b \in C$, where $a \neq b$. Each term in $T(C)$ denotes a set of labeled undirected graphs. Since any two graphs denoted by the same term t are isomorphic, one can also consider that t defines a unique abstract graph.

The following definitions are given by induction on the structure of t. We let $val(t)$ be the set of graphs denoted by t.

If $t \in T(C)$ we have the following cases:

1. $t = a \in C$: $val(t)$ is the set of graphs with a single vertex labeled by a;
2. $t = t_1 \oplus t_2$: $val(t)$ is the set of graphs $G = G_1 \cup G_2$ where G_1 and G_2 are disjoint and $G_1 \in val(t_1)$, $G_2 \in val(t_2)$;
3. $t = \rho_{a \to b}(t')$: $val(t) = \{\rho_{a \to b}(G) | G \in val(t')\}$ where for every graph G in $val(t')$, the graph $\rho_{a \to b}(G)$ is obtained by replacing in G every vertex label a by b;

4. $t = \eta_{a,b}(t') : val(t) = \{\eta_{a,b}(G)|G \in val(t')\}$ where for every undirected labeled graph $G = (V, E, \gamma)$ in $val(t')$, we let $\eta_{a,b}(G) = (V, E', \gamma)$ such that $E' = E \cup \{\{x, y\}|x, y \in V, x \neq y, \gamma(x) = a, \gamma(y) = b\}$;

For every labeled graph G we let

$$cwd(G) = min\{|C||G \in val(t), t \in T(C)\}.$$

A term $t \in T(C)$ such that $|C| = cwd(G)$ and $G = val(t)$ is called optimal *expression of G* [15] and written as $|C|$-expression.

3   Computing *cwd* of Two Simple Intersected Cycles

Let $G = (V, E)$ be a connected graph with $n = |V|$, $m = |E|$ and such that $\Delta(G) \geq 2$. Let $\mathcal{C}$ be the set of fundamental cycles of G. If $C_i, C_j \in \mathcal{C}$ and $E(C_i) \cap E(C_j) \neq \emptyset$ then $C_i \triangle C_j = (E(C_i) \cup E(C_j)) - (E(C_i) \cap E(C_j))$ forms a composed cycle, where $\triangle$ denotes the symmetric difference operation between the set of edges in both cycles. We show how to compute the clique-width of what we call simple intersected cycles and then we generalize the result.

Definition 1. *Let C_i, C_j be two fundamental cycles of a graph G, let v, w be two vertices in both C_i and C_j, the set of edges $path(v, w)$ is said to be a* join set *of both C_1 and C_2 only if $path(v, w) = E(C_1) \cap E(C_2)$.*

Definition 2. *Let G be a graph and $\mathcal{C}$ its set of fundamental cycles. Let C_1 and $C_2 \in \mathcal{C}$ such that $E(C_1) \cap E(C_2) \neq \emptyset$. It is said that C_1 and C_2 form a* simple intersected cycle *if and only if there is not a third fundamental cycle $C_3 \in \mathcal{C}$ such that $E(C_1) \cap E(C_2) \cap E(C_3) \neq \emptyset$.*

Figure 2 shows an example of a graph that consists of a simple intersected cycle $C_6 \triangle C_8$, where the dashed vertices are the ones that are part of the joint.

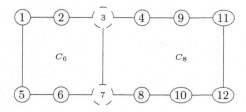

Fig. 2. A graph that consists of a simple intersected cycle, where the dashed vertices are the ones that are part of the joint.

It is well known that that clique-width of a fundamental cycle C_i is smaller or equal than 4, being exactly 3 when $i < 6$ and 4 otherwise. However, the k-expression is unique up to isomorphism in the following sense.

Lemma 1. *Let $v_1, v_2, v_3 \ldots v_{i-1}, v_i$ be the vertices that form the cycle C_i where $i \geq 6$. The 4-expression of C_i is as follows (up to isomorphism):*

- *The labels of v_1, v_{i-1} and v_i are different.*
- *The vertices $v_2, v_3 \ldots v_{i-2}$ have the same label.*

Hence, using a 4-expression, it is not possible to swap the label of a vertex v_h, $2 \leq h \leq i - 2$ with one of the labels of v_1, v_{i-1} or v_i. The following lemma establishes the clique-width of simple intersected cycles depending of the number of vertices in the intersection.

Lemma 2. *Let $G = C_i \cup C_j$ be a graph where C_i and C_j are two fundamental cycles such that $E(C_i) \cap E(C_j) \neq \emptyset$.*

1. *if $|E(C_i) \cap E(C_j)| = 1$ then $cwd(G) \leq 4$*
2. *if $|E(C_i) \cap E(C_j)| > 1$ then $cwd(G) \leq 5$*

Proof

1. Let $vw = E(C_i) \cap E(C_j)$, from Lemma 1 the 4-expression of C_i can be built starting from v and ending at w, hence v and w are assigned different labels. One of the remaining labels is used for v_{i-1} and the other for the set of vertices $\{v_2, v_3, \ldots, v_{i-2}\}$. (*) The label of vertex v_{i-1} can be renamed to the label of the set $\{v_2, v_3, \ldots, v_{i-2}\}$ since it can not be further connected, call a to the freed label. So we built the 4-expression of C_j starting from w and ending at v. Let $w = w_1, w_2, \ldots, w_j = v$ be the vertices of the cycle C_j. Since the edge vw has been built when the 4-expression of C_i was built, only the k-expression of the path from w_1 to w_j has to be constructed. It is well know that the clique with of a path is smaller or equal than 3, so the free label a together with the labels of v and w are used to built the 3-expression of the path. Hence only 4 labels are needed to build the 4-expression of G.
2. Let $path(v, w) = E(C_i) \cap E(C_j)$, where v, w are the ends. We built the 4-expression of C_i using Lemma 1 starting at v, when the vertex w is reached, we use a new label, let say a for w, so 5 labels are used to built C_i. Since v and w have unique labels, the proof is the same from (*) in 1.

Algorithm 1 summarizes the computation of the $(4, 5)$-expression of two intersected fundamental cycles.

4   Computing the Clique-Width of Polygonal Trees

Let G be a polygonal tree, hence each l-gon of G represents a node of the tree and a l-gon K_i is a child of another l-gon K_j only if $|E(K_i) \cap E(K_j)| = 1$. The leaves of the tree are the l-gons which belong to simple intersected cycles, i.e. those l-gons which intersect exactly one l-gon. Each (l-gon) interior node of the tree may have at most $\lfloor l/2 \rfloor - 1$ children and 1 father, so we show that the clique-width of polygonal trees is 5 and as a consequence it is the clique-width of hexagonal trees.

Algorithm 1. Procedure that computes the $(4,5)$-expression(G) when G is decomposed in a intersected simple fundamental cycles

---

1: **procedure** k-EXPRESSION(G)
2: **let** (C_n and C_m be simple fundamental cycles G)
3: **let** ($n \geq m$)
4: **if** $|E(C_n) \cap E(C_m)| \geq 1$ **then**
5:     Identify the joint edge vw and choose let say v, make a label $b(v)$ and begins to build the C_n expression from it {The last vertex is labeled with c}
6:     **let** (d, e be the free allowed labels to be used)
7:     Build the k-expression of the intersection $C_n \cap C_m$
8:     Build the $k - expression$ of the $path(v, w)\backslash w$
9:     Make an edge $\eta_{c,d}(k)$ {Close the cycle C_n}
10:     **let** (d be the free allowed label to be used)
11:     Build the k-expression of C_m beginning from the joint vertex v
12:     Create a label $d(u)$ where $u \in V(C_m)$ and $vu \in E(C_m)$ and make an edge between b and d, e.g. $\eta_{b,d}$
13:     Rename b by a, e.g. $\rho_{b \to a}$
14:     **let** (The free labels are b and d.)
15:     Build the $k - expression$ of the $path(u, w)\backslash w$
16:     $\eta_{c,d}(k)$ {Close the cycle C_m}
17: **else**
18:     Identify the joint edge vw and choose let say v, make a label $b(v)$ and begins to build the C_n expression from it {The last vertex is labeled with c}
19:     Make an edge between b and c, e.g. $\eta_{b,c}$ {Close the cycle C_n}
20:     **let** (d be the free allowed label to be used)
21:     Build the k-expression of C_m beginning from the joint vertex v
22:     Create a label $d(u)$ where $u \in V(C_m)$ and $vu \in E(C_m)$ and make an edge between b and d, e.g. $\eta_{b,d}$
23:     Rename b by a, e.g. $\rho_{b \to a}$
24:     **let** (The free labels are b and d).
25:     Build the $k - expression$ of the $path(u, w)\backslash w$
26:     $\eta_{c,d}(k)$ {Close the cycle C_m}
27: **end if**

Definition 3. *Let* $G = K_1 \cup K_2 \cup \ldots \cup K_r$ *be a polygonal tree where:*

- *each K_i, $1 < i < r$ is a l-gon*
- *$|E(K_1) \cap E(K_i)| = 1$ for each $2 < i < r$.*
- *$E(K_i) \cap E(K_j) = \emptyset$ for each $2 < i, j < r$, $i \neq j$.*

We call to these graphs simple polygonal trees whose root is K_1 and each K_i, $1 < i \leq r$ are leaves.

We now show how to compute the clique-width of simple polygonal trees.

Lemma 3. *If G is a simple polygonal trees then $cwd(G) \leq 5$.*

Proof. Each l-gon is a fundamental cycle. We begin building the 5-expression in a bottom up manner of the polygonal tree, i.e. we begin with the leaves.

Let G be built as Definition 3, let $v_2 w_2 = E(K_1) \cap E(K_2)$. The 4-expression of K_2 is built beginning at v_2 and ending at w_2 so that the labels of v_2, w_2 are unique. As in Lemma 2 the vertices in $path(v_2, w_2)$ different from v_2 and w_2 can be named with the same label, lets call this label a, hence a label from the 4-expression can be freed and only 3 labels are used to built K_2. Let $v_3 w_3 = E(K_1) \cap E(K_3)$, independently of the 4-expression of K_2, built the 4-expression of K_3 as follows: one label for v_3, another label for w_3 and the label a for the vertices in $path(v_3, w_3)$ different from v_3 and w_3. In summary, 5 labels are used $b(v_2), c(w_2), d(v_3), e(w_3)$ and a for the rest of the vertices. Joint the 4-expressions of K_2 and K_3 using $\oplus$ and add an edge from $b(w_2)$ to $c(v_3)$. Now, the labels b and c can be freed since each edge with ends either w_2 or w_3 has been built. The 4-expression of K_4 is built similar to K_3 using the labels b and c for the joints with K_1. The process is repeated until K_r is reached. The last step joins w_r with v_2 via an edge. The cycle $v_2, w_2, v_3, w_3, \ldots, v_r, w_r, v_2$ is K_1, so 5 labels are used to built a simple polygonal tree.

Now we show that the graph which results from joining a l-gon to $\lfloor l/2 \rfloor - 1$ independent simple polygonal trees has clique-width smaller or equal than 5.

Lemma 4. *If $G = G_1 \cup G_2 \cup G_3 \cdots \cup G_r$ where each $G_i, i \in \{1, \ldots r\}$ is a simple polygonal trees and such that $|E(G_1) \cap E(G_i)| = 1$ for each $2 < i < r$ and $E(G_i) \cap E(G_j) = \emptyset$ for each $2 < i, j < r$, $i \neq j$ then $cwd(G) \leq 5$.*

Proof. Built the 5-expression of G_2 using Lemma 4 starting at the vertex which connect it to G_3. Rename the vertices of G_2 with the same label except the one which connects it with G_3 and G_1, so 2 labels are freed. The same proof of Lemma 4 applies substituting K_i with G_i, $2 \leq i \leq r$.

There is a last topology in polygonal trees, that in which a l-gon has less than $\lfloor l/2 \rfloor - 1$ children, which means that between at least two l-gon children there is a path containing more than one edge. Lemma 4 shows that in this last case the clique-width is also smaller or equal than 5.

Lemma 5. *If*

$$G = G_1 \cup G_2 \cup G_3 \cdots \cup G_r \bigcup_{i=2}^{r-1} (V(path(w_i, v_{i+1})), path(w_i, v_{i+1}))$$

$$\cup (V(path(w_r, v_2)), path(w_r, v_2))$$

where each $G_i, i \in \{1, \ldots r\}$ is a simple polygonal trees and such that $E(G_1) \cap E(G_i) = v_i w_i$ for each $2 < i < r$ and $E(G_i) \cap E(G_j) = \emptyset$ for each $2 < i, j < r$, $i \neq j$ then $cwd(G) \leq 5$.

Proof. The proof proceeds according to the cardinality of $path(w_i, v_{i+1})$. If $|path(w_i, v_{i+1})| = 1$ for each $2 < i \leq r$ then G is exactly the graph of Lemma 4. Let $path(w_2, v_3) > 1$, it means that there is a sequence of edges $w_2 w_{2_1}, w_{2_1} w_{2_2}$, $\ldots w_{2_p} v_3$ in G that connect G_1 with G_2 for some $p < l$. We show that a

5-expression is enough for building $G_1 \cup G_2 \cup (V(path(w_2, v_3)), path(w_2, v_3))$. Built the 5-expression of G_2 as in Lemma 4 starting at the vertex v_2 and ending at w_2. Relabel each vertex of G_2 with the same label except v_2 and w_2, so 2 labels are freed. Since the clique-width of a path is 3, used the 2 free labels and the label of w_2 to built the k-expression of $path(w_2, v_3) \backslash w_{2_p} v_3$. The k-expression of the remaining G_j, $2 < j < r$ are built and joined similarly.

Theorem 1. *If G is a polygonal tree the $cwd(G) \leq 5$.*

Proof. Inductively apply Lemmas 4 or 5 from the leaves to the root according to the structure of the l-gons.

If G is a hexagonal tree, i.e. decomposed by fundamental cycles of length 6, that have the property that every two contiguous hexagons most be intersected in exactly one edge. Because of the structure of the hexagonal tree we have the following consequence.

Corollary 1. *If a graph G is a hexagonal tree then $cwd(G) \leq 5$.*

Proof. Hexagonal trees are special cases of polygonal trees.

5   Example

We present an example of the application of Theorem 1. Let us consider the graph G of Figs. 3 and 4.

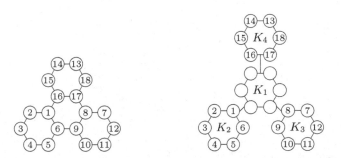

Fig. 3. G **Fig. 4.** An hexagonal tree of G

According to the procedure, we will build each $K_i \in G$ as follows

The k-expression of K_2 is:

$$\eta_{c,b}(\rho_{d\to c}(\rho_{c\to a}(\eta_{c,d}(\rho_{d\to a}(\eta_{d,c}(\rho_{c\to a}(\eta_{c,d}(\eta_{a,c}(\eta_{b,a}(b(1) \;\oplus\; a(2)) \;\oplus\; c(3)) \;\oplus\; d(4))) \oplus c(5))) \oplus d(6)))))$$

The k-expression of K_3 is:

$$\eta_{c,b}(\rho_{d\to c}(\rho_{c\to a}(\eta_{c,d}(\rho_{d\to a}(\eta_{d,c}(\rho_{c\to a}(\eta_{c,d}(\eta_{a,c}(\eta_{b,a}(b(9) \;\oplus\; a(10)) \;\oplus\; c(11)) \;\oplus\; d(12))) \oplus c(7))) \oplus d(8)))))$$

The k-expression of K_4 is:

$$\eta_{c,b}(\rho_{d\to c}(\rho_{c\to a}(\eta_{c,d}(\rho_{d\to a}(\eta_{d,c}(\rho_{c\to a}(\eta_{c,d}(\eta_{a,c}(\eta_{b,a}(b(16) \;\oplus\; a(15)) \;\oplus\; c(14)) \;\oplus\; d(13))) \oplus c(18))) \oplus d(17)))))$$

Now, we make the union of K_2 and K_3. The k-expression of $K_2 \cup K_3$ is:

$$\rho_{d\to a}(\rho_{c\to a}(\eta_{c,d}(\rho_{c\to e}(\rho_{b\to d}(k_{K_3})) \oplus k_{K_2}))).$$

Later, we joint K_3 and K_4 the k-expression of G, finally K_4 is joined with K_2 whose 5-expresion is:

$$\eta_{d,b}(\eta_{e,c}(\rho_{b\to d}(k_{K_4}) \oplus k_{K_2 \cup K_3})).$$

As can be seen 5 labels are only used. The next figure shows the labels assigned to each vertex.

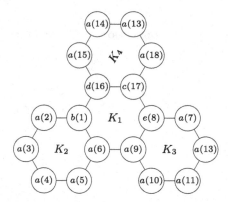

6   Conclusions

We have shown that the clique-width of polygonal trees is smaller or equal than 5 and an algorithm to built the 5-expression has been presented. To identify leaves and interior nodes of the polygonal tree, a spanning tree together with its cotree can be built. A worst case algorithm to do so runs in $n \times m^2$ using the adjacent matrix. The 5-expression is built traversing the spanning tree from leaves to the root whose algorithm has a time complexity of $n \times m$. Hence, the worst case time complexity is given by $n \times m^2$. As a consequence, we have shown that a special class of polygonal trees called hexagonal trees, commonly use in chemistry, can be built also with a 5-expression.

Acknowledgment. The author would like to thank CONACYT for the scholarship granted in pursuit of his doctoral studies. This work has been supported by the Cuerpo acadmico of Algoritmos Combinatorios and Aprendizaje (CA-BUAP-257) of the BUAP.

References

1. Courcelle, B., Engelfriet, J., Rozenberg, G.: Handle-rewriting hypergraph grammars. J. Comput. Syst. Sci. **46**(2), 218–270 (1993)
2. Fellows, M.R., Rosamond, F.A., Rotics, U., Szeider, S.: Clique-width is NP-complete. SIAM J. Disc. Math. **23**(2), 909–939 (2009)
3. Oum, S.I., Seymour, P.: Approximating clique-width and branch-width. J. Comb. Theory Ser. B **96**(4), 514–528 (2006)
4. Langer, A., Reidl, F., Rossmanith, P., Sikdar, S.: Practical algorithms for MSO model-checking on tree-decomposable graphs. Comput. Sci. Rev. **1314**, 39–74 (2014)
5. Fomin, F.V., Golovach, P.A., Lokshtanov, D., Saurabh, S.: Intractability of clique-width parameterizations. SIAM J. Comput. **39**(5), 1941–1956 (2010)
6. Corneil, D.G., Rotics, U.: On the relationship between clique-width and treewidth. In: Brandstädt, A., Le, V.B. (eds.) WG 2001. LNCS, vol. 2204, pp. 78–90. Springer, Heidelberg (2001). doi:10.1007/3-540-45477-2_9
7. Golumbic, M.C., Rotics, U.: On the clique—width of perfect graph classes. In: Widmayer, P., Neyer, G., Eidenbenz, S. (eds.) WG 1999. LNCS, vol. 1665, pp. 135–147. Springer, Heidelberg (1999). doi:10.1007/3-540-46784-X_14
8. Corneil, D.G., Habib, M., Lanlignel, J.-M., Reed, B., Rotics, U.: Polynomial-time recognition of clique-width ≤ 3 graphs. Disc. Appl. Math. **160**(6), 834–865 (2012). Fourth Workshop on Graph Classes, Optimization, and Width Parameters Bergen, Norway, October 2009 Bergen 09
9. Gurski, F.: Graph operations on clique-width bounded graphs. CoRR, abs/cs/0701185 (2007)
10. Johansson, Ö.: Clique-decomposition, NLC-decomposition, and modular decomposition - relationships and results for random graphs. Congr. Numer. **132**, 39–60 (1998)
11. Gurski, F., Wanke, E.: The tree-width of clique-width bounded graphs without Kn,n. In: Brandes, U., Wagner, D. (eds.) WG 2000. LNCS, vol. 1928, pp. 196–205. Springer, Heidelberg (2000). doi:10.1007/3-540-40064-8_19
12. Wagner, S., Gutman, I.: Maxima and minima of the Hosoya index and themerrifield-simmons index. Acta Applicandae Math. **112**(3), 323–346 (2010)
13. Gutman, I.: Extremal hexagonal chains. J. Math. Chem. **12**(1), 197–210 (1993)
14. Harary, F., NATO Advanced Study Institute: Graph Theory and Theoretical Physics. Academic Press, London (1967)
15. Courcelle, B., Olariu, S.: Upper bounds to the clique width of graphs. Discrete Appl. Math. **101**, 77–114 (2000)

A New Approach to Weakening and Destruction of Malicious Internet Networks

Mark Korenblit[✉]

Holon Institute of Technology, Holon, Israel
korenblit@hit.ac.il

Abstract. Models and algorithms for weakening and destruction of malicious complex internet networks are widely studied in AI in recent years. These algorithms must detect critical links and nodes in a dynamic network whose removals maximally destroy or spoil the network's functions. In this paper we propose a new approach for solution of this problem. Instead of removal of corresponding key segments of networks we initiate intentional misrepresentation in important sites leading to wrong network evolution that in fact is equivalent to weakening/destruction of the network. Specifically, we cause and study artificial decentralization and artificial fragmentation in the network. For simulation of these phenomena, we apply and develop a network model based on nonuniform random recursive trees, so called one-max constant-probability network.

1 Introduction

Many papers on network survivability are devoted to detecting critical areas in a network whose damage or elimination seriously degrades the overall performance of network services [1, 3, 4, 9–11]. Specifically, the *critical node problem* (CNP) consisting of finding a set of k nodes in the graph whose deletion results in the maximum network fragmentation, is discussed in [1]. Adaptive algorithms for detecting critical links and nodes in a dynamic network whose removals maximally destroy the network's functionality are presented in [11]. Optimization problems related to assessing network vulnerability are solved in [3, 4].

In principle, the objective of these investigations is to provide a network's reliability by protection and restoration of its critical areas. However, information about these areas may also be used for struggle with a malicious (specifically, terrorist) network. Identifying key players in the terrorist network can help to prevent terrorist attack and destroy the terrorist network completely [8].

Algorithms for weakening and destruction of malicious complex internet networks are widely studied in AI in recent years. Specifically, the algorithms proposed in [1] are tested in the same paper on a model of the terrorist network. The initial graph simulating the network and the resulting graph obtained in accordance with the optimal solution of CNP are illustrated.

The adaptive algorithm that allows to remove the critical edges (links) from the terrorist network is described in [11]. The special algorithm in [12] provides a means of

© Springer International Publishing AG 2017
O. Pichardo-Lagunas and S. Miranda-Jiménez (Eds.): MICAI 2016, Part II, LNAI 10062, pp. 460–469, 2017.
DOI: 10.1007/978-3-319-62428-0_37

identifying various enemy combatants for elimination in a manner that will destroy the terrorist network system.

In this paper we propose a new approach. Instead of removal of corresponding key segments of networks (as done in most other works) we initiate intentional misrepresentation in important sites leading to wrong network evolution that in fact is equivalent to destruction of the network. Our intention is to demonstrate this approach for some network models. In the framework of these models, we show using computer simulation how transient interference in the network operation leads to significant changes in its further behavior and structure.

2   A Network Model

According to the well-known Barabási-Albert model [2], *scale-free networks* are characterized by two main mechanisms: continuous growth and preferential attachment. That is, (a) the networks expand continuously by addition of new vertices, and (b) there is a higher probability that a new vertex will be linked to a vertex already having many connections (high-degree vertex). Vertex degrees in a scale-free network are distributed by a power law. Most vertices have only a few connections while there are a few highly connected hubs. Vertices of a scale-free network are the elements of any system and its edges represent the interaction between them. For example, the World-Wide Web forms a large graph (network), whose vertices are documents (sites, pages, etc.) and edges are links pointing from one document to another. Actually, many other systems have topology similar to the Web's topology since the mechanism of growth and the mechanism of preferential attachment are common to a number of complex systems, including the Internet and the Web, real networks (communication, business, social, transportation, biological), etc. Thus irrespective of the nature, many complex systems may be simulated using scale-free networks.

The Barabási-Albert random graph model is described as follows:

Starting with a small number m_0 of vertices, at every time step we add a new vertex with $m \leq m_0$ edges that link the new vertex to m different vertices already present in the system. To incorporate preferential attachment, we assume that the probability Π that a new vertex will be connected to vertex i depends on the degree d_i of that vertex.

The mechanism of preferential attachment is assumed to be linear in the model, i.e., $\Pi(d_i)$ is proportional to d_i [2]. However, as noted in the same work, in general relationship between $\Pi(d_i)$ and d_i could have an arbitrary form and, therefore, different types of preferential attachment may be considered.

It is of interest to consider a special case when in every step a new vertex is connected to only one of the old vertices ($m = 1$). In this case the resulting graph is a tree known as a *nonuniform random recursive tree* [6]. The probability of linking to its vertex depends on its degree. When the probability of linking to a vertex is proportional to its degree, this gives a *random plane-oriented recursive tree*.

Nonuniform random recursive trees have a number of applications. Specifically, they may be convenient for simulation of scale-free networks with m_0 close to 1 in which m does not exceed 1 in most of steps. Decentralized networks of hubs to which a new node (e.g., personal computer or server, Web page or media file) may always be added, present the example of such networks. In a special case when a decentralized network is reduced to the centralized one created by "winner take all" scenarios, we have a star topology with a central.

In our paper we apply and develop a network model based on nonuniform random recursive trees, so called *one-max constant-probability network* introduced in [7]. This model is characterized by the following features: (i) each new vertex may be connected to at most one old vertex, i.e., in every time step at most one new edge appears in the network; (ii) any connection event is realized with the same probability p due to external factors; (iii) the probability Π that a new vertex will be connected to vertex i depends not directly on its degree d_i but on the place of d_i in the sorted list of vertex degrees.

The mechanism of preferential attachment is not linear in the model and, for this reason our network is not exactly scale-free.

The proposed network model is rather realistic because in real life the choice of an object may be determined not by an absolute characteristic of the object but by a relative status of this object among other objects. The status itself depends, in its turn, on the objects' characteristics. Besides, this model explicitly defines the order of priorities in the search of appropriate connection and, therefore, it allows not just to analyze the topology of networks, but also to examine the network dynamics step-by-step.

As noted in [5], one of disadvantages of commonly used techniques for the random generation of graphs is their lack of bias with respect to history of the evolution of the graph. Our model being functionally similar to the model [5] introduces an explicit dependency of the graph's topology on its previous evolution. Specifically, we study the genesis of networks using the NodeXL environment which being intended for real network analysis, may be also successfully applied for modeling of network evolution and prediction of various network effects. These effects are then justified analytically.

3   Simulation of One-Max Constant-Probability Network

The network is presented as an undirected graph consisting of a vertex set V and an edge set E. In accordance to the model, the list of existing vertices is kept sorted in decreasing order of their degrees so that the vertex with a maximum degree is in the top of the list. When a new vertex arrives, the list is scanned from the top and the new vertex is connected to the first vertex v which "is allowed to be connected by the probability p". The degree of vertex v is incremented by 1 and this vertex is moved toward the top of the list to find a proper new place for it. The new vertex's degree is assigned to 1 and this vertex is inserted into the list above vertices with degrees 0 (*isolated vertices*) if it has been connected to any vertex.

Therefore, the vertex with the 1-st largest degree will be "chosen for connection" by a new vertex with probability p, the vertex with the 2-nd largest degree - with probability $(1-p)p, \ldots$, the vertex with the i-th largest degree - with probability $(1-p)^{i-1}p$ (for equal degrees, the degree of a vertex checked earlier is quasi larger). For n existing vertices, the probability that the new vertex will connect to no vertex is equal to $(1-p)^n$.

Diagrams of two 100-vertex networks simulated for different values of p are presented in Fig. 1. Three the largest degrees in a network are indicated (degree of vertex arrived in time step t is denoted by d_t).

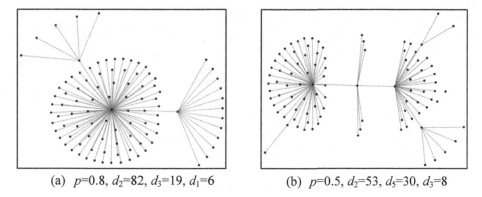

(a) p=0.8, d_2=82, d_3=19, d_1=6   (b) p=0.5, d_2=53, d_5=30, d_3=8

Fig. 1. 100-vertex one-max constant-probability networks

One can see that for relatively large p, vertices which take the lead at the beginning of the formation of the network remain in the top of the list in the future and, therefore, most new vertices are connected to them.

Complex networks are characterized by their own laws of evolution. However, in this paper we intent not only to use these laws but also to influence them by means of short-term periodic external impacts.

4 Artificial Decentralization of a Network

As noted above, there are few nodes of high degree in scale-free and one-max constant-probability networks. These the most connected nodes are, as a rule, network's centers. Their elimination or damage seriously degrades the overall performance of network services.

In accordance to our approach we do not directly remove the most connected vertices but prevent occurrence of high-degree vertices in the malicious network. This is achieved by the periodical interventions in the mechanism of the network formation. Each intervention is swapping of the vertex that is in the top of the list of vertex degrees with a random vertex in the list. As a result, a random vertex is wrongly interpreted as the highest-degree vertex and is a most likely for connecting with a new vertex. Real centers of the network which are leader vertices turn out in the middle of the list, and eventually cease to be leaders. New top vertices are also swapped, in turn, in next steps and thus this way allows to take the lead to no vertex.

Finally, the network is divided into many domains with local centers. The number of these domains (level of decentralization) depends on the frequency of swapping operations.

A strongly centralized network with one center or a small amount of centers is the most vulnerable to these swapping operations. For example, a 100-vertex star-topology network ($p = 1$) is illustrated in Fig. 2(a). A 100-vertex network ($p = 1$) in which a swapping operation between the first and the random vertex is performed every ten time steps is shown in Fig. 2(b).

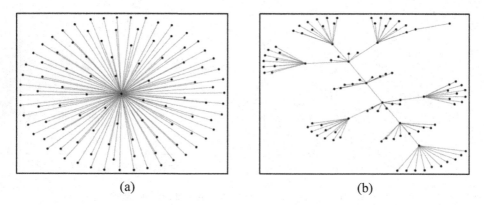

(a)   (b)

Fig. 2. 100-vertex one-max constant-probability networks ($p = 1$): (a) without decentralization; (b) decentralized every ten time steps.

Figure 3 presents the same networks for $p = 0.1$. One can see that now there is no significant difference between networks with and without artificial decentralization. However, the described swapping operations in any case may be useful for shuffling and making confusion in the malicious network.

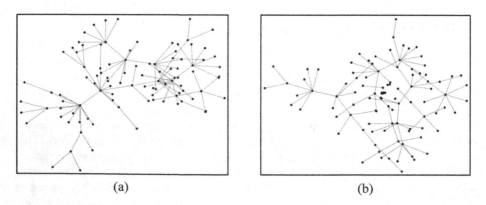

(a)   (b)

Fig. 3. 100-vertex one-max constant-probability networks ($p = 0.1$): (a) without decentralization; (b) decentralized every ten time steps.

As noted in [7], given an n-vertex one-max constant-probability network which starts with one vertex, the lower bound of the expected number of the maximum degree in the network is equal to $p(n - 1)$. The artificial decentralization leads to decrease of this characteristic which is now a function of p and the frequency of swapping operations.

It should be noted that the proposed procedure is quite simple and cheap. The algorithm requires only minor periodical updates in the network database.

However, not always all the information about node connections is open (especially, when it comes to the enemy network). There may be only the set of supposed vertices with maximum degrees. In this case the procedure of the artificial decentralization is to be complicated. For instance, the most likely leader vertices will be swapped with random vertices in the sorted list of vertex degrees.

5 Artificial Fragmentation of a Network

The approach presented in the previous section leads to weakening of center nodes in the malicious network. However, it does not break down the network into separate fragments.

In order to disconnect the network into separate parts we also use the evolutionary method, i.e., we attempt to do so that autonomous subnetworks form themselves in the course of the network's growth. To achieve this we should understand how these independent subnetworks are created naturally.

As shown in [7], in the first steps of creating a one-max constant-probability network, isolated vertices connected with no other vertices may appear. In the next steps new vertices can connect to these isolated vertices. Another possibility is that isolated vertices which are in the bottom of the list of vertex degrees will forever remain separated from the network. In any case, isolated vertices appear only at the beginning of the formation of the network because with the increase of the number of vertices, the probability that a new vertex does not join any of the existing ones tends to zero.

Therefore, an isolated vertex is a start vertex of a new autonomous part in the network. The number of connected components (including isolated vertices) in the network is equal to the number of vertices which were isolated some time, i.e., to the number of appearances of isolated vertices.

Proposition 1. Given an n-vertex one-max constant-probability network, the expected number C_n of the number of connected components (including isolated vertices) in the network is defined recursively as follows:

$$C_1 = 1$$
$$C_{n+1} = C_n + (1-p)^n$$

Proof. For $n = 1$, it is clear that the only vertex is a connected component. In the general case, consider an n-vertex network. There are two possible events in time step $n + 1$:

1. Vertex $n + 1$ is connected to one of old vertices. The probability of the event is $1 - (1-p)^n$. In this case, the number of connected components after step $n + 1$ does not change, i.e., it equals C_n.
2. Vertex $n + 1$ is connected to no of old vertices. The probability of the event is $(1-p)^n$. As noted above, appearance of a new isolated vertex means appearance of

a new connected component. In this case, the number of connected components after step $n + 1$ increases by 1, i.e., it equals $C_n + 1$.

Therefore,

$$
\begin{aligned}
C_{n+1} &= (1 - (1 - p)^n)C_n + (1 - p)^n(C_n + 1) \\
&= [1 - (1 - p)^n + (1 - p)^n]C_n + (1 - p)^n = C_n + (1 - p)^n.
\end{aligned}
$$
  □

Corollary 1. Given a network discussed in Proposition 1, the expected number C_n of connected components (including isolated vertices) in the network is expressed explicitly as follows:

$$
C_n = 1 + (1 - p)\frac{1 - (1 - p)^{n-1}}{p}.
$$

Proof. As follows from Proposition 1,

$$
\begin{aligned}
C_n &= C_{n-1} + (1 - p)^{n-1} = C_{n-2} + (1 - p)^{n-2} + (1 - p)^{n-1} \\
&= C_{n-3} + (1 - p)^{n-3} + (1 - p)^{n-2} + (1 - p)^{n-1} = \cdots \\
&= C_{n-(n-1)} + (1 - p)^{n-(n-1)} + (1 - p)^{n-(n-2)} + \cdots + (1 - p)^{n-1} \\
&= C_1 + (1 - p)^1 + (1 - p)^2 + \cdots + (1 - p)^{n-1} \\
&= 1 + \sum_{k=1}^{n-1}(1 - p)^k = 1 + (1 - p)\frac{(1 - p)^{n-1} - 1}{1 - p - 1} \\
&= 1 + (1 - p)\frac{1 - (1 - p)^{n-1}}{p}.
\end{aligned}
$$
  □

Corollary 2. Given a network discussed in Proposition 1, with increase of n, the expected number C_n of connected components (including isolated vertices) in the network tends to $\frac{1}{p}$.

Proof. According to Corollary 1,

$$
\begin{aligned}
\lim_{n\to\infty} C_n &= \lim_{n\to\infty}\left(1 + (1 - p)\frac{1 - (1 - p)^{n-1}}{p}\right) \\
&= 1 + (1 - p)\frac{1 - 0}{p} = \frac{1 - p + p}{p} = \frac{1}{p}.
\end{aligned}
$$
  □

Thus in order to create the network consisting of more than $\frac{1}{p}$ connected components which appear not only in the first steps, we must achieve an appearance of artificial isolated vertices.

This could be done by short-term periodic external disturbances in the network. That is, p temporarily becomes zero, and, as a result, few new vertices will connect to no of existing ones.

However, appearance of new isolated vertices is not sufficient for appearance of new autonomous subnetworks. These vertices characterized by zero degrees will be in the bottom of the list and their chance "to be found" by new vertices is negligible. Formally, every isolated vertex is a connected component. However, really a vertex itself that does not begin a new autonomous part of the network is not of interest.

For this reason, a disturbance is followed by a swapping operation similar to the operation described in the previous section. This time, the top vertex or the most likely leader vertices are swapped with recently coming vertices which probably are isolated. As a result isolated vertices may become start vertices of new autonomous parts and the network is divided into unconnected islands.

Figure 4 illustrates an example of artificial fragmentation of the network ($p = 0.8$). The network after 100 time steps is presented in Fig. 4(a). This network consists of the 99-vertex connected component and one natural isolated vertex that appeared in the first steps. Figure 4(b) presents the same network and three artificial isolated vertices

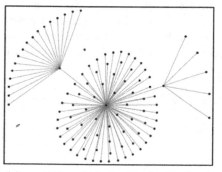

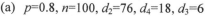

(a) p=0.8, n=100, d_2=76, d_4=18, d_3=6

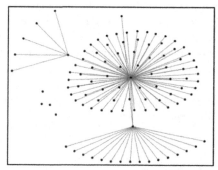

(b) p=0, n=103, d_2=76, d_4=18, d_3=6

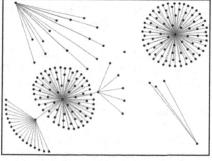

(c) p=0.8, n=203, d_2=76, d_4=18,
d_3=6, d_{101}=83, d_{102}=14, d_{103}=3

Fig. 4. Artificial fragmentation of the network.

created by means of a short-term disturbance in time steps 101, 102, 103. The same network after 100 new time steps is shown in Fig. 4(c). Vertices 101, 102, 103 which are now in the top of the list are start vertices of the new three connected components and, consequently, the network consists of four connected components and one isolated vertex. In all figures n is a number of vertices in the network.

6   Conclusion and Open Problems

We proposed a new approach for struggle with malicious networks. According to this approach, a wrong network development is forced using laws of network evolution and by means of short-term information distortions. Specifically, we simulated artificial decentralization and artificial fragmentation in some networks and studied their structure and behavior.

We plan to extend the proposed approach to more complicated models describing complex real networks (specifically, non-tree-like networks) and to develop the mechanism of its realization. We are going to evaluate our method using different characteristics and to compare it with other algorithms.

We intend to formalize these studies by solving the following optimization problems: (i) To minimize the number of vertices in a network whose degree exceeds a specified threshold; (ii) To maximize the number of connected components in a network whose size exceeds a specified value. The problems will be reformulated as mixed-integer mathematical programs with stochastic input data and will be solved by the new fast discrete algorithms.

Acknowledgment. The author warmly thanks Eugene Levner for his helpful advises and interesting comments.

References

1. Arulselvan, A., Commander, C.W., Elefteriadou, L., Pardalos, P.M.: Detecting critical nodes in sparse graphs. Comput. Oper. Res. **36**(7), 2193–2200 (2009)
2. Barabási, A.-L., Albert, R.: Emergence of scaling in random networks. Science **286**(5439), 509–512 (1999)
3. Dinh, T.N., Xuan, Y., Thai, M.T., Park, E.K., Znati, T.: On approximation of new optimization methods for assessing network vulnerability. In: INFOCOM 2010, Proceedings of the IEEE Browse Conference Publications, pp. 1–9, San Diego, CA, March 2010
4. Dinh, T.N., Xuan, Y., Thai, M.T., Pardalos, P.M., Znati, T.: On new approaches of assessing network vulnerability: hardness and approximation. IEEE/ACM Trans. Netw. **20**(2), 609–619 (2012)
5. Gustedt, J.: Generalized attachment models for the genesis of graphs with high clustering coefficient. In: Fortunato, S., Mangioni, G., Menezes, R., Nicosia, V. (eds.) Complex Networks. Studies in Computational Intelligence, vol. 207, pp. 99–113. Springer, Berlin (2009). doi:10.1007/978-3-642-01206-8_9
6. Katona, Z.: Levels of a scale-free tree. Random Struct. Algorithms **29**(2), 194–207 (2012)

7. Korenblit, M., Talis, V., Levin, I.: One-max constant-probability models for complex networks. In: Contucci, P., Menezes, R., Omicini, A., Poncela-Casasnovas, J. (eds.) Complex Networks V. SCI, vol. 549, pp. 181–188. Springer, Cham (2014). doi:10.1007/978-3-319-05401-8_17
8. Li, M., Gao, L., Zhou, W.: S-Kcore: a social-aware Kcore decomposition algorithm in pocket switched networks. In: IEEE/IFIP 2010: Proceedings of the IEEE/IFIP 8th International Conference Embedded and Ubiquitous Computing 2010, IEEE, Piscataway, N.J., pp. 737–742
9. Molisz, W., Rar, J.: End-to-end service survivability under attacks on networks. J. Telecommun. Inform. Technol. **3**, 19–26 (2006)
10. Peixoto, T.P., Bornholdt, S.: Evolution of robust network topologies: emergence of central backbones. Phys. Rev. Lett. **109**, 118703 (2012)
11. Shen, Y., Dinh, T.N., Thai, M.T.: Adaptive algorithms for detecting critical links and nodes in dynamic networks. In: 2012 IEEE Military Communications Conference Browse Conference Publications, MILCOM 2012, pp. 1–6, Orlando, FL, 29 October–1 November 2012
12. Thompson, K.R.: Phoenix Algorithm: A Behavior-Predictive Algorithm. http://educology.indiana.edu/Thompson/Phoenix%20Algorithm.pdf

Intelligent Learning Environments

Toward Optimal Pedagogical Action Patterns by Means of Partially Observable Markov Decision Process

Manuel Mejía-Lavalle[1]([⊠]), Hermilo Victorio[1], Alicia Martínez[1], Grigori Sidorov[2], Enrique Sucar[3], and Obdulia Pichardo[2]

[1] Centro Nacional de Investigación y Desarrollo Tecnológico (CENIDET), Cuernavaca, Mexico
{mlavalle,hvictoriom,amartinez}@cenidet.edu.mx
[2] Instituto Politécnico Nacional (IPN), Ciudad de México, Mexico
sidorov@cic.ipn.mx, ayilina@hotmail.com
[3] Instituto Nacional de Astrofísica Óptica y Electrónica (INAOE), Puebla, Mexico
esucar@inaoep.mx

Abstract. Good pedagogical actions are key components in all learning-teaching schemes. Automate that is an important Intelligent Tutoring Systems objective. We propose apply Partially Observable Markov Decision Process (POMDP) in order to obtain automatic and optimal pedagogical recommended action patterns in benefit of human students, in the context of Intelligent Tutoring System. To achieve that goal, we need previously create an efficient POMDP solver framework with the ability to work with real world tutoring cases. At present time, there are several Web available POMDP open tool solvers, but their capacity is limited, as experiments showed in this paper exhibit. In this work, we describe and discuss several design ideas toward obtain an efficient POMDP solver, useful in our problem domain.

Keywords: Partially Observable Markov Decision Process · Intelligent Tutoring Systems · Automatic pattern generation · Optimal pedagogical actions · Statistical & structural pattern

1 Introduction

Intelligent Tutoring Systems (ITS) help students in their learning process, expressed as the acquisition of knowledge and skills. There are many ways of conceptualize, design and develop services that provide ITS and e-learning [1, 2]. The special ITS feature is their adaptability to personal state of the student and thus, knowledge representation is an element of special importance.

Student Model is the ITS component that contains needed information for customized adaptability expressed as learning tasks related to current situation. There are different approaches to Student Model representation and they are applied to different learning features and/or personal student features. Ideally, it should contain as much

© Springer International Publishing AG 2017
O. Pichardo-Lagunas and S. Miranda-Jiménez (Eds.): MICAI 2016, Part II, LNAI 10062, pp. 473–480, 2017.
DOI: 10.1007/978-3-319-62428-0_38

knowledge as possible about the cognitive and affective states and the student's evaluation as the learning process goes on.

The Domain Model (also called Expert Knowledge) contains the concepts, rules and strategies of problem solving domain to be learned. It can fulfill various functions: as a source of expert knowledge, a standard for evaluating student performance or to detect errors, etc.

The Tutor Model receives information from Student Model and Domain Model and makes decisions about the tutorial strategies or pedagogical actions. Based on the received knowledge it must make decisions such as whether to intervene or not, and if so, when and how. The planning and delivery of content are also part of the functions of the Tutor Model [2]. Correct pedagogical actions are fundamental components in all learning-teaching process. Automate that is an important ITS objective. There are several proposed approaches to accomplish that objective.

For example, Bayesian methods reason about the likelihood of future events, given their past and current situation. They are based on the fact that the world is full of uncertainty and often not suitable for clean statistical tests. Bayesian Networks allow computers to combine new information with prior beliefs about the data, making subjective decisions about how strongly weighed prior beliefs and provide a policy to retain new information in perspective (Leonhardt, 2001, as cited [1]).

Markov models (that include Markov chains, Markov Hidden Models, Markov Decision Processes and Partially Observable Markov Decision Processes) are a particular form of Bayesian models. In Markov models, each next state of the world (an instantiation of variables that build the model) depends only of the current state and not of its complete past history (this is known as the Markov property). Markov property releases the system of the need to store potentially great quantities of information related to complete behavior history model. It is of special ITS interest modeling method known as Partially Observable Markov Decision Processes (POMDP) [3]. POMDP consider that true states are not fully visible, but they are partially evidenced from observations; also, POMDP include, among its model components, a set of actions that will try to change the model to an advanced state guided for expected rewards (another model's component) [4, 5]. Due to these attractive characteristics we chose applying POMDP technique.

POMDP consist of tuple $(S, a, P(s'|s, a), R(a, s), O, P(o|s, a))$ where S are states, a are actions, $P(s'|s, a)$ represent transition probabilities, $R(a, s)$ are for rewards, O is an observation set and finally $P(o|s, a)$ is a set of emission probabilities (Fig. 1).

We propose to apply POMDP in order to obtain automatic and optimal pedagogical recommended action patterns in benefit of human students, in the context of Intelligent Tutoring System. To achieve that goal, we need previously create an efficient POMDP solver framework with the ability to work with real world tutoring cases, which include tens of states, actions, rewards, transitions, observations and so on. At present time, there are several Web available POMDP open tool solvers, but their capacity is limited, as experiments showed in this paper exhibit. In this work, we describe and discuss several design ideas toward obtain an efficient POMDP solver, useful in our problem domain (see Sect. 3).

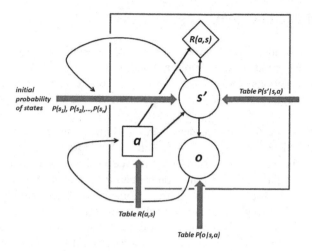

Fig. 1. POMDP graphic representation

The rest of this work is organized as follows: Sect. 2 describes research problem to solve; Sect. 3 is devoted to present our research methodology and main contributions of this work; Sect. 4 shows results achieved and Sect. 5 offers conclusions and discuss future work.

2 Problem to Solve

Our main research problem is to automate the recommendation of optimal (or best possible) pedagogical actions to benefit a human student and form consequently, recommended action patterns. And we propose the use of POMDP as computer approach to achieve that research goal, in the context of ITS.

Then, our hypothesis can be formulated as:

> "POMDP can effectively contribute to automate the recommendation of optimal pedagogical action patterns, in an ITS context."

But to achieve this main research problem, before we need to design and developed ideas focused on the creation of a POMDP solver with the ability of work over tens of variables, because is the case of real world pedagogical problems.

Although there are several Web available POMDP open tool solvers, their capacity is limited, as experiments showed in Sect. 4 of this paper exhibit.

So, we need to tackle this intermediate research problem. And is in this scenario that we are searching for design ideas which effectively attack the combinatorial problem observed in traditional POMDP implementations. In Sect. 3 we addressed and proposed several ideas to solve that problem. For this intermediate research problem to solve, hypothesis can be:

> "There are POMDP algorithm modifications that can reduce computational complexity and, therefore, allow solve real world pattern recommendations of optimal pedagogical actions".

3 Proposed Methodology

To obtain a general idea over POMDP solvers, we design several experiments. For example, generate random models were designed with $2 \times 2 \times 2$ size (i.e.: 2 states, 2 actions and 2 observations), and so on $3 \times 3 \times 3, 4 \times 4 \times 4, 5 \times 5 \times 5, 6 \times 6 \times 6,$ $10 \times 10 \times 10$ and $20 \times 20 \times 20$ (in Tables 1 and 2 they are labeled as *2aleat, 3aleat* and so on).

Also POMDPs models that consider a half of efficiency in learning were designed, with size $2 \times 2 \times 2, 3 \times 3 \times 3, 4 \times 4 \times 4, 5 \times 5 \times 5$ and $6 \times 6 \times 6$ (in Tables 1 and 2 they are labeled as *2ef, 3ef* and so on). We designed a model that considers $10 \times 10 \times 10$ POMDP removing transition probabilities and observation probabilities to less than 0.05 (5% threshold), that is, transition to 0.0. After changing these probabilities the rest of the row values are normalized to sum 1.0.

The proposed models in the current tests consider an action by state. Ideally it is assumed that *a1* action applied in the state *s1* generated by the transition to state *s2*, etc.

It is considered a uniform reward distribution (all states have the same value or ratio). From the above, the reward (calculated as a percentage) to apply the action i in the state i of a model of n states is $r = 100/(n - 1)$. It is divided by $(n - 1)$ because it is assumed that the last state is the goal and no rewards for implementing additional actions in this state. Any action x different from i applied in state i will not generate reward (0). Although the models could be considered "punishment" or costs (negative "rewards") to implement actions that generate transitions to undesirable states.

In our research we want to reduce the model POMDP complexity in three aspects:

- Elimination of state transitions (or combinations of transition*reward; or reward*transition*observation) under minimum established thresholds.
- Classify states within a maximum of three groups: backward (rewards lower than those obtained in the present state), stable (rewards equal to those obtained in the present state) and forward (rewards greater than those obtained at present sate). Additionally consider variations in granularity levels (sublevels of the three major groups, to expand range of search).
- Solutions like POMDP different hierarchical levels compared vs. monolithic models.

  There are two main expected contributions:

- Create a modified POMDP algorithm which can manage real world ITS problems.
- Recommend optimal pedagogical actions by means of that modified POMDP algorithm, in direct benefit of human students and ITS area.

4 Experiments and Obtained Results

POMDP-Solve software v5.3 [6–16] was used to calculate the exact solutions (Enumeration, Twopass, Witness and Incremental Pruning algorithms) and the approximate method FiniteGrid.

The software package ZMDP v1.1.7 [17] running the approximate algorithms *Heuristic Search Value Iteration* (HSVI) and *Focused Real-Time Dynamic Programming* (FRTDP) was also used. In addition, the APPL v0.96 [18] package applies the approximate algorithm *Successive Approximations of the Reachable Space under Optimal Policies* (SARSOP). We used versions of the aforementioned software generated by a Cygwin version of 64-bit Windows 8 64-bits. A portable computer was used with Intel Core i5 at 2.40 GHz and 4 GB RAM, Windows 8 of 64 bits. Table 1 shows the results obtained using exact solution methods and Fig. 2 shows the same results graphically.

Table 1. Experiments with POMDP exact solvers

CASO	ENUMERATION			TWO PASS			WITNESS			INCREMENTAL PRUNING		
	t (seg)	obs.	Lim. Inf.	t (seg)	obs.	Lim. Inf.	t (seg)	obs.	Lim. Inf.	t (seg)	obs.	Lim. Inf.
2aleat	6.240		717.017	0.560		717.017	0.520		717.017	6.730		717.017
2ef	0.450		419.355	0.590		419.355	0.480		419.355	2.050		419.355
3aleat	0.860		247.012	0.770		247.012	0.730		247.012	2.060		247.012
3ef	6.610		278.979	3.740		278.979	1.880		278.979	2.930		278.979
4aleat	11.510		162.834	12.940		162.834	4.170		162.834	17.420		162.834
4ef	320.370		168.118	278.510		168.118	28.180		168.118	36.040		168.118
5aleat	> 1200.000	3 épocas *	40.275	> 1200.000	3 épocas *	40.275	> 1200.000	4 épocas *	45.990	> 1200.000	8 épocas *	63.780
5ef	> 1200.000	3 épocas *	47.773	> 1200.000	3 épocas *	47.773	> 1200.000	4 épocas *	55.221	> 1200.000	4 épocas *	55.221
6aleat	> 1200.000	2 épocas *	27.064	> 1200.000	2 épocas *	27.064	> 1200.000	3 épocas *	31.920	> 1200.000	3 épocas *	31.920
6ef	> 1200.000	2 épocas *	31.700	> 1200.000	2 épocas *	31.700	> 1200.000	3 épocas *	39.206	> 1200.000	3 épocas *	39.206
10u05	> 1200.000	1 época *	1.982	> 1200.000	2 épocas *	2.345	> 1200.000	2 épocas *	2.345	> 1200.000	2 épocas *	2.345
10aleat	> 1200.000	1 época *	1.866	> 1200.000	2 épocas *	2.175	> 1200.000	2 épocas *	2.175	> 1200.000	2 épocas *	2.175
20aleat	mem. agot.	1 época *	0.525	> 1200.000	1 época *	0.525	> 1200.000	1 época *	0.525	mem. agot.	1 época *	0.525
t(2 a 4)	346.040			297.110			35.960			67.230		

* épocas resueltas

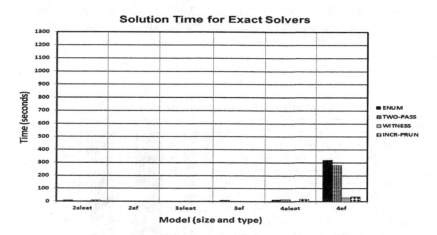

Fig. 2. Results from Table 1 shown graphically

Note that only full exact solutions were obtained for model size 2 to 4. For the remaining models partial solutions were obtained and, in some cases, memory lack stops the process. Better solution was obtained with Witness method, respect to processing time. The worst times were obtained with the Enumeration method.

Table 2 shows the results obtained using approximate solution methods and Fig. 3 shows the same results graphically (we used the same scale in Figs. 2 and 3 for equality comparison purposes).

Table 2. Experiments with POMDP approximate solvers

CASO	FINITE GRID		HSVI				FRTDP				SARSOP			
	t (seg)	obs.	t (seg)	Lim. Inf.	Lim. Sup.	precisión	t (seg)	Lim. Inf.	Lim. Sup.	precisión	t (seg)	Lim. Inf.	Lim. Sup.	precisión
		Lim. Inf.												
2aleat	1.490	717.017	0.000	717.018	717.018	0.0000767	0.000	717.018	717.018	0.0000767	0.000	717.018	717.018	0.0000767
2ef	1.470	419.355	0.000	419.355	419.355	0.0000773	0.000	419.355	419.355	0.0000773	0.000	419.355	419.355	0.0000773
3aleat	1.530	247.012	52.000	247.012	247.013	0.0009991	59.000	247.012	247.013	0.0009999	2.265	247.012	247.013	0.0009989
3ef	2.740	278.979	1200.000	278.979	278.981	0.0021507	.	.	.	err. descon.	1200.200	278.979	278.981	0.0018238
4aleat	3.000	162.834	1200.000	162.835	162.883	0.0487897	1255.000	162.835	162.978	0.1434480	1200.060	162.834	162.870	0.0356065
4ef	5.670	168.118	1200.000	168.118	168.186	0.0681463	1213.000	168.118	168.314	0.1959010	1205.110	168.118	168.168	0.0505067
5aleat	49.200	97.665	1200.000	97.665	97.813	0.1484820	1201.000	97.665	97.978	0.3126630	1201.470	97.665	97.797	0.1323930
5ef	247.490	118.904	1200.000	118.904	119.754	0.8497500	1200.000	118.904	120.249	1.3447500	1200.910	118.904	119.567	0.6628640
6aleat	678.960	75.013	1200.000	75.013	76.180	1.1670700	1200.000	75.013	77.224	2.2107800	1203.250	75.013	76.158	1.1452600
6ef	> 1200.000 47 épocas *	94.970	1200.000	95.507	97.855	2.3472800	1200.000	95.507	99.102	3.5949900	1201.130	95.507	97.591	2.0840600
10u05	> 1200.000 15 épocas *	4.062	1200.000	3.113	3.325	0.2117600	1213.000	3.113	3.493	0.3797950	1202.080	3.113	3.319	0.2059780
10aleat	1245.000	4.190	1200.000	2.748	2.909	0.1614160	1209.000	2.748	3.033	0.2856130	1205.750	2.748	2.906	0.1584260
20aleat	> 1200.000 5 épocas*	0.647	1200.000	0.898	0.815	0.1169550	1269.000	0.697	0.901	0.2032100	1255.920	0.697	0.854	0.1563630
t(2 a 4)	15.900		3652.000				2527.000				3607.635			

* épocas resueltas

From Table 2, it is observed that FiniteGrid method gets the best solution times for models size 2 to 5, and *6aleat* variant; however, no complete solution for most size models were obtained. Other than this, there is very little difference in time among the three HSVI solution, FRTDP and SARSOP methods. A slight advantage is observed in the solution for SARSOP times and in most of the solutions increased accuracy (estimation approximation to the optimal solution).

The principal conclusion from these experiments is that, for both, exact and approximate solvers, there is a time explosion when we try to model problems with relatively few variables. So, for more real problems (with more variables), it is clear that it would be impractical to apply these solvers due to excessive computing processing times.

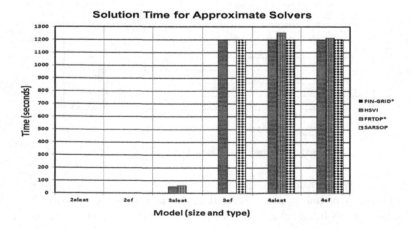

Fig. 3. Results from Table 2 shown graphically

5 Conclusions and Future Work

We are proposing to apply POMDP in order to obtain automatic and optimal pedagogical recommended action patterns in benefit of human students, in the context of Intelligent Tutoring System and Distance Learning [19].

To achieve that goal, we need previously create an efficient POMDP solver framework with the ability to work with real world tutoring cases.

At present time, there are several Web available POMDP open tool solvers, but their capacity is limited, as experiments showed in this paper exhibit in Sect. 4: exact and approximate solvers exhibit time explosion when we try to model problems with relatively few variables.

We describe and discuss several design ideas toward obtain an efficient POMDP solver, useful in our problem domain.

Further implementations and experiments are needed to validate our hypothesis. It is necessary further analysis of POMDP solver techniques and reports which are their main advantages and disadvantages. We think that with a theoretical analysis it is possible to say which are more competitive, and support our conjectures with experimental results. We also need to improve the state of the art and clarify the idea of how we will use the POMDP for recommending optimal pedagogical actions.

References

1. Woolf, B.: Building Intelligent Interactive Tutors. Student-Centered Strategies for Revolutionizing e-learning. Morgan Kaufmann, Burlington (2009)
2. Nkambou, R., Bourdeau, J., Mizoguchi, R.: Introduction: what are intelligent tutoring systems, and why this book? In: Nkambou, R., Bourdeau, J., Mizoguchi, R. (eds.) SCI 2010, vol. 308, pp. 1–12. Springer, Heidelberg (2010). doi:10.1007/978-3-642-14363-2_1
3. Folsom-Kovarik, J.T., Sukthankar, G., Schatz, S.: Tractable POMDP representations for intelligent tutoring systems. ACM Trans. Intell. Syst. Technol. **4**(2), Article ID 29 (2013)
4. Folsom-Kovarik, J., Sukthankar, G., Schatz, S.: Integrating learner help requests using a POMDP in an adaptive training system. In: Proceedings of the Twenty-Fourth Innovative Applications of Artificial Intelligence Conference (2012)
5. Cassandra, A.: Exact and approximate algorithms for partially observable Markov decision processes. Ph. D. thesis. Brown University. Providence, Rhode Island (1998)
6. The POMDP Page. http://www.pomdp.org/
7. Hauskretch, M.: Value-function approximations for partially observable Markov decision processes. J. Artif. Intell. Res. **13**, 33–94 (2000)
8. Paquet, S., Chaibdraa, B., Ross, S.: Hybrid POMDP algorithms. In: Proceedings of the Workshop on Multi-Agent Sequential Decision Making in Uncertain Domains (MSDM-2006) (2006)
9. Ross, S., Pineau, J., Paquet, S.: Online planning algorithms for POMDP. J. Artif. Intell. Res. **32**, 663–704 (2008)
10. Rafferty, A.N., Brunskill, E., Griffiths, T.L., Shafto, P.: Faster teaching by POMDP planning. In: Biswas, G., Bull, S., Kay, J., Mitrovic, A. (eds.) AIED 2011. LNCS, vol. 6738, pp. 280–287. Springer, Heidelberg (2011). doi:10.1007/978-3-642-21869-9_37

11. Rafferty, A.: Applying Probabilistic Models for Knowledge Diagnosis and Educational Game Design. Technical report no. UCB/EECS-2014-61. Electrical Engineering and Computer Sciences. University of California at Berkeley (2014)

12. Theocharous, G., Beckwith, R., Butko, N., Philipose, M.: Tractable POMDP planning algorithms for optimal teaching in SPAIS. In: Workshop on Plan Activity, and Intent Recognition (PAIR). IJCAI (2009)

13. Zhang, P.: Using POMDP-based reinforcement learning for online optimization of teaching strategies in an intelligent tutoring system. Master of Science thesis. University of Guelph. Guelph, Ontario, Canada (2013)

14. Wang, F.: POMDP framework for building an intelligent tutoring system. School of Computer Science, University of Guelph. Guelph, Canada (2014)

15. Sondik, E., Smallwood, R.: The optimal control of partially observable Markov processes over a finite horizon. Oper. Res. **21**(5), 1071–1088 (1973)

16. POMDP-solve. http://www.pomdp.org/code/

17. ZMDP software for POMDP and MDP planning. https://github.com/trey0/zmdp

18. Approximate POMDP Planning Software. http://bigbird.comp.nus.edu.sg/pmwiki/farm/appl/

19. Salinas, J.G.M., Stephens, C.R.: Applying data mining techniques to identify success factors in students enrolled in distance learning: a case study. In: Lagunas, O.P., Alcántara, O.H., Figueroa, G.A. (eds.) MICAI 2015. LNCS, vol. 9414, pp. 208–219. Springer, Cham (2015). doi:10.1007/978-3-319-27101-9_15

Data-Driven Construction of a Student Model Using Bayesian Networks in an Electrical Domain

Yasmín Hernández[1(✉)], Marilú Cervantes-Salgado[2],
Miguel Pérez-Ramírez[1], and Manuel Mejía-Lavalle[2]

[1] Gerencia de Tecnologías de la Información,
Instituto Nacional de Electricidad y Energías Limpias, Reforma 113,
62490 Cuernavaca, Mexico
{myhp,mperez}@iie.org.mx
[2] Computer Science Department, Centro Nacional de Investigación y Desarrollo
Tecnológico, Interior Internado Palmira s/n, 62490 Cuernavaca, Mexico
{marilu.cersa,mlavalle}@cenidet.edu.mx

Abstract. The student model is a key component of intelligent tutoring systems since enables them to respond to particular needs of students. In the last years, educational systems have widespread in school and industry and they produce data which can be used to know students and to understand and improve the learning process. The student modeling has been improved thanks to educational data mining, which is concerned with discovering novel and potentially useful information from large volumes of data. To build a student model, we have used the data log of a virtual reality training system that has been used for several years to train electricians. We compared the results of this student model with a student model built by an expert. We rely on Bayesian networks to represent the student models. Here we present the student models and the results of an initial evaluation.

Keywords: Bayesian networks · Educational data mining · Student model · Virtual reality · Training systems

1 Introduction

Over the last decades, intelligent tutoring systems (ITS) have evolved and proved to be a successful application of artificial intelligent techniques. A part of the intelligence of these systems resides in knowing students and, consequently, in responding to individual needs of students. This adaptation process is based on the student model, which is a structure storing knowledge about student such as errors, misconceptions, trials, and also it can store information about personality, emotions, self-efficacy and motivation.

There is extensive research in student modeling [1–4], and a novel approach is concerned in to analyze data from educational environments to understand learning and students. This emerging field is called Educational Data Mining (EDM). The EDM have emerged as a result of the growing usage of educational environments, such as e-learning systems and ITS, which produce an amazing volume of data about the student-system interaction and how the learning process is advancing. EDM exploits

© Springer International Publishing AG 2017
O. Pichardo-Lagunas and S. Miranda-Jiménez (Eds.): MICAI 2016, Part II, LNAI 10062, pp. 481–490, 2017.
DOI: 10.1007/978-3-319-62428-0_39

statistical, machine-learning and data mining algorithms [5], and it is defined as an emerging discipline, concerned with development of methods for exploring the unique types of data that come from educational settings, and using those methods to understand students, and the settings in which they learn [6].

We developed a non-immersive virtual reality training system for electrical maintenance. This system has been used for several years as a complementary tool to certify electricians in maintenance procedures to medium tension power lines. We want to build a student model based on the data log of this system.

Bayesian networks have been used in ITS to model student knowledge, predict student behavior and make tutoring decisions due to their strong mechanisms for managing the involved uncertainty [7]. We rely on Bayesian networks to probabilistically relate behavior and actions of the students with their current knowledge. The tree augmented naive Bayes algorithm [8] and the GeNIe software package [9] were used to learn the Bayesian model from the data from the system for electrical training. We conducted an initial evaluation comparing the data-driven student model with a student model built with expert knowledge.

Here we describe the process to build the data-driven student model and the results of the initial evaluation. The rest of this paper is organized as follows: Sect. 2 presents the Virtual Reality System for Electrical Training that we have used as study-case. Section 3 describes the procedure to build the data-driven student model. Section 4 presents the results of the initial evaluation of the student model. Finally, conclusions and future work are presented in Sect. 5.

2   Virtual Reality System for Electrical Training

We have developed several non-immersive virtual reality systems for training. The Virtual Reality System for Electrical Training (SRV) is one of them and it includes lessons and practices for 43 maintenance procedures (MP) to medium tension power lines which are a rigorous sequence of steps. Figure 1 shows the SRV while a trainee is performing a MP.

Fig. 1. Virtual reality system for training on maintenance procedures to medium tension power lines. The MP "change of a pin insulator using bucket truck" is being performed.

Each MP is composed by a different number of steps, and in turn each step is composed by a different number of sub steps. At the beginning of each MP the system also includes a training section where students should learn all the materials, equipment, safety gear and tools needed to perform the MP. Thus, each MP includes two sections, namely, selection of tools and development of a MP throughout a series of steps and sub steps. The system provides students with facilities for these two sections to be learnt, practiced and evaluated. In Table 1, a MP step which consists of six sub-steps is described. Each sub-step consists of the description of the sub-step and the instruction; the instruction is an action to be executed by the trainee. The MP described in Table 1 corresponds to the MP shown in Fig. 1.

Table 1. Example of a step of the maintenance procedure "change of a pin insulator using bucket truck". The step consists of six sub-steps.

	Sub-step	Instruction
1	Place the new pin insulator and screw it to the crossarm	Select the 13PC pin insulator from menu of materials
2	The lineman places the pin insulator in the crossarm. The isolator is previously climbed up using the errand bucket	Click on the 13PC pin insulator
3	Proceed to screw and fix the insulator using the ½" reversible ratchet with a 15/16" socket. Then the insulator base and the crossarm are covered back with the rubber blanket	Click on the ½" reversible ratchet
4	Proceed to remove the rubber blanket covering the auxiliary support and the medium tension line. Then the new insulator just placed is covered with the same blanket. See Chapter 100, Sect. 119, Paragraph L, for more details on the importance of covering the operating point	Click on the clamp clip or the rubber blanket
5	Once the insulator is covered, the floor lineman releases the moorage holder made in the rope restrainer. So the lineman on the pole can place the medium tension live line back on the new insulator just placed	Click on the polypropylene rope
6	Once it is released the errand rope from the support for restraining rope, medium tension line (the one covered), is placed on the new insulator	Click on the medium voltage line (the one covered)

Evaluations are organized in two separate sub evaluations: (a) practical test, which consist in selecting tools and development of the MP visiting the two mentioned learned sections and (b) theoretical test, which consist of questionnaires of multiple choice questions selected from a database, and they are marked automatically by the system.

During the evaluation process, the system generates relevant data such as approved MP, errors during tools selection, errors made in specific steps and correct and incorrect answers. The errors are classified according their impact on learning. Table 2 shows the type of errors in the performance of the MP and Table 3 shows the type of errors in the tools selection.

Table 2. Error types in the performance of a maintenance procedure.

Error type	Description
1	The trainee is trying to guess because he clicked on the wrong element in the virtual environment
2	The trainee is trying to guess because he selected a tool which is not required for the MP
3	This error is moderate. The trainee is unfamiliar with the interface; he clicked on an element when it was asked to interact with the menu
4	This error is weak. The trainee was distracted because he selected a tool when a scene interaction was required

Table 3. Error types in the tools selection section of a maintenance procedure.

Error type	Description
5	The trainee is trying to guess because he selected a tool which is not required for the MP
6	The trainee has incomplete knowledge because he selected the corrected tool but he selected a wrong number of items
7	The trainee was distracted because he selected a tool already selected

3 Data Mining for Student Modeling

Human teachers and tutors know students by means of interaction and observation, and in this way they adapt their instruction to particular needs of students. The interaction between students and teachers provide data about student knowledge, goals, skills, motivation, and interests. In an intelligent tutoring system this information is recorded in the student model to ensure that the system has principled knowledge about each student, and hence it can respond effectively, engage students and promote learning [1].

It is likely that educational data mining and machine learning techniques will play larger role in augmenting student models automatically. Machine learning is concerned with the ability of a system to acquire and integrate new knowledge through observations of users and with improving and extend itself by learning rather than by being programmed with knowledge [1, 10]. These techniques organize existing knowledge and acquire new knowledge by intelligently recording and reasoning about data. For example, observations of the previous behavior of students will be used to provide training examples that will form a model designed to predict future behavior [1, 11].

The SRV has been used in several training courses by hundreds of trainees since 2006. During this time it has produced a big sum of data that can be exploited to understand the electrical training and to know the trainees. This new knowledge could be useful to improve the learning process and also could be worthwhile for the training politics of the electricity company.

Data mining or Knowledge Discovery in Databases is the field of discovering novel and potentially useful information from large amounts of data [12]. Educational data mining methods are often different from standard data mining methods, due to the need to explicitly account for the multi-level hierarchy and non-independence in educational data [6].

As a first attempt to take advantage of the data produced by the SRV, we decide to build a student model by mining the data about the performance of trainees in the SRV. As we mentioned, the SRV includes 43 MP, every MP is different from the others as they contains different numbers of steps and sub-steps. Therefore we decided to mine the data about each MP separately. Consequently, in this exercise we mined the data related with only one MP. Also we just take the data of a division; we believe that we could find differences in training among divisions of the company.

In order to obtain a sample, we analyzed the different tables at the databases of the SRV. As we mentioned, the SRV only keeps track the errors in the performing of the MP and a mark for the theoretical evaluation. Some examples of the records of errors are shown in Table 4.

Table 4. Examples of the errors stored in the SRV database.

Evaluation id	Trainee id	MP id	No. step	No. sub-step	Error id
32	93713	1	5	1	1
32	67856	1	3	1	1
23	YF022	1	5	1	1
23	YF022	1	5	1	1
23	YF022	1	5	1	1

After several attempts to prepare and to mine this data, we obtained a data sample which consisted of 518 registers of 100 trainees in 67 courses. However, after analyzing the completeness and correctness of the data, we found only 157 useful records. For the learning process we use 100 records and for the evaluation, we used 57 records. Examples of resultant registers after preprocessing are shown in Table 5. The attributes for the MP, step and sub-step are not included because the data mining algorithms did not find a relationship with the other attributes.

Table 5. Examples of resultant registers after preprocessing the errors in the SRV database.

Mark	EPT1	EPT2	EPT3	EPT4	EMT5	EMT6	EMT7
87	8	0	0	0	7	4	5
100	3	0	0	0	5	0	0
80	0	0	0	0	0	3	3
90	0	0	0	0	5	3	3
70	3	0	0	0	1	0	0

The database contains the errors in the performance of the MP and the mark in the theoretical test, however there is not a field which tells us if the trainee is qualified in the MP, because the system is not intended to certify trainees. To get a classification of the records, we used an unsupervised learning approach by applying the *k-means* algorithm in Weka [13], the popular suite of machine learning software. The *k-means* algorithm allows us to group a set of objects in such a way that objects in the same cluster are more similar (in some sense or another) to each other than to those in other clusters [14]. As we need to know if the trainee is skilled in the MP, we used two classes: *trained* and *untrained*. The Table 6 shows the results of the *k-means* algorithm. An expert decided which cluster corresponds to trained participants and which cluster corresponds to untrained participants.

Table 6. Results of the *k-means* clustering algorithm with a sample of 100 records.

Class	Number of records classified
1 (Trained)	87
0 (Untrained)	13

Then, we analyzed the fields in the database to select the adequate attributes for building the Bayesian network representing the student model. We selected eight attributes related with the errors during the performance of the MP and the mark of the theoretical evaluation. The Table 7 describes the selected attributes. The description of each type of error can be found in Tables 2 and 3.

Table 7. Selected attributes to be included in the learning process of the Bayesian network.

Attribute	Description	Values
Trained	Competency of the trainee in the MP	1, 0
Mark	Mark of the trainee in the theoretical test	0–100
EPT1	Number of type 1 errors made by the trainee in the MP	$0-n$
EPT2	Number of type 2 errors made by the trainee in the MP	$0-n$
EPT3	Number of type 3 errors made by the trainee in the MP	$0-n$
EPT4	Number of type 4 errors made by the trainee in the MP	$0-n$
EMT5	Number of type 5 errors made by the trainee in the MP	$0-n$
EMT6	Number of type 6 errors made by the trainee in the MP	$0-n$
EMT7	Number of type 7 errors made by the trainee in the MP	$0-n$

Since the data are continuous (except the attribute *trained*, the class) a preprocessing was needed in order to discretize them. The discretization of the attributes is shown in Tables 8 and 9.

After the processing, the data was ready to be used to find patterns and learn a Bayesian network which represents the student model. We rely on the tree augmented naive Bayes algorithm of the GeNIe software package. GeNIe is the graphical interface to SMILE, a fully portable Bayesian inference engine implementing graphical decision-theoretic methods, such as Bayesian networks and influence diagrams and structural equation models [9].

Table 8. Discrete values for the attribute mark.

Value	Description
Between 0–10	A mark between 0 and 10 was obtained by the trainee
Between 11–20	A mark between 11 and 20 was obtained by the trainee
Between 21–30	A mark between 21 and 30 was obtained by the trainee
Between 31–40	A mark between 31 and 40 was obtained by the trainee
Between 41–50	A mark between 41 and 50 was obtained by the trainee
Between 51–60	A mark between 51 and 60 was obtained by the trainee
Between 61–70	A mark between 61 and 70 was obtained by the trainee
Between 71–80	A mark between 71 and 80 was obtained by the trainee
Between 81–90	A mark between 81 and 90 was obtained by the trainee
Between 91–100	A mark between 91 and 100 was obtained by the trainee

Table 9. Discrete values for the attributes representing the errors.

Value	Description
Between 0–10	A number of errors between 0 and 10 was made by the trainee
Between 11–20	A number of errors between 11 and 20 was made by the trainee
Between 21–30	A number of errors between 21 and 30 was made by the trainee
Between 31–40	A number of errors between 31 and 40 was made by the trainee
Between 41–50	A number of errors between 41 and 50 was made by the trainee
Between 51–60	A number of errors between 51 and 60 was made by the trainee
Between 61–70	A number of errors between 61 and 70 was made by the trainee
Between 71–80	A number of errors between 71 and 80 was made by the trainee
Between 81–90	A number of errors between 81 and 90 was made by the trainee
More than 90	A number of errors greater than 90 was made by the trainee

To select the data-driven techniques to apply to a particular class of problems is a function of the nature of the data and the problem to be solved [15]. There are several interesting alternatives; we tried the algorithms within GeNIe in order to get the data-driven model. These algorithms are Bayesian search, PC, essential graph search, greedy thick thinning, tree augmented naive Bayes, augmented naive Bayes, and naive Bayes. However, the only one which found beliefs and dependencies that we were looking for was the tree augmented naive Bayes algorithm [16]. We are looking for dependencies such as: class node given errors nodes. Thus, the network obtained with tree augmented naive Bayes algorithm is the one that found this kind of relation-ship. For this exercise, we chose node EMT3 as network class node because this type of error shows knowledge on both sections: tools selection and maintenance procedure.

The tree augmented naïve Bayes network is an extension of the naïve Bayes network. Similar to naïve Bayes, the root node is the class node, and it is causally connected to every evidence node. The tree augmented naïve Bayes network structure relaxes the assumption of independence between the evidence nodes, and allows most evidence nodes to have a second parent, which can be a related evidence node. This maintains the directed acyclic graph requirements and produces a tree that captures relationships among the evidence [15]. The resultant network of this algorithm is presented in Fig. 2.

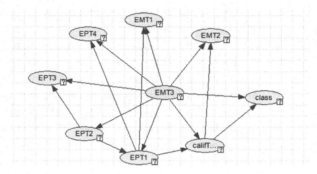

Fig. 2. Bayesian network learned from the data by the tree augmented naïve Bayes algorithm. This network represents the student model.

In the learned Bayesian model we can see the relevance of EMT3 node (which represent no severe errors when selecting tools) to classify the trainee as *trained* or *untrained* in the MP. This relationship confirms that knowing the tools is important to knowing the performance of the MP.

4   Results

In order to evaluate the data-driven model, we built a student model with base on expert knowledge. We asked an expert instructor to assert relationships between the factors of a MP, namely, steps, sub-steps, tools, errors, theoretical test. The expert built the model presented at Fig. 3.

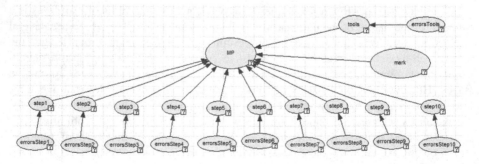

Fig. 3. Bayesian network representing the student model built by the expert.

As it can be observed, the expert considers that errors have impact on each step. The values for step nodes are the types of errors. The expert stated the conditional probabilities with base on the type of errors and on the number of them. Namely, the probability of knowing a step depends on the number of errors and its severity. This means that the trainee make errors type 1, the probability of knowing that step decreases more than the error is type 3.

To evaluate the data-driven model we compared the results of the classification of both models. The results of this evaluation are presented in Table 10; also, some examples of the 47 records are presented. As it can be observed the precision of the data-driven model is around 50%. We need more experimentation and a more principled evaluation in order to have a comprehensive result.

Table 10. Comparison between the data-driven model and the model built by the expert.

Trainee	Data-driven model		Expert model		Difference between models
	Trained	Untrained	Trained	Untrained	
1	50%	50%	62%	38%	12%
2	75%	25%	80%	20%	5%
3	88%	13%	80%	20%	8%
4	88%	13%	85%	15%	3%
5	75%	25%	84%	16%	9%
Precision in cases with difference $\geq$ 5%					50%
Precision in cases with difference $\geq$ 10%					70%
Precision in cases with difference $\geq$ 20%					80%

5   Conclusions and Future Work

We have presented a student model built with base on data of a training system. We evaluate the model comparing its results of classification with the results of a student model built by an expert. In an initial evaluation, we obtained encouraging results since in most cases the classification by the data-driven model coincides with the classification made by the model built by the expert. However, more experimentation is needed before to integrate the model into the system for training. We need to build the structure for the rest of the MP. Also we want to apply other EDM algorithms that we did not consider for this experiment. Additionally, we would like to compare the results of the data-driven model with the opinions of the trainees, in this way the trainee could evaluate the assessment of the model and give us his own opinion.

In the integration of a student model to the SRV there several alternatives. One of them is to use the model for adapting the instruction to the trainee learning necessities. Another alternative is using it as an open student model; namely, to show the model to instructors and trainees. The trainee could see what are the topics and steps he ought to practice. The instructor could use the model to help the student to learn and also to plan the lessons and to prepare his own teaching. Also, the student model can be useful to design new courses, and to design the instructional material. These potential applications of the student model in turn will improve the learning process.

Acknowledgments. Authors would like to thank CFE experts for many useful advises in the definition of the model. MCS wants to thank INNEL for all the support in the development of this experiment.

References

1. Woolf, B.P.: Student modeling. In: Nkambou, R., Bourdeau, J., Mizoguchi, R. (eds.) SCI 2010, vol. 308, pp. 267–279. Springer, Heidelberg (2010). doi:10.1007/978-3-642-14363-2_13
2. Sosnovsky, S., Brusilovsky, P.: Evaluation of topic-based adaptation and student modeling in QuizGuide. User Model. User-Adapt. Interact. **25**(4), 371–424 (2015)
3. Conati, C., Samad, K.: Student modeling: supporting personalized instruction, from problem solving to exploratory, open-ended interactions. AI Mag. **34**(3), 13–26 (2013)
4. Mitrovic, A.: Modeling domains and students with constraint-based modeling. In: Nkambou, R., Bourdeau, J., Mizoguchi, R. (eds.) SCI 2010, vol. 308, pp. 63–80. Springer, Heidelberg (2010). doi:10.1007/978-3-642-14363-2_4
5. Romero, C., Ventura, S.: Educational data mining: a survey from 1995 to 2005. Expert Syst. Appl. **33**, 135–146 (2007)
6. Baker, R.S.J.D.: Mining data for student models. In: Nkambou, R., Bourdeau, J., Mizoguchi, R. (eds.) SCI 2010, vol. 308, pp. 323–337. Springer, Heidelberg (2010). doi:10.1007/978-3-642-14363-2_16
7. Pearl, J.: Causality: Models, Reasoning, and Inference. Cambridge University Press, Cambridge (2000)
8. Jiang, L., Zhang, H., Cai, Z., Su, J.: Learning tree augmented naive Bayes for ranking. In: Zhou, L., Ooi, B.C., Meng, X. (eds.) DASFAA 2005. LNCS, vol. 3453, pp. 688–698. Springer, Heidelberg (2005). doi:10.1007/11408079_63
9. Druzdzel, M.: SMILE: structural modeling, inference, and learning engine and GeNIe: a development environment for graphical decision-theoretic models. In: Proceedings of the 11th Conference on Innovative Applications of Artificial Intelligence, pp. 902–903 (1999)
10. Shapiro, S.: Encyclopedia of Artificial Intelligence, 2nd edn. Wiley, Chichester (1992)
11. Webb, G., Pazzani, M., Billsus, D.: Machine learning for user modeling. User Model. User-Adapt. Interact. **11**, 19–29 (2001). Netherlands
12. Witten, I.H., Frank, E.: Data Mining: Practical Machine Learning Tools and Techniques with Java Implementations. Morgan Kaufmann, San Francisco (1999)
13. Hall, M., Frank, E., Holmes, G., Pfahringer, B., Reutemann, P., Witten, I.H.: The WEKA data mining software: an update. SIGKDD Explor. **11**, 10–18 (2009)
14. Kanungo, T., Mount, D.M., Netanyahu, N.S., Piatko, C.D., Silverman, R., Wu, A.Y.: An efficient k-means clustering algorithm: analysis and implementation. IEEE Trans. Pattern Anal. Mach. Intell. **24**, 881–892 (2002)
15. Mack, D.L.C., Biswas, G., Koutsoukos, X.D., Mylaraswamy, D.: Using tree augmented naive Bayes classifiers to improve engine fault models. In: Uncertainty in Artificial Intelligence: Bayesian Modeling Applications Workshop (2011)
16. Friedman, N., Geiger, D., Goldszmidt, M.: Bayesian network classifiers. Mach. Learn. **29**, 131–163 (1997)

Strategic Learning Meta-model: A Selection Model of Learning Activities

Rafaela Blanca Silva-López and Oscar Herrera-Alcántara$^{(\boxtimes)}$

Universidad Autónoma Metropolitana Unidad Lerma, Av. de las Garzas No. 10,
Col. El Panteón Lerma de Villada, Lerma, Estado de México, Mexico
r.silva@correo.ler.uam.mx, oha@correo.azc.uam.mx

Abstract. In this work we present a Selection Model of Learning Activities
(SMLA) in a Personalized Virtual Learning Environment. The SMLA consists
of a model to evaluate and classify academic activities based on its difficulty, so
the *difficult* or *easy* activities are replaced with other with intermediate difficulty.
The SMLA is part of a Strategic Learning Metamodel that is conformed by three
layers: (*i*) the intelligent layer that includes a personalized virtual learning
environment, (*ii*) the infrastructure layer based on the Cloud Computing, and
(*iii*) the regulation model that provides a control of the activities assigned to the
learners based on the Full-Brain theory. We develop four experiments that
implement the SMLA, and we observed that the model with activities with
difficulty between 0.2 and 0.85 produces an enhancement int the academic
performance of the students.

Keywords: Learning activities · Personalized Virtual Learning Environment ·
Cloud Computing · Strategic Learning · Virtual Learning Environment

1 Introduction

The Strategic Learning Metamodel (SLM) is divided in three layers: the infrastructure
layer, the intelligent layer and the reactive layer. The infrastructure layer is based in the
Cloud Computing technologies. The intelligent layer combines a Selection Model of
Learning Activities (SMLA), a Personalized Virtual Learning Environment (PVLE)
and an Ontological Model (OM). The reactive layer has a regulation model that controls the activities that are assigned to the learners.

The integration of a selection model (such as SMLA) in the intelligent layer is
relevant because it modifies the academic performance and consequently it becomes a
useful tool in the assignment of activities to the students according to its difficulty
index.

In particular, we consider that the assignment of activities with an intermediate
index of difficulty allows to increase his or her academic performance, without detri-
ment of the academic quality.

The SMLA evaluates the difficulty of the activities to classify them in three categories: *difficult*, *easy*, and *intermediate*. The *difficult* and *easy* activities are replaced
with other of intermediate index in order to enhance the academic performance.

O. Pichardo-Lagunas and S. Miranda-Jiménez (Eds.): MICAI 2016, Part II, LNAI 10062, pp. 491–500, 2017.
DOI: 10.1007/978-3-319-62428-0_40

Our experiments support these ideas. We applied SMLA along several periods of three months, and we observed an enhancement in the academic performance, once the students started with 29/100 and reached 68/100 in the last period.

The paper is organized as follow: In Sect. 2, we present a conceptual framework that supports the development of the SLMA. In Sect. 3, we present our methodology that considers the design of the Selection Model of Learning Activities (SMLA). In Sect. 4, we present cases of study that describe the relationship between the difficulty index of activities and the percentages of the academic performance of undergraduate students enrolled in language programming courses. In Sect. 5, we present experimental results, and finally, in Sect. 6 we present our conclusions and comment about future work.

2 Antecedents

Recently, in the context of learning environments, a relevant research area has been the *test analysis* that has been focused on the evaluation of questions to determine its difficulty. For example, the Test of Fundamental Knowledge and Abilities (called EXHCOBA[1]) has been applied in Mexico and several reports about the quality of the test have been published [1]. These reports include *question analysis* from the point of view of difficulty and discrimination capacity of the test. The results show that the EXHCOBA questions have an intermediate average level and good discriminative capacity [1].

However, in all cases of EXHCOBA, the cases of study are focused on the level of difficulty of the test questions, and do not consider the difficulty of activities of the courses.

2.1 The Conceptualization of Question Analysis

The *study of quizzes* with *question analysis*, often considers two relevant concepts: (i) the difficulty index, and (ii) the discrimination index. The former is defined as the proportion of participants with a correct answer in a quiz respect to all the participants that attempts to answer the question [1, 2]. As higher the proportion, the difficulty index will be lower [3, 4]. The difficulty index range is [0.0, 1.0]. When nobody answers the question, the difficulty index has a value of 1.0, and when all the participants give the correct answer the difficulty index has a value of 0.0.

When both of the test and the question measure the same ability or capability, is natural to expect that a student with high score in a test achieves a high probability of getting a correct answer, and viceversa. So, a *good reactive* must provide a good discriminative capacity between the students with high scores in the test, and those with low scores [1]. Consequently, the discrimination index measures how each question differentiate students with high and low scores [3].

---

[1] EXHCOBA in Spanish: "Examen de Habilidades y Conocimientos Básicos".

The discrimination index can be calculated as the difference between two groups, the first that considers the proportion of correct answers divided by the number of participants with high score, and the second that considers the proportion of correct answers divided by the number of participants with low score. A question is considered as good when its discrimination index has a value greater than 0.30 [4].

2.2 Reliability Coefficient, Typical Error and Discrimination Index

Some authors (see [5] and [2007]) use the G-Theory as a mechanism to develop a single psychometrics testing with the estimation of multiple variability sources.

Other authors (see [6–12]) have proposed equations to calculate the reliability coefficient, and the typical error for test questions.

In [13] and [14] a mechanism is presented to calculate the discrimination index. However, all the authors deal with the problem of difficulty from the point of view of individual questions and testing, and not from the point of view of learning activities.

2.3 Statistical Models of the Discrimination Index

Several statistical models to analyze the learning evaluation have been considered in previous works. A first model is the linear regression model of the Classical Measure Theory [15–17] that has been applied in psychometric testing [18]. Its main drawback relies on the fact that the characteristics of the questions depend of the group of participants, and the score of a single participant depends of the question ensemble.

An alternative model called the *generalizabilidad* is provided by Cronbach [19], that applies a specific variance analysis and allows to analyze several error sources associated with the scoring.

Other model was proposed by Sympson and Haladyna [20] and is based on the linear combination of several answer for the questions of a test [1].

Additionally, the Answer to the Question Theory AQT [18, 21] is focused on the question properties of the test from an individual point of view. This model considers that a *good question* must discriminate between participants with high scores and other with low scores.

Finally, other mathematical model has been proposed by Rasch [22] that is easier to apply than the AQT, once it provides a solution to calibrate the evaluation testing where the artefact to measure considers the participants and the questions of the test; and also considers that the student scoring and the question difficulty determines the probability of choosing the correct answer.

We remark that that these models are strongly focused in the questions of the test, but in our approach we refer to a model that determines the difficulty indices of learning activities.

2.4   Strategic Learning Metamodel

In this section, we present the architecture of the Strategic Learning Metamodel (SLM) [23]. The SLM integrates the principles of the Mediator Evaluation [24], the learning activities customization, the assessment, the supervised and personalized attention, as well as the collaborative work in the learning communities that aims to provide the reinforcement of abilities for the workgroup, the leadership and the trading, among others. The SLM optimizes the physical and human resources from an institution in order to increase the academic performance.

In Fig. 1, we show the meta-model that includes the three SLM layers: the infrastructure layer, the intelligent layer and the reactive layer.

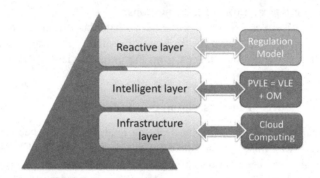

Fig. 1. Strategic Learning Metamodel (SLM) [27]

The infrastructure layer is based on the cloud computing [25]. The intelligent layer includes a Personalized Virtual Learning Environment (PVLE = VLE + OM) that merges a Virtual Learning Environment (VLE) with the customization of learning activities supported by an ontological model [26] (OM). The Regulation Model is focused in the assessment, the monitoring, the feedback and the motivation of the students [27].

As we pointed, several works have been published related with the difficulty of questions, but we are focused on the difficulty of learning activities. In our intelligent layer, a main contribution is the incorporation of a model that determines the difficulty level of learning activities. In this sense, we present the methodology in Sect. 3.

3   Methodology

Our methodology considers:

1. The empirical referent
2. The design of the ontology used to recommend activities to the students
3. The design of the architecture of the regulation model
4. The design of a mathematical model for classification of question difficulty

The empirical referent describes the context of the learning environment. In this case, it corresponds to Language Programming courses for undergraduate students of the Metropolitan Autonomous University, in Mexico.

The design of an ontology was developed and it was used as a recommendation system of learning activities that applies the Graphical Ontology Design Methodology (GODeM) [28], as well as the notation of Onto Design Graphics (ODG) [29]. The ontological model has been applied in the customization of learning activities for specific courses.

The architecture of the Regulation Model (RM) is inspired by the Ned Herman Whole Brain Theory and considers the next components: (i) the teacher, (ii) the learner, (iii) the process facilitator, (iv) the emotional and motivational facilitator, (v) the content, and (vi) the learning activities [27].

The main goal of the Selection Model of Learning Activities (SMLA) is to identify activities with an intermediate index (0.2 to 0.85) that can be considered in the assignment of actitivies to the participants of a course. The difficulty index is determined from the results of the last course.

The questions classified as *easy* and those classified as *difficult* are diminished, and they are replaced with other of intermediate index of difficulty. The lower bound and the upper bound are parameters that can be adjusted by the teacher.

4 Case of Study

The case of study consists of experiments that involves undergraduate students enrolled in Structured Programming courses of the Faculty of Engineering at the Autonomus Metropolitan University in Mexico, Mexico. The main goal is to increase the academic performance, that is calculated by considering the number of students with a scoring greater o equal to 60/100 and the total number of students.

We developed four experiments with a duration of three months: at winter 2014 (14I), at spring 2014 (14P), at winter 2015 (15I), at spring 2015 (15P). To validate the proposed model and the architecture, the courses were registered with the modality called *Cooperative Learning System (CLS, 50% online, 50% cooperative),* with a capacity between 40 and 100 students.

The SMLA was applied in the experiments. The students developed the predetermined activities of a course and the results were reviewed in order to determine the difficulty level to choose the activities with a difficulty index in the interval (0.2 to 0.85). The non-selected activities were replaced with new activities.

4.1 Difficulty Index of Learning Activities

The difficulty index of a learning activity is determined with the percentage of students that solves an activity. If at least 85% of the students approve the same activity (score $\geq$ 0.6) it is considered an *easy activity*. If 20% of the students do not approve the same activity (score < 0.6) it is considered as a *difficult* activity. When the percentage of students that approves an activity is greater than 21% and lower than 84% the activity is considered of *intermediate* index.

We developed a *concept test* for the periods "11O", "12I", "12P", "12O", "13I", "13P" and "13O" with no activity recommendation.

Also, we consider test cases with activity recommendation for the periods 14I, 14P, 15I and 15P. The experimental data show the enhancement of the academic performance when we apply the SLMA to regulate the difficulty index of the learning activities.

4.2 Academic Performance

e academic performance is defined by considering the students with a score greater than 60/100 divided by the total number of students (with score between 0/100 and 100/100). Note that there exists the possibility that some students have a scoring equals to zero when they are inscribed in the course, but they do not attend the course activities neither the course assistance.

The academic performance is calculated as:

$$R = \frac{Ap}{At}$$

where:

R is the academic performance

Ap is the number of students with scoring greater or equal to 60/100

At is the number of students with scoring lower than 60/100

5 Experiments

We develop four experiments along three-months periods identified as "14I", "14P", "15I" and "15P" with the SLMA. In these experiments we selected the learning activities according to their difficulty index. The participants developed the learning activities, and the results were valuated with the score.

The difficulty index was calculated and the learning activities with intermediate difficulty index in range (0.2 to 0.85) were chosen. Then the experiments were developed again and the academic performance was calculated.

As a first stage, the *concept-proof* was developed without learning activities customization in different periods denoted by "11O" and "12I". As a second stage, the customization of learning activities appealing to the ontological model and the thinking style of the students was developed in the periods "12-P", "12O", "13I", "13P" and "13-O". At this point, we observed that the academic performance was not increasing as we expected because the questions tends to be more difficult, so we considered to include a selection model of the activities.

Consequently, as a third stage, we apply the SMLA in the periods "14I", "14P", "15I" and "15P".

6 Results

In the test cases we calculate the average difficulty of activities for eleven periods (see Fig. 2). From these results we identify a maximum in the average of difficulty of learning activities in the period "13O".

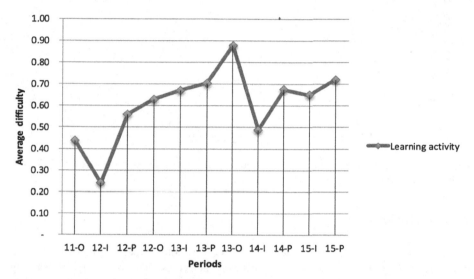

Fig. 2. Average of the difficulty level for learning activities in language programming courses.

Then we apply our model SMLA in the periods (14I, 14P, 15I and 15P) and it was possible to moderate the difficulty index of the activities for these courses. We observed that the average of the difficulty index was effectively taken to the range (0.20, 0.85), which produced an enhancement in the academic performance indicator.

From the data shown in Table 1 we observed that in the periods "14-I", "14-P", "15-I" and "15-P" the academic performance R increases, in comparison with the values of the period "13O" that reaches the highest difficulty index for the activities and a lower academic performance (R value).

Table 1. Average of the academic performance indicator.

Period	Academic performance (R)
13-O	0.298
14-I	0.538
14-P	0.545
15-I	0.636
15-P	0.680

Finally, in Fig. 3, we illustrate graphically the increment of the academic performance after applying our SMLA successfully.

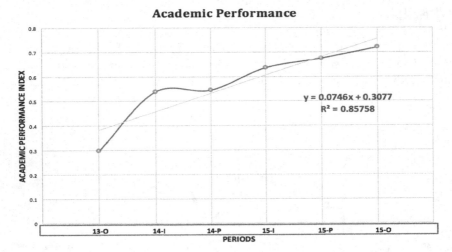

Fig. 3. Academic performance for the language programming courses in the periods 13-O, 14-I, 14-P, 15-I and 15-O.

7   Conclusions

We have successfully implemented the SMLA in four experiments by involving teachers, undergraduate students, and learning activities. The difficulty of learning activities was regulated to values in the interval (0.2 to 0.85) and the easiest and the most difficult activities were replaced.

The experimental results show the enhancement of the academic performance indicator of the students enrolled in this courses, that is consistent with one of the most important goals of our research.

We can conclude that the SMLA has a positive relevance in the academic performance of the students, and in the institutional indicators.

Our main contribution is the incorporation of the SMLA as other regulation factor included in the Intelligent Layer of the Strategic Learning Metamodel.

Now, the SMLA is part of the intelligent layer in the Strategic Learning Model, which constitute a learning solution based on Cloud Computing.

As future work, we consider to automatize the SMLA and to incorporate the feedback coming from the analysis of previous scorings of learning activities, as well as the teacher experience in order to moderate the difficulty level to appropriate intervals.

References

1. Backhoff, E., Larrazolo, N., Rosas, M.: Nivel de dificultad y poder de discriminación del Examen de Habilidades y Conocimientos Básicos (EXHCOBA). Revista Electrónica de Investigación Educativa, **2**(1), 11–28 (2000). Consultado el día de mes de año en el World Wide Web: http://redie.ens.uabc.mx/vol2no1/contenido-backhoff.html

2. Backhoff, E., Tirado, F., Larrazolo, N.: Ponderación diferencial de reactivos para mejorar la validez de una prueba de ingreso a la universidad. Revista Electrónica de Investigación Educativa, 3(1), 21–31 (2001). Consultado el día 1 de julio de 2016 en el World Wide Web: http://redie.ens.uabc.mx/vol3no1/contenido-tirado.html

3. Morales, P.: Estadística aplicada a las Ciencias Sociales La fiabilidad de los tests y escalas. Universidad Pontificia Comillas, Madrid Facultad de Ciencias Humanas y Sociales. Recuperado en 18 de enero de 2015, de http://web.upcomillas.es/personal/peter/estadisticabasica/Fiabilidad.pdf

4. Casart, Y., Fang, F.P., Trías, M.: Complejidad de la tarea cognitiva y nivel de dificultad de preguntas en evaluación de comprensión de lectura en Inglés Científico y Técnico (ICT). Paradígma, 32(2), 23–38 (2011). Recuperado en 22 de enero de 2015, de http://www.scielo.org.ve/scielo.php?script=sci_arttext&pid=S1011-22512011000200003&lng=es&tlng=es

5. Montero-Rojas, E., Zúñiga-Brenes, M.E.: Teoría G: un futuro paradigma para el análisis de pruebas psicométricas. Actualidades en Psicología, 21, 117–144 (2007). Recuperado de http://www.redalyc.org/articulo.oa?id=133212641006

6. Thorndike, R.: Applied Psychometrics, Applied Psychometrical Measurement Inc. Boston, Houghton Mifflin. 7(2), 241–245 (1982)

7. Traub, R.E., Rowley, G.L.: Understanding reliability. Educ. Meas.: Issues Pract. 10(1), 37–45 (1991)

8. Nunnally, J.C., Bernstein, I.H.: Psychometric Theory, 3rd edn. McGraw-Hill, New York (1994)

9. Traub, E.: Reliability for the Social Sciences: Theory and Applications. Sage, Newbury Park (1994)

10. Moss, P.A.: Can there be validity without reliability. Educ. Res. 23(2), 5–12 (1994)

11. Cronbach, L.J., Shavelson, R.J.: My current thoughts on coefficient alpha and succesor procedures. Educ. Psychol. Measur. 64(3), 391–418 (2004)

12. Burton, R.F.: Multiple choice and true/false tests: reliability measures and some implications of negative marking. Assess. Eval. High. Educ. 29(5), 585–595 (2004)

13. Mehrens, W.A., Lehmann, I.J.: Measurement and Evaluation in Education and Psychology, 3rd edn. Holt, Rinehart and Winston, New York (1984)

14. Black, T.R.: Doing Quantitative Research in the Social Sciences. Sage, London (1999)

15. Spearman, C.E.: The proof and measurement of association between two things. Am. J. Psychol. 15, 75–101 (1904)

16. Stevens, S.S.: On the theory of scales of measurement. Science 103, 667–680 (1946)

17. Muñiz, J.: Introducción a la Teoría de Respuestas a los Ítems. Pirámide, Madrid (1997)

18. Embretson, S.E., Reise, S.P.: Item Response Theory for Psychologists. LEA, Mahwah (2000)

19. Cronbach, L.J.: Test validation. In: Thorndike, R.L. (ed.) Educational Measurement, 2a edn. Consejo Americano en Educación, Washington (1971)

20. Sympson, J.B., Haladyna, T.M.: An evaluation of "polyweighting" in domain referenced testing. Trabajo presentado en la Reunión Anual de la American Educational Research Association, Nueva Orleans, EE.UU (1988)

21. Hambleton, R.K., Swaminathan, H.: Item Response Theory: Principles and applications. Kluwer-Nijhoff Publishing, Boston (1985)

22. Rasch, G.: Probabilistic models for some intelligence and attainment tests. Danish Institute for Educational Research, Copenague (1960)

23. Silva-López, R., Méndez-Gurrola, I., Sánchez-Arias, V.: Strategic learning, towards a teaching reengineering. Res. Comput. Sci. 65(2013), 133–145 (2013)

24. Hoffmann, J.: Evaluación mediadora. Una propuesta fundamentada. In: Anijovich, R.W., De Camilloni, A., Cappelleti, G., Hoffmann, J., Katzkowicz, R., Mottier, L. (eds.), La evaluación significativa. Voces de la educación, pp. 73–102. Paidós, Buenos Aires (2010)

25. Silva-López, R.B., Méndez-Gurrola, I.I., Herrera, O.: Metamodelo de aprendizaje estratégico (MAE): arquitectura de la capa de infraestructura, solución basada en la Cloud Computing. Res. Comput. Sci. **93**(2015), 175–188 (2015)
26. Silva-López, R.B., Méndez-Gurrola, I.I., Alcántara, O.H., Silva-López, M.I., Fallad-Chávez, J.: Strategic Learning Meta-model (SLM): Architecture of the Personalized Virtual Learning Environment (PVLE) based on the cloud computing. In: Lagunas, O.P., Alcántara, O.H., Figueroa, G.A. (eds.) MICAI 2015. LNCS, vol. 9414, pp. 183–194. Springer, Cham (2015). doi:10.1007/978-3-319-27101-9_13
27. Silva-López, R.B., Herrera-Alcántara, O., Fallad-Chávez, J.: Strategic Learning Meta-model (SLM): Architecture of the Regulation Model (RM) based on the cloud computing. In: Sucar, E., Mayora, O., Muñoz de Cote, E. (eds.) Applications for Future Internet. LNICSSITE, vol. 179, pp. 172–184. Springer, Cham (2017). doi:10.1007/978-3-319-49622-1_19
28. Silva-López, R.B., Silva-López, M.I., Méndez-Gurrola, I., Bravo, M., Sánchez, V.: GODeM: a graphical ontology design methodology. Res. Comput. Sci. **84**(2014), 17–28 (2014)
29. Silva-López, R.B., Silva-López, M., Méndez-Gurrola, I.I., Bravo, M.: Onto Design Graphics (ODG): a graphical notation to standardize ontology design. In: Gelbukh, A., Espinoza, F.C., Galicia-Haro, Sofía N. (eds.) MICAI 2014. LNCS, vol. 8856, pp. 443–452. Springer, Cham (2014). doi:10.1007/978-3-319-13647-9_40

CodeTraining: An Authoring Tool for a Gamified Programming Learning Environment

María Lucía Barrón-Estrada$^{(\boxtimes)}$, Ramón Zatarain-Cabada,
and Mario Lindor-Valdez

Instituto Tecnológico de Culiacán, Juan de Dios Bátiz no. 310 pte., Col.
Guadalupe, 80220 Culiacán, Sinaloa, Mexico
{lbarron, rzatarain, m05170485}@itculiacan.edu.mx

Abstract. We have developed a novel authoring tool for a programming learning environment that incorporates Gamification as a means of motivation named CodeTrainig. This tool focuses on improving students' programming skills, and it offers authors not only authorship of resources but also of Gamification associated with them. An author can create courses composed by several resources. Resources are formed, in its finer grain, by programming exercises which have a description of the problem to be solved, a set of test cases, and game elements. Students can participate on courses by solving its programming exercises. As they solve exercises they earn points and rise in a leader board. Moreover, the environment let students enable or disable game components, since some of them might dislike the competitive nature of Gamification. We present some experiments we have made with the authoring tool.

Keywords: Gamification · Authoring tool · Intelligent learning environment

1 Introduction

To improve programming skills, students need to practice on a regular basis. In order to do so, students must be highly motivated; unfortunately, this is not an easy task. The role of motivation is very important, and has been identified as valuable on the learning process [1, 2]. Jenkins presented motivation as one factor that make learning to program a complicated skill to master; students might need a particular form of motivation. He found that students are motivated to succeed, and proposed that they can learn in a new way as long as this need is addressed and appreciated [3]. Other difficulty that students face is that they only understand the surface knowledge of a program. Knowing the syntax and semantics of each statement of a program is not enough; they must know how to effectively combine them to write a valid program [4]. Therefore, the concepts that require understanding larger portions of a program are the most difficult to learn. Furthermore, student's biggest problem is how to apply the learned concepts to solve new problems [5].

To overcome this problems, in [6] is recommended that teachers should put special emphasis on teaching how to apply the basic concepts of computer programming to

© Springer International Publishing AG 2017
O. Pichardo-Lagunas and S. Miranda-Jiménez (Eds.): MICAI 2016, Part II, LNAI 10062, pp. 501–512, 2017.
DOI: 10.1007/978-3-319-62428-0_41

design a basic program. Also, in the work of [5], it's highlighted the importance of practical learning. Both, teachers and students agreed that practical learning was very useful, and that it allows understanding the concepts. They concluded that the more practical the learning situations are; the more learning takes place. Also, in [7] is said that programming is best learned by practice and that an instructor key role is to persuade students to do that. Practice, thus, becomes an essential part of learning computer programming. But, if students are to learn effectively, they must be motivated so they will engage properly.

An authoring tool for a gamified learning environment will allow teachers to provide learning materials that highly promotes practical learning instead of focusing only in theory, even though is also very important. But, at the same time, motivation is also considered. In the past few years, Gamification has emerged as a way to engage and motivate users within a large spectrum of domain. Not only does research show that education is one of the top fields for Gamification, but also there is empirical work that supports its positive effects [8]. In this work, we present an authoring tool for a learning environment that features several gamification elements as a mean of motivation, which is used to reinforce positive user behavior.

Desired behavior from students will range from solving most of the programming exercises presented on the learning environment to doing in an efficiently way by using a minimum number of solution attempts. A programming exercise is defined by a description of a problem, and an example of a valid test case (a desired output given a particular input). Students will have to provide a valid programming code as a solution to solve the problem. Each student will have the possibility of gaining points by solving these exercises. The more failed attempts they submit, the few points they get. By using this mechanic, we expect students to carefully inspect their code before trying to use it as a suitable solution as each failed attempt will mean fewer points earned. Students will also be able to customize game elements according to their needs. This means that they can fully enable or disable any game mechanism that they like or not.

The organization of this article is as follows. Section 2 contains an overview of gamification related literature. The description of the proposed system and its requirement and architecture is found in Sect. 3. Section 4 contains how both type of users use the system: students and authors. Section 5 contains the conclusions.

2   Related Works

2.1   Gamification on Education

There are several cases of study that cover the topic of gamification being applied on different education domains. One example of this is the work of [9]. They developed a gamification plugin for the Blackboard e-learning platform with the goal of increase the student motivation. Its experiment showed mixed results, since the experimental group got better scores on practical assignments but lower performance on written assignments. Li et al. [10] developed GamiCAD, a gamified in-product, with an interactive tutorial system for first time AutoCAD users. GamiCAD focuses on helping users through missions, scoring, game levels, time pressure, and mini-games. Results revealed an increase in engagement and performance among naïve users.

Guiding residents in initial American Board of Internal Medicine certification preparation have to attend 'board review conferences'. However, sometimes due to patient care or duty-hour restrictions, residents might be unable to attend. To meet this learner need, [11] developed an online quiz system that emphasized multiple adult learning principles and was constructed using popular concepts of gamification. The authors speculate that the gamified features promoted quiz engagement.

In the work of [12], a gamified smartphone application was developed to introduce new students to the campus. Results indicated that user engagement was improved, and suggested that there is value in adding game elements in the way it was implemented.

In [13] the impact of gamification on student's investigation in a reverse engineering activity is explored. They created a game in which students are awarded achievements by completing various activities. The study suggests that there was a significant improving on the learning process.

Landers et al. [14] developed an online social network with gamification to motivate students in a Psychology Department in order to motivate students to complete optional multiple-choice quizzes. They conducted a study on order to know if students learn more by completing tests than when studying, and that students can be motivated to complete those test by offering them social rewards. Results showed that 29% of students opted to complete gamified optional quizzes. Furthermore, students found gamified quizzes enjoyable and rewarding.

The research found in [15] evaluated the process and outcomes of converting a library orientation tutorial into a game in a cornerstone design in the Engineering Science Program at the University of Toronto. The idea of a gamified tutorial aimed to create incentives for learning was one of the goals of their study. Game elements included in the system were achievement levels. Among its findings, research suggested that gamification offered motivation in the educational setting that activated the competitive nature of engineering students.

2.2 Learning Environments for Teaching Programming

In [16] a blended learning implementation supported with intelligent learning environments is described. One of the intelligent learning environments is CTutor, which allows students to resolve C programming exercises. CTutor is described as problem-solving environments that can diagnosis students' knowledge level in order to provide feedback to help students to understand and reinforce learned concepts. In CTutor, students must develop solution for given exercise, but these solutions are restricted to a special form. The system interface allows building programs by means of a drag and dropping feature, which limits the actions that can be done.

The work of [17] presented an Intelligent Tutor System named CSTutor. The system was designed to help students learn to program in the C# language. It uses a learning approach called anchored learning. This approach place each student in a role-play that obliges him/her to write C# programs to solve given tasks. Students can write correct programs in many ways. In CSTutor, to check if the program is correct, it extracts facts and actions from students' code. These are used to determine if the proposed code satisfies the given exercises' goal.

I-Han Hsiao et al. [18] developed QuizJET system, which is able to generate and assess parameterized Java programming questions. The work explores the impact of adaptive navigation support on student work with parameterized questions in the domain of object-oriented programming. In order to do so, they developed JavaGuide System, which enhances QuizJET questions with adaptive navigation support.

In [19] an online learning environment that analogues the dynamic that exists between tutor and student in a real-world programming workshop is described. The system use online delivery and automated assessment, and is also suggested that if used correctly, this tools can deliver flexible, self-paced learning in a discipline that is fraught with pedagogic difficulties.

2.3 Gamification on Learning Environments

The work of [20] proposed a design of an e-learning platform, aimed at programming education for students. The proposed design makes use of a number of gamification concepts. It is expected to increase students' engagement in learning by awarding individual work and also stimulating rivalry and teamwork.

In [21], the learning effectiveness and engagement appeal of a gamified learning activity targeted at the learning of C-programming language is studied. The work inquired into which gamified learning activities were more appealing to students. The results showed positive effects on the engagement of students toward the gamified learning activities and a moderate improvement in learning outcomes.

Most works on education used gamification to improve the learning process by motivating users through a variety of game mechanics. While some opted for the competitive nature that gamification offers, others focused on individual student engagement trough achievement as rewards. The main contribution of our work, is offering a novel-authoring tool oriented to teach and motivate students to learn a programming course, by incorporating several elements of gamification. The proposed system allows educators to provide learning materials that encourage students to practice their programming skills. Also, since most of the literature highlights how important motivation is on the learning process, we used a gamification approach to properly engage students on learning activities. At the same time, special attention is put at how gamification is embedded in the system, since we are aiming at offering a customizable experience. To the best of our knowledge, this is the first authoring tool used to teach programming courses incorporating gamification.

3 CodeTraining: Requirements and Architecture

CodeTraining is composed by two major applications: the authoring tool for teachers, and the training platform aimed at students. The authoring tool is a web application, which will give educators the instruments that will allow them to publish complete programming courses. In the first place, instructors are able to create and edit new programming exercises. Relevant data associated with such exercises range from how the exercises are described (a brief description of the problem to solve) to how they are evaluated. For example, to evaluate a programming exercise, the system requires that the author provides the solution in form of programming code and one or more (in some circumstances) test cases in order to know if the solution is correct.

In the second place, students can take available courses and try to solve its programming exercises on the training platform. They are allowed to compile and run code through the web interface, and received instant feedback: compile or runtime errors when are found, or if the solution submitted is valid or not. Additionally, they can adjust all gamified elements incorporated on the system.

3.1   Logical Architecture

The system user interface is web-based and works with Google Chrome and Mozilla Firefox web browsers. The client was developed using HTML, JavaScript and the following JavaScript libraries: jQuery, React and Underscore. The web server was developed with Python and the Pyramid Web Framework. The evaluation module was written in Java, since is the initial language supported by the system. Besides, in order to communicate both, the web server and the evaluation module, RabbitMQ and Redis were used. Finally, PostgreSQL was chosen as reliable database management system.

We implemented a Service Oriented Architecture (SOA) that provides a well-defined form of exposition and invocation of services. The standard used is REST (Representational State Transfer), which through the http protocol provides an API, which enables operations between the client and the web service. All presentation logic resides in the client and the server handles the persistence of data and assessment of the programming exercises.

Figure 1 shows the SOA architecture for CodeTraining.

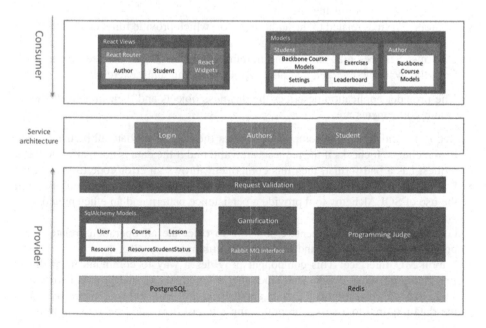

Fig. 1. Architecture of CodeTraining

The consumer is the application that can make use of the services from one or more providers. In the context of CodeTraining, it describes our training platform. Each component is described below:

- React Views: These components were created with the React library developed by Facebook. They contain all the presentation logic to create user interfaces in form of HTML, and include the logic related to the behavior of how the view changes in response to user interaction.
- React Router: It is used to map each view of the web site to a specific URL.
- Author Views: These views are used by the authoring tool aimed at teachers. For example, they allow them to create and publish programming courses.
- Student Views: The views used on the training platform for students. These allow students to take courses and to solve exercises.
- Widgets Views: These are views that can be reused by other components to provide basic interaction, for example: pop-up modals or message alerts.
- Models: These components were created with the JavaScript Backbone library. The goal of these models is to give structure to the web application by providing a connection for an existing API over a RESTful JSON interface. In the architecture described, our JSON interface will be the service architecture composed by the login, author, and student components.

The service architecture exposes three major services which are used by the consumer application: login, author, and student. This provides a bridge between the consumer and the provider application. Each set of services is described below:

- Login: These services provide functionality for registration on the web site as well for log in or log out of the site.
- Authors: Services related to the authoring tool, which provide functionality to create resources: courses, lessons, and programming exercises.
- Students: Services related with the training platform. These are used to get data from the available courses, and also to solve programming exercises.

The provider application describes the business objects and their implementations. The main components are:

- Request Validation: This component handles the task of validate all requests made by the clients. It checks if the requests are valid and if the data is not malformed. If a request has a bad format, then this component throws an error code to the client.
- SqlAlchemy Models: This component contains all the data models which through the use of SQLAlchemy tool provide a persistence pattern and an efficient and high performing database access.
- Gamification: The component responsible to calculate all operations related with points earned by students and leaderboard rankings.
- Rabbit MQ Interface: This component provides a way to communicate with the Programming Judge component; since the judge is an external program written in Java, and the web server is a Python application. It uses a message queue and sends the data required to assess a programming exercise formatted on JSON format.

- Programming Judge: This component has the task of assessing programming exercises. It receives the data of such exercises from a message queue owned by RabbitMQ. This component compiles and runs the code sent by students in order to find compile or runtime errors.

4 Functionality of CodeTraining

4.1 Case Study: Creation and Publishing of an Exercise on the Authoring Tool

Let suppose that an author wants to create and publish a programming course. The first step to do is sign in on the system. Next, to create a course the author has to follow the next steps:

- In the home page, an author creates a course by specifying only its name. Once the course is created, an author has the possibility to add lessons and exercises. The interface also shows all other courses previously created and can be filtered by course name. An author can select any course to see its details.
- The author selects the created course on the previous step to show the course edit page. In this interface the author adds or edits the courses' description and its availability for students. Furthermore, it shows all lessons and resources added to the course.
- The author selects option "Add lesson…" and specifies the lessons name.
- The author proceeds to select the option "Add Exercise…" on the previous created lesson. The author creates a programming exercise by filling the fields required. There are three tabs containing all the information of the exercise: details, gamification and shared options.
- On the details tab, the author specifies the following: the title, description, code needed to validate it against a set of test cases and how many test cases will be showed to the students as an example. When the author tries to save the exercise, the code will be proved against all specified test cases, and if the program results are equal to the output of the test cases, only then, the exercise can be saved (see Fig. 2).
- On the gamification tab the author sets the difficulty of the exercise. At the moment, there are three options: normal, hard, and advanced. The points granted to students are based on those difficulties levels. The author can also indicate the time and attempts restrictions to award bonus points. (see Fig. 3)
- Finally, an author can choose if the exercise will be public or private to other authors; public resources can be added to other courses owned by different authors.

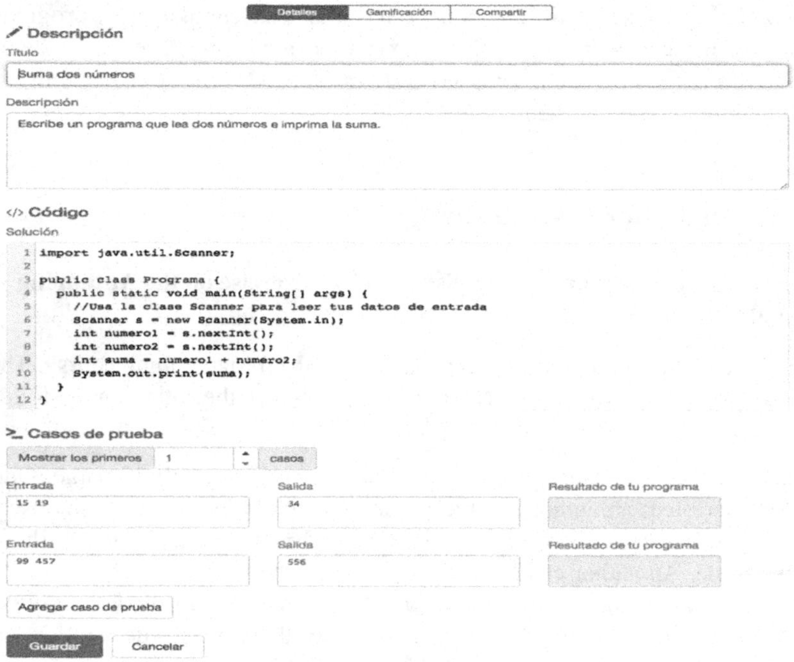

Fig. 2. Creating a programming exercise with test cases.

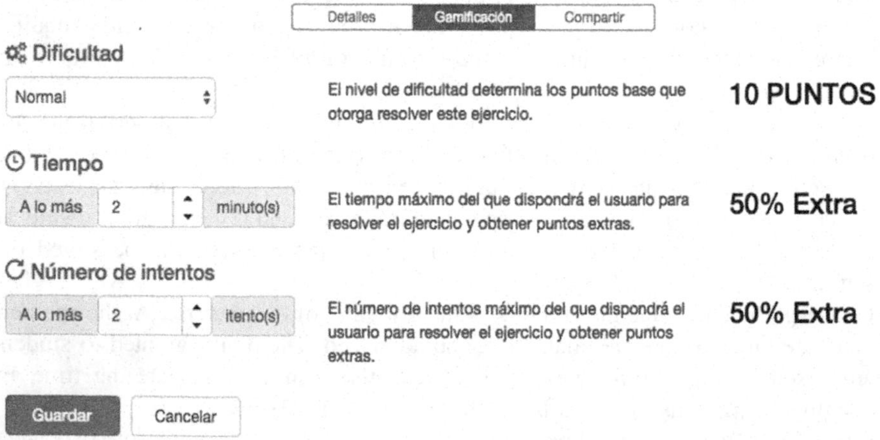

Fig. 3. Adding gamification elements to an exercise.

4.2 Case Study: Using the Training Platform

When a student chooses an exercise, CodeTraining shows the exercise page. In this page, the problem statement of the exercise is showed along with one or more test cases as an example for the student. At the middle of the page, there is a text area box for the student to begin writing java-programming code. Below the code area, there is another text box used for testing purposes (see Fig. 4).

Fig. 4. A programming exercise.

Students can run the code without being evaluated. When this happens, the code is sent to the server and it is compiled and executed. If errors are found, this page shows the exact message thrown by the compiler, otherwise the system prints the output of the program. When students are sure that they have found the correct solution for the problem, they can submit the code for evaluation with the button "submit". This process is exactly as when they just test the code, but this time, besides looking for compile or runtime errors, the system evaluates if the student's code is one the possible valid solutions for the problem. In case of the code being valid, the system shows the user how many points has earned and how many attempts and time was required to solve it. Otherwise the system only informs that the code submitted is not a valid solution and no further details are showed.

When a student correctly solves an exercise, it is marked as solved and it cannot be solved again in an effort to gain more points. Students can also see how well they are performing on the site. The leaderboard page shows ranked users by how much points they have earned. There are two types of leaderboards: course-leaderboard (see Fig. 5) which filters users by course and a global-leaderboard which shows all ranked students considering the total points earned across the several courses.

In the other hand, if students find the gamification options not suitable for them, they can change the settings on the Gamification Settings page. This page allows students to customize gamification settings. For instance, if the point option is disabled, the system will not show the points earned. Also, when a student resolves a problem,

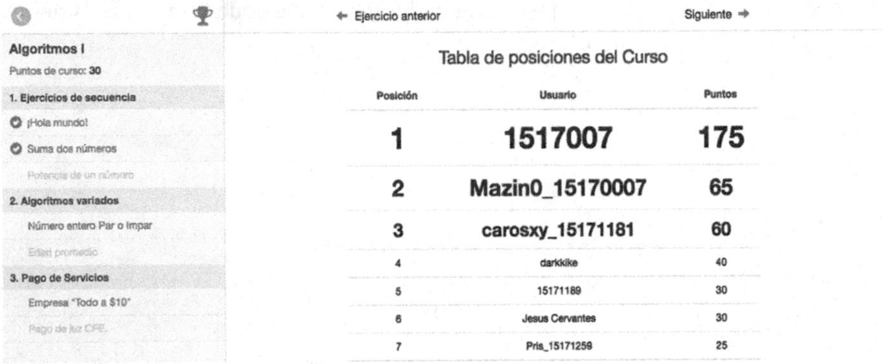

Fig. 5. Course-leaderboard.

the response message will not show any information related with the points; the message will be limited to only inform that the solution was correct. On the other hand, when the leaderboard option is not enabled, all links to the leaderboards will be hidden to the student. In this way, the student might not be concerned about being at bottom of the ranks, if that's the case. The system also offers the choice of make students more comfortable if they actually don't like being on the leaderboards for any reason. A student profile can be made private, when this happens, students will not appear on the leaderboards.

5 Conclusions

In order to evaluate the effectiveness of the system, we are actually running some tests involving 40 students from the Instituto Tecnológico de Culiacán, belonging to a group that attends the course Programming Fundamentals. Prior to the start of the experiment, a complete session was devoted to explain the operation of the system, to the students. The main goal was to get them familiarized with the system prior using it seriously. The experiment was conducted using a course with 10 exercises as a pre-test, then a test period of use in which students could attend any course of the tool they wanted. For this purpose, there were already 3 courses registered on the system. Finally, another course was designed as a post-test. We expect to have results soon from this experiment.

In this work we presented the development of an authoring tool, which aims to provide a learning environment for newbies programmers which allows them to test their theoretical knowledge and programming skills acquired for the solution of problems through programs written in the Java programming language.

The system was developed as a web application with a services-oriented architecture, and an experiment was designed to evaluate the effectiveness of the system. The experiment was carried out using a course like pre-test, a period of trial use, and a new course as post-tests. The results of this experiment will enable us to obtain valuable data with which to determine the effectiveness of the tool in student learning.

It is expected that the elements of Gamification will strongly motivate the students and that their knowledge will be reinforced and therefore they will able to become more proficient.

References

1. Portelli, J.P., McMahon, B.: Engagement for what? Beyond popular discourses of student engagement. Leadersh. Policy Sch. **3**(1), 59–76 (2004)
2. De Freitas, S.: Learning in immersive worlds a review of game-based learning prepared for the JISC e-learning programme. JISC eLearn. Innov. **3**(3), 73 (2006)
3. Jenkins, T.: On the difficulty of learning to program. Lang. (Baltim) **4**, 53–58 (2002)
4. Winslow, L.E.: Programming Pedagogy - a Psychological Overview. ACM SIGCSE Bull. **28**(3), 17–22 (1996)
5. Lahtinen, E., Ala-Mutka, K., Järvinen, H.-M.: A study of the difficulties of novice programmers. ACM SIGCSE Bull. **37**(3), 14 (2005)
6. Robins, A., Rountree, J., Rountree, N.: Learning and teaching programming: a review and discussion. Comput. Sci. Educ. **13**(2), 137–172 (2003)
7. Feldgen, M., Clua, O.: Games as a motivation for freshman students to learn programming. In: 34th Annual Frontiers in Education, FIE 2004, pp. 1079–1084 (2004)
8. Seaborn, K., Fels, D.I.: Gamification in theory and action: a survey. Int. J. Hum.-Comput. Stud. **74**, 14–31 (2014)
9. Domínguez, A., Saenz-De-Navarrete, J., De-Marcos, L., Fernández-Sanz, L., Pagés, C., Martínez-Herráiz, J.J.: Gamifying learning experiences: practical implications and outcomes. Comput. Educ. **63**, 380–392 (2013)
10. Li, W., Grossman, T., Fitzmaurice, G.: GamiCAD: a gamified tutorial system for first time AutoCAD users. In: UIST 2012 - Proceedings of the 25th Annual ACM Symposium on User Interface Software and Technology, pp. 103–112 (2012)
11. Snyder, E., Hartig, J.R.: Gamification of board review: a residency curricular innovation. Med. Educ. **47**, 524–525 (2013)
12. Fitz-Walter, Z., Tjondronegoro, D., Wyeth, P.: A gamified mobile application for engaging new students at university orientation. In: Proceedings of the 24th Australian Computer-Human Interaction Conference - OzCHI 2012, pp. 138–141 (2012)
13. Foster, J.A., Sheridan, P.K., Irish, R.: Gamification as a strategy for promoting deeper investigation in a reverse engineering activity. In: Proceedings of the 2012 ASEE Annual Conference, pp. 1–15 (2012)
14. Landers, R.N., Callan, R.C., De Freitas, S., Liarokapis, F.: Casual social games as serious games: the psychology of gamification in undergraduate education and employee training. In: Ma, M., Oikonomou, A., Jain, L.C. (eds.) Serious Games and Edutainment Applications, pp. 399–423. Springer, Heidelberg (2011). doi:10.1007/978-1-4471-2161-9_20
15. Spence, M., Foster, J.A., Irish, R., Sheridan, P.K., Frost, G.S.: 'Gamifying' a library orientation tutorial for improved motivation and learning. In: ASEE Annual Conference and Exposition, Conference Proceedings, no. 2007 (2012)
16. Kose, U., Deperlioglu, O.: Intelligent learning environments within blended learning for ensuring effective C programming course. arXiv Prepr arXiv1205.2670 (2012)
17. Hartanto, B.: Incorporating anchored learning in a C# intelligent tutoring system (2014)

18. Hsiao, I.-H., Sosnovsky, S., Brusilovsky, P.: Adaptive navigation support for parameterized questions in object-oriented programming. In: Cress, U., Dimitrova, V., Specht, M. (eds.) EC-TEL 2009. LNCS, vol. 5794, pp. 88–98. Springer, Heidelberg (2009)
19. Neve, P., Hunter, G., Livingston, D., Orwell, J.: NoobLab: an intelligent learning environment for teaching programming. In: 2012 IEEE/WIC/ACM International Conference on Web Intelligence and Intelligent Agent Technology, pp. 357–361 (2012)
20. Swacha, J., Baszuro, P.: Gamification-based e-learning platform for computer programming education. In: World Conference on Computers in Education, no. 2012, pp. 122–130 (2013)
21. Ibanez, M.-B., Di-Serio, A., Delgado-Kloos, C.: Gamification for engaging computer science students in learning activities: a case study. IEEE Trans. Learn. Technol. 7(3), 291–301 (2014)

Generating a Logical Structure for Virtualizing Physiotherapy Instructions Through NLP

Sandeep Kumar Dash[1], Partha Pakray[1(✉)], and Alexander Gelbukh[2]

[1] Department of Computer Science and Engineering,
National Institute of Technology, Aizawl, Mizoram, India
{sandeep.cse,partha.cse}@nitmz.ac.in
[2] Centro de Investigación en Computación (CIC),
Instituto Politécnico Nacional (IPN), Mexico City, Mexico
gelbukh@gelbukh.com

Abstract. We describe a framework for virtualizing the documented physiotherapy instructions. This paper tries to bridge the gap between human understanding and the written manuals of instructions for physiotherapy through a pipeline of language processing techniques. As mapping of text to action needs accurate synchronization between the sequence of commands and generation of action, a structure has been developed that reflects the modeling techniques followed by some of the important action rendering systems. The idea is to put the semantic information into the proposed structure and add the implicit knowledge related to the domain. It eases the process of manual mapping of wearable sensor data of human body movements to rather a simple analysis of textual instructions. The Natural Language Processing pipeline will involve among others some of the main concepts as semantic and spatial information processing as these carries vital importance in this approach.

1 Introduction

The General human tendency is to visualize a scenario while going through any document or text. By means of visualization it relates both implicit and explicit information in text. For human understanding it seems easy to co-relate both but when it comes to virtual representation through computer system it asks for a lot of further details such as placement of objects with respect to others, relating the entities with one another and also carving out all necessary information for a proper representation. For any kind of instruction related to a domain, the domain specific terms are often important for shaping the representation. These are often expressed in terms of knowledge base or ontology in language processing terminologies. Hence the task of converting input natural language text into virtual action holds much importance with respect to the complexity faced mainly in understanding of written manuals, simulation of production line, story description for students as an aid in literacy and in other such applications.

Natural Language text made to describe a scene is much easier than complex manipulation interfaces through which objects are constructed and precisely positioned within scenes. The complexity lies with natural language in which both linguistic and real-world knowledge, in particular knowledge about the spatial and functional

O. Pichardo-Lagunas and S. Miranda-Jiménez (Eds.): MICAI 2016, Part II, LNAI 10062, pp. 513–523, 2017.
DOI: 10.1007/978-3-319-62428-0_42

properties of objects; prepositions and the spatial relations they convey is often ambiguous. Also verbs and how they resolve to poses and other spatial relations [1] as well needs to be analyzed in the input text for a proper scene building. Furthermore, implicit facts about real world has also to be analyzed from the text which is rarely mentioned therewith. Apart from these another necessary part of this research is to analyze the synchronization of multiple action sequences that can be described through the proposed structure. Therefore an action representation task is often heavily constrained by the synchronization factor.

Physiotherapy is one such area where textual descriptions of the exercises are difficult to interpret. The various body parts, joints and their angle along with direction of movement carries utmost importance while carrying out specific physiotherapies, mainly because a lot of information are kept implicit making it complex for normal understanding and implementation. This is one of the challenging areas where interpretation of textual content has to be perfect or else consequences can be damaging for health.

In this paper we are introducing a structure for representing text describing different body part movements during physiotherapy exercises. The structure will carry sequence wise information for some specific action. We will describe how the input textual description of a physiotherapy exercise can be converted into a virtual action describing the same. The method is proposed for some of the therapies only which can be extended for others after further research.

2 Related Work

There has been a great number of work which implements natural language text as input for generating 3D scene as a virtual scenario. Researchers have utilized various text processing methods in order to build structures which can be made to generate the scene. Mainly these systems follow basic four steps. First is to parse the input text into a structure or template establishing spatial relation between the different objects mentioned in it. Secondly using real world knowledge find any implicit constraints also which is not mentioned in the text. In third step the scene templates are converted into geometric 3D scene. Lastly optimize the placement of objects as per the templates. These type of work are influencing in our research in the sense that the spatial information about the objects mentioned in the sentence carries importance as it can also be different body parts placement during a physiotherapy along with the items used during this as balls, chairs, wall, floor, sitting mat etc.

As spatial information retrieval is one of the key area for converting text to action representation, a lot of researchers have developed novel techniques for representing objects or items mentioned in the text along with the involvement of other alongside objects derived from real world knowledge. The main aim of this is to create a peoper scene even without even the explicitly mentioned information. The pioneering work in this area was carried out by [1]. They developed an automatic text-to-scene conversion system named WordsEye. Their first system was designed with a large library of 3D objects to depict scenes from input text. Whereas their current system contains 2,200 3D objects and 10,000 images and a lexicon of approximately 15,000 nouns. It supports language-based control of objects, spatial relations, and surface properties (e.g., textures and colors); and it handles simple Co-reference resolution, allowing for a variety of ways of referring to objects [1]. They have utilized a self-designed lexical knowledge base called SBLR (Scenario-Based Lexical Resource), which consists of an ontology and lexical semantic information extracted from WordNet [2] and FrameNet [3]. Their system works by first tagging and parsing the input text, using Church's (1988) part of speech tagger [4] and Collins' (1999) parser [5]. The parser output is then converted into a dependency structure which is processed to resolve anaphora and other Co-references. The dependency structure is utilized to create semantic nodes from which the semantic relations of lexical items are formed with the help of information in the SBLR. These semantic relations are then converted to a final set of graphical constraints representing the position, orientation, size, color, texture, and poses of objects in the scene. This final structure was then utilized to create the 3D scene with the help of a graphic rendering software.

Research by [6] has shown an approach of finding the implicit spatial relationship between objects described in a scene. They considered the output scene to be generated as a graph whose nodes are objects mentioned either implicitly or explicitly in the text and the edges as the semantic relationships among them. The semantics of a scene were described using a 'scene template' and the geometric properties using a 'geometric scene'. In their approach scene template is a triplet $T = (O, C, C_s)$, which consists of object descriptions O, constraints C on the relationships between the objects and a scene type C_s. Here object description provides information about the object as category label, basic attributes such as color and material, and number of occurrences in the scene. Spatial relations between objects were expressed as predicates of the form supported_by(o_i, o_j) or left(o_i, o_j) where o_i and o_j are recognized objects. Geometric Scene represents concrete geometric representation of a scene. It consists of a set of 3D model instances – one for each object – that capture the appearance of the object. To exactly position the object they also derived a transformation matrix that represents the position, orientation, and scaling of the object in a scene. A scene template was generated by selecting appropriate models from a 3D model database and determining transformations that optimize their layout to satisfy spatial constraints.

The system [7] creates a visual action design environment that improves action design for intelligent toy robot. The environment automatically creates action sequence files in terms of txt or xml from given action sequences [7]. Action sequences are nothing but set of aggregated arrays of actions as per their time of occurrences. These actions may be parallel actions with complete or in-part synchronous with time, linear action or repeated serial actions; see Fig. 1.

These action sequences can be created in the visualized design environment and the action sequence file can be automatically generated thereafter. These files contain action sequences in terms of tags and data blocks as shown in Table 1.

In the above the tag "Begin LinearAction/End LinearAction" represents linear action, tag "Begin ParallelAction/End ParallelAction" represents parallel action and the tag "Action/End Action" represent data block which represents information about a particular action [7]. The intelligent toy robots are limited to only rotational freedom. Hence any action is defined logically as A_i (Joint, Angle, Axis, Absolute, Time, StartTime, Isparallel). The parameters respectively represent joint that exerts action, angle of rotation, axis of rotation, absolute or relative value of angle, and timeline for

516 S.K. Dash et al.

adjusting & harmonizing the coherent action sequence, order of size of action and finally whether the node is an action node or substitute node. Further they have used the queue data structure to store the action files as per their order of StartTime. Finally virtual action was generated by matching action sequence files into corresponding joints of intelligent toy robot model. They used Eon studio for virtual simulation purpose.

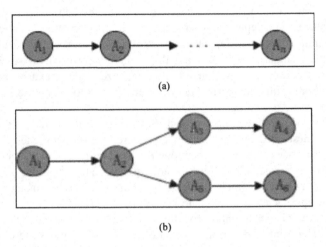

(a)

(b)

Fig. 1. Types of action sequences (a) linear action (b) parallel action (Mo et al. [7])

Table 1. Tags and data blocks for action sequences. Source: Mo et al. [7]

Begin	Action
Begin	...
LinearAction	End Action
Action	End LinearAction
...(action	Begin
Information)	LinearAction
End Action	Action
Action	...
...	End Action
End Action	Action
Begin	...
ParallelAction	End Action
Begin	End LinearAction
LinearAction	End ParallelAction
Action	End LinearAction
	End

In another innovative research funded by EU named MUSE (Machine Understanding for interactive Storytelling) [8] project, the aim is to bring texts to life by developing an innovative text-to-virtual-world translation system. It mainly evaluates two scenarios: story-telling and patient education materials. The idea involves semantic role recognition of a sentence, spatial relations between objects and chronology of events.

The above works mostly relates to text-to-scene conversion system which draws similarity with the proposed system with respect to the static positioning of objects. However for virtual action representation it is important to form the structure first which will signify the detailed information for agents or avatars for representing the action. In this direction few novel structures has been proposed. Lexical Conceptual Structure (LCS) [9] is a semantic representation proposed by Jackendoff (1990). He explains that conceptual structure is made up of a set of entities (conceptual primitives or ontological categories) that combine to perform a number of meaning functions. As per this the semantic structure of "John went towards the house" is represented as:

[EVENT go [THING JOHN], [PATH towards [THING HOUSE]]]

As per him the decomposition of word meaning into smaller semantic elements allows specification of a generative, compositional system which constrains the way such elements can be related and thereby constrains the ways in which sentences can be constructed, i.e. to prevent semantically anomalous sentences.

A work by [10] has introduced a structure named Parametrized Action Representation (PAR) for virtual agents; see Fig. 2. They have categorized two different types of PAR; UPAR (Uninstantiated PAR) and IPAR (Instantiated PAR). A UPAR contains default applicability conditions and preconditions for the action, and also points to the executable actions that actually drive the embodied character's movements. An IPAR is a UPAR instantiated with information or pointers to a specific agent, physical object(s), manner, and termination conditions. The syntactic representation of PAR explains the various structural information along with synchronization information.

Ma et al. [11] has proposed Lexical Visual Semantic Representation (LVSR) which is a necessary semantic representation between 3D visual information and syntactic/semantic information. They have introduced the notion of visual valency and Level-Of-Detail for language visualisation. An automatic word sense disambiguation approach for mapping verbs to Lexical Conceptual Structure (LCS) entries using frequency information of WordNet senses, thematic grids and lexical-semantic representations from the LCS database has been used. They have proposed nine ontological categories of concept such as: OBJ, HUMAN, EVENT, STATE, PLACE, PATH, PROPERTY, TIME, and AMOUNT. The LVSR representation for some of the statements are as follows:

(i) John pushed the door

```
[EVENT push ([HUMAN john], [OBJ door])]
[EVENT go ([OBJ door], [PATH away_from ([PLACE at ([HUMAN john])])])]
```

(ii) John lifted his hat

```
[EVENT lift ([HUMAN john], [OBJ hat])]
[EVENT go ([OBJ hat], [PATH from [PLACE on [OBJ john.head]]])]
```

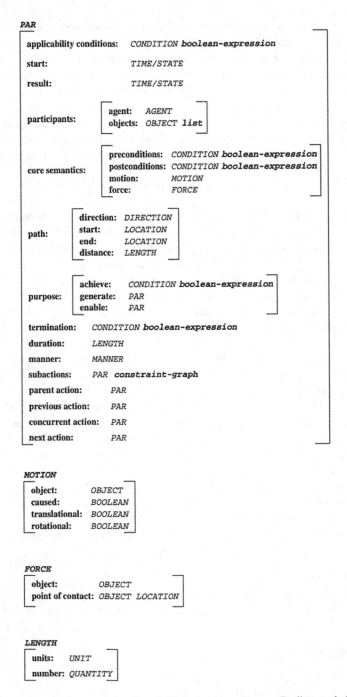

Fig. 2. Syntactic representation of PAR structure. Source: Badler et al. [10]

3 Brief Dataset Description

The dataset contains textual manuals for different types of physiotherapy instructions which are simple sentences. Each instruction involves either explicit or implicit body parts as Hand, Foot, Neck, Back, Shoulder, Knee etc. For example knee may involve exercises as 'Knee squats', 'Leg cross', 'Leg stretch', 'Sitstands', 'Step ups' etc are each maintained as different text manuals (Table 2).

Table 2. Names of instructions

Body part	Instructions
Knee	Leg stretch
	Leg cross
	Knee squats
	Sit stands
	Step ups
Neck	Neck stretch
	Neck tilt
	Neck turn
Shoulder	Door lean
	Door press
	Pendulum exercise
	Shoulder stretch
Foot	Achilles tendon and plantar
	Plantar fascia stretch
	Sitting plantar fascia stretch
Back	Back stretch
	Deep lunge
	Knees to chest
	One-leg stand (front)
	Pelvic tilt

The instructions are mostly categorized into three different types as simple, medium level and complex instructions. The simple instructions carry explicit details about the necessary information. Medium level instruction requires anaphora resolution and name entity identification techniques to be applied for resolving any implicit mention of terms. Finally the complex instruction category requires the knowledge repository for forming the structure. The quality of virtual action to be generated will definitely be affected by the semantic information retrieved from the instruction description. As in literature review stage of our research we did not find mention of any such dataset that involves textual description of exercise related activities, we have developed the dataset of which 70% of the instructions will be used for training the system and 30% will be used as test set.

The following are the three different levels of instructions considered in our system:

(i)   Simple Instruction: *Lying on back, pull one knee up and hug toward chest.*
(ii) Middle Level Instruction: *Keep the other leg flat on floor.*
(iii) Complex Instruction: *With legs together and straight, move legs apart from each other and return to the neutral Position.*

In the simple instruction the body parts such as 'back', 'knee', 'chest' can easily be identified, whereas in second type anaphora resolution will be required to identify 'other leg' with respect to the previous instruction. Finally in the third type the term 'neutral position' for legs has to be identified which is implicit in the instruction. For this the knowledge repository can be looked into.

4   The Framework

The proposed framework involves a pipeline of natural language processing techniques such as part-of-speech tagging, name entity recognition and semantic parsing for identifying different role labels related to physiotherapy instructions with the required world knowledge gathered from the knowledge base. The system diagram described below shows the stepwise process of converting the written manual instruction into action representation (Fig. 3).

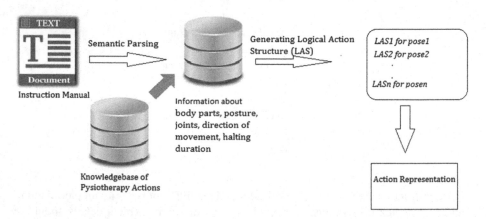

Fig. 3. Proposed framework of logical action representation

In the proposed framework the knowledge base to be used, will contain information about type of posture each therapy generates by involving the joints of the respective parts, the prescribed angle between joints, type of movements and the necessary time duration of halting in the pose, also the number of times the action is to be repeated. This information is collected in consultation with the expert. Further each action structure can be appended to the previous one, as there is synchronization factor that is a vital information during rendering process. This helps to have the implicit information produced for a better action representation. In the initial stage the following information will be incorporated in the system.

Type of Body Planes. For describing the structural positions and directions of functional movement of the body, the standard posture is, body facing forward, the hands at the sides of the body, with the palms facing forward, and the feet pointing straight ahead. Body planes are derived from dimensions in space and are oriented at right angles to one another. The median sagittal plane, also called the midsagittal plane, divides the body into right and left halves. The coronal plane is vertical and extends from side to side. The transverse plane is a horizontal plane and divides a structure into upper and lower components. We will use these three types of planes for representing different postures.

Axes of Movements. Axis represents a line around which movement will occur. The system will consider three types of movements possible around each joint rotation, translation, and curvilinear motion. All movements that occur about an axis are considered rotational, whereas linear movements along an axis and through a plane are called translational. Curvilinear motion occurs when a translational movement accompanies rotational movements.

Type of Joints. The three types of joints that will be considered are mainly based upon how much movement they allow. A synarthrosis joint permits no movement as the gomphoses that connect the teeth to the skull. An amphiarthrosis joint allows a slight amount of movement at the joint. For ex. pubic symphysis of the hips. The third type is the diarthrosis joint. Diarthroses have the highest range of motion of any joint and include the elbow, knee, shoulder, and wrist.

Type of Movements. Table 3 presents list of possible movements of body parts. It shows the various manner in which some or all the bodypart can be moved while performing any of the action implementation.

Table 3. Movements

Types	Description
Flexion	Bending parts at a joint so that the angle between them decreases and the parts come closer together (bending the lower limb at the knee)
Extension	Straightening parts at a joint so that the angle between them increases and the parts move farther apart (straightening the lower limb at the knee)
Hyperextension	Excess extension of the parts at a joint, beyond the anatomical position (bending the head back beyond the upright position)
Eversion	Turning the foot so the sole faces laterally
Inversion	Turning the foot so the sole faces medially
Protraction	Moving a part forward (thrusting the chin forward)
Retraction	Moving a part backward (pulling the chin backward)
Elevation	Raising a part (shrugging the shoulders)
Depression	Lowering a part (drooping the shoulders)

This work introduces LAS (Logical Action Structure) that describes logically each pose for a particular therapy. The structure is suitable mainly for carrying semantic role-wise information from the mentioned textual instruction data. It will involve information about body planes, axes, type of movement mentioned in the described text. These details will be used to form the action representation for each pose, thereby helping to form action sequences. LAS can be explained by the help the following format of an instruction (Table 4).

Table 4. Example of LAS Format

```
<Action>
  <Posture>
    <Bodypart id='12' >Hand</Bodypart>
    <Plane_of_movement>Transverse</Plane_of_movement>
  </Posture>
  <Relative_Bodypart>Shoulder</Relative_Bodypart>
  <Joint>Diarthroses</Joint>
  <Movement_type>Flexion<Movement_type>
  <Duration>5sec</Duration>
</Action>
```

The above format represents information such as type of joint involved and the movement type, which are often not mentioned in the instruction but has to be incorporated while constructing the action representation. As action is consisting of different body movements, each structure should carry a particular label as 'Duration', through which proper synchronization can be maintained between the rendered action sequences. The mentioned implicit information can be derived from the knowledge base given the action and body part along with other explicit information. The 'Relative_Bodypart' explains the movement of any other body part with movement of main bodypart for the action. Finally through efficient text processing methods along with implicit information incorporation from the developed knowledge base of different therapy poses, each structure can represent its logical action which can lead sequentially to generate the exact virtual action prescribed in the written manuals.

5   Conclusion

Virtual Action Generation from textual content involves various techniques of Natural Language Processing. This work has proposed a structure that can carry the semantic information for representing instructions in virtual action format. The information can further be processed in terms many other formats such as this newly introduced LAS, which can be efficiently mapped to virtual action generation system. Initially though the system considers limited number of therapies and its associated movements, the structure will be well extensible to variety of instructions. Developing the knowledge repository about the domain entities and identifying semantic roles is a future task of this work.

Another foremost consideration will be to disambiguate posture related phrases mentioned in the instructions as the case with disambiguation of spatial tags for scene representation. Finally, as representing humanoid kinematics is a main task in animation generation, the most convenient and efficient program will be taken into consideration for rendering of the logical structure in to virtual action.

Acknowledgements. This research was partially supported by DST-DAAD Project Based Personnel Exchange Programme: an Indo-German Joint Research Collaboration (No. INT/FRG/DAAD/P-15/2016). Authors also acknowledge Department of Computer Science & Engineering, National Institute of Technology Mizoram, India, for supporting the research.

References

1. Coyne, B., Sproat, R., Hirschberg, J.: Spatial relations in text-to-scene conversion. In: Computational Models of Spatial Language Interpretation, Workshop at Spatial Cognition (2010)
2. Fellbaum, C.: WordNet: An Electronic Lexical Database. MIT Press, Cambridge (1998)
3. Baker, C., Fillmore, C., Lowe, J.: The Berkeley FrameNet project. In: COLING-ACL (1998)
4. Church, K.W.: A stochastic parts program and noun phrase parser for unrestricted text. In: Proceedings of the Second Conference on Applied Natural Language Processing, pp. 136–143 (1988)
5. Collins, M., et al.: A statistical parser for Czech. In: Proceedings of the 37th Annual Meeting of the Association for Computational Linguistics on Computational Linguistics. Association for Computational Linguistics (1999)
6. Chang, A.X., Savva, M., Manning, C.D.: Learning spatial knowledge for text to 3D scene generation. In: EMNLP, pp. 2028–2038 (2014)
7. Mo, J., He, H., Zhang, H.: Virtual simulation of intelligent toy robot driven by the action sequence files. In: 2012 IEEE International Conference on Computer Science and Automation Engineering (CSAE), vol. 1, pp. 401–404. IEEE (2012)
8. De Mulder, W., Do Thi, N.Q., van den Broek, P., Moens, M.F.: Machine understanding for interactive storytelling. In: Proceedings of KICSS 2013: 8th International Conference on Knowledge, Information, and Creativity Support Systems, pp. 73–80 (2013)
9. Jackendoff, R.S.: Semantic Structures. Current Studies in Linguistics, vol. 18. MIT Press, Cambridge (1990)
10. Badler, N.I., Bindiganavale, R., Bourne, J.C., Palmer, M., Shi, J., Schuler, W.: A parameterized action representation for virtual human agents (2000)
11. Ma, M.: Automatic conversion of natural language to 3D animation. Ph.D. dissertation, University of Ulster (2006)

Building a Corpus and a Local Binary Pattern Recognizer for Learning-Centered Emotions

Ramón Zatarain-Cabada[1(⊠)], María Lucía Barrón-Estrada[1],
Francisco González-Hernández[2], Raúl Oramas-Bustillos[1],
Giner Alor-Hernández[2], and Carlos Alberto Reyes-García[3]

[1] Instituto Tecnológico de Culiacán, Culiacán, Sinaloa, Mexico
rzatarain@itculiacan.edu.mx
[2] Division of Resarch and Postgraduate Studies,
Instituto Tecnológico de Orizaba, Orizaba, Veracruz, Mexico
galor@itorizaba.edu.mx
[3] Instituto Nacional de Astrofísica, Óptica y Electrónica (INAOE) Luis Enrique
Erro no. 1, Sta. Ma. Tonanzintla, 72840 Puebla, Mexico
kargaxxi@inaoep.mx

Abstract. Studies investigating the effectiveness of affect detection inside intelligent learning environments (ILEs) have reported the effectiveness of including emotion identification on learning . However, there is limited research on detecting and using learning-centered data to investigate metacognitive and affective monitoring with ILEs. In this work we report the methodology we follow to create a new facial expression corpus from electroencephalography information, an implementation of an algorithm and a training of an SVM to recognize learning-centered emotions (frustration, boredom, engagement and excitement). Also, we explain changes realized in a fuzzy logic system into an intelligent learning environment. The affect recognizer was tested into an ILE for learning Java programming. We present successful results of the recognizer using our corpus face database and an example test using our ILE.

Keywords: Face expression databases · Face expression recognition · Intelligent tutoring system · Intelligent learning environment

1 Introduction

Traditionally, teaching and learning have been related to school only. Usually, lessons are taught in a classroom where students dedicated hearing their teachers passively. Previous investigation have discovered that emotions play an important role in students during their learning tasks because they affect different aspects like the cognitive mechanisms of storage and retrieval of information [1, 2]. This means that the influential of emotions can affect students in a negative or positive sense.

Previous works have studied the so-called basic emotions which are known to be spontaneous and expressive; some examples of basic emotions are anger, happiness, sadness, and fear which express human reactions in different situations of daily life [3]. However, there are other kind of emotions which emerge when students are working in

© Springer International Publishing AG 2017
O. Pichardo-Lagunas and S. Miranda-Jiménez (Eds.): MICAI 2016, Part II, LNAI 10062, pp. 524–535, 2017.
DOI: 10.1007/978-3-319-62428-0_43

their learning tasks. These emotions are presented in complex tasks and they involve not only reactions from students but also their cognitive process at that moment. Some of these emotions are confused, boredom, frustration, engagement, and excitement; They are called learning-centered emotions [4, 5]. Learning-centered emotions unlike basic emotions emerge during deep learning activities.

Various developed technologies have been created to face up the necessity of integrating emotions in learning and teaching process. These systems are known as intelligent tutoring systems (ITS) and intelligent learning environments (ILE) which manage to capture and identify emotions. These systems try to recognize emotions in students by means of features obtained from the face, voice, corporal expressions, heart rates, etc. However, most of these systems work only with basic emotions [6, 7]. That is way, the main contribution of this work is first, the creation of a new Face-expression database with learning-centered emotion frustration, engagement, excitement, and boredom, second, the implementation of a classifier algorithm for recognizing learning-centered emotions; and last the integration of both elements (face-expression database and emotion recognizer) into the our ILE for programming learning called Java Sensei.

2 Related Works

2.1 Face Expression Databases

Face expression databases are a dataset of images wherein people often poses to represent something and some conditions are controlled like illumination conditions, head-pose variations, and nature of expressions. Important databases are explained below.

CK [8] is a dataset of 486 sequences from 97 positioned persons. The database seeks to represent the image sequence inside the Facial Action Coding System (FACS) [9]. Each expression begins like a neutral expression and then move to a peak expression. Each time a neutral expression changes it is turned into a peak expression. In this way, each expression can receive an emotion label. CK includes basic emotions as well as AU (Action Units) annotations. CK+ [10] as the name implies is an extension of original CK (version 2). This version includes in addition to posed expressions, non-posed (spontaneous) expressions recording from 84 novel subjects and more metadata information. Spontaneous expressions were taken at one or more times between tasks. Number of posed expression increased 22% with respect to initial version; the target of each expression is yet completing FACS coded. RaFD [11] contains an image set of 49 models in two subsets: 39 Caucasian Dutch adults and 10 Caucasian Dutch children. All model expressed eight facial expressions (anger, happiness, fear, sadness, contempt, surprise, disgust, and neutral) with three gaze directions and five camera angles. These expression represented Ekman basic emotions. They obtained a total of 120 images per model which had to comply various requisites like wearing a type of shirt or no hair on the face. The database reached the overall 82% agreement rate. Contempt was a complicated expression to detect. GEMEP [12] is the first dataset used in an analysis challenge known as FERA2011 (a challenge of recognition expression). The database is coded for FACS AUs as target and display of 18 portrayed discrete emotions by 10 professional French-speaking theater actors who were trained by a professional director. The corpus is comprised of over 7000 audiovisual emotion representations. They have 18 emotion categories which are 12 non-basic emotions (e.g. joy, amusement, pride, pleasure, relief, interest, admiration) and 6 basic emotions (sadness, surprise, anger, fear, disgust, contempt). Emotions were labeled by arousal (high or low) and valence (negative or positive) and they indicate the intensity of an emotion; e.g. anger with high arousal and negative valence is equivalent to rage. GEMEP offers a dataset for investigating theoretical prediction concerning of nonverbal expressions of emotions. SEMAINE [13] is a database that includes high-quality, multimodal recordings. The recording were generated when people were talking with an automatic system which simulates emotions to observe whether participants had emotional reactions. The recordings showed people engaged with the system. In database-building, they investigated the concept known as dimensional emotions where six basic emotions were founded. The dimensions of an emotion are Valence, Activation, Power, and Anticipation/Expectation. This database can be useful for investigation of non-verbal signal components in conversations.

As it can see, the investigations about face expression databases have been focused on the research of basic and non-basic emotions. However, the effort of these investigations has not relation with emotions expressed in learning settings. Our work contribution is facing this problem.

2.2 Face Expression Recognition

Some techniques to recognize expression was analyzed. Low-Level Histogram Representations was the kind of method selected; it fulfills the requirements such as working while a webcam is taking photographs and having little computational cost. These methods transforms an image for clustering its local features into regions and finally pool the features of each region with local histograms. The representations are obtained by concatenating all local histograms. Histograms can be normalized to increase the validity of the general representation. Next, we present three of the most important low-level (based appearance) methods.

Local Binary Pattern (LBP) is a method that takes the pixel value of the image center as the threshold. Each pixel value is compared against the threshold; if the threshold is bigger than the pixel value then the resulted is 0, otherwise, it is 1. The last step creates a sequence of binary numbers which is converted into its decimal representation. The method has two input parameters; a P value which works like the number of points to calculate, and an R value which works as the number of separation points of the pixel in the center. This technique was applied to identify face expressions [14], and the results were satisfactory. In order to identify a face expression, the whole face must be divided into blocks (usually 9×9 blocks); the histogram of each LBP operator is extracted, and each histogram is concatenated forming a feature vector. This vector normally exceeds 2,000 values. LPQ is a method that works for blur insensitive texture classification through local Fourier transformation neighborhood by computing its local Zernike moments. The process generates LPQ codes which are collected into a histogram. This descriptor is ideal for image blurring. Some works have proven LPQ can be used for expression recognition with FACS [15]. Histograms can reach up to 25,000 features so that indicates that LPQ covers an extension area of the face. Gabor [16] is a representation of a convolving of an input image using a set of Gabor filters with various scales and orientations. Gabor filters encode componential information, and depending on the registration scheme, the overall representation may implicitly convey configurable information. This technique can be used with simple dimensionality reduction techniques such min, max and mean grouping. The representation is robust to registration errors to an extent as the filters are smooth and the magnitude of filtered images are robust to small translation and rotations. The feature amount can reach up to 165,000 values.

The three methods work with low-level features, and they create a representation from the image. However, we need to consider covering an important aspect that is the performance. While LPQ and Gabor have proved to have a better result for classification, both methods generate a set of features computationally costly. However, LBP has a much better performance and its accuracy normally is above 90% with a computational cost lower than the other two.

3 Building a New Face Expression Database

In order to recognize facial expression in learning environments, we decided to build our own facial database. The database should contain faces expressing emotions directly related to learning. Every face in the database is labeled to one of the learning-centered emotions *frustration, boredom, engagement*, and *excitement*. This set of emotions have proven to be always presented during the process of deep learning [4, 17]. In order to accomplish this task, we used a mobile electroencephalography (EEG) technology called Emotiv Epoc. Emotions were captured during one learning process where a student solve a problem by coding a Java program.

EEG Signals is a measure of brain electrical activity of a set of neurons in cerebral cortex. Neurons contain physical information, physiologic, and pathology. In order to be measured encephalograms are needed. Emotiv Epoc is a human-computer interface of scientific context used to capture brain activity. The device has 14 principal channels and 2 reference points.

3.1 Building and Filtering of Database

First, we used a methodology to build the database which can seem to be simple; however, the goal is to search inducing ideal situations wherein students express emotions related to education. The methodology proposed is as follows:

- A subject performs programming (coding) activities in a programming environment.
- Meanwhile, the Emotiv EPOC device captures brain activity and a webcam takes a photograph every 5 s.

- Every user photograph is labeled with the user emotion obtained from the Emotiv EPOC device. Both objects (photograph and emotion) are saved into the Face expression Database.

In this way, brain activity represents affective states of users and images represent facial expression of subject while the subject performs exercises. Figure 1 shows how the process is performed by users.

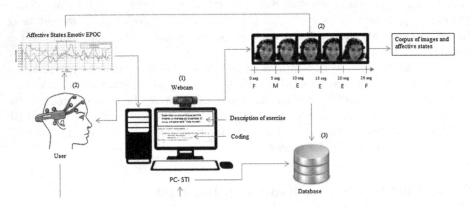

Fig. 1. Methodology to take photographs for face expression database

At the end we obtain a database containing a total of 7,019 photographs. However, many photographs and their corresponding emotions had not a matching consistency. We proceed to filtering the database by eliminating those incorrect registers (face-emotion mismatch) using the human judge obtaining a final database of 730 photographs. In order to test our face expression database, we performed a verification using our face expression recognizer which it is explained at next section. Figure 2 shows some photographs from the face expression database.

Fig. 2. Emotions expressed during sessions

4 Building a Face Expression Recognizer

Previously, we mentioned the need for creating our own face expression recognizer. There are many reasons why it is a good choice creating your own recognizer, where the main reason is that this approach gives you more control over how to adapt the recognizer to your specific conditions. This is especially important because we are working with our own face expression database and we are going to integrate the recognizer to our ILE. We selected the method LBP for working in our recognizer. LBP solves many requirements we have to take into consideration (performance and variations of light). We founded and selected the work made by Happy [18]. In that work, they introduce an extension of LBP techniques to reduce the number of features necessaries to recognize face expressions by locating active facial patches. Figure 3 shows our modified process of selecting regions of the face. The face image is transformed into grayscale (for better presentation, in Fig. 3, we show the image in colors). The nose is located, it works like reference point to search other regions. The mouth is located under the noise and the eyes are located above the noise. Two regions are located above the eyes; these regions are known like "candidate regions" and they are areas where we assumes positions of eyebrows.

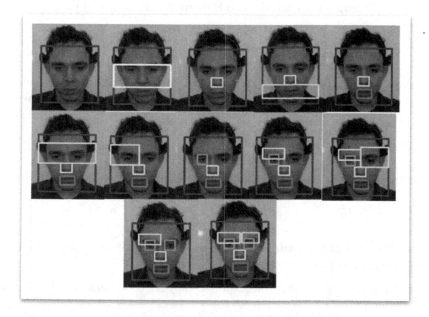

Fig. 3. Selecting regions of the face to locate key points. (Color figure online)

- The next filters are applied in the following order: Gaussian Blur, Sobel, Otsu's Threshold, Binary Dilation, and Removing Small Objects to right and left eyebrows and mouth (Fig. 4a).
- The last pixels to left and right ends from eyebrows and mouth are established; in the case of nose and eyes, central positions are established (Fig. 4b).
- Using key points on face, facial active patches are established. These facial patches has a proportion of one sixteenth of face width (Fig. 4c).

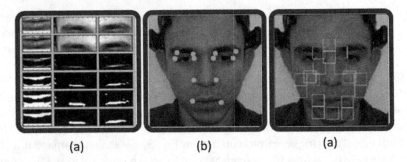

(a)   (b)   (a)

Fig. 4. (a) Applying of filter; (b) Location of key points; (c) Location of activate facial patches.

- LBP uniform operator is applied to each active facial patch. This operator generates a binary number by comparing neighborhood pixel values against the center pixel value. The pattern with 8 neighborhoods (normal size) is given by

$$LBP(x, y) = \sum_{n=0}^{7} s(i_n - i_c)2^n$$

Where i_c is the pixel value at coordinate (x, y) and i_n are the pixel values at coordinates in the neighborhood of (x, y). The binary number is established by

$$s(x) = \begin{cases} 1, x \geq 0 \\ 0, x < 0 \end{cases}$$

The histograms of LBP image are utilized as features descriptors, given by

$$H_i = \sum_{x,y} \{LBP(x, y) = i\}, \quad i = 0, 1, \ldots, n - 1$$

Where n is the number of labels produced by LBP operator. For instance, LBP with 8 neighboring points produces 256 labels.

- Each histogram is generated with 256 bins. They are concatenated and normalized in a vector.
- A support vector machine (SVM) classifier receives the histogram. We used scikit-learn [19] like a support tool to create the SVM. The kernel used was "Linear". Scikit-learn already uses a one-vs-the-rest scheme to take multi-class decisions.

5 Fuzzy Logic System

Java Sensei [20] uses a module which contains fuzzy rules for managing pedagogic aspects of student. We adapted the module for integrating the learning-centered emotions. Two teaching experts built the rules considering the emotions and other aspects such as quality answer or global ability. As a result, we obtained a total of 495 rules. The rules are wrote using Fuzzy Control Language (FCL) and the implementation was supported with the library JFuzzyLogic [21].

5.1 Determination of Input and Output Variables

The inputs for the fuzzy logic system are emotions and cognitive aspects of student. The emotional value is extracted from our recognizer; this value is generated from by photographs taken by the ILE. The cognitive values are generated by calculates of completed tasks and incorrect/correct answers in the ILE. The outputs variables are reactions and answers can do the tutor in the ILE; some of reactions are positive/ neutral/negative feedback messages about the progress of the student or their level of care.

5.2 Fuzzification

Linguistic variables were established by two expert teachers in java and teaching. The variables are a representation of a state; in the case of cognitive states are bad or good; in the case of emotional states are a linguistic variable by each emotion (Table 1).

Table 1. Linguistic variables

Name	Type	Fuzzy values
Currentemotion	Input	Engagement; excitement; frustration; boredom;
Previousemotion	Input	Engagement; excitement; frustration; boredom;
Abilityglobal	Input	Bad; good;
Qualityanswer	Input	Bad; good;
Expression	Output	Delighted; neutral; surprised; compassionate; skeptical;
Feedback	Output	Positive; neutral; negative
Intervention	Output	Yes; no;

Respectively, membership functions are shown in Fig. 5 after running an evaluation. These memberships were established by the same experts. They determined the relation between real value and fuzzy value.

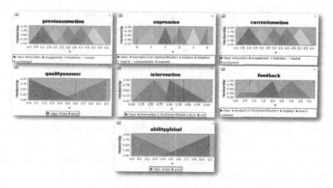

Fig. 5. Membership functions (input and output) for fuzzy logic system.

An example of a fuzzy logic rule is shown below. This rule is defined using FCL. It follows a structure typical of a fuzzy rule which contains number of rule, a section *if* with two types of conditions (and, or) and a section *then*.

```
RULE 1:
IF lastemotion IS frustration AND currentemotion IS engage-
ment AND globalability IS bad AND qualityanswer IS bad
    THEN feedback IS neutral;
```

6   Experiments and Discussions

We present two experiments, the first is a test on face databases using our recognizer, and the second is an example of integration on the ILE Java Sensei.

6.1   Experiments of Face Databases Using the Recognizer

We proposed a method in which the faces of databases are validated and tested in the recognizer we built. The idea is training the classifier of recognizer using 90% of the face database and 10% remaining for testing. The test is a ten-fold validation cross. Finally, the recognizer generates a confusion matrix using metric tools of scikit-learn library [19].

We applied our recognizer to all photographs, this only works if the photograph has all regions of the face distinguishable. After applying the recognizer, we obtained a total of 118 photographs recognized of 730 available. Distribution of emotion instances (photograph) shows in Table 2.

Table 2. Distributions of instances.

Emotion	Boredom	Engagement	Excitement	Frustration
Instances	13	56	35	14

The calculated accuracy was 80% with 2% of standard deviation. The confusion matrix is presented in Table 3.

Table 3. Confussion matrix using posposed method

	Boredom	Engagement	Excitement	Frustration
Boredom	**71%**	0%	0%	17%
Engagement	0%	**93%**	0%	0%
Excitement	0%	0%	**100%**	0%
Frustration	29%	7%	0%	**83%**

As it can see, various faces do not accomplish requirements needed, we found out some head or eyes were far away from the webcam. Also, we found out as well that eyes are the region most complicated to detect, maybe by their small sizes. Nevertheless, we obtained an accuracy of 80%, in addition to obtain successful results for engagement and boredom emotions, what we can say we obtain a result significantly higher. We searched works to compare results in this work; however, we found only very few works related to research topic; the most of researches are investigations about basic emotions; In [17] tested a methodology to evaluate different dimensions for learning-centered emotions, their results are compared against ours with comment that excitement is named as delighted (Table 4).

Table 4. Results in [17] about learning-centered emotoins in wild context

Emotion	Boredom	Engagement	Delighted (Excitement)	Frustration
Accuracy	64%	64%	83%	62%

Their results are visibility lower than ours in all classes although they used a methodology distinct. We can say that our method using face expression has capabilities to detect learning-centered emotions. Also, we can say that our face expression database represents clearly those emotions.

6.2   Using Java Sensei with Learning-Centered Emotion Recognizer

Java Sensei is an ILE to learn Java programming language. In order to achieve goals of an ILE, it needs to understand emotions of students. The ILE captures photographs from them while they do their programming activities. This process occurs as follows:

- The student accesses Java Sensei via an authentication mechanism of Facebook.
- Once the student has been authenticated, the ILE remembers the user positioning its face on webcam center.
- The user selects an exercise on ILE menu. When the ILE loads exercise, the ILE starts to take photographs from the student.
- The server receives the last three photographs taken when the user selects an option on exercise.
- The server sends the recognizer the photographs; the recognizer then sends the emotion to the fuzzy logic system which provides the pedagogic results for ILE (Fig. 6).

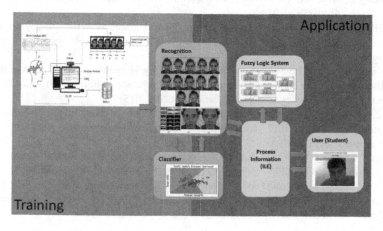

Fig. 6. Process to recognize emotions in the ILE.

7   Conclusion

We introduced the building and validation of a new face expression database focused on learning-centered emotions, the building of an appearance-based LBP recognizer which provides information about how the low level representations can give significant results to working with this kind of emotions. Also, we showed the coupling of both objects to an ILE called Java Sensei. The test validates the work performed had successful results despite not having several works to compare it. This work can be used as a method to build face expressions databases with educational approach. The database can be found through the next URL: ftp://javasensei.ddns.net/corpus.rar.

8   Future Work

They are many slopes that can be resolved later. Increase the amount of subjects ones for the database. It decreases the features necessaries to recognizer. It enhances recognizer of face parts with new photographs acquired. Testing the ILE with new improvements. All this is taken into consideration to improve next works.

References

1. Pekrun, R.: The impact of emotions on learning and achievement: towards a theory of cognitive/motivational mediators. Appl. Psychol. **41**(4), 359–376 (1992)
2. Pekrun, R., et al.: Academic emotions in students' self-regulated learning and achievement: a program of qualitative and quantitative research. Educ. Psychol. **37**(2), 91–105 (2002)
3. Ekman, P.: An argument for basic emotions. Cogn. Emot. **6**(3–4), 169–200 (1992)
4. Baker, R.S., et al.: Better to be frustrated than bored: the incidence, persistence, and impact of learners' cognitive–affective states during interactions with three different computer-based learning environments. Int. J. Hum. Comput. Stud. **68**(4), 223–241 (2010)
5. D'Mello, S., Graesser, A.: Dynamics of affective states during complex learning. Learn. Instr. **22**(2), 145–157 (2012)
6. D'Mello, S., et al.: AutoTutor detects and responds to learners affective and cognitive states. In: Workshop on Emotional and Cognitive Issues at the International Conference on Intelligent Tutoring Systems (2008)
7. Wiggins, J.B., et al.: JavaTutor: an intelligent tutoring system that adapts to cognitive and affective states during computer programming. In: Proceedings of the 46th ACM Technical Symposium on Computer Science Education. ACM (2015)
8. Kanade, T., Cohn, J.F., Tian, Y.: Comprehensive database for facial expression analysis. In: Proceedings of Fourth IEEE International Conference on Automatic Face and Gesture Recognition. IEEE (2000)
9. Ekman, P., Friesen, W.: Facial Action Coding System: A Technique for the Measurement of Facial Movement. Consulting Psychologists Press, Palo Alto (1978)
10. Lucey, P., et al.: The extended cohn-kanade dataset (CK+): a complete dataset for action unit and emotion-specified expression. In: 2010 IEEE Computer Society Conference on Computer Vision and Pattern Recognition-Workshops. IEEE (2010)

11. Langner, O., et al.: Presentation and validation of the radboud faces database. Cogn. Emot. **24**(8), 1377–1388 (2010)
12. Bänziger, T., Mortillaro, M., Scherer, K.R.: Introducing the Geneva multimodal expression corpus for experimental research on emotion perception. Emotion **12**(5), 1161 (2012)
13. McKeown, G., et al.: The semaine database: annotated multimodal records of emotionally colored conversations between a person and a limited agent. IEEE Trans. Affect. Comput. **3**(1), 5–17 (2012)
14. Ahonen, T., Hadid, A., Pietikainen, M.: Face description with local binary patterns: Application to face recognition. IEEE Trans. Pattern Anal. Mach. Intell. **28**(12), 2037–2041 (2006)
15. Jiang, B., et al.: A dynamic appearance descriptor approach to facial actions temporal modeling. IEEE Trans. Cybern. **44**(2), 161–174 (2014)
16. Wu, T., et al.: Action unit recognition transfer across datasets. In: 2011 IEEE International Conference on Automatic Face & Gesture Recognition and Workshops (FG 2011). IEEE (2011)
17. Bosch, N., et al.: Automatic detection of learning-centered affective states in the wild. In: Proceedings of the 20th International Conference on Intelligent User Interfaces, IUI 2015 (2015)
18. Happy, S., Routray, A.: Automatic facial expression recognition using features of salient facial patches. IEEE Trans. Affect. Comput. **6**(1), 1–12 (2015)
19. Pedregosa, F., et al.: Scikit-learn: machine learning in python. J. Mach. Learn. Res. **12**, 2825–2830 (2011)
20. Cabada, R.Z., et al.: An affective learning environment for java. In: 2015 IEEE 15th International Conference on Advanced Learning Technologies. IEEE (2015)
21. Cingolani, P., Alcalá-Fdez, J.: jFuzzyLogic: a java library to design fuzzy logic controllers according to the standard for fuzzy control programming. Int. J. Comput. Intell. Syst. **6**(sup1), 61–75 (2013)

Affective Learning System for Algorithmic Logic Applying Gamification

Ramón Zatarain-Cabada^(✉), María Lucia Barrón-Estrada,
and José Mario Ríos-Félix

Instituto Tecnológico de Culiacán, Juan de Dios Bátiz 310 Pte., Col. Guadalupe,
80220 Culiacán, Sinaloa, Mexico
{rzatarain,lbarron,mario_rios}@itculiacan.edu.mx

Abstract. The growing demand for software tools that encourage and support students in learning design and algorithm implementation, has allowed the creation of such software systems. In this paper we present a new and innovative affective tutoring system, for logic and algorithmic programming, based on block techniques. Our approach combines the Google Blockly's interface with gamification techniques and exercises that are monitored according to the emotional state of the student. Depending on the expressed emotion (boring, engagement, frustration, and neutral), the system evaluates a number of variables to determine whether the student requires assistance. Tests have shown that the detection of the emotional state of the student, affect favorably the student evaluations.

Keywords: Affective Computing · Intelligent tutoring systems · Algorithmic logic · Programming Languages

1 Introduction

Learning to program remains one of the most demanding tasks for most students. Programming courses are held every year to new generations of students. Even study fields outside the computer science include in its curriculum basic programming courses.

Today there are many tools that aim to support students in their arduous task of learning computer-related topics, because computer science is not just about programming, but a whole way of thinking [1]. We can classify these tools depending of their orientation. Some of these software tools are e-learning or CAI (Computer Assisted Instruction) systems, programming intelligent tutoring systems (ITS), and serious games that teach programming topics.

E-learning tools for programming intend to facilitate learning using preset frameworks that simplify the implementation of algorithms and programs to students. Within this classification, we highlight the authoring tools, which allow users to design and build their own interactive stories, animations, simulations or even games. Within the authoring tools, we include those that seek to instruct students in what is known as "Computational Thinking". Computational thinking is a series of skills that make problem solving, systems design, and human behavior understanding, based on the fundamental concepts of computing [2].

© Springer International Publishing AG 2017
O. Pichardo-Lagunas and S. Miranda-Jiménez (Eds.): MICAI 2016, Part II, LNAI 10062, pp. 536–547, 2017.
DOI: 10.1007/978-3-319-62428-0_44

On the other hand, ITS are computerized learning environments that incorporate computational models of cognitive science, learning science, computational linguistics, artificial intelligence, and other fields. An ITS provides tracking of psychological states of students in the fine details; a process called student modeling [3]. Within the family of ITS, there exist the affective tutoring systems (ATS), which are intelligent systems that incorporate the ability to recognize the emotional state of the students, that allow users to interact with exercises that stimulate their emotional state.

Finally, serious games are those games that more than entertain, aim to teach through a game. Consequently, they attract and retain students more easily than other teaching tools. From the idea of games, it arises what is known as gamification. Basically, gamification is a term used to describe those characteristics of an interactive system that aim to motivate and engage end users through the use and mechanics of stimuli commonly included in games, such as trophies, levels and leaderboards [4].

Our system *EasyLogic* is a tool that combines the previously described technologies (e -learning tools for teaching programming, affective-intelligent tutoring systems, and gamification) that allows a student to design and implement algorithms in a simple way but powerful at the same time. The main contribution of this work, is the combination of emotional and motivational aspects, in a tool that teaches the difficult process of construction of algorithms and programs.

This paper is organized as follows: Sect. 2 describes the related work. Section 3 presents the structure and functionality of the tool (EasyLogic). Section 4 shows a working session with EasyLogic. Section 5 presents the experiments with the software tool and the student results. Finally, in Sect. 6 the conclusions and future work are described.

2 Related Work

This section describes research work in areas related to our investigation.

2.1 E-Learning Tools for Programming

Among the most important programming tools we can mention Greenfoot [5], an integrated development environment that combines Java programming with an interactive graphical interface. Greenfoot focuses to facilitate the teaching of courses for object oriented programming. Another important tool is Alice [6], in which novice students can program 3D games using predefined object models.

On the other hand, in recent years different research groups have developed tools to learn mobile programming, as is the case of MIT App Inventor [7], which allows design and build fully functional mobile applications for Android. With this tool, developers focus on logic and algorithm solution, rather than syntax of the programming language.

2.2 E-Learning Support Tools

Specific authoring tools that address concepts of algorithmic thinking and basic programming are: Scratch [8, 9], a community of online creative learning, where users can interact and upload their projects to encourage the code reuse and enable remixing them. To create a project, graphic blocks are used, where each block represents an element of the programming language, such as: control structure, operators, variables, and functions.

Another case is Scalable Game Design Arcade (AgentSheets) [1, 10], which allows students to create games easily, for which they use pedagogical agents using gamification techniques. Another important tool is Code Studio [11], which is presented through a home page with online courses created by Code.org, and represents a community where a student can learn different subjects from computer science.

Finally, PseInt [12] is a tool to assist a student with a simple and intuitive pseudo-language in Spanish, complemented by a flowchart editor, that allows to focus on the fundamental concepts of programming logic and the use of control structures.

2.3 Affective and Intelligent Tutoring Systems

Our main interest are those intelligent tutors who perform an intervention depending on the emotional state of the student.

Among the most recent affective ITS are Gaze tutor, an intelligent tutor for the biology area that through eye tracking detects if students are bored, engaged/motivated, or distracted. The tutor uses textual dialogues through a pedagogical agent to try to redirect the student's attention [13]. Another example is Gerda, an ITS for operating system topics, which through a dialogue (questions and answers), analyzes the affective state of students using dictionaries of words with emotional annotations [14].

Perhaps the most important affective ITS is Affective AutoTutor, an extension of AutoTutor (an ITS that helps students learn complex technical content in different areas of knowledge), which adds capabilities to recognize and manage emotions by detecting student affective states, using facial expressions, body motion sensors, and textual conversations [15].

2.4 Serious Games

Two of the most interesting serious games are Program your robot [16] and Cargo-bot [17]. The first focuses on the teaching of algorithmic thinking and the second presents a new methodology of teaching the technique of recursion through a game. Both games are very well implemented, and they catch users who do not realize they are learning as they play.

2.5 Current Panorama

One of the main weaknesses of this kind of tools focused on learning computational thinking topics, and in specific algorithmic logic, is that they only target K12 students mainly, and even younger, and do not consider the student affective state when they use them. Immordino-Yang and Damasio established that emotional processes act as a "rudder" in the transfer of knowledge and skills, and that emotions play an important and necessary role in decision making, as is the crossing point between cognition leading to potentially developing creativity [18].

In addition, as argued by M. Kölling and J. Maloney in Scratch and Greenfoot, the philosophy that is used to teach is as follows: first, we must let students play; then create something; next, include motivation to be creative, and finally explain what really is happening. They conclude that a person using Scratch can continue his enrichment of skills through Greenfoot and then migrate to any IDE (Scratch → Greenfoot → IDE) [19].

To date, there is no a comprehensive system in which students can learn and master the elements of algorithmic and programming logic progressively, and also take into account the emotional state of the student. To handle this challenge, the tool should handle 3 stages:

(a) To act as tutor to develop a computational thinking.
(b) To practice algorithmic logic knowledge.
(c) To guide the student toward a transition to a programming language.

The main contribution of EasyLogic, is to have an ITS for teaching algorithmic logic, at a university level in addition to using gamification techniques, allowing to recognize and manage the emotional state of students, as support for cognitive elements used in the personalization of student's teaching/learning.

3 EasyLogic

EasyLogic is a web system, which acts as an affective ITS in the process of learning algorithmic logic and programming. Our system is made up of 3 main sections: (a) Learn: Provides various courses, which include a series of exercises, to give a lesson to each of the different control structures that exist in programming. These exercises supervise the affective state that the student is presenting. (b) Imagine and creates: This section allows student to design their own algorithms and then execute them. You can also generate code in a programming language associated with the developed algorithm. (c) Code: In this section students can program directly in JavaScript instead of using the graphic blocks (still in development).

Like many modern authoring and programming tools, EasyLogic uses graphic blocks. The interface is achieved using Blockly, a Google's library [20]. Blockly is a JavaScript library that besides being free, is customizable and extensible, so new suitable blocks for various exercises were created.

3.1 PREMOC

For affect recognition, a Multimodal Emotion Recognition Platform (PREMOC, by its Spanish acronym), which is being developed in the Laboratory of Affective Computing from Instituto Tecnológico de Culiacán was used. PREMOC consists of a web service that takes as input, facial expressions, audio signals, text dialogs, and electroencephalography signals (EEG), which are processed to deliver as an output the current student emotion(s).

PREMOC has 3 integration modes: Single mode, Multimode, and Student mode. In the Single mode, the response sent, is the detected emotion for each input read by the recognizer. For example, in case of sending data from a facial image, and EEG data signals, the response will be 2 independent emotions; one for the face image and one for the EEG signals. In Multimode, the user response is multimodal, that is to say, the web service sends only one emotion to the user, integrating all emotions detected by each recognizer. This is achieved using an integrator implemented in fuzzy logic. In Student mode, unlike using Ekman's basic emotions, the user will get learning-oriented emotions (engaged, bored, frustrated and neutral). Figure 1 shows the structure and operation of PREMOC.

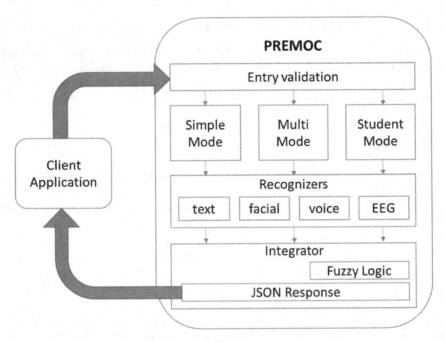

Fig. 1. PREMOC's structure.

For the current version of the system, the student mode is used, and information of facial images is sent. PREMOC's image recognizer consists of two phases: Training and Execution. The training phase consisted in training a neural network responsible of the image classification. To this, images from RAFD corpus were used as training data (955 images were used) [21]. Of each of the images a vector of 10 features was extracted, where each feature is a Euclidean distance between different points of the face. With these data, a back-propagation neural network was trained, using the Weka library for Java. The emotion recognition phase is showed in Fig. 2.

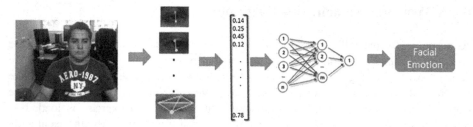

Fig. 2. Facial emotion recognizer algorithm.

3.2   Interventions

Once the user proceeds to perform an exercise, the system starts capturing the student faces to be sent continuously to PREMOC. After the images are analyzed, an emotion state is obtained (bored, engaged, confused, or neutral); then the system stores the emotion state of the user. Every 30 s, EasyLogic evaluates different variables such as the time spent in the exercise, the number of program executions, and the student emotion state to determine if the student needs some assistance.

Interventions consists of different pop-ups that are displayed automatically when the system detects that the user needs a help or a hint. The interventions are divided into three types: initial, informative and motivational. Figure 3 describes each of the interventions used by EasyLogic.

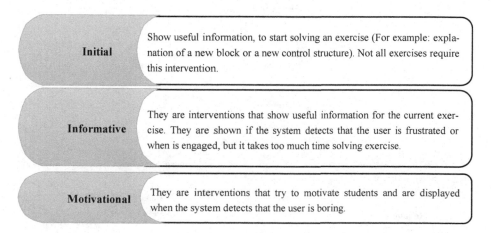

Fig. 3. Types of interventions used in EasyLogic.

EasyLogic implements gamification techniques to motivate students, providing them with trophies and points as they progress in their course. Because the tool is intended for use in real courses, students must select the group they belong at registration. Each student can view the score that each of his classmates have so far and the trophies they have achieved. This is intended to motivate the student competition.

4   A Working Session with EasyLogic

At home screen the following information is shown: access to courses, access to the area for creating algorithms, and access to the programming area. To access the courses, users must log in using their email and password. Once selected the course, the system will automatically load the next unsolved exercise by the student. Some exercises are associated with an initial intervention; once the exercise is loaded, if initial assistance is required, is shown. To not bore the student with assistances already read, the system saves information of all previously provided interventions to the student, when confirmed that the information has been read.

Once the exercise is loaded, the system let the student to work for a specified time. If the exercise is solved, points earned are calculated based on the time spent in the exercise and the amount of program executions. If a new trophy is just obtained, it is displayed to the student. In case the student hasn't solved the exercise, user data (elapsed time, emotional state, and number of executions) are analyzed to verify if the user needs some intervention (informative or motivational). If so, an intervention is obtained from a database for the current exercise. In Fig. 4 the process previously described is shown.

The main interface (Spanish) to solve the exercises is shown in Fig. 5, which consists of an option bar to redirect to other screens (1), the name of the course being conducted (2), the current exercise level (3), the classification of the graphic blocks (4),

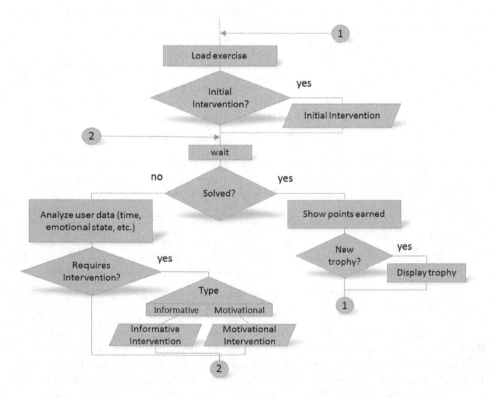

Fig. 4. Flowchart showing the process followed by the courses in EasyLogic.

an area to create the algorithm by blocks (5), the game to be animated once executed the algorithm (6), the current number of blocks used (7), and a button to run the algorithm and another to see the associated code to the created algorithm (8).

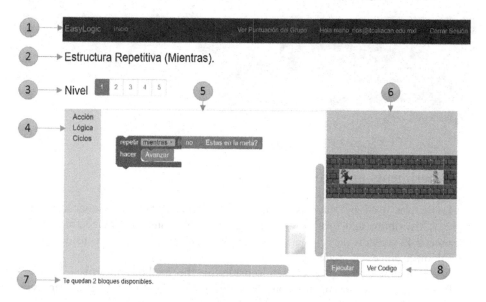

Fig. 5. Interface for solving exercises.

Figure 6 shows an example of an informative help for the repetitive structure "For".

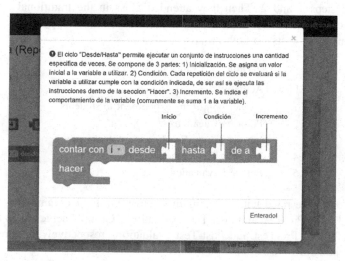

Fig. 6. Informative intervention example.

In the section "Imagine and creates" students can create any kind of algorithms using graphic blocks. It is particularly focused to solve exercises commonly used by teachers in the classroom. Once developed the algorithm, students can visualize the associated JavaScript code. An example of an algorithm is shown in Fig. 7. When executed, the student will have to enter a number from the keyboard and the system will display a text message indicating if the student is adult or underage.

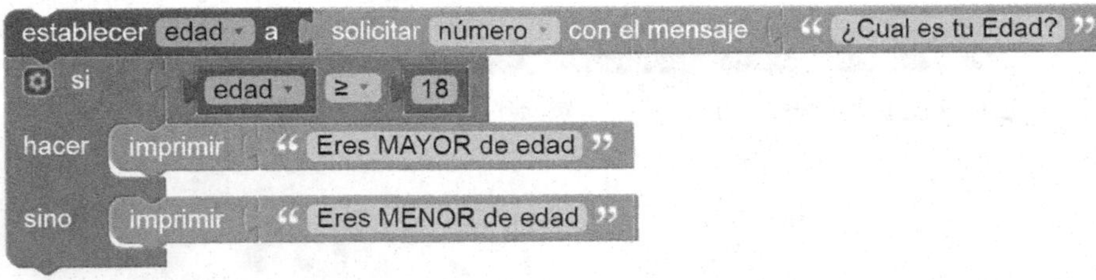

Fig. 7. Example of an algorithm created in EasyLogic.

5 Experiments and Results

EasyLogic was used by students of the Instituto Tecnológico de Culiacán, in the course: "Algorithms and Programming Languages" of Industrial Engineering. In the experiment 42 students participated, separated in 2 groups of 21 each considering the grade-point averages of students.

An evaluation design was chosen considering the methods described by Beverly P. Woolf [22], which mainly considered the goals of the tool. The chosen evaluation method was: *Pre-Test + Intervention + Post-Test*.

EasyLogic tests were conducted between March and May 2016. These tests involved the students of Group 1. Activities shown in Table 1 were carried out. Group 2 performed steps 1 and 2. Then they attended class in the traditional way, where algorithmic control structures topics were studied. Finally, we applied the same tests (Pre-Tests and Post-Tests) to both groups.

Table 1. Evaluation activities.

Phase	Activity
1	Explanation of the experiment to students
2	Pre-test evaluation
3	Introduction to EasyLogic environment
4	Usage of EasyLogic by students
5	Post-test evaluation

Evaluations were rated with a maximum of 100. Group 1 obtained an average of 82.19 and 83.57 in Pre-Test and Post-Test evaluations. Group 2 achieved an average of 84.28 and 82.95 in Pre-Test and Post-Test evaluations respectively. Figures 8 and 9 shows the results of both Groups.

Based on the above results we can see that in both groups the average of the tests is similar. If we compare the results of the Post-Test in both test groups, we can see a difference of 0.62%, combined with a higher average in the Pre-Test for Group 2, against the Group 1 evaluation, which means that the Group 2 has a negative trend related to the group average, compared to Group 1.

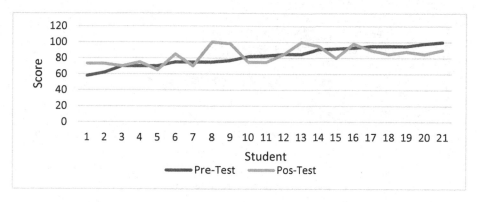

Fig. 8. Pre-test and Post-test evaluation results for Group 1.

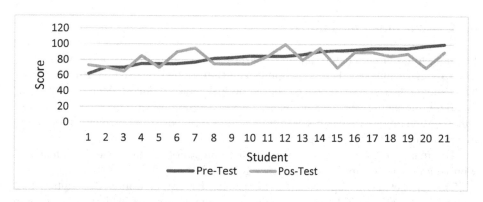

Fig. 9. Pre-test and Post-test evaluation results for Group 2.

5.1 Emotional Results

During the experiment with Group 1, the tool EasyLogic constantly monitored the emotional state of the students. It was decided to use the tool with 2 configurations:

(a) With full features (emotional detection, application of gamification with trophies and scoreboard), where 10 students worked like this.
(b) Emotional detection and part of gamification was disabled, so that interventions showing points and trophies were omitted (only initial and informative interventions were shown), where 11 students used the tool with this configuration.

Comparing the results obtained by the tool as shown in Fig. 10, better results were observed with students who used Configuration 1, in relation to the time it took to solve the exercises. However, there was no difference in the average of all exercises done by students. Also, a positive trend in increasing the level of learning of the students who used configuration 1 was observed. Averages in Fig. 10 refers to the average results of: minimum and average time needed to solve an exercise, the amount of solved exercises, and the displayed tool interventions for each student.

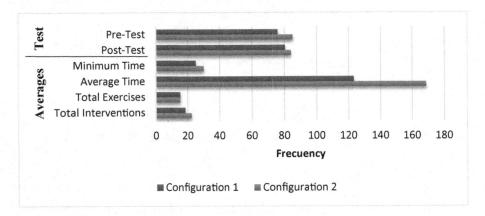

Fig. 10. Comparison of Group 1 based on configurations.

6   Conclusions and Future Work

Learning to program remains a demanding task for students. In this paper, we present EasyLogic, an affective ITS for learning algorithmic and programming logic. Tests have shown that the detection of the emotional state of the student, it influences favorably on having been used to realize an intervention, in case the student needs it, either redirecting the student's attention if they are bored or showing informative interventions when they are frustrated.

The main contribution of this work is the unification of gamification techniques, with technologies of artificial intelligence for the detection of emotions.

This project has a huge potential to be used by any educational institution that requires to teach Algorithms and/ or Programming topics. To achieve this, it must consider a few points like:

- Add more courses, which should consider specific topics as: multiple conditionals, functions, and recursion.
- Conclude the development of the Programming section, which because of the scope of the project was not completed.
- Consider other affective recognition sources, such as: the position and movement recorded by the accelerometer in mobile devices.
- Allow to work in collaborative mode, where more than one student can create the algorithm/ code in real time.

References

1. Ioannidou, A., Bennett, V., Repenning, A., Koh, K.H., Basawapatna, A.: Computational thinking patterns **2** (2011, online submission)
2. Wing, J.: Computational thinking. J. Comput. Sci. Coll. **24**(6), 6–7 (2011)
3. Graesser, A.C., Conley, M.W., Olney, A.: Intelligent tutoring systems. In: APA Educational Psychology Handbook: Application to Learning and Teaching, vol. 3, pp. 451–473. American Psychological Association, Washington (2012)

4. Seaborn, K., Fels, D.I.: Gamification in theory and action: a survey. Int. J. Hum. Comput. Stud. **74**, 14–31 (2014)
5. Kölling, M.: The greenfoot programming environment. ACM Trans. Comput. Educ. (TOCE) **10**(4), 14 (2010)
6. Werner, L., Campe, S., Denner, J.: Children learning computer science concepts via alice game-programming. In: Proceedings of the 43rd ACM Technical Symposium on Computer Science Education, pp. 427–432 (2012)
7. Crawford, S., Dominguez, J.J.: MIT App Inventor: enabling personal mobile computing. arXiv preprint arXiv:1310.2830 (2013)
8. Resnick, M., Maloney, J., Monroy-Hernández, A., Rusk, N., Eastmond, E., Brennan, K., Millner, A., Rosenbaum, E., Silver, J., Silverman, B., Kafai, Y.: Scratch: programming for all. Commun. ACM **52**(11), 60–67 (2009)
9. Brennan, K., Resnick, M.: New frameworks for studying and assessing the development of computational thinking. In: Annual Meeting of the American Educational Research Association, Vancouver, BC, Canada, pp. 1–25 (2012)
10. Repenning, A., Webb, D.: Scalable game design and the development of a checklist for getting computational thinking into public schools (2010)
11. Code Studio (2016). https://studio.code.org. Accessed Apr
12. Loyarte, H., Novara, P.: Desarrollo e implementación de un Intérprete de Pseudocódigo para la Enseñanza de Algorítmica Computacional. In: I Congreso de Tecnología en Educación y Educación en Tecnología (2006)
13. D'Mello, S., Olney, A., Williams, C., Hays, P.: Gaze tutor: a gaze-reactive intelligent tutoring system. Int. J. Hum. Comput. Stud. **70**(5), 377–398 (2012)
14. Landowska, A.: Affective computing and affective learning – methods, tools and prospects. Stara strona magazynu EduAkcja **5**(1) (2013)
15. D'Mello, S., Graesser, A.: AutoTutor and affective AutoTutor: learning by talking with cognitively and emotionally intelligent computers that talk back. ACM Trans. Interact. Intell. Syst. (TiiS) **2**(4), 23 (2012)
16. Kazimoglu, C., Kiernan, M., Bacon, L., MacKinnon, L.: A serious game for developing computational thinking and learning introductory computer programming. Procedia - Soc. Behav. Sci. **47**, 1991–1999 (2012)
17. Tessler, J., Beth, B., Lin, C.: Using cargo-bot to provide contextualized learning of recursion. In: Proceedings of the Ninth Annual International ACM Conference on International Computing Education Research - ICER 2013, p. 161 (2013)
18. Butler-Kisber, L.: Mind, brain, and education: implications for educators. Learn. Landsc. **5**(1), 1–266 (2011)
19. Utting, I., Cooper, S., Kölling, M.: Alice, greenfoot, and scratch–a discussion. ACM Trans. **10**(4), 1–11 (2010)
20. Fraser, N.: Google blockly-a visual programming editor (2016). https://developers.google.com/blockly/. Accessed Apr 2013
21. Langner, O., Dotsch, R., Bijlstra, G., Wigboldus, D.H., Hawk, S.T., Van Knippenberg, A.D.: Presentation and validation of the Radboud Faces Database. Cogn. Emot. **24**(8), 1377–1388 (2010)
22. Woolf, B.P.: Building Intelligent Interactive Tutors Student-Centered Strategies for Revolutionizing E-learning. Morgan Kaufmann, Burlington (2010)

Author Index

Printed in the United States
By Bookmasters